AN INTRODUCTION TO THE HISTORY
OF THE PRINCIPAL KINGDOMS
AND STATES OF EUROPE

NATURAL LAW AND
ENLIGHTENMENT CLASSICS

Knud Haakonssen
General Editor

Samuel Pufendorf

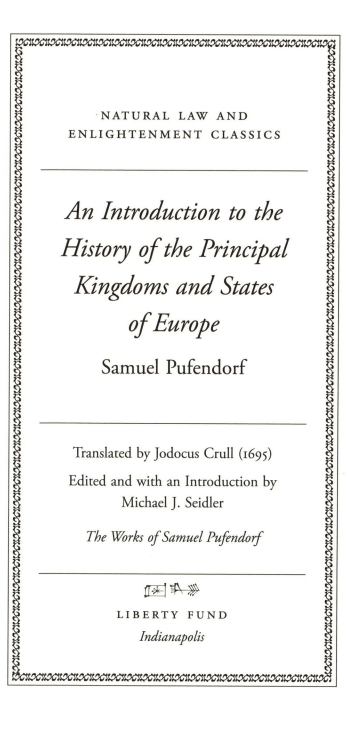

An Introduction to the History of the Principal Kingdoms and States of Europe

Samuel Pufendorf

Translated by Jodocus Crull (1695)

Edited and with an Introduction by
Michael J. Seidler

The Works of Samuel Pufendorf

LIBERTY FUND

Indianapolis

This book is published by Liberty Fund, Inc., a foundation established to encourage study of the ideal of a society of free and responsible individuals.

Introduction, annotations, charts, appendixes, bibliography, index
© 2013 by Liberty Fund, Inc.

C   10   9   8   7   6   5   4   3   2   1
P   10   9   8   7   6   5   4   3   2   1

Frontispiece: The portrait of Samuel Pufendorf is to be found at the Law Faculty of the University of Lund, Sweden, and is based on a photoreproduction by Leopoldo Iorizzo. Reprinted by permission.

Library of Congress Cataloging-in-Publication Data
Pufendorf, Samuel, Freiherr von, 1632–1694
[Einleitung zu der Historie der vornehmsten Reiche
und Staaten so itziger Zeit in Europa sich befinden.
English]
An introduction to the history of the principal
kingdoms and states of Europe
Samuel Pufendorf; translated by Jodocus Crull (1695);
edited and with an introduction by Michael J. Seidler.
page cm.   (Natural law and Enlightenment classics)
Includes bibliographical references and index.
ISBN 978-0-86597-512-5 (hardcover: alk. paper)
ISBN 978-0-86597-513-2 (pbk.: alk. paper)
1. Europe—History.   I. Crull, Jodocus,   –1713? translator.
II. Seidler, Michael J., 1950–   editor.   III. Title.
D103.P97 2013
940—dc23   2013003026

LIBERTY FUND, INC.
8335 Allison Pointe Trail, Suite 300
Indianapolis, Indiana 46250-1684

CONTENTS

EDITOR'S INTRODUCTION

In the early twentieth century when his main natural law works were reissued in the Carnegie Classics series,[1] Samuel Pufendorf was known as a theorist of international law; toward the latter end of the century, when he became more familiar to the Anglo-American world, he was studied mainly as a moral and political theorist.[2] However, in his own time in the late seventeenth and early eighteenth centuries, Pufendorf was known and respected primarily as a historian.[3] Though these roles may now seem distinct and the subject of different professional literatures, they intersected or coincided in that earlier period. Thus, contrary to interpretations that segment Pufendorf's life and thought in either topical or temporal ways, or that seek to prioritize one or another function,[4] his roles as international jurist, natural lawyer, and historian must be seen in active relation to one another. They are present at all stages of his career.

Samuel Pufendorf was born in 1632, at the height of the Thirty Years' War, to a Lutheran pastor in Lower Saxony whose family experienced firsthand some of the terrors of that formative period in European history. When he died in 1694, he was royal historian to both Sweden and Brandenburg, an ennobled international figure whose services were also desired in Vienna to record the history of the empire and its Turk-

1. Pufendorf (1927a), (1927b), (1931a), (1931b), (1934a), (1934b).
2. Krieger (1965); Denzer (1972); Tuck (1981), (1987); Schneewind (1987), (1998); Haakonssen (1996).
3. Döring (1995), "Einleitung" to "Epistolae duae . . . ," in Pufendorf (1995), p. 460; and Döring (1994), p. 214 (on the funeral sermons after Pufendorf's death).
4. Krieger (1965), pp. 201–3, 209; Meinecke (1925), pp. 286–88.

ish wars.[5] His older brother, Esaias (1628–87), who often furthered his career and remained close despite eventual political differences, was an experienced and well-connected European diplomat; and Samuel himself held the posts of secretary to Hedwig Eleonora—widow of Charles Gustav, dowager queen of Sweden, and mother of Charles XI—and of privy councillor in Berlin. Throughout his career, he maintained close ties to members of the Swedish ruling class, whose sons he taught during his university periods at Heidelberg (1660–68) and Lund (1668–76). Indeed, as a historian who emphasized the importance of modern history, Pufendorf was throughout his life appropriately in the thick of things.

Like Esaias before him, Samuel began his formal education in 1645 at the ducal school at Grimma, where his studies included the Greek and Latin classics, especially the ancient historians. This was also a personal passion that he indulged voraciously on the side and that would provide a basis for his broad historical and political understanding. He continued his study of classics, or philology, at the University of Leipzig (1650–58) where, an early biographer reports, his favorite subjects were "divine and natural law" and the associated study of "history, politics, and civil law."[6] Equally important at the time was his membership in the Collegium Anthologicum, an extracurricular academic society where he gave many lectures on historical topics, including church history and the Holy Roman Empire.[7] In 1658 Samuel followed Esaias into Swedish service by becoming tutor to the household of Peter Julius Coyet, Sweden's envoy to Denmark. The renewed war between these countries led to an eight months' long imprisonment in Copenhagen, during which Pufendorf composed the *Elements of Universal Jurisprudence* (1660), his first and structurally most formal natural law

5. Döring (1996b), p. 92, note 57; letter to von Seilern (March 5, 1690), Pufendorf (1996), #175, p. 261, and p. 263, note 1; *Hamburgische Bibliotheca. . . . Die zehnte Centuria,* Art. 37, p. 128; and Moraw (1962), pp. 168–69, 172.

6. Adlemansthal [Dahlmann], "Vita, Fama, et Fata Literaria Pufendorfiana . . . ," in *Samuels Freyhrn. von Puffendorff kurtzer doch gründlicher Bericht von dem Zustande des H. R. Reichs teutscher Nation . . .* (Leipzig: Gleditsch und Weidmann, 1710), #3, p. 650.

7. See Pufendorf (1995), pp. 21–86; Döring (1992b), pp. 165–68, 174; and Döring (1988).

work. Notably, that same experience also led to a lesser-known political tract, *Gundaeus Baubator Danicus* (1659), which explored the status and rights of ambassadors in the context of international law.[8]

The *Elements* was published in the Netherlands, where Pufendorf was secretary to Coyet while also studying at Leiden University and editing several classical texts. Its dedication to Karl Ludwig, the reinstated Elector Palatine, soon secured for him a chair at Heidelberg in philology and international law (*ius gentium*).[9] There he cultivated close ties with a number of young Swedish aristocrats,[10] in part through a series of important theses (written by himself and defended by students), which were later included in his *Select Academic Dissertations [Dissertationes academicae selectiores]* (1675). These early pieces focused on topics (for example, patriotism, systems of states, irregular states) that remained central to his thought and elaborated the bare theoretical framework of the *Elements* through a rich analysis of historical examples, thereby creating the foundation for his main natural law treatise, *On the Law of Nature and of Nations* (1672). At Heidelberg, Pufendorf also composed a historically based justification of the Elector's disputed population politics (the *Wildfangstreit*),[11] he wrote a short history of the fifteenth-century Albanian folk hero George Kastrioti Skanderbeg (who had led a successful resistance against the Turks),[12] and he produced (under the pseudonym Severinus de Monzambano) his notoriously irreverent, or

8. Pufendorf (1995), pp. 125–55.

9. See Döring (2006) on Pufendorf's Heidelberg period.

10. These included Otto Wilhelm von Königsmark, who later secured for Pufendorf the post of secretary to Ulrike Eleonora. Königsmark entered imperial service in the 1680s during the joint European effort against the Turks, and Pufendorf's history of Skanderbeg (see note 12, below) was dedicated to him. See Döring's biographical entry in Pufendorf (1996), p. 399.

11. *Prodromus solidae et copiosae confutationis mox secuturae scripti . . .* (Heidelberg, 1665), in Pufendorf (1995), pp. 187–93; and the Introduction to Pufendorf (2007), pp. 11–12.

12. *Georgii Castriotae Scanderbeg vulgo dicti Historia, compendio tradita* (Stade, 1664). This piece indirectly supported the empire's defensive war against the Ottomans, which occupied the imperial diet of Regensburg (1664), and it was commissioned by Karl Ludwig or Johann Philipp von Schönborn, elector of Mainz. However, it was not published until 1684, after the Turkish attack on Vienna (1683). See Döring (1992a), pp. 200–201, and Palladini (1999a), #1346, p. 316.

realistic, account of the Holy Roman Empire, *The Present State of Germany* (1667), which also foreshadowed many of his later works, including the *Introduction*.

In 1668 Pufendorf left Heidelberg for a chair in natural law at the newly established University of Lund, in Sweden. There he completed *On the Law of Nature and of Nations* and its shorter pedagogical compendium, *The Whole Duty of Man* (1673), vigorously defending them against the fierce attacks of Lutheran and Neo-Aristotelian critics in both Sweden and Germany. When renewed hostilities with Denmark forced the closure of the university in 1676, he became royal Swedish historian in Stockholm. In that capacity he produced two long histories of Sweden, including *Twenty-six Books of Commentary on Swedish Affairs, from the Expedition of Gustavus Adolphus into Germany to the Abdication of Christina* (1686), and its sequel, *Eight Books of Commentary on the Achievements of Charles Gustav, King of Sweden*, which appeared posthumously in 1696 even though it was essentially completed when Pufendorf was loaned to Brandenburg in 1688. In Berlin he quickly completed his *Nineteen Books on the Achievements of Frederick William, the Great Elector of Brandenburg* (1695) and then turned to the unfinished (and, until 1784, unpublished) fragment, *Three Books of Commentary on the Achievements of Frederick III, Elector of Brandenburg*, which is notable for its detailed account of the English Revolution of 1688.[13]

While still in Sweden, Pufendorf collected the lectures on European history that he had given at Lund, and perhaps Heidelberg, and issued them in 1682 as *An Introduction to the History of the Principal Kingdoms and States of Europe*. Ironically in view of its immediate success, this was a forced publication. Because an unauthorized Swedish translation based on circulating student manuscripts had appeared in 1680, Pufendorf was compelled to publish an official version in order to assert his authorship ("than to suffer that another should rob me of it").[14] To remedy the absence of a separate chapter on Sweden in

13. Seidler (1996).

14. Preface, p. 6. Martinière, "Eloge historique" (1753), p. xv, says that the *Introduction* was circulated in manuscript form to the young people Pufendorf was teaching, and Siebenkäs (1790), p. 52, that Pufendorf was forced to publish.

the manuscript version—whose pedagogical aim had been to educate young Swedes about the rest of Europe—Pufendorf followed up with his *Continued Introduction to the History of the Principal Kingdoms and States of Europe, Wherein the History of the Kingdom of Sweden and Its Wars with Foreign Crowns Are Especially Described* (1686), a work as long as the much wider ranging original. That same year, before leaving Sweden for Brandenburg, Pufendorf also issued his *Scandinavian Quarrel* (*Eris Scandica*), a collection of polemical essays defending his natural law theory against a variety of critics. And in Berlin, before his death in 1694, he published two important works on religion that addressed church-state relations, religious unification, and toleration.[15] At the same time he was preparing the second edition of *The Present State of Germany,* which he had substantially revised to reflect current European conditions.

The Introduction—Background, Content, and Reaction

Pufendorf's original *Introduction* consisted of a preface and twelve chapters, each devoted to a different European state. The relatively short chapter I pays tribute to the ancient historians as "equally usefull and pleasant,"[16] and continues to adhere formally to the traditional four-monarchies scheme (Assyria, Persia, Macedonia, and Rome) associated with Daniel 2:31–44. However, that framework is not employed in the unified, millenarian fashion of universal history, and Pufendorf subjects each ancient empire (especially Rome) to the same realistic, reason-of-state analysis as the rest of the work. Subsequent chapters

---

15. Pufendorf (2002b) and (2002c).

16. This comment is from the Preface, pp. 5–6, which also says: ". . . that the History of later Times is so much neglected is a great Mistake and want of Understanding in those to whom the Education of Youth is committed; for I lay down this as a Principle, That we are to study those things in our Youth, which may prove usefull to us hereafter, when we come to riper Years, and apply our selves to Business. Now I cannot for my life apprehend, what great Benefit we can expect to receive from Cornelius Nepos, Curtius, and . . . , as to our Modern Affairs, tho' we had learned them by heart, . . ."

all focus on the supposedly neglected but more useful study of modern history (i.e., the recent history of modern states), where the fourth monarchy—the Holy Roman or German Empire (chapter VIII)—appears merely as one political entity among others. The twelfth chapter, which is devoted to the papacy or the court of Rome, had appeared separately already in 1679 under the pseudonym of Basileus Hypereta and was neatly folded into the larger work.[17] The missing thirteenth chapter, as it were, as found in the later English and Latin versions, was not by Pufendorf himself but is most likely Crull's condensation of the *Continued Introduction.*[18]

According to the Preface, Pufendorf's respective accounts of individual states were based on their own historians, which made for some differing perspectives that he explicitly chose not to "reconcile or decide."[19] Moreover, as literary historians report, he relied mainly on one main source in each case,[20] including the following authors: Mariana (Spain), Vasconcellus (Portugal), Vergilius (England), Aemylius (France), Grotius (United Provinces), Simler (Switzerland), Lehmann (Germany), Pontanus (Denmark), Neugebauer (Poland), Herbsteiner (Russia), and Messenius (Sweden—in the *Continued Introduction*).[21]

17. [Pufendorf, Samuel] *Basilii Hyperetae historische und politische Beschreibung der geistlichen Monarchie des Stuhls zu Rom* (Leipzig: Wittigau; Franckfurt: Knoch, 1679). Niceron (1732), p. 284, does not identify the changes made to this work when it was incorporated into the *Introduction* in 1682. He notes, though, the appearance of a similar (also anonymous) work a few years later, *Theodosii Gibellini Caesaro-Papia* (Franckfurt, 1684), which some had attributed to Esaias Pufendorf. This latter work saw further editions in 1691 and 1720. Adlemansthal (1710), p. 800, notes its close similarity to *Basilii Hyperetae.* . . .

18. See Appendix 1, Publication History, pp. 606–7 (at notes 17–20) below.

19. Preface, p. 7.

20. Meusel (1782), p. 198, probably drawing on Ludwig, "Eulogium" (1721), pp. 480–81.

21. Juan de Mariana [1536–1624], *Historiae de rebus Hispaniae libri XXX, editio nova, ab auctore recensita, & aucta . . .* (Mainz, 1619); Diogo Mendes de Vasconcellos [1523–1599], *Deliciae Lusitano-Hispanicae: in quibus continentur De magnitudine Hispanici Imperii relatio: novi orbis regionum a Lusitanis subactarum brevis descriptio. De Lusitania ceterae Hispaniae adiuncta historia* (Cologne, 1613); Polydorus Vergilius [ca. 1470–1555], *Anglicae historiae libri vigintisex, ab ipso autore postremùm iam recogniti, adque amussim, salva tamen historiae veritate, expoliti Simon Grynaeus lectori* (Basel, 1546); Paulus Aemilius Veronensis [ca. 1455–1529], *De rebus gestis Fran-*

The controversial account of the papacy relied on "an anonymous Frenchman" and, perhaps, a student manual on church history by the Lutheran theologian Hieronymus Kromayer, who had taught the subject at Leipzig during Pufendorf's residency there.[22] Basileus Hypereta's preface (1679)—not transferred to the *Introduction*—also refers to church histories by M. Antonius de Dominis and Petrus Suavis but deems these unhelpful because of their focus on doctrinal disputes and clerical matters of little interest to politicians.[23] In general, the *Intro-*

corum, a Pharamundo primo rege usq[ue] ad Carolum octavum libri X, editio ultima superioribus emendatior (Basel, 1601); Hugo Grotius [1583–1645], *Annales et historiae de rebus Belgicis* (Amsterdam: Blaev, 1657); Josias Simler [1530–76], *De Helvetiorum republica, pagis, foederatis, stipendiariis oppidis, praefecturis, foederibus tum domesticis, eorumque origine ac legibus, tum externis, pagorumque singulorum privata reipublicae ratione, libri duo. Quibus etiam Helvetiorum res gestae, domi forisque, a Rodolphi ad Caroli V. Imperium exponuntur . . .* (Paris, 1577); Christoph Lehmann [1568–1638], *Chronica der freyen Reichs-Statt Speyer: . . . Zum andern, von Anfang und Auffrichtung deß Teutschen Reichs . . .* (Franckfurt am Mayn: Daniel Fievet, 1662); Johannes Isaac Pontanus [1571–1639], *Rerum Danicarum historia libris X* (Hardervici Gelrorum, 1631); Salomon Neugebauer [1611–54], *Historia rerum Polonicarum concinnata . . . libris decem* (Hannover, 1618); Sigismund von Herberstein [ca. 1486–1566], *Rerum Moscoviticarum commentarii . . . quibus Russiae ac Metropolis eius Moscoviae descriptio, chorographicae tabulae, religionis indicatio, modus excipiendi & tractandi oratores, itineraria in Moscoviam duo, & alia quaedam continentur . . .* (Basel, 1571); Johannes Messenius [ca. 1579–1636], *Historia suecorum gothorumque, per . . . Ericum Olai . . . concinnata, res commemorans LXVII potentissimorum regum, tertia marique gloriosissime gesta, primordio capto ab anno restauratae salutis humanae primo, ad MCDLXIV hoc thema continuans, . . .* (Stockholm, 1615).

The composition of the *Continued Introduction* (1686) took place concurrently with Pufendorf's *Twenty-six Books of Commentary on Swedish Affairs* (1686), which rested on thorough archival research. Also, his accounts made use of other sources at various points, including William Temple's *Observations upon the United Provinces of the Netherlands* (London, 1673) at note 39, p. 302, and note 50, p. 308, below.

22. Hieronymus Kromayer [1610–70], *Ecclesia in politia. Id est historiae ecclesiasticae centuriae XVI . . .* (Leipzig, 1666). See Döring's Introduction to "Brevis commentatio . . ." (1675), in Pufendorf (1995), p. 201. Palladini (1984) shows also that Pufendorf's account relied on Guicciardini.

23. Marco Antonio de Dominis [1560–1624], *De republica ecclesiastica libri X* (Heidelberg, 1618); and Paolo Sarpi [1552–1623], *Petri Suavis Polani* [pseud.] *historiae Tridentini libri octo: ex Italicis summa fide ac cura Latini facti*, editio quinta & ultima (Gorinchem, 1658). Also see Pufendorf's letter to Thomasius (December 30, 1688), in Pufendorf (1996), #158, pp. 235–36, where Pufendorf comments on the proper

duction relies on other authors mainly for the older, distant histories of individual states, but as the respective accounts approached his own time Pufendorf made more use of his own experience and research; for here, according to Ludwig, he held "the chief place."[24]

The final sections of each chapter, which were termed "politick remarks" or "politische Anmerckungen" by later authors, are of special note. Comprising Pufendorf's "Observations . . . concerning the good and bad Qualifications of each Nation, . . . as also what concerns the Nature, Strength and Weakness of each Country, and its form of Government"[25]—a kind of political commentary already found in *The Present State of Germany*[26]—they applied the Preface's distinctions about different types of state's interest (*ratio status*) to the peculiar form and condition of each country. Pufendorf was not the first to offer a history of individual European states as such, and others had lectured on the topic before, including Hermann Conring (1606–81) at Helmstedt and Johann Andreas Bose (1626–74), professor of history at Jena (since 1656) with whom Pufendorf was personally acquainted.[27] There

---

way to write ecclesiastical history and suggests that the results will differ in the case of a theologian and an honest man.

24. Ludwig, "Eulogium" (1721), p. 481.

25. Preface, p. 7. Note that Pufendorf refers to such observations "as are generally made" in this regard, suggesting that the approach was not new or unique to him. See note 57, p. xxiv, below.

26. See chapter VI on the form, and chapter VII on the strength and diseases, of the German Empire.

27. Hammerstein (1972), p. 239; Döring (1992b), pp. 159–60, note 473; and Valera (1986), 119–43, especially 122–26. Bose studied with Johann Heinrich Boecler (at Strassburg), a leading German Tacitist, before returning to Leipzig and then Jena, where he would have met Pufendorf. His *Introductio generalis in notitiam rerum publicarum orbis universi. Accedunt eiusdem dissertationes de statu Europae . . .* (Jena 1672, though based on lectures held already in 1662) is considered an early example of what became, in the eighteenth century, the science of *Statistik*, a historical and empirical study of individual states similar to that of Pufendorf in the *Introduction*. Conring had lectured on such topics already in 1660, also under the title of "notitia rerum publicarum." These lectures were issued against his will by two students in 1668, and they appeared at Geneva in 1675 under the title *Thesaurus rerum publicarum totius orbis*. See Behnen (1987), p. 77, note 3, and p. 83; and Pasquino (1986), especially p. 163, note 64, and pp. 164–65, note 70. Achenwall—one of the

were also contemporary analyses of Europe in terms of state's interest, such as Petrus Valckenier's *Das verwirrte Europa* (1677) and Christian Widemann's *Academia status* (1681).[28] The "new moment" in Pufendorf's approach was the emphasis on modern history and, especially in these sections, the concrete assessment of individual states and their external relations in terms of a normative notion of interest rooted in his natural law theory.[29] That is, it was the unusual combination of Pufendorf's philosophical theory of the state with his practical observations of contemporary political affairs that gave the work its pull.

Like many of Pufendorf's other works, the *Introduction* was well received and soon translated into other European languages (see Appendix 1, Publication History, p. 603). According to Ludwig (1695/1700), it gained many adherents (*Liebhaber*) and served as a "manual in history" for almost everyone.[30] Siebenkäs (1790) also referred to its popular, handbook status and noted its "important influence on the teaching of history," to which it had given "a new direction."[31] Brockwell (1702) considered it one of Pufendorf's "most Compleat and Perfect Pieces" and called him a "prophet" on the basis of its political analyses.[32] The Dedication of Etienne de la Chambre's (Bruzen de la Martinière's) grand 1721 French revision of the *Introduction* describes it as "the chief

---

eighteenth-century inheritors of this tradition—explicitly traced the origin of the term *Statistik* to the Italian notion of *ragio di stato*. More generally on the study of history at Protestant universities in Germany, see Scherer (1927), pp. 135–213; Bödeker (1986); and Boockmann (1987). Also see p. xxiv, note 57, below, and Appendix 1, p. 603, note 3.

28. Meinecke (1925), pp. 287–88, note 3. Petrus Valckenier, *Das verwirrte Europa. Oder, politische und historische Beschreibung, der in Europa . . . seither dem Jahre 1664 entstandenen . . . Kriegen, und leidigen Empörungen, nebenst deroselben Ursachen und Gründen, . . . in vier Teilen* (Amsterdam, 1677; the German edition); and Christian Widemann, *Academia status, ad status Europae cognoscendos* (Jena, 1681). Niceron (1732), pp. 165ff., lists many other works on Europe (under *Universal-Historie*) in the early eighteenth century.

29. Hammerstein (1972), p. 240.

30. Ludwig (1700), Preface, p. 19.

31. Siebenkäs (1790), p. 52.

32. Brockwell, Preface, in Pufendorf (1976).

work of a wise man who is regarded as the oracle of politicians."[33] These and other estimations were not confined to those with a vested interest in the work, such as its translators, editors, and commentators, but they also issued from the new scholarly journals in which Pufendorf's works, including his histories, were often reviewed.[34] Two such reviews are of particular note since Pufendorf replied to them in print—with his fictive "Two Letters . . . to Adam Rechenberg" (*Epistolae duae . . . ad Adamum Rechenbergium,* 1688).[35] The first appeared in the *Journal des Savants,* where the Abbé de La Rocque made minor corrections to Pufendorf's account—in *Twenty-six Books of Commentary on Swedish Affairs* (1686)—of France's role during the Thirty Years' War, evoking from the latter (in his first "letter") not only a complaint about La Rocque's pro-French and pro-Catholic bias[36] but also some valuable observations on the writing of history. The second, by Jean Le Clerc in the *Bibliotheque universelle et historique,* focused directly (via Cramer's 1688 Latin translation) on Pufendorf's *Introduction,* particularly its comments about religious freedom in the United Provinces (chapter VI).[37] This initial exchange with Le Clerc about the appropriate degree of religious toleration in a state continued with the latter's response to Pufendorf's "Two Letters," and with Pufendorf's *The Divine Feudal Law* (1695), which Le Clerc also reviewed some years later.[38]

33. Dedication, in Pufendorf (1721), vol. 1.

34. See the Reviews section of the Bibliography, pp. 647, and also Zurbuchen (1991), pp. 180–82; Palladini (1978), pp. 64–66; and Döring, in Pufendorf (1995), p. 462, note 43, and p. 467, note 59.

35. See Pufendorf (1995), pp. 488–506.

36. Abbé Jean-Paul de La Rocque, in *Journal des Savants* 15 (1687), pp. 112–20; see Döring's Introduction to Pufendorf's *Epistolae duae,* in Pufendorf (1995), pp. 460–67.

37. See VI.21, p. 308, and note 61, p. 178, below. Le Clerc reviewed Cramer's 1688 Latin translation of the *Introduction* in his *Bibliotheque universelle* 7 (1687), pp. 205–11. On background, see Döring's Introduction to "Epistolae duae," in Pufendorf (1995), pp. 467–71. Also see Appendix 2 in this book, p. 625, note 15.

38. Jean Le Clerc, *Bibliotheque universelle* 12 (1689), pp. 472–86. Le Clerc reviewed Pufendorf's *The Divine Feudal Law* in *Bibliotheque choisie* 7 [1705], p. 392. See Döring's Introduction to "Epistolae duae," in Pufendorf (1995), p. 467, note 59, and p. 477, note 80.

Pufendorf as Historiographer

What reviewers like Le Clerc, Rechenberg, Bayle, and (Henri) Basnage de Beauval appreciated about Pufendorf's historical writing matched his own assessment of what mattered.[39] Most important was the reliance on documentation and first-hand reports, rather than hearsay or speculation. As royal historiographer in Stockholm and Berlin, Pufendorf made thorough use of the archives to which he had privileged access. He also travelled in Europe to obtain source materials, and he attempted sometimes to obtain important records through personal connections—even from parties otherwise unlikely to provide them, such as the court of Rome.[40] Indeed, Pufendorf's principled reliance on archival materials—that is, his writing of "public" rather than "private" history[41]—sometimes provoked complaints that he had revealed state secrets and led to censorship of certain works for this reason.[42] Other commendations of Pufendorf's historiographical method noted his avoidance of speculation about the motives of historical actors, and his self-limitation to what he took to be the implications of the documentary evidence. Moreover, it was said, he did not ascribe malicious motives to the adversaries of those who had commissioned his works,

39. For more details on individual reviewers' comments, see Piirimäe (2008), pp. 246–48, and Piirimäe (unpublished manuscript), pp. 15–16, and 11–12.

40. On Pufendorf's work in the archives, see his letters to the Austrian councillor Johann Friedrich von Seilern (March 5, 1690), in Pufendorf (1996), #175, p. 262, ll. 34–35; and to Landgraf Ernst von Hessen-Rheinfels (mid-November 1690), #194, pp. 293–94, ll. 12–14; on his gathering of materials at Cassel, to von Hessen-Rheinfels (March 29, 1690), #176, p. 264, ll. 23–30; and on his approaches to Christina, Salzer (1904), p. 6, note 15.

41. Moraw (1962), p. 173.

42. On the posthumous censorship of Pufendorf's *Nineteen Books on the Achievements of Frederick William, the Great Elector of Brandenburg* (1695), see Adlemansthal [Dahlmann] (1710), #42, pp. 786–87, and #43, p. 795; Seidler (1997), p. 215; and Palladini (2003) and—for Leibniz's role—(1999b). On Swedish attempts to censor or control Pufendorf's work, see Piirimäe (unpublished manuscript), pp. 11–13. Some Swedes were upset by Pufendorf's ethnographic characterization of them in the *Continued Introduction* (1686), which was summarized by Crull in XIII.18. See p. 599, and note 40, in the text below, and also note 57 in the Editor's Introduction.

and he left moral judgment about events to the reader. In Tacitean fashion (*sine studio et ira:* "without bias or malice," *Annals* I.1), he sought explicitly to avoid interpolating personal emotion or prejudice into his accounts.[43]

By avoiding both "the writing of falsehoods and the concealment of truths" the historian is distinguished, so Pufendorf, from a fabulist and a flatterer. His role also differs from those of an advocate (lawyer) and a judge. The former is essentially a special pleader or propagandist for his clients, seeking in every way to advance their cause, even by distorting the record; while the latter presumes to render verdicts from an acontextual or disinterested meta-perspective, a view from nowhere, as it were. The historian, instead, should describe things as he finds them and leave judgment to the reader. However, this does not preclude the expression of a particular view. On the contrary, as Pufendorf somewhat misleadingly observed, a historian also plays the tune of the one who pays or feeds him, and so (the former) Queen Christina's complaint (at Rome) that his account of Sweden's involvement in the Thirty Years' War had displeased Catholics was to him "ridiculous." What he meant by such statements was better expressed, perhaps, by two other similes: the historian as secretary or architect who fashions a literary or physical edifice for a ruler by using the latter's own materials and plans. Thus, two historians can write ". . . the history of two hostile princes . . . with the same appearance of truth [*pari specie*], as long as each adjusts himself to the opinions, impressions, and interests of his own prince." Indeed, Pufendorf remarked, waxing autobiographical, the same skillful individual can write both histories, build the same information into both accounts, and even have one borrow from the other, as long as the general perspectives are different. In fact, this describes his own histories of Frederick William and Charles Gustav, respectively, and to some

---

43. In his posthumous *Seven Books of Commentary on the Affairs of Charles Gustav, King of Sweden* (Pufendorf [1696]), I.1, p. 5, Pufendorf says that "the only commendation I expect for my work from reasonable people is that I have drawn it honestly from reliable sources, without any admixture of emotion or prejudice."

extent the various accounts in the *Introduction,* where the same events are treated in the context of differing national histories.[44]

Historically, the early modern historiographer was situated between two more general or (apparently) less partial roles: that of the so-called universal (or salvation) historian and that of later, more disaffiliated historians purporting to work only for the party of humanity.[45] Despite clear continuities with the classical, "rhetorical" tradition that high-lighted virtuous exemplars and ideal types,[46] his own accounts were "pragmatic" in the sense of focusing on the concrete interconnected-ness of actual events.[47] In fact, the historiographer's role evolved along with its subject matter, which was the early modern states and rulers in need of legitimating narratives to maintain their internal sovereignty, external independence, and relative claims upon one another. Arising in the late fifteenth and sixteenth centuries, in Iberia and Italy, the formal office of royal historiographer moved gradually from there into northern Europe, where it culminated in the seventeenth century to-gether with the process of state-building.[48] Despite or perhaps because of its overt nationalistic function, the role was international in charac-ter. That is, not only was it shared or iterated in many states, which had their own historiographers, but it also became professionalized or bu-reaucratized, with the individuals filling it often switching their employ like diplomats, soldiers, and other state officers.[49] Most significantly, historiographers' works were mainly aimed at an international audi-ence, including a state's or ruler's antagonists. In Pufendorf's terms, the

44. For detailed supporting references for ideas in this paragraph, see Seidler (1997).

45. See Meinecke (1925), pp. 293 and 300–301.

46. There is much in Pufendorf's dedications and prefaces about the exemplary value of history. See Seidler (1997), pp. 209–10.

47. See Reill (1975), pp. 41–43, and Krieger (1965), pp. 172–73, for the distinction and the evolving meaning of "pragmatic." Martinière's "Avertissement" to Pufendorf (1721) refers to the *Introduction* as a new kind of "universal history." Also see Simo-netti (1746), in Blanke (1991).

48. Piirimäe (unpublished manuscript), pp. 2–8, and (2008), pp. 242–44; Moraw (1962), p. 166.

49. Meinecke (1925), p. 299.

historiographer was a kind of "public interpreter"[50] whose task it was to lay before the world the case of the political actors he represented and to defend their claims and policies in terms of rational and moral criteria. The crucial and, perhaps, paradoxical assumption was that this could be done without sacrificing truth.

History, Natural Law, and Interest

By recording, portraying, and analyzing political agency as such (as exhibited in the diplomacy, negotiations, treaties, alliances, and other strategic decision-making that were Pufendorf's main concern), history facilitated the extension of natural law reasoning from individuals to the collectives that they comprised or represented. And by articulating the concrete interests of competing states, it allowed their association with the obligations of rulers, thereby linking international to natural law, and politics to morality. This seems to be the meaning of the statement in the "Eloge historique" prefixed to the 1753 French edition of the *Introduction:* that without history, *On the Law of Nature and of Nations* would have been nothing but "abstract speculation," and that Pufendorf composed the *Introduction* as a guide for young people so that they would not be misled by the theoretical treatise.[51] Of course, the *Introduction* and other works were not simple, textbook applications of the latter's principles. Still, they were presumed to be consistent with these in the same way that Pufendorf's historical knowledge about political affairs, both ancient and modern, gave substance and intelligibility to the natural law theory that it in a sense generated. That is, the theory not only emerged from practice as depicted in history, but it also guided it in turn.

The prime directive of Pufendorf's natural law theory, the law of sociality, enjoins humans "inasmuch as [they] can, [to] cultivate and maintain toward others a peaceable sociality that is consistent with the

---

50. Letter to von Seilern (March 5, 1690), in Pufendorf (1996), #175, p. 262, l. 49.
51. "Eloge historique," p. xiv, in Pufendorf (1753). The "Eloge" is an expanded version of the "Mémoires" prefixed to Pufendorf (1721), where the same observation is made.

native character and end of humankind in general."[52] It is dictated by the realities of humans' so-called natural state or condition, which reveals them to be self-interested, imperfect, vulnerable, and, accordingly, insecure beings. To escape from this undesirable condition, which also impedes further enculturation and moralization, the sociality law compels humans to establish states, namely, composite moral persons, which so unify their members' disparate wills that a common peace and security can be achieved.[53] However, states can be effective vehicles for individual self-preservation only if they meet certain formal requirements, specifically if they are "regular" in the sense of having clearly defined, undivided, and supreme or inexorable command structures, or sovereignty, toward those that establish and compose them. Furthermore, to realize their purpose, states (or their rulers) must correctly identify and pursue their own interests, as determined by their particular characteristics and also their relation to other states with whom they interact.[54] For this they require accurate historical knowledge (especially of recent affairs) and acute political analysis, such as is provided by Pufendorf's *Introduction* and other historical works, which are in effect governing "manuals" for rulers.

The *Introduction*'s Preface[55] provides a brief anatomy of state's interests that underlies Pufendorf's analytical historiography in general, and also his natural law assessment of particular states' concretely conditioned obligations toward their own citizens and competing powers. There are three basic distinctions, the first between real and imaginary interests. The latter are self-defeating in that, if pursued, they damage the state. To exemplify this, Pufendorf refers to the striving for hegemonic superiority or "universal monarchy," which other states are both inclined and compelled (given their obligations to their own citizens) to oppose with all their might, thus producing a counterproductive,

---

52. *On the Law of Nature and of Nations,* II.3.15; translation emended from Pufendorf (1994), p. 152. See note 85 below.

53. *On the Law of Nature and of Nations,* VII.2.13.

54. *On the Law of Nature and of Nations,* VII.8.1–4: rulers must subsume their personal interests to those of their states.

55. See pp. 5–9 below.

international state of war. The former are subdivided into perpetual and temporary interests, the first of which depend on internal characteristics of states such as their location, geography, natural resources, type of people, and the like; the second are determined by a state's relation to its neighbors and their relative strengths and weaknesses. It is clear from these descriptions that a state's real and imaginary interests may change depending on its current international setting, and that such changes may warrant shifts in its internal and external policies, including alliances and treaty obligations. A third distinction, between private and public interest, is equally significant, and it applies both to in-state factions seeking to undermine the state's authority and to sovereigns who put their personal concerns above the civic welfare.

The long historical accounts that constitute the bulk of the *Introduction* (and the *Continued Introduction*) actually make scant formal use of these distinctions but consist instead, as Meinecke put it, of "a rather primitive and conventional treatment of materials."[56] Still, the varying fortunes of the different historical personae encountered there, both individual and collective, clearly invite such analysis. Moreover, the cumulative impact of the political opportunism, treachery, organized violence, and other contingencies reviewed—that is, the actual history of European states—facilitates Pufendorf's comparative assessment of each state's current interests at the end of the respective chapters. These final sections, which were a major reason for the popularity of the work, follow a general pattern in each case, addressing things like the following: the peculiar characteristics (negative as well as positive) of a state's people; its natural resources, geographical advantages and disadvantages, and form of government; and its external relations to other states whose actions could affect its own.[57] Here one clearly

56. Meinecke (1925), p. 295. Given the work's range, this is almost inevitable. In his accounts of individual states Pufendorf still uses an explicitly annalistic style, even listing successive years in the margins.

57. Such and other concrete, empirical details were also central to Conring's and Bose's "notitia rerum publicarum," and to the eighteenth-century tradition of *Statistik* whose historical-political studies began (in Germany) to "replace" Pufendorf's *Introduction* in the early 1730s. See Behnen, p. 92; also pp. xvi–xvii, note 27 above, and Appendix 1, pp. 603–4, note 3, below.

Pufendorf's national characterizations were sometimes resented, and as his letter sees the distinctions among interests at work, particularly permanent and temporary ones. As noted before, the great attraction of the *Introduction* for all sides was its move beyond a general and even stylized reason-of-state analysis to a detailed examination of specific states' concrete interests,[58] for this not only gave everyone a better sense of how the game was played but also allowed them to tailor their policies so as to avoid conflict and reap (mutual) advantage. The separate end-of-chapter accounts amounted, in short, to a kind of political advice in each case, if not on how to alter or improve a particular state's international situation then certainly how best to maneuver and survive in it.

These features of the *Introduction* also link it with Pufendorf's activities as political advisor and apologist—a role inevitably involving the consideration of different types of interest. Since early modern territorial and dynastic claims were often historical in nature—besides searching for deeper or broader justifications like those provided by natural law—broadly competent scholars like Pufendorf were regularly entrusted with this role.[59] Thus, the latter produced a number of political tracts justifying the policies of his current employers, both at Heidelberg and at Stockholm. These include the aforementioned *Prodromus* and the piece on Skanderbeg, which exhibit the different levels on which such arguments were offered: the former tract defended the particular claims of Karl Ludwig's Palatinate against other powers within the empire, while the latter represented the interests of Christian Europe as a whole against the Turks.

More instructive here, however, are two later pieces produced by

---

to Friese (October 26, 1692), in Pufendorf (1996), #222, p. 347, ll. 3–7, reveals, the Swedes in particular were incensed by his comments in the *Continued Introduction*. (Also see *Introduction*, XIII.18, p. 599 below, and note 42 above.) His anthropological or ethnographical descriptions were rooted in the study of classical antiquity and already evident in Heidelberg dissertations such as *De Phillipo Amyntae filio* (1664), where they provide the background to his political analysis of Macedonian, Phocian, Athenian, Spartan, and other peoples' affairs.

58. Dufour (1996), p. 117.

59. Toyoda (2011), p. 94, and note 45, suggests that Leibniz's failure to complete his history of the Welf (Guelph) dynasty was deeply frustrating to Georg Ludwig, who sought to rely on it in his pursuit of electoral status, and that it helps to explain Leibniz's political isolation at court, especially toward the end of his life. See VIII.7, p. 332, note 7, below.

Pufendorf for Charles XI of Sweden.[60] The *Discussion of Certain Writers of Brandenburg* (1675), written while he was professor of natural law at Lund, defends Sweden's attack (in December 1674) on Brandenburg, then allied with the emperor against France (Sweden's ally). It argued that Brandenburg (which banned the tract in 1677) was acting against its own interests by maintaining its imperial alliance, pursuing, in a word, an imaginary or "chimerical" rather than a real interest.[61]

In 1681, when the situation in Europe and Sweden alike had changed, with France supplanting Austria as the most likely threat of a "universal monarchy," Pufendorf (now royal historiographer in Stockholm) published another political pamphlet, *On the Occasions When Sweden and France Have Been Allied,* which once again defended Sweden, though now for its more recent, anti-French policy. Significantly, the latter work was commissioned by the new chancellor, Bengt Oxenstierna, who had supplanted the pro-French Magnus de la Gardie at the Swedish Court and whose policy differences with Pufendorf's brother, Esaias, led eventually to the latter's resignation from Swedish service and his condemnation (*in absentia*) to death for treason. Pufendorf himself left Sweden for Brandenburg in 1688, albeit only temporarily (on loan) and on friendlier terms.[62]

The upshot of these difficult and complicated affairs was, as Pufendorf expressly repeated in the *Discussion,* that states' interests are not immutable but depend rather on "the change of events . . . and alterations in one's own and one's neighbors' affairs."[63] This meant that rulers had to orient themselves by current realities and not maintain policies

---

60. "Discussio quorundam scriptorum Brandeburgicorum . . . ," in Pufendorf (1995), pp. 236–80 (Döring's Introduction) and 281–336 (text); and "De occasionibus foederum inter Sueciam et Galliam et quam parum illa ex parte Gallia observata sint," at pp. 338–59 (Döring's Introduction) and pp. 360–85 (text). The full title of the latter work suggests the justification for Pufendorf's shift in view: ". . . and how little those alliances have been observed on the part of France."

61. Pufendorf (1995), p. 266.

62. Samuel also disagreed with Esaias about William III's overthrow of James II; he approved of this action (which was actively supported by Brandenburg) while Esaias opposed it. See Pufendorf (1995), p. 357, note 32.

63. Pufendorf (1995), p. 288; also Preface, p. 8, below.

and alliances that might endanger their state.[64] Moreover, given the layers of human identification and commitment, the interests of historians themselves could change, raising difficult questions about loyalty or patriotism, and about personal versus public interest.[65]

Finally, it is worth noting that Pufendorf's end-of-chapter discussions are genuinely interesting and informative, not only about the respective states canvassed but also his general view of Europe. Judgments—or, as he might say, observations—abound. Thus France (chapter V) is said to be swarming with people who are collectively characterized as warlike, good at fortifications, of a merry disposition, lecherous, and economically savvy at attracting others' wealth. Its military power is land-based, its government an absolutist monarchy, and its clergy in possession of half the nation and relatively independent of Rome. As the most powerful state in Europe, France need fear no one except Germany, although only hypothetically because of the latter's irregularity or divided sovereignty.[66] In contrast, the United Provinces (chapter VI) is also populous for its size, is a sea power, and is generally incapable of land service and thus dependent on mercenaries in this respect. Its people are open-hearted and honest, parsimonious and punctual, and both eager and fit for trade. Magistrates there are generally merchants, and commoners are prone to become a dangerous rabble. The different provinces are divided by jealousies and rivalries, and thus are but imperfectly joined into a loose confederacy or system held together by necessity and interest. The irregularity and instability of this form of government are further increased by the role of the Prince of Orange, though it remains in his interest as well to maintain the status quo. The latter includes a toleration of many religions, which Pufendorf (disagreeing with Le Clerc) regards as a political weakness,

64. See *On the Law of Nature and of Nations,* V.8.3–4 (on economic partnerships), and VIII.6.14 (on the priority of a state's own citizens).

65. See Seidler (2005).

66. See note 26 above, and *On the Law of Nature and of Nations,* VII.5.14–15; also the Heidelberg dissertation, "Samuels von Puffendorff gründliche Untersuchung von der Art und Eigenschaft eines irregulairen Staats . . ." [*De republica irregulari,* 1668, in Pufendorf (1675), pp. 381–452], in Adlemansthal (1710).

even though he also mentions positively that the Dutch rarely hate and persecute one another on account of their beliefs. As for security, the Dutch must maintain their naval strength and keep France at bay by supporting Spain's claims to the Spanish Netherlands. They have a strong interest in maintaining freedom of commerce around the globe, where they have a growing commercial empire.[67] These and the other accounts are detailed, piquant, and bold (reminding readers of Monzambano's unabashed account of Germany), albeit according to the general rules of historiography described earlier. They offered readers a compelling primer of European power politics at the time.

The Popish Monarchy

The challenge of organized religion to early modern statecraft explains the inclusion of the long chapter on the papacy. The Protestant Reformation had loosed many bonds within Christendom, dissolving former wholes and turning internal into external conflicts in both the religious and the secular spheres. Protestants, while politically liberated from Rome in some areas, remained threatened by Catholic powers in and out of the empire, well through the end of the seventeenth century. Pufendorf traced the problem—at least in its latest configuration—to the election of Charles V, whose combined roles as king of Spain and Holy Roman Emperor had given the pope and ecclesiastical princes inordinate power in the empire.[68] This remained so at the Westphalian negotiations (1648), which the papacy could not prevent but nonetheless obstructed.[69] At the heart of the conflict was the issue of secular sovereignty in increasingly complex and pluralistic societies over which the papacy still claimed a spiritual dominion, and the associated question of concrete control over so-called ecclesiastical benefices or goods, which had important fiscal and political ramifications. Unlike Luther,

67. On France, see V.25–29, pp. 262–71, and on the United Provinces, VI.19–22, pp. 300–312.
68. XII.38, pp. 509–10. Meinecke (1925), pp. 290–92.
69. See Baena (2007), p. 628, on how the pope's refusal to renounce "spiritual sovereignty" over all lands affected the concrete negotiations between Spain and the United Provinces in 1647.

whose opposition to Catholicism had been mainly doctrinal, Pufendorf worried more about the papacy's worldly ambitions and interpreted its spiritual claims largely as a front for these.[70] In his view, ". . . since the beginning of the World, there has not been set up a more artificial Fabrick than the Popish Monarchy," whose maintenance has required all the more craftiness and deception as its ends have differed from those of other states, namely the security and peace of subjects.[71] Indeed, because its claims challenged secular sovereignty and thereby endangered both intra- and international peace, which were divinely sanctioned,[72] political Catholicism was for Pufendorf a false religion.[73] Like the *Introduction*'s other chapters, his historical and political account of the papacy was intended as an instructive exposé. Even if it did not succeed in getting the pope to recognize his own state's true interest, the account could help secular (Protestant) rulers to protect their states and fulfill their natural law duties toward their subjects.

Unsurprisingly, the papacy chapter earned (in 1692) the *Introduction* a place on the *Index of Forbidden Books,* and an earlier ban in Vienna, though everyone there read it anyway.[74] This was because the tide had already begun to turn, and people recognized the truth of Pufendorf's

70. Döring's Introduction to "Brevis commentatio," in Pufendorf (1995), pp. 197, 203 note 17, 213–14; also see Friedeburg (2008).

71. XII.30, pp. 482–86, below; and already in *The Present State of Germany* (2007), VIII.8, p. 233.

72. *On the Law of Nature and of Nations,* VII.3.2.

73. For the distinction, see "De concordia verae politicae cum religione Christiana" (1673), §18, in Pufendorf (1675), pp. 581–82. Also, in *Of the Nature and Qualification of Religion in Reference to Civil Society,* §35 [36], in Pufendorf (2002c), pp. 80–81, Pufendorf says that Catholic theological interests are too much linked to the popish monarchy and thus takes a dim view of reconciliation. This is the same position that he held in *The Present State of Germany* (Pufendorf, 2007), VIII.8, pp. 230–37.

74. The *Introduction*'s first listing on the *Index* was in 1692, in the form of Rouxel's first (1687) French edition; it was placed there a second time in 1736, in the form of Cramer's third (1702) Latin edition. See DeBujanda (2002), pp. 731–32. Pufendorf reports in an earlier letter to Rechenberg (October 20, 1688), in Pufendorf (1996), #148, pp. 213–14, that while the *Continued Introduction* was sold without incident in Vienna, the *Introduction* was forbidden there. The importance of the papacy tract to Pufendorf himself emerges from the fact that it is mentioned more often in his correspondence than any of his other works. See Döring at Pufendorf (1995), p. 202, note 16. Pufendorf refers to the Index at XII.35, p. 504, below.

concluding observation about the divergence of political and religious interests: just as two states of the same religion could be opposed because of their respective secular interests, the latter could also make allies of states with different religious colorations. The former situation was exhibited by the rivalry between France and Spain and that between England and the United Provinces; and something like the latter obtained when emperor and pope alike allowed William of Orange and his Protestant allies to overthrow the Catholic James II of England because of fears about his French alliance and its possible disturbance of the European balance of power.[75] Second, various elements of Pufendorf's case had already been rehearsed in several earlier works and were therefore not unfamiliar to his European audience. One source of its ideas was the eighth chapter (titled "On the German Empire's Reason of State") of *The Present State of Germany* where, in the 1667 edition, Pufendorf had first a Catholic and then a Protestant speaker offer trenchant criticisms of the Catholic church in terms later iterated by the *Introduction*.[76] Another precedent was Pufendorf's "Brief Commentary on the Bull of Clement IX on the Suppression of Religious Orders," which appeared (along with the already rare bull itself) in Pufendorf's *Dissertations* (1675). Clement's bull (issued on December 6, 1668) had dissolved—because their founding missions were supposedly no longer served—the religious orders of the Jesuates (*sic*) and Hieronymites, so that their confiscated resources could be used to assist the Venetian defense of Crete against the Turks. Although the bull was quickly suppressed upon the belated realization that it might also justify Protestant attempts to appropriate church goods for secular purposes, Pufendorf used the opening to reject papal claims of authority and to criticize clerical interference in state affairs.[77] Another work in the *Dissertations* volume, "On the Agreement of True Politics with Religion" (1673) also helped lay the basic groundwork for Pufendorf's analysis in the papacy chapter.

75. See below at XII.41, pp. 520–21, and Seidler (2001), p. 349.
76. Pufendorf (2007), VIII.5–8, pp. 221–37; and VIII.9–10, pp. 237–46.
77. The entire bull and Pufendorf's commentary thereon appeared in Pufendorf (1675), pp. 632–72. For the commentary alone, and Döring's discussion thereof, see Pufendorf (1995), pp. 196–233.

Two decades after Pufendorf's death the work was deconfessional-
ized by Christian Thomasius in his commented edition of 1714. The
latter did not hesitate to criticize his friend and mentor in the extensive
notes and introduction accompanying the text, where he argued that
Lutherans labored under the same kinds of prejudices or "remnants
of the papacy" as the Catholics whom Pufendorf so mistrusted. Specifically, he claimed that Lutherans also permitted useless speculation
and excessive abstraction to occlude the true doctrine of salvation; they
considered themselves to have the only true religion and condemned
Catholics and other Protestants as heretical and wicked; and they used
the power of secular authorities to suppress revelations of religious error and impropriety in their own case.[78] After Thomasius, the work
was often reprinted in the eighteenth century as part of the *Introduction,* albeit with strategic omissions and alterations to appease Catholic
sensibilities.[79] Its final appearance (before the present edition)—again
as an independent tract—came in mid-nineteenth-century Germany
(1840), ironically amid the revived confessional conflicts following the
Napoleonic era, which were induced in part by a redrawing of territorial boundaries that created religiously more mixed populations.[80]
The irony is compounded by the fact that one of the key disputes that
led to the so-called crisis year of 1837 was the increasing number of
mixed marriages between Protestants and Catholics—an issue that had
evoked one of Thomasius' early essays[81] and one into which the papacy

78. Dedicatory letter by Thomasius, in Pufendorf (1714).

79. See Meusel (1782), p. 199, on the Martinière edition of 1743–48. Martinière's
"Eloge historique," in Pufendorf (1753, vol. 1), p. xix, has a negative view of the
popedom chapter, even while the edition still includes it. Also, there is a clear effort
to avoid antagonizing Catholics starting with the seventh (1711) edition of Crull's
translation (see Appendix 1, Publication History). Pufendorf himself provided the
model for such judicious alterations by removing various anti-Austrian and anti-
Catholic remarks from the second, posthumous edition (1706) of *The Present State
of Germany.*

80. See Drury (2001), especially pp. 110–31, and Kraus (2007).

81. Christian Thomasius, *A Legal Discussion of the Question, Whether Two Noble
Persons in the Roman Empire, One of Whom Is Lutheran and the Other Calvinist, May
Marry One Another in Good Conscience [Rechtmäßige Erörterung der Ehe- und Gewis-
sensfrage, Ob zwey Fürstliche Personen im Römischen Reich, deren eine der Lutherischen*

again inserted itself. Thus Weise's thematically appropriate resurrection of Pufendorf as a supporter of the "friends of truth," whose work might still be useful in opposing the growing "system of darkness."[82] The conflict between confessions continued into the latter part of the century, including Bismarck's *Kulturkampf,* which sought the cultural assimilation of Catholics into a Protestant Prussia. However, despite Pufendorf's resonance with the strongly antipapalist tenor of that debate, there is no further evidence of Weise's edition, nor of any other subsequent reprint of the work.

History, Natural Law, and International Law (*Ius Gentium*)

As noted above, the consideration of states' interests is continuous with the analysis of their natural law foundation. The latter is an internal, constitutive matter involving a state's legitimate claim to sovereign authority over its members, while the former is externally oriented and concerns the effective performance of its natural law obligations (particularly security) in an international context, on which the claim to internal sovereignty rests. In short, a state's *raison d'état* is rooted in its *raison d'etre.* To be sure, the reality of separate states pursuing their own interests presents an interstate coordination problem, as it were, in the same way that the so-called state of nature did or does for individuals.[83] And its resolution depends in both instances on how the natural law is conceived (for example, as compatible with or antithetical to selfish-

---

die andere der Reformirten Religion zugethan ist, einander mit gutem Gewissen heyra-then können?] (Halle, 1689). Though Thomasius's essay was about inter-Protestant marriages only, the fact does not undermine the anticonfessional thrust of his piece.

82. Weise's Preface to Pufendorf (1839), p. iv. Cf. Hobbes, *Leviathan,* part IV, chap. 44.

83. On Pufendorf's comparison of individual and international states of nature, see Seidler, "Introduction to Pufendorf" (1991), pp. 40–42, and 53. In this dissertation ("De statu hominum naturali," 1674; also in Pufendorf [1675], pp. 582–632), Pufendorf models the latter state on the former. Christov (2008), pp. 95–102, claims that the modeling is actually the reverse, as does Tuck (1999), p. 140.

ness) and on the kind of (real or apparent, permanent or temporary) and the manner in which self-interest is pursued.

Conflicts of interest among states are regulated by international law (the law of nations, *ius gentium*), which Pufendorf conceives and designates, following Hobbes, as "the natural law of states."[84] It rests like natural law in general on "considerations of our need [*indigentiae nostrae*], which is relieved, as much as can be, by sociality," and it straddles Pufendorf's distinction between absolute and hypothetical precepts of the natural law, where the former applies to all humans as such while the latter presupposes certain human institutions like speech, property, or civil society.[85] Hypothetical natural laws are no less constraining than absolute ones, but are merely contingent upon the prior establishment of certain institutions under or within which the natural law's general dictates are instantiated. Thus, there are broad, strategic absolutes in international law such as the prohibition on unnecessary wars, as well as other, equally stringent hypothetical rules like those pertaining to the manner in which wars are waged (they may not make peace impossible). Both of these differ from other, tactical requirements originating in the legislation of particular states, from custom, or from tacit agreements: such as specific methods of property acquisition, types of contract, and conflict etiquette. These Pufendorf calls the "voluntary or positive law of nations"—which falls outside of what is required for "the security, interest, and safety of nations" and, more important, is not really a "law" at all because there is no (human) superior to enforce it.[86]

---

84. *On the Law of Nature and of Nations,* II.3.23, in Pufendorf (1934b), p. 226; cf. Hobbes, *On the Citizen,* 14.4–5.

85. *On the Law of Nature and of Nations,* II.3.23 (translation by MJS), and II.3.24. Note the important qualification ("as much as can be" [*quam maxime*]), which matches that ("inasmuch as he can" [*quantum in se*]) within the general law of sociality itself. See note 52 above. That is, sociality is no panacea or perfectionist command, only the best possible solution under given circumstances; there is a fundamental realism or conditioned character in Pufendorf's natural law theory at all levels.

86. *On the Law of Nature and of Nations,* II.3.23, in Pufendorf (1934b), pp. 226 and 228; also I.6.4, pp. 89–90.

Likewise excluded from international (and thus natural) law as such, says Pufendorf, are "special agreements of two or more peoples, usually defined by leagues and agreements of peace,"[87] for these are infinite in number and usually temporary. By contrast (and, no doubt, mindful here of *Gundaeus Baubator Danicus*), the law of embassies or the inviolability of ambassadors clearly is an instance of international law, for "such persons are necessary, in order to negotiate, preserve, and strengthen by treaties and agreements that peace which the law of nature itself commands men to embrace by all honourable means." The final condition points to the duties of ambassadors (and their hosts) and limits their activities, preventing them, for instance, from spying on one another—unless this is typically assumed or mutually accepted by the parties involved.[88] Just as natural law commands humans only to form states as such rather than particular kinds of states, a similar, justified flexibility applies to interstate arrangements. And just as citizens are not perpetually bound to particular states in many instances, so states themselves need not always continue their associations or honor their commitments, at least within certain limits (typically procedural, involving notification requirements and such). The concrete interests of states, both permanent and temporary, depend on many real-world factors such as those described in the *Introduction*'s "political remarks," and it is the duty of rulers, for their citizens' sake, to adapt to these. This has some controversial consequences in areas like immigration policy, the duty of hospitality, freedom of religion, the right of transit, trade policy, and preemptive war—in each of which Pufendorf seeks to develop a qualified position that privileges a state's own security and

87. *On the Law of Nature and of Nations,* II.3.23, in Pufendorf (1934b), p. 229.

88. *On the Law of Nature and of Nations,* II.3.23, in Pufendorf (1934b), p. 228. Also, according to *The Whole Duty of Man,* II.16.5, in Pufendorf (2003), p. 239, wiles and deception are acceptable, though an outright violation of one's faith is not. On the origin of and need for embassies (I.20), and the problem of ambassadorial spying (II.4), also see Alberico Gentili, *De legationibus libri tres* (Hanau: Wilhelm Antonius, 1594). Pufendorf cites Gentili (in his *Dissertationes academicae selectiores* and *On the Law of Nature and of Nations*), but not this particular work, even though he owned the second edition (1607). See Palladini [1999a], #651, p. 155.

welfare while seeking also to respect that of others, as well as the absolute, universal, and humanitarian dictates of natural law.[89]

In a dangerous world of imperfect and self-interested states, one duty of rulers or governments is to equip their states with "innocent means of defense" (such as geographical advantages like ports and passes, and resources for possible wars); others are to get themselves appropriate and timely allies and "carefully [to] observe the undertakings of others."[90] The latter is Pufendorf's final recommendation in the chapter on the duty of supreme sovereigns in *On the Law of Nature and of Nations*: ". . . the plans and undertakings of neighboring nations should be carefully ascertained and observed (an end which is served to-day by permanent representatives at their courts . . .), while friendships should be assiduously cultivated, and prudent alliances contracted."[91] Of course, such friendships and alliances are always conditional and must yield to the primary interests of one's own subjects, and one who thinks otherwise does so at his peril.[92] That is why, precisely, the role of observers is so important. The early modern historiographer was, like ambassadors and other legates, a reporter of the affairs of others, past and present, and thus a servant of his own state's interests. This is clearly true of the *Introduction* itself, which usefully mapped the political geography of Europe. However, in this work Pufendorf also contributed to a more general interest by sharing his relative assessment of states' disparate histories and current conditions with all the major

89. *On the Law of Nature and of Nations*, III.3, on the general duties of humanity. Pufendorf had a more limited view of trade and economics as a force in international affairs than later natural law thinkers such as Vattel, and he was more willing to limit others' access to trading opportunities based on considerations of a state's own interest. See Hont (2005).

90. *On the Law of Nature and of Nations*, II.5.6, in Pufendorf (1934b), p. 273.

91. *On the Law of Nature and of Nations*, VII.9.13, in Pufendorf (1934b), p. 1127.

92. *On the Law of Nature and of Nations*, VIII.6.14, p. 1306; and VII.1.8, p. 963: the probity of others is liable to change; VIII.9.5, pp. 1334–35. In the latter passage Pufendorf emphasizes the concomitant duty to warn one's ally of one's intent to change one's allegiances. On the temporality and contingency of alliances, also see "De occasionibus foederum inter Sueciam et Galliam et quam parum illa ex parte Gallia observata sint," in Pufendorf (1995), especially pp. 384–85.

parties. In this way, the work might be said to transcend—albeit not undermine—its partisan purpose. Perhaps this was so because it began life as a pedagogical instrument rather than a formal monument of statist historical remembrance.

Shared knowledge can create a more-even playing field, it can restrain hegemonic aspirations and encourage political caution, and by describing the actual complexities of human affairs it can support a general balance of power. This, along with an emphasis on alliances and state systems,[93] was Pufendorf's preferred solution to the opposed problems of international anarchy and universal monarchy—not some kind of inclusive international counterpart to the sovereign state. For as he noted in the early *Elements of Universal Jurisprudence*, ". . . that one body, in such huge dimensions, would be threatened through internal disturbances by the same inconveniences as those which exercise the human race, and almost greater ones, divided, as the race is, into a larger number of smaller sovereignties."[94] That is, a *de facto* cosmopolis in the human sphere would only transform external conflicts into internal ones less amenable to solution. The continued appeal of the *Introduction* in the eighteenth century was due precisely to such considerations rather than the details of its rough and annalistic historical accounts. And the many corrections, continuations, additions, deletions, and other alterations made to the work by others merely sought to ensure its utility for a changing Europe.[95] It would have been easy

93. Dufour (1996), pp. 109ff. See *On the Law of Nature and of Nations*, VII.2.2 and VII.5.16–18, on the importance of confederacies or state systems for mutual protection; and Pufendorf's dissertation *On State Systems* [*De systematibus civitatum*, Heidelberg, 1667, in Pufendorf [1675], pp. 264–330). Meinecke (1925), p. 281, says that Pufendorf did not sufficiently appreciate the possibility of a confederated state (*Bundestaat*) as opposed to a confederacy of states (*Staatenbund*).

94. II.5.1, in Pufendorf (2009), p. 368.

95. Thus, Martinière says in his "Avertissement" to Pufendorf (1721) that he has corrected Pufendorf's work in three ways: (1) by giving an account of all the ruling houses of Germany and Italy that might be of current importance, (2) by continuing Pufendorf's chapters up to the present, and (3) by indicating in the notes such changes as Pufendorf could not have foreseen. Moreover, to reflect this broadening of Pufendorf's work, and because the new edition includes as well a French translation (from the German translation) of Crull's *An Introduction to the History of the*

to let the work lapse gradually into historical irrelevance if its purpose had been a purely historical one. However, its continual adaptation to new circumstances indicates that it was also a sort of political treatise, a scholarly intervention into real states' affairs that sought to make history and not merely to report it.

On J.C.M.D.

Jodocus Crull (d. 1713) was born in Hamburg, earned a medical degree at Leiden (1679), and soon after emigrated to England, where he became a fellow of the Royal Society (1681) and a licentiate of the Royal College of Physicians (1692).[96] His absence from the rolls of the Royal Society suggests that he could not pay the dues, a fact that may help to explain his busy literary career as translator, compiler, and author—a role sometimes difficult to trace because his books were often anonymous or attributed only by initials (such as J.C.M.D.). Crull translated two of Pufendorf's works: the present *Introduction,* which appeared in 1695 and saw ten more editions through 1753, and *Of the Nature and Qualification of Religion in Reference to Civil Society* (1698), whose original had appeared in 1687 shortly after Louis XIV's revocation (1685) of the Edict of Nantes.

Other translations include Dellon's *Voyage to the East-Indies* (London, 1698), and *The Present Condition of the Muscovite Empire . . . in Two Letters . . . with the Life of the Present Emperor of China, by Father J. Bouvet* (London, 1699). Among works composed by Crull himself are *The Antient and Present State of Muscovy, Containing an Account of All the Nations and Territories under the Jurisdiction of the Present Czar* (London, 1698), *The Jewish History . . . Being an Abridgment of Sr. Roger l'Estrange's*

Kingdoms and States of Asia, Africa and America (see note 97 below), Martinière changes its title to *Introduction à l'histoire generale et politique de l'univers.* More generally, Pufendorf's *Introduction* also prompted other works of the same genre, particularly by Johann Peter Ludwig and Jacob Paul Gundling. On these, see Hammerstein (1972), pp. 234–44.

96. On Crull, see Goodwin, (1993), Bedford (2004), and Zurbuchen's Introduction to Pufendorf (2002c), pp. xvii–xix.

Josephus (London, 1702), *With a Continuation* (1708), and *The Complete History of the Affairs of Spain* (London, 1707). This listing is significant because its mention of the East-Indies, Muscovy (Russia), China, [Israel], and Spain support the attribution to Crull of another work associated with Pufendorf's *Introduction,* namely *An Introduction to the History of the Kingdoms and States of Asia, Africa and America, both Ancient and Modern, According to the Method of Samuel Puffendorf . . .* (London, 1705). That work became the official Part 4 of Pufendorf's (wider) *Introduction* in the eighteenth century, when it was also reprinted a number of times.[97]

While Crull was a competent translator of Pufendorf,[98] other estimations of his literary work have been more dismissive, perhaps unfairly and anachronistically so. These include designations like "wretched composition" for Crull's *The Antiquities of St. Peter's, or the Abbey Church of Westminster . . .* (London, 1711), and "crypto-pornographer" for his detailing of Ivan the Terrible's cruelty and sexual deviancy in *The Antient and Present State of Muscovy.* Crull is also described as a "hack" for "plunder[ing]" other authors and opportunistically "catching the market," as after Czar Peter the Great's visit to London in 1698. Some of these practices might be expected of an "impecunious *émigré*" with a "primary and overriding need to produce a vendible book," while others seem less objectionable than they might today, given the early modern activity of "cultural translation," where notions of literary ownership and intellectual property were less stringent, and perhaps more realistic, than in later periods.[99]

97. Crull also authored the condensation of Pufendorf's *Continued Introduction,* which appears as chapter XIII of his translation of the *Introduction.* See p. xiv above, and the Publication History below, at (1) pp. 606–7 and (2) pp. 624–25. Interestingly, Crull's volume on Asia, Africa, and America has no "political remarks" at the end, which is in accord with Gundling's comment (see Hammerstein [1972], p. 243) that only those histories are of interest that have a bearing on current European conditions. Accordingly, Franckenstein did add such comments to his own 1706 supplement on Italian states (that is, Part 3 of the eighteenth-century *Introduction*), but only up to the year 1678—in order to stay in line with Pufendorf's own chapters.

98. See the "Note on the Text," pp. xlii–xliv.

99. Goodwin (1993), p. 262, and Bedford (1996), pp. 210, 207, and 211. On early modern translation practices, see Burke (2007).

Early English readers and translators of Pufendorf were of various political leanings, making it difficult to maintain that the latter was drafted by one side or the other. For instance, Edmund Bohun (translator of *The Present State of Germany,* 1696) was a Tory who attacked Algernon Sidney (in *A Defense of Sir Robert Filmer,* 1684) and edited Filmer's *Patriarcha* (1685),[100] while Locke's friend, James Tyrrell, included significant portions of Pufendorf's *Of the Law of Nature and of Nations* in his *Patriarcha non Monarcha* (1681) as an example of a nonabsolutist position that rejected divine right (being in turn criticized for this by Bohun).[101] Crull's situation is more ambiguous. To be sure, his translation of Pufendorf's *Of the Nature and Qualification of Religion* was dedicated to William, Lord Craven, a Royalist and financial supporter of both Charles I and Charles II, and a member of James II's privy council. However, in the 1690s Craven was also a patron of letters who received many dedications from a variety of authors desperate for employment. Moreover, although Crull's political sympathies in *The Antient and Present State of Muscovy* may have differed from Milton's, whose *A Brief History of Moscovia* (1682) he excerpted, he notes in the same Dedication to Lord Craven Pufendorf's caution to young lawyers—in the appendix to that work, which criticized the monarchical absolutism espoused by the Dutch Hobbesian, Adrian Houtuyn—that "under the Pretense of maintaining the Prerogatives of Princes, they should not be prodigal of their Liberty and Property," adding his own assurances that Pufendorf's aim was "very remote from maintaining an Arbitrary Power in the State."[102]

Crull also wrote two works on Denmark: *Denmark Vindicated . . .* (London, 1694), and *Memoirs of Denmark . . .* (London, 1700).[103] Nei-

---

100. See the editor's Introduction to Pufendorf (2007), pp. xxiii–xxvi.

101. Seidler (2001), pp. 329–30. More generally, see Saunders and Hunter (2003).

102. Bedford (1996), p. 208; and Crull's "Introductory Epistle" in Pufendorf (2002c), pp. 3–6.

103. [Jodocus Crull], *Denmark Vindicated: being an answer to a late treatise called, An account of Denmark, as it was in the year 1692, sent from a gentleman in the country, to his friend in London* (London: Newborough, 1694), and [Jodocus Crull], *Memoirs of Denmark, containing the life and reign of the late K. of Denmark, Norway, &c. Christian V. together with an exact account of the rise and progress of those differences*

ther was as such of particular note, but the former is significant as a spontaneously offered rebuttal to Robert Molesworth's *An Account of Denmark as It Was in 1692* (London, 1694), a flamboyant Whiggish critique of Denmark's monarchical institutions and national characteristics that greatly irritated the Danes.[104] Whether Crull's reply to Molesworth indicates his own political leanings or, again, only another attempt to "catch the market" (he seems to have expected some reward from the Danish delegation in London) is unclear. Either way, the work also links him to the Danish playwright, essayist, and composer Ludvig Holberg, who later responded to Molesworth by way of Pufendorf. Holberg's *Introduction to the Histories of the Foremost European States* (1711) was essentially a Danish version of Pufendorf's *Introduction* that served as a general preparation for his *Description of Denmark and Norway* (1729). This latter work offered a systematic, subtle, and detailed defense of Danish institutions against Molesworth's critique, situated within a larger historical and philosophical context. Holberg returned (through Danish history) to Pufendorf's natural law theory and its rationale of common security as the basic purpose of states— rejecting the divine right justification that Molesworth had attributed to the Danes—and he defended the limited sovereignty of the Danish monarchy in comparison to other forms of government.[105] This was essentially Tyrrell's position, and it may also have been Crull's.

---

now on foot betwixt the two houses of Denmark and Holstein Gottorp; with all the remarkable circumstances thereunto belonging taken from authentick letters and records (London: John Nutt, 1700).

104. Olden-Jorgensen (2007), pp. 68–87.

105. Of course, there had been divine right justifications of the Danish monarchy, particularly a controversial work by the Danish court preacher Hector Gottfried Masius, whose *The Importance of Lutheranism for Princes* [*Interesse principum circa religionem evangelicam*] appeared in 1687, shortly before Molesworth's ambassadorial stay in Copenhagen (1689–92). Masius's arguments were rejected by both Pufendorf and Christian Thomasius. On this complex episode, see Grunert (2004), pp. 119–74.

A NOTE ON THE TEXT

The text of this Liberty Fund edition reproduces *An Introduction to the History of the Principal Kingdoms and States of Europe, by Samuel Puffendorf, Counsellor of State to the Present King of Sweden, Made English from the Original* (London: Printed for M. Gilliflower at the Spread-Eagle in Westminster-Hall, and T. Newborough at the Golden Ball in St. Paul's Church-Yard, 1695). It has been checked against the first (1682) and second (1684) German editions (see Appendix 1 at the end of this volume), mainly to detect omissions and additions but also, especially in the chapter on the papacy (chapter XII), for the accuracy and consistency of Crull's translation, whose variations are indicated in the text or notes.

In Crull's original, Pufendorf's Preface is followed by an alphabetical index called "The Table." This has been moved to the rear as "Index I" (see p. 661), followed there by the modern "Index II." In its place at the front of the work I have inserted a "List of Chapters" referenced to the pagination of the present, Liberty Fund edition. Thus, the page numbers in Index I refer to Crull's original—shown in the text by horizontal angle brackets < . . . >—while those in Index II refer to the pagination of the current, edited reprint. Also, Crull's original enumeration contains some errors, the most serious at p. 292, which is followed by p. 273 instead of p. 293, thus repeating the sequence 273–92. This error is negotiated in the angle bracket enumeration, and in Index I, by marking the repeated page numbers with a lowercase "r": thus one finds both <275> and <r275> (= <repeated p. 275>) in the text.

Like[+] Pufendorf's German original, Crull's translation contains relatively few paragraph divisions within the numbered sections of each chapter. Since those sections are often quite long and dense, I have inserted many additional breaks in order to make the narrative more accessible and to give relief to contemporary readers. Given their quantity, these breaks are inserted without notice. However, Crull's original divisions are also retained, and identified by a superscripted "plus" sign after the first word, as at the beginning of this paragraph.

The marginal dates in Crull's shoulder notes mostly overlap with Pufendorf's, except that the latter inserted his dates into the text itself, preceded by A., An., or Anno ("in the year"). Since Pufendorf's dates are more accurately associated with the events to which they refer, I have used them as my guide, instead of following Crull's (or his typesetter's) often vague and sometimes erroneous marginal placements. Indeed, for reasons of accuracy, consistency, and fluidity, I have also followed Pufendorf's practice by placing all marginal dates back into the text itself. There, Crull's marginal dates are enclosed in backslashes, such as \A. xxxx\. Where Crull omits a date found in Pufendorf, I have inserted it by using the standard designators for such additions from Pufendorf's text, for example, {A. xxx}. In those few instances where Crull inserts a marginal date not reflected in Pufendorf's text, I have not distinguished it from Crull's other marginal dates: that is, it too appears as \A. xxxx\.

In the case of discrepancies between Crull's and Pufendorf's dates, especially where the difference is slight, I have followed the latter. However, in the case of more significant divergences, and where Crull is more obviously correct, I have followed his dates instead. I have not checked all of the dates against the historical record, and so they should be used with caution. Moreover, as will be obvious, there are many other dates in the manuscript besides the reinserted marginal dates; these remain without special indication. That is, backslashes \A. . . .\ and braces {A. . . .} are used exclusively for marginal dates in Crull and their in-text counterparts in Pufendorf.

Crull's translation is accurate and reliable on the whole: as a native of Hamburg he had no difficulty with Pufendorf's German, including its many colloquialisms (which he sometimes converted into English counterparts and more often ignored, thus losing some of the flavor of Pufendorf's text). Still, he worked quickly, and this sometimes gives his translation a run-on character, especially when compared with Pufendorf's stylistically more measured German. Such awkwardness is most noticeable when Crull bridges or conflates two or more of Pufendorf's sentences—where, it seems, he is in too much of a rush to search for a more suitable accommodation for the varying periodicities of English and German, and where, occasionally, he loses the thread or actually misunderstands Pufendorf's meaning. Such passages are merely identified and clarified in the notes, and I have not otherwise altered or rearranged the translation. The archaic punctuation and capitalization are also retained, except where (as also indicated) it has been necessary to divide sentences (in accord with Pufendorf's original) in order to accommodate newly introduced paragraph divisions. In such instances, the change typically involves no more than different end-of-sentence punctuation and capitalization of the next word.

More generally, I have as a rule (with some exceptions) not corrected, modernized, or standardized Crull's language. The latter was often careless with the spelling of names, and even when he hit upon suitable equivalents in English, he did not use them consistently. Sometimes he pronominally personified or depersonified referents in Pufendorf's German (for example, "France" for "the Frenchman," or the reverse), which makes for some awkward passages that are difficult to clarify. Moreover, his vocabulary is typically less colorful than Pufendorf's, sometimes more opinionated, and often not as technical or philosophically self-conscious. Thus Crull freely interchanged terms like "papacy," "papal chair," "popish monarchy," "the pope," and "church of Rome," as well as political terms like "sovereignty," "state," and "commonwealth"—either as he pleased or to suit his adoptive English audience.[1] Specifically, he substituted "ecclesiastical" for Pufendorf's "spiritual," "civil" for "worldly," and "monarchy" for "sovereignty." Since all these reflect significant distinctions in Pufendorf, I have inserted bracketed in-text substitutions and clarifications throughout and have added explanatory footnotes in the case of longer expressions. Brackets

1. See Saunders and Hunter (2003) on the transformation of Pufendorf's text in early English translations.

are also utilized in places where Crull's translation seems clearly off the mark; there, the expression being corrected is enclosed within single quotation marks. Occasionally, too, where Crull's expressions may be misleading or obscure (albeit technically not wrong), I have added more-apt or contemporary English terms. Finally, where it may seem to a current reader that Crull's text is lacking a word, I have inserted it to preserve continuity in thought or style. That is, despite seeking to respect Crull's text as such, I have treated it mainly as a vehicle to Pufendorf rather than a work in its own right.

The following in-text symbols are used:

> ⁺ = Crull's own paragraph divisions
>
> {. . .} = text *omitted* by Crull, including marginal dates
>
> <. . .> = text *added* by Crull (including pleonasm, periphrasis, elaboration)
>
> |[. . .]| = text *changed* by Crull from the original (intentionally or not)
>
> [. . .] = editorial substitutions, clarifications, insertions, or corrections
>
> '. . .' = translated text *corrected* in the subsequent [. . .]

\A. . . .\ = marginal or shoulder dates reinserted into the text

It may be noted here that John Chamberlayne translated Pufendorf's chapter XII (on the papacy) as a separate work in 1691. This translation also seems reliable, though I have not made a complete or systematic comparison with Crull. As there is no translator's preface to Chamberlayne's text, it remains unknown whether he translated Pufendorf's long essay in its earlier, separately issued form (1679), or the basically identical chapter XII of the *Introduction* (1682). Christian Thomasius's annotated German text (1714) of the same chapter matches Pufendorf's original. However, Weise's nineteenth-century preface (1839) to the same work admits that, for the sake of readability, he has "softened" (*gemildert*) some of Pufendorf's terms (*Formen*), replaced antiquated expressions and constructions, and substituted German equivalents for foreign usages.[2]

Finally, Pufendorf's works are listed by title in a special subsection ("Works by Pufendorf") of the Bibliography, ordered there by date of publication. Thus, Pufendorf (1995) refers to *Kleine Vorträge und Schriften* . . . , and so on. Other bibliographical entries are listed separately by their authors' names.

2. See Appendix 1, Publication History, p. 613.

ACKNOWLEDGMENTS

For access to their collections and/or providing copies/microforms of original works, I am grateful to the following libraries: British Library, Herzog August Bibliothek Wolfenbüttel, Kungliga Biblioteket (National Library of Sweden), Universitäts- und Landesbibliothek Sachsen-Anhalt (Martin Luther Universität Halle-Wittenberg), Staatsbibliothek Berlin (SBB) Preussischer Kulturbesitz, Württembergische Landesbibliothek Stuttgart, University of Helsinki Library, Library of Congress, Northwestern University Library, Syracuse University Library, University of Virginia Library, and University of Florida Library.

In addition, I would like to thank the following persons for various kinds of assistance: Kari Saastamoinen (University of Helsinki) for procuring copies of texts from the Helsinki University Library; Petter Korkman (formerly, University of Helsinki) for Swedish translation and reminding me of Le Clerc's review of the *Einleitung;* Pärtel Piirimäe (University of Tartu) for introducing me to the *Hamburgische Bibliotheca* in the reading room at Wolfenbüttel, and for additions to the Publication History; Hugh Phillips (Western Kentucky University) for translating Russian bibliographical entries; Åsa Soderman for obtaining microfilms in Stockholm; Fiammetta Palladini (Berlin) and Peter Schröder (University College London) for comments on my introductory essay and the publication history; Mark Somos (University of Sussex), Hans Blom (Erasmus University Rotterdam), Blake Landor and Matthew Loving (University of Florida) for help with references and biography; and Knud Haakonssen for checking Brask's version of the *Einleitung,* for inviting my participation in this series, and for his editorial support throughout the project. Finally, I am grateful to the careful Liberty Fund editors for making helpful suggestions and, of course, corrections. All these individuals have improved the work and made it easier for me, alone, to accept responsibility for any remaining deficiencies.

AN

INTRODUCTION

TO THE

HISTORY

Of the Principal

Kingdoms and States

OF

EUROPE.

By *SAMUEL PUFFENDORF,*

Counsellor of State to the present King of *Sweden*.[1]

Made English from the Original.

LONDON,

Printed for *M. Gilliflower* at the *Spread-Eagle* in
Westminster-Hall, and *T. Newborough* at the *Golden
Ball* in *St. Paul's Church-Yard.* MDCXCV.

1. Charles XI (1655–97).

To His EXCELLENCY,

CHARLES

Duke of Shrewsbury:

His Majesty's Principal
Secretary of State;

Knight of the most Noble
Order of the Garter, &c.

And one of the Lords Justices
of England.[2]

SIR,

I Should scarce have had the boldness to prefix your great Name to this
Book: had I not been fully persuaded that the extraordinary worth of
my Author would strongly plead for me to your Excellencies Generosity. For, since my intention was, that the *Sieur Puffendorf*'s Introduction to the History of *Europe* should appear in no less Lustre in this
Kingdom, than it has heretofore done in most parts of *Europe;*[3] I could
not, without injuring a Person so famous for his Learning, and the rank

2. Charles Talbot, duke and twelfth earl of Shrewsbury (1660–1718), was raised
a Catholic but converted to Protestantism in 1679. He was one of seven English
lords who invited William III of Orange to invade England in 1688. Made a duke in
1694, he served as William's secretary of state during 1689–90 and 1694–99. He also
worked for the recognition of Georg Ludwig (1660–1727) of Hannover as George I
in 1714.

3. There had been editions in several other languages before Crull's 1695 translation appeared. See Appendix 1, Publication History, and Appendix 2, List of Early
Modern Editions and Translations.

he bears in one of the Northern Kingdoms,[4] submit his Treatise to the Protection of any other Person, than your Excellency, whose judging Power is so universally acknowledged: If it endures this Test, it must pass current [be accepted] in this Nation. The high Station in which you are now plac'd by the choice of the wisest and bravest of Kings,[5] having put your Merits above the Praises of a private Person; I shall rather admire than pretend to enumerate them, wishing, that as your Actions have hitherto been most effectual in preserving your Country's Liberty, so your Counsels may for the future prove as fatal to the *French,* as the Swords of your glorious Ancestor's in former Ages.[6] Thus recommending my self to your Excellencies Protection, I beg leave to subscribe my self,

Your Excellencies,
Most devoted Servant,

J.C.M.D.

4. Apparently Crull did not know of Pufendorf's move from Sweden to Brandenburg in 1688, nor of his death in 1694, when he wrote this Dedication.

5. See note 2, p. 3 above.

6. In 1694, England was at war against France in league with other European powers (Spain, the United Provinces, and the Holy Roman Empire) in what is alternately called the Nine Years' War, the War of the Grand Alliance, or the War of the League of Augsburg (1689–97), which ended with the Treaty of Ryswick (1697).

THE PREFACE TO THE READER

That History is the most pleasant and usefull Study for Persons of Quality, and more particularly for those who design for Employments in the State, is well known to all Men of Learning.[1] *It is therefore requisite, that young Gentlemen should be exhorted early to apply themselves to this Study, not only because their Memory is vigorous, and more capable to retain what they then learn, but also because it may be concluded, that he who has no Relish for History is very unlikely to make any Advantage of Learning or Books.*[2]

It is a common Custom as well in Publick as Private Schools, to read to their Scholars some ancient Historians; and there are a great many who employ several Years in reading of Cornelius Nepos, Curtius, Justin[us] *and* Livy, *but never as much as take into their Consideration the History of later Times. 'Tis true, and it cannot be deny'd, but that we ought to begin with the ancient Historians, they being equally usefull and pleasant; but that the History of later Times is so much neglected is a great Mistake and want of Understanding in those to whom the Education of Youth is committed; for I lay down this as a Principle, That we are to study those Things in our Youth, which may prove usefull to us hereafter, when we come to riper Years, and apply our selves to Business. Now I cannot for my life apprehend, what great Benefit we can expect to receive from* Cornelius Nepos, Curtius, *and the first Decad of* Livy,[3] *as to our Modern Affairs, tho' we had learn'd them*

1. For Pufendorf's views on the study of history, see the Editor's Introduction, pp. xix–xxii.
2. On the importance of both ancient and modern history in the education of noble youth, see Pufendorf's "Unvorgreiffliches Bedencken wegen Information eines Knaben von Condition," in Pufendorf (1995), §§5–6, pp. 544–57.
3. Livy's books on Roman history were divided (probably by later copiers) into decades or groups of ten. The first decade begins with the foundation of Rome and covers some 460 years.

by Heart, and had, besides this, made a perfect Index *of all the Phrases and
Sentences that are to be found in them: Or if we were so well vers'd in them,
as to be able to give a most exact account, how many Cows and Sheep the*
Romans *led in Triumph when they had conquer'd the* Aequi, *the* Volsci,
and the Hernici.[4] *But what a considerable Advantage it is to understand
the Modern History as well of our Native Country, as also its neighbouring
Nations, is sufficiently known to such as are employ'd in States Affairs.*

*But it is not so easie a matter to acquire this Knowledge, partly because
those Histories are comprehended in large and various Volumes; partly because they are generally publish'd in the native Language of each Country;
so that he who intends to apply himself to this Study must be well vers'd in
Foreign Languages.[5] To remove in some measure this Difficulty, I did some
Years ago, for the Benefit of some young Gentlemen in* Swedeland, *compile
a Compendium, in which was comprehended the History of such States as
seem'd to have any Reference unto this Kingdom, with an Intention only to
give them the first tast[e] of those Histories fitted chiefly for their Improvement. But after this rough Draught had fallen into other Hands, I had
some reason to fear, lest some covetous Bookseller or another might publish
it imperfect, as I have known it has happen'd to others, whose Discourses
scarce premeditated, have been publish'd against their Will and Knowledge.
Wherefore I saw my self oblig'd, notwithstanding I had but little Leisure,
to revise the said Work, and after I had render'd it somewhat more perfect,
rather to publish it, such as it is, than to suffer that another should rob me
of it.[6] I hope therefore, that the Discreet Reader will look favourably upon
this Work, not as a Piece design'd for Men of great Learning, but adapted*

4. These were three ancient peoples in central Italy.
5. On Pufendorf's sources for the individual chapters, see the Editor's Introduction, notes 21–24, pp. xiv–xvi.
6. There was a Swedish translation of Pufendorf's *Introduction* two years before
his own (German) version appeared in 1682, viz., *Samuelis Pufendorf Inledning til
historien, angående the förnähmste rijker och stater, som för tijden vthi Europa stå
oprätte,* translated into Swedish by Petrus Brask (Stockholm, 1680); presumably this
is the unauthorized work that Pufendorf refers to here. Little is known of Brask (ca.
1650–ca. 1690) other than that he was from Linköping; if he was not a student of
Pufendorf at Lund, he probably got hold of a set of class notes from another student.
See "Brask, Petrus" under Biographical Entries, in the Bibliography, p. 649.

*to the Apprehensions and Capacities of young Men, whom I was willing to
shew the Way, and, as it were, to give them a tast[e], whereby they might be
encouraged to make a further search into this Study.*

*I must here also advertise the Reader, That because I have taken the
History of each Kingdom from its own Historians, a great Difference is to
be found in those several Relations, which concern the Transactions of some
Nations that were at Enmity, it being a common Observation, That their
Historians have magnify'd those Factions which have prov'd Favourable to
their Native Country, as they have lessen'd those that prov'd Unfortunate.
To reconcile and decide these Differences was not my Business, but to give a
clearer insight into its History. I have added also such Observations as are
generally made concerning the good and bad Qualifications of each Nation,
nevertheless, without any Intention either to Flatter or Undervalue any; as
also what concerns the Nature, Strength and Weakness of each Country, and
its form of Government:[7] All which I thought might be an Inducement to
young Gentlemen when they Travel or Converse with Men of greater Experience in the Affairs of the World, to be more inquisitive into those Matters.
What I have related concerning the Interest of each State, is to be consider'd
as relating chiefly to that Time when I compos'd this Work. And, tho' I must
confess, that this is a Matter more suitable to the Capacity of Men of Understanding than young People, yet I could not pass it by in Silence, since this
is to be esteemed the Principle, from whence must be concluded, whether
State-Affairs are either well or ill managed.[8]*

*I must also mention one thing more, which may serve as an Instruction
to young Men,* viz. *That this Interest may be divided into an Imaginary
and Real Interest. By the first I understand, when a Prince judges the Welfare of his State to consist in such things as cannot be perform'd without dis-
quieting and being injurious to a great many other States, and which these
are oblig'd to oppose with all their Power: As for Example, The Monarchy*

7. Such a comparison of sovereign states was already a feature of Pufendorf's *The
Present State of Germany* (1667), chapter VII, where he discussed the "strength and
diseases" of the German Empire in relation to its neighbors.

8. The changing interests of states in response to altered historical circumstances
motivated the frequent updating and revision of the *Introduction* by others during
the following century.

of Europe, *or the universal Monopoly, this being the Fuel with which the whole World may be put into a Flame.* Num si vos omnibus imperare vultis, sequitur ut omnes servitutem accipiant? If you would be the only Masters of the World, doth it thence follow, that all others should lay their Necks under your Yoke?[9] *The Real Interest may be subdivided into a Perpetual and Temporary. The former depends chiefly on the Situation and Constitution of the Country, and the natural Inclinations of the People; the latter, on the Condition, Strength and Weakness of the neighbouring Nations; for as those vary, the Interest must also vary. Whence it often happens, that whereas we are, for our own Security, sometimes oblig'd to assist a neighbouring Nation, which is likely to be oppress'd by a more potent Enemy; we at another time are forc'd to oppose the Designs of those we before assisted; when we find they have recover'd themselves to that degree, as that they may prove Formidable and Troublesome to us.*[10]

But seeing this Interest is so manifest to those who are vers'd in State-Affairs, that they can't be ignorant of it; one might ask, How it often times happens, that great Errors are committed in this kind against the Interest of the State. To this may be answer'd, That those who have the Supream Administration of Affairs, are oftentimes not sufficiently instructed concern-

9. Tacitus, *Annales* XII.37.7–9. In the first edition of *The Present State of Germany* (1667), Pufendorf worried about Austria's aspirations to universal monarchy; by the late 1680s, when he was preparing the second (posthumous, in 1706) edition, the threat was embodied by France. This mandated significant revisions, especially in chapter VIII.

10. Such shifts in states' interests often involved a concomitant change in personal loyalties. Like other early modern scholars in the employ of princes, Pufendorf's duties at Heidelberg and in Sweden included the defense of his respective lords' interests. Thus, he played an active, publicist's role in the so-called Wildfangstreit that pitted Karl Ludwig against his neighbors. See the Introduction to *The Present State of Germany*, pp. x–xii. Later, at Lund, he penned the "Discussio quorundam scriptorum Brandenburgicorum" (1675) at the request of Charles XI, justifying Sweden's unprovoked attack (in support of its French alliance) on Brandenburg during the Franco-Dutch War (1674–79). In 1681 he published another political pamphlet, the "De occasionibus foederum inter Sueciam et Galliam," which again defended Sweden, though now for its more recent, anti-French policy. His earlier, anti-Brandenburg stance understandably caused him some apprehension when he transferred to Berlin in 1688. On this, see the Editor's Introduction, pp. xxv–xxvii. Also, see Seidler (2005), pp. 349–50, on the relation of such changes in states' interest and personal commitments to Pufendorf's notion of patriotism.

ing the Interest both of their own State, as also that of their Neighbours; and yet being fond of their own Sentiments, will not follow the Advice of understanding and faithfull Ministers. Sometimes they are misguided by their Passions, or by Time-serving Ministers and Favourites. But where the Administration of the Government is committed to the Care of Ministers of State, it may happen, that these are not capable of discerning it, or else are led away by a private Interest, which is opposite to that of the State; or else, being divided into Factions, they are more concern'd to ruin their Rivals, than to follow the Dictates of Reason. Therefore some of the most exquisite parts of Modern History consists [sic] in this, that one knows the Person who is the Sovereign, or the Ministers, which rule a State, their Capacity, Inclinations, Caprices, Private Interests, manner of proceeding, and the like: Since upon this depends, in a great measure, the good and ill management of a State. For it frequently happens, That a State, which in it self consider'd, is but weak, is made to become very considerable by the good Conduct and Valour of its Governours; whereas a powerfull State, by the ill management of those that sit at the Helm, oftentimes suffers considerably. But as the Knowledge of these Matters appertains properly to those who are employ'd in the management of Foreign Affairs, so it is mutable, considering how often the Scene is chang'd at Court. Wherefore it is better learn'd from Experience and the Conversation of Men well vers'd in these Matters, than from any Books whatsoever.[11] And this is what I thought my self oblig'd to touch upon in a few Words in this Preface.

---

11. Pufendorf notes in the Dedication (to the young Charles XII of Sweden) of his *Continued Introduction* (1685) how William II de Croy (1458–1521), lord of Chièvres and guardian of the young Charles V (1500–1558), would not allow his charge to be instructed in history by his tutor, Adrian of Utrecht (later Pope Adrian VI) but reserved this task for himself, because the use of history to discern one's true interests "tends not to be learned in universities" but through practical experience. Ironically—given the severe criticism in the *Anhang* (1688; see Appendix 1, Publication History, p. 606)—this anecdote is attributed in the shoulder note to Antoine Varillas's *La pratique de l'education des princes, ou histoire de Guillaume de Croy . . . gouverneur de Charles d'Autriche qui fut Empereur Cinquième du nom* (Amsterdam, 1684), which Pufendorf owned (see Palladini, [1999a], #1762, p. 415). Pufendorf's opinion of Varillas was apparently changed by the intervening *Histoire des revolutions arrivées dans l'Europe en matière de religion* (Paris, 1686).

An Introduction to the History of the Principal Kingdoms and States of Europe

LIST OF CHAPTERS

An Introduction to the History of
the Chief Kingdoms and States
now in *EUROPE.*

✜ CHAPTER I ✜

Of the Ancient Monarchies, and more especially of the Roman, *out of whose Ruines arose several Kingdoms and States.*

§1. No Man of Common Sense, imagines, that at the first Propagation of Mankind, there were such Governments as are among us at this time. But in those Times each Father, without being Subject to any Superiour Power, governed his Wife, Children and Servants, as a Sovereign. Nay, it seems very probable to me, that even to the time of the Deluge, there was no Magistracy, or any Civil Constitution; but that the Government was lodged only in each Father of his Family. For it is scarce to be imagined, that such abominable Disorders could have been introduced, where the Power of Magistrates and Laws was exercised: And it is observable, that after once the Rules of Government were Constituted, we do not find that Mankind in general did run into the same Enormities, of which God Almighty was obliged to purge the World by an Universal Punishment, though the Root of the Evil was remaining as well after as before the Deluge. It seems also, that for a Considerable time after the Deluge this Paternal Government continued in the World. <2>

§2. But the reason why the Fathers of Families left this Separate way of living, and joyned in a Mutual civil Society, seems to be, That among the Neighbouring Families, sometimes Quarrels used to arise, which being often decided by Force, drew along with them very great Inconveniencies, to prevent which, it was thought necessary for the Preservation of Peace and Quietness among Neighbours, to referr the Decision of such Matters to the Judgment of some of the wisest and most Considerable among them. After the increase of Mankind, it was also easily to be observed, how difficult it would prove for a Single Family to defend itself against the Joint Conspiracy of a malicious Party, to Oppose which, the Neighbours living so near, as to be able to assist one another in case of Necessity, did enter into a Society Mutually to defend themselves against their Common Enemies. That they might do this with the better Success, the Administration of the whole Society was committed to him, who appeared most Considerable for his Wisdom and Valour. It is also very Probable that such as by Common Consent sought out new Habitations, chose a Leader, who both in their Journey, and in the Country, which they possessed themselves of, had the chief Direction of Affairs: And this office of a Judge, Head, or Leader by degrees degenerated [changed] into that sort of Government, which *Aristotle* calls *Heroical,* which is nothing else but a *Democracy* under the Authority of one of the Citizens, who has a Power rather to Advise than to Command the rest. And this seems to be the most ancient Form of *Republicks:* for the Fathers and Rulers of their Families could not so soon forget their Liberty, as not to Reserve to themselves a share in the Government by which their Consent was required to be given unto all Matters, which were to be decreed in the Name of the whole Society.

§3. But at what time precisely these Societies were first Instituted, and which of them is to be esteemed the most Ancient, is not easie to be determined; for though commonly the *Assyrian* Empire is taken for the first Monarchy,[1] yet it is not from hence to be con-<3>cluded, that

---

1. A reference to the millenarian four monarchies (Assyrian/Babylonian, Persian, Macedonian, Roman) scheme of human history based on chapters 2 and 7 of the Old Testament book of Daniel.

the same was the first civil Society; since it is evident that this Empire acquired its Greatness by swallowing up Lesser States. And those Wars which the *Assyrian* Kings waged against other States, do abundantly testifie, that besides the *Assyrian,* there were also other Civil Societies even at that time in the World. And here is to be observed, that as all human Affairs do not come immediately to Perfection, so were the first Institutions of Civil Society very simple and imperfect, till by degrees the Supreme Civil Power, together with such Laws and Constitutions as were requisite for the maintaining of a Civil Society, were instituted. The first Common-wealths also were very small, and their Territories of a very little extent, so that it was easie for the Citizens to assemble, either to Consult or to Defend themselves against a Foreign Power. It is evident out of History, that the deeper you search into the most ancient Times, the more Separate small Common-wealths [*Staaten*] you will meet withal, out of the Union of which great Empires in Process of time did arise, some of those Uniting themselves by common Consent, others being Subdued by the more Powerfull.

The first States were very small and imperfect.

§4. Among these great Empires, the *Assyrian* is commonly reckoned the most Ancient, the reason of which may probably be, That those Parts were Sooner, and More Inhabited than other places, which being later possessed had Fewer Inhabitants. Wherefore the *Assyrians* might without much difficulty overcome one small Common-wealth after another, and by Subduing some, make way for an Entire Conquest over the rest, that had not then learned the advantage of a joint Power and Confederacy. The vast Armies with which *Ninus* and *Semiramis* (the first Founders of this Monarchy) did over-power far distant Nations, make the common Chronologies very doubtfull: But to settle this is not to our present purpose. But by what means the Kings of this vast Empire did bridle the Conquered Nations, ought to be remembred, Two of them being most remarkable.[2]

The Assyrian Empire.

The First was, That they intending to imprint an Extraordinary Character of their Persons into the Minds of the People, they always

By what means this Empire was maintained.

2. This is a good example of how Pufendorf derives philosophical lessons from historical accounts.

kept them-<4>selves very close in their Palaces, and being seldom to be seen by any but their nearest Servants, they never gave Answer to their Subjects Petitions but by them. Whereby they possessed [persuaded] the People that they were much above the Common Rank of Mankind. The Second was, That every Year they used to draw a certain number of Souldiers out of each Province, and these being Quartered in and about the place of their Residence, and Commanded by such a one as was thought most faithfull, these Forces struck Terrour both into the Subjects at Home and the neighbouring Nations Abroad. This Army was again Disbanded every year, and another drawn out of the Provinces, that the General by the Authority he had with the Soldiers, might

Its Fall.   not be in a condition to Invade the Empire. The Ruin of this Empire under *Sardanapalus,* is not so much to be ascribed to his Effeminacy, as to this, That the Kings allowed too much Power to the Governours of Provinces of so vast an extent. These grew at last too Powerfull for the Kings themselves, who being lull'd asleep by Voluptuousness (the effects of Peace and Plenty) did not, as they used to do formerly, by great Actions endeavour to maintain their Authority among the People.

Out of the Ruins of the *Assyrian* Empire two new Kingdoms were erected; *Arbactes* taking upon himself the Sovereignty of *Media,* where he was Governour, as the Lord Lieutenant of *Babylon* did the same in his Province, both which were afterwards re-united under the *Persian* Monarchy.

The Persian   §5. *Cyrus* the first Founder of the *Persian* Empire, did, besides what
Empire.   formerly belonged to *Media* and *Babylon,* also Conquer a great part of
              the Lesser *Asia.* This Prince, besides other remarkable Constitutions,
By what   did wisely institute this, as a most necessary one to preserve the Peace of
means it was his Empire; That in all Provinces, where he sent his Lords Lieutenants,
maintained.   he Constituted Governours of the Fortresses chosen out of the Commons, who being not under the Jurisdiction of the Lords Lieutenants, had their dependence immediately on the King. These therefore living in continual Jealousies, served as a Bridle <5> to one another. The Lords Lieutenants, without the Assistance of the Governours of the Fortresses, were not in a Capacity to Mutiny against the King, who not only Ob-

served all their Actions, but also frequently Informed the King concerning their Behaviour. From the Governours of the Fortresses nothing was to be feared, because, being of Mean Condition and a very Limited Power, they were not capable of making any great Factions, or drawing any considerable Party after them.

Cambyses annex'd *Egypt* to the *Persian* Empire. But whenever the Kings of *Persia* did undertake to extend their Conquests further, it always proved fruitless. *Cambyses* did in vain Attack the *Aethiopians,* as *Darius Hydaspes* did the *Scythians.* And *Xerxes* was shamefully beaten by the *Greeks:* But the following Kings, *Artaxerxes Longimanus, Darius Nothus,* and *Artaxerxes Mnemon,* did Manage their Affairs with more Wisdom against the *Greeks,* whom they did not Attack; but leaving them at rest, they quickly saw Intestine Wars kindled amongst themselves [the Greeks]; wherein they so well knew how to play their Game, that by always affording Assistance to the weaker Side, they rather protracted than finished these intestine Wars, till the *Greeks,* quite tired and exhausted, were obliged to accept of such Conditions of Peace as were projected by the *Persians,* whereby each City being declared free and independent of one another, *Greece* was disabled hereafter to undertake any thing of Moment.[3] Notwithstanding *Macedon,* an obscure Nation of *Greece,* proved the Ruin of the *Persian* Monarchy, through a defect of Policy in their Kings, in not early Opposing the Growing Power of *Philip,* by raising Powerfull Enemies in *Greece,* against him and his Son *Alexander,* (which for great Summs of Money they might easily have done,) and thus have cut out so much Work for these two Warlike Princes at Home, that they could not have had leisure so much as to have entred on the thoughts of Invading *Persia:*[4] In the same manner,

3. The Persian kings after Xerxes ruled in the latter half of the fifth century B.C., including the time of the Peloponnesian War. Pufendorf applied these historical lessons about the importance of unified agency to his analysis of sovereignty and the defensive needs of Germany in the late seventeenth century. See *On the Law of Nature and of Nations,* VII.4, and *The Present State of Germany,* VII.6–7 and VIII.4, especially the *editio posthuma* additions focusing on the French threat.

4. On the rise of Philip II of Macedon, see Pufendorf's dissertation "De rebus gestis Philippi, Amyntae filio" (Heidelberg, 1664), which was republished in Pufendorf (1675), pp. 109–95.

as formerly the *Persians* had obliged *Agesilaus* quickly to return into *Greece*.[5] But being over secure in their own Strength, and despising Others, they drew upon themselves their own Destruction. <6>

Greece. §6. *Greece* was in ancient times divided into a great many petty Common-wealths, every one of these being governed by its own Laws. Among those in Process of time, *Athens* grew most famous, whose Citizens for Ingenuity, Eloquence, and the knowledge of Arts and Sciences, surpassed all the rest; their Glory increased exceedingly after they had signalized themselves so bravely against the *Persians*. After this, by adding of the Harbour of *Pyreum* [Piraeus] to their City, they made it very commodious for Shipping, and acquired such vast Riches, that by their naval Strength they subdued the Isles of the *Aegean* Sea and the Coasts of the Lesser *Asia*. But being puffed up with their good Success, they drew upon themselves the hatred of their Allies: and after they once attempted to be sole Masters of *Greece,* the *Peloponnesians,* headed by the *Spartans* (who especially envied the *Athenians*) united together to chastise the insolence of *Athens.* Yet the *Athenians* behaved themselves so bravely, that the War was carried on for a considerable time with near equal Success, till at last being vanquished in a Battle in *Sicily,* they also lost their whole Fleet on the Coast of *Thrace;* then the *Lacedaemonians* becoming Masters of *Athens* constituted thirty Governours, who tyrannized most cruelly over such of the Citizens of *Athens* as survived the Storming of their City; yet *Thrasibulus* having expelled the same with the assistance of some of the banished *Athenians,* restored the City to its former Liberty. After this, though the *Athenians* did recover themselves a little, yet were they never able to arrive at the former Grandeur of their Common-wealth, and being afterwards too forward in making head against *Philip,* they were severely chastised by him.

It was therefore the immoderate Ambition of the *Athenians,* and their desire of conquering more than they were able to defend, which occasioned their Ruin. For the number of the Citizens of *Athens* did not

5. Agesilaus, king of Sparta from 400–359 B.C., was forced to halt his campaigns in Persia because of an uprising in Boeotia in 395 B.C. See §6, p. 19.

exceed ten thousand, and they rarely receiving others as Citizens among them, great Cities and Provinces, could not be kept in obedience by such a number, and with one unfortunate Blow their whole power was struck down without Recovery. And consider-<7>ing that such Cities are better fitted for their own Defence, than making Conquests upon others, it is more adviseable for them to mind the advantage of their own Trade, than to inter-meddle too much in foreign Affairs, and rather to keep safe their own Walls, than to invade their Neighbours.

Next to *Athens, Lacedaemon* was famous in *Greece,* whose Citizens by the constitutions and rigorous Discipline introduced by *Lycurgus,* seem'd to be most fitly qualified for warlike Achievements. This City having not any powerfull Neighbour to contest withall, was strong enough to defend its Liberty against the Neighbouring Common-wealths. And the *Spartans,* as long as they, according to their Laws and Institution, despised Riches, had no great occasion to invade others: But as soon as they began to aim at higher matters,[6] they found by experience, that it was a quite different case to conquer Kingdoms, than to defend their own City. For having had the good Fortune of subduing *Athens,* they fell into the same folly which had been the Ruin of the *Athenians,* and were not only for conquering the *Asiatick* Sea Coasts, but also under the Conduct of *Agesilaus* they invaded *Persia.* But it was easie for the King of *Persia* to find out means to chastise their Insolence, who caused a diversion to be made by the {other} *Greeks,* that envied the Success of the *Spartans,* so that they were quickly obliged to recall *Agesilaus* to defend themselves at home. Not long after their Fleet being beaten by *Conon, Epaminondas* defeated their Army by Land in the Battle of *Leuctra,* whereby they were so weakened, that they were scarce able to defend their own Walls.

Next to these two Cities, *Thebes* was for a while famous, through the Valour and Wisdom of *Epaminondas,* who so well knew how to head his Countrymen, that they humbled the *Spartans,* and as long as he lived, were the most flourishing State of *Greece.* But after his death, this City

Sparta.

---

6. Rather: "But when they wanted to fly higher than their feathers would allow them, . . ." Pufendorf's colloquial witticisms are often lost in Crull.

returned to its former State, and making head against *Philip,* was severely chastised by him, and quite destroyed by his Son *Alexander.* <8>

Macedon. §7. *Macedon* was before the times of *Philip* an inconsiderable Kingdom, and so exposed to the Incursions of its Neighbours, that it was scarce able to defend it self, this Nation being then esteemed the most despicable of *Greece.* But by the Military Virtue of two Kings, this Nation did show it self so considerable, that it conquered a great part of the World. The circumstances wherein the neighbouring Nations of *Macedon* were at that time, and the good Conduct of *Philip,* whereby he so settled the Kingdom at home, that it quickly became the chiefest in all *Greece,* gave the first opportunity to lay the Foundation of this Monarchy. For on one side it had for its Neighbours the *Thracians, Triballians,* and *Illyrians,* very barbarous Nations; these were easily kept in awe by a neighbouring, wise and brave King. On the other side, was *Greece* and its Cities, which, though they were much fallen from their ancient Glory, yet, were all together still too hard for the *Macedonians.* Against those he made use of this Artifice, That by setting them together by the Ears among themselves, he so weakened them with intestine Wars, that they were afterwards not able to hold out long against him. And because *Philip* used only to attack one of those Cities at a time, and the rest were not forward enough unanimously to hinder his growing Greatness, he was upon a sudden, before they were aware of it grown too strong and potent for them all.

The Politick Conduct and great Actions of Philip.

Philip seemed particularly endowed with great qualifications for this enterprize: For besides the Vivacity of his Spirit, he was push'd on by an extraordinary Ambition to make himself famous by great Actions. What real Vertues were wanting in him, he endeavoured to supply with pretending to the same; wherefore tho' he did nothing without a fair Pretence; yet did he never stick at any thing, provided he could obtain his ends, and was never sparing in Promises or Oaths, if he thought he could thereby deceive such as he intended to overcome. He was an absolute Master of his Passions, and knew how to keep his Counsels secret, how to set Friends together by the Ears, and by pretending Friendships to both Parties, to deceive them by vain hopes. He being al-<9>so very Eloquent, knew how to insinuate himself with every body; and as for

Money, he made no other use of it, than to advance his designs. He was a most experienced Warriour, and had made the *Macedonians* so excellent Souldiers, that the *Macedonian* Phalanx, first invented by him, was terrible, even to the *Romans.* And, because he was always at the Head of his Armies, continually exercised his Souldiers, and punctually paid them, there were no better Souldiers, in his days, than the *Macedonians.* Being arrived to this Greatness, so that he was chosen by the common consent of *Greece* their General against the *Persians;* and being busie in making preparations for this expedition, he was barbarously murthered, leaving his Son *Alexander* the glory of pursuing it.

§8. There is scarce in all History to be read of an Expedition more famous than that of *Alexander* the Great, wherein he, with thirty odd thousand Men, conquer'd so vast and potent Kingdoms, and by his victorious Arms extended his Empire from the *Hellespont* to the *Indies.* If we enquire into the causes of so uncommon and happy progresses; it is undeniable that, besides the Providence of God Almighty, who has put bounds to all Kingdoms upon Earth, the incomparable Valour of *Alexander* himself had a great share in the same; who having an Army of chosen Men, fell upon his Enemy's Army with such swiftness and vigour, that it was impossible for any new levied Forces, though never so numerous, to resist him. Yet *Darius* committed a grand mistake, when he offered Battel to *Alexander;* it being evident, that the *Persians* never were equal to the *Greeks* in Pitch'd Battels. Besides this, the *Persians* having lived for a considerable time in Peace, had few experienced Souldiers among them; so that the greater the number was of such undisciplined Souldiers, the sooner were they brought into disorder at the time of Battel. *Darius* was ignorant of that great Art of protracting the War, and by posting himself advantageously, and cutting off the Provisions from his Enemies, to take off the edge of fierce *Alexander.* And because he had neg-<10>lected to give him a diversion at home with the assistance of the *Greeks,* who envied his Greatness, no other Event could reasonably be expected, than what afterwards followed.

§9. But the untimely Death of *Alexander* robb'd both him and his young Children of the fruits of his Victories. For these, being young,

Alexander the Great.

He dies young.

lost not only their Father's Kingdom, but also the fatal Wars carried on after his Death betwixt his Generals, brought the conquer'd Nations under great Calamities, who else would have been in hopes to have changed their {former} Kings for a much better and greater Prince. But that it seem'd was next to an impossibility, that these so suddenly conquered Countries should so soon be united in one Kingdom. Since a firm Union betwixt so many Nations could not be established without a singular Prudence of their supream Head, and a considerable time. We find also that a sudden Greatness is rarely lasting, there being no less ability required to maintain, than to acquire a thing of this nature.

The Conquests therefore of *Alexander* being of so vast an extent, that the small number of his *Macedonians* was by no means sufficient to keep them in awe; and to make those Provinces dependent on the *Macedonian* Empire, there was no other way to maintain such vast Conquests, than to treat the conquered Nations in the same manner with his native Subjects, and not to oblige them to recede from their ancient Laws and Customs, or to turn *Macedonians,* but rather for him to turn *Persian,* that the conquered might not be sensible of any other change, but what they found in the Person of their King. *Alexander* understood this very well; wherefore he not only used [accustomed] himself to the *Persian* Customs and Habit, but also married the deceased King's Daughter, and had a *Persian* Guard about him. Those Writers, who reprehend *Alexander*'s Conduct in this matter, only discover their own indiscretion. But to settle a right understanding betwixt the Conquerours and Conquered, did require a considerable time; to effect which, *Alexander* seemed to be the fittest Man in the World, as being endowed with a more than <11> ordinary Valour, Magnanimity, Liberality and Authority. If he had left a Son behind him not unworthy of so great a Father, the *Persian* Throne would questionless have been entailed upon his Family.

§10. The Death of *Alexander* the Great was the occasion of long and bloody Wars; For the Army, puff'd up with the Glory of its great Actions, esteemed no body worthy of the supream Command; And the Generals refusing to obey one another, were grown too potent to live as private persons. 'Tis time *Arideus* had the name of King; but this poor

Great Troubles after the Death of Alexander.

Man wanted both Authority and[7] Power to bridle the Ambition of so many proud and great Men. Wherefore all spurr'd on by their hopes, some of obtaining the whole Empire, some of getting a considerable share, they waged a most bloody and long War among themselves, till their number was reduced to a few, from a great many, who first pretended to the Empire. Five of them took upon themselves the Title of Kings, and the Sovereign Dominion of their Provinces, *viz. Cassander, Lysimachus, Antigonus, Seleucus* and *Ptolemy.* But only the three last transmitted their Kingdoms to their Families. There were then no more than three Kingdoms remaining in the power of the *Macedonians;* viz. That of *Syria, Egypt* and *Macedon;* That part of the *Persian* Empire which lay Easterly beyond the River *Euphrates,* being become a vast new Kingdom under the name of the *Parthian* Empire.

The above-mentioned three Kingdoms were afterwards swallowed up by the *Romans,* and the Kingdom of *Macedon* was the first, as lying nearest unto *Italy.* For the *Romans,* after having subdued all *Italy,* began to extend their Conquests beyond the Seas; and perceiving that *Philip,* an active King,[8] bid fair for the Conquest of all *Greece;* they did not think it advisable to let him grow more Powerfull, he being so near to them, that in time he might easily prove troublesome to *Italy.* They entring therefore into a League with the same Cities of *Greece,* which were Attack'd by *Philip,* under that pretence made War upon *Philip;* and having driven him back into *Mace-* <12> *don,* restored Liberty to all *Greece.* By which means the *Romans* at the same time divided their [the Greeks'] Strength, and gain'd their Affections; at length they Conquer'd *Perseus,* and with him the Kingdom of *Macedon:* Then they turn'd their Arms against *Syria,* and took from *Antiochus* the Great, all that part of *Asia* which extends as far as Mount *Taurus.*[9] And though this Kingdom did hold out for a while after, yet being miserably torn to pieces by the

The Fall of the Macedonian Empire.

7. Rather: "Although one gave the name of king to Aridaeus, this naive man had neither Authority nor." Arrhidaeus or Philip III (359–317 B.C.) was the half-brother of Alexander and ruled Macedon after the latter's death in 323 B.C.

8. Philip V (238–179 B.C.) of the Antigonid dynasty was succeeded by his son, Perseus, who ruled Macedon from 179–168 B.C. After his defeat by the Romans, Macedon became a Roman province.

9. Antiochus III the Great (241–187 B.C.) was ruler of the Seleucid Empire.

Dissentions, which were risen in the Royal Family, it Surrendred it self to *Tigranes*, King of *Armenia*. But he being Conquered by *Pompey*, the Whole was made a Province of the *Roman* Empire. *Egypt* at last could not escape the Hands of the *Romans*, after the Emperour *Augustus* had defeated *Cleopatra* and her Galant *Mark Antony*.

Carthage. §11. Before we come to *Rome*, we must say something of *Carthage*. This City having long contested with *Rome* for the Superiority, so that 'the *Roman* Government' [Rome] did not think it self well secured, as long as this City was in Being. This City, though it was rather fitted for Trade than War; yet having acquired vast Riches by its Traffick, and being vastly encreased in Power and Inhabitants, forced not only the next adjacent Countries in *Africa* to pay them Tribute, but also sent vast Armies into *Sicily, Sardinia* and *Spain*. This occasioned the Wars betwixt them and the *Romans;* the two First they maintain'd with extraordinary Resolution and Valour, but in the Third they were brought to utter Destruction. If they had avoided to meddle with the *Roman* Affairs, they might in all probability have been able for a great while to defend their Liberty.

Ambition therefore was the chief Cause of their Ruin, since the Constitution of their Government was such, as being Adapted for Trade, did not require any great Possessions, except a few Lands for the use of their Citizens, and some Sea-Ports in *Spain* and *Sicily*, for conveniency of Commerce and Shipping. But the Conquests of large Countries were more hurtfull than profitable to them. For those Generals who Commanded their Armies abroad, proved at last dangerous to them, thinking it <13> below themselves after so much Glory and vast Riches obtained, to be put in the same Rank with their Fellow Citizens. The Inhabitants besides, of this City, were not so well fitted for Land-service; so that they being obliged to fill up their Armies with Mercenary Souldiers, collected out of several Nations, these were a vast and certain Charge to them, the hopes of the Benefit remaining uncertain. And besides this, their Faith was very inconstant, and the Conquered places could scarce be trusted to those, whose Faith might easily be bought by Money. After their first War with the *Romans*, they

Experienced almost to their utter Ruin, how dangerous it is to wage War altogether with Foreign and Mercenary Souldiers. And therefore they could not possibly hold out against the *Romans,* who fought with a much greater Constancy for their Native Country, than these Foreign Mercenaries did for their Pay.[10]

'Twas a Capital Errour in the *Carthaginians,* that they did not take care in time, so to Establish their Power at Sea, that they needed not to have feared any thing from the *Romans* that way: But after they had once let the *Romans* become Masters at Sea, they could not but expect them one time or another at their City-gates. At the time when *Hannibal* had such prodigious Success against the *Romans,* it proved also a fatal Neglect in them, that they did not timely send fresh Supplies to Re-inforce him so that he might have prosecuted the War to the Destruction of *Rome.* For after they had once given leisure to the *Romans,* to recollect themselves, they, conscious of their former danger, never rested till they had rased *Carthage* to the ground.

§12. It is worth the while to trace the Common-wealth of *Rome* back to its Original, because none ever yet Equall'd it in Power and Greatness, and because young Students are first Entred and best Read in the *Roman* History. This City was perfectly made for War, from whence she first had her Rise, and afterwards her Fall. Its first Inhabitants were a sorry Rabble of Indigent People, <the very Dregs of *Italy,*> being ignorant of what belonged to Commerce, and <14> not expert in any Handy-craft's Trade. For the carrying on of the first, *Rome* was not Commodiously Situated; and the Latter was at that time unknown in *Italy.* That small parcel of Ground which at first they had possess'd themselves of, was not sufficient to maintain a considerable Number of People; nor was there any vacant Ground in the Neighbourhood, which could be Tilled for their use. If therefore they would not always remain Beggars, nothing was left them but their Swords, wherewith to cut out

Rome a War-like City.

10. See *The Present State of Germany,* VII.9, p. 206, where Pufendorf criticizes Germans for serving as mercenaries to all of Europe instead of defending their fatherland. Also see VIII.16, p. 231, and VIII.18, p. 233.

their Fortune. And truly *Rome* was nothing else but a Den of Wolves, and its Inhabitants, like Wolves, always thirsting after their Neighbour's Goods and Blood, living by continual Robberies.

By what means
Rome became
so populous.

It was then necessary for a City, under these Circumstances, to keep up a constant Stock of Valiant Citizens. To effect this the better, *Romulus* commanded, that no Child should be kill'd, except such as were very Deformed; which barbarous Custom was also then very common among the *Grecians*. Besides this, he ordered that all Slaves at *Rome*, together with their Liberty, should have the Privilege of the City, from whom afterwards descended great Families, their Posterity being ambitious by great Deeds, to Efface the Memory of their base Original. But above all, one thing did mightily contribute towards the Increase of *Rome*, that *Romulus* did not suffer the Men to be put to the Sword, in such places, as were taken by force by the *Romans*, nor would let them be sold for Slaves; but receiving them into *Rome*, granted them the same Privileges with the rest of the Citizens. The *Roman* Writers give this for one reason, why *Athens* and *Sparta* could not so long maintain their Conquests, as *Rome* did; since they seldom Naturalized Strangers; whereas *Romulus* frequently used to receive the same as Citizens of *Rome* in the Evening, with whom he had fought in the Morning. For War cannot be carried on without a good Stock of Men; nor can Conquests be maintain'd without a considerable Number of Valiant Souldiers, upon whose Faith the Government can rely in case of an Attack. But that the Conquered places might not be left destitute of Inhabitants, and *Rome* might not <15> be fill'd up with too much Rabble, they used only to Transplant the best and richest Men of the Conquered places to *Rome*, filling up their places with the poorest of the *Roman* Citizens; who setling a continual good Correspondence betwixt the Conquered and the *Romans*,[11] served also for a Garrison in these places. By these means the most Valiant and Richest Inhabitants of the Neighbouring Countries were drawn to *Rome*, and the poorest among the *Romans* obtained thereby, in those places, large Possessions.

But although Necessity gave an Edge to the *Roman* Valour, 'twas not that alone that made them so War-like a People; for the Courage of

11. That is, they made those places well disposed toward Rome.

their Kings, who instructed them in Military Affairs, and hardned them to Dangers, had a great share in it; though, the thing rightly considered, it is not always adviseable, to lay the Foundation of a State upon Military Constitutions; since the Changes of War are uncertain, and then it is not for the Quiet of any State that Martial Tempers should prevail too much in it. Wherefore Peaceable times did never agree with the *Romans;* and as soon as they were freed from the Danger of Foreign Enemies, they sheath'd their Swords in each other's Bowels.[12]

§13. There 'were' [are] also other things worth our Observation, which did greatly advance the Military Affairs of *Rome*. One of the chiefest was, That their King *Servius Tullius* had ordered, that only the most able and wealthy Citizens should do Service as Souldiers, and Equip themselves either with light Arms or compleat Armour, according to their Ability: And, whereas formerly every body, without distinction, was obliged to serve the Publick in the Wars at his own Charge; the poorer sort afterwards were never made use of, but upon Extraordinary Occasions. And though Riches do not make a Man the more Valiant, yet was it but reasonable, since every body was obliged to serve without Pay, that those, who were scarce able to maintain themselves, should be spared as much as could be: But besides this, their Wealth was a Pledge of their Fidelity. For he that has nothing to lose but his Life, carries all along with him, and has <16> no such strict Obligation to face Death; besides, that he may easily be brought to desert his own Party, if he meets with a prospect of a better fortune among the Enemies. On the contrary, a wealthy Man fights with more Zeal for the Publick Interest, because in defending That, he secures his own, and is not likely to betray his Trust; For if he deserts, he leaves his Possessions behind him, with uncertain hopes of a recompence of his Treachery from the Enemy. And, though this Custom grew out of fashion under the Emperours, yet, in lieu of that, they always kept part of their Arrears [soldiers' wages] behind, to assure themselves of their Fidelity; and these {being stored in camp near the flags,}[13] were never paid, till they were dismiss'd.

Several other Military Institutions.

12. Rather: ". . . the citizens got into each other's hair."
13. The flags were near the general's tent.

It is also remarkable, that, though the *Romans* have been often Sig-
nally beaten in the Field, yet did they never despair or accept of any disadvantageous Conditions of Peace, except what they did with *Porsena,*
and [with] the {Senonian} *Gauls* <call'd the Terrour>; to the first they
were fain to give Hostages, upon condition, that they should not make
any Iron-work, except what was requisite for Tilling the Ground. Of
which shamefull Peace, the *Roman* Historians have cautiously avoided
to speak in their Writings. And the *Gauls* were within an Inch of having
put a period to the very Being of *Rome,* if they had not been bought off
with Money, to Raise the Siege of the *Capitol,* reduced to the utmost extremity by Famine. For what is related, that *Camillus* coming up just at
the time of the weighing out of the Gold, and drove the *Gauls* from the
Capitol, some look upon as a fabulous Relation.[14] Upon all other occasions they have always born their publick Misfortunes with an extraordinary Constancy. For, notwithstanding that *Hannibal* in the second
Punick War had reduced them to the last Extremity, yet was not a word
of Peace mentioned at *Rome.* And when their Generals by *Claudius* and
Numantia had agreed upon shamefull Conditions with the Enemies,
they chose rather to deliver up the Generals to the Enemies, than Ratifie the Treaty. They used also commonly to have but a small regard, and
rarely to redeem such as were made Prisoners among them, to teach
thereby the *Roman* Souldiers, to <17> expect no deliverance but from
their own Swords. As this Custom did oblige the Souldiers to fight till the
last, so did their Constancy stand them in great stead among other Nations. For he that shows himself once fearfull of his Enemy, must expect
to be Attackt by him, as often as opportunity presents it self.

Of the Reli-
gion of the
Romans.
§14. It is also worth the while to touch a little upon the Religion of the
Ancient *Romans,* which, though it was derived from the *Greeks,* yet the
Romans knew much better how to Accommodate it to the advantage of
their State. It was therefore from the very beginning a constant Rule at

14. Marcus Furius Camillus (ca. 446–365 B.C.). The Gallic siege of the Roman
Capitol ca. 387 B.C. is recounted by Livy V.47–49. Lars Porsena was an Etruscan
king of Clusium who came to the aid of the expelled Tarquinius Superbus around
508 B.C.

Rome, not to begin any publick Affairs of moment, without good Indications or Presages: Because that the Event [*Ausgang*] of things is commonly supposed to happen according to the Approbation of God. And therefore such as think themselves assured of the good Will of God, undertake and effect things with a greater Courage. These Indications were commonly taken from Birds. Which being a very ancient Superstition, which took its Rise from an Opinion of the Heathens, that the Gods having their place of Residence immediately above the Region of the Air, did make use of the Creatures of the next adjoyning Element for their Interpreters. These Indications also were thought particularly usefull, because the same were at hand at all times, and the Motions and Chirpings of the Birds might be variously interpreted according to the Exigency of the Times, and the Affairs of the State. The cunning Augurs or Sooth-sayers made use of these Predictions from the flight of Birds, to inspire the ignorant Multitude either with Hopes or Despair, Valour or Fear, according as it seem'd most suitable and convenient to the publick Affairs. Wherefore *Cato* the Elder, who was an Augur himself, did not stick to say; *He did wonder, how one Augur, meeting another, could forbear laughing, because their Science was built upon so slight a foundation.*[15]

What the *Romans* did call Religion, was chiefly instituted for the benefit of the State, that thereby they might the better be able to Rule the Minds of the People, according to the Conveniencies <18> and Exigencies of the State; quite in another manner, than the Christian Religion does, which is instituted for the benefit of the Soul, and the future Happiness of Mankind.[16] Wherefore there were no certain Heads or Articles of Religion among the *Romans,* whence the People might be instructed concerning the Being and Will of God, or how they might regulate their Passions and Actions so as to please God: But all was involved in outward Ceremonies; *viz.* What sort of Sacrifices was to be made, what Holy-days and Publick Games were to be kept, *&c.*

15. See Cicero, *De divinatione* II.24.51–52.

16. On the nature of the Christian religion and its relation to the state, see XII.4–7, pp. 418–24, below.

For the rest, the Priests were unconcerned, as to what the People did believe or not believe of Divine Matters; or, whether after this Life the Vertuous and Wicked were to expect Rewards according to their several deserts; or, whether the Souls perish'd together with the Bodies. For we see, that the Heathens have spoken very dubiously concerning these Matters, and the wisest of them have taken these things for Inventions wherewith to keep the People in awe. But in their Ceremonies they were most exact, performing the same with great pomp and outward show, and rarely admitting of the least alteration to be made in the same.

All this was instituted to please the humour of the Multitude, which is most moved with those things, which dazle the Eyes, and strike strongly on the Senses. Wherefore their Temples and Sacrifices were not only extraordinary Magnificent, but the Priests also were chosen out of the most Noble Families, which served to increase the Reverence of the People, that commonly judges of the Value of things, according to the quality of such as are employed about them. Yet besides this, there was another Mystery in it. For, because they made use of their Religion only as an Instrument of State, to make the People pliable to the Intentions of their Rulers; it was by all means necessary, that such Priests were made use of, as understood the Interest of the State, and did themselves also sit at the Helm of the Common-wealth. On the contrary, if the meaner sort had been employed as Priests, they might easily, out of Ambition, have, with the assistance of the People, raised a Faction contrary to the Governours, since <19> the Multitude commonly depends on those of whose Sanctity they have an Opinion; or else out of ignorance of the publick Affairs and the present Exigencies they might chance to influence the People in another manner, than was consistent with the present state of Affairs. They prevented also by this way, that the Priests could not form a particular Estate in the Common-wealth, and thereby either cause a mischievous Division, or else strive to get the Power into their own hands.[17]

17. This is in contrast to the clerical estate in the German Empire. See *The Present State of Germany,* II.10, pp. 68–72.

§15. After *Rome* had been governed for Two hundred forty and two Years by Kings, another Form of Government was introduced, *Sextus Tarquin* having at that time ravish'd *Lucretia*. Whether *Junius Brutus* had sufficient reason, upon this account, to expell the King, may very well admit of Dispute. For on one side the Fact was most abominable, and of such a nature, that a brave Man would rather venture at any thing, than bear such an affront. And there are a great many Examples, that Princes, who, to satisfie their brutish Lusts, have Violated the Chastity of their Subject's Wives and Daughters, and thereby lost both their Lives and Crowns. But on the other hand, it is to be considered, that a Fact, though never so Criminal, committed by a Son, without the Knowledge and Consent of his Father, ought not to be prejudicial to the Father and Family; much less could it be a pretence to depose a King from a Throne, which he lawfully possessed; Especially, since to take Vengeance of Criminals does belong only to the King, and not the Subjects. And *Brutus* and *Collatinus* would have had reason to complain, after the King had denied them just satisfaction for the Fact [rape] committed by his Son, or if he had in any ways approved of the same. But it is commonly observed, that in Revolutions things are seldom carried according to the 'New' [exact] form of the Rules of Justice. And as there is commonly some injustice committed at the first Settlement of a new Form of Government;[18] so Ambition and Envy, covered with Pretences of the Faults and Male-Administration[19] of the Prince, are the true Motives of Dethro-<20>ning the same.

But not to insist further upon this, it is certain that Kingly Government could not be durable at *Rome;* For such States as are comprehended in one great City are more fit for an *Aristocratical* or *Democratical* Form of Government; whereas a Monarchy is fittest to be erected in Kingdoms, where the Subjects are dispersed in a considerable Tract and Extent of Land.[20] The true Reason of this is, That Mankind in general, politically considered, is like wild unruly Creatures, ready upon all oc-

The Expulsion of their Kings and the Erection of a new Form of Government.

18. Rather: "at the acquisition of new sovereignties (*Herrschaften*)."
19. That is, mal-administration, from *male* (badly).
20. See *On the Law of Nature and of Nations,* VII.5.22.

casions to shake off the Bridle of Civil Obedience, as often as Matters do not suit with its humours. Besides, this Man cannot be kept in Obedience without the assistance of Men. From whence it may rationally be concluded, why a King, who Commands only over one great populous City, is immediately in danger of losing all, as soon as his Subjects are disgusted at him, or another can insinuate himself into their favour, except he is fortified with a strong Guard of Foreigners, and a considerable Fort; though these Remedies are very odious, and oftentimes very uncertain. For when in such a Government the Prince comes to be odious, the Hatred is quickly communicated to all his Subjects, as living close together, and having consequently an opportunity of uniting themselves easily against him. But where the Subjects of a Prince live at a distance from one another, it is easie for him to keep so many of them inclined to his side, as are sufficient to suppress the mutinous Party. Wherefore also they are not so much to be feared, as being not able to meet so soon, and to unite themselves in one Body. But it is more especially very dangerous to Command over Subjects living in one place, of a fiery Temper, and exercised in Arms. For Common sense tells us, that he who will controul another, ought to have more force than him.

In the mean while, this is most certain, that this Alteration of the Government mainly contributed towards the Encrease of *Rome;* it being not credible, that under the Monarchical Government it could have arrived to that Greatness; partly, because the Kings would have been obliged for their own security to suppress, in some measure, the Martial Spi-<21>rit of their Citizens; partly, because the Negligence or Unskilfulness of some Kings must needs have proved disadvantageous to the Common-wealth.

Reasons of the fall of the Roman Greatness. §16. Above all, it is worth our Consideration, by what means the *Roman* Empire, which extended it self over so considerable a part of the World, was destroyed, and became a prey to the Northern Nations, after it had been broken by its own Intestine Troubles. The Causes of which we will enquire into from their first beginning. The People of *Rome* then being naturally of a fierce and martial Spirit, and enclosed together within the Walls of one City, their Kings had no way left to secure their

Obedience, but by gaining their Affections with the gentleness and moderation of their Government, since they had not sufficient Power to balance the Forces of so vast a City. Wherefore the six first Kings kept the People in Obedience, rather by their good Inclinations than Fear. But as soon as *Tarquin* the Proud began to oppress the People with new Impositions, whereby he had so alienated the Hearts of his Subjects from him; it was easie for *Brutus,* under pretext of the Fact committed upon *Lucretia,* to stir up the discontented People, and to shut the City-gates against the King.

But as all sudden Changes of Government, that are carried on before things have been maturely considered, and all Emergencies provided against, are commonly accompanied with great Defects: So also was this at *Rome,* where some things were admitted, and others left undone; not so much because they conduced to the advantage and safety of the State, but because the present Juncture of Affairs would not suffer them to be otherwise. There were also many Over sights committed in the beginning, which left a Gap open for future Evils and Troubles. It seems to be evident, that *Brutus* and his Associates, after they had expell'd *Tarquin,* did intend to introduce an *Aristocratical* Form of Government: For it is scarce credible that they, being Noble-men, with the peril of their Lives should have expelled *Tarquin* on purpose to subject themselves to the Government of the Common people; but because no Wise man is willing to exchange his <22> present condition with another, without hopes of amending the same: Therefore the chief Authors of this Revolution were obliged, not only to render the Kingly Government odious to the People, but also by Mildness and Concessions to make the People in love with the New Government. For if the Common people had not been made sensible of the benefit they received from the Government of the Nobility, they might easily have opened the Gates again to *Tarquin.* Wherefore *Valerius Papicola* did strive to please the People, especially in letting down the Rods or *Fasces* (the Ensigns of Authority) before them, and allowing Appeals to the People, as a tacit Confession that the Supreme Power of *Rome* did belong to them.

It was by all means requisite, if the Noble-men did intend to maintain the newly acquired Authority, to have a particular care of these two

The Defects of the Roman Commonwealth.

things. First, To take heed that they did not exasperate the Common people with their Pride; And, Secondly, To find Means to maintain the poorer sort, that they might not be forced to seek for Remedies against their Poverty and Debts by disturbing the Publick. But neither of them were sufficiently regarded by the Nobility. There being at that time no written Laws at *Rome,* and the Nobility being in possession of all publick Offices, Justice was oftentimes administered according to Favour and Affection, the poorer sort being often, though unjustly, oppressed by the more Powerfull. And because the Citizens were obliged to serve in the Wars at their own Charge at that time, when little was to be got, they were thereby miserably exhausted; so that they had no other remedy left them but to borrow Money from the Richer sort. These used such as were not able to satisfie their Creditors in so barbarous a manner, by Imprisoning, laying of them in Chains, and other Cruelties, that the Commons, quite put into despair, unanimously retired out of the City; neither could they be persuaded to return, before the Senate had agreed to constitute Magistrates, called *Tribunes of the People,* who were to protect the Commons against the Power of the Nobility. <23>

Two distinct Bodies in Rome. §17. This was the Original and Cause of the Division of the *Romans* into two 'Factions' [bodies]; *viz.* One of the Nobility, and the Other <two Parties> of the Common people: The continual Jealousies of which did afterwards minister [furnish] perpetual fewel [fuel] for Civil Dissentions. It seem'd at first sight but equitable and of no great consequence, that the Commons might have for their Heads some, who could upon all occasions protect them against the Nobility: But in this the Nobles did commit a grand Errour, that they allowed to the Common people, which made the major part of the City, a protection independent of the Senate; making thereby the Body of the Common-wealth as it were **Factious Tribunes.** double-headed.[21] For the *Tribunes,* spurr'd on by Ambition, and the Hatred, which is common in the *Plebeians* against the Nobility, were not satisfied with affording their Protection to the People against the

---

21. See XII.6, p. 422, below, and *The Present State of Germany,* VII.9, in Pufendorf (2007), p. 205.

Nobility; but also were always endeavouring to be equal in Power, nay even to surpass the Senate in Authority. And first by their continual Contests they obtained a Privilege for the Commons to intermarry with the Nobles; Afterwards they forced also the Nobility to consent that one of the Consuls should be chosen out of the Commonalty. They took upon themselves the Power of a Negative Voice, so as that no Decree of the Senate could pass into a Law without their consent, nay and even without the consent of the Senate to make Laws, and to exercise the other Acts of Sovereign Authority.

The Senate, 'tis true, to divert and employ the People, continually engaged them in one War or another, that they might not have leisure to contrive any thing against the Government. This, though it did very well for a while, and the Power and Territories of *Rome* were mightily thereby increased, yet did arise from thence some other inconveniencies, which did not a little contribute towards the indisposition of the State. For whereas the conquered Lands ought to have been given to the poorer sort of the people, whereby the City would have been freed from a great many needy Citizens; the Nobles, under pretence of Farming the same, took them into their own possessi-<24>on; and what with these Revenues, and the great Booty which fell in the Wars almost all to their share, as being Commanders in Chief, the Riches of the Nobles encreased prodigiously; whereas a great many of the *Plebeians* had scarce wherewithall to maintain themselves. The Commonalty being for these Reasons extreamly dissatisfied with the Senate, there were not wanting some of the Nobility, and others, of an ambitious Spirit, who having taken distaste at some Transactions of the Senate, did, under pretence of maintaining the Liberties of the People, make a considerable Party among them, though, in effect, their chief aim was, with the assistance of the *Plebeians,* to carry on their ambitious designs. Those being by force opposed by the Senate, it came quickly to a Civil War, and they sheath'd their Swords in each other's Bowels.[22]

22. Rather: ". . . , one began in the city to resort to fisticuffs, and citizens started breaking one another's necks." Crull repeats his earlier metaphor (see note 12, p. 27) here; his use of "civil war" is more definitive than Pufendorf's colloquial description.

Citizens too
powerfull.

§18. In the mean time, partly by the vast Increase of the *Roman* Empire, partly by Inadvertency of the Senate, another Evil had taken root; *viz.* That vast and rich Provinces, together with great Armies, were committed to the Government of some of the *Roman* Citizens, and that for several years. From which, as it created in them an aversion to a private life, so it gave an opportunity to have whole Armies at their Devotion [service]. It is not adviseable for any State whatsoever to let any of its Citizens mount to that degree of Power. For he that has a potent Army at his Devotion, will scarce be able to resist the temptation, but will be apt to attempt to make himself Sovereign. It is evident that the Ambition and great Power of *Marius, Sulla, Pompey* and *Caesar* did spur them on, by Intestine Wars, to suppress the Liberty of their native Country; and after *Rome* was quite broken by them, to introduce an alteration in its Government. There was scarce any remedy left against this Evil, after the Citizens had once laid aside the respect due to the Senate, and the Souldiers had tasted the Sweets of the Booty got by Civil Commotions. Wherefore this Common-wealth at the very time when it was arrived to the pitch of its Greatness, it return'd a-<25>gain to a Monarchy, but not of the best kind, where the Army exercised Sovereign Authority.

The Constitution of the Roman Monarchy.

Augustus was the first Founder of this Monarchy, which he by his wise and long Reign, seem'd to have establish'd pretty well: And truly this new introduc'd form of Government, did for a while promise very fair, since *Augustus* assum'd only the Title of Prince, and maintaining the Senate and the rest of the great Officers in their Stations, took upon himself no more than the administration of Military Affairs. But in effect, this Monarchy was not founded so much upon the consent of the Senate and People, as upon the Power of the Souldiery, by whose assistance it was introduc'd and maintain'd. And because the ancient Nobility could not brook to be commanded by one single person, and was always for recovering its former Liberty, the Emperours left no Stone unturn'd either to diminish, or quite to extinguish the Splendour of the ancient Nobility; so that within the space of 200 Years, very few were left, in whose places new Favourites of the Emperours were created, who were willing to submit themselves to their Commands.

§19. But this Monarchy being founded upon the Souldiery, could not The Roman Monarchy could not be of a long continuance. be of a long continuance; for as soon as the Souldiers had once learn'd this Secret, that they being the Supporters of the Monarchy, could dispose of the Empire at pleasure, and that the Senate and People were now empty Names; the Emperours were not only oblig'd with double Pay and great Presents to purchase their Favour; but they also began to kill such Emperours as were not pleasing to them, and to fill up their room with such as could obtain their Favour. And because one Army did claim the same Prerogative as well as the other, not only the *Pretorian* Bands, but also other Armies, which were on the Frontiers, undertook to do the same. Hence came nothing but Misery and Confusion in the *Roman* Empire, the Life of each Emperour depending on the Will of the covetous and unruly Souldiers, so that no Emperour was assur'd to leave the Empire to his Posterity. Oftentimes the bravest Princes were <26> murther'd, and in their room others set up of the meanest Rank and Capacity. Oftentimes two or more were declared Emperours, who used to make horrid slaughters among the Citizens in deciding their Titles to the Empire. And this was the reason why not only very few of the ancient Emperours died a natural death, but also the Power of this vast Empire, was diminish'd to that degree by these intestine Wars, that it did appear no otherwise than a Body without its Nerves.[23]

Constantine the Great did also hasten its fall, when he transferr'd the Imperial Court from *Rome* to *Constantinople,* and sent away the Veterane Legions which guarded the Frontiers of the Empire, along the *Danube* and the *Rhine,* to the Easterly Parts, whereby the Western Provinces, destitute of their Guards, became a prey to other Nations. Besides this, *Theodosius* divided the Empire betwixt his two Sons, giving to *Arcadius* the *Eastern,* to *Honorius* the *Western* parts; which division did not a little contribute towards the destruction of the Empire. The *Western* Parts became a prey to the *Germans* and *Goths,* who about that

---

23. More usually, Pufendorf compares the relation of unified sovereignty and the state to a body-soul relationship: *On the Law of Nature and of Nations,* VII.4.1 and 4.12; and *The Present State of Germany,* VI.8 and VII.7.

time came in prodigious numbers, to change their poor Habitations for the pleasant and rich Provinces of the *Romans. England* the *Romans* left of their own accord, as being not in a capacity to defend it against the *Scots,* and having occasion for their Troops to defend *France. Spain* fell to the share of the *West-Goths.* The *Vandals* settled themselves in *Africa.* The *Goths, Burgundians* and *Francks* divided *France* betwixt them. *Rhaetia* and *Noricum* was conquer'd by the *Suevians* and *Bavarians.* A great part of Pannonia and Illyricum was possessed by the *Huns.*[24] The *Goths* settled a Kingdom in *Italy,* and did not think *Rome* worthy to make it the place of Residence of the *Gothick* Kings.

The Imperial Seat in Constantinople. §20. Though the *Western* parts of the *Roman* Empire fell to the share of Foreign Nations, yet the *Eastern* Provinces, whose Capital City was *Constantinople,* remain'd for a great many hundred years after. But this *Eastern* Empire was neither in Power nor Splendour to be compar'd to the Ancient *Roman* <27> Empire. And *Agathias* the Vth. says, That *whereas heretofore the* Roman *Forces consisted of 645.000 Men, the same did amount in the times of* Justinian *scarce to 150.000.*[25] 'Tis true, under the Reign of this *Justinian,* the Empire began to recover something of its former Power, *Belisarius* having destroyed the Empire of the *Vandals* in *Africa,* as *Narses* did that of the *Goths* in *Italy,* because these Nations were grown Effeminate, and overcome with the deliciousness of a plentifull Country: Yet did it again decrease by degrees, the neighbouring Nations taking away one piece after another, the Emperours were partly in fault themselves, some of them being sunk in pleasures, and grown quite effeminate; others in continual Divisions, destroying each other.

One part was subdu'd by the *Bulgarians.* The *Saracens* conquer'd *Syria, Palestine, Egypt, Cilicia,* and other neighbouring Countries, and

24. Rhaetia was a Roman province in the modern region of east-central Switzerland and Bavaria; to its east lay Noricum, covering the area of Austria and Slovenia. Illyricum stretched along the eastern Adriatic, covering modern Croatia and Serbia, while Pannonia was to its north in the modern area of Hungary, bordering on its western side upon Noricum.

25. Justinian was emperor during 527–65. Agathias (ca. 532–ca. 580) continued Procopius's (ca. 500–ca. 565 A.D.) *History of the Wars* (of Justinian) in his own *Histories,* in five books.

ravaging the rest, besieged *Constantinople;* which City was once taken by Count *Baldwin* of *Flanders,* but his Forces were obliged to quit it not long after.[26] The City also of *Trebisond,* with the neighbouring Countries withdrawing from the Obedience of the rest of the Empire, set up an Emperour of their own choosing.[27] At last the *Turks* entirely subdu'd this Empire, who did not only conquer the *Saracens,* but also afterwards swallow'd up the Remnants of the *Eastern* Empire of *Constantinople; Greece* having before withdrawn it self from the Obedience of the Emperours, was govern'd by its own petty Princes; making, thereby, the Conquest of the *Turks* over them the easier; till, at last, the City of *Constantinople* being taken by Storm by the *Turks* \A. 1453\, was afterwards made the place of Residence of the *Ottoman* Emperours. <28>

26. Baldwin (1172–1205) of Flanders was a leader of the fourth Crusade, which never made it to the Holy Land but sacked Constantinople instead. As Baldwin I, he became the first emperor of the Latin empire of Constantinople.

27. Trebizond, a city on the Black Sea, became the capital of one of three smaller empires that emerged after the sack of Constantinople in 1204.

✪ CHAPTER II ✪

Of the Kingdom of Spain.

§1. *Spain* was in ancient Times divided into a great many States, inde-
pendent of one another, which was at that time the condition of most
other Countries of *Europe.* But, by reason of this Division, this otherwise
War-like Nation was very instrumental to its being conquer'd by foreign
Enemies. To this may be added, That the *Spaniards* did want good and
understanding Generals, under whose Conduct they might easily have
resisted the Power of their Enemies. For not to mention how the *Celts*
pass'd out of *Gaul* into the next adjacent parts of *Spain,* who being mixt
with the *Iberians,* were from thenceforward call'd *Celtiberians;*[1] neither
how the *Rhodians* built *Roses,* the Citizens of *Zante Saguntum,* the *Phoe-
nicians Cadiz, Malaga* and other Cities,[2] the *Carthaginians,* above the
rest, immediately after the first *Punick* War with the *Romans,* began to
conquer a great part of *Spain.* Wherefore in the second *Punick* War the
Romans did at first send their Forces into *Spain,* where they fought so
long with the *Carthaginians,* till at last, *Scipio,* afterwards sir-nam'd the
African, made a great part of it a *Roman* Province; the other parts were
subdu'd by degrees, till *Augustus* at last entirely subduing the *Cantabri-
ans,* who live next to the *Pyrenean* Mountains, joined all *Spain* to the
Roman Empire, under whose Protection it was peaceably govern'd for a
considerable time, except that the *Spaniards* now and then were drawn
in to take a part in the Civil Wars among the *Romans.*

The ancient
State of Spain.

1. The term is used by Diodorus Siculus, Appian, and Martial. The Celtiberi
sided with Hannibal during the Second Punic War and were subdued by the Romans thereafter.

2. All of these are cities on the southeastern shore of Spain.

West Goths
Conquer
Spain.
§2. But the *Western* parts of the *Roman* Empire declining, the *Van-dals, Suevians, Alani* and *Silingi* made an inrode into *Spain,* and after many bloody Battels fought, divided it betwixt them; which Conquests nevertheless they did not enjoy long; for the *Vandals* passing over into *Africa,* the *Alani* were quite <29> routed by the *Suevians,* who having also subdu'd the *Silingi,* were in a fair way of becoming Masters of all *Spain,* if they had not been prevented by the *West Goths;* who, after they had under the Conduct of their King *Alarick,* ransack'd *Italy* and *Rome* it self, settled themselves {under King Araulff} upon the Borders lying betwixt *Spain* and *France,* making *Narbonne* the Seat of their Kings, who at first had under their Jurisdiction *Catalonia* and *Languedock,* but soon after extended their Power over other Provinces of *Spain.* Among these was particularly renown'd their King *Euric,* who took from the *Ro-mans* all what was left them in *Spain,* except *Gallicia,* which remained under the Power of the *Suevians:* He also conquer'd several Provinces in *France.* But *Clodoveus,* King of the *Francks,* having defeated the Son of *Euric,* retook from the *Goths,* what they had conquer'd before in *France,* under the Reign of *Agila* and *Athanagildas* \A. 554\; the *Romans,* who had before rescu'd *Africa* from the hands of the *Vandals,* retook a part of *Spain,* but were chac'd from thence, for the most part, under the Reign of *Levigildis* \A. 572\, who also did quite root out the *Suevians* in *Gal-licia* \A. 586\.[3] Under the Reign of his Son *Recaredus,* the Empire of the *Goths* was arriv'd to its highest pitch of greatness, as comprehending not only some neighbouring Provinces of *France,* and a part of *Mauritania,* but also all *Spain,* except a small part possess'd as yet by the *Romans;* from whence they were quite chased afterwards by King *Suinthila.* King *Wamba* subdu'd the *Gothick* Rebels in *France* \A. 646\ with great suc-cess, and beat the Fleet of the *Saracens* \A. 677\, who much infested

The Ruine of
the Gothick
Empire in
Spain.
those Seas; but under *Witiza* the *Gothick* Empire began to decline from their ancient Valour, the *Goths* being much degenerated, till under the Reign of *Roderic* it was quite extinguish'd.

The King himself contributed greatly to its sudden downfall; for

---

3. Liuvigild (ca. 525–86 A.D.) was a Visigoth king; the Suevians, or Suebians (cf. *Schwaben*), were a Germanic tribe. See p. 332, note 7, below.

having ravish'd a certain Court Lady call'd *Cava,* the Daughter of Count *Julian,* Governour of that part of *Mauritania* which belong'd to the *Goths,* as also over that tract of *Spain* which lies near the Streights of *Gibraltar;* he to revenge himself for this affront, first stirr'd up a great many of the King's <30> Subjects against him, and afterwards persuaded the *Saracens* to pass out of *Africa* over into *Spain.* These to try their Fortune, first pass'd over with a small number, but quickly encreasing by continual Supplies of Men sent from home, they vanquish'd such Forces as *Roderic* sent in hast against them \A. 713\. After this Success the treacherous *Julian* understanding that *Roderic* did intend to bring into the Field the whole Forces of his Kingdom, which consisted of 100.000 Men, brought more *Saracens* over into *Spain,* who being joined with the rest, did in a most memorable Battle intirely rout this Multitude of unexercised and ill arm'd Souldiers, who were surpriz'd to see one of their own party call'd *Oppas,* with the Troops under his Command, went over to the Enemy, and fell into their Flanck, together with the Forces of *Julian.* Thus all was given over for lost, and in this one Battle fell the whole Power and Splendour of the *Goths,* which had been famous in *Spain* for three hundred Years, *Roderic* himself being kill'd in the flight \A. 714\, so that the *Goths* being without a Head were quite dispers'd, and all the great Cities, partly by force of Arms, partly upon Articles, fell into the Hands of the Enemy within the space of three Years. Only *Asturia, Biscay,* a part of *Gallicia* and some Countries next adjacent to the *Pyrenean* Mountains remain'd under the *Goths,* rather, because the Enemies did not think it worth their while to drive them from these Mountainous places, than that the *Goths* trusted to their own Strength to defend themselves against them. Into these parts also retir'd such Christians as had escap'd the Sword of the Enemies. But all the rest of *Spain* was inhabited by the *Saracens* and *Jews.*

The Saracens conquer Spain.

§3. To free *Spain* from this Tyranny, was first undertaken by *Pelagius,* who (as 'twas said) was descended from the Race of the *Gothick* Kings. This Man being chosen King {A. 726}, did recollect the remaining Forces of this unfortunate Nation; and having brought together an Army, obtained a signal Victory against the *Moors;* and in the mean

Kings in Oviedo. Pelagius.

while that the *Saracens* were weakening their Strength in *France,* took
Favila.   from them <31> the City of *Leon,* and several others. His Son *Favila,*
Alfonso I.   who succeeded him, did nothing worth mentioning. But *Alfonso* the
Catholick re-took several Places from the *Moors* \A. 737\, and reigned
Favila.   till the Year 757. Whose Son 'Favila' [Froila] also Valiantly defended his
Kingdom, vanquishing the *Moors* in a great Battle. He was killed in the
Aurelius.   Year 768: But his Successor *Aurelius* made a shamefull Peace with the
Moors, by virtue of which he was obliged to give them a yearly Tribute
of a certain Number of Virgins. He died in the Year 774. His Succes-
Silo.   sor *Silo* did also nothing worth mentioning, and died in the Year 783.
Alfonsus II.   After him reigned *Alfonso,* the Son of 'Favila' [Froila], against whom
Mauregatus taking up Arms, forced him out of the Kingdom; who,
to settle himself the better in the Empire, craved assistance from the
Moors, promising them a yearly Tribute of 50 Noble Virgins, and as
many others {of common status}. He died in the Year 788. His Suc-
Veremundus.   cessor *Veremundus* did nothing Praise-worthy, except that he recalled
Alfonso [son of Froila], Sir-named *the Chaste* \A. 791\; who refusing to
pay the Tribute of the Virgins to the *Moors,* gave them several signal
Defeats: But having no Children, he made an agreement with *Charles*
the Great, that he should assist him in driving the *Moors* out of *Spain;*
in recompence of which, he was to be his Heir in the Kingdom of
Spain. Charles therefore sent his Son *Bernard* with a Puissant Army into
Spain, but the *Spaniards* not liking the agreement, as being not willing
to be under the Command of the *French,* arose unanimously, and falling upon the *French* near *Ronceval;* just as they were entring into *Spain,*
entirely routed them; in which Battle the famous *Rowland* was slain.
Thus it is related by the *Spanish* Historians, but the *French* do not agree
with them in the relation.[4]
Ramirus.   *Alfonso* died in the Year 844, whose Successor *Ramirus* most gloriously usher'd the *Spanish* Liberty. For the *Moors* demanding the Tribute
according to the agreement made with *Mauregatus,* he defeated them

4. The battle of Ronceval or Roncesvalles (in 778 A.D.) was immortalized in *The
Song of Roland* (ca. 1100), which has the (Christian) Franks being defeated by the
Muslims. In fact, they were ambushed by the (Christian) Basques.

in a great Battle, but could not take from them many of their strong Holds, being with-held partly by Intestine Commotions, partly by an Inrode the *Normans* made upon him. He died in the Year 851. <32> After him succeeded his Son *Ordonius,* who reigned with great applause; he obtain'd a Victory over the *Moors,* and took some of their strong Holds. He died in the Year 862, whose Son and Successor *Alfonso,* Sirnamed *the Great,* fortunately overcame the Rebels at home, and the *Moors* abroad. But by laying too heavy Impositions upon the People, he drew the hatred of a great many upon himself, and was therefore robb'd of the Crown by his Son *Garsias.* This King Valiantly attackt the *Moors* \A. 910\, but died soon after. His Brother {Ordonius} also was Victorious against the *Moors* \A. 913\; transferring the Seat of the *Spanish* Kings from *Oviedo* to *Leon.* He died in the Year 923. `Ordonius I.` `Alfonso III.` `Garsias.`

But besides this Kingdom of *Oviedo,* there arose several other Governments in *Spain.* For *Garsias Semenus* erected a new Kingdom in *Navarre;* and *Aznar,* Son of *Eudo,* Duke of *Aquitain,* having taken several Places from the *Moors,* took upon himself, with consent of the before-mentioned *Garsias,* the Title of Earl of *Arragon.* *Lewis* also, Son of *Charles* the Great, taking *Barcelona,* constituted a Governour there, whose Name was *Bernard,* a *Frenchman,* from whom descended the Earls of *Barcelona.* About the time also of the above-mentioned Kings there were several Earls or Governours of *Old Castile,* who acknowledged the foresaid Kings for their Soveraigns. These Earls being once suspected by King *Ordonius,* he call'd them together; who appearing {and anticipating nothing bad}, were all kill'd by his Order. Wherefore the Old *Castilians,* under the Reign of his Son '*Favila*' [Froila], a cruel Tyrant, with-drawing themselves from the Kingdom of *Leon,* chose two Governours, under the Name of *Judges,* who were to administer all Civil and Military Affairs. But this Form of Government did not last long among them. `The Origin of the Kingdom of Navarre and Arragon.` `Favila II.`

§4. After '*Favila*' [Froila] *Alphonso* the IVth. obtained the Kingdom {of Leon}, under whose Reign *Ferdinand Gonsalvo,* Earl of *Castile,* perform'd great things both against the *Moors,* and *Sanctius Abarcus,* and his Son *Garsias,* Kings of *Navarre,* whom he vanquish'd. But *Alfonso* himself be- `Alfonso IV.`

Ramirus II. ing unfit to Govern the Kingdom, surrendred it \A. 931\ to his Brother *Ramirus;* who, with the assistance of the before-mentioned *Ferdinand,* beat the <33> *Moors* in several Places. He died in the Year 950, and was

Ordonius III. succeeded by his Son *Ordonius,* [who was] a Valiant Prince, but did

Sanctius. not Reign long, leaving the Kingdom [*Reich*] to his Brother *Sanctius* [Sancho] *Crassus* {A. 955}. He [the latter] was Banish'd by *Ordonius,* Sir-named *the Wicked* \A. 955\; but soon restored by the help of the *Moors.* It is said that by certain Articles made betwixt *Sanctius* and *Ferdinand,* Earl of *Castile,* it was agreed \A. 965\, that *Castile* after that time should not be obliged to acknowledge any dependance on [subjection to] the

Ramirus III. Kings of *Leon.* He [Sanctius] was succeeded by *Ramirus* \A. 967\, who, in his Minority, was under Womens tuition; and {also} when grown up {and on his own}, proved very useless to the Publick.[5] For, under his Reign, partly by civil Commotions, partly by the In-roads made by the *Moors,* the Kingdom was considerably weakened, and in great danger of losing more, several Places being taken from the *Christians.* Under

Veremund II. *Veremund* [Bermudo] II. also {who acquired the kingdom A. 982}, the *Moors* did considerable mischief <in those Parts>, taking and plunder-ing, besides a great many others, the City of *Leon;* to which Misfortunes the civil Commotions did greatly contribute. But at last *Veremund* [Ber-mudo] entring into a Confederacy with the King of *Navarre,* and [with] *Garsias,* Earl of *Castile,* forced the *Moors* out of his Kingdom. Him

Alfonso V. [Bermudo] succeeded his Son *Alfonso* V. \A. 999\ under whose Reign there were great Intestine Commotions in *Castile,* whereby the *Moors* were encouraged to attack it with such vigour, that they over-threw *Garsias,* and took him Prisoner, whose Son *Sanctius* [Sancho] revenged himself afterwards upon the *Moors.*

After this, great Dissentions being arisen among the *Moors,* their Empire was divided into several Parts, each Governour of its Province

Veremund III. assuming the Name of King. *Alfonso* succeeded his Son *Veremund* III.[6] \A. 1025\ under whose Reign there happened a great Revolution in

5. Literally: "good for nothing" (*zu nichts taugete*).
6. That is, Alfonso V was succeeded by Bermudo III.

Spain. For *Garsias,* Earl of *Castile,* being upon the point of being married to the King's Sister at *Leon,* was there 'barbarously' [treacher-
ously] murthered by some of his Vassals. *Castile* therefore falling to
Sanctius, King of *Navarre,* who had married the Sister of *Garsias,* ‖[he   Castile made
took upon him the Title of *King of Castile.*]‖[7] This *Sanctius,* Sir-named   a Kingdom.
Major, also waged War against *Veremund,* who had no Children, taking
from him, by force of Arms, a considera-<34>ble part of the Kingdom.
Whereupon a Peace was concluded, whereby it was agreed, that *Sanctius* should keep what he had taken before, but that his Son *Ferdinand*
should Marry *Sanctia,* the Sister of *Veremund,* she being Heiress to her
Brother, and to succeed him in the Kingdom of *Leon.* In this manner
was *Leon, Navarre* and *Castile,* United in one House:

But in the mean while that *Sanctius Major* was in the Field against   Sanctius II.
the *Moors,* a great Misfortune happened at Home. He had particularly   Major.
recommended to the Care of his Queen a very fine Horse, which *Garsias,* her Eldest Son, had a mind to have, and would have obtained it
from the Mother, if the Master of the Horse had not opposed it, telling them, that his Father would be greatly displeased at it. This denial
wrought so upon the Son, that he accused his Mother of committing
Adultery with the Master of the Horse. The Matter being examined,
the King's Natural[8] Son, *Ramirus,* profered to justifie the Innocency of
the Queen in a Duel with *Garsias,* and the King being uncertain what
to do, a Priest did at last enforce the Confession of the Calumny cast
upon the Queen from *Garsias;* whereupon *Garsias* being declared incapable of succeeding his Father in *Castile,* which did belong to him by
his Mother's side, and *Ramirus* obtained the Succession in the Kingdom
of *Arragon* as a recompence of his Fidelity. This *Sanctius Major* died in
the Year 1035.

7. Rather: "was henceforth designated a kingdom."
8. According to Jacob and Wilhelm Grimm, *Deutsches Wörterbuch* (Leipzig:
Hirzel, 1854–1960), 32 vols., vol. 24, col. 445, the German *unecht* (inauthentic) is
related to *unehaft* and *unehelich* (outside of marriage), and thus suitably reflected
in Crull's "natural"—in the sense of (merely) biological rather than "legal" or
"legitimate."

§5. Thus all the Provinces of *Spain,* which were possess'd by the *Chris-*
tians, being joined in one House, it seem'd an easie matter to root out
the *Moors,* divided among themselves, and to restore *Spain* to its former
state, if the same had remained under one 'Head' [king]. But the division made by *Sanctius Major* occasion'd most bloody and pernicious
Wars. This before-mentioned *Sanctius* had four Sons: To the Eldest
Garsias, he left *Navarre* and *Biscay;* to *Ferdinand, Castile;* to *Gonsalvo,*
Suprarbe and *Ripagorsa;* and to *Ramirus* his Natural Son, *Arragon,* giving to each of them the Title of *King.* These being all ambitious to
be equal in Power and Greatness to their Father, and thinking their
Bounds too narrow, fell quickly together by the <35> Ears. For whilest
Garsias was gone in Pilgrimage to *Rome, Ramirus* endeavoured to make
himself Master of *Navarre;* but the other returning home, chased him
out of *Arragon.* There arose also a War betwixt *Ferdinand* of *Castile*
and his Brother-in-law *Veremund,* King of *Leon;* wherein the latter being slain in Battle \A. 1038\, *Ferdinand* became Master of *Leon,* which
did by Right of Succession belong to him {in any case}. He also took
from the *Moors* a great part of *Portugal.* After the Death of *Gonsalvo,*
the Third Son of *Sanctius Major, Ramirus* made himself Master of his
Territories, and endeavoured also to recover, by force of Arms, *Arragon*
from the King of *Navarre* \A. 1045\. Not long after *Ferdinand* of *Castile,*
and *Garsias* of *Navarre,* waged War together about a certain Tract of
Ground, wherein *Garsias* was slain in a Battle \A. 1053\. By his Death
Ramirus got an opportunity of recovering *Arragon.*

    Ferdinand, Sir-named *the Great,* died in the Year 1065, dividing the
Empire, to the great detriment of *Spain,* among his three Sons. The
Eldest *Sanctius* had *Castile, Alfonso, Leon, Garsias Gallicia,* and a part of
Portugal, with the Titles of *Kings. Sanctius* waged War with *Ramirus* of
Arragon, whom he slew in a Battle \A. 1067\, but was beaten back again
by *Sanctius,* Son of *Ramirus,* and the King of *Navarre.* Afterward having
driven *Alfonso* out of his Territories, and taken *Garsias* Prisoner, he took
possession of the Territories belonging to his Brothers, but was slain in
the Siege of *Camora,* which City he endeavour'd to take from his Sister.
Then *Alfonso* his Brother, who had hitherto dwelt with the *Moorish*
King of *Toledo,* made himself Master of *Castile* and *Leon* \A. 1073\. And

took from the *Moors* \A. 1085\, besides some other Places, the City of *Toledo,* which was in those days esteemed impregnable. But the *Moors* in *Spain* having received fresh Re-inforcements out of *Africa,* got new Courage, and falling upon the *Christians,* defeated them in two Battles, till *Alfonso* got an entire Victory over them, obliging the *Moorish* King of *Corduba* to pay him a yearly Tribute. Nevertheless he was afterwards again over-thrown in a Battle <sought> with the *Moors,* where he lost his only Son, *Sanctius,* whose Death he revenged soon after <36> upon them. He died in the Year 1109.

Urraca his Daughter was Heiress to the Kingdom, she being Married to *Alfonso* King of *Arragon;* Which Marriage, under pretence of too near a Consanguinity and Adultery committed by the Queen, was afterwards dissolved again. But, because *Alfonso* would nevertheless keep *Castile* as the Dowry of the Queen, it caused great Intestine Wars and Divisions. For *Alfonso* VIII. Son of *Urraca* by *Raymond* of *Burgundy,* her first Husband, who was come out of *France* to assist her Father in the Wars against the *Moors,* was proclaimed King of *Castile,* in the mean while that *Alfonso* of *Arragon* was busied in taking, besides some other Places, the City of *Saragossa* from the *Moors* \A. 1118\. At last a Peace was concluded betwixt *Arragon* and *Castile* \A. 1122\. Afterwards *Alfonso* of *Castile* made War against the *Moors* with great Success, taking from them divers Places of Note.

But \A. 1134\ *Alfonso* of *Arragon* being slain in a Battle, <sought> with the *Moors,* and leaving no Children behind him, those of *Navarre* chose for their King *Garsias,* who was of the Race of their former Kings: But the *Arragonians* conferr'd the Crown upon *Ramirus,* Brother to the deceased King, who had been a Monk. *Alfonso* of *Castile,* in Opposition to both, pretending to have a Right to these Kingdoms, conquered a great part of them, causing himself, with consent of Pope *Innocent* II. who was supposed to do it in spite to the *German* Emperours, to be proclaimed Emperour of *Spain.* But this difference was also at last composed, it being agreed that *Ramirus* should give his only Daughter, together with the Kingdom, to *Raymond* Earl of *Barcelona,* by which means *Catalonia* and *Arragon* were United \A. 1137\; then *Alfonso* entring into a Confederacy with the Kings of *Navarre* and *Ar-*

Alfonso VII.

Alfonso VIII.

ragon, Attack'd again the *Moors*, taking from them the City of *Almeria*, which in those days was a great Sea-port and Harbour for Privateers. *Raymond* {also} took from the *Moors Tortosa*, *Lerida*, and other strong Holds. *Alfonso* died in the Year 1157.

Sanctius IV.   §6. The same *Alfonso* (though *Spain* had suffered sufficiently by its being divided into so many Govern-<37>ments) left to his Son *Sanctius*, *Castile*; to *Ferdinand*, *Leon* and *Gallicia*. *Sanctius*, who did nothing, that is remarkable, except that he beat twice those of *Navarre*, died in

Alfonso IX.   the Year 1158, leaving his Son *Alfonso* IX. a Child of four years of Age. During the time of his Minority, there were great Disturbances in *Castile*, occasioned partly by the Divisions among the Nobility, partly by the Wars with *Ferdinando* of *Leon*, and *Sanctius* of *Navarre*, who took several Places from the *Castilians*. But coming to his riper years, he did extricate himself, though not without great difficulty, out of those Troubles. In the War against the *Moors*, who always kept the *Spanish* Kings in Exercise, he suffered extreamly, so that he was obliged to make a Truce with them, because the Kings of *Navarre* and *Leon* at the same time fell upon him. At last there was a Confederacy made betwixt these Kings, with a certain agreement, how such Places should be disposed of as should be taken from the *Moors*. In the Year 1210, a most Memorable Expedition was undertaken against the *Moors*, where presented themselves a great many Foreigners, who came to Signalize themselves; but a great many of them being soon tired out, returned home. At that time was fought the famous Battle of *Lasa*,[9] where 200.000 *Moors* being slain, they lost all their Strength. In this Battle *Sanctius* King of *Navarre*, breaking first through a Chain which surrounded the *Moorish* Army, he afterwards bore a Chain with an Emerald in his Shield. In this War was taken from the *Moors*, besides other Places, the City of *Calatrava*. The King of *Leon* took *Alcantara*.

Henry.   *Alfonso* died in the Year 1214, leaving behind him his Son *Henry*, whose Minority occasioned great disturbances in the Kingdom; he died

---

9. The battle of Las Navas de Tolosa, in 1212, was a turning point in the eventual decline of Moorish power in Spain.

without Issue in the Year 1217. He had two Sisters, the Eldest *Blanch* was Married to *Lewis* VIII. Son of *Philip Augustus,* King of *France:* The second, *Berengaria,* was Married to *Alfonso,* King of *Leon.* The Crown, by Right of Succession, did belong to the Eldest, and her Heirs: But out of a hatred the States [estates] bore to Strangers, they conferr'd the Kingdom upon *Ferdinand,* Sir-named *the Holy,* Son of *Berengaria,* who <38> with all speed imaginable, possess'd himself of it, before he could be prevented by his Father {Alfonso}, surmounting all the difficulties which were rais'd against him, partly by his Father, partly by some of the Nobility. It is related by some, That *Blanch* was not the eldest Sister, but that some of the *Castilian* Noblemen did dispute the right of *Berengaria* to the Crown, because the Pope had declar'd her marriage with *Alfonso* void, and their Children illegitimate, as being too near in Bloud.

    By the death of *Alfonso* \A. 1230\, *Leon* and *Castile* were reunited under *Ferdinand,* at what time the *Moors* suffer'd extreamly in their Affairs. King *James* of *Arragon* took from them *Majorca,* in the Year 1232. *Minorca* in the Year 1234. *Yvica* in the Year 1238. The City and Kingdom of *Valencia, Ferdinand* took from them {A. 1238}, besides other places, in the Year 1230, *Merida* and *Badajoz.* In the Year 1236, the City and Kingdom of *Corduba: Murcia* surrender'd it self to the protection of *Castile* \A. 1240\. In the Year 1248, *Jaen, Sevile,* and the greatest part of *Andalusia.* But whilst he was making Preparations to carry the War into *Africa,* he died in the Year 1252.

§7. The History of the next following Years is full of Troubles and Divisions. *Alfonso* {X.}, 'tis true, was famous in foreign Countries for his Wisdom and great skill in Astronomy, so that it is reported of him, that he used to say, *That if God would have advised with him at the time of the Creation of the World, the World should have been made more uniform;* yet he was unfortunate at home, and hated by his Subjects.[10] The first occasion of which was, that he being desirous to fill his Treasury, which was exhausted, he caus'd the current Coin to be diminish'd,

Ferdinandus Sanctus.

Alfonso X.

---

    10. For an interesting use of Alphonso X's (1221–84) philosophical views, see Neiman (2002), chap. 1, pp. 14ff.

which enhanc'd the price of every thing, and whilst to prevent this, he set certain rates on all Commodities, which occasion'd a general scarcity of all things, the people not being willing to sell at his rates. He was by some of the Electors chosen *Roman* Emperour \A. 1256\, but because his Children were then very young, and great Divisions arose among his Nobles, he delay'd for a great many Years <39> to go thither, and to receive the Imperial Crown, till in the Year 1275, a fancy took him all on a sudden, to go and take possession of the Empire, though *Rudolf* of *Habsburgh* was already got into the Imperial Throne.[11] But his Journey was ended in *Provence,* he returning from thence home by the persuasion of the Pope, who afterwards excommunicated him, and obliged him also to renounce the Title of Emperour. After the death of *Ferdinand,* his eldest Son, *Sanctius* {*V.*}, the younger Brother, did aim at {and receive} the Succession, tho *Ferdinand* had left Children behind him. This rais'd a Jealousie betwixt the Father and Son, who rose in open Rebellion against his Father, being assisted by the major part of the States [estates], which Commotion however ceas'd with the death

Sanctius V.   of *Alfonso* \A. 1284\. Under the Reign of this King many Battels were fought against the *Moors* with various success.

The Sicilian   In the Year also 1282 happened the *Sicilian* Vespers, by which means
Vespers.   *Peter* [III.] King of *Arragon* obtain'd the Kingdom of *Sicily,* he having before a pretence to it, as having married *Constantia* the Daughter of *Manfred.*[12] Against this *Sanctius* [V.] the Son{s} of *Ferdinand,* his elder Brother, rais'd several disturbances, which he overcame all by his Wisdom: he dyed in the Year 1295. During the time of the Minority of

Ferdinand IV.   his Son *Ferdinand* IV. the Kingdom of *Castile* was overwhelm'd with trouble. After he came to Age, he undertook an Expedition against the

11. Rudolph I of Habsburg (1218–91) became King of the Romans in 1273 and was eventually acknowledged as such by Alphonso X, who had been elected to the role (but not crowned) in 1256. See note 23, p. 60, and note 28, p. 67.

12. The Sicilian Vespers was the name of a rebellion in Sicily, so named because of the timing (at Vespers) of the first violence against the French troops. See V.8, note 15, p. 205, below. Manfred, son of Frederick II of the Hohenstaufen dynasty, was king of Sicily from 1258 to 1266.

Moors, taking from them *Gibraltar,* and died in the flower of his Age \A. 1312\. Under the Reign of this King \A. 1297\ *James* King of *Arragon* was presented with the Kingdom of *Sardinia,* by the Pope, who pretended to have a right of disposing of it;[13] and those of *Pisa* being then in possession of the same, were afterwards \A. 1324\ beaten out by the *Arragonians.*

The Minority also of *Alfonso* XI. was full of troubles. At that time the *Moors* had again received a great Reinforcement out of *Africa,* the *Castilians* nevertheless obtain'd a most signal Victory over them in the Year 1340 {near Tarissa}, in which Battel, 'tis said 200.000 were slain on the side of the *Moors,* and but only 25.000[14] *Spaniards.* At that time *Al*{*gi*}*zira* was taken, and a Peace concluded with the King of *Granada,* under condition that he should be tributa-<40>ry to *Castile.* This King died \A. 1350\ in the Siege of *Gibraltar,* which he had lost before. His Son *Pieter,* sir-named *The Cruel,* reigned very tyrannically. He drew the hatred of most of his Subjects upon himself by parting from his Queen *Blanch,* whom he afterwards, tho Innocent, for the sake of a Concubine, caus'd to be murther'd. This occasion'd a Plot against him, which he suppress'd with a great deal of Bloudshed. In the mean while a War arose betwixt him and *Pieter* IV. King of *Arragon,* who assisted the Rebels in *Castile,* who had set up for their King, *Henry* the King's Brother, begotten on a Concubine call'd *Eleonora Gusman:* With him also join'd a great many *French* Voluntiers; so that falling upon *Pieter* of *Castile* \A. 1366\, {where many of the cities fell to him,} he forc'd him to flee into *Aquitain.* But he [the latter] having rais'd there a considerable Army, return'd into *Spain,* defeated *Henry,* and obliged him to flee into *France,* but did not desist from his Tyranny, whereby he quite lost the Affection of his Subjects: And *Henry* having gather'd another Army in *France* return'd into *Castile;* where being assisted by the *Castilians* he vanquish'd *Pieter,* and in the flight kill'd him with his own Hands \A. 1369\.

Alfonso XI.

Peter the Cruel.

13. Pufendorf's original is unclear: "which the popes assigned to them [*ihnen zueigneten*] from olden times." Boniface VIII granted James II of Aragon the title "king of Sardinia and Corsica."

14. The German has "25." Spanish casualties.

Henry II. §8. Out of the Race of this *Henry* II. sirnam'd *The Bastard,* sprang afterwards Princes who prov'd very mischievous to *Spain.* *Henry* himself did at first labour under great difficulties, the neighbouring Nations attacking him every where, yet he surmounted them, and at last made Peace with them all. But the Favour of his Nobles he bought with John II. Money. He died in the Year 1379. His Son *John* endeavour'd to obtain the Crown of *Portugal,* of *Ferdinand* its King, whose Daughter he had married. But the *Portugueses,* out of a hatred against the *Castilians,* set up for their King, *John* natural Son to *Pieter* King of *Portugal,* who maintained himself against the *Castilians,* routing them near to *Aliunbaret;* which Victory the *Portugueses* mightily boast of in their Histories. *Castile* was at that time in great danger, the *English* siding with the *Portugueses,* under the Duke of *Lancaster,* who having married *Constantia,* the Daughter <41> of *Pieter* sirnamed *The Cruel,* pretended to the right of that Crown, bearing also the Title and Arms: But the business was at last compos'd, by marrying the Daughter of the *English* Duke to the Prince of *Castile;* after which also a Peace was concluded with *Portugal.*

Henry III. *John* died by a fall from his Horse \A. 1390\. His Son *Henry* III. was a sickly Prince, under whose Minority great Divisions arose in the Kingdom. During the time of his Reign he did nothing remarkable, except that he restor'd the Revenues which the Nobles had alienated from the John II. Crown. He died in the Year 1407, leaving behind him *John* II. a Child of two Months old. The tuition of this Prince was, besides his Mother, committed to *Ferdinand* his Uncle, to whom the States [estates] did offer the Kingdom, which he generously refusing to accept of, he obtain'd afterwards the Crown of *Arragon.* This King [John II.] being under the tuition of his Mother grown very Effeminate, only addicted to Voluptuousness, having no Genius nor inclination for publick Business, committed the whole management to his Favourite *Alvarez de Luna,* an ambitious Man, which occasion'd great Jealousies in his Nobles against him. This King taking his Favourite's part against the Nobility, an open War ensu'd betwixt them, the Rebels being headed by his own Son, and the City of *Toledo* declar'd against the King. At last the King being tir'd with the many Inconveniencies, cut this Favourite's Head off \A. 1453\;

but died himself in the Year next following. Under the Reign of this King a War broke out betwixt the *Spaniards* and those of *Granada,* wherein the first signaliz'd themselves to their advantage.

In the Year 1420 King *Alfonso* {*V.*} of *Arragon* was adopted by *Joan* Queen of *Naples* {as her son}; but a difference arising betwixt *Joan* and *Alfonso,* she declar'd the said Adoption void and null, receiving in his stead *Lewis* Duke of *Anjou;* which afterwards occasion'd bloody Wars betwixt *France* and *Spain:* Yet *Alfonso* at last kept the upper hand, making himself Master of *Naples* \A. 1442\, and leaving the same to his natural Son *Ferdinand.*

In the Kingdom of *Castile* succeeded *John* {*II.*} his Son *Henry* IV. the scandal to the *Spanish* Nation. He being incapable of be-<42>getting Children, to take away this suspicion, hired one *Bertrand Corva,* who for this service was made Earl of *Ledesma,* to lie with the Queen, who having brought forth a Daughter call'd *Joan, Henry* caus'd her to be proclaim'd Heiress to the Crown. What confirm'd this the more was, that the Queen afterwards had another Bastard begotten by another person. To remove this shame, and to exclude *Joan* from the succession of the Crown, the Nobles of *Spain* enter'd into an Association; and putting the Image of *Henry* upon a Scaffold, they there formally accus'd him, and afterwards, having taken off his Ornaments, threw it from the Scaffold, at the same time proclaiming *Alfonso,* Brother of *Henry,* their King. From hence arose most pernicious intestine Wars which ended in bloudy Battels. During these troubles *Alfonso* died \A. 1468\: About the same time, *Ferdinand* Son of *John* II. King of *Arragon,* whom his Father had declar'd King of *Sicily,* propos'd a Marriage with *Isabella, Henry's* Sister, to whom the rebellious *Castilians* had offer'd the Crown, and forc'd *Henry* to confirm the right of *Isabella* to the Crown; whereupon the Nuptials were celebrated, but privately \A. 1469\: Yet would *Henry,* by making this Concession void, have afterwards set up again the Title of *Joan,* whom he had promis'd in marriage to *Charles* Duke of *Aquitain,* Brother to *Lewis* XI. King of *France;* but he dying suddenly, *Henry* at last was reconcil'd to *Ferdinand* and *Isabella,* and died in the Year 1472.

Henry IV.

§9. From this match of *Ferdinand* (whom the *Castilians* call *The V.* or *The Catholick*) with *Isabella,* sprang the great Fortune and Power of *Spain,* it under his Reign arriving to that pitch of Greatness, which ever since has made it both the Terrour and the Envy of *Europe.* This *Ferdinand* also met with some obstacles at the beginning of his Reign, the States of *Castile* having limited his Power within too narrow Bounds: And *Joan,* the late King *Henry's* suppos'd Daughter, having contracted a match with *Alfonso* King of *Portugal,* who entring *Castile* with a puissant Army, caus'd her to be proclaim'd Queen; but the <43> *Portugueses* being soundly beaten, the whole design vanish'd, and *Joan* retiring into a Monastery, the civil Commotions were totally suppress'd. The next care of *Ferdinand* was to regulate such Disorders as were crept into the Government in the former Reigns; wherefore he caus'd that Law-book to be compil'd, which from the City of *Toro,* where it first was publish'd, is call'd *Leges Tauri.*[15]

In the Year also 1478, the famous *Spanish* Inquisition was first instituted by him against the *Moors* and *Jews,* who having once profess'd themselves Christians, did afterwards return to their Idolatry and Superstitious Worship.[16] This Court of Inquisition is esteemed an inhuman and execrable Tribunal among other Nations, and carries the greatest Injustice with it, in ordering the Children to bear the Guilt of their Parents, nor permitting any body to know his Accusers to clear himself against them: But the *Spaniards* ascribe to this Inquisition, the benefit which they enjoy of one Religion, the variety of which has brought great Inconveniencies upon other States: 'Tis true, by those means you may make Hypocrites, not sincere Christians.[17]

After he had order'd his Affairs at home, and after the death of his Father \A. 1479\, taken upon him the Government of *Arragon,* he undertook an Expedition against the *Moors* of *Granada* \A. 1481\, which

---

15. The Laws of Toro (1505).

16. Both Pufendorf and Crull reserve the term "Marrano" for Muslims, who are distinguished from Jews. See §§11, 12, and 15 of this chapter.

17. See Pufendorf (2002c), §35, p. 78, and §48, p. 104, a work originally published in 1687, in response to Louis XIV's revocation of the Edict of Nantes. Also see V.22, p. 248, and XII.41, p. 518, below.

[margin notes]

Ferdinand the Catholick and Isabella. The Kingdom of Castile and Arragon united.

The first beginning of the Spanish Inquisition.

lasted ten Years, wherein the *Spaniards* were routed near *Mallaga*
\A. 1483\, but quickly reveng'd themselves upon their Enemies, taking
from them one place after another, till they at last besieg'd the City of
Granada with 50.000 Foot and 12.000 Horse, and having forc'd the   Granada
King *Boabdiles* to a surrender \A. 1492\, they put an end to the King-   taken.
dom of the *Moors* in *Spain,* after it had stood there for above 700 Years:
And to prevent the possibility of their ever encreasing again in *Spain,*
he banish'd 170.000 Families of *Jews* and *Moors* out of *Spain,* by which
means, the Kingdom nevertheless was despoil'd of vast Riches, and of a
great number of Inhabitants. After this he took from them *Mazalquivir,*
Oran, Pennon de Velez and *Mellilla,* situated upon the Coast of *Barbary.*
Ferdinand also made use of this opportunity to teach his Nobles, who
were grown overpowerfull, their due <44> Respect and Obedience to
the King, and took upon himself the Sovereign Disposal of all the *Span-*
ish Orders of Knighthood, which were grown to that excess of Riches
and Power in *Spain,* that they were formidable to its Kings.

Much about the same time \A. 1494\ *Christopher Columbus, a Gen-*   America
ouese, discover'd *America,* after his Offers had been refus'd by the Kings   discover'd.
of *Portugal* and *England;* and after he had been seven Years solliciting at
the Court of *Castile* for a supply to undertake the Voyage: At last 17.000
Ducats were employed in equipping three Vessels, out of which Stock
such prodigious Conquests and Riches have accru'd to *Spain,* that ever
since it has aim'd at the Universal Monarchy of *Europe.* How easily the
Spaniards did conquer these vast Countries, and with what Barbarity
they us'd the Inhabitants, is too long to be related here.[18]

Not long after a War was kindl'd betwixt *Spain* and *France,* which has
been the occasion of inspeakable Miseries in *Europe;*[19] after these two
Warlike Nations were freed from that Evil which had hitherto diverted
them from medling with Foreign Affairs, the *French* having rid them-   The first rise
selves from the *English,* and the *Spaniards* from the *Moors.* For, when   of the War
Charles VIII. King of *France,* undertook an Expedition against the King-   and Spain.

---

18. Pufendorf owned a copy of Bartholomaeus de Las Casas, *Regionum indi-*
carum per Hispanos olim devastarum accuratissima descriptio, editio nova (Heidelberg: Walter, 1664). See Palladini (1999a), #969, p. 232.

19. The Italian Wars (1494–1559).

dom of *Naples* {A. 1494}, *Ferdinand* did not judge it for his Interest, to let the *French,* by conquering this Kingdom, to become Masters of *Italy;* especially, since by marrying his Daughters he was in aliance with *England, Portugal* and the *Netherlands,* and besides the then Kings of *Naples* descended from the House of *Arragon:* And tho *France* lately enter'd with him into a Confederacy, by vertue of which the *French* gave up *Roussilion* to *Spain,* hoping thereby to bring over *Ferdinand* to their Party; nevertheless, when he perceiv'd, That by all his Intercessions he could not disswade him [the French] from undertaking of this Expedition, he enter'd into a Confederacy with the Pope, Emperour, *Venice* and *Milan* against *France.* He also sent to the assistance of the *Neapolitans, Gonsalvus Ferdinand de Cordua,* afterwards sirnam'd *The Grand Captain,*[20] under whose Conduct the *French* were beaten out of the *Neapolitan* <45> Territories, whilst he himself made an inrode into *Languedock.*

In the Year 1500 the *Moors* living in the Mountains near *Granada* rebell'd, and were not without great difficulty appeas'd. Afterwards an Agreement was made betwixt *Ferdinand* and *Lewis* XII. King of *France,* concerning the Kingdom of *Naples,* under pretence, to make War from thence against the *Turks;* which being soon conquer'd by their joint Power, they divided it according to their Agreement. But because each of them would have had this delicious Morsel for himself, they fell at variance concerning the Limits and some other matters which interven'd betwixt two Nations that had an animosity against one another: Wherefore they came quickly to Blows, and *Gonsalvus* routed the *French* near *Ceriniola,* took the City of *Naples,* beat them again near the River *Liris* or *Garigliano,* and taking *Cajeta,* drove the *French* a second time out of the Kingdom of *Naples:* But *Gonsalvus* was not rewarded by *Ferdinand* according to his Deserts, for he not only lessen'd his Authority at *Naples,* but also being suspicious, that he either intended to keep that Kingdom for *Philip,* Son-in-law to *Ferdinand,* or else for himself, *Ferdinand* undertook a Journey in Person to *Naples,* on purpose to bring *Gonsalvus* handsomly away from thence; and taking him along with him into *Spain,* he treated him ill for his great deserts.

20. Gonzalo Fernandez de Cordoba (1453–1515). See V.16, note 32, p. 224, below.

In the mean time died the Queen *Isabella* \A. 1504\, which occasion'd some Differences betwixt *Ferdinand* and his Son-in-law *Philip* the *Neth-* erlander, *Ferdinand* pretending, according to the last Will of *Isabella,* to take upon him the Administration of *Castile.* And to maintain his Claim the better, he enter'd into a Confederacy with *France,* by marrying *Germana de Foix,* Sister to *Lewis* XII. hoping thereby to obtain a powerfull Assistance, in case *Philip* should come to attack him: But *Philip* coming into *Spain,* and taking upon him the Administration of the Government in the name of his Lady *Joan, Ferdinand* retir'd into *Arragon.* But *Philip* died soon after \A. 1506\, whose Queen *Joan* being not in her right Wits, yet undertook the Administration of the Government, not without the opposition of some <46> of the chief of the Nobility; wherefore, the Administration of the Government was by common consent committed to *Ferdinand* after his return from *Naples,* notwithstanding the Emperour *Maximilian* did pretend to it, in the right of his Grandson *Charles.*[21]

In the Year 1508 *Ferdinand* enter'd into a Confederacy against the *Venetians,* whereby he regain'd the Cities of *Calabria, Brindisi, Otranto, Trazo, Mola* and *Polignano,* which the *Venetians* had formerly obtain'd for some Services done to the *Neapolitans.* But as soon as *Ferdinand* perceiv'd that the *Venetians* were like to be swallow'd up by the Emperour and *France,* the Pope and he left the Confederacy, thinking it more convenient to preserve the State of *Venice;* since by adding the Territories of *Venice* to those of *Milan,* which were then possess'd by the *French,* they would have grown too powerfull in *Italy.* Hence arose a War, in which *John d' Albert,* King of *Navarre,* taking part with the *French,* was upon instigation of *Ferdinand* excommunicated by the Pope; under which pretext *Ferdinand* took an opportunity \A. 1512\ to possess himself of that part of the Kingdom, which lies on the *Spanish* side of the *Pyrenean* Mountains; which since that time the *French* have in vain indeavour'd to recover. In the Year 1510 the *Spaniards* took *Bugia*

Philip.

Ferdinand
conquer'd
Navarre.

---

21. Charles V (1500–1558) was Maximilian's grandson through his father, Philip the Fair (that is, the Netherlander; 1478–1506), who was married to Ferdinand and Isabella's daughter, Joan of Castile (1479–1555).

and *Tripolis* upon the Coast of *Barbary;* but were routed in the Island of *Gerbis*. This wise King died in the Year 1516.[22]

Charles. §10. Him succeeded his Grandson by his Daughter, *Charles,* the fifth Emperour of that Name, who, with the assistance of the Cardinal *Ximenes,* immediately took upon himself the {complete} Administration of the Government, his Mother, {Joanna,} to whom the same [the empire] did belong, being incapable of Administring it. This Prince, who, since *Charles* the Great, was the most Potent Prince that hath been in *Europe,* spent the greatest part of his Life in Travels and Wars. In the very beginning of his Reign, there were some Commotions in *Spain,* which were soon appeased. *John D' Albert* also made an Inrode into the Kingdom of *Navarre,* in hopes to recover it, but was quickly repul-<47>sed. But with the *French,* during his whole Life, he waged continual Wars. For, though in the Year 1516, he made a League with King *Francis* I. whereby the Daughter of *Francis* was promised to him in Marriage; yet was this Tie not strong enough to withhold the Animosity of these two 'courageous' [ambitious] Princes. *Charles,* who was flush'd up with the great Success of his House, had always in his Mind his Motto, *Plus ultra* [still further]. But *Francis,* who was surrounded every-where by so potent a Prince, did oppose his Designs with all his Might, fearing, lest his Power should grow too strong both for him and all the rest of *Europe*.

Charles obtain'd a most particular advantage, when the Imperial Dignity[23] was conferr'd upon him \A. 1519\; to obtain which for himself, or some-body else, *Francis* had labour'd with all his Might, but in vain.

22. Ferdinand (like Philip of Macedon) was one of the monarchs respected by Pufendorf for their executive ability and constructive use of sovereign power. He employed ratio status in the best interest of his own state and exhibited the kind of realistic flexibility required for this.

23. Literally: "the dignity of a Roman King." "King of the Romans" was the title of an emperor after he had been elected (by the Electors) but not yet crowned (by the pope). It also came to mean emperor-elect, as when it was conferred on an emperor's expected heir or successor. Charles V was elected in 1519 but not crowned by Clement VII until 1530. See note 11, p. 52, and note 28, p. 67; also, Pufendorf (2007), IV.9, pp. 109–110.

Robert de Mare [von der *Marck*], Lord of *Sedan,* withdrawing him-
self from the Emperour, and putting himself under the Protection of
France, with whose assistance he attack'd the Lord of *Emmerick,* who
was under the Emperour's protection, administer'd new matter of jealousie, which quickly broke out into an open flame in the *Netherlands.*
In which War the *French* lost *Tournay* and *St. Amant,* but beat the
Imperialists from before *Meziores. Charles* also did intend to drive the
French out of *Milan* upon instigation of Pope *Leo* X. *Charles* pretending
that *Francis* had neglected to receive this Dutchy in fief of the Empire,
beat the *French* near *Bicoque. Fonterabie* also, which they had taken
by surprize, was re-taken by force from the *French.* It proved also very
disadvantageous to them, that the Constable *Charles* of *Bourbon,* sided
with the Emperour; and entring *Provence* \A. 1524\, besieged *Marseilles;*
Which nevertheless he was forced to quit, as soon as *Francis* march'd
with all his Forces that way into *Italy* to recover the *Milaneze.* Where
he took the City of *Milan,* but at the Siege of *Pavia* was Attack'd by the
Imperial Generals, who totally routed his Army; and having taken him
Prisoner, carried him into *Spain* \A. 1525\.

The King himself was in part the occasion of this loss, he having
sent a great part of his Army towards *Naples* and *Savona;* and those that
remained with him, <48> were most *Italians, Swiss* and *Grisons,*[24] who
did not perform their Duty in the Battle; and most of his Generals were
of opinion, to avoid the hazard of a Battle, by retiring under the City
of *Milan.* The *French* also succeeded ill in the Diversion, which they
endeavour'd to give the Emperour; <for> by the help of *Charles* Duke
of *Geldres,* and the *Friselanders,* for they were at that time worsted by
Charles's Forces. There were some that advised *Charles,* to set *Francis* at
liberty without any Ransome, and by this Act of Generosity to oblige
him for ever: But he followed the Counsels of such as did advise to
make advantage of so great a Prisoner. He therefore imposed very hard
Conditions upon him, which *Francis* refusing to accept of, out of discontent fell into a dangerous Sickness, so that *Charles* himself went to
visit and comfort him; Though he was advised to the contrary by his

24. Grisons or Graubünden refers to the most eastern canton of Switzerland.

Chancellour *Gallinaca,* who alledged that such a Visit, where he did not intend to promise the Prisoner his liberty, would rather seem to proceed from Covetousness, and fear of losing the advantage of his Ransome, than from any civility or good inclination towards him. And this Sickness was the real cause, why at last the Treaty, concerning his Liberty, which had been so long on foot, was finish'd, the Emperour fearing that his Discontent might plunge him into another Sickness, or Death itself.

In the mean time, the prodigious Success which attended the Emperour, did raise no small jealousie among other Princes; and by instigation of Pope *Clement* VII. three Armies were raised to maintain the Liberty of *Italy.* To prevent this Storm, and especially to withdraw the Pope from the Confederacy, the Emperour's Generals marched directly against *Rome,* which they took by Storm, (where *Charles* of *Bourbon* was slain,) and for several days together plunder'd the City, and committed great Out-rages. The Pope himself was besieged in the Castle of *St. Angelo;* and *Charles,* at the same time that the Pope was enclosed {by} his own Forces[,] caused {public} Prayers to be made {in Spain} for 40 days together, for his deliverance;[25] at last \A. 1527\, forced by Famine, he was forced to Surrender, and to renounce the above-men-<49>tion'd League.

Rome taken
by Charles V.

The Conditions, on which *Francis* had obtain'd his Liberty, were, That *Francis* should surrender the Dukedom of *Burgundy;* to renounce the Sovereignty over *Flanders* and *Artois;* quit all his pretences upon *Naples* and *Milan;* to marry the Emperour's Sister *Eleonora,* and to give his two Sons as Pledges for the performance of these Articles. But as soon as he got into his own Kingdom he protested against the Treaty, which was extorted from him during his Imprisonment: And making a League with the Pope, *England, Venice,* the *Suiss* and *Florence,* sent an Army into *Italy* under the Command of *Odet de Foix,* Lord of *Lautree.* This occasion'd not only that very gross words pass'd betwixt these two

---

25. Charles's troops had mutinied because they had not been paid, and the sack was not ordered by Charles. Thus, the public prayers for the pope's "deliverance" (*Erledigung*) were likely a way to assert his impotence in the matter, or to cover his embarrassment. The German *erledigen* can also mean "to finish off," but if that meaning is also intended the irony would be Pufendorf's, not Charles's or Crull's.

Princes, but they also gave one another the lye, and a Challenge pass'd
betwixt them: But *Lautree,* who had at first great success, being destroy'd
with his Army by Sickness in the Siege of *Naples,* a Peace was at last concluded at *Cambray,* in the Year 1529, by virtue of which *Francis* paid for
his Sons 2.550.000 Rixdollars [*Reichsthaler*], renounc'd his Pretensions
to *Flanders, Artois, Milan,* and *Naples,* and marry'd *Eleonora,* Sister to
the Emperour; out of which Marriage, if a Son should be born, he was
to be put into the possession of the Dukedom of *Burgundy.*

A Peace made at Cambray.

In the Year 1530, *Charles* 'was' [had himself] Crowned by Pope *Clement* VII. at *Bononia* [Bologna], whereby he obtained from the Emperour, that the Common-wealth of *Florence* should be made a Principality, and the said City was by force obliged to admit this Change.
Alexander de Medicis being constituted Duke, to whom the Emperour
married his natural Daughter *Margaret.* In the same Year the Bishop of
Utrecht resign'd the Soveraignty of that City, and the Province of *Over-
yssel,* into the Hands of *Charles,* and the Provinces of *Geldren, Zutphen,
Groningen;* the *Twente* and *Drente* also fell into his Hands. In the Year
1535, he went with a puissant Army into *Africa,* took *Tunis* and *Goletta,*
restoring the Kingdom of *Tunis* to *Muleassa,* who was banished before
by *Haradin Barbarossa,* but in *Goletta* he left a Garrison.

In the Year 1537, another War broke out betwixt *Charles* and *Francis:*
For the latter could not digest the loss of *Milan;* and being advised <50>
by the Pope, that when-ever he intended to Attack *Milan,* he should
first make himself Master of *Savoy;* and *Francis Sforzia* dying at the
same time, he fell upon *Charles* Duke of *Savoy;* and under pretence,
that he defrauded his Mother of her Dowry, drove him quite out of
Savoy, and conquered a great part of *Piedmont.* But the Emperour, who
was resolved to annex the Dutchy of *Milan* to his Family, came to the
assistance of the Duke of *Savoy,* and at the Head of his Army, entring
Provence, took *Aix,* and some other Places; but his Army being much
weakned with Sickness, for want of Provisions, he was forced to retire
again. In the *Netherlands,* the *Imperialists* took St. *Paul* and *Monstrevil,*
killing great Numbers of the *French.* Through Mediation of the Pope,
Paul III. a Truce of 10 Years was concluded at *Nissa* in *Provence* \A. 1538\;
after which these two Princes had a friendly Interview at *Aigues Mortes.*

And in the next following Year, the Emperour, against the advice of his friends, ventured to take his way through the very heart of *France,* being desirous with all possible speed to compose the Disorders, which were arisen at *Ghent.* Yet had he before by the Connestable *Anna{n} Montmorancy,* cajolled *Francis* into a belief, that he would restore to him the Dutchy of *Milan,* which however he never intended to perform.

In the Year 1541, he undertook an Expedition against *Algiers* in *Africa,* at the latter end of the Year, against the advice of the Pope and others <of his friends>, who 'persuaded' [advised] him to stay [wait] till next Spring. He there Landed his Army with good success; but a few days after such prodigious Storms and Rains did fall, which dispersed his Ships, and spoiled the Fire-locks of the {foot}Souldiers, that the Emperour was obliged, with the loss of one half of his Army, to return into *Spain.* In the Year next following \A. 1542\, *Francis* broke with him again, under pretence that his Ambassadours *Caesar Fregosus* and *Anthony Rinco,* which he had sent through the *Milanese,* by the way of *Venice,* to go to the *Ottoman* Port, were upon the River *Po* Murthered by Orders of the Governour of *Milan.* Wherefore *William* Duke of *Cleves* entring *Brabant* on one side, the Duke of *Orleans* on <51> the other side, took *Luxemburgh* and some other places. The *Dauphin* besieg'd *Perpignan,* but was oblig'd to raise the Siege: The famous Pirate *Barbarossa,* did by the instigation of *Francis,* great mischief on the Seacoasts of *Calabria,* destroying *Nissa* in *Provence* by Fire.

Charles seeing himself at once attack'd in so many places, setting aside the Differences which were arisen about the Divorce betwixt *Henry* and his Aunt *Catherine,*[26] made a League with *Henry* King of *England,* wherein it was agreed, That the Emperour should force his way through *Champaigne,* whilst *Henry* enter'd into *Picardy,* that so they might, by joining their Forces, ruine the whole Power of *France.* The Emperour therefore, with an Army of 50.000 men, beat the Duke of *Cleves* in the *Netherlands,* forcing him to surrender *Guelderland;* and after having recover'd the places in *Luxemburgh,* taken before by the *French,*

---

26. The reference is to Henry VIII and Catherine of Aragon, who was the youngest child of Ferdinand and Isabella, and aunt of Charles V.

enter'd into *Campaigne,* taking by force *Lygny* and *Disier: Francis* kept with his Army on the other side of the River *Marne,* and not daring to fight the Imperialists, contented himself to ravage the Country which they were to march through, to endeavour to cut off their Provisions: Nevertheless the Imperial Army found a sufficient quantity at *Espernay* and *Chasteau Thierry.* This occasion'd such a Terrour and Confusion in *Paris,* that the Citizens were for leaving the City, if the King, by his Presence, had not encourag'd them to stay. And if, on the other side, King *Henry* had acted according to the Agreement, they might easily have got the *French* Army betwixt them, and in all likelyhood, would have put a period to the *French* Greatness. But *Henry* being detain'd at the Sieges of *Bologne* and *Monstrevil,* sent word to the Emperour, That he would not stir further, till he had made himself Master of these two places. *Charles* then began to suspect the King of *England,* whom he perceived meerly to be for his own Interest, and did not think fit to trust any longer; considering also with himself what vast charges he was at in this War, and how thereby his Designs were retarded which he had projected against the Protestants in *Germany;* as also, that his Forces had receiv'd a considerable overthrow <52> in *Italy,* near *Carizola,* from the *French,* he made thereupon a Peace with *Francis* at *Crespy* in the County of *Valois* {A. 1544}.

Peace made at Crespy.

Then *Charles* undertook to subdue the Protestants, entring, for that purpose, into a League with Pope *Paul* III. which War he carried on with such success, that without great trouble he overthrew them \A. 1547\, making their chief Heads, the Elector of *Saxony* and *Landsgrave* of *Hesse,* Prisoners: The Emperour made use of this Policy, in fomenting Divisions betwixt Duke *Maurice* and his Cousin, the Elector of *Saxony;*[27] and refusing to fight with them at first, he thereby protracted the War, foreseeing, that a Confederacy under so many Heads would not last long, and that the Cities, which contributed the most towards it, would grow quickly weary of the Charges of the War. *Francis* also,

Charles wages War against the Protestants in Germany.

27. Maurice (1521–53) of Albertine Saxony and his cousin, John Frederick (1503–54) of Ernestine Saxony, a cofounder of the Protestant Schmalkaldic League (1531–47).

and *Henry* VIII. were both of them lately dead, who else, questionless, with all their Power, would have oppos'd his designs of oppressing the Protestants, thereby to make himself absolute Master in *Germany.* The Heads also of the Protestant League did greatly contribute to their own Misfortune, they having let slip several opportunities, especially, at first, before the Emperour had rightly settled his Matters, when they might have done him considerable mischief; nevertheless *Charles* was no great gainer by these Victories, because he used the Conquer'd, whom he was not able to keep in Obedience by force, with too much rigour, keeping the Captive Princes in too close an Imprisonment. He also disobliged *Maurice* Elector of *Saxony,* after his Father-in-law the *Landtgrave* of *Hesse,* had by his persuasions surrender'd himself to the Emperour. The Elector therefore being persuaded by the Prayers of his Children and others, who objected to him, That by his Assistance their Religion and Liberty were in danger of being lost, he fell unawares upon *Charles* \A. 1550\, whom, under favour of the Night and a Fogg, he forc'd to retire from *Inspruck.* After this exploit a Peace was concluded by the Me-

Treaty at Passaw. diation of King *Ferdinand,* where, in the Treaty at *Passaw,* the Protestant Religion was establish'd. In the mean while *Henry* II. King of *France,* coming to the assistance of <53> the Protestants, had taken *Metz, Toul* and *Verdun.* The Emperour attackt *Metz* again with great fury, but having been fain to leave it after a considerable loss sustain'd, he discharg'd his Fury upon *Hesdin* and *Tervanne,* which he levell'd with the Ground. In *Italy* the *Imperialists* took *Siena* \A. 1554\, which afterwards *Philip* II. gave to *Cosmus* Duke of *Tuscany,* reserving to himself the Sovereignty and some Sea-ports.

At last, *Charles* tir'd with the Toils of the Empire, and the Infirmities of his Body, resigned the Imperial Crown to his Brother *Ferdinand,* who would not consent that the same should come to his Son *Philip.* But to *Philip* he gave all his Kingdoms and Territories, except those

Abdication of Charles. in *Germany* (which fell to *Ferdinand*'s share) reserving to himself only a yearly allowance of 100.000 Ducats. He had made a little before, a Truce of five Years with *France,* which was soon broke by the persuasions of the Pope, who endeavouring to drive the Family of *Colonna* out of their Possessions; and they being upheld by the *Spaniards*, the *French* sided with the Pope. But this War prov'd very unfortunate to the *French*, they being routed at St. *Quintins*, lost that City, and the Mareschal *de Thermes* was also soundly beaten near *Gravelin*. At last \A. 1559\ a Peace was again concluded at *Chateau en Chambrasis*, by virtue of which, the *French* were obliged to restore all what they had taken in *Italy*, which had been the occasion of some Blood-shed by *Francis* and *Henry*. But under-hand it was agreed, That both the King of *Spain* and *France* should endeavour to root out the Hereticks (as they call'd them) which succeeded afterwards very ill both in *Spain* and *France*. In the Year before this, *viz.* 1558, died *Charles* in the Convent of St. *Justus* in *Spain*, where he spent his last days in quiet. His last Will and Testament (tho never so rational) was so far from being pleasing to the Inquisition, that it wanted but little of having been burnt as Heretical. But his Father Confessour and the rest of the Monks in that Convent, who had been present, were forc'd to undergo the severe Judgment of this Court. <54>

§11. Under the Reign of *Philip* II. the {extraordinary} greatness of the *Spanish* Monarchy began to be at a stand; neither had its Kings the same success, as formerly, to get vast Kingdoms by Marriages. For from the match of *Philip* with *Mary* Queen of *England*, came no Children. And truly, in my Opinion, the *Spanish* Greatness receiv'd the first shock at that time, when *Charles* V. surrender'd his Dominions in *Germany* to his Brother *Ferdinand* [of Austria], and afterwards had him elected King of the *Romans;*[28] by which means the Power of this House was divided, and the Imperial Crown separated from the *Spanish* Monarchy. *Charles* would fain have afterwards persuaded *Ferdinand* to transfer the Succession of the Imperial Crown upon *Philip;* but he being persuaded by his Son *Maximilian* to keep what he had got, would in no ways part with it. He was also much belov'd by the *Germans*, whereas they had an aversion against *Philip;* who being a meer *Spaniard*, did not as much as understand the *German* Tongue: And *Ferdinand* and his Successours

Peace betwixt Spain and France.

Charles dies.

Philip II.

28. See note 11, p. 52, and note 23, p. 60.

|[prov'd very good Princes, who were not fond of the *Spanish* methods of Governing.[29]]|

But that which gave the greatest shock to the *Spanish* Greatness, were the Troubles arisen in the *Netherlands*. The reason why this 'Evil' [cancer] grew incurable, was, because *Philip* being over fond of his ease, would rather sit still in *Spain,* than by his Presence endeavour to stop the current before it ran too violent, tho' his Father did not think it too much, to venture himself at the Discretion of *Francis* his {greatest} Rival, to appease the Tumults arisen only in the City of *Ghent*.[30] Another reason was, That he took the most violent course, by sending the Duke of *Alva,* a cruel Man, among the *Netherlanders,* who being us'd to a mild sort of Government, were thereby put into despair; especially when they were inform'd, That the Inquisition had declar'd Criminal, not only those who were guilty of the Rebellion, and pulling down the Images, but also all such Catholicks as had not made resistance against them. The Saying of *Anthony Vargas,* a *Spanish* Minister, is as famous as ridiculous; *Haeretici diruerunt templa, boni nihil fecerunt contra, ergo omnes debent patibulari;* i.e. *The Here-<55>ticks demolish'd the Churches, the Catholicks [boni] did not oppose them, wherefore they ought all to be hang'd.* Besides this, the *Spaniards* were much hated by the *Netherlanders,* not only because of the great differences there was betwixt the Manners of these Nations, but also, because these latter had been in great esteem with *Charles* V. who was very like them in all his Behaviour: On the contrary, *Philip* |[only encourag'd the *Spaniards*]|,[31] who having an extraordinary conceit of their own Abilities, and taking the *Netherlanders* for Cowards, did not think they had Courage enough to oppose their Designs. The *Spaniards* also were well pleas'd to see the *Netherlanders* to begin first, hoping the King would thereby take an opportunity to clip their Privileges, and by making them all alike obtain an absolute Dominion over them: This done, they hoped to make these Countries their Armory and Store-house, from whence they

29. Rather: "were men [*Herren*] of a calm disposition, and did not always wish to dance according to the Spanish pipe [flute]."

30. See §10, p. 64, above.

31. Rather: "esteemed only his Spaniards."

might with more ease invade *France* and *England,* and raise the *Spanish* Monarchy to the highest degree of Greatness. But the *Netherlanders,* on the other side, were resolv'd not to part with their Liberty, nor to be treated as a conquer'd Nation. And when *Philip,* at his departure, would leave *Spanish* Garrisons in the *Netherlands,* and to soften the matter, constituted the Prince of *Orange* and Earl of *Egmont,* Generals over them, yet could they not be persuaded to accept of the same, alledging, That the *Netherlanders* had got but very small Advantages by the Peace with *France,* which they had procur'd by their own Valour, if they now should be in danger of being subdu'd themselves by a foreign Power.

The neighbouring Princes also, but especially *Elizabeth,* Queen of *England,* took an opportunity by these troubles to empty the vast Treasures of *Spain,* and to exhaust its Strength. The Protestant Princes also of *Germany,* who hated the *Spaniards,* were glad of this opportunity, and assisted the Prince of *Orange* upon all occasions. And the Emperours thought it more convenient to be at quiet and to please the *Germans,* than to be too forward to assist their Cousins. These Commotions in the *Netherlands* did also occasion the War betwixt *Philip* and *Elizabeth,* Queen of <56> *England,* she not only affording assistance to the *Netherlanders,* but also the *English* Privateers doing considerable mischief to the *Spanish West-India* Ships; and the famous *Francis Drake* plunder'd the very Southern Coast of *America.* On the other side, *Philip,* by supporting the Rebels in *Ireland,* proved very troublesome to Queen *Elizabeth.* At last *Philip* did resolve with one stroke to put down the whole Strength of *England;* to which purpose he was equipping a great Fleet for several Years together, which he call'd *The Invincible,* the like never had been seen before those times. The Fleet consisted of 150 Sail of Ships, which carried 1600 great pieces of Brass Cannon, and 1050 of Iron; 8000 Seamen, 20.000 Souldiers, besides Volunteers; the Charge amounted daily to 30.000 Ducats, but the whole Preparations to twelve Millions of Ducats. The Pope *Sixtus* V. also excommunicated Queen *Elizabeth,* assigning her Kingdom to *Philip.* But all these Preparations came to nothing, the greatest part of this Fleet being destroy'd, partly by the *English* and *Dutch,* partly by Tempests, few return'd home, and that in a most miserable condition, so that there was scarce a Noble

War with England.

The Spanish Armada destroyed.

Family in *Spain* but went into Mourning for the loss of some Friend or another. But the evenness of Temper is much to be admir'd in *Philip*, who receiv'd this bad news \A. 1588\ without the least alteration, giving only this Answer, *I did not send them out to fight against the Winds and Seas.* Afterwards the *English* and *Dutch* Fleets being joined, beat the *Spanish* Fleet near *Cadiz*, taking from the *Spaniards*, not only a great many Ships richly laden, but also the City of *Cadiz* it self; which nevertheless was again left by the *English* General, the Earl of *Essex*, after he had plunder'd it, to the great dishonour of the *English*, who might from thence have done a great deal of mischief to the *Spaniards*.

Neither did *Spain* get any advantage by having entangled it self \A. 1596\ in |[the Troubles, and (as it was call'd) *the holy League*, made in *France*.]|[32] *Philip*, 'tis true, propos'd to himself to have met with a fair opportunity, by excluding the *Bourbon* Family[,] to annex the Crown of *France* to his House, or by raising <57> Divisions in this Kingdom to swallow up one piece or another, or to assist one of his Creatures in obtaining that Crown; or, at least, by dividing it into so many Factions, so to weaken its Strength, as that it should not be able to recover it self for a considerable time. But by the Courage and good Fortune of *Henry* IV.[33] all these Measures were broke, and he declaring himself a Catholick, took away the Foundation whereupon the League was built. Thus *Philip* lost his vast Expences; and besides this, suffer'd extreamly in his Affairs; for in the mean time that he sent the Duke of *Parma*, Governour of the *Netherlands*, to the assistance of the League in *France*, the Confederate *Netherlanders* had leisure given them to put themselves and their Affairs into a good posture: *Philip* acted in this business according to the old proverb; *That he who hunts two Hares at once, commonly catches neither of them:* Besides, *Henry* IV. after he had restor'd his Affairs in *France*, declar'd War against *Philip* \A. 1594\; which was nevertheless carried on in the *Netherlands* with 'various' [dubious] success,

---

32. Rather: "the troubles caused by the so-called Holy League in France."

33. Henry of Navarre (1553–1610), whose conversion to Catholicism and accession to the French crown (in 1589) ended the religious wars. His Edict of Nantes (1598) granted Huguenots a measure of religious freedom in France until the edict was revoked by Louis XIV in 1685.

the Count *de Fuentes* taking *Cambray* in the Year 1595, and in the Year next following, the Archduke *Albert, Calais.* On the other side, *Henry* recover'd *Fere* from the *Spaniards.* In the Year 1597, the *Spaniards* took *Amiens* by surprise, which *Henry* recover'd not without great difficulty. At last, a Peace was concluded in the same Year betwixt *France* and *Spain* at *Vervin,* because *Philip* was unwilling to leave his Son, who was but young,[34] entangl'd in a War with so great a Captain as *Henry* was; and *Henry* was sensible, that the Kingdom of *France* being enervated did greatly want a Peace.

Peace made at Vervin.

Philip also waged several Wars against the *Turks;* for the Pyrate *Dragutes* had taken from the *Spaniards Tripoli* \A. 1551\, after they had been in possession of it for forty Years. To retake this, *Philip* sent a strong Army \A. 1560\, which took the Isle of *Gerbis;* but being afterwards beaten by the *Turkish* Fleet, he lost, together with the Island, 18.000 Men and 42 Ships. In the Year 1564 *Philip* retook *Pegnon de Velez.* In the Year 1566 *Maltha* was besieg'd by the *Turks* during the space of four Months, which was reliev'd by *Philip,* he forcing the *Turks* to raise the Siege with great loss. <58> In the Year 1571 the Confederate Fleet of *Spain, Venice,* and other *Italian* States, under the Command of *Don John* of *Austria,* did obtain a most signal Victory over the *Turkish* Fleet near *Lepanto,* whereby the *Turkish* Naval Strength was weaken'd to that degree, that they were never afterwards so formidable in those Seas, as they were before. But else the *Spaniards* had got no great Reputation in this War; for by their delays that considerable Island of '*Rhodes*' [Cyprus] was lost <before>. In the Year 1573 *Don John* of *Austria* pass'd with an Army into *Africa,* to retake *Tunis,* which succeeded so well, that he forc'd the City, and added a new Fortification to it. But in the Year next following, the *Turks* sent a puissant Army thither, and retook the City, its Fortifications being not quite perfected, as also *Goletta* which being not very well provided with all Necessaries, was lost by the unskilfulness and Cowardice of the Governour; so that the whole Kingdom of *Tunis,* to the great prejudice of the Christians, fell into the Hands of the *Turks.*

34. Philip II died in September 1598, leaving the kingdom to his twenty-year-old son, Philip III, who had little interest in governing.

At home *Philip* had a War with the *Marans* of *Granada*,[35] who re-belling against him, were supported by the *Algerines,* and could not be subdu'd but with great difficulty; and if the *Turks* had been quick enough in giving them timely assistance, it might have prov'd very dangerous to *Spain*. This Rebellion did not end till the Year 1570, after it had continued for three years. There were also some Commotions among the *Arragonians* \A. 1592\; who 'pretended to take part with' [took the side of] *Anthony Perez,* who |[standing upon his privilege against the Process that was made]|[36] him for having upon the King's Orders, 'murther'd' [executed] *Escovedo,* an intimate Friend of *Don John* of *Austria. Philip,* by this intended to purge himself of the Infamy of the fact, and at once to revenge himself upon *Perez,* who had been unfaithfull to him in some Love Intrigue, aiming at that himself which he had undertaken to procure for the King. And tho this did not much redound to the honour of *Philip,* yet by this he took an opportunity to retrench the Privileges of the *Arragonians.* In the Year 1568, *Philip* caus'd his Son *Charles* to be 'kill'd' [executed], under pretence that he had endeavour'd to kill his Father; and not long after, the <59> Queen *Isabella* also, *Charles*'s Step-mother, died, not without suspicion of having been poison'd. But a great many are of opinion, that some Love Intrigues were the occasion of their death, which is the more probable, because the said *Isabella* being intended for the Bride of *Charles,* had been taken by the Father in spite of his Son.[37]

Portugal falls to Spain.

Henry King of *Portugal* dying \A. 1579\, there were several pretend-ers to that Crown, among whom was *Philip,* as being born of *Isabella, Emanuel* King of *Portugal*'s Daughter, who maintain'd his Right by the Sword; and under the Conduct of the Duke of *Alva* conquer'd the

35. Crull does not translate Pufendorf's reference to the Moorish Marranos as "riff-raff" (*Gesindel*).

36. Rather: "sought to protect himself with that kingdom's privileges from the suit brought against."

37. The reference is to Elisabeth of Valois (1545–68), daughter of Henry II of France and Catherine de Medici, and Philip II's third wife, who was initially be-trothed to Don Carlos (Philip's son from his first marriage, to Maria Manuela of Portugal). The legend of a tragic love between Carlos and Elizabeth (eventually, his stepmother) became the theme of Schiller's play, and Verdi's opera, *Don Carlos.*

Kingdom, forcing *Anthony,* the Bastard, who had caus'd himself to be proclaim'd King, to fly into *England,* and from thence into *France,* where he died {miserably} an Exile in *Paris* \A. 1595\: Only the Island of *Tercera* held out for some time longer, which the *French* intending to relieve, were totally routed by the *Spaniards.* And thus *Philip* became Master, both of the *East* and *West Indies,* the two greatest Mines of Riches in the World. Nevertheless, the *French, English* and *Hollanders* had found out a way to ease him of these prodigious Revenues. For *Philip,* just before his death, did confess, That the War with the *Netherlands* only, had cost him 564 Millions of Ducats. And truly, it is very probable, that trusting to his vast Riches he was thereby prompted to his ambitious Designs and to undertake more than prov'd beneficial to him. He died in the Year 1598.

§12. *Philip* the IIId's Father had left him the Kingdom in Peace with *France,* but the *Dutch* War grew every day the heavier upon the *Spaniards.* The *Spaniards* did hope, that after *Philip* II. in his latter days had married his Daughter *Clara Eugenia* to *Albert* Archduke of *Austria,* giving her the *Netherlands* for a Dowry, the *Dutch* would become more pliable, and reunite themselves with the rest of the Provinces in the *Netherlands,* as having now a Prince of their own, and not liable to the *Spanish* Government. But because the *Hollanders* did by no means like this bait, and at the Siege of *Ostend* gave a tast to the *Spani-*<60>*ards,* both of their Strength and firm Resolution, that they were resolv'd to stand it out with them, the *Spaniards* resolv'd to make Peace with them; especially since the *Hollanders* had found out the way to the *East Indies,* where they made great progress; *France* also enjoying a peaceable Government under *Henry* IV. and encreasing in Power, it was fear'd, That if the *French* should fall upon *Spain* with fresh Forces, which had been tir'd out by this tedious War, it might prove fatal to *Spain.* They were also in hopes, that the fear of a foreign Enemy ceasing, the *Hollanders* in time of Peace might fall into Divisions among themselves; or at least, that Peace and Plenty might abate their Courage. The *Spaniards* did sufficiently shew their eagerness for a Peace with *Holland,* by setting the Treaty on foot in the *Hague,* by sending *Ambrosius Spinola*

Philip III.

himself,[38] among others, thither as Ambassadour, and by granting and
allowing them the *East India* Trade. Whereas the *Hollanders* 'carried
it very high' [were tough and arrogant during the negotiations], and
Truce with would not abate an ace of their Proposals. At last \A. 1609\, a Truce for
Holland. twelve Years was concluded with *Holland.*

In the Year next following, *Philip* banish'd 900.000 *Marans* (the Off-
spring of the ancient *Moors,* who had profess'd themselves Christians
only for a shew) out of *Spain,* because they intended to raise a Rebellion, and had underhand crav'd Assistance from *Henry* IV. In the same
Year the *Spaniards* took the Fortress of Arache, situated on the Coast
of *Africa;* as they had likewise possess'd themselves before of the Harbour of *Final,* near *Genoua,* in the Year 1619. Those of the *Valtelins* did
withdraw themselves from the *Grisons.* The *Spaniards* sided with the
former, in hopes to unite them with the Dukedom of *Milan.* But *France*
taking part with the *Grisons,* the business was protracted for a great
many years, till at last matters were restor'd to their former state. This
difference did rouse up all *Italy,* and the Pope himself took part with the
Grisons, tho Protestants, assisting them in the recovery of the *Valtelins.*
The War being broken out in *Germany,* the *Spaniards* sent *Ambrose
Spinola* out of the *Netherlands* into the *Palatinate,* part of which was
subdu'd by them. *Philip* III. died in the Year 1621. <61>

Philip IV. §13. His Son *Philip* IV. at the very beginning of his Reign made great
alterations in the Court, sending away the Creatures of the Duke *de
Lerma,* the Favourite of his Father: He himself foreseeing what was
likely to befall him, did timely obtain a Cardinal's Cap, fearing the
King should aim at his Head. With the beginning of the Reign of this
King, the Truce with *Holland* being expir'd, the War was rekindled, in
which *Spinola* was forc'd \A. 1622\ to raise the Siege of *Bergen op Zoom,*
because *Christian* Duke of *Brunswick,* and General *Mansfeld,* having
before routed the *Spaniards* near *Fleury,* came to the assistance of the

---

38. Ambroglio Spinola (1569–1630), an Italian, was at the time the respected
leader of Spain's forces in the Southern (Spanish) Netherlands.

Hollanders. Pieter Heyn surpris'd the *Spanish* Silver Fleet[39] \A. 1628\, with a Booty of 12 Millions of Gilders. At the same time the *Hollanders* did settle themselves in *Brasile,* taking the City of *Olinda.* In the Year 1629, the *Spaniards* being in hopes to make a considerable Diversion, and to put the *Dutch* hard to it, made an Inrode into the *Velaw,* and took *Amersfort,* whilst the *Hollanders* were busied in the Siege of *Hertogenbusk Bois le Duc,* but the *Hollanders* taking *Wesel* by surprise, they were oblig'd to retreat with all speed over the River *Yssel,* for fear, that their retreat should be cut off by the *Dutch.*

In the Year 1639, a great Fleet was sent out of *Spain* into the Channel, under the Command of *Don Oquendo,* which was destroy'd by *Martin Tromp,* in the *Downs,* in the very sight of the *English.* What the Intention was of sending so great a Fleet this way, was not generally known at that time; but afterwards it was divulged, that the same was intended against *Sweden,* and that there were 20.000 Men ready in *Denmark,* which, as soon as this Fleet should have appear'd before *Gothenburg,* were to have join'd them and enter'd *Swedeland.* Afterwards the War was protracted, but most to the disadvantage of the *Spaniards,* till the Year 1648, when the *Spaniards* concluded a Peace with the *Hollanders* at *Munster,*[40] declaring them a free People, renouncing all their pretences over them, and leaving to them all the places which they had taken from them. And notwithstanding *France* did its utmost to hinder the conclusion of this Peace, at least so long, till that Kingdom might also make a Peace <62> with *Spain;* but the *Hollanders* did not think it adviseable to stay their leisure, fearing, that if *Spain* was brought too low, the *French* would thereby be enabled to swallow up the [Spanish] *Netherlands,* and become their immediate Neighbours, which they foresaw would prove fatal to their State. It was also alledged, and that with good reason, That it was time to put up the Sword, when all those things might be obtained by fair means for which it was drawn at first;

39. The annual fleet transporting Spain's precious metals from its American colonies to Spain. The shipment was crucial to the Spanish economy.
40. This was part of the Westphalian settlement ending the Thirty Years' War.

and that the Province of *Holland* had contracted considerable Debts. *Spain* also perceiving, that the *Dutch* were not to be overcome by force, was willing to agree to those Conditions, being glad to be rid once [and for all] of so troublesome an Enemy, that they might |[have the more leisure to be even with]|[41] *France* and *Portugal*. It is reported, that this War cost the *Spaniards* <above> One thousand five hundred Millions of Ducats.

In the Year 1628, *Vincent* II. Duke of *Mantua,* dying, the Emperour endeavour'd to exclude *Charles* Duke of *Nevers,* he being a Frenchman born, from the succession of that Dukedom, under pretence of having neglected some Matters appertaining to it, as being a Fief of the Empire. The *Savoyards* also took this opportunity to renew their Pretensions upon *Montserrat,* and the *Spaniards,* in hopes of getting something in the Fray, besieged *Casal.* On the other side, the *French* took part with the Duke of *Nevers,* raised the Siege of *Casal,* and put the Duke of *Nevers* into possession of the Dukedom of *Mantua,* which did much weaken the Reputation of the *Spaniards* in *Italy.*

In the Year 1635, the *French* denounced War against *Spain,* under pretence, that they had taken prisoner *Philip Christopher* Elector of *Treves,* he being under the protection of the King of *France,* and that they had driven the *French* Garrison out of *Treves,* and possess'd themselves of that City; but the true reason was, that it was thought high time to bridle the Ambition and Power of the House of *Austria,* which after the Battel of *Nordlingen,* and the Peace concluded at *Prague,*[42] was grown very formidable, and *France* being well settled at home, began to be in a very flourishing condition. The *French* therefore, af-<63>ter they had beat the Prince *Tomaso* near *Avennes,* enter'd the *Netherlands* with a great Army, but the Success did not answer Expectation; the *Dutch* especially being unwilling, that *France* should make any considerable Conquests on that side: Neither did the *French* gain any thing in *Italy.* In the Year next following the Prince of *Conde* was forc'd to raise the

---

41. Rather: "be better able to handle."
42. In 1635, Sweden's first great defeat in Germany after the death of Gustavus Adolphus, in 1632. See XIII.15, p. 590.

Siege of *Dole;* and the *Spaniards* entring *Picardy* fill'd *Paris* it self with Terrour and Confusion. *Gallas* also, the Imperial General, endeavoured to enter *Burgundy* with his Army, but did not advance much.

In the Year 1637 the *Spaniards* lost *Landresi.* In the next Year they were forced to retire from before *Leucate* with great loss; but the Prince of *Conde,* on the other hand, had the same ill fortune before *Fonterabia;* \A. 1639\ the *Spaniards* beat the *French* soundly near *Thionville,* but lost *Hesdin, Salses* and *Satins;* and in the Year following, the strong City of *Arras,* they being besides this, routed near *Casal:* Nor could they with all their Strength force the Earl of *Harcourt* from before *Turin.* In the same Year also the *Catalonians* did revolt, they being first dissatisfy'd at the Pride of the Duke *d'Olivarez,* the King's Favourite, against whom they had made great complaints, but were nevertheless sorely oppress'd by him. These discontents encreased after the *Catalonians,* endeavouring the relief of *Salses,* were beaten, they pretending that they were not duely assisted by the *Castilians,* and therefore left the Army and march'd home. *Conte Duca* taking this opportunity, represented them very ill to the King, and caused their Privileges to be considerably diminished, and their Country to be oppress'd with their quartering of Souldiers. This put them in open Rebellion, and *Barcellona* beginning first, they drove the *Spaniards* out of *Catalonia.* Then seeking Aid from *France,* they at last, after the *Spaniards* had cut off by their Cruelty, all hopes of Mercy, put themselves under the Protection of that Kingdom: And it was eleven Years before the *Spaniards* could quite recover *Catalonia,* the intestine Commotions in *France* presenting them with a fair opportunity; for *Barcellona,* being not timely reliev'd, was forc'd to surrender {again} to <64> the *Spaniards* \A. 1651\.

But the *Portugueses* withdrawing themselves from the Obedience of the *Spaniards* \A. 1640\, gave a great shock to the *Spaniards. Philip* II. tho he had conquered this Kingdom, yet had always endeavour'd by mildness, and by preserving their Privileges, to mitigate the hatred which the *Portugueses* bore to the *Castilians,* which were grown to that height, that the Priests used to insert it in their Prayers, *That God would be pleased to deliver them from the* Castilian *Yoak:* But after his death the *Spanish* Ministers had not been so carefull by maintaining their Privi-

Catalonia rebels.

Portugal falls off from Spain.

leges, to keep the affection of the *Portugueses,* but rather had treated them as a conquered Nation; which so exasperated the *Portugueses,* that as soon as they saw *Spain* begin to decline, immediately \A. 1636\ some places in *Portugal* did rebel, but were soon after reduced to their former Obedience. The *Spaniards* therefore thought it adviseable, that to bridle this People, nothing could be more proper, than by employing the [Portuguese] Nobles as well as the Commoners in the [Spanish] Wars, to purge the superfluous ill Humours of this Nation. In the mean while the *Catalonians* falling into Rebellion, the *Portuguese* Nobles were ordered to go into the Field, which they did not relish well; having besides this, some other reasons to be dissatisfy'd with the *Spaniards:* And, because the *Portugueses* had a great affection for the Duke of *Braganza,* the *Spaniards* try'd all ways to entice him to come to Court, and supposing that they had cajoll'd him sufficiently with fair promises, invited him very courteously to go in person with the King into the Field; which invitation, nevertheless he knew how to decline very dex-

The **Portugueses.** terously. At last the *Portuguese* Nobility being hard press'd to serve in the Expedition against the *Catalonians,* which they would in no ways consent to, unanimously agreed to shake off the *Castilian* Yoak, and secretly sounded the Inclinations of the Duke of *Braganza.* As soon as he, upon the persuasions of his Lady, had resolv'd to accept of the Crown, they broke loose, and surprising the Garrison in the City, Palace and Fort, seiz'd the Ships, kill'd the Secretary of State *Vasconcello,* who had

Duke of Braganza proclaimed King of Portugal. carried himself very proudly a-<65>mong them, and proclaimed the Duke of *Braganza* King, under the Name of *John* IV. purging the whole Kingdom within eight days of the *Castilians,* and that with the loss only of two or three persons. Which may serve as a remarkable instance to convince the World, how easily a Kingdom is lost, where the Peoples Inclination is averse to the supream Head.

Thus the *Spanish* Monarchy received a great blow, and its Power being distracted, it could not act effectually on all sides. They also lost *Perpignan* \A. 1642\; tho the *French* could not go further into *Spain,* for the Prince of *Conde* besieged *Lerida* in vain \A. 1647\. In the Year 1641 {, as well}, the Prince [of] *Monaco* driving the *Spanish* Garrisons out of his Territories, put himself under the protection of *France.* There also happen'd {A. 1647} a most dangerous Rebellion at *Naples,* the Head of which was a poor Fisherman, whose Name was *Massanello;* who might have put the whole Kingdom into a flame, if the *French* had been at hand to give him timely assistance; but by the prudent management of the Governour, the Earl of *Ognato,* the Tumult was appeased. *Spain* then being forc'd to quench the flames on all sides, it could not be so mindfull of *Holland,* as the most remote, having all hands full, to resist the dangers threatning them nearer home. And the *Spaniards* had the good fortune to reduce, as we said before, *Catalonia,* under their Subjection, and \A. 1650\ to chase the *French* out of *Piombino* and *Porto Longone;* but the *English* took from them the Island of *Jamaica* in the *West Indies.* At last *France* being re-established in its former Tranquility, the *Spaniards* thought it most convenient to make Peace with that Crown: Which was concluded betwixt the two great Ministers of State, the Cardinal *Mazarini* and *Don Lewis de Haro,* in the *Pyrenean* Mountains {A. 1659}:[43] By vertue of which *France* got *Roussilion,* and several considerable places in the [Spanish] *Netherlands.*

Spain having thus concluded a Peace with all the rest of its Neighbours, it began in earnest to make War against *Portugal.* The *Spaniards* therefore enter'd *Portugal* with a great Force, taking from the *Portugueses* several places, but were also at several places soundly beaten. The Battel near <66> *Entremos* \A. 1662\, where *Don Juan,* and that near *Ville Viciosa* \A. 1665\, where *Cavacena* received a fatal Defeat, are most famous: The obtaining of which two Victories on the *Portuguese* side is chiefly ascribed to the *French* General *Schamberg.*[44] *Philip* IV. died in the Year 1665.

§14. He had for his Successour his Son *Charles* II. a Child of four years of age, who under the Tuition of his Mother, negligently prosecuted the War against *Portugal,* and at last \A. 1668\, by the Mediation of *England,* was forc'd to make Peace with that Crown, renouncing his right

Right margin notes:

Massanello's Rebellion at Naples.

The Pyrenean Treaty.

Charles II.

Peace with Portugal.

---

43. The Treaty of the Pyrenees (1659).

44. Frederick Hermann, duke of Schomberg (1615–90). A Calvinist, Schomberg later left France for Brandenburg and accompanied William III to England, dying in Ireland at the Battle of the Boyne. See Glozier (2005).

to the same; because the *French* at that time made a grievous havock in the *Netherlands*. For tho' *Mary Teresia*, Daughter of *Philip* IV. at the time when she was married to the King of *France* had renounc'd all her right of Succession to her paternal Inheritance, yet the *French* taking the opportunity of their flourishing condition, and the decay'd state of *Spain, England* also and *Holland* being engaged in a War with one another, who would else not have left the *Netherlands* to be devoured by them; they enter'd *Flanders* with a vast Army, using among other things, for a pretence, that which in *Brabant* is called, *Jus devolutionis,* by which the real Estates of private persons, fall to the Children born during the time of the first marriage, as soon as the Father marries again. The *French* took in this War, without much resistance, a great many considerable Cities and Forts, *viz. Charleroy, Tournay, Lisle, Donay, Oxdenarde,* and some others; they conquer'd also the whole *Franche Compte,* which hastened the Peace betwixt *England* and *Holland,* and occasioned the

The Tripple Alliance.

Tripple Alliance, as it is called, made {A. 1667} betwixt *England, Sweden* and *Holland,* for the preservation of the *Spanish Netherlands.* In the fol-

Peace made at Aix la Chapelle.

lowing Year *France* made a Peace with *Spain* at *Aix la Chapelle,* restoring to *Spain* the *Franche Compte,* but keeping what places 'he' [it][45] had taken in *Flanders.* But when *Holland,* in the Year 1672, was attack'd by the *French, Spain* sided with the *Dutch,* knowing that the loss of the *United Provinces* must draw after it that of the *Spanish Netherlands:* So it came again to an open War, wherein, at first, <67> *Spain* lost *Burgundy.* The rebellious *Messineses* threw themselves under the protection of *France,* but were afterwards deserted by them. *France* also got *Limburgh, Conde, Valencienne, Cambray, Ypres, St. Omer, Aeth* and *Ghent:*

Peace made at Nimmegen.

But \A. 1679\ a Peace was concluded at *Nimmegen,* by virtue of which *France* kept the *Franche Compte,* and most places taken in the *Netherlands,* restoring only to *Spain, Limburgh, Ghent, Cortryck, Oudenarde, Aeth* and *Charleroy.*

---

45. Crull is probably thinking of "the Frenchman," a usage silently accepted elsewhere in this edition where it does not create inconsistencies, as here. See note 64, p. 93, below.

§15. Having thus given a brief History of the Kingdom of *Spain*, we will also add something concerning the Genius of the *Spaniards*, and the extent of their Territories, as also of the Strength and Weakness of this Kingdom, and its Condition in reference to its Neighbours: The *Spanish* Nation therefore is commonly esteem'd to be very 'wise' [sensible], and to take remote prospects, throughly weighing a thing before it undertakes it. Whereby, nevertheless the *Spaniards*, being overcautious and exact in their Counsels, do often lose the opportunities of action. Besides this, the *Spaniards* are very constant to their Resolutions; and tho' they fail once in an Attempt, they will try their Fortune again, endeavouring to overcome its frowns by their Constancy. They are very fit for War, and not only brave at the first attack, but also will hold out till the last; their sober way of living, and spare Bodies make them fit to bear Hunger and Thirst, and to be very watchfull: But this the *Spaniards* are extreamly blamed for, that they maintain their Gravity by high-flown Words and a proud Behaviour. Tho' those that converse with them, do declare, that this Gravity which appears so odious, is not so much the effect of their Pride, as of a melancholy Constitution and an ill Custom, they never being fond to converse much with Foreign Nations.

They are in general, very zealous for the *Roman Catholick* Religion, and abominate all others. They are seldom fit for any Trade or Business where any hard labour is required; such as Husbandry, or any Handycraft Trades; wherefore these are chiefly managed among them by Foreigners. It is credibly reported, That in *Madrid* alone, there <68> are above 40.000 *Frenchmen,* being for the most part, Merchants, Artists, Handycrafts men and Labourers, who go under the Name of *Burgundians,* thereby to avoid the hatred, which the *Spaniards* naturally bear against the *French.* And such is the *Spanish* pride, that tho' they think it below themselves to meddle with those trifles, yet they do not think much to be a poor Centinel in some Fort or another all their life time, the honour of the Sword, and hopes of becoming in time an Officer, making them amends for what hardship they endure. Their Pride, 'Covetousness' [miserliness] and 'rigorous proceedings' [severity] make

them hatefull to all such as are under their Command; which are very
unfit Qualifications for the maintaining of great Conquests. For no
body is willing to be despised by Foreign Governours.

Spain being mightily exhausted of Men, and therefore incapable of
raising great Armies within it self, is very unfit to maintain vast Countries, for which several reasons may be given. For the Women here are
not so fruitfull as in the Northern parts, which is to be attributed to
the heat of the Climate, and the constitution of their 'spare' [dry] Bodies. Those parts also which are remote from the Sea-shore, are not well
peopled, some of these Grounds being very barren, not producing any
thing for the subsistance of Mankind. Whoring also being publickly
allowed of here; a great many of them will rather make shift with a
Whore than to maintain a Wife and Children. These also, who have
taken upon them holy Orders, of whom there is a great number, are
obliged not to marry. The Wars which they have waged against so many
Nations, but especially in *Italy* and the *Netherlands,* have devoured a
great many *Spaniards.* A vast number have transplanted themselves into
'*America*' [*the West Indies*] {and have filled that land with new domi-
ciles [*Wohnstädten*]}, being glad to go to a place where they may with
a small beginning come to live very plentifully. {On the other hand,}
before the discovery was made of '*America*' [the West Indies], *Ferdinand*
the *Catholick,* had <at> once before the City of *Granada,* an Army of
50.000 Foot and 20.000 Horse, tho' *Arragon* did not concern it self in
that War, and *Portugal* and *Navarre* were at that time not united with
Castile. At last this Country was mightily dispeopled, <69> when *Ferdi-*
nand, after the taking of *Granada,* and *Philip* III. banished a great many
thousands of *Jews* and *Marans,* who could not be kept in obedience in
Spain; these settling themselves in *Africa,* retain to this day their hatred
against the Christians, robbing their Ships in those Seas.[46] But this is
evident enough, that the *Spaniards* could never have made a Conquest
of those vast Countries, by force of Arms, if the greatest part of them
had not fallen into their Hands by easier ways.

46. Pufendorf does not mention the emigration of Jews to the United Provinces.

§16. Concerning those 'Countries' [regions, *Landschafften*] which are The Con-
under the Jurisdiction of this Nation; *Spain* is large enough in extent stitution of
the Spanish
for the number of its Inhabitants, but it is not fertile alike in all places; Countries.
for the most remote parts from the Sea-coasts are many of them barren,
not producing any thing for the subsistance of Men or Beasts: But for
the most part, nearer to the Sea-side, it is very fine and fruitfull. There
is abundance of Sheep here. They have also very fine Horses, but not
in very great quantities, having scarce enough for their own use. This
Kingdom is very well situated for Trade, having on the one side the
Ocean, and on the other side, being almost surrounded by the Mediterranean, where they have most excellent Harbours. The product of their
Grounds and Commodities fit for Exportation, are especially Wooll,
Silk, Wine, Oyl, Raisons, Almonds, Figs, Citrons, Rice, Soap, Iron,
Salt, and such like. In former times the *Spanish* Gold-mines were most
famous, but now-a-days, neither Gold nor Silver, as far as I know, is
digged out in *Spain:* Some will alledge for a reason, That it is forbidden
under severe penalties, to keep it as a reserve in case of a great extremity.
But I am rather apt to believe, That those Gold-mines have been long
a-goe quite exhausted by the Avarice of the *Spaniards.*

§17. The greatest Revenue of *Spain* comes from the '*East*' [West] *Indies,* The Spanish
from whence Gold and Silver, like Rivulets are conveyed into *Spain,* West Indies.
and from thence into the other parts of *Europe.* At what time, and by
whom this Country, which had been so long un-<70>known to the
Europeans, was first discover'd, we have already mentioned.[47] Tho' there
are [those] that pretend, That *America* was discovered in the Year 1190,
by one *Madoc,* Son to *Owen Gesnerb,* a Prince in *Wales,* who they say,
made two Voyages thither; and having built a Fort in *Florida* or *Virginia,* or as some say, in *Mexico,* died in *America:* And this is the reason
why in the *Mexican* Tongue abundance of *British* words are to be met
withall; and that the *Spaniards,* at their first coming into *America* did
find the remnants of some *Christian* Customs among the Inhabitants:

47. See §9, p. 57, above.

From whence some inferr, That if the first discovery of a Country, gives a good Title of Propriety to the Discoverers, *England* would have as good, if not a better Title to *America* than *Spain;* but this we will leave to be decided by others.[48]

But it is not so evident, from whence *Spain* could claim a right of subduing that Countrey by force of Arms. For, what is alledged among other pretences, concerning the Bull of *Alexander* VI.[49] wherein he did grant those Countries to *Spain,* this does not only seem ridiculous to us, but also to those *Barbarians* themselves, who have ridicul'd it, saying, *The Pope must be a strange sort of a Man, who pretended to give away that which was none of his own:*[50] But let this be as it will, the *Spaniards* think it sufficient that they are in possession of it; and if an exact scrutiny should be made into other matters of this nature, it would appear, that the Titles to most conquered Countries were none of the best.[51] But <some of> the most conscientious *Spaniards* do not justifie what Cruelties, their Country-men committed in the beginning against those poor People, of whom they kill'd, without any provocation given, a great many hundred thousands; or destroyed them by forcing them to undergo intolerable hardships, and making the rest their Slaves: Tho' afterwards *Charles* V. being informed of their miserable condition, ordered all the rest of the *Americans* to be set at liberty.[52]

But the *Spaniards* are not Masters of all *America,* but only of the

48. The Madoc legend began in the Middle Ages but became more popular during the Elizabethan era, when it was used to support English claims in the New World. It survived into the mid-twentieth century.

49. The Bull of Alexander VI in 1493 effectively partitioned the newly discovered Americas between Spain and Portugal, though America was still thought to be part of the East Indies at the time rather than a new continent.

50. This statement may be quoted from Las Casas. See §9, note 18, p. 57, above.

51. In relation to this general question, see *On the Law of Nature and of Nations,* VIII.6, on the law of war.

52. Even though, in 1518, he had granted a license to a Flemish nobleman for the annual importation of 4,000 African slaves into the West Indies, Charles V was prompted by Las Casas in 1542 to enact the so-called New Laws forbidding enslavement of native Americans. Colonial opposition soon weakened them, however, and they were generally ignored in the Americas.

middle part of it, *viz.* The Kingdoms of *Peru* and *Mexico*, and those vast Islands of *Hispaniola*,[53] *Cuba* and *Porto Ricco, Jamaica* having been taken <71> from them by the *English*. These parts of *America* are now-a-days inhabited by five several sorts of People: The first are the *Spaniards,* who come thither out of *Europe;* these are put in all Offices. The second are called *Crioliens* [Creoles], who are born in *America* of *Spanish* Parents: These are never employ'd in any Office, as being ignorant of the *Spanish* Affairs, and too much addicted to love their native Country of *America;* wherefore the King is cautious in giving them any Command, fearing, lest they should withdraw themselves from the Obedience of *Spain,* and set up a Government of their own; especially, because these *Crioliens* bear a great hatred against the *European Spaniards.* For this reason also the Governours are changed every three Years, to take away the opportunity of strengthening their Interest too much; who after their return into *Spain* are made Members of the Council for the *Indies,* as being esteemed the most proper to advise concerning the preservation of that Country. The third sort are called *Metiffs* [Mestizos], who are born of a *Spanish* Father and an *Indian* Mother, are in no esteem among them. Those who are brought forth of the marriage of a *Spaniard* with a *Metiff,* or of a *Metiff* and a *Spanish* Woman, are called *Quatralvos,* as having three parts of a *Spaniard,* and one of an *Indian:* But such as are born of a *Metiff* and an *Indian* Woman, or of an *Indian* Man and a *Metiff* are called *Tresalvos,* as having three parts of an *Indian* and one of a *Spaniard.* The fourth sort are the remnants of the ancient Inhabitants, of whom a great many are to be met with, especially in the Kingdoms of *Peru* and *Mexico,* who are not so Barbarous as some may imagine, there having been found among them such excellent Laws and Constitutions as would make some *Europeans* blush. The fifth sort are the *Moores,* or, as the *Spaniards* call them, *Negroes,* who being bought in *Africa* are sent thither to do all sorts of drudgery. These are generally very handy, but very perfidious and refractary, wherefore they must always be kept

Several sorts of Inhabitants in the Spanish West Indies.

53. Hispaniola designated the island now occupied by Haiti and the Dominican Republic.

under a strict hand.[54] Such as are born of a *Negro* and an *Indian* Woman are called *Mulats* [Mulattos].

Yet is that part of *America,* considering its bigness, not <72> very well stock'd with People, since the *Spaniards* did in a most cruel manner root out the most of its ancient Inhabitants: And if I remember well, *Hieronymus Benzonus* says, *That all the Cities in* America, *which are inhabited by the* Spaniards, *joined together, were scarce to be compared, for number of People, with the Suburbs of* Milan:[55] Yet there are some who talk 'largely' [specifically] concerning *Mexico, viz.* That it has betwixt 30 and 40.000 *Spanish* Citizens, who are most of them very wealthy, so that it is reported, there are 18.000 Coaches kept in that City.

The *Spaniards* are not easily to be beaten out of *America;* because most places which are in their possession, are hard to come at, and it is very difficult to transport such a number of Souldiers out of *Europe,* as can be sufficient to attack any of these places: Besides this, the great difference of the Climate, and Diet could not but occasion mortal sicknesses among them: But in *Peru,* especially, they are very well settled, there being scarce any access by Land, and by Sea you are obliged to go round the South and remotest parts of *America,* or else to come from the *East Indies;* both which are such long Sea-voyages, which an Army can scarce undergo without running the hazard of being destroy'd by Sickness.

Riches of America. Concerning the Riches of *America,* 'tis true, the *Spaniards* at their first coming thither did find no coined Gold or Silver, that being unknown in those days to the Inhabitants; but an inconceivable quantity of uncoined Gold and Silver, and abundance of Gold and Silver Vessels made without Iron Tools, all which the *Spaniards* carry'd into *Spain,* except what the Seas swallowed up in their Voyages, which was very

54. Pufendorf formally rejects the notion of natural slaves, though he allows that some people are better off submitting themselves to others for their own welfare. See *On the Law of Nature and of Nations,* III.2.8.

55. Hieronymus (Girolamo) Benzoni (1519–70) wrote *La historia del mondo nuovo* (Venice, 1572). Pufendorf's library contained a French version thereof: *Histoire nouvelle du nouveau monde . . . , extraite de l'italien de M. Hierosme Benzoni Milanois . . .* par M. Urbain Chauveton (Geneva, 1579). See Palladini (1999a), #186, pp. 44–45.

considerable: But now-a-days those Rivers which formerly used to carry a Golden Sand, are most exhausted; and what is found there now is all dug up out of the Mines; especially the Silver Mines of *Porost* [Potosi] in *Peru*, do {still} afford an incredible quantity of Silver, which is yearly, together with some other Commodities, transported in a Fleet into *Spain:* Nevertheless a great part of this Silver |[belonging to]|[56] *Italian, French, English* and *Dutch* Merchants, the least part of it remains in *Spain;* so that the *Spaniards* keep the Cow, <73> but others have the Milk: Wherefore, when \A. 1563\ the *French* and *Spanish* Ambassadours at *Rome* quarrel'd about Precedency, and the latter, to represent his Master's Greatness, spoke very largely of the vast Riches of *America*, the *Frenchman* answered, *That all* Europe, *but especially* Spain, *had been a considerable loser by them: The* Spaniards *having employed themselves in searching after the Treasures of* America, *were thereby become idle, and had dispeopled their own Country. The King of* Spain *trusting to his great Riches, had begun unnecessary Wars.* Spain *being the fountain from whence vast Riches were derived to other Nations, did receive the least benefit of all by them, since those Countries that furnish'd* Spain *with Souldiers and other Commodities did draw those Riches to themselves.*

Formerly there were also Emeraulds in *America*, and Pearls were found, but that Stock is long since, by the Avarice of the *Spaniards*, quite exhausted. There is besides this, a great quantity of Commodities in *America*, which are used in Physick and Dying Colours. There is also great quantities of Sugars and Hides, as appears in that in the Year 1587 the *Spanish* Fleet transported 35.444 Hides from St. *Domingo*, and 64.350 from *New Spain:* For the Oxen and Cows, which were first transported from *Spain* into *America*, are grown so numerous, that they shoot them for their Hides sake only throwing away the Flesh, which is scarce eatable. And as *America* is the best Appendix of the *Spanish* Kingdom, so the *Spaniards* take all imaginable care to prevent its being separated from *Spain*. They make, among other things, use of this Arti-

---

56. Rather: "is acquired by." This remark reflects mercantilist assumptions, according to which economic wealth was measured in terms of precious metals acquired through commerce. See IV.34, p. 185, below.

fice, That they will not allow any Manufactory to be set up in *America*, so that the Inhabitants cannot be without the *European* Commodities, which they do not suffer to be transported thither in any other Ships but their own.

The Canary Islands.

§18. Besides this, the *Canary Islands* are in the possession of the *Spaniards*, from whence are exported great quantities of Sugar and Wine; it is credibly reported, That *England* alone transports above 13.000 Pipes of Canary, at 20 *l. per* Pipe.[57] The Island of <74> *Sardinia* also belongs to the *Spaniards*, which Isle is pretty large, but not very rich, its Inhabitants being for the most part *Barbarians*. The Isle of *Sicily* is of much greater value, from whence great quantities of Corn and Silk are to be exported; but the Inhabitants are an ill sort of People, who must be kept under, according to the old Proverb, *Insulini quidem mali, Siculi autem pessimi.*[58] Unto *Sicily* does belong the Isles of *Maltha* and *Goza,* which was given in Fief from *Charles* V. to the Order of the Knights of *Rhodes. Spain* also has a great part of *Italy* in its possession, *viz.* The Kingdom of *Naples,* who's Capital City is scarce bridled [kept obedient] by three Castles. The Sovereignty of *Siena,* and a great many strong Sea-ports, and the Sea-coasts of *Tuscany,* viz. *Orbitello, Porto Hercule, Telemone, Monte Argentario, Porto Langone,* and the Castle of *Piombino;* besides that noble Dukedom of *Milan,* which is the Paradise of *Italy,* as *Italy* is commonly called the Paradise of *Europe:* They have also the Harbour of *Final* upon the *Genouese* Coast. In the City of *Milan,* Trade and Manufactory flourishes extreamly, and this Dukedom is much valued by the *Spaniards,* because they have thereby a convenient Correspondence with the House of *Austria.*

Sardinia.

Sicily.

Naples.

Milan.

The Netherlands.

As long as *Burgundy* and the *Netherlands* were united, they might be compared to a Kingdom; but now *Burgundy* is lost, the seven united Provinces have separated themselves from the rest of the *Netherlands,* and *France* has conquered a great part of the remainder. And tho' in

57. In German: "13000. Pipen Canarie secc, die Pipe zu 20. Pf. Sterling." A pipe is a hollow tube or cylinder, so the reference is to containers of (dry, *secc*) wine.

58. "Islanders are [always] bad, but Sicilians are the worst." The saying is typically identified as a Latin or Italian proverb, though always without precise attribution.

the *Spanish Netherlands* there are very fair and strong Cities left, yet
nevertheless it seems, that the greatest benefit which *Spain* receives
from them amounts to this, That by them the *French* Arms are diverted
from the other *Spanish* Territories, that they commonly draw the Seat
of War thither, and serve to take off the edge of the *French* Fury. In
the *East Indies* the *Philippine* Islands belong to the *Spaniards,* whose   The Philippine
Capital City being *Manilla,* was taken by them in the Year 1565: but   Islands.
these Islands are so inconsiderable, that it has been often under debate, whether it were not most convenient to abandon them: Yet some
Indian Commodities, which from <75> several places, and especially
from *China* are brought to *Manilla,* are from thence transported to
New-Spain and *Mexico,* whereby there is kept a constant Communication betwixt the *Spanish West* and *East Indies.*

§19. From what has been said it is evident, that *Spain* is a potent King-   Strength and
dom, which has under its Jurisdiction, rich and fair Countries [*Länder*],   Weakness of
abounding with all Necessaries, not only sufficient for the use of its   Spain.
Inhabitants, but also affording a great overplus for Exportation. The
Spaniards also do not want Wisdom in managing their State Affairs,
nor Valour to carry on a War: Nevertheless this vast Kingdom has its
Infirmities, which have brought it so low, that it is scarce able to stand
upon its own Legs: Among those is to be esteemed one, the want of
Inhabitants in *Spain,* there being not a sufficient number both to keep
in obedience such great Provinces, and at the same time to make Head
against a potent Enemy; which want is not easily to be repaired out of
those Countries which are under their subjection, since it is the Interest
of *Spain,* rather to restrain the Courage of these Inhabitants, for fear
they should one time or another take Heart, and shake off the *Spanish* Yoak. And whenever they raise some Souldier in these Provinces,
they cannot trust them with the defence of their Native Country, but
are obliged to disperse them, by sending them into other Parts, under
the Command only of *Spaniards: Spain* therefore is scarce able to raise
within it self, a sufficient number of Souldiers for the Guard and Defence of its frontier places: Wherefore, whenever *Spain* happens to have
War with other Nations, it is obliged to make use of Foreign Souldiers,

and to raise those, is not only very chargeable but also the King is not so well assured of their Faith, as of that of his own Subjects.[59] The want of Inhabitants is also one reason, why *Spain* cannot now-a-days keep a considerable Fleet at Sea, which nevertheless is extreamly necessary to support the Monarchy of that Kingdom.

Another weakness is, That the *Spanish* Provinces are mightily disjoined, they being divided <76> by vast Seas and Countries: These therefore cannot be maintained and governed without great difficulty; for the Governours of the Provinces being remote from the sight of the Prince, he cannot take so exact an account of their Actions; and the oppressed Subjects want often opportunity to make their Complaints to the King; besides that, Men and Money are with great charge and danger sent out of *Spain* into these Provinces, without hopes of ever returning into the Kingdom. Their Strength cannot be kept together, as being obliged to divide their Forces. The more disjoined these Provinces are, the more frontier Garrisons are to be maintained; all which may be saved in a Kingdom, whose parts are not so much dis-joined. They are also liable to being attack'd in a great many places at once, one Province not being able to assist another: Besides this, *America* being the Treasury of *Spain,* is parted from it by the vast Ocean, whereby their Silver Fleets are subject to the hazard of the Seas and Pyrates. And if it happens that such a Fleet is lost, the whole Government must needs suffer extreamly by the want of it, the Inhabitants of *Spain* being so exhausted, as not to be able to raise sufficient Summs to supply the Publick Necessities.

The *Spaniards* are also mighty deficient in regulating their *West India* Trade, which is so ill managed, that the greatest part of those Riches are conveyed to other Nations, whereby they are empoured to chastise *Spain* with its own Money. After the death of *Philip* II. it has also proved very prejudicial to *Spain,* that by the carelessness of the succeeding Kings, and during the long Minority of this present,[60] the Nobles

59. On mercenaries, see I.11, pp. 24–25, above.
60. Since Charles II (1661–1700), son of Phillip IV (1605–65), was physically and mentally disabled, the kingdom was mostly governed by his mother and others. His failure to produce an heir led to the War of the Spanish Succession (1702–13).

have so increased their Power, that they are now very backward in duely
assisting the King, and by impoverishing the King and Commonalty
have got all the Riches to themselves. It is also a common Disease in
all Governments, where the Popish Religion has got the upper hand,
That the Popish Clergy is very rich and potent, and yet pretends, by
a Divine Right, to be exempted from all publick burdens, except that
some of them in the utmost extremity vouchsafe to contribute some
small portion for the defence of the whole, <77> but that not without
consent of the Pope:[61] Yet the King of *Spain* has that Prerogative, which
he obtained from Pope *Hadrian* IV. that he has the disposal of all the
chief Church Benefices in his Kingdom; and he is also Head and Master
of all the Ecclesiastical Orders of Knighthood in *Spain.* And because
the Kings of *Spain* have hitherto pretended to be the most zealous Protectours of the Papal Chair and Religion, they have thereby so obliged
the Zealots of the *Roman Catholick* Religion, and especially the *Jesuits,* that these have always been endeavouring to promote the Interest
of *Spain.*

§20. Lastly, It is also worth our observation, how *Spain* does behave
it self in relation to its Neighbours, and what Good or Evil it may
again expect from them. *Spain* therefore is opposite to the Coast of
Barbary, having also several Forts on that side, *viz. Pegnon de Velez,
Oran, Arzilla,* and would be [even] better [off] if they had also *Algiers*
and *Tunis.* From hence *Spain* need not fear any thing now, since it
has quite freed it self from the very Remnants of the *Moors:* But the
Pyracies committed by those *Corsaires* is not so hurtfull to *Spain,* as to
other Nations, who traffique with *Spain, Italy* or *Turky;* for the *Spaniards* seldom export [transport] their own Commodities into the other
parts of *Europe,* but these are exported by other Nations.[62] The *Turks*

In what condition Spain is in, in reference to its Neighbours, and especially as to Barbary.

Turky.

61. See XII.30, pp. 483–85. The fiscal strength of the Catholic Church, especially
in relation to the financial needs of Protestant states, was a prime concern of Pufendorf. This essentially political dispute over income-producing properties was similar
to that between monarchs and the nobility, as in Sweden, where the matter was
resolved by the so-called absolutist Reduktion of the early 1680s.
62. That is, the shipping is done by other nations.

seem to be pretty near to the Islands of *Sicily* and *Sardinia,* and to the Kingdom of *Naples:* Yet are they not much feared by the *Spaniards,* the Sea which lies betwixt them being an obstacle against making a Descent with a considerable Army in any of those Parts; and if an Army should be landed, its Provisions, which must come by Sea, might easily be cut off: For in such a case all the States of *Italy* would be obliged to side with the *Spaniards* to keep this cruel Enemy from their Borders, and their Naval Strength joined together, much surpasses the *Turks* in every respect.

Italian States.   From the *Italian* States, the *Spaniards* have little to fear, it being a maxim with them, to preserve the Peace of *Italy,* thereby to take away all opportunity from *France* to get a footing in *Italy,* <78> which is also a general maxim among all the States of *Italy:* Nevertheless this is most certain, That if *Spain* should endeavour to encroach upon the rest of the *Italian* States, they would unanimously oppose it; and if they should find themselves too weak to oppose their Designs, they The Pope.   might be easily wrought upon to call *France* to their aid. The Pope, perhaps, might be willing enough to be Master of the Kingdom of *Naples,*[63] *Spain* holding the same in Fief of the Papal Chair, and thereby the Popes might have a fresh opportunity to enrich their Kindred: But the Pope wants Power to execute such a Design, and the rest of the States of *Italy* would not be forward to see so considerable a Country added to the Ecclesiastical State; and the Pope's Kindred are more for gathering of Riches out of the present Ecclesiastical Revenues, than to bestow the same upon an uncertain War. On the other side, *Spain* having found it very beneficial for its Interest, to pretend to the chief Protectorship of the *Roman* Religion, and that the Pope's good or bad Inclinations towards it, may either prove advantageous or disadvantageous, *Spain* has always endeavoured by all means to keep fair with the Popes. *France,* on the contrary, having taken part with the *Protestants,* whom *Spain* and the House of *Austria* have sought to oppress,

---

63. Pufendorf's language is more crass: "the pope's mouth [*Maul*] may water after [that is, salivate in anticipation of] Naples." Cf. p. 333, note 8.

has demonstrated sufficiently to the *Roman* Court, that it is not so fond of that Religion, as to neglect an opportunity to enrich himself with the Possessions of the *Protestants*, and to make way for attaining to the so long projected Design of the <Universal> Monarchy; which done, he [it] might easily make the Pope his [its][64] Chaplain: Wherefore the chief aim of the wisest Popes has been, to keep the Power of *Spain* and *France* in an equal Balance, this being the most proper method to keep up the Authority and provide for the Security of the Popedom.

It being the principal maxim of the *Venetians,* to [p]reserve their Liberty and State, by maintaining the Peace of *Italy, Spain* has no reason to be 'jealous of' [worried about] them as long as it undertakes nothing against them. It is also the Interest, as well of them as of all the other *Italian* States, that the *Spaniards* remain in possession of *Milan,* for <79> fear, if *France* should become Master of this Dukedom, it might thereby be put in a way to conquer all the rest of *Italy.* On the other side, if *Spain* should shew the least Inclination to undertake any thing against the Liberty of *Italy,* it cannot expect, but that the *Venetians,* if not by an open War, at least, by their Counsels and Money would oppose it: For the rest, this State endeavours to remain Neuter betwixt *France* and *Spain,* and to keep fair with both of them, as long as they do not act against their Interest; *Genoua* is of great consequence to the *Spaniards,* from which, depends in a great measure, the Security and Preservation of the *Milaneze:* Wherefore, when *Charles* V. could not effect his Intention of building a Castle (being opposed therein by *Andreas Doria*) whereby he intended to make the *Genoueses* dance after his Pipe, the *Spaniards* found out another way to make them dependent on their Interest, by borrowing vast Summs of Money from the *Genoueses* upon the security of the King's Revenues in *Spain.* Besides this, they are possess'd of the Harbour of *Final* on the Coast of *Genoua,* whereby they have taken away the power from them of cutting off the Correspondency betwixt *Spain* and *Milan. Spain* has great reason to

Venice.

Genoua.

64. See note 45, p. 80, above.

Savoy. live in a good Correspondency with *Savoy;* for if that Prince should side
with *France* against it, the *Milaneze* would be in eminent danger of being lost. But because it would be very pernicious for *Savoy,* if the King
of *France* should become Master of *Milan,* since *Savoy* would be then
surrounded on all sides by the *French,* it is easie for *Spain* to maintain
a good Correspondency with *Savoy. Florence* and the rest of the *Italian*
Princes have all the reason to be cautious not to offend *Spain,* yet, as
much as in them lies, they would scarce suffer *Spain* to encroach upon
any of them.

The Suiss.   It is also of consequence to the *Spaniards* to live in friendship with
the *Suiss,* partly because they must make use of such Souldiers as are
[en]listed among them; partly because they may be very serviceable
in preserving the *Milaneze;* and their Friendship is best preserved by
Money. But, because the *Suiss* are of several Religions, *Spain* is in greater
Authority with <80> the *Roman Catholick Cantons,* but *France* with the
Protestant Cantons, which being the most potent, yet have, either cajolled by fair Words, or Money, or out of Fear, conniv'd at the *Frenches*
becoming Masters of the 'County' [earldom, *Grafschaft*] of *Burgundy*
in the last War, whereas formerly they used to take effectual care for its
preservation.

Holland.   The *Hollanders* were before the Peace of *Munster* the most pernicious
Enemies to *Spain;* but since the Conclusion of that Peace there is no
cause that *Spain* should fear any thing from them, since I do not see any
reason, why these should attack *Spain,* or endeavour to take any thing
from them, having enough to do to maintain what they have already
got. And, if they should be tempted to attempt any thing against the
West Indies, they would not only meet with great resistance from the
Spaniards there, but also *France* and *England* would not easily suffer,
that both the *East* and *West Indies,* the two Fountains from whence
such vast Riches are derived, should be in possession of the *Dutch:* And
the *Dutch,* as for their own Interests, [are] obliged to take care, that
France, by swallowing up the rest of the {Spanish} *Netherlands,* may not
become their next Neighbour on the Land, or that it should obtain any
considerable advantage against *Spain.*

The Power of *Germany* *Spain* may consider {almost} as its own, ‖[as far as the same depends on the House of *Austria*.]|[65] And it is not long ago, since the States [estates] of *Germany* were persuaded to take upon them afresh the Guaranty of the Circle of *Burgundy*;[66] whereby *Spain* hoped to have united its Interest with that of the *German* Empire against *France;* since, whenever a War happens betwixt these two Crowns, it is scarce possible, that this Circle should escape untouch'd, it being the most convenient place where they may attack one another with vigour. *England* is capable of doing most damage to the *Spaniards* at Sea, and especially in the *West Indies:* But *England,* in all likelyhood, would be no great gainer by it, since the *English* have a vast Trade with the *Spanish* Sea-ports, and their Trade in the *Levant* would suffer extreamly from the *Spanish* Privateers; but also *Holland* could not look with a good Eye upon these Conquests of the <81> *English. Portugal,* by it self, cannot much hurt *Spain,* but in conjunction with another Enemy, it is capable of making a considerable Diversion at home. But the *Portugueses* could not propose any considerable Advantages to themselves thereby; and it might easily happen, that *Holland* siding with *Spain* might take from hence an opportunity to drive the *Portugueses* quite out of the *East Indies.*

The King of *France,* therefore, is the capital and most formidable Enemy to *Spain,* who wanting not Power, not only longs to devour the rest of the *Netherlands,* but also aims at the Conquest of other parts of *Spain.* But if the old Maxims of Policy are not grown quite out of date, it is to be 'hoped' [assumed], that all who have any Interest in the preservation of *Spain,* will with all their power endeavour to prevent, that <the ruin of *Spain,*> the Liberty and Possessions of all the States in *Europe* may not depend on the Pleasure and Will of one single person.[67] But what <Revolution> may happen in *Spain* if the present

Germans.

England.

Portugal.

France.

---

65. Rather: "insofar as Austria can dispose over it."

66. The Holy Roman Empire was divided into ten quasi-autonomous administrative regions or "circles" in 1512. See *The Present State of Germany,* II.15, in Pufendorf (2007), pp. 78–79. The circle of Burgundy included the Spanish Netherlands.

67. That is, Louis XIV.

What may be the conse- quence of the Extinction of the Royal Family.

Royal Family, which has no Heirs yet, should fail, is beyond Human Understanding to determine or foresee; because it is to be feared, that upon such an occasion, not only *France* would do its utmost to obtain it, but also, because several States which were annexed to *Spain,* by the Royal Family, might take an opportunity to withdraw themselves from the same.[68]

68. See note 60, p. 90 above.

Of Portugal.

§1. *Portugal,* which comprehends the greatest part of that Province which the *Romans* called *Lusitania,* fell, with the rest of *Spain,* under the last *Gothick* King *Roderick,* into the Hands of the *Moors,* who were in possession of it for a long time; but 'in' [about] the Year 1093, *Alfonsus* VI. King of *Castile* and *Leon,* arming himself with all his Power to attack the <82> *Moors;* and craving also the Assistance of Foreign Princes, among others, also, came one *Henry,*[1] to signalize himself in this War, whose Pedigree is variously related by the Historians. For some will have him descended out of the House of *Burgundy,* and have made him a younger Son of *Robert* Duke of *Burgundy,* whose Father was *Robert* King of *France,* Son of *Hugh Capet.* Others derive his Pedigree from the House of *Loraine,* alledging, That the reason of his being called a *Burgundian* was, because he was born at *Besanson.* To this *Henry,* King *Alfonsus* VI. gave in marriage his natural Daughter *Theresia,* as a reward of his Valour, giving unto him for a Dowry, under the Title of an Earldom, all that part of *Portugal* which was then in the possession of the Christians; which comprehended that part of the Country, where are the Cities of *Braga, Coimbria, Visco, Lamego,* and *Porto,* as also that tract of Ground which is now called *Tralos Montes,* granting to him also a power to conquer the rest of that Country, as far as to the River of *Guadiana,* and to keep it under his Jurisdiction; yet with these conditions, That he should be a Vassal of *Spain,* repair to the Dyets of that Kingdom, and in case of a War, be obliged to serve with 300 Horse.

The Origin of the Kingdom of Portugal.

Henry Earl of Portugal.

---

1. Henry of Burgundy (1066–1112 A.D.).

CHAPTER III

Alfonsus I.
King of
Portugal.

Henry died in the Year 1112. leaving a Son whose name was *Alfonsus*, being then very young: His Inheritance was, during his Minority, usurp'd by *Ferdinand Potz* [*Pacz*],[2] Count of *Trastamara*, his 'Father-in-law' [stepfather], he having married his Mother {who could not control her lust [*unzüchtig*]}. But as soon as he was grown up, he took up Arms against his 'Father-in-law' [stepfather], beat him out of *Portugal*, but his Mother he put in Prison; who calling to her aid *Alfonsus* VII. {king of Castile,} [s]he promised to dis-inherit her Son, and to give him all *Portugal*. But *Alfonsus* of *Portugal* defeated the *Castilians* in a Battel, by which Victory he pretended to have freed himself from the '*Spanish*' [Castilian] Subjection \A. 1126\. This *Alfonsus* undertook \A. 1139\ an Expedition against King *Ismar*, who had his Kingdom on the other side of the River *Taio*, who being joined by the Forces of 'four' [five] other petty *Moorish* Kings, drew out against him. *Alfonsus* was then in his Camp near *Cabebas* [*Cabecas*] *des Reyes* proclaimed King, thereby to animate his Souldiers; and get[ting] a <83> most signal Victory, [and] taking the five Standards of those Kings, <whence> he put five Shields in the [coat of] Arms of *Portugal*, and retained ever after the Title of King. He took afterwards a great many Cities from the *Moors;* and among the rest, with the assistance of the *Netherland* Fleet the City of *Lisbon* in the Year 1147. This *Alfonsus* was taken Prisoner \A. 1179\ near *Badajoz*, by *Ferdinand* King of '*Egypt*' [Leon], who gave him his Freedom without any other Ransom, than that he was to restore <to him> some Cities, which he had taken <from him> in *Gallicia*. After he had reigned very gloriously, and greatly enlarged the Limits of his Kingdom, he died in the 91st Year of his Age \A. 1185\.

The Origin of
the five Shields
in the Arms
of Portugal.

Sanctius I.

§2. Him succeeded his Son *Sanctius*, who built a great many Cities, and fill'd them with Inhabitants. He took from the *Moors* the City of *Selva* [*Salva*], being assisted in that Expedition, by a Fleet |[sent out of the *Netherlands*]|[3] to the *Holy Land*. He was, during his whole Reign, always in action with the *Moors*, and died in the Year 1212. After

2. Fernando Pérez de Traba (ca. 1090–1155).
3. Rather: "from the Netherlands, which continued after the war."

him reigned his Son *Alfonsus* sirnamed *Crassus*, who did nothing worth   Alfonsus II.
mentioning, but that, with the help of the *Netherlanders*, who went to
the *Holy Land*, he took from the *Moors* the City of *Alcassar*. He died
in the Year 1223. His Son *Sanctius*, sirnamed *Capellus*, succeeded him;   Sanctius II.
who being very careless, and ruled by his Wife, was excluded from the
Administration of the Government by the *Portugueses*, who conferr'd
it on *Alfonsus* his Brother. *Sanctius* died {miserably} an Exile in *Toledo*
\A. 1246\. The *Portugueses* have made this observation concerning him,
that he was the only *Portuguese* King who died without leaving either
Legitimate Children or Bastards behind him. *Alfonsus*, the Brother of   Alfonsus III.
Sanctius, parted from his Lady *Mathildis*, Countess of *Boulogne*, she
being somewhat Ancient and Barren, and married *Beatrice*, Daughter
to *Alfonsus* X. King of *Castile*, with whom he had for a Dowry <the
County of> *Algarbia;* but the Pope being dissatisfy'd with this Divorce,
excommunicated both him and the whole Kingdom. He reigned very
laudably {otherwise}, and united a great many Cities to his Kingdom,
and died in the <84> Year 1279.

The extraordinary Virtues of his Son *Dionysius*, especially, Justice,   Dionysius.
Liberality and 'Constancy' [truthfulness], are highly extoll'd by the *Por-*
tugueses: He having also adorn'd the Kingdom with a great many publick
Buildings {and foundations [*Stiftungen*]}, among which is the Academy
of *Conimbria* [Coimbra], first founded by him. There is an old Proverb
concerning him, used among the *Portugueses, El Rey D. Denys, qui fiz*
quanto quin: King *Dionysius*, who did |[whatsoever he pleased.]|[4] He
died in the Year 1325; his Son *Alfonsus* IV. sirnamed *the Brave*, was very   Alfonsus IV.
glorious for his Atchievements both in Peace and War; but he {unfairly
persecuted and} banished his Bastard Brother, who was greatly beloved
both by his Father and the People; and caused *D. Agnes de Castro*, a very
beautiful Lady, who was without his consent married to his Son *Pieter*,
barbarously to be murthered; which so exasperated *Pieter*, that he taking up Arms against the Father, did considerable mischief, till at last the
business was composed. He died in the Year 1357. His Son *Pieter* was   Pieter.

4. Rather: "everything that he wanted." The proverb suggests accomplishment,
not arbitrariness.

commonly called *the Cruel,* tho' some will have this rather to have been spoken to his praise, as having {only} been an exact observer of Justice, never sparing any Offender. He died in the Year 1368.

Ferdinand.   His Son *Ferdinand* contended with *Henry* the Bastard, who had murthered his Brother *Pieter,* sirnamed *the Cruel,* King of *Castile,* about the Kingdom of *Castile,* because the [Ferdinand's] Mother *Beatrice* had been Daughter of *Sanctius* IV. King of *Castile;* and a great many of the Nobility and some Cities of that Kingdom declaring for him, he waged {a difficult} War against the forementioned *Henry.* But he [Henry] being too strong for him, he could not maintain his Pretensions, but was obliged to make Peace. However the War broke out afresh again betwixt them \A. 1373\, because *Ferdinand* had protected some who were banished out of *Castile* for High Treason, neither would, upon demand, surrender them. To revenge this, *Henry* made an inrode into *Portugal,* and finding no resistance, over-ran the greatest part of the Country. After the death of *Henry, Ferdinand* made a Peace with his Son *John,* but the same was soon violated again by the *Portugueses,* who encouraged the Duke of *Lancaster,* that [had] married *Constantia* Daughter <85> of *Pieter* King of *Castile,* to pretend to the Crown of *Castile:* He came with a good Army into *Portugal;* but the *English* being quickly grown weary of the War in *Spain,* and living very disorderly in *Portugal,* a Peace was concluded on both sides. At last *Ferdinand* married his Daughter *Beatrice* to *John* of *Castile,* under condition, that such Children as were born of their Bodies, should succeed in the Kingdom of *Portugal;* which was afterwards the occasion of {further} bloody Wars. This *Ferdinand,* who by his frequent Wars had proved very pernicious to *Portugal,* died in the Year 1383, being the last of the true 'Race' [*Stamm*] of the Kings of *Portugal.*

Interregnum.   §3. After the death of *Ferdinand* great Troubles arose in *Portugal,* most of the *Portugueses* not being able to brook living under the Subjection of the *Castilians,* whom they mortally hated. It was, 'tis true, agreed on in the Articles of Marriage made betwixt the King of *Castile* and *Beatrice* Daughter of *Ferdinand,* That her Mother *Eleonora* should have the Administration of the Government in *Portugal,* till such Children

as should be born of this Marriage should be of age: But this *Eleonora,*
leaving all to the management of the Count of *Ancira,* her much
suspected Favourite, she drew upon her self the hatred of the *Portugueses. John,* therefore, natural Son of *Pieter* King of *Portugal,* privately
murther'd him, whereby he got both the Favour of the people, and
encreased the hatred against the Queen Dowager: But some of the *Portugueses* being much dissatisfy'd at these proceedings, begg'd the King of
Castile, to take upon him the Crown of *Portugal;* which he might in all
likelyhood have obtained, if he had been quick enough, either by fair
means or by force, to have put himself into full possession of the same:
But he being uncertain in his Resolutions, gave by his delays, time
and opportunity to the adverse Party to strengthen it self. Wherefore,
he coming without an Army into *Portugal,* his Mother-in-law resign'd
to him the Government, but he found but an indifferent Reception
among the *Portugueses,* they being very averse to him <86> because he
used very rarely to speak or converse with them: Nevertheless a great
many of the Nobility and some Cities did side with him; but most out
of a hatred to the *Castilians,* chose for their Leader *John* the *Bastard,* a
wise and brave Man, and much belov'd by the People. The *Castilians*
thereupon besieged *Lisbon,* but their Army being for the most part
destroyed by the Plague, they were obliged to leave it without having
got any advantage.

    In the Year next following \A. 1385\, the *Portugueses* declar'd this *John*
their King, who very courageously attack'd those places, which had declared for the *Castilians,* and subdued the greatest part of them. The
Castilians then entred with an Army into *Portugal,* but were entirely
routed by this new King near *Aliubarotta,* which Victory is yearly celebrated to this day among the *Portugueses.* After this Battel, all the rest
of the Cities did without more adoe surrender themselves to the new
King. The *Portugueses* also calling unto their aid, the Duke of *Lancaster,*
unto whom they had promised the Crown of *Castile,* they enter'd into
that Kingdom with an Army: But the *English* having suffer'd extreamly
by Sickness, the Duke of *Lancaster* thought it most convenient to conclude a Peace with the *Castilians,* whereupon it was agreed, That the
Son of the King of *Castile* should marry his only Daughter *Catharine,*

Some call in
the King of
Castile.

John the
Bastard.

which he had by *Constantia,* Daughter to *Pieter* King of *Castile.* A Truce
was also made betwixt *Portugal* and *Castile* at that time; but the War
soon breaking out again, at last, an everlasting Peace was concluded
betwixt both Kingdoms \A. 1399\; so that *John* had the good fortune to
maintain himself in the possession of the Crown of *Portugal,* and reign'd
with great applause. After he was quietly settled in the Throne, he undertook an Expedition into *Africa,* and took the City *Ceuta* \A. 1415\;
whose Son also \A. 1420\ first found out the Isle of *Madera.* This King
died in the Year 1433, and left a Memory that is to this day dear to the
Portugueses.

Edward. §4. His Son *Edward* was a very Virtuous Prince, but did not reign long;
for at that time, *Portugal* being over-run with the Plague, he got the
Infection by a <87> Letter, and died in the Year 1438. During his Reign,
his Brothers undertook a most unfortunate Expedition into *Africa,*
where being themselves taken Prisoners before *Tangier,* they promised
to restore to the *Moors Ceuta* for a Ransom, leaving *Don Ferdinand* as
a Hostage behind them. But the States of *Portugal* refusing to stand
Alfonsus V. to the Contract, the Hostage was forc'd to end his days in Prison. *Alfonsus,* Son to this *Edward,* was but six years old when his Father died,
whose Tuition was committed, by his Father's last Will, to his Mother.
But the States, refusing to submit themselves to the Government of a
Foreign Woman, conferr'd the Administration of the Kingdom on *Don
Pedro* Duke of *Conimbria* [Coimbra], Brother to King *Edward,* but he
received a very slender Recompence for his Services; for being falsely
accused before the new King [i.e., Alfonsus], he was slain as he was going with some Troops to the King to justifie himself.

Alfonsus V. was else a very good Souldier and a brave Prince, under
whose Reign the *Portugueses* took several places on the Coast of *Africa,*
viz. *Tangier, Arcilla, Alcassar,* and some others. Good store of Gold was
also transported out of *Guinea* into *Portugal,* which he employ'd in coin-
ing of Cruisadoes.[5] After this *Alfonsus* had great contests with *Ferdinand*

5. *Crusados* (or *cruzados*) were Portugese coins made of gold, with a cross (thus,
the name) on the rear.

the *Catholick* and *Isabella,* there being a promise of marriage made betwixt him and *Johanna,* the supposed Daughter of *Henry* IV. King of
Castile; but, as it was reported, begotten in Adultery; but the Marriage
was not consummated, she being *Alfonsus's* Sister's Daughter, tho', at
last, the Pope gave his Dispensation, which he had refused at first. *Alfonsus,* under this pretence, took upon himself the Title and Arms of *Castile,*
'surprising' [overcoming] several Cities, assisted by some of the Nobility
of *Castile,* who sided with him: *Lewis* XI. also, King of *France,* sent him
some Auxiliaries, but these were not sufficient to enable him to undertake any thing of moment: Wherefore, *Ferdinand* retaking all the places
from the *Portugueses,* routed them also near *Toro* \A. 1476\ and near
Albuhera \A. 1479\; so that *Alfonsus* despairing of obtaining his Ends,
concluded a Peace with *Ferdinand,* wherein he renounced both *Castile*
and the Bride *Johanna,* she being promised in <88> marriage to *John*
Son of *Ferdinand,* who was then a Child: But she, perceiving that this
was only done to 'elude' [mislead] her, went into a Nunnery \A. 1479\.

Portugal sustained considerable losses in this War, and *Alfonsus* died
in the Year 1481, as it is supposed, out of Grief, because he had lost the
hopes of his Bride and the Crown of *Castile.* Him succeeded his Son
John II. against whom a most horrid Conspiracy was discovered, for   John II.
which *Ferdinand* Duke of *Braganza,* and *James* Duke of *Visco* lost their
lives, the latter being kill'd by the King's own Hand. This King *John* was
the first, who found out the way to sail into the *East Indies,* having not   A Project of
only ordered an exact Survey to be made of the *African* Coast, as far as   sailing to the
to the *Cape of good hope,* but also sent some by Land into the *East Indies,*   East Indies.
to inform themselves concerning the Condition of those Countries. He
built also the Castle of *Mina* on the Coast of *Guinea:*[6] But before this
intended Voyage to the *East Indies* could be begun, this King died in
the Year 1495, leaving no Heirs behind him.

§5. *John* II. was succeeded by his Cousin *Emanuel,* Son of *Ferdinand*   Emanuel.
Duke of *Viseo,* Grandchild of King *Edward.* With him contended for

6. Pufendorf might also have noted that John continued, in all this, the work of
his great-uncle, Henry the Navigator (1394–1460).

the Succession the Emperour *Maximilian,* whose Mother *Eleonora* was a Daughter of King *Edward:* But the *Portugueses* declared for *Emanuel,* who for his extraordinary Qualifications both of Body and Mind, was extreamly beloved by them. He, the better to establish himself at home, married *Isabella,* eldest Daughter of *Ferdinand* the *Catholick,* out of which marriage a young Prince was born, whose Name was *Michael,* who, if he had lived, would have been Heir to all the *Spanish* Kingdoms, except that of *Navarre.* To please his Bride, he [Emanuel], by his Proclamation, banish'd all the *Jews* and *Moors* out of *Portugal* by a prefix'd time, under penalty, for all such as should stay behind, to be made Slaves for ever.[7] Whereupon the *Moors* immediately {and without restrictions} retir'd into *Africa;* but from the *Jews* they took their Children which were under the Age of fourteen, and baptized them against their Will: And as for the old ones, they were so plagued and vexed <89> every where, and stopp'd or hinder'd in their Journeys, that most, to be rid of these Vexations, and to avoid the danger of Slavery, were baptized, retaining, nevertheless, in their Minds, their ancient Superstition:

    Under the Reign of this King, *Portugal* arrived to the highest pitch of its 'Greatness' [fortune], the design of the *East-India* Voyage round *Africa,* which was projected by the former King, being now accomplish'd by *Vascus de Gama,* who first arrived at *Calicut* \A. 1497\. As soon as the *Portugueses* began to draw into their Country the Trade of Spices, they were opposed, especially by the Sultan of *Egypt,* because formerly these Commodities used to be conveyed through *Egypt* to *Venice,* and from thence to other parts of *Europe,* from which both these Countries drew vast Profit. Wherefore the *Venetians* stirred up the Sultan, sending him great stores of Metal to make Cannons of, and Shipwrights to build Ships; by which means they hoped to drive the *Portugueses* out of the *Indies:* But the *Portugueses,* who did not much trust the *Barbarian* Kings of the *Indies,* began to build Forts and strong Holds in the most convenient places; wherein they met with little opposition, partly because the *Indians* were terrify'd by the vastness of the Ships, and the thunder

Moors and Jews banish'd out of Portugal.

The first Sea-voyage into the East Indies.

The reason why the Venetians opposed the Portugueses settling themselves there.

7. This was in 1496; Ferdinand and Isabella had expelled the Jews from Castile in 1492. See II.9, p. 56.

of the Cannons of the *Europeans;* partly because they were not aware of what consequence they might prove one day against them. The Duke of *Albuquerque,* specially, did mightily advance the Power of the *Portugueses* in the *Indies,* who took the Cities of *Ormuz, Malacca, Cochin* and *Goa;* the latter of which is the place of Residence of the *Portuguese* Governour in the *Indies.* And thus the *Portugueses* engrossed to themselves the whole Trade and Commerce of *Africa* and the remotest parts of *Asia,* having possessed themselves of all the most commodious Ports and Places not only on the *Western* side of *Africa,* in *Mauritania, Guinea, Congo, Angola,* in the Isle of St. *Thomas,* and some others, but also on the *East* side, in *Manzambique, Melinde, Mombazo, Zafala,* and from the mouth of the *Red Sea,* as far as *Japan;* from whence incredible Riches were conveyed into *Portugal.* Besides all this did *Pieter Alvanus* [*Alvarus*] *Capralis,* or as some <90> will have it *Americus Vesputius* discover the Country of *Brasile* in *America,* whither the *Portugueses* sent {A. 1500} 'several' [many] Colonies.

The Progress of the Duke of Albuquerque in the East Indies.

The discovery of Brasil in America.

And under the Reign of this King *Emanuel,* who died in the Year 1521, *Portugal* increased to that degree, that his Reign was called, *The Golden Age.* After him reigned his Son *John* III. under whose Reign *Portugal* continued in the same flourishing condition. This King sent *Francis Xavier,* and some other Jesuites into the *East Indies,* who were to settle the Christian Religion among the *Barbarians.* The Jesuites commonly boast of great numbers of Heathens converted by them, but whether they deserve an intire credit in this, or whether, perhaps, a great many of these have not rather taken upon them the Name, than the Faith of Christians, those are best able to judge, who have been conversant in those places. He died in the Year 1557.

John III.

The Jesuites sent to the Indies.

§6. *John* III. had for his Successour his Grandson *Sebastian,* a Child of three Years of age, whose Tuition was committed to the Cardinal *Henry,* his Uncle, because his Grandmother was not willing to take upon her the burthen of the 'Government' [guardianship]. Through the over-forwardness of this young Prince, *Portugal* receiv'd such a blow, that it fell from the Pinacle of its Greatness: For some of his Court Favourites did put this magnanimous and ambitious Prince, upon such

Sebastian.

Enterprizes as were far surpassing both his Age and Power, and were in no ways suitable to the present juncture of Affairs, so that his whole Mind was bent upon Warlike Exploits, and how by Martial Exercises, to revive the ancient Valour of his Subjects, which by Peace and Plenty, having been more addicted to Commerce, was of late much decay'd. He undertook, therefore, an Expedition into the next adjacent parts of *Africa,* intending, by light Skirmishes to try his Enemies. He proposed, afterwards, a Voyage into the *Indies,* but his Council opposing it, it was agreed upon, that he should undertake an Expedition into *Africa,* an occasion presenting it self at that time; for that *Muley Mahomet,* King of *Morocco,* being banish'd by his Uncle *Muley Malucco,* craved the as-<91>sistance of King *Sebastian:* Wherefore, notwithstanding the

His fatal Expedition into Africa.

good Counsels of *Philip* King of *Spain,* and others, who dissuaded him from it, he in person, with a great but unexercised Army enter'd *Africa,* and advancing, against all Reason, too far into the Country, was obliged, in a disadvantageous place, to fight against a much more numerous Army; wherefore the success of the Battel was answerable to the rash attempt; his Army, wherein was the flower of the Nobility of *Portugal,* being miserably routed, and the Souldiers all either cut to pieces or made Prisoners. This Battel is famous, because three Kings fell, *viz.* King *Sebastian,* the banish'd *Muley Mahomet,* and *Muley Malucco,* King of *Morocco,* who during the time of the Battel, died of a Fever. This happened in the Year 1578.

Henry.

Him succeeded his Uncle *Henry* the Cardinal, a very old Man, under whose Reign there happened nothing worth mentioning, but that perpetual contests were set on foot concerning the Succession. Wherefore, he dying in the Year 1580, *Philip* II. King of *Spain,* thought it the most efficacious way, to dispute with the Sword in hand; and perceiving that the *Portugueses,* out of that hatred which they bare to the *Castilians,* were inclined to *Anthony* Son of *Lewis de Beya,* natural Son to King *John* III. he sent the Duke *d' Alba* with a great Army into *Portugal,*

Portugal united to Spain.

who quickly chased away *Anthony,* and in few days became Master of the whole Kingdom, all being forced soon to submit, except the Isle of *Tercera,* which was not reduced till after the *French,* who came to its relief, were beaten.

As the *Portugueses* did not, without great reluctancy, bear the Government of the *Castilians;* so this Union with *Castile* proved very prejudicial to them afterwards. For *Philip,* who was for bringing the *Netherlanders* again under Obedience, thought that nothing could do it more effectually, than to stop their Trade and Commerce with *Spain* and *Portugal:* For hitherto they had traded no further, being used to fetch away their Commodities from thence, and to convey them into the more Northern parts of *Europe.* Wherefore *Philip* concluded, that if this way of getting Money were once stop'd, they <92> would quickly grow poor, and thereby be obliged to submit themselves. But this design had a quite contrary effect; for the *Hollanders* being themselves excluded from Trade with *Spain* and *Portugal,* try'd, about the end of the latter Age [century], to sail to the *East Indies.* And as soon as, after a great many difficulties, they had once gotten footing there, they greatly impaired the *Portugueses* Trade, who hitherto had 'only' [alone] managed the same, and afterwards took from them one Fort after another. And \A. 1620\ the *English,* with the assistance of *Abbas* King of *Persia,* forced from them the famous City of *Ormutz.* Nor was this all, for \A. 1630\ the *Hollanders* took from them a great part of *Brasile,* and several places on the Coast of *Africa;* which the *Hollanders,* in all probability, would have had no reason to undertake, if *Portugal* had remained a Kingdom by it self, and had not been annexed to *Spain.*

The Dutch sail to the East Indies.

§7. But in the Year 1640, the *Portugueses* took an occasion to shake off the '*Spanish*' [Castilian] Yoak. For *Philip* IV. then summoned the *Portuguese* Nobility to assist him in the War against the *Catalonians,* who had rebelled against him. Being therefore armed, and finding an opportunity to consult with one another, concerning those Troubles in which *Spain* was involv'd at that time; they agreed to withdraw themselves from the Subjection of *Spain,* proclaiming for their King, the Duke of *Braganza,* who stiled himself *John* IV. whose Grandmother had stood in competition with *Philip* II. for that Crown [of Portugal]. The *Spaniards* committed a gross mistake in this, that they did not in time secure the Duke, whom they knew to have a fair pretence to that Crown; to be extreamly beloved by that Nation, and to be in possession of the fourth

The Portuguese shake off the Yoak of Spain.

The Duke of Braganza proclaimed King. John IV.

part of the Kingdom. The *Spaniards* being at that time entangled in Wars against *France, Holland* and *Catalonia;* the *Portugueses* had thereby good leisure given them, to settle their Affairs. They made also a Peace with *Holland,* by virtue of which, both Parties were to remain in possession of what they had gotten. But this Peace did not last long; for, these places which were in the possession of the *Hollanders,* <93> in *Brasile,* revolted to the *Portugueses,* which the *Hollanders* looking upon as done by contrivance of the *Portugueses,* denounced War against them. And tho' they did not retake *Brasile,* yet did they take a great many other places from them in the *East Indies,* viz. *Malacca,* the places on the Coast of the Isle of *Zeylon,* on the Coast of *Cormandel,* and on the Coast of *Malabar, Cochin, Canaror, Cranganor,* and some others; and if they had not clapt up a Peace with them \A. 1661\, they would in all likely hood have also driven them out of *Goa* it self.

John IV. died in the Year 1656, leaving the Kingdom to his Son *Alfonsus,* who was under Age, but the Administration of the Government was in the mean time lodged with his Mother. After the *Pyrenean* Treaty was concluded,[8] out of which *Portugal* was excluded by the *Spaniards,* it being besides this agreed with *France,* not to send any Assistances to the *Portugueses,* the *Spaniards* fell upon the *Portugueses* in good earnest: But these defended themselves bravely, and notwithstanding the Articles of the *Pyrenean* Treaty, the *French* King did give leave to the Earl of *Schombergh,*[9] and a great many other *Frenchmen* to enter into the Service of the *Portugueses,* who routed the *Spaniards* in several Encounters, but more especially, near *Extremos* and *Villa Vitrosa.* At last \A. 1668\, the *French* entering with a great Army into the *Netherlands,* the *Spaniards* were willing to conclude a Peace with the *Portugueses,* who were also glad to be once disentangled out of so tedious a War. By virtue of this Peace *Spain* did resign all its Pretensions upon *Portugal.*

In the mean time *Alfonsus* was grown up a wild and awkward sort of

[Marginal notes:]
A League between Portugal and Holland.

A War breaks out betwixt them.

A Peace.

Alfonsus VI.

8. The Treaty of the Pyrenees (1659) ended the war between France and Spain and fixed the border between them. See II.13, p. 79, above.

9. On Schomberg, see II.13, p. 79, above.

a Man, as *Don Pedro*'s 'Friends' [patrons][10] have represented him to the World; who, besides this, by a Distemper which he had in his tender Age, was so disabled both in his Body and Mind, that he was neither fit to rule nor marry: Yet he taking from his Mother \A. 1666\ the Administration of Affairs upon himself (who quickly after died) married a Princess of *Nemours*, descended from the House of *Savoy*; who having lived with him about sixteen Months, retired {A. 1667} into a Monastery, desiring to be divorced from him: She alledged, That <94> *Alfonsus* was not only incapable of Matrimony, but also that he had endeavoured, to have one of his Favourites get her with Child, thereby to secure the Crown to his Family. There was, besides this, so strong a Jealousie betwixt the King and his Brother *Don Pedro*, that the latter thought his Life to be in danger, if he did not prevent the Designs of his Brother and his Favourites: He therefore, bringing the Nobility and People over to his Party, forced *Alfonsus* to surrender to him the Administration of the Kingdom, reserving for his Maintenance only the yearly Revenue of 270.000 Livers, as also the Palace of *Braganza*, with all its Appurtenances. *Don Pedro* would not take upon himself the Title of King, but chose rather to be called Regent of *Portugal*, in the name of his Brother *Alfonsus*, he being incapable of Administring the Government: He married also upon the desire of the *Portugueses*, and with the Dispensation of the Pope, his Brother's Wife. And because *Alfonsus* should not be in a capacity of raising any disturbances, he was under a good Guard conducted into the Island of *Tercera*. But *Don Pedro* has hitherto administred the Government in peace, and to the general satisfaction of the People.

Don Pedro.

§8. And to say something {now} concerning the Genius of the *Portugueses*, and the Strength and the Nature of the Country. The *Portugueses* are not inferiour to the *Spaniards* in Pride and Haughtiness; but are not esteemed so Prudent and Cautious as these, but are over-secure in

The Humours of the Portugueses.

10. Pedro, Duke of Beja (1648–1706), became regent in 1668 and succeeded his brother (Alfonso VI) as king (Peter II) in 1683.

Prosperity, and in time of danger rash and fool-hardy. Where they get the upper-hand they are very rigorous and cruel. They are mightily addicted to be Covetous, and love Usury, and |[have searched after Money in all corners of the World]|.[11] Some also will have them to be very Malicious, which they say is the remnant of the *Jewish* Blood, which is intermingled with that of the *Portuguese* Nation. This Country, considering its bigness, is very populous, as is evident by the number of *Portugueses,* which have settled themselves in *Brasile,* on the Coast of *Africa,* and in the *East Indies:* Yet are <95> they not in a capacity to raise a numerous Land Army without Foreign help, or to man out a mighty Fleet of Men of War; but they have enough to do, to Garrison their frontier Places well, and to keep Convoys for their Merchant Ships.

Fruitfulness of Portugal. §9. Concerning the 'Countries' [lands] which belong now-a-days to *Portugal.* The Kingdom of *Portugal,* by it self considered, is neither very large nor very fruitfull, the Inhabitants living most upon such Corn as is imported: Yet is the Country full of Cities and Towns, and has a great many commodious Sea-ports. The Commodities 'of the growth of' [produced in] *Portugal,* [and] fit for Exportation, are Salt, of which a great quantity is from *Setubal* or St. *Hubes* transported into the Northern Countries: As also Oyl, some Wine, and all sorts of Fruit. The other Commodities which are brought from thence they first have from those Provinces that belong to them. The Silver Mine called *Guacaldane* [Guadacanal], is said to be of the yearly value of 178 Quentoes of Silver (each Quent being reckoned to amount to 2673 Ducats, 8 Reals, and 26 *Marvedoes.*)[12]

Brasile. Among those Countries that now belong to *Portugal* the chiefest is *Brasile,* being a long tract of Land in *America,* extended all along the Sea side, but very narrow, and famous for the wholsomness of the Air, and its Fertility. Here abundance of Sugar is made, from whence arises

---

11. More literally: "have crawled into every nook and cranny of the world to scrape money together."

12. The Guadalcanal mine was located in Portugal itself, in the area of present Sierra Morena.

the main Revenue of the Country, the *Portugueses* making use of the same in preserving those excellent Fruits as grow both in *Portugal* and *Brasile*. *Brasile* also affords Ginger, Cotton, Wooll, Indigo and Wood for the Dyers. But because the Natives of this Country are naturally lazy, who cannot by any ways be forced to hard labour, the *Portugueses* buy upon the Coast of *Africa,* and especially in *Congo* and *Angola,* Negroes, whom they use for Slaves, buying and selling them in *Brasile* as we do Oxen; they are employed in all sorts of hardships and drudgery.

The Trade of the *Portugueses* on the *West* side of *Africa* is not now of any great consequence, since the *Hollanders* have interfered with them; and those places which they are possess'd of on the *East* side of *Africa* <96> only serve to enrich their Governours. What the *Hollanders* have left them in the *East Indies* is ||[of no final consequence]|[13] to them; for *Goa* {especially} is a very large City, where there is a great Trade among People of all Nations: But the wiser sort do not approve of the *Portuguese* Government in the *East Indies;* the *Portugueses* there are given to Voluptuousness, and neglecting Military Affairs, are so presumptuous, as to imagine, that nevertheless with their haughty Carriage they can out-brave [*pravirten*] others. Hence it was that the *Hollanders* found it so easie to drive this Nation out of the greatest part of the *Indies,* which was grown hatefull to them all: Yet the *Portugueses* enjoy one Privilege which the *Dutch* have not, that they are allowed a free Trade with *China,* where they have the City of *Macao* in an Island not far distant from the Continent; and they have understood so to mis-represent the *Hollanders* with the *Chineses,* that they, hitherto, as far as I know, <they> have not been able to obtain a free Commerce with *China.*

Formerly the *Portugueses* had a great Interest in *Japan,* which was chiefly procured by means of the Jesuites, who made it their business to convert the *Japoneses* to the Christian Religion. It is related, that above 400.000 of them were baptized, not without hopes, that all the rest would at last have followed their example. But about thirty years ago, the *Dutch,* by their Practices and Artifices, render'd the *Portugueses*

Africa.

The East Indies.

A horrible Persecution raised on the Christians of Japan, and the occasion of it.

13. Rather: "still of some importance."

suspected to the Emperour of *Japan,* having intercepted a Letter from the Jesuits to the Pope, wherein they promised to bring, ere long, the whole Kingdom of *Japan* under the Obedience of the *Roman* See. The *Hollanders* interpreted this Letter in such a sense, as if the Jesuits, with the assistance of the new Converts, did intend to dethrone the Emperour; telling him, That the Pope pretended to an Authority of disposing of Kingdoms at his pleasure, and that the King of *Spain* who was then Master of *Portugal,* was in great esteem with him. The 'jealous' [suspicious] *Japoneses* were easily persuaded hereof, when they considered with what Respect and Kindness the Jesuits were treated by the new Christians; those [Jesuits] being also very ready to accept of what these good natur'd <97> People offered them. And the Governours were sensible, and complained, that their usual Presents from the Subjects decreased daily, since the new Converts gave so much to their Priests. The *Hollanders* also shew'd the Emperour of *Japan* in a Mapp, how the Conquests of the King of *Spain* did extend on one side as far as *Manilla,* on the other side as far as *Macao,* so that by subduing of *Japan,* he would have an opportunity of uniting his Conquests. This occasioned a most horrible Persecution against the Christians, the *Japoneses* endeavouring by incredible Torments to overcome the Constancy of a Nation, which is naturally one of the most obstinate. Neither did they cease, till there was not one Christian left in *Japan,* and the *Portugueses,* upon pain of death, were for ever banish'd the Country. And the *Hollanders,* when afterwards they sent any Ships to *Japan,* used to forbid their Subjects, to shew the least appearance of Religious Christian Worship, but if they were ask'd, *Whether they were Christians,* to answer, *They were not, but they were* Hollanders. Lastly, To *Portugal* belong also the Isles called *Azores,* whereof *Tercera,* and the Isle *Madera,* which are tolerably fruitfull, are the principal.

The Strength
of Portugal.
§10. From what hath been said, it is apparent, that the welfare of *Portugal* depends chiefly on their Commerce with the *East Indies, Brasile* and *Africa;* whereby also it is evident enough, that the Strength and Power of *Portugal* in comparison of the rest of the more potent States of *Europe*

is not to be esteemed such, as to be able to attack any of them, or gain any thing upon them. It is therefore the Interest of this Crown to take care how to preserve it self in the same condition as it is in now, and to be very cautious of engaging it self in a War with any Nation that is potent at Sea, which perhaps might undertake something against their Provinces abroad.

But as for its Neighbours in particular; *Portugal* is for the most part nearest unto *Spain,* so that it is easie for the *Spaniards* to enter *Portugal,* yet is the Power of *Spain* not very dreadfull to the *Portugueses,* partly, because the *Spaniards* can-<98> not conveniently keep an Army of above 25.000 Men on foot on that side, by reason of the scarcity of Provisions; the like number the *Portugueses* also can bring into the Field; partly, because *Spain* cannot man out a considerable Fleet of Men of War wherewith to attack the *Portuguese* Provinces: Besides, *Portugal* in case of such an attack might certainly expect to be assisted either by the *French* or *English,* who as much as in them lies, will not suffer *Spain* to become again Master of *Portugal.* Neither does it appear for the Interest of *Portugal,* upon the Instigation of *France* or some other Foreign Power, to engage it self without a pressing necessity in a War with *Spain,* since it is not probable that it could gain any thing considerable, but would only weaken it self without the hopes of any advantage:

Portugal has, in all probability, not much to fear from *France,* they lying at a considerable distance from one another; besides this, the Naval Strength of *France* is not come, as yet, to that height, as to be in a capacity to be hurtfull to a Nation that has settled it self very securely in the *East* and *West Indies;* and more especially, since these two Nations have not any pretensions on each other: And it rather concerns *France* that *Portugal* may stand secure against *Spain* and *Holland.*

The *Hollanders* have hitherto proved the most pernicious Enemies to *Portugal,* they being in a capacity not only to disturb their Trade on the Coast of *Portugal,* but also may prove very troublesom to them both in the *East* and *West Indies:* And it seems, that it would be no difficult matter for the *Hollanders,* by taking from the *Portugueses* the City of *Macao,* on the Coast of *China,* and some other places on the Coast of *Malabar,*

How it stands with regard to Spain.

To France.

To Holland.

quite to destroy their Trade in the *East Indies*.[14] But it is probable, that, in case of a War betwixt the *Portugueses* and *Hollanders, England* would assist the former against the latter, since it has not been without great Displeasure to the *English,* to see what progresses the *Hollanders* have made in the *East Indies,* whereby they have acquired such vast Riches, that they have bid defiance to *England* and all the rest of *Europe.* <99>

14. It was the Dutch seizure of the Portuguese vessel *Sta. Catarina,* in the Straits of Singapore, during February 1603, that led Grotius (then employed by the Dutch East India Company) to write his *De rebus Indicis* (or *De jure praedae/ Commentary on the Law of Prize and Booty,* 1604), including the separately published chap. 12, titled *Mare Liberum/ On the Free Sea* (1609). For an account of these events see the editor's Introduction to Grotius (2006), pp. xiii–xxvii.

CHAPTER IV

Of England.

§1. In Ancient Time, *Britainy*, which was then esteemed the biggest Island of the World, was not ruled by one Prince, but divided into a great many petty States [*Republicquen*],[1] 'each' [most] of them govern'd by its own King; but this multitude of petty Princes, as it caused great Divisions among them, so it exposed them to the danger of being overcome by their Foreign Enemies. This Island was scarce known to the *Greeks* and *Romans* till *Julius Caesar's* time, who, after he had conquer'd the greatest part of *France,* undertook an Expedition into this Island, hoping, as 'tis suppos'd, to meet there with great Booty and Riches. But he enter'd not very far into the Country, and after some Skirmishes with the Inhabitants, returned again without leaving a Garrison, or exacting any Contributions.

The ancient State of England.

After this *Britainy* was not attack'd again by the *Romans,* till under the Reign of the Emperour *Claudius,* who bent his Arms against it in good earnest, and the Inhabitants being divided among themselves, and not joined in a mutual defence against the common Enemy, he, without great difficulty, conquer'd part of it. At which time *Britainy* was made a *Roman* Province, a constant Army being maintained here by the *Romans,* who by degrees conquered one part after another, yet not without receiving some Defeats. At last, under the Reign of *Domitian, Julius Agricola* marched with his victorious Army through the whole Island,

The Romans conquer England.

---

1. Pufendorf uses the term *republic* for all kinds of regular and irregular states. See VI.11, note 25, p. 291; VIII.20, note 29, p. 349; XII.33, note 171, p. 500; and Seidler (2011), p. 171, and p. 254, note 77.

and giving a signal overthrow to the *Caledonians,* who are now called the *Scots,* subdued them; tho' the *Romans* could never entirely conquer the utmost parts of *Britainy,* being almost inaccessible. Wherefore, afterwards the Emperours *Adrian* and *Severus,* by building a Wall cross the Island from Sea to Sea, divided them from the *Roman* Province, hoping thereby to stop their Incursions. But the *Romans* never came into *Ireland.* After the *Britains* had been <100> above 400 Years under subjection to the *Romans,* the Northern 'Nations' [peoples] at that time over-running the Western parts of the *Roman* Empire, the *Romans* left this Island voluntarily, being obliged to recall their Legions, which were posted in *Britainy,* to oppose their Enemies.

The Saxons come into Britainy,

§2. *Britainy* being thus without 'an Army' [Roman assistance], and besides this, mightily exhausted in its Strength, for that the *Romans* had made use of their young Men in their Wars, the *Picts* and *Scots,* from their barren Country, made an Inrode into these plentifull Provinces, destroying all before them. The *English,* to make the better Head against them, had chosen one *Vortigern* for their King; but he perceiving himself to be no ways able to resist their Power; and Assistance being denied him from the *Romans,* called in the *Angles,* a *Saxon* Nation, living then in *Holstein:* One part of which retains that Name to this day,[2] tho' some will have them to have been *Frieslanders,* others *Goths;* it being certain, that the modern Language of the *Frieslanders* has a great affinity with the ancient *English* Tongue. These *Angles,* under their Leaders *Hengist* and *Horsa,* coming with some thousands of Men to the assistance of the *Britains,* beat out the *Scots* \A. 450\. But they being mightily taken with the Fruitfulness of the Country, resolved to subdue it, and to lay the Yoak upon the *Britains,* who had called them in to deliver them from it. As soon as the *Britains* perceived what their Intention was, they endeavour'd to drive them out of the Island; but these taking up Arms, and calling in a great many thousands of their Country-men to their assistance, first took from the *Britains* the Eastern parts of the

2. The region of Angeln, southeast of Flensburg, in the north-German province of Schleswig-Holstein.

Island. And the Western parts, which were yet in the possession of the *Britains,* being afterwards extreamly wasted by Plague and Famine, so that the *British* King *Cadwalladar* retired into the *lesser Britainy:*[3] The *Saxons* took hold of this opportunity, conquering all the rest of *Britainy,* except the Province of *Wales,* which being surrounded with Mountains, they were not able to subdue. This abovementioned *Cadwalladar* was the <101> last King of the ancient *British* Race, who, perceiving that he was no ways able, any longer, to resist the Power of the *Saxons,* retired to *Rome,* into a Convent [monastery] \A. 689\. But *Britainy* received the Name of *Anglia,* or *England,* from the *Angles.*

§3. These *Saxons* erected seven Kingdoms, which however had not their beginning all at one time, but according as they had taken one part after another from the Inhabitants: At last they fell together by the ears among themselves, till one having swallowed up another, all were united into one Kingdom; which, how it happened we will briefly relate. The first Kingdom, then, was that of *Kent,* which began in the Year 455, and during the Reigns of seventeen Kings, lasted till the Year 827, when it was subdued by the *West Saxons.* The second was the Kingdom of *Sussex,* which began in the Year 488, and, under five Kings, lasted till the Year 601, when it was likewise made a Province by the *West Saxons.* The third was that of the *West Saxons* [Wessex], which began in the Year 519, and lasted, under nineteen Kings, 561 Years. The Eleventh of these Kings named *Ino,* did order, That each Subject that was worth 'ten' [nineteen] Pence, [and] should yearly give one Penny [*Pence*] to the Pope of *Rome,* which Tax was first called *the King's Alms,* and afterwards *Peter's Pence.* The fourth Kingdom was that of *Essex,* which began in the Year 527, and lasted, under fourteen Kings, till the Year 808, when it was also conquered by the *West Saxons.* The fifth was that of *Northumberland,* which began in the Year 547, and lasted, under three and twenty Kings, till the Year 926, when it also was brought under subjection by the *West Saxons.* The sixth Kingdom was that of the *Mercians,* which had its beginning in the Year 522, and lasted, under twenty Kings, till

The Saxon Kings in England.

The Saxon Heptarchy.

Peter's Pence.

3. Brittany, or Bretagne, across the Channel in France.

the Year 724, when it also fell into the Hands of the *West Saxons.* The seventh was that of the *East Angles,* which began in the Year 575, and lasted, under fifteen Kings, till the Year 928, when under its King *Athelstan* it was united with the rest.

The Kingdom of England. But \A. 818\ after *Egbert,* King of the *West Saxons,* had either |[subdued the rest]|,[4] or forced <102> their Kings to acknowledge him for their Supream Head, he and his Successours were henceforward called **Danes first come into England.** no more Kings of the *Saxons,* but of *England.* Under his Reign the *Danes* first enter'd *England,* as they continued to do under the following Kings, tho' in the beginning they were at several times bravely repuls'd: Nevertheless they got footing, at last, in the Northern parts of *England,* where they lived for a while pretty quietly under the Protection of the Kings of *England.* But in the time of King *Ethelred,* who began his Reign in the Year 979, the *Danes* made Inrodes into the Southern parts of *England,* forced the *English* to pay them great Summs of Money, ravish'd their Women, and committed such outrages, that they got the Name of *Lord Danes.* And tho' the *English* conspir'd [united] against the *Danes* \A. 1002\, and cut them all off [down], yet the *Danish* King [Sueno] return'd the next Year, and made prodigious havock among the *English,* their great Preparations which were made against the *Danes,* being by the Craft of the Traitor *Edrick* (notwithstanding *Ethelred* had made him Duke of *Mercia,* giving him his Daughter for a Wife) render'd ineffectual; so that *Ethelred* was obliged to leave his desolate Kingdom, and to retire into *Normandy. Sueno,* while he was busie in plundering the Nunnery of St. *Edmund* {in Suffolk}, having been kill'd by a Sword which no body knew from whence it came, **The Danes driven out, but return again.** *Ethelred* return'd out of *Normandy* into *England,* and forced *Canute, Sueno's* Son, to retire out of *England* into *Denmark;* but he return'd quickly with a much greater Force, and *Ethelred* making all imaginable Preparations against him, died in the Year 1016, whose Son *Edmund,* sirnamed *Ironside,* did defend himself with great Bravery against the *Danes,* and might have obtained several Victories over them, if he had not been therein prevented by that Traitor *Edrick.* At last it was agreed,

4. Rather: "made the rest into provinces".

That both Kings should make an end of the War by a single Combat, in which, tho' *Edmund* had the advantage of giving *Canute* a dangerous stroke, yet was he persuaded to finish the Combat, by dividing the Kingdom with the *Danes;* and was afterwards, as he retired privately to ease Nature, treacherously murther'd by *Edrick.* <103>

King Edmund treacherously murther'd.

§4. After the death of *Edmund, Canute* called together the *English* Lords, and asked them, Whether at the time, when the Kingdom was divided, there was any thing mentioned concerning the right of Succession of the Brothers and Sons of *Edmund;* and the *English,* out of fear, answering *there was not,* he received Homage from them, and was crowned King of *England.* After he had rid himself of all that were left of the Royal Race \A. 1017\, he, to curry favour with the People, married *Emma,* the Widow of King *Ethelred,* sent most of his *Danes* home, and reigned with great applause. Some of his Parasites, who pretended to attribute to him something above a Humane Power, he ridicul'd, by causing a Chair to be set near the Sea-side, commanding the Seas not to wet his Feet; but the Tide rolling on the Waves as usually, he told them, That from thence they might judge of what extent was the Power of all worldly Kings. He died in the Year 1035.

Canute, the Dane, King of England.

His Son *Harald* succeeded, by reason of his nimbleness sirnamed *Harefoot:* He did nothing worth mentioning, but that he caused his Stepmother *Emma,* and her Sons, whom he had, with fair words, persuaded to come over out of *Normandy,* to be miserably murther'd. He died in the Year 1039, leaving no Children behind him. After his death the great Men of the Kingdom called out of *Denmark, Hardiknut* his Brother, born of *Emma* and *Canute,* who was famous for nothing but his greedy Appetite, he being used to keep Table four times a day. His Subjects were so averse to him, that when he happened to die at a Feast, after he had reign'd but two Years, the *English* made publick Rejoicings in the Streets, which they called *Hocks-tide;* [5] the *Danes,* after his death, growing so despicable to the *English,* that the *Danish* Government in

Harald.

Hardiknut.

5. The feast of "hock-tide" was celebrated on the second Monday and Tuesday after Easter.

England expired, after they had ravag'd *England* for the space of 240, tho' they possessed the Throne but 26 Years.

Edward, the Confessor.

After the death of *Hardiknut, Edward* sirnamed the *Confessor,* Son of King *Ethelred* and *Emma,* Brother of *Hardiknut* on the Mother's-side, who had sought Sanctuary in *Normandy,* was called in to be King of *England:* He was crowned in the <104> Year 1042; and to gain the Affection of the People, he remitted a Tax called *Danegeld,* which had been constantly paid for forty Years last past. He reigned very peaceably, except, that he was now and then pester'd with the *Irish* and *Danish* Pirates, whom, nevertheless, he quickly overcame. He was the first to whom was attributed that Virtue, which even to this day the Kings of *England* are said to have, to heal by touching, that Disease which in *England* is called *the King's Evil.*[6] He died without Children \A. 1066\. He intended to have left the Kingdom to his Cousin *Edgar Atheling,* Grandson of King *Edmund Ironside;* but he being very young, *Harald,* Son of *Goodwin* Earl of *Kent,* who had the Tuition of *Edgar,* put the Crown upon his own Head, but did not enjoy it above nine Months, being slain in a Battel by *William* Duke of *Normandy,* whereby the Crown of *England* was transferr'd to the *Norman* Family.

William the Conquerour.

§5. This *William,* sirnamed *the Conquerour,* was Son of *Robert* Duke of *Normandy,* who was descended from *Rollo,* a *Dane,* who about the Year 900, with a great number of his Country men and *Norwegians,* fell into *France,* and ravaging the Country without resistance, *Charles* the *Simple,* the then King of *France,* thought it the best way to set him at quiet, by putting him into possession of the Province of *Neustria,* which afterwards was called *Normandy,* and giving to him in Marriage his Daughter *Geisa,* under condition that he should become a Christian. *Rollo* had a Son whose Name was *William,* sirnamed *Long-sword;* whose Son was *Richard,* sirnamed *the Hardy;* who was the Father of *Richard* II. sirnamed *the Good,* who was succeeded by his Son *Richard* III. as he was by his Son *Richard* IV. But he dying without Issue, after him *Rob-ert* became Duke of *Normandy.* This *Robert* was Father to *William the*

6. That is, scrofula or struma, a bacterial disease that causes swelling of the lymph glands of the neck.

Conquerour, whom he had by one *Arlotte,* a Furrier's Daughter, with whom, 'tis said, he fell in love, seeing her dance among other Maids in the Country, and afterwards married her. And notwithstanding this *William* was a Bastard, yet his Father made him his Successour, <105> and got the Nobility to acknowledge him as such when he was but nine Years of Age, and died soon after. This *William* met with great Troubles and Dangers in his younger Years, which he had the good fortune to overcome by his Valour, and acquired thereby great Reputation.

After the death of *Edward the Confessour, William* understanding that *Harald* had made himself King, resolv'd to demand the Crown of *England,* as belonging to him by virtue of the last Will of King *Edward,* who, he pretended, had left the same to him, as an acknowledgment for the great Favours he had received from his Father *Robert.* There are others, who say, That *Edward* did only promise this by word of mouth; and that *Harald* being then in *Normandy,* was forc'd to engage by Oath, to help him in obtaining the Crown of *England.* It is possible, this was only made use of as a pretence. But however it be, *William* landed without resistance with a great Army, compos'd of *Normans, French* and *Netherlanders,* whilst the Fleet of *Harald* was sailed to the Northern Coast of *England,* to oppose his Brother and *Harald Harfager* King of *Norway,* who were enter'd *England* on that side, and both vanquish'd by him; but thereby he left open the Door to *William* to enter into the Kingdom, and brought his Souldiers back much weakened and fatigued by their great Marches: Yet having reinforc'd his Army as well as he could, he offer'd Battel to *William* near *Hastings* in *Sussex* \on 14. October 1066\; which Battel was fought on both sides with great obstinacy; till *Harald* being mortally wounded by an Arrow, the Victory and Crown of *England* remain'd to *William; England,* without any further resistance, acknowledging him for a King.

The *English* were at first extreamly well satisfy'd with his Government, he leaving each in possession of what was his own, and only giving the vacant Lands to his *Normans;* partly, also, because he was related to the former Kings of *England,* partly, because he was greatly recommended to them by the Pope.[7] He was also very strenuous in securing

Willam conquers England.

---

7. Alexander II, pope from 1061 to 1073, supported William's invasion.

himself, commanding all the Arms to be taken from the People, and
to prevent Nocturnal Assemblies and Commoti-<106>ons, he ordered,
That after the Bell had rung at eight in the Evening, no Fire nor Candle
should be seen in their Houses: Besides this, he built several Forts in the
most commodious places. Notwithstanding all this, *Edgar Atheling* being with some of the Nobility retir'd into *Scotland,* and being assisted by
the *Danish* Pirates, continually ravag'd the Northern Parts of *England,*
burning the City of *York* it self, wherein all the *Normans* were put to
the Sword; but he [William] forced them afterwards thence. There was
also a dangerous Conspiracy set on foot against him {A. 1076}, which
was happily suppress'd by him, before the Conspirators could join their
Forces. His Son *Robert* also, endeavoured to take from him *Normandy,*
against whom his Father led a great Army out of *England,* and the
Father and Son encountring one another in the Battel, the first was
dismounted by the latter, but he discovering him to be his Father by his
voice, immediately dismounted, embraced him, and begg'd his pardon,
and was reconcil'd to his Father, who freely pardon'd all past Injuries.

This King also forc'd *Wales* to pay him Tribute, and King *Malcolm* of
Scotland to swear Fealty to him. But perceiving that this new-conquer'd
People would not be govern'd altogether by Mildness, he began to act
more severely, taking away out of the Convents what Gold and Silver
he could meet with, of which there was great store convey'd thither,
as into Sanctuaries.[8] He also imposed heavy Taxes, he appropriated to
himself a great part of the Lands of *England,* ||[which he gave unto
others, reserving to himself out of them]|[9] a yearly Revenue. He took
upon him the Administration of the Goods and Possessions of all Minors, till they came to the 21st Year of Age, allowing them only so much
as was requisite for their Maintenance: He revised all their Privileges,
introduced new Laws in the *Norman* Tongue; whereby a great many,
that did not understand that Language, fell under severe Penalties: He
erected new Courts of Judicature, and employed great tracts of Ground
for the conveniency of his Hunting. This King introduced first the use

The Curfew Bell.

Edgar Atheling makes an escape.

His Son Robert Rebels.

He acts as a Conqueror.

8. Those seeking to secure their wealth had hidden it there.
9. Rather: "and out of those he gave to others, he reserved to himself."

of the long Bow in *England*, whereby he had chiefly obtained the Victory against *Harald*, <107> and whereby afterwards the *English* did great mischief to the *French*, and gained many Battels from them.

At last, *Philip* I. King of *France*, by stirring up his [William's] Son *Robert* against him, endeavouring to raise Disturbances in *Normandy*, he went in person over into *Normandy*, where the Son was quickly reconcil'd to the Father. But being obliged to keep his Bed at *Roan* [Rouen], by reason of an Indisposition in his Belly, which was very gross, the King of *France* ridicul'd him, asking, *How long he intended to lie in;* to whom *William* sent this Answer, *That as soon as he could go to Church after his lying in, he had vow'd to sacrifice a thousand 'Candles'* [lights] *in* France;[10] and he was as good as his word, for he was no sooner recover'd, but he invaded *France*, and burnt all where ever he came: But he having overheated himself he fell ill and died \A. 1088\, leaving by his last Will, to his eldest Son *Normandy*, but to the second, called *William*, the Crown of *England*.

Robert Rebels again.

§6. *William* II. sirnamed *Rufus*, met, at first, with some {internal} Disturbances, occasioned by his Brother *Robert*, who pretending to the Crown, was back'd by a great many of the Nobility: but he appeased him, by promising to pay him yearly, the Summ of 3000 Marks, and that he should succeed him after his death. But the Nobles, who had dispersed themselves up and down in the Country, he partly by 'fair means' [assurances], partly by force, reduced to Obedience. This Rebellion proved very beneficial to the *English*, the Rebels being most of them *Normans*, wherefore the King afterwards rely'd more upon the *English*, as the most faithfull. He waged War twice with *Malcolm* King of *Scotland*, whom he forced in the first to swear him Fealty, but in the last, he killed both him and his eldest Son. He also subdued the Province of *Wales*. Among other Inventions to get Money one was remarkable; for he summon'd together 20.000 Men, under pretence to go with them into *Normandy*, but when they were just agoing to be shipp'd off, he caused Proclamation to be made, that every one who was willing to

William Rufus.

10. That is, he would set France ablaze.

pay ten Shillings, should have leave to stay at home, unto which every one of them readily con-<108>sented. He was kill'd by a random shot in hunting {by his servant} \A. 1100\.

Henry I.   Him succeeded his younger Brother *Henry,* who being present when the King died, seized upon his Treasures, whereby he procured himself a great many Friends, so that he was preferr'd before *Robert* his elder Brother, who at that time assisted in the taking of *Jerusalem,* which proved no less than the loss of a Crown to him. For *Henry,* the better to establish himself in the Throne, remitted not only several Taxes, which were laid upon the People by the former Kings, but also secured unto his Interest the King of *Scotland, Edgar,* his most dangerous Neighbour, by marrying his Sister *Maud.* 'Tis reported, that this *Maud* had vow'd Chastity, and that when her Brother forced her to marry, she wish'd, that such Children, as should be born out of this Marriage, might never prove fortunate; which wish was afterwards sufficiently fulfilled in her Children, and a great many of their Posterity. Notwithstanding this, *Robert* landed a great Army in *England,* but *Henry* and *Robert,* by the mediation of some Friends, and a Promise of a yearly Pension to be paid to *Robert* from *Henry,* were reconcil'd, which Pension also afterwards *Robert* remitted to *Henry.* But afterwards repenting of what he had done, *Henry* was so exasperated against him, that he made a Descent in *Normandy* with a great Army, and vanquish'd him in a bloody Battel, wherein he took him Prisoner. He kept him not only a Prisoner all his life time, but also, at last, put his Eyes out, uniting *Normandy* to the Crown of *England.*

Robert makes a Descent in England.

Normandy annexed to the Crown of England.

But King *Lewis* of *France,* sirnamed *Crassus,* being very jealous of the Greatness of *Henry,* undertook, with the assistance of *Fulco* Earl of *Anjou,* and *Baldwin* Earl of *Flanders,* to restore unto *William,* Son of *Robert,* the Dukedom of *Normandy;* whereupon a bloody War ensued, which was at last composed under this condition, That *William,* Son of *Henry,* should swear Fealty to *France,* for this Dukedom of *Normandy.* And it obtained afterwards as a Custom, That the King's eldest Son, was called *Duke of* Normandy, as long as this Province was united to *England.* The new Duke of *Normandy* did also mar-<109>ry the Daughter of the Earl of *Anjou:* And *William,* Son of *Robert,* being then made Earl of *Flanders,* and endeavouring a second time to regain *Normandy,* was slain in that War.

It is related by some, tho' others contradict it, That this King [Henry] was the first who admitted the Commons [*Bürgerschaft*] unto the Grand Council [*Berathschlagung*] of the Kingdom, unto which the Nobility and Bishops only were admitted before it came to be divided into the Higher and Lower House. His Son *William,* being by the carelessness of a drunken Master of a Ship drowned at Sea, with a great many other persons of Quality of both Sexes, as they were coming back from *Normandy* to *England,* he endeavoured to settle the Crown upon his Daughter *Maud,* and her Heirs, she being at first married to the Emperour, *Henry* IV.[11] by whom she had no Children, and afterwards to *Geoffrey Plantagenet,* Son to *Fulk* Earl of *Anjou.* Her Father made the States of *England* take Oaths of Fealty to her in his life time. He died in the Year 1135, and with him ended the Male Race of the *Norman* Royal Family in *England.*

The Norman Race extinct.

§7. After the death of *Henry,* *Stephen* Earl of *Boulogne, Henry's* Sister's Son, did by great Promises obtain the Crown of *England,* notwithstanding that both he and the States [estates] had taken the Oaths to acknowledge *Maud* for their Sovereign, which they endeavoured by a great many frivolous pretences to prove to be of no force. The better to establish himself in the Throne, he gained the Affection of the States with Presents, and discharged the People of several Taxes, giving Authority to the Nobility to build fortify'd Castles, which afterwards proved very mischievous to him. He also married his Son *Eustace* to *Constantia,* the Daughter of *Ludovicus Crassus,* King of *France.* This King's [Stephen] Reign was overwhelmed with continual Troubles. For the *Scots,* at first, and afterwards a great many of his Nobles, trusting in their strong Castles, raised great Disturbances; yet he bridled the Insolence of the *Scots,* giving them a signal overthrow. But his greatest Contest was with the Empress *Maud;* for she landing in *England* was

Stephen.

Maud makes War on him.

11. Actually, Matilda or Maude of Anjou had been married to Emperor Henry V (1086–1125), who acceded to the Concordat of Worms (1122).

re-<110>ceived by a great many, and King *Stephen* in a Battel fought
near *Chester,* was taken Prisoner. But she refusing to restore to the *Londoners,* King *Edward*'s Laws, they sided with her Enemies, and besieged
her very closely in the City of *Oxford,* from whence she narrowly escaped; and King *Stephen* also got an opportunity to get out of Prison.

These Troubles continued till *Henry,* Son of *Maud,*[12] came to the
nineteenth Year of his age, who, being Lord of four large Dominions,
as having inherited *Anjou* by his Father's, *Normandy* by his Mother's
side, *Guienne* and *Poictou* by his Wife *Eleonora,* Daughter and Heiress
of *William,* the last Duke of *Guienne,* he also endeavoured to obtain
the Crown of *England;* for which purpose he landed with an Army in
England. But he obtained his End without any great opposition; for
Eustace, King *Stephen*'s Son dying suddenly, an Agreement was made
betwixt them, whereby *Stephen* adopted him, and constituted him his

Henry II.   Heir and Successour, and died not long after in the Year 1154. *Henry* II
therefore succeeded him, who, among other memorable Actions, demolish'd such fortify'd Castles of the Nobility and Bishops, as were built
with the consent of King *Stephen.*

After he had reigned near eighteen Years in Peace and Quietness, he
had a mind to have his Son *Henry* crowned, the better to secure the
Succession, he received him as his Copartner in the Government; but
he being married to *Margaret,* the Daughter of *Lewis* the younger King
of *France,* this proved the cause of great Disturbances afterwards. For
some persuaded young *Henry,* That his Father having abdicated himself
from the Government, had committed thereby the same to his management. *France* envy'd that a King of *England* should have such vast
Possessions in *France.* The *Scots* wish'd for nothing more, than to have
His Son, with   an opportunity of committing Depredations in *England.* Wherefore the
the French   *French* and *Scots,* joining with young *Henry,* fell upon *Henry* II. all at
and Scots,
join in a War   one time, but were as vigorously repulsed by him; the *Scots,* especially,
against him.   suffered the most in this War, and lost all *Huntingtonshire.* A Peace was
also concluded with *France; Adela,* Daugh-<111>ter of *Lewis* King of
France, being promised in marriage to *Richard,* second Son of *Henry.*

12. Henry II (1133–89).

But the old King, as 'tis reported, falling in love with her, privately kept her company, and therefore opposed the consummation of the marriage betwixt her and his Son *Richard.* This so exasperated *Richard,* who, after the death of his eldest Brother *Henry,* was now the next Heir to the Crown, that he made Head against his Father; and *Philip Augustus,* King of *France,* taking hold of this opportunity, took the City of *Muns* [*Le Mans*]. King *Henry* seeing himself, besides this, deserted by his Friends, Wife, and Children, died in few days of Grief \A. 1189\.

This *Henry* also conquer'd *Ireland,* and united it to *England,* which he and his Successours govern'd under the Title of *Lords of* Ireland, till the time of *Henry* VIII.[13] who, after he had withdrawn himself from the Obedience of the Pope, to nettle him the more, assumed the Title of *King of* Ireland; because the Pope pretends to the sole right to bestow the Title of King in Christendom, and that none ought to take it upon him without his consent; wherefore the Pope, afterwards, to make his Pretence the more plausible, freely gave the same Title to *Mary* Queen of *England. Henry* also had some differences with *Thomas Becket,* Archbishop of *Canterbury,*[14] who pretended it was derogatory to the Glory of God, that the Priests, according to the King's Commands, should be subject to the Civil Judicatures. There is a fabulous Relation concerning this Archbishop *Thomas,* That he riding a Horse-back, one time, through a Village, the Country Fellows cut off the Tail of his Horse, and that their Children, afterwards, were born with such Tails.

§8. *Richard* I. who succeeded his Father *Henry* in the *Kingdom,* did, out of a preposterous Zeal [ill-considered devotion], undertake an Expedition into the *Holy Land,* with 35.000 Men, being accompanied by *Philip Augustus,* King of *France.* In this War he took the Island of *Cyprus,* which he gave to *Guido Lusignanus,* who in consideration thereof resigned his Right to *Jerusalem;* and in the Year 1192, he was present at the taking of *Pto-*<112>*lemais,* where the Standard of Duke *Leopold* of *Austria* being set up first, he pull'd it down again, putting his own in the

Ireland conquered.

Richard I.

He makes an Expedition into the Holy Land.

13. Henry VIII (1491–1547).
14. Thomas Becket (1118–70).

place. But when they were in great hopes of gaining *Jerusalem, Philip* returned home engaging himself by a solemn Oath, that he would not injure *Richard* in any of his Dominions. {*Odo* or} *Hugo,* Duke of *Burgundy,* afterwards followed his example, which greatly encouraged *Saladin:* And *Richard* understanding that the *French* were fallen into *Normandy,* he also made a Peace with *Saladin;* and taking his way by Land *incognito,* was discovered in his Journey through *Austria,* where Duke *Leopold,* remembring the affront done to him near *Ptolemais,* took him Prisoner, and delivered him to the Emperour, who after fifteen Months Imprisonment, made him pay 100.000 Pounds for his Ransom. After his return home, he found every thing in confusion, the *French* having not only ravaged *Normandy,* and other Provinces belonging to him, but also his Brother had made a Pretension to the Crown; but he obliged the latter to implore his Pardon, and beat the *French* back into their own Country. He died not long after \A. 1199\, of a wound which he received in a Siege of some inconsiderable place in *France.*

After his death his Brother *John* took upon him the Crown of *England,* who was opposed by *Arthur* Earl of the *lesser Britainy,* his elder Brother's Son; who finding himself alone not strong enough, sought for Aid of the King of *France,* who was ready upon all occasions to create Troubles in *England.* He took a great many Cities in *Normandy* and *Anjou.* Wherefore King *John* was obliged to make a dishonourable Peace with him, giving in marriage, to *Lewis,* King *Philip*'s Son, *Blanch* Daughter of *Alfonsus,* King of *Castile,* and of his Sister *Eleonora,* to whom he gave as a Dowry, all the Cities which *Philip* had taken from him, except *Angiers.* Then he married *Isabella,* Daughter and Heiress of the Earl of *Angoulesme,* who was promised before to *Hugh* Earl of *Marche.* He, to revenge this affront, join'd his Forces with the King of *France* and Prince *Arthur* of *Britainy,* and fell into *Touraine* and *Anjou.* But King *John* falling upon them unawares, routed the <113> Enemy, and took Prince *Arthur* Prisoner, who died not long after a Prisoner in *Roan.* But *Constantia,* the Mother of *Arthur,* made her Complaints to *Philip* King of *France,* whose Vassal King *John* was, on the score of such Provinces as he was possess'd of in *France,* and the King of *France* summon'd King *John* to appear before him, and to answer for the death

In his return he is taken Prisoner.

John.

His Nephew Arthur opposes him.

of *Arthur.* But he not appearing, it was declar'd, that King *John* had forfeited what Fiefs he was posses'd of in *France,* and King *Philip* took from him *Normandy* 316 Years after *Rollo* the *Norman* had conquered the same.

The King of France dispossesses him of Normandy.

But the *French* afterwards attack'd also *Angiers,* where they were repulsed with great loss by King *John,* whereupon a Truce was concluded betwixt them for two Years: During which time he routed the *Scots,* and suppressed the Rebels in *Ireland* and *Wales.* The Truce being expired, the War began afresh with *France,* and King *John's* Army being routed, he made another Truce with *France.* But this ill success had much diminished his Authority among his Nobles, who also hated him, because he had imposed heavy Taxes upon them; wherefore they, with joint consent, demanded from him the restitution of their ancient Privileges; but perceiving that he only intended to give them fair Words for Deeds, they called to their aid, *Lewis,* Son of *Philip* King of *France,* who landing with a great Army in *England,* was received with a general applause, and whilst King *John* endeavoured to make Head against him, he died overwhelm'd with Troubles \A. 1216\.

The Dauphin invited by the Barons, invades England.

§9. Him succeeded his son *Henry* III.[15] whose tender Age wrought Compassion on most, and extinguish'd the Hatred which had been conceiv'd against his Father. And the Earl of *Pembroke,* to whose Tuition he was committed, having totally routed the *French* near *Lincoln,* and destroyed the *French* Forces at Sea, that were sent to their assistance, *Lewis* did renounce all his Pretensions upon the Crown of *England,* and retir'd into *France.* This King's Reign was very long, but also very troublesom, occasion'd chiefly by the great concourse of Foreigners into *England;* who <114> crept into all places of profit: For the Pope sent at one time 300 *Italians,* who being admitted into Church Benefices, did so lay about them, that their yearly Rents amounted to 60.000 Marks of Silver, which was a greater Revenue than the Crown had at that time.[16]

Henry III.

The Dauphin is forced home again.

15. Henry III (1207–72) became king in 1216, at the age of nine, though regents ruled in his stead until 1227.

16. Henry III was in fact a strong supporter of the papacy and welcomed many Italians into positions of influence in England.

And by reason of the Prodigality of the King, tho' constantly burthening the People with Taxes, he was always in great want of Money. He married, besides this, the Daughter of the Earl of *Provence,* who having abundance of poor Kindred, they enrich'd themselves out of the Treasury of the King. This caused, at last, an open War betwixt the King and the principal Men of the Kingdom, in which *Henry* resign'd to the King of *France,* all his Pretensions upon *Normandy, Anjou, Poictou, Touraine* and *Mans,* in consideration of the Summ of 300.000 pounds paid him by the *French* King, and he was himself taken Prisoner in the first Battel: But his Son, Prince *Edward,* gathered another Army, and killed the General of the Rebels, *Simon* of *Monfort* Earl of *Leicester;* delivering thereby his Father, and suppressing the whole Rebellion. He [Henry] did nothing worth mentioning abroad, except that he undertook two Expeditions into *France,* both which prov'd fruitless. He died in the Year 1272.

A War with the Barons.
He quits his Pretensions on Normandy for a Summ of Money.

Edward I.

Him succeeded his Son *Edward,* who was at that time in the *Holy Land;* and tho' he did not come into *England* till a Year after his Father's death, yet took quiet possession of the Crown. This King entirely united the Principality of *Wales* to the Crown of *England,* the last Prince, *Lyonel,* being slain in a Battel. Under his Reign also began a bloody War, and an implacable hatred was raised betwixt the *English* and *Scotch* Nations, which for 300 Years after caused abundance of bloodshed betwixt both Nations. The occasion was thus: After the death of *Alexander* III. King of *Scotland,* who died without Heirs, there were several that pretended to the Crown of *Scotland,* wherefore King *Edward* took upon him the Arbitration of this matter, that Crown having depended on his Predecessours, and the *Scots* being still obliged to do Homage to the King of *England.* The matter being examined, it so proved, that *John Baliol* Earl of <115> *Galloway,* and *Robert Bruce,* were found to have the best Title to that Crown. But these two having contested for the same during the space of six whole Years, *Edward* sent under hand to *Bruce,* telling him, That he would decide the difference concerning the Crown of *Scotland* in favour of him, if he would swear Fealty to *England,* which *Bruce* refused, answering, That he was not so fond of the Crown, as to purchase the same with the prejudice of the Liberty of his Native Country. But *John Baliol* receiving the same offer, was made King of *Scotland.*

The causes of the Differences betwixt the English and Scots.

There was about that time a capital Quarrel in *Scotland*, betwixt the Earl of *Fife* and the Family of *Alberneth*, who had kill'd the Earl's Brother, and the King of *Scotland* had by his Sentence absolv'd the latter. The Earl, therefore, appeal'd to the *English* Court, whither King *Baliol* was called to appear, and to sit with the King in Parliament: But as soon as this matter came under debate, he was admonished to rise from his Seat, and to give an account concerning his Sentence. He pretended to answer by his Advocate, which being denied him, he was obliged to answer in person from the same place, where others used to plead their Causes: Which both he and the *Scots* resented as so signal an affront, that, no sooner was he returned home, but he renounced his Oath to King *Edward,* pretending the same to have been unjust, and that it was not in his power to make such a promise; and renewing the ancient Alliance with *France,* he denounced War against *England*. King *Edward,* therefore enter'd *Scotland* with an Army, took the best strong Holds, and forced the *Scots* and their King to swear fealty to him; their King he sent a Prisoner into *England,* leaving considerable Forces in *Scotland,* which were, nevertheless, soon after beaten out of *Scotland* by the *Scots,* under the Conduct of a Gentleman of a mean Fortune, whose name was *William Wallis* [Wallace].[17] But King *Edward* soon returned, kill'd 40.000 *Scots* in a Battel near *Torkirke,* and forced them to swear Fealty to him a third time. Notwithstanding all these Oaths, *Robert Bruce,* who had been *John Baliol's* Competitour, took upon him the Crown, <116> who was several times worsted, but also beat the *English* at other times, particularly when King *Edward* going with an Army against *Robert,* in person, fell sick and died \A. 1307\.

    This King *Edward* had also had some Differences before with *France.* For some of his Subjects in *Aquitain,* having done considerable mischief by Privateering on the Coast of *Normandy,* King *Philip* sirnam'd *the Handsome* summon'd *Edward* to appear at his Court as his Vassal, and to answer the same, which *Edward* refusing to do, he declared all his Possessions which he held from the Crown of *France* to be forfeited; taking from him by force of Arms *Bourdeaux* and some other places; against whom *Edward* enter'd into a Confederacy with the Earl

A War with Scotland.

With France.

17. William Wallace (1270–1305), the national hero of Scotland.

of *Flanders* and the Emperour *Adolphus*. But coming into *Flanders* with an Army, and finding every thing in confusion and disorder, he made a Truce with King *Philip* \A. 1297\, promising, That his Son *Edward*

He banishes the Jews.

should marry *Isabella, Philip*'s Daughter. This King caused, likewise, all the *Jews* to be banished out of *England*, not allowing them to carry away any thing more than what they could carry themselves.

Edward II.

§10. Him succeeded his Son *Edward* II. who at the very beginning of his Reign, married *Isabella*, Daughter of *Philip* sirnamed *the Handsom*, with whom he had for a Dowry '*Guienne*' [*Aquitaine*], and the County of *Ponthieu*, the greatest part whereof had been taken from

Unsuccessfull in his War with Scotland.

his Father by the *French*. This King was very unfortunate in his Wars against the *Scots*, who in the Battel fought near *Bannoksborough*, with an Army of 30.000 Men defeated 100.000 *English*, which struck such a terrour among them, that 100 *English* durst scarce face three *Scotchmen:* And the *English* were continually beaten by the *Scots* (except in *Ireland*, where they beat the *Scots* out, who had enter'd that Kingdom) so that

His Troubles at home.

Edward was at last obliged to make a Truce with them. He met also with great Disturbances at home, the great Men of the Kingdom pressing him without intermission, to leave to their Mercy, his Favourites *Gaveston*, and after him the *Spencers*, which he refusing to consent to, they fell into open Re-<117>bellion, in which they proving unsuccessfull, several of the Nobility paid with their lives for it. But the Queen, pretending that the *Spencers* had diverted the King's Love from her, retir'd first into *France*, and from thence into *Hainault*, and returning with an Army, took the King Prisoner, and caused the *Spencers* to be executed. The King was carried from place to place, and greatly abused during his Imprisonment, having been forced before by the Parliament, to resign the Kingdom to his Son *Edward*. At last, about six Months after his Deposition, he was miserably murther'd \A. 1327\.

Edward III.

§11. *Edward* III. was very young when the Crown was conferr'd upon him, wherefore the Administration of the Government was, during his Minority committed to his Mother, and managed under her chiefly by her Favourite *Roger Mortimer*. She immediately, at the beginning, made a dishonourable Peace with *Scotland*, whereby *Edward* renounced the Sovereignty and all other Pretensions upon that Kingdom; and the *Scots* renounced their Title to *Cumberland* and *Northumberland*. This and some other matters laid to their charge, was the reason why, some Years after, the Queen was condemned to a perpetual Imprisonment, and *Mortimer* was hanged.

Afterwards a most cruel War broke out betwixt *England* and *France*; for *Lewis*, *Philip* and *Charles*, all three Sons of *Philip* sirnamed the *Handsom*,[18] dying without Issue, *Edward* did pretend a right to the *French* Crown, as being the late King's Sister's Son; alledging, That if his Mother, as being a Woman, might be thought incapable of governing the Realm, the same ought not to be prejudicial to him, as being a Man. But *Philip de Valois*,[19] notwithstanding he was a degree farther of[f], as being the late King's Father's Brother's Son, yet prevailed with the States, who under pretence of the *Salick* Law,[20] and the hatred they bore to a Foreign Sovereign; being, besides this, encouraged thereunto by the Earl of *Artois*, set him upon the Throne. *Edward* being afterwards summon'd by *Philip*, to come in person, and to do Ho-<118>mage for the Dukedom of *Aquitain*, went thither in person, he being then but young, and *England* full of intestine Commotions, notwithstanding this seemed to be very prejudicial to his Pretensions: And King *Edward* appearing in the Church at *Amiens* with the Crown upon his Head, his Sword and Spurs on, was ordered to lay them aside, and to take the Oath upon his Knees; which so exasperated *Edward*, that *France* afterwards felt the effects of it.

His Pretensions to the French Crown.

Not long after, *Edward Baliol*, Son of *John Baliol*, made pretensions to the Crown of *Scotland* against the young King, being assisted by King *Edward*, notwithstanding King *David* of *Scotland* had married his Sister. During which Commotions the *English* recovered *Barwick* upon *Tweed*, and in one Battel killed 30.000 *Scots*, whereupon *Edward*

He is successfull against Scotland.

18. Philip IV (1268–1314).
19. Philip VI (1293–1350), the first king of France from the house of Valois.
20. The Salic Law was a disputed rule of royal succession that excluded females and their descendants from certain titles and roles. Originally it focused only on land or property, thus the "pretence" [*Vorwand*]. See V.9, p. 207, below.

Baliol did do Homage to the King of *England* for the Crown of *Scotland.* By this time King *Edward* being come to his riper years, upon His Expedition the instigation of *Robert* Earl of *Artois,* undertook an Expedition into into France. *France,* and taking upon him the Title and Arms of *France,* renewed his Pretensions to that Crown. In this Expedition \A. 1340\ he entirely routed the *French* Fleet near *Sluys,* which was sent to hinder his landing, and defeated 30.000 Men, and after he had besieged *Tournay* he made a Truce with them for twelve Months. In the mean while the *English* were engaged in a War with the *Scots,* who, under the Conduct of their former King *David,* had driven out *Edward Baliol.* The time of the Truce being expir'd, the War began afresh in *France,* where, among other places, the *English* took *Angoulesme.* King *Edward* himself came with a great Army into *Normandy,* and took, both there and in *Picardy,* The Battel a great many places from the *French:* At last a bloody Battel was fought near Crecy. betwixt them near *Crecy* in *Picardy,* wherein the *English,* tho' but 30.000 strong, fought against 60.000 *French,* killing 30.000 upon the spot, among whom were 1500 persons of Quality. The next day after 7000 *French* were cut to pieces by the *English,* who, not knowing what had happened the day before, were upon their march to the *French* Camp. In this Battel \A. 1346\ no Quarter was given on either <119> side. Much about the same time King *David* of *Scotland* enter'd *England* with an Army of 60.000 Men, to make a Diversion in behalf of *France;* The Scotch but he was defeated in a great Battel, and himself taken Prisoner. The defeated. *English* had no less success the same Year in *Britainy* and *Guienne.* In He takes the Year next following King *Edward* took the City of *Calais,* which he Calais. fill'd with *English* Inhabitants.

Prince *Edward,* Son to *Edward* III. whom his Father had sent with an Army into *Guienne* \A. 1356\, behaved himself very valiantly, making great havock where-ever he came. *John* King of *France* drew out an Army against him of 60.000 Men, tho' the Prince was not above 8000 strong; upon this the King, thinking he had catch'd the Bird in the Net, would not accept of any Conditions, tho' never so advantageous. But Prince *Edward* having posted his Men betwixt the Bushes and Vineyards, from thence so gall'd the *French* Horse with his long Bows, that they being repulsed, put all the rest in confusion; King *John* himself was taken Prisoner, as also his youngest Son, and above 1700 persons of Quality were slain. This Battel was fought about two Leagues from *Poictiers.* At last, after King *Edward* had with three Armies over-run the greatest part of *France,* a Peace was concluded by the Mediation of the Pope, at *Bretaigny,* not far from *Chartres:* The Conditions of this Peace were, That *England,* besides what it had before in *France,* should be put in possession of *Poictou, Zaintogne, Rochelle, Pais d'Aulnis, Angoumois, Perigord, Limoisin, Quercy, Agenois,* and *Bigorre,* with an absolute Sovereignty over the same; besides this, the City of *Calais,* the Counties of *Oye, Guisnes,* and *Ponthieu,* and three Millions of Crowns were to be given as a Ransom for the King; and that King *John* should give his three younger Sons, his Brother, and thirty other persons of Quality as Hostages for the payment of the said Summs. But that on the other side, the *English* should restore all the other places which they had taken from the *French,* and renounce their Right and Title to the Crown of *France.*

The Peace being thus concluded, Prince *Edward,* to whom his Father had given the Dukedom of *Aquitain,* <120> restored *Peter* King of *Castile* to his Kingdom. But in his Journey, the Souldiers being very mutinous for want of Pay, he levyed an extraordinary Tax upon his Subjects, which they complaining of to the King of *France,* he summon'd the Prince to appear before him, who answer'd, He would <suddenly> appear with an Army of 60.000 Men; therefore *Charles* V. King of *France,* denounced War against the *English,* pretending, that the promised Sovereignty, at the last Peace, was void, because the Prince had not fulfilled the Articles of the same, and had committed Hostilities against *France.* But whilst Prince *Edward* was busie in making great Preparations against *France,* he died suddenly, and with him, the *English* good Fortune; for the *French* took from them all the Dukedom of *Aquitain,* except *Bourdeaux* and *Bayonne.* The King was so troubled at the loss both of so brave a Son and his Conquests in *France,* that he died within ten Months after his Son \A. 1377\.

§12. Him succeeded *Richard* II. Son of that brave Prince *Edward,* who being but eleven Years of Age when he came to the Crown, was despised

The Battel near Poictiers.

A dishonourable Peace to France.

Another War with France.

Richard II.

by the *French,* who burnt several places on the *English* Coast. The *Scots*
also made an Inrode on the other side of *England,* and the War being
carried on with various Fortune, after several Truces expired, a Peace
was at last concluded.

A Peace with France.

Troubles at home.

    There were also great Commotions in the Kingdom under this King's
Reign: For in *Kent,* and other neighbouring Counties, there was an Insurrection of the Rabble, occasioned by the Insolence of one of the Re-
ceivers of the Poll Tax: This Rabbles Intention was to have murthered
both the Nobility and Clergy, except the *Mendicant* Fryars; but were
soon restrained by the King's Valour. But there were continual Discontents betwixt the King and the Lords, the King being resolved to rule
according to his Pleasure, and to maintain his Favourites against the
Lords, who were for removing his Favourites, and bringing his Royal
Power into a more narrow compass by the Authority of the Parliament.
But it was the King's custom, as soon as the Parlia-<121>ment was dissolved, to reverse all that was concluded upon before; yet once the Parliament got him at an advantage, when it forced him to permit most
of his Favourites to be either kill'd or banish'd; and obliged him by an
Oath to promise, That he would administer the Government according to the Advice of his Lords. Not long after, a Conspiracy among the
Lords was discovered against him, a great many of them paid for it with
their Heads, the King seemed at last to have master'd his Enemies; but

The occasion of his Ruin.

he was, nevertheless, ruin'd at last, which was occasioned thus: *Henry*
Duke of *Lancaster* accused the Duke of *Norfolk,* as if he had spoken ill
of the King; and the latter giving the lye to the former, they challenged
one another, but the Duel was prevented by the King's Authority, who
banish'd them both out of the Kingdom. *Henry* of *Lancaster* retired
into *France,* raising there a Faction against the King, by inviting all
dissatisfy'd persons to him, who promised to set him on the Throne of

Henry Duke of Lancaster invades England.

England. He landed but with a few in *England,* but at a time, as King
Richard's ill Fortune would have it, when he was in *Ireland;* and the
Wind proving contrary, he could not have notice of his Enemies arrival
in *England* till six Weeks after, which gave them opportunity and leisure
to strengthen their Party. The King also committed a great errour, for
that he afterwards, against his Promise, tarry'd so long in *Ireland,* which

was the cause, that such Forces as were brought together by his Friends, whom he had sent before, were again dispersed before his arrival in *England*. Coming afterwards in person into *England*, and being informed how powerfull his Enemies were, he despair'd of his Affairs, and having dismiss'd his Forces, that were ready to fight for him till the last gasp, he was made a Prisoner. *Henry* of *Lancaster* calling, immediately hereupon, a Parliament, a great many things were objected to *Richard*, and he was declared to have forfeited the Crown. But before this Resolution was published, he resign'd himself, and was not long after miserably murthered in Prison \A. 1399\. <122>

§13. Thus *Henry* IV. of the House of *Lancaster*, came to the Crown, he being after the Deposition of King *Richard* declared King by the Parliament, tho', if the Pretensions of *Henry*, together with the Power of the Parliament, be duely examined, the Title of *Henry* IV. to the Crown of *England*, will be found to have a very ill Foundation. For what some pretend, that *Edmund*, from whom the House of *Lancaster* descended, was the eldest Son of *Henry* III. and that he being very deformed, was obliged to give way to his Brother *Edward* I. is rejected as a frivolous Fable by the *English* Historians. This King did labour under great difficulties at the beginning of his Reign, all which he at last overcame: For the Design of the *French* to restore *Richard* ended with his death. And a Conspiracy of some Lords against him was discover'd, even before *Richard* died. The *Scots*, who made War on him, got nothing but blows. The *Welshmen* also, in hopes of having met with an opportunity to shake off the *English* Yoke, joined with a discontented Party out of *England*, and rebell'd against him; but before they could join all their Forces, the King came suddenly upon them, and overthrew them in a great Battel, wherein, 'tis said, the King kill'd six and thirty with his own Hands. Yet the discontented Party did not rest, but enter'd into a third Conspiracy against him, which was soon discover'd. A great many of them retir'd afterwards into *Scotland*, where they stirr'd up the *Scots* against *England* (for these never used to miss an opportunity of being troublesome to *England*) but they got nothing but blows again for their pains. This King died in the Year 1413.

§ *Henry* IV. of the House of Lancaster.

§ He had great Difficulties which he surmounted.

Henry V.   §14. After him reigned his Son *Henry* V. who in his younger Years did not promise much, but after he came to the Crown, shew'd himself one of the most valiant Kings the *English* ever had. And as he was very Aspiring and Ambitious, so he thought he could not meet with a better opportunity of gaining Glory, than by entring into a War with *France,* and renewing the ancient Pretensions upon that Crown. He sent, therefore, his Ambassadours to *Charles* VI. to <123> lay claim to that Crown, and to make this Proposition to him, That if he would resign to him the Crown of *France,* he would marry his Daughter *Catharine.* But it being not usual that Princes are persuaded to part with a Crown thus, the next

He invades France to prosecute his claim of the Crown.   way was to try their Fortune by Arms. *Henry* therefore enter'd *France* with an Army, took *Harfleur,* and obtained afterwards a most signal Victory near *Agincourt* in *Picardy* against the *French,* who (according to the *English* Historians) were six times stronger than the *English.* Ten

The Battel near Agincourt.   thousand of the *French* were kill'd upon the spot, and as many taken Prisoners, not above some Hundreds being slain of the *English:*[21] Yet at that time *Henry* did not pursue his Victory. But not long after, the *French* Fleet having first been beaten by the *English* near *Harfleur, Henry* made a second Descent upon *France,* taking one place after another in *Normandy,* and at last the City of *Roan* it self \A. 1419\.

He met with very little opposition in *France* at that time, because all was in confusion at the *French* Court, the King, *Charles* VI. being not in his right Wits, and the Queen being fallen out with her Son, the Dauphin, who had taken from her all her Jewels and Money, alledging, That they might be better employ'd upon the Souldiery: Which was the reason that the Queen siding with *John* Duke of *Burgundy,* did promote him to the place of chief Minister of *France;* who was more intent to maintain his private Interest and Greatness, against the Dauphin, than to make Head against the *English.* A Congress was proposed to be held betwixt the two Kings, but this Design was frustrated by the cunning of the Dauphin, who gave the Duke hopes of an entire Reconciliation to

21. The Battle of Agincourt took place on October 25, 1514, the celebrated St. Crispin's Day of Shakespeare's Henry V (act 4, scene 3). The English success was largely due to the effectiveness of the longbow against the French cavalry, which was greatly impeded by the terrain.

be made betwixt them both. And *Monterau* being named for the place where they should meet, the Duke of *Burgundy* was there, (questionless, by instigation of the Dauphin) miserably murther'd. For this reason his Son, Duke *Philip,* being resolved to revenge his Father's death, declared openly for the *English,* and by his Mediation obtain'd, That King *Henry* should marry the Princess *Catharine,* and during the life of his Wife's Father, administer the Government in his name, but after his death, <124> should succeed him in the Throne. The Nuptials were afterwards celebrated at *Troyes* in *Champaigne* \A. 1420\.

The Admin-
istration of
France to be
in Henry dur-
ing Charles's
life, and after
his death the
Crown to de-
scend to him.

After the Treaty had been confirmed by solemn Oaths on both sides, which was also ratify'd by the three Estates assembled in *Paris,* where the Dauphin was summon'd to appear, to answer concerning the death of the Duke of *Burgundy:* But he not appearing, Sentence was given against him, That he should for ever be banish'd out of *France.* There were also some who design'd to make him away [do away with him], and he was forced to go from place to place, but his common place of Residence was *Bourges,* wherefore they used to call him, by way of ridiculing, *The King of* Bourges. In the mean time the *English* took one place after another from him. At last, King *Henry* being upon his March to raise the Siege of the City of *Cosne* on the *Loire,* which was besieged by the Dauphin, he fell sick in his Journey thither, and being carried to *Bois de Vicennes,* there died in the flower of his Age and Felicity \A. 1422\, leaving the Administration of *France* to his Brother, the Duke of *Bedford,* and the Administration of *England* to his second Brother, the Duke of *Gloucester.*

§15. Him succeeded his Son *Henry* VI. a Child of eight Months old; who, after he was grown up, degenerated from his Father's Martial Valour, and by his ill management, lost what his Father had got, eclipsing thereby the *English* Glory. He was, after the death of *Charles* VI. who died not long after *Henry* V. proclaimed King of *France* in *Paris.* In opposition to him, the Dauphin, *Charles* VII. also declared himself King of *France,* with whom sided the Bravest among the *French,* and a great many *Scots* were sent to his assistance. But *Philip* Duke of *Burgundy,* and *John* Duke of *Britainy,* held to the Confederacy with the

Henry VI.

Proclaim'd
King of
France.

English, which was renewed at that time. And then they began to fall upon one another with great fury: For the *French* received a great Defeat near *Crevant* in *Burgundy* \A. 1423\, and were soundly beaten near *Verneuil* {in the following year}. In the Year 1425 {as} the *French* had besieged St. *'Jaques'* [*James*] *de Beuveron* with Forty <125> thousand Men, the Garrison being reduc'd to great extremity, prayed with a loud voice to St. *George* of *Salisbury:* The Besiegers hearing the name of *Salisbury* very frequently among the Besieged, supposed that the Earl of *Salisbury* was coming to raise the Siege; whereat the *French* were so terrify'd that they ran away for fear of his Name {as the English historians purport}.

This is certain, that the *English,* for a while, were Masters where-ever they came, but before *Orleans* the carreer of their Fortune was first stopt. For, tho, during that Siege, they beat the *French,* who came to cut off their Provisions (which Battel is commonly called *the Battel of the* Flemmings [herring])[22] and the City would have surrender'd it self to the Duke of *Burgundy,* which the *English* would not accept of; yet did they not only lose in that Siege the brave Earl of *Salisbury,* but also the *French,* being encouraged by a Maid called *Joan,* that was born in *Lorraine,* {successfully} beat the *English* from before *Orleans.* This Maid did several great exploits against the *English,* and led, her self in person, King *Charles* to his Coronation in *Rheims.* At last she was taken Prisoner by the *English* in an Encounter, who carried her to *Roan,* where they burnt her for a Witch. But because the *English* perceived, that after the Coronation of *Charles,* a great many Cities sided with him, they also called over their King *Henry* out of *England,* and crowned him King of *France* in *Paris* \A. 1432\.

About the same time, a Truce was concluded by Mediation of the Pope, for six Years; but it lasted not long, for the *French,* during the time of the Truce, possess'd themselves of several places, which they had brought over to their side by cunning Insinuations, pretending, That any thing gained without open violence did not violate the Truce. And

The Maid of Orleans.

He was crowned in Paris.

22. An episode, in 1429, before the besieged city of Orleans, where the French and Scottish defenders attacked an English supply convoy that carried, among other things, barrels of herring. This action involved one of the first uses of gunpowder artillery in the war. See V.13, at note 24, p. 217, below.

King *Charles's* Maxim was, *Not to fight with the* English, *but to strive to get Advantages over them rather by Policy* [*Geschwindigkeit*] *than open force.* But that which gave a great blow to the *English,* was, That the Duke of *Burgundy* having taken a distaste at the *English* upon some slight occasion, was reconciled to King *Charles.* There were some small Differences arisen betwixt the Duke of *Bedford* and the Duke of *Burgundy;* to compose which, a meet-<126>ing was appointed at St. *Omer* [Omar]: But the time being near at hand, a Dispute arose, which of them should appear there first; it being supposed, that he who should come first, did thereby yield the Precedency to the other; wherefore the Duke of *Bedford* refused to come first, alledging, That he being Regent of *France,* ought not in that Quality to give preference to a Vassal of *France.* But the Duke of *Burgundy* stood upon his right of being Sovereign of the place where they were to meet; so that the meeting being set aside, the Duke of *Burgundy* broke quite off with the *English,* and afterwards assisted King *Charles* against them. The death of the Duke of *Bedford* \A. 1435\, proved another Misfortune to the *English.* For the Duke of *Somerset* and the Duke of *York* both pretended to his place; and tho' the latter did obtain it, yet did the first always oppose his Designs, so that, before the new Regent arrived, *Paris,* which had been seventeen Years in the possession of the *English,* and a great many other Cities, did surrender themselves to King *Charles* \A. 1436\. Yet did the Duke of *Gloucester* beat the Duke of *Burgundy* before *Calais,* making great havock in *Flanders, Artois* and *Hainault;* and the brave *Talbot* did considerable mischief to the *French.*

But when afterwards, by a Truce made with *France,* the fury of the War ceased for a little time, there was a Foundation laid in *England* for intestine Commotions. The King had promised marriage to the Daughter of the Earl of *Armagnac,* to prevent which, the *French* King had made both the Earl and his Daughter Prisoners. The Earl of *Suffolk,* who was then Ambassadour in *France,* did propose thereupon, without having received any Instructions to that purpose from the King, a Match betwixt the King and *Margaret* Daughter of *Rene,* Duke of *Anjou* and King of *Naples* and *Sicily,* and afterwards persuaded the King to ratifie the same. This Match was mightily opposed by the Duke of

The English decline in France.

The Duke of Burgundy leaves the English and is reconciled to Charles.

The occasion of the Troubles in England.

Gloucester, the King's Uncle, who alledged, That her Father had only the bare Titles of King and Duke; and that besides this, great Injury was done thereby to the first Bride, *viz.* to the Daughter of the Count of *Armagnac.* Notwithstanding this, the Match went forward, and to <127> obtain the Bride of the *French, Anjou* and *Maine* were given them as a Recompence. The King being thus 'led away' [ruled] by the Queen and his Favourites,[23] her first design was to revenge her self upon the Duke of *Gloucester,* whom she accused of Male Administration,[24] and after she had got him committed to Prison, caused him privately to be murther'd. The death of so innocent a Man did afterwards fall heavy

The English driven out of France. upon the King: For the *French,* not long after \A. 1449\, took from them all *Normandy,* the *English,* by reason of a Rebellion in *Ireland,* not being in a capacity to send thither speedy and sufficient Relief. They were also beaten out of *Aquitain,* so that they had nothing left them in *France,* but *Calais,* and some neighbouring places; neither could they, afterwards, ever get footing again in *France.*

The occasion of this sudden loss. This sudden loss was occasioned by the carelessness of the *English* Garrisons, that were not provided with able Governours, as also by the Pride of the *English,* whereby they were become hatefull to the *French* Subjects: But the chief cause was, *Richard* Duke of *York,* who had underhand raised intestine Commotions in *England:* For he being sensible of the King's Weakness, and how ill satisfy'd the People were with the Queen's management of Affairs, hoped, by fomenting and raising Troubles in the Kingdom, to make way for himself to obtain the Crown; and this he did, principally, because he pretended to have the best right to the Crown, being descended, by his Mother's side, from *Lionel* Duke of *Clarence,* third Son of King *Edward* III. whereas *Henry* was descended from *John* of *Gaunt,* fourth Son of the said *Edward* III.[,] but publickly he profess'd, That his Intention was only to remove from the King's Person his pernicious Favourites, and especially the Duke of *Somerset.* Having therefore got an Army on foot, he fought with the

23. In German: "den [the] Favoriten"; that is, they might be hers instead of his, which is more likely here.
24. Cf. the Latin *male* (badly).

King's Forces, in which Battel the Duke of *Somerset* was slain, and the Duke of *York* thereupon declared Protector of the King's Person and the Kingdom. But this Agreement did not last long, and things came quickly again to an open War, wherein the Duke of *York* being worsted, was forced to fly into *Ireland.* But not long after <128> the Earl of *Warwick* did beat the King's Army, and taking him Prisoner, the Duke of *York* was again declared Protector of the King and Kingdom, and lawfull Heir of the Crown; under condition that *Henry* should retain the Title of King during his life. But Matters did not remain long in this condition, for the Queen, who was fled into *Scotland,* marched with a great Army against the Duke of *York,* who was kill'd in the Battel, and all the Prisoners were executed. But his Son, in conjunction with the Earl of *Warwick,* raised another Army, and marching up to *London,* the young Duke of *York* was there \A. 1460\ proclaimed King by the Name of *Edward* IV.

§16. Thus *Edward* IV. came to the Crown, but could not maintain it without great difficulty: For *Henry* had got together a very powerfull Army in the *North,* against whom *Edward* fought the most bloody Battel that was ever fought in *England,* there being 36.796 Men killed upon the spot, because *Edward* knowing his Enemies to be superiour in number, had ordered, not to give Quarter to any of them: After which Battel *Henry* retired into *Scotland,* from whence he returned with another Army, and being again defeated, with much adoe got safely into *Scotland.* But returning again *incognito* into *England,* he was taken Prisoner and committed to the *Tower.* This Prince, would have made a better Priest than a King of such a Nation, |[that was distracted by the Animosities of several Factions]|.[25]

Edward IV. of the House of York.

A bloody Battel betwixt *Edward* and *Henry.*

But the Tragedy did not end here: The King [*Edward* IV.] had sent the Earl of *Warwick* into *France,* to conclude a Match betwixt him and *Bona* the Daughter of *Lewis* Duke of *Savoy.* But the King having in the mean time suddenly married *Elizabeth,* the Widow of *John Gray,* the

25. Rather: "where there are so many contrary dispositions [*widerwertige Köpfe*]"—referring to the character of the English.

Earl was so dissatisfy'd at it, that he declared for King *Henry;* and having brought over to his Party the Duke of *Clarence,* the Brother of King *Edward,* he fell upon a sudden upon *Edward,* and took him Prisoner; but by the carelessness of his Keepers he escaped not long after. And tho' an Agreement was then made betwixt them, yet was it of no long continuance, for the <129> Earl of *Warwick's* Forces were routed, and he forced to fly into *France.* As soon as he had recover'd himself a little, he returned into *England,* where he was so well received, that he forced King *Edward* to fly into the *Netherlands* to *Charles* Duke of *Burgundy:* And King *Henry,* after he had been nine Years a Prisoner in the *Tower,* was again set upon the Throne.

Henry taken out of Prison and set on the Throne.

But *Edward* having received some Assistance from the Duke of *Burgundy,* returned again into *England;* but perceiving that but few came in to him, he made an Agreement with King *Henry,* which he confirm'd with a solemn Oath, That he would not undertake any thing against him, but be contented with his own Estate: Yet notwithstanding his Oath, he underhand gathered what Forces he could. The Earl of *Warwick* therefore marched towards him, when the Duke of *Clarence,* being reconcil'd to his Brother King *Edward,* went over with all his Forces to him. This gave a signal blow to the Earl of *Warwick,* who being now not strong enough to oppose him, was forced to let him march up to *London,* where he was joyfully received by the *Londoners,* to whom, as 'tis said, he owed much Money, and was very acceptable to their Wives;[26] but King *Henry* was committed again to the *Tower* \A. 1471\. Then King *Edward* attack'd the Earl of *Warwick,* where a bloody Battel was fought, the Victory seeming, at first, to incline on the Earl's side: But some of his Troops, by reason of a thick Fogg, charged one upon another, which lost him the Battel, he remaining, with a great many other persons of Quality, slain in the Field. There happened also this misfortune, That King *Henry's* Lady and his Son *Edward* having got together very considerable Forces in *France,* could not come [in] time

Edward returns into England.

Henry a second time Prisoner, and murther'd by the Duke of Gloucester.

26. In German: *"und bey ihren Weibern gute partes hatte."* George, Duke of Clarence, had a reputation as a heavy drinker, which may have led to the story (still alluded to by Shakespeare, *Richard III,* I.4) that he drowned in a barrel of wine rather than being executed in the Tower.

enough to his assistance, having been detained by contrary Winds; and coming afterwards into *England*, she was taken Prisoner, and her Son kill'd; and King *Henry*, also, was murthered by the Hand of the bloody Duke of *Gloucester*.

England being thus restor'd to its Tranquility at home, *Charles*, Duke of *Burgundy*, who was in hopes of getting an advantage by a War betwixt *England* and *France*, stirr'd up King *Edward* against *Lewis* XI. King of <130> *France*. But King *Lewis*, who was not ignorant how mischievous the Confederacy of *England* and *Burgundy* might prove to him, did endeavour to detain the *English* King with fair words, and to render the Duke of *Burgundy* suspected to him; which had the design'd effect with *Edward*, who considered with himself, That *Charles* Duke of *Burgundy* having besieged *Nuys*, did not send him the promised Succours; so that the Peace was easily concluded, ||[the *French* having been very liberal to the *English*]||.[27] To confirm this Peace, King *Lewis* proposed a Congress to be held betwixt him and *Edward* at a certain place, where he, without making any further difficulty, appeared first in person,[28] and bestowed a good quantity of Wine upon the *English* Souldiers, who soon after returned with their King, who had got but little Honour in this Expedition[,] into *England*, {to the great displeasure of the Burgundian}. But he behaved himself better against the *Scots*, to whom he did considerable mischief. In the mean time the Duke of *Gloucester* had rid himself of his elder Brother, the Duke of *Clarence*, thereby to advance himself one step nearer to the Crown. At last King *Edward* being now resolved to enter again into a War with *France* (since King *Lewis* made a very slight account of what he had promised in the last Peace, after he was once rid of his Enemy) he fell sick, and died in the Year 1483.

§17. After the death of *Edward* IV. his Son *Edward* V. a Child of eleven Years of Age was proclaimed King, but scarce enjoyed this Title ten Weeks. For his Uncle *Richard*, Duke of *Gloucester*, the most bloody

Edward V.

27. Rather: "because Edward's associates [*Leute*] had been well rewarded by the French"—suggesting bribery.

28. That is, he allowed Edward the honor of arriving last, and waited for him. Cf. above at §15, p. 141.

and wicked Man that ever the World beheld, immediately made it his business to set the Crown upon his own Head. Wherefore he first of all secured to himself the Tuition of the King's and his Brother's Persons, by making away their most trusty Friends. Afterwards, by the help of some Impudent 'Priests' [preachers],[29] he got it spread abroad, That *Edward* IV. was born in Adultery, and that consequently the Crown did of right belong to himself, as being the most like his Father. At last, the Duke of *Buckingham* did insinuate into the Lord Mayor of *London,* That the Crown ought to <131> be offered to *Richard;* and his Proposal being approved by the Acclamations of a few 'Villains' [boys] set on for that purpose, it was divulged, That the {whole} People had conferr'd the Crown upon *Richard.* Having by these {shameless} Intrigues obtain'd the Crown, *Richard* III. got himself proclaimed King \A. 1483\; and having been crowned, he caused the innocent <King> *Edward* V. and his Brother, miserably to be murthered.

Richard III.

Murthers his
Nephews.

But soon after his Coronation a difference arose betwixt him and the Duke of *Buckingham,* who had been chiefly instrumental in helping him to the Crown. He therefore leaving the Court, began to make a Party against the King, with an intention, to set the Crown upon the Head of *Henry* Earl of *Richmond,* who was then an Exile in *Britainy.* And tho' the Duke of *Buckingham's* Plot was discovered, and he beheaded, yet was not the Design stopt. For the Earl of *Richmond* set sail with a great Fleet out of *Britainy* {A. 1484}, but being driven by contrary Winds on[to] the Coast of *Normandy,* he sought Aid of *Charles* VIII. King of *France,* which he readily granted him. A great many *English,* also, went over to him, who swore Allegiance to him, he promising them upon Oath, That he would marry the Princess *Elizabeth,* Daughter of *Edward* IV. But *Henry* was within an ace of having been delivered up to *Richard* by the Treachery of one *Pieter Landois,* Treasurer of the Duke of *Britainy,* who had received a great Summ of Money from *Richard* for undertaking it, for which reason he was afterwards

29. Specifically, the claim was made in a sermon by one Ralph Shaa (sometimes called John Shaa, d. 1484), a British theologian and half-brother to the mayor of London.

hang'd by his Master's order. *Richard* also had an Intention of marrying the Princess *Elizabeth*, and therefore had privately made away [secretly murdered] his former Lady, but was obliged to delay the consummation of the Match, by reason of the approaching danger from *Henry:* Who to prevent this intended Match, did in all haste sail out of *France*, and landing in *Wales*, was kindly received by most. Not long after he gave Battel to *Richard*, where *William Stanley*, with some thousands of Men, went over to *Henry*; and besides this, a great many of *Richard*'s Souldiers refusing to fight, *Richard* himself was slain in the Field, and the Crown being immediately <132> there put upon *Henry*'s Head, he was proclaimed King \A. 1485\.

§18. Hitherto *England* had been miserably torn to pieces by the bloody Wars betwixt the Houses of *York* and *Lancaster*, the first whereof bore a White, the latter a Red Rose in their Shields. For *Henry* IV. of the House of *Lancaster*, had driven *Richard* II. from the Throne; *Edward* IV. of the House of *York*, dethroned again his [Henry's] Grandson *Henry* VI. And *Henry* VII. of the House of *Lancaster*, took from *Edward* the IVth's Brother, *Richard* III. both his Crown and Life. This King *Henry* marrying the Daughter of *Edward* IV. united the Red and White Roses, and by his singular Wisdom, did again settle the State of the Kingdom.

Yet was he not altogether free from Disturbances at home. For first of all, one *Lambert Symnel*, Son to a Baker, taking upon him the Name and Person of *Edward* Earl of *Warwick*, caused himself to be proclaimed King in *Ireland*. This Comedy was first invented by a Priest, and encouraged by *Margaret*, the Widow of *Charles* Duke of *Burgundy*, Sister to *Edward* IV. who, to spite *Henry*, gave them all the Assistance she could. This *Symnel* transported an Army out of *Ireland* into *England*, but was routed by *Henry*; and being taken Prisoner, was made a Turnspit in the King's Kitchin.

In the Year 1491 *Henry* undertook an Expedition against *France*, and besieged *Bologne*.[30] But the Emperour *Maximilian* failing in his promises of giving him Assistance, he in consideration of a good Summ of

He murthers his Wife.

Henry Earl of Richmond invades England.

Henry VII.

He united the White and Red Roses.

Lambert Symnel.

He makes an Expedition into France.

---

30. Boulogne-sur-Mer, in northern France.

Money made a Peace with *France*. In the mean time, *Margaret* Dutchess Dowager of *Burgundy*, had set up another Impostor, whose Name was *Perkin Warbeck*. He pretended to be *Richard*, a younger Son of King *Edward* IV. and knew so well how to act his part, that he got a considerable Party in *Ireland*. From thence he went to *Paris*, where he was very well received, *France* being then engaged in a War with *England:* But a Peace being concluded betwixt them, he retir'd to the Dutchess *Margaret's* Court. From thence he returned into *Ireland*, and afterwards came into *Scotland*, <133> where being splendidly received by that King, he was married to one of his Kinswomen, and enter'd *England* with a considerable Army. This business might have proved very dangerous to *England*, since there were, at the same time, great Tumults in *England*, arisen about some new Taxes. But the Rebels were beaten, and the *Scots* obliged to retire with great loss into *Scotland*. The *Scots* made thereupon a Peace with *England*, promising, among other things, not to uphold, by any ways, the Impostor *Perkin*, who fled from thence into *Ireland*, and so came into *Cornwall*, where he caused himself to be proclaimed King: But perceiving that few came over to his side, and the King's Forces coming upon him, he took sanctuary in a Church, and surrender'd himself to the King, who committed him a Prisoner to the *Tower;* but he having twice made an attempt to escape, was at last hang'd 'according to his demerits' [as he had long deserved].

In the Year 1501, a Marriage was concluded betwixt *James* IV. King of *Scotland*, and *Margaret* the Daughter of *Henry*, which afterwards united *England* and *Scotland* under one King. *Arthur*, also, eldest Son of *Henry*, married *Catharine* Daughter of *Ferdinand the Catholick*.[31] But the Prince dying a few Weeks after the Wedding, in the sixteenth Year of his Age, and *Henry* being unwilling to give back the Dowry, and desirous to maintain the new Alliance with *Ferdinand*, married the said *Catharine* to his second Son *Henry*, who was then but twelve Years of Age, having obtained a Dispensation from Pope *Julius* II. under pretence that there had been no carnal knowledge betwixt them; which

Perkin Warbeck.

He marries his Daughter Margaret to the King of Scotland.

---

31. Catherine of Aragon (1485–1536), youngest surviving child of Ferdinand and Isabella.

afterwards proved the cause of great Alterations. This King [Henry VII] is reckoned among the wisest of his Age, and the only thing which is reprehended in him, is, That he had a way, by false Accusations against the rich, to squeeze out of them great Summs of Money from them. He died in the Year 1509.

§19. *Henry* VIII. immediately upon his first accession to the Throne, celebrated the Nuptials with his Brother's Widow [Catherine of Aragon], more to fulfill his Father's Will than out of his own Inclination; yet as long as he <134> lived with her in Wedlock he govern'd the Realm very laudably, and in the Court nothing was seen but Plays and Diversions. As to his Transactions abroad, upon the persuasions of Pope *Julius* II. and *Ferdinand the Catholick*, he enter'd \A. 1512\ into a Confederacy with them against *France*, which Confederacy was pretended to be made for the defence of the Holy See. *Ferdinand* also put him in hopes of recovering *Guienne;* wherefore *Henry* sent an Army into *Biscay,* to fall in conjunction with the *Spaniards* into *Guienne*. But *Ferdinand* having rather his Eye upon *Navarre,* and being negligent in sending timely Succours to the *English,* they returned home without doing any thing.

> Henry VIII.
>
> He enters into League with Ferdinand and the Pope.
>
> His Expedition against France.

In the Year 1513 *Henry* enter'd *France* with a great Army, where he lost his time in the taking of *Terovane* and *Tournay,* which [Therouanne] was wholly destroyed in spight of all the Attempts of the *French* to relieve it, tho' *Tournay* was {later} redeemed by *Francis* I. with a good Summ of Money. But at that time *Henry* did not pursue his Advantage, partly out of carelessness, incident to young Men, partly, because he had carried on this War, not so much for his own Interest, as in favour of the Pope, and so returned into *England*. During the absence of *Henry, James* IV. King of *Scotland,* upon instigation of the *French* invaded *England,* but received a great overthrow, himself being killed in the Battel. In the Year next following [1514], *Henry* perceiving that his Father-in-law *Ferdinand* did only impose upon him, concluded a Peace with *France,* giving his Sister *Mary* in marriage to King *Lewis* XII.

> A Second.
>
> An Invasion of the Scots.

In the Year 1522 *Henry* again denounced War against *Francis* I. and sent considerable Forces into *France,* which, nevertheless, both in the

> He makes a second War against France.

same and next following Year did nothing of moment; and the *Scots,* on the other side, obtained not any advantages against the *English.* But after *Francis* was taken Prisoner near *Pavia,*[32] it seem'd that *Henry* had met with a fair opportunity to give a great blow to *France,* more especially, since he had before prepared a Fleet, which lay ready to make a Descent in *Normandy,* yet he left *Charles* and made Peace with *France.* And <135> *Charles,* after he thought he had obtained his aim, did not make any great account of *England,* leaving the Princess *Mary,* Daughter of *Henry,* to whom he had promised Marriage, for the Princess of *Portugal,* whom he married. And whereas he used formerly to write to the King with his own Hand, and subscribe himself, *Your Son and trusty Friend;* he now caused his Letters to be writ by his Secretary, subscribing only his Name, *Charles.* And truly it seemed very necessary for *Henry* to keep a little the Ballance. Tho' a great many are of opinion, That Cardinal *Woolsey* {who was then in charge of Henry's affairs} had a great hand in this business, who was no great Friend of *Charles* V. because he had not promoted him to the Papal Dignity, and had denied him the Archbishoprick of *Toledo,* of which he had put him in hopes at first;[33] neither did he subscribe himself any more *Your Son and Cousin,* as he used to do. But however it be, *Henry* at that time saved *France* from an imminent danger.

The Divorce of Henry VIII.

After he had lived very peaceably and well with his Queen for the space of twenty Years, he began to have a scruple of Conscience, Whether he could lawfully live in Wedlock with his Brother's Widow; which scruple he pretended was raised in him first by the President of *Paris,* who was sent to treat concerning a Marriage betwixt *Mary* Daughter of *Henry,* and the second Son of *Francis.* Some say, that he being weary of her, was fallen in love with *Anna Bullen* [Anne Boleyn], and found out this way to be rid of her. Yet this seems not so probable

---

32. Francis I (1494–1547) was captured at the battle of Pavia, Italy, in 1525 by the armies of Charles V (1500–1558), with whom Henry VIII was then allied. See II.10, p. 61, above.

33. Charles V opposed Wolsey's aspirations to the papacy during the conclave of 1521 and also denied him the promised archbishopric of Toledo (and its revenues). This supposedly encouraged Wolsey (see Shakespeare's *Henry VIII,* II.i) to support Henry's divorce from Catherine (Charles's aunt).

to some, since he did not marry the said *Anna Bullen* till three Years
after he pretended to the scruple of Conscience; whereas the heat of
Love does not usually admit of such delays. Some will have it, that
Cardinal *Woolsey* raised this scruple first in him, on purpose to nettle
Charles V. and to please *Francis* I. in hopes, after this Divorce, to make
up a Match betwixt *Henry* and the Dutchess of *Alenson,* Sister of *Francis.* But however it be, the business was brought before the Pope, who
gave a Commission to the Cardinal *Campegius,* to enquire, in conjunction with *Woolsey,* into the matter: 'Tis said, That the Pope was willing
to gratify *Henry,* and for that purpose had sent a Bull to *Campegius,*
yet with this <136> caution, to keep it by him till further order. But
when he afterwards saw *Charles* V. to prove so successfull, he durst not
venture to do any thing that might displease him, wherefore he ordered
Campegius to burn the Bull, and to delay the business to the utmost.
The Queen also refused to answer to their Commission, but appealed
to the Pope in person; besides, *Charles* V. and his Brother *Ferdinand*
had protested against this Commission. *Woolsey* did also perceive, that
the King was fallen in love with *Anna Bullen,* which being likely to
prove prejudicial to his Authority, he persuaded the Pope underhand,
not to give his consent unto this Divorce. *Henry* being informed what
Intrigues the Cardinal was carrying on against him, humbled the great-   The fall of
ness of this haughty Prelate, who died in the Year next following in   Woolsey.
great misery.

And *Henry* being made sensible, that the Pope regarded more his
own Interest than the merits of the Cause, he forbid, that any body
should hence forward appeal to *Rome,* or send thither any Money for
Church Benefices. He therefore sent to several Universities in *France*
and *Italy* to define their Opinions in this matter, who all unanimously
agreed in this, That such a Marriage was against the Laws of God; and
having once more, by his Ambassadours, sollicited the Pope, but in
vain, to decide the matter, the King had the same adjudged in Parliament, and divorced himself from her \A. 1532\, yet conversed with her
in a very friendly manner ever after till her death, except, that he did
not bed with her since the time when this scruple first arose. Some
Months after he was married to *Anna Bullen,* by whom he had *Eliza-*   He marries
beth, who was afterwards Queen.   Anna Bullen.

He abrogates
the Pope's
Supremacy.
Anno 1535 the King caused himself to be declared *Supream Head of the Church of* England, abrogating thereby all the Pope's Authority in that Kingdom, and *John Fisher* Bishop of *Rochester,* and *Thomas Moor* the Lord Chancellour, refusing to acknowledge him as such, it cost them their Heads. Yet would *Henry* never receive the Doctrine of *Luther* or *Zwinglius,* but continued in the *Roman* Communion, because he was mightily exasperated against *Luther.* For *Henry* had formerly got a Book to be published <137> under his Name against *Luther* in favour of the Pope, for which he acquired the Title of *Defender of the Faith,* which Title the Kings of *England* retain to this day. But *Luther* setting aside all the Respect due to a King, writ an Answer to the same, full of Heat

Monasteries
demolished.
and bitter Reflections.[34] Yet because he esteemed the Monks as a sort of people that were not only useless, but also such as depending on the Pope, might prove very pernicious to him at home, he gave free leave to all Monks and Nuns to go out of the Convents and Nunneries; and by degrees converted unto his own use the Revenues of all Nunneries and Convents, Colleges and Chappels, as also those of the Order of the Knights of St. *John* of *Jerusalem;* nevertheless he employed some part of them in erecting six new Episcopal Sees, and Cathedral Churches, and to the advancing of Learning in the Universities. A great part also he gave away or sold for a little Money to great Families, intending thereby to oblige them for the future to maintain the alterations he had made. It is reported, that these Church Revenues which were so reduced, did amount yearly to 186.512 *l.* or as some others will have it, to 500.752 *l.* He also abolished the superstitious worship of Images, and made some other alterations in Religious Worship, so that, in effect, he

Protestants
and Papists
executed.
laid the Foundation of the Reformation. Nevertheless *England* was at that time in a miserable condition; for a great many *Roman* Catholicks, that would not acknowledge the King for the Supream Head of the *English* Church were executed: And a great many more Protestants received the same punishment, because they would not own the Corporal

---

34. Henry's Defense of the Seven Sacraments (*Assertio Septem Sacramentorum,* 1521), was dedicated to Leo X. Luther replied with *Contra Henricum Regem Angliae* (1522), generating a defense of Henry by Thomas More.

presence of the Body of Christ in the Sacrament; tho' this effusion of blood was not so much caused by the King as by the Bishops, who had first brought in use such rigorous Laws, and now executed them with as much severity.

In the Year 1543, another War happened with the *Scots,* who making an Inrode into *England* were beaten by a few *English;* which did grieve King *James* V. to that degree, that he died for trouble [grief], leaving behind him one only Daughter *Mary,* whom *Henry* would have engaged to his Son *Edward,*[35] there-<138>by to unite these two Kingdoms; and the business was like to have succeeded very well, if the Archbishop of St. *Andrews* had not opposed it. *Henry* also enter'd into a League with the Emperour against *France,* wherein it was agreed, to join their Armies of 80.000 Foot and 22.000 Horse near *Paris,* to plunder that City, and to ravage the whole Country as far as the *Loire.* But neither of them acted according to the Agreement, for *Henry* wasted his time in the Siege and taking of *Boulogne,* which he afterwards, by the Peace concluded in the Year 1546, promised to restore to *France* within the space of eight Years, in consideration of the Summ of 800.000 Crowns to be paid him for the same; which was performed accordingly under *Edward* VI. \A. 1550\. Neither do I believe that *Henry* was in good earnest by ruining the *French* to give such great advantages to *Charles* V.

After his Divorce with *Catharine* of *Arragon,* he was very unfortunate in his Marriages; for *Anna Bullen* was beheaded for Adultery and Incest, tho' some are of opinion, that it was more the Protestant Religion than the Crime which proved fatal to her. It is certain, that the Protestant Princes of *Germany* did so resent this matter, that whereas they intended to have made *Henry* the Head of their League, they afterwards would hold no correspondency with him. After *Anna Bullen* he married *Jane Seymour,* Mother to *Edward* VI. who died in Child-bed. Then he married *Anna* of *Cleves,* whom he also pretending I know not what bodily infirmity in her, quickly dismiss'd. The fifth was *Catharine Howard,* who was beheaded for Adultery. The sixth *Catharine Parre,* Widow of the Lord *Latimer,* who outlived him. *Henry* died in the Year 1547.

War with Scotland.

He enters into a League with the Emperour against France.

Anna Bullen beheaded.

His other Wives.

35. Edward VI (1537–53) succeeded in 1547.

Edward VI. §20. *Edward* VI. was nine Years of age when he came to the Crown, during whose Minority his Uncle, the Duke of *Somerset* had the Administration of Affairs. His first design was to force the *Scots* to agree to a Match betwixt *Edward* and their young Queen *Mary*, wherefore he fell into *Scotland*, and overthrew them near *Muskelborough* in a great Battel. Nevertheless he miss'd his aim, for the *Scots* sent their <139> Queen into *France*, who was there married to the Dauphin, afterwards King of *France* by the Name of *Francis* II. Under this King *Edward* the Reformed Religion was publickly established in *England*, and the Mass quite abolished; which occasioned great disturbances in the Kingdom, which were nevertheless happily suppress'd. In the Year 1550 there was a Peace concluded betwixt *England, France* and *Scotland*, when also *Boulogne* was restor'd to the *French*. But King *Edward* falling sick, the Duke of *Northumberland*, who had before destroyed the Duke of *Somerset*, persuaded King *Edward*, under pretence of settling the Protestant Religion, to exclude by his last Will and Testament his two Sisters, *Mary* and *Elizabeth* (for of the Queen of the *Scots* they made but little account at that time) from the Succession of the Crown, and to settle it upon *Jane Grey*, Daughter of the Duke of *Suffolk*, whom he had by *Mary* Daughter of *Henry* VII.[36] which afterwards proved fatal both to {the good} *Jane* and the Author [Northumberland]. For after the death of *Edward* \A. 1553\, the Duke of *Northumberland* caused

Lady Jane Grey proclaimed Queen.   *Jane* to be proclaimed Queen in the City of *London;* but *Mary* eldest Sister of *Edward* did immediately lay claim to the Crown in her Letters to the Privy Council: And Letters proving ineffectual, they began to come to blows; but most of the Nobility, unto whom *Mary* promis'd not to make any alteration in Religion, did side with her; and a part of the Army and Fleet, most of the Privy Counsellors, and the City of *London*, taking her part proclaimed her Queen. *Northumberland* himself being now willing to go with the tide, did proclaim *Mary* Queen in *Cambridge*, notwithstanding which he afterwards lost his Head.

36. Actually, Jane Grey was the daughter of Frances Brandon, who was the daughter of Mary Tudor.

§21. Queen *Mary* caused the *Roman* Catholick Religion and Mass, which were abolished in her Brother's time, as also the Pope's Authority to be restor'd in *England,* she used the Protestants very hardly, of whom a great many were punished with death, Yet was she not able to restore the Church Revenues, for fear of exasperating the greatest Families, who had them in their possession. The Pope did also send Cardinal <140> *Poole* [Pole], to re-unite the Kingdom to the holy See of *Rome.*

Mary. Restores Popery.

This Queen *Mary* was married to *Philip* Son of *Charles* V. who was afterwards King of *Spain,* yet under these Conditions, That she should have the sole disposal of all Offices and Revenues of the Kingdom, and if a Son was born, he should, besides the Crown of *England,* inherit *Burgundy* and the *Netherlands: Don Carlos,* who was born of a former Wife, should be Heir of *Spain* and all the *Italian* Provinces, and in case he died without Issue, this [son of Mary] should also inherit his part. But no Children came of this marriage, *Mary* being pretty well in Years, for she was thirty Years before proposed in Marriage. And there were some, who being dissatisfy'd at this Match, raised Tumults; among whom was the Duke of *Suffolk,* Father of *Jane* [Grey], who had hitherto been a Prisoner in the *Tower,* but she and her Husband *Guilford,* and her Father, paid with their Heads for it. It was within an ace but that *Elizabeth,* who was afterwards Queen, had also undergone the same fate, if *Philip* and the *Spaniards* had not interceded for her, not out of any affection to her person, but because they knew, that after her, the next Heir to the Crown of *England* was *Mary* Queen of *Scotland,* who being married to the Dauphin of *France,* they feared, lest by this means *England* and *Scotland* might be united with *France.*

Marries Philip of Spain.

Lady Jane, &c. beheaded.

The reason why Philip interceded for the Lady Elizabeth.

Among other Articles in the Marriage Contract of Queen *Mary,* it was agreed, That she should not be obliged to engage her self in the Wars which her Husband, *Philip,* should carry on against *France:* Notwithstanding which, when *Philip* afterwards was engaged in a War with *France,* she sent to his assistance some of her best Forces, who by their Bravery chiefly obtain'd the Victory near St. *Quintin;* for which reason *Philip* gave the City to be plundered by the *English. Henry* II. King of *France,* taking hold of this opportunity, assaulted the City of *Calais,* under the Command of the Duke *de Guise,* which being not well

The Battel of St. Quintin.

Calais lost.

Garrison'd he took in a few days, and obliged all the Inhabitants to quit the City, and to leave behind them all their Gold, Silver and Jewels. He also took afterwards the two Castles of *Guisnes* and <141> *Hammes,* and thereby drove the *English* quite out of *France.* Not long after this loss Queen *Mary* died \A. 1558\.

Elizabeth. §22. *Elizabeth,* who after the death of her Sister, was unanimously proclaimed Queen, maintain'd her Authority, and govern'd with great Prudence and Glory in the midst of a great many threatning dangers to the very end. In the beginning *Philip* endeavoured by all means to keep
Philip *England* on his side, for which reason he proposed a Marriage betwixt
desires her in *Elizabeth* and himself, promising to obtain a Dispensation from the
marriage. Pope, which was nevertheless opposed by the *French* in the Court of *Rome. Elizabeth* was very unwilling to disoblige so great a Prince, who had well deserved of her; yet on the other side, the same scruple which had caused her Father to be divorced from *Catharine* of *Arragon,* by a parity of reason, did remain with her;[37] she considered, especially, that the said Divorce must needs be esteemed unjust, if the Pope's Dispensation was allowed of; since it had been alledged as a fundamental reason of the said Divorce, that the Pope had no power to dispense in any cases which were contrary to God's Law: She resolved therefore not to have any further concerns with the Pope, and to give a friendly refusal to *Philip.*

Then she, by an Act of Parliament, constituted the Protestant Episcopacy, yet not at once, but by degrees, taking away from the Papists the free exercise of their Religion, and under several Penalties and Fines obliged every one to frequent the Protestant Churches on *Sunday.* Every body also was obliged by a solemn Oath to acknowledge her the Supream Governour in *England,* even in Spiritual Matters; which Oath was among 9400, who were possess'd of Church Benefices, taken by all, except 189 who refused the same, among whom were fourteen Bishops. She kept stedfast to the established Episcopal Church Government,

---

37. The scruple was whether she could marry her dead sister's widower. See §§18–19, pp. 148–51, above.

tho' she met with great opposition from two sorts of people, *viz.* the Papists and Puritans. These having conceived a great hatred against Episcopacy, and all other Ceremonies which had the least resemblance of <142> Popery, were for having every thing regulated according to the way of *Geneva*.[38] Tho' their number increased daily, yet the Queen kept them pretty well under. But the Papists made several attempts against her Life and Crown; for her envious Enemies did erect several Seminaries or Schools for the *English* Nation in foreign Countries; *viz.* at *Douay,* at *Rheims,* at *Rome* and *Valedolid;* all which were erected for the Instructing of the *English* Youth in these Principles, *viz.* That the Pope had the Supream Power over Kings, and as soon as a King was declared a Heretick by him, the Subjects were thereby absolved from their Allegiance due to him, and that it was a meritorious work to mur-ther such a King.[39] Out of these Schools Emissaries and Priests were sent into *England,* whose business was there to propagate the *Roman* Catholick Religion; but more especially, to instruct the People in the abovementioned Doctrines. To these associated themselves some Des-perado's, who, after Pope *Pius* V. had excommunicated the Queen [in 1570], were frequently conspiring against her Life. But most of them got no other advantage by it, than to make work for the Hang-man, and occasioned that the Papists were stricter kept than before.

Mary also, Queen of *Scotland,* raised abundance of troubles against Queen *Elizabeth;* she being the next Heiress to the Crown of *England,*[40] did, with the assistance of the Duke of *Guise,* endeavour to have Queen *Elizabeth* declared by the Pope Illegitimate (which the *Spaniards* under-hand [secretly] opposed) and both she and the Dauphin assumed the

38. A reference to Calvin's mode of church government in Geneva, which re-jected rule by bishops in favor of elected assemblies composed of clergy and elders (presbyters), which also had considerable power over civic affairs. See at note 48, p. 166, below.

39. The doctrine of regicide was historically associated with the Jesuits, specifi-cally Juan de Mariana, *De rege et regis institutione* (Toledo, 1599). Pufendorf men-tions Mariana in *On the Law of Nature and of Nations,* but only his *Historia de rebus Hispaniae libri XX* (Toledo, 1592).

40. Mary Stuart was daughter of James V of Scotland (1512–42) and wife of Francis II of France (1544–60).

Arms of *England*, which undertaking proved afterwards fatal to Queen *Mary*. For *Elizabeth* sided with the Earl of *Murray*, natural Brother of Queen *Mary*,[41] whose main endeavour was to chase the *French* out of *Scotland*, and to establish there the Protestant Religion, both which he effected with the assistance of Queen *Elizabeth*. This Queen *Mary* being after the death of *Francis* II. returned into *Scotland*, was married to her Kinsman *Henry Darley*, one of the handsomest Men in *England*, by whom she had *James* VI. But her Love to him grew quickly cold; for a certain *Italian* Musician, whose name was *David Ritz* <143> was so much in favour with the Queen, that a great many persuaded *Henry*, that she kept unlawfull company with him. He being thus animated, with the assistance of some Gentlemen, pull'd *David Ritz* out of the Room where he was then waiting upon the Queen at Table, and kill'd him immediately. From whence King *James*, with whom Queen *Mary* was then big with Child, had this natural infirmity, That he could not see a naked Sword, his Mother having at that time been frighted with

The Queen of Scots married Bothwell, who murthered her Husband.

naked Swords. This so exasperated the Queen against her Husband, that he soon after, as was suppos'd, was in the Night time murthered by *George Bothwell*, who was afterwards married to the Queen. The Earl of *Murray*, with some others, did publish, That this Murther was committed by the instigation of the Queen, and *George Buchanan*, a Creature [*sic*] of the Earl's, does boldly affirm the same in his Writings.[42] Yet there are some, who say, That the Calumnies as well concerning *David Ritz*, as also concerning the death of *Henry Darley*, were raised against the Queen by the Artifices of the Earl of *Murray*, thereby to defame and dethrone her.

But however it be, there was an Insurrection made against the Queen, and *Bothwell*, whom she had married, was forced to fly the

---

41. James Stuart (1531–70), first earl of Moray, was Mary's half-brother by James V.
42. George Buchanan (1506–82), author of *De jure regni apud Scotos* (written 1567–68, published 1579), defended the deposition of Mary Stuart by her brother, James Stuart, and distinguished kings from tyrants—who might be opposed. On such grounds he was later called a "monarchomach" by the Gallican monarchist, William Barclay (ca. 1546–1608). Pufendorf's library contained a later imprint of Buchanan's *Rerum Scoticarum historia* (1582). See Palladini (1999a), #310, p. 76.

Land (who died, in *Denmark* some Years after in a miserable condition) and she being made a Prisoner, made her escape in the Year 1568.
But the Forces which she had gathered being routed, she retir'd into
England, where she also was made a Prisoner. There she enter'd into
a Conspiracy against the Queen *Elizabeth,* with the Duke of *Norfolk,*
whom she promised to marry, hoping thereby to obtain the Crown
of *England.* But the Plot being discover'd, the Duke was made a Prisoner, but was afterwards released. And being again discover'd to have
afresh pursued his former design, paid for it with his Head \A. 1572\.
Queen *Mary* was confined to a more close Imprisonment. Several Treaties were set on foot to procure her Liberty, but no sufficient security
could be given to Queen *Elizabeth.* Wherefore Queen *Mary* growing at
last impatient, and being overcome by ill Counsellours, enter'd into a
Conspiracy with *Spain,* the Pope, and <144> the Duke of *Guise* against
Elizabeth: Which Plot having been long carried on privately, did break
out at last \A. 1586\, and some Letters of her own hand writing having been produced among other matters, a Commission was granted
[set up] to try the Queen; by vertue of which she received Sentence of
Death; which being confirm'd by the Parliament, great application was
made to the Queen for Execution, which Queen *Elizabeth* would not
grant for a great while, especially, because her [Mary's] Son *James* and
France did make great intercessions in her behalf. At last the *French* Ambassadour *d'Aubespine,* having suborned a Ruffian to murther Queen
Elizabeth, her Friends urged vehemently to hasten the Execution, which
she granted, and signed the Warrant, commanding, nevertheless, Secretary *Davidson* to keep it by him till farther order: But he advising thereupon with the Privy Council, it was order'd, that Execution should be
done upon her immediately \A. 1587\. Queen *Elizabeth* seemed much
concerned there-at, and removed *Davidson* from his place. King *James*
also was grievously exasperated, and some of his Friends advised him to
join with *Spain* and to revenge his Mother's death. But Queen *Elizabeth*
found a way to appease his Anger, and there was ever after a very good
understanding betwixt them to the very last.

    The Duke of *Guise* and his party were great Enemies to Queen *Eliza-*
beth in *France,* and she, on the other hand, assisted the *Huguenots* with

[margin notes:]
She was made
a Prisoner in
England.

Beheaded.

Queen Eliza-
beth assists the
Huguenots.

Men and Money, who surrender'd into her Hands as a pledge, *Havre de Grace* \A. 1562\, but her Forces were obliged to quit the same in the Year next following. Neither could she ever get *Calais* restored to her, tho' in the Peace concluded at *Chasteau en Cambresis* \A. 1559\, the same was promised to her. With *Henry* the IVth.[43] she lived in a good understanding, sending frequently to his assistance both Men and Money. But with *Spain* she was at variance about the Rebellious *Netherlanders,* to whom she not only granted a safe retreat in her Country and Harbours, but also assisted them, first underhand, and afterwards openly, both with Men and Money, they having surrender'd unto her

The Sovereignty of the Netherlands twice offered her.

as a pledge, *Flushing, Brill* and *Rammeken:* <145> But she would never accept of the Sovereignty of the *Netherlands,* which being twice offered her, she refused as often, out of weighty and wise Considerations. She sent, however, the Earl of *Leicester,* her Favourite, thither as Governour, who did not acquire much Reputation; but having put things rather in confusion, he was recalled in the second Year. She did also great damage to the *Spaniards* on their Coasts, and in the *West Indies,* by Sir *Francis Drake* and others, and the Earl of *Essex* took from them *Cadiz* \A. 1595\; but quitted it immediately after. On the other side, *Spain* was continually busie in raising Commotions and Conspiracies against her. And because the *Spaniards* were of Opinion, That *England* might be sooner conquer'd than the *Netherlands,* and that the latter could not be subdued without the other, they equipp'd a Fleet which they called *the Invincible Armado,* wherewith they intended to invade *England* [in

The Armado defeated.

1588]. Which Fleet, to the Immortal Glory of the *English* Nation being partly destroy'd by them, and many miserably torn to pieces by Tempests, did return home in a very miserable condition.

Spain also supported constantly the Rebels in *Ireland,* who were very troublesome to Queen *Elizabeth,* tho' they were generally beaten by her Forces, except in the Year 1596, when they soundly beat the *English.* Wherefore the Queen sent thither the Earl of *Essex,* who did nothing

43. Henry of Navarre (1553–1610) became Henry IV of France in 1589. Born Catholic but raised as a Protestant, he converted (back) to Catholicism in 1593 in order to end the continuing struggles for the crown. His Edict of Nantes (1598) granted limited toleration and civil rights to Huguenots.

worth mentioning. And after his return, the Queen giving him a severe Reprimand, and ordering him to be kept a Prisoner, he was so exasperated at it, that tho' he was reconcil'd to the Queen, he endeavoured to raise an Insurrection in *London,* which cost him his Head. Tho' the *Spaniards* were twice repulsed and chased out of *Ireland* with considerable loss, yet the Rebellion lasted till the very end of her life. Neither could a Peace be concluded betwixt her and the *Spaniards* as long as she lived: For tho' a Treaty was appointed to be held at *Boulogne* \A. 1600\, by the Mediation of *Henry* IV. yet the same was immediately broke off, because the *English* did dispute Precedency with the *Spaniards.* Essex beheaded.

This Queen could never be brought to take a Resolution to marry, tho' <146> her Subjects did greatly desire it, and she had great Offers made her; amongst whom were, besides *Philip, Charles* Archduke of *Austria, Eric* King of *Sweden,* the Duke *de Anjou,* and his Brother the Duke *de Alenson,* the Earl of *Leicester,* &c. It was her custom not to give a flat denial to such as sued for her in Marriage, but she used to amuse them with hopes, whereby she made them her Friends: For she treated with *Charles* Archduke of *Austria* for seven Years together, and with the Duke of *Alenson* she was gone so far, as that the Marriage Contract was made, yet was it so drawn as that a way was found to annul the same afterwards.

Under her Reign the *English* Trade was first established in *Turkey* and the *East Indies,* the finest Coin, as also the Manufactury of Serges and Bays[44] was settled in *England* about the same time. This Queen also brought first into Reputation the *English* Naval Strength, which she was so jealous of, that, tho' she supported the *Netherlanders* against the *Spaniards,* yet would she never consent, that the *Netherlanders* should so augment their Sea Forces, as that thereby they might be able to contest with *England* at Sea. This Maxim, which seem'd so necessary for *England,* was not regarded by King *James* [*I.*], he being a lover of Peace: And King *Charles* I. having always his Hands full with his Rebellious Subjects, was not in a capacity to observe it; wherefore the *Dutch* Power at Sea, could neither by *Cromwel,* nor by *Charles* II. be brought She was jealous of her Power at Sea.

44. Serge and bayes are types of woven textiles.

down again. This most glorious, and by her Subjects, extreamly beloved Queen died in the Year 1602, having before appointed *James* VI. King of *Scotland*, for her Successour.

James I. §23. After the death of *Elizabeth, James* VI. King of *Scotland*, was with an unanimous applause proclaimed King [James I] of *England*. His Title to this Crown was derived from *Margaret* Daughter of *Henry* VII. who was married to *James* IV. King of *Scotland;* whose Son *James* V. left one only Daughter, who was Mother of *James* VI. He at first shewed himself pretty favourable to the Papists, fearing, lest they might in the beginning of his Reign raise some Commotions <147> against him.

Cobham's Conspiracy. Notwithstanding which, immediately after his Coronation \A. 1603\ the Lord *Cobham, Gray*, and others, enter'd into a Conspiracy against him: Their main design was to root out the Line of *James*, and to put in his place the Marchioness *d'Arbelle*,[45] she being also descended from the abovesaid *Margaret* Daughter of *Henry* VII. This Lady [Margaret] was after the death of her Father married to *Archibald Douglass*, by whom she had *Margaret*, who was married to *Matthias* Earl of *Lenox;* and this *Arbella* being the Daughter of *Charles Lenox*, the third Son of this Earl, was, by the intercession of *Spain*, to have been married to the Duke of *Savoy*, and by this means the Popish Religion was again to be introduced into *England:* But the whole Plot being discover'd, the Ring-leaders were punish'd, yet not with that Severity as the hainousness of their Crime did deserve; tho' in the Year next following, all the Jesuits and Popish Priests were, by a severe Proclamation, banish'd out of *England*.

The Powder Plot. In the Year 1605, some Popish Villains had hir'd a Vault under the Parliament House, which being fill'd up with a great many Barrels of Gunpowder, they intended to have blown the King, the Prince, and the whole Parliament into the Air. But this devilish Design was discover'd, for one of the Accomplices, by a Letter that was obscurely written, and deliver'd by an unknown person to a Footman of the Lord *Mounteagle*, did intreat him not to come the next day into the Parliament House:

45. Arbella Stuart (1575–1615).

Which causing a suspicion in the King, all the Vaults were search'd, and the Powder found. Hereupon the Parliament made an Act, *That all Subjects, by a solemn Oath, should acknowledge* James *for their lawfull Sovereign; neither, that the Pope had any Authority to Dethrone Sovereigns, or to absolve Subjects from their Allegiance.*

He concluded a Peace with *Spain* \A. 1604\, and was afterwards one of the Mediators of the Truce made betwixt *Spain* and *Holland.* His Son-in-law, the Elector *Palatine* being banish'd out of his Territories,[46] he assisted only with sending of Ambassadours and proposing of an Agreement, all which the *Spaniards* render'd ineffectual. His Son Prince *Charles* was sent into *Spain* \A. 1626\ <148> to marry the Infanta, where the Marriage Contract was concluded and confirmed by Oath, but the Nuptials were deferred till the next year, the *Spaniards* being willing to gain time, and to see how things would be carried on in *Germany* for the House of *Austria.* But when, after the Prince's return into *England,* the *English* would needs have the Restitution of the Elector *Palatine* inserted in the Articles, the Match was broke off, and, tho' the Parliament voted a Subsidie to be employed towards the restoring of the Elector *Palatine,* yet the Design came to nothing.

Under this King there was a period put to the Differences and Wars betwixt *England* and *Scotland,* which hitherto had created abundance of Troubles to this Island. And that nothing of jealousie might remain betwixt these two Nations about Preference in the Royal Title, he introduced the Name of *Great Britain,* which comprehends both the Kingdoms. There was also set on foot a Treaty to unite both Kingdoms into

46. Frederick V (1596–1632), Elector Palatine during 1610–23, was married to Elizabeth Stuart, the eldest daughter of James I. In 1619 he accepted the crown of Bohemia from its Protestant estates but was defeated by the Hapsburgs a year later in the battle of White Mountain (thus his designation as "the Winter King"), losing his lands and electoral status. Frederick and Elizabeth's many childen included Karl Ludwig (1617–80), who was restored (to a newly created electorate) in 1648 and called Pufendorf to teach at Heidelberg in 1660; and also Prince Rupert (1619–82), who fought for his uncle, Charles I (1600–1649), during the English civil war. Their youngest daughter, Sophie (1630–1714), became electress of Hannover and was, by the Act of Settlement in 1701, next in line to the English throne after Queen Anne. Thus, her son, Georg Ludwig, the elector of Hannover, became George I of England in 1714. See Pursell (2003).

one Body, but it did not succeed, because the *Scots* would not be Infe-
Foreign riour to the *English*. Under this King's Reign Colonies were established
Plantations. in *Virginia*, *Bermudos* and *Ireland;* by which means the *English* have
extended their Dominions, but there are some, who believe that this has
weakened the *English* at home, and that in all probability, it would have
been more profitable for *England* to have employed those people in
Manufactury and Fishing of Herrings, which produce such vast Riches
to the *Dutch* in the very sight of the *English*. Yet some are also of Opinion, That it is good for the publick repose, that the unruly Multitude
do not grow too numerous in *England*.[47] The *East India* Trade was also
greatly promoted at that time, but the *English* could not come there in
competition with the *Dutch,* these having been before hand with them.
This King died in the Year 1625.

Charles I. §24. His Son *Charles* I. succeeded him, who, after the *Spanish* Match
was broke off, married *Henrietta* Daughter of *Henry* IV [of France].
War with \A. 1626\ He equipp'd out a great Fleet against the *Spaniards,* the *En-*
Spain. *glish* landed near *Cadiz,* but being repulsed with loss, returned with-
<149> out doing any thing, and all Commerce was prohibited betwixt
War with *Spain* and *England.* He also broke with *France,* and because the *French*
France. Merchants had been ill treated by the *English,* all Commerce was also
prohibited betwixt these two Nations. The *English* thereupon endeavoured to send Aid unto the City of *Rochelle* {A. 1627}, and landing
in the Isle of *Rhee* [Ré], besieged the Fort of St. *Martin,* which being
valiantly defended by one *Toyras,* the *English* were repulsed with great
loss. In the Year next following, they undertook to relieve *Rochelle,* but
A Peace in vain. Whereupon *Charles* concluded a Peace with *France* in the Year
concluded 1629, and in the Year next following with *Spain,* having by this War,
with both. waged against these two Nations, which were not so easie to be attack'd
by one at the same time, gained no Reputation to the dissatisfy'd Subjects, and vast Debts.
    Under this King arose very violent Divisions betwixt him and the
Parliament, which produced a most strange [*wunderliche*] Revolution

47. This was a Roman tactic. See I.12, p. 26, above.

in that Kingdom. It will be very well worth our while, to enquire a little more narrowly into the true causes thereof. That wise Queen, *Elizabeth,* held it for a constant maxim, to oppose the growing power of *Spain* with all her might, whereby she weaken'd *Spain,* and not only enrich'd her Subjects, but also exercised them in Sea Affairs, wherein consists the chief Strength and Security of this Kingdom: Wherefore she always kept a good Correspondency with all such as were Enemies of the House of *Austria;* she assisted *France* against the Designs of the *Spaniards,* favoured the Protestant Princes in *Germany,* upheld the *Dutch* against the *Spaniards,* thereby the better to weaken so formidable a Neighbour, looking upon the *Netherlands* as the Out-work of her Kingdom. Besides this, she finding continual employment for her Subjects abroad, did not a little contribute towards the preserving the Health of the State; for by this means a great deal of corrupt and inflamed Blood being taken away, it prevented intestine Diseases in the State. But King *James* took quite another course, and perceiving that the *United Provinces* were grown strong enough, not only to support themselves against *Spain,* but also to dispute <150> the Dominion of the '*Narrow Seas*' [Ocean] with *England,* he left them to themselves, and concluding a Peace with *Spain,* establish'd a lasting Tranquility at home, for his Inclinations were more for Books than Arms. And because Subjects in general are apt to follow the Inclinations of their Sovereigns, the People laid aside all Warlike Exercises, and fell into such Weaknesses and Vices, as are commonly the product of Plenty and Peace: And the King hoped, when these Nations applyed themselves only to Trade and Commerce, they would {become womanly [*Weibisch*] and thus} be diverted from having any thoughts of opposing his Authority.

He made it also his main endeavour to unite the Minds of the *Scots* and *English,* by Naturalizing the *English* in *Scotland,* and the *Scots* in *England,* and by joining the great Families by Marriages: But he was more especially carefull of establishing one Form of Religious Worship in both Kingdoms. For tho' there was no great difference in the Articles of Faith, yet the Ceremonies and Church Government were very different. For Queen *Elizabeth,* when she established the Protestant Religion retained many Ceremonies, which were anciently used in the Primitive

Margin notes:

Causes of the intestine Commotions in England.

The different Conduct of Queen Elizabeth and King James as to the State.

The Occasions that were taken from Religion.

Church, as also used by the Papists afterwards; she maintained also the Authority of the Bishops, yet under the Royal Power; supposing that this Constitution was most suitable to a Monarchy, considering that the Bishops had some dependence on the King, and had their Votes in Parliament. And it used to be the saying of King *James, No Bishop, no King.* But this Constitution did not agree with those of the Reform'd Religion in *Holland, Switzerland* and *France,* partly because these Nations were used to a Democratical Liberty, and therefore loved an Equality in the Church-Government as well as the State; partly because they had suffered from some Kings and Bishops, and therefore both were equally hated by them. These would not allow of any Superiority among the Clergy, but constituted the outward Church-Government by Presbyteries, Classes and Synods; neither would they admit any Ceremonies, believing, that the perfection of the Reformed Religion did consist in not having so much as anything, tho' never so indifferent, common <151> with the Papists.[48]

And according to this Form the Church of *Scotland* being establish'd, the number of such as were of the same Opinion increased daily in *England,* who were commonly called Presbyterians or Puritans. And the Capriciousness of those who were of several Sentiments proved the more dangerous, because these Nations[49] being of a melancholy temper used to adhere stedfastly to their Opinions, not to be removed from them. King *James* being besides a great Enemy of the Puritans, thought to have found out a way to suppress them in *Scotland,* by inserting it among the Royal Prerogatives, which was to be confirmed by the Parliament of *Scotland, That he had the Supream Power both in Spiritual and Temporal Affairs in the same manner in* Scotland *as in* England. By this means he hoped to model, without any great difficulty, the Church of *Scotland* according to that of *England.* And tho' this Proposition was opposed by a great many in the Parliament of *Scotland,* yet the King's party prevailed, and a new Form of Church-Government was established in *Scotland.* But the King had no sooner turned his back and was

48. See IV.22, note 38, p. 157, above.
49. That is, England and Scotland.

return'd into *England*, but the common people made an Insurrection against the Bishops in *Scotland*, who began to introduce there the Ceremonies of the Church of *England*.

§25. Tho' King *Charles* I. was of a more war-like temper than his Father, yet was he obliged, tho' against his Will, according to the Maxims of his Father, to preserve Peace abroad, to avoid the danger of being oblig'd to depend on the Capricious Humours of his Subjects. And because he, as well as his Father, had a great dislike of the Power of the common people, and of <the Temper and Principles of> the Puritans, all his Thoughts were bent to find out ways how to secure himself from the danger of both: And because the King could not impose any extraordinary Taxes without the consent of the Parliament, *Charles* chose rather to controul his own Inclinations, which were bent for War, than to fawn upon the Parliament; in hopes that its |[Heats, which was for limiting <152> the King's Power]|,[50] would by degrees diminish, if it was not called together for a considerable time. It is supposed, that the Lord Treasurer *Weston* did confirm him in this Opinion, who did expect to be call'd to an account by the Parliament.

    The Parliament used anciently to provide a certain yearly Revenue for the King, towards maintaining his Court and Fleet, to secure the Commerce of the Kingdom, which Revenue was not hereditary to the next Successour. The first Parliament which was called by *Charles* I. had settled the Customs, as part of his Revenue, but when he afterwards, having dissolved the same |[against the Opinion of the Male Contents,]|[51] his Revenues also began to be call'd in question, it being their Opinion, that nothing could so soon oblige the King to call a new Parliament, as if what was necessary for his and the Courts Subsistence, were withheld from him. But the King, however, {took no notice and}

The Conduct of Charles I.

50. Rather: "its authority [*Autorität*], which greatly circumscribes the king's power."

51. Rather: "in disgust, in order to annoy him." Against long tradition, Parliament restricted Charles's receipt of customs revenues to one year only, because it was worried about his foreign policy, including the war against Spain in support of his sister Elizabeth's effort to regain the Palatinate.

did not only receive [collect] the same Customs as his Predecessours
had done, but also augmented them with new Impositions to the yearly
value of '800.000' [80.000] *l.* by which means the King, who was {in
any case} firm in his Opinion, was thought to have a Design to alter
the ancient 'Constitution of the Government' [manner of ruling], and
to maintain himself without a Parliament; which however was look'd
upon as an impossibility by the 'generality of them' [people]: For King
James had left above 1.200.000 *l.* Debts, which were since increased by
Charles 400.000 *l.* more, which Money was expended in the {futile}
Wars against *France* and *Spain;* it was therefore not visible, how he
could extricate himself out of these Debts without the assistance of
a Parliament, since according to the fundamental Constitutions[52] of
the Realm he could not levy any Taxes upon the Subjects, and to force
them [illegally] to pay any, was beyond his Power, having no Forces on
foot, but the Militia of the Kingdom. And it was impossible to bring
in such a Foreign Force, as could be supposed to be able to make Head
against the dissatisfy'd people{, though he considered for some time,
the recruitment of some German troops}. Notwithstanding all which
the King pursued his Resolution, and having ask'd the Opinion of {a
few} Men skill'd in the Law, who told him, *That it was allowable, for
the publick benefit, to levy Money by his own Authority;* he imposed several new <153> Taxes, whereby he augmented his yearly Revenue from
500.000 *l.* to 800.000 *l.* Besides this, he laid a Tax {on all households,
according to each's means, on the pretext} for maintaining of a Fleet,
which amounted to 200.000 *l.*[53] All which caused great dissatisfaction
among the Subjects against the King:

52. Pufendorf refers often in his works to the "fundamental laws" of limited
monarchies, including in his history of the English Revolution. See *On the Law of
Nature and of Nations,* VII, 2.10 and 6.9–10, and *On the Affairs of Fredrick III (De
rebus gestis Friderici Tertii,* Berlin, 1784), I.77, in Pufendorf (1695b), pp. 88–89.

53. Here Crull omits the following passage: "Next he resorted to the old claim
about the forests, which had of old belonged to the crown, but which had through
logging been turned into acreage and pasture. Under this pretext he cast doubts on
most people's land-holdings. The province of Essex was forced to purchase satisfaction of this claim for 300.000 *l.*, and only the incipient disturbances prevented the
other provinces from being dealt with in the same way."

Besides, the King was thought by the Puritans, to deal {too} hardly with them and too mildly with the Papists (by the Counsel of Archbishop *Laud* {of Canterbury}, a 'Man of great Resolution' [hothead]<, who at that time apprehended, that Faction very dangerous both to Church and State>) which was by the Puritans interpreted, as if the King was resolved, by suppressing of them, to introduce Popery; [and] to insinuate this into the Multitude, abundance of Libels and scurrilous Papers were scatter'd abroad against the King and the Bishops, and Commissioners being appointed to inquire into them, they [the Multitude] were rather exasperated than appeas'd by its [the Commission's] Severity.

§26. Both Nations being therefore full of Discontents, the Flame first broke out in *Scotland:* For the King endeavouring to root out Puritanism there, to establish the Authority of the Bishops, and an Uniformity in Religion, he order'd a Church Liturgy to be composed, abrogating all Presbyteries, Classes and Provincial Synods, and enjoining every one under severe penalties, to conform to the same; there was a general Insurrection raised by 'that party' [the priests] in *Scotland* \A. 1637\. There was also another reason; for, at the time of the first Reformation the Revenues of a great many Church Benefices were appropriated to the use of the Crown, but without any remarkable advantage; for they were lett out, for the most part, to younger Brothers of Noble Families. These having found the benefit of them, had, by getting from time to time the Survivorship, continued the same in their Families, and kept them as their own Propriety. Nay, they did more than this, for during the Minority of King *James* VI. {around the Year 1567} they had obtained the Titles of Lordships for some of the most considerable of these, or some lesser Benefices joined together. King *James* afterwards perceiving, that thereby they had bound him up from rewarding such with these Benefices as deserved well of him, would have recall'd the beforesaid <154> Grants \A. 1617\, but met with such opposition in the Nobility, that he desisted from it. But the King [Charles I] undertook the business effectually \A. 1633\, employing the said Revenues towards the augmenting of the Salaries of the Clergy. These therefore who had

Troubles in Scotland and England.

been losers by this Revocation joined with such Ministers as were mortal Enemies of the *Liturgy,* [and] did, with all their might, help to stirr up the Rebellion.

Alexander Lesley, also, who had been a Commander in the *German* Wars {under the Swedes}, and having refused to serve under *John Banniers* there, was returned into his native Country, ||[in hopes to make his advantage of these Troubles.]|[54] He put himself at the Head of the Rebellious Party, and by persuading the Nobility, that the King intended to take away their ancient Privileges, stirr'd up a great many against the King. And to make a fair shew to the common people, they made use of the Religious Cloak of Conscience, ordering a Directory to be compos'd by the Ministers quite opposite to the former *Liturgy.* They thereupon enter'd into an Association confirm'd by solemn Oaths, That they would maintain the same against all, even the King himself: This Association was called *the Covenant,* which being subscrib'd by the greatest part of the Nobility and Clergy, a Council was constituted, unto whom was committed the supream direction of their Affairs.

The Scotch Covenant.

To suppress these Commotions, the King sent the Marquiss of *Hamilton* into *Scotland,* who dealing mildly with them, only encouraged the adverse party: For the King calling a Parliament in hopes to remedy these Disorders, the Covenant was by its Authority confirm'd, the Episcopal Authority quite abolish'd, and Puritanism establish'd ||[in defiance of]|[55] the Royal Authority. There being then no other way left to reduce the Rebellious Party to 'Obedience' [reason] but force, and the King being in want both of Money and a sufficient number of faithfull Subjects, he was forc'd to make some use of the Papists to obtain both, wherefore he did not only raise an Army, wherein were some Papists, but also was assisted by them with some Summs of Money, all which, however, was in no ways sufficient to supply the want of the King; and a Supply being demanded <155> from the Subjects, very few, except the King's Servants and Officers were for contributing any thing. And it being divulged, that a great many thousand of *Irish* Papists and

---

54. Literally: "hoping to fish in the murky waters there." Johan Banér (1596–1641) was one of the main Swedish commanders who continued the Thirty Years' War after the death of Gustavus Adolphus in 1632. See XIII.15, pp. 591–93, below.

55. Rather: "to the great detriment of."

Germans were ready for the King's Service, to try, whether by this way the Subjects could be frightened out of some Money, it served only to exasperate the Minds of the people.

Yet the King's Forces might in all probability have been successfull against the *Scots,* if they had fallen upon them immediately. But because they had leisure given them, they did not only settle a Correspondency with *France* and *Holland,* from whence they were supply'd with Money and Ammunition; but also sent their Deputies into *England,* who so well knew there to represent the state of their Affairs, that the King being persuaded by the *English,* made a dishonourable Agreement with them [the Scots]: Which nevertheless did not last long, the Court being asham'd of the Agreement, and the *Scots* not trusting the King, the King had in the mean while intercepted a Letter, wherein the *Scots* had sollicited for some Officers and Money to be sent them from *France;* this he hoped might prove an inducement to the *English* to oppose the Treachery of the *Scots,* and to furnish him with some Supplies, of which he stood in great need at that time. He calling therefore a Parliament, the Letter was read, but to no great purpose, the Members of the House of Commons being most of them Puritans, who were great friends of the *Scots,* so that the Parliament was a little while after dissolv'd by the King's Authority. The King had caused to be made Prisoner in *London* the *Scotch* Commissioner, who had subscribed the abovementioned Letter, whereupon the *Scots* took up Arms, and took the Castle of *Edinburgh.* The King having with great difficulty, for want of Money, got together an Army, went in person against the *Scots,* but as <a party of> his Army endeavouring to force their passage was beaten back with loss, which augmented the Discontents of his Subjects, the Souldiers for want of Pay, 'being' [having] to be maintained by those Counties where they were quartered. Besides this, ten thousand Men, which were raised by the <156> Parliament in *Ireland* for the King's service, were forc'd to be disbanded for want of Pay. There was then no other remedy left but to make a Truce with the *Scots,* and to call a new Parliament in *England,* which began to sit in *November* in the Year 1640.

§27. But in the Session of this Parliament, the Ulcer [*Übel*] which had been long gathering in the Minds of the people broke out: For the

A Letter intercepted, wherein the Scots desire Succour from France.

The Parliament is factious, and favours the Scots.

The Parlia-
ment of En-
gland directly
oppose the
King.
Parliament, in lieu of assisting the King against the *Scots,* enter'd into
a Confederacy with them, promising a monthly Subsidy towards the
maintaining of the *Scottish* Army, which was to be ready at the *English*
Parliament's command. Then they began to reform the |[States]|,[56] to
clip the King's Authority, to punish his Ministers and Servants, and
to take away the Bishops, Liturgy, and fall upon Papists. The better to
obtain their aim, they forced the King to consent, that he would not
dissolve the Parliament, till all such as were criminal were punished, and
the State were entirely reformed: In a word, that they should have the
liberty to sit as long as they pleased. Which in effect put an end to the
Royal Authority. To try the King's Patience, and their own Strength,
they brought the Earl of *Strafford,* Lord Deputy of *Ireland,* to his Tryal,
who, notwithstanding he made a good Defence, and the King did his
utmost to preserve his beloved and faithfull Minister, yet the Rabble
of *London,* then encouraged by the House of Commons, making an
Insurrection, he received Sentence of Death in the House of Lords. And
the King refusing to sign the Warrant for his Execution, was obliged
thereunto, partly by the importunity of the Parliament, partly by the
Insurrection of the Rabble of the City of *London,* and partly by a Letter
from the Earl, desiring him to do it.

Then the rest of the King's Ministers went to rack [and ruin], some
of them saving themselves by flight, some being imprisoned. The Bishops were excluded from the House of Lords. The Star-chamber, the
Authority of the Privy Council, and the High Commission were suppressed: the Customs and power over the Fleet were taken away from
the King. Some of these and <157> some other things, which proved
very prejudicial to him, the King was forced to grant them, in hopes
thereby to heal the ulcerated Minds of the people. He went also in
person into *Scotland,* where he granted them all what they could desire.
About the same time a horrid Conspiracy broke out among the *Irish*
Papists, who pretended to maintain the Popish Religion, and to redress
some Grievances by force of Arms, which occasioned afterwards a most
cruel slaughter.

56. Rather: "government [*Regiment*]."

At last \A. 1642\ it came to an open Rebellion: For the Parliament not ceasing to encroach daily more and more upon the Royal Authority, the King resolved to assert his Authority; wherefore he summoned five Members of Parliament, whom he accused as Traitors, and authors of all the Differences: And the House of Commons taking their part, the King went into the House accompanied with some Officers, and spoke to them with a due resentment of their Behaviour, which however they made but little account of, being not ignorant of his want of Power, of which he seem'd to betray himself, when he immediately afterwards condescended and came nearer their Expectations. The House of Commons thereupon stirr'd up the neighbouring Counties, and especially the *London* Apprentices, who made such an Insurrection, that the King, not thinking himself safe in *London,* retir'd into the Country. And the Parliament order'd all the Governours of the Sea-ports, not to obey the King's Commands. It was certainly a great errour in the King, that in such troublesome times, he had not taken care to secure to himself the Sea-ports, by which means he might have hoped for some assistance from abroad: For, when the King intended to possess himself of the Fort and Harbour of *Hull,* 'he' [his envoy] was not admitted; so that there was nothing left, but that the Parliament had not as yet taken from the King {completely} the disposal of Offices. But for the rest it was evident, that their Intention was, to abolish totally the Royal Power, and to introduce a Democracy. And after the King had once given his Assent to the exclusion of the Bishops from the House of Lords, where they had six and twenty votes, and the rest of the King's Friends had once absented themselves from both <158> Houses, it was easie for the remainder quite to abolish the Authority of the House of Lords.

Thus, after there had been long contests by Words and Writings betwixt both parties, the King now as well as the Parliament began to Arm themselves: And the King having at several times, at first, beat the Parliament Forces, the Parliament stirr'd up the *Scots,* entring with them into a Confederacy. Whereupon the *Scots* came with a considerable Force to the assistance of the Parliament, which turned the Scale, the King's Forces being routed near *York,* and he obliged, for want of Men and Money, to give himself up to the protection of the *Scots,*

The Rebellion begins.

Their Behaviours.

The King made a Prisoner.

who nevertheless did surrender him to the *English* for the Summ of 400.000 *l.* under condition that he should not be abused by them. The King was afterwards carried a Prisoner from place to place for a considerable time.

The Indepen-
dents become
Masters.

§28. By these means the Puritans or Presbyterians, had, under the pretext of Religion, overthrown the Royal Power: But that they could not long enjoy their usurped power, was occasioned by a certain Sect that called themselves *Independent,* because they would not depend on any certain form of Faith, or Spiritual, or Temporal Constitutions, nor acknowledge any of the same, whereby they opened a door for all sorts of Fanaticks, to come under their Protection. These, under pretence of a particular holy Zeal, had not only got a great sway in the Parliament, and had been against any peaceable accommodation, propos'd by others; but also by their cunning insinuating way crept into the chief Civil and Military Employments: For in the place of the Earl of *Essex,* *Thomas Fairfax* was made General, and *Oliver Cromwell* Lieutenant General over the Army, the last of which was the Head of the Independents, a sly and cunning Fox. And out of this party all vacant places were supply'd in Parliament.

The Presbyterians therefore perceiving that the Independents began to be very strong in the House, and that most Military Employments were in their Hands, proposed in the House, That one part of the Army should be sent into *Ire-*<159>*land,* that some Forces only should be kept in *England,* and the rest be disbanded. *Cromwell* made use of this to stirr up the Souldiers, telling them, that they were likely to be disbanded without pay, or else to be starv'd in *Ireland.* Thereupon the Souldiers enter'd into an Association among themselves, taking upon them not only the Military, but also all the Civil Power, they took the King from the Parliament into their own custody, pretending they would give him his liberty, but made themselves Masters of the City of *London,* and acted in every thing at discretion. For they quickly after broke off the Treaty with the King, and a great many of the Subjects, who were not able to bear their Tyranny, taking up Arms were dispers'd by *Cromwell,* who also beat the *Scots* that were come into *England* to the assistance of the King, making their General *Hamilton* a Prisoner.

But during the absence of *Cromwell*, the Parliament had re-assumed the Treaty with the King, and the business was carried on so far, that there was no small hopes of an Accommodation, when the Souldiers, headed by *Ireton*, Son-in-law to *Cromwell*, broke off the Treaty, taking Prisoners such Members of the House as did oppose them: So that there were not above forty Members left in the Parliament, and those were either Officers, or at least, favourers of the Army. These decreed, *That no Treaty should be set on foot for the future with the King; That the Supream Power was to be lodged in the People, which was represented by the House of Commons; But the Regal Power, and the Authority of the House of Lords should be quite abolished.* Then they order'd a Court of 250 [150] persons to be erected, by whose Authority the King was to be summoned, sentenced and punished, notwithstanding that the generality of the people look'd upon this Court as an abominable thing, <some> Presbyterian Ministers cry'd out aloud against it in the Pulpits; the *Scots* protested against it, and the *Dutch* Ambassadours, and other Princes did their utmost to oppose it. Before this Court, where sat among the rest, a great many of very mean Extraction [*Lumpenhunden*], the King was accused of High Treason, Tyranny, and of all the Murthers and Robberies committed since <160> the beginning of these Troubles. And the King, as in justice he ought to do, refusing to acknowledge its Authority {and to answer its charges}, was sentenced to be beheaded, tho' there were but 67 of these pretended Judges present, the rest abominating the fact, had absented themselves, among whom was *Fairfax*. But the King, having been miserably abus'd by the Souldiers, was beheaded with an Ax upon a Scaffold erected for that purpose before *Whitehall* \A. 1649\. The King is sentenced to death and executed.

§29. After the death of the King the outward shew of the Supream Power was in the Parliament, but in effect it was lodged in the Generals of the Armies. Their first design was to banish the King's Son and the whole Royal Family, and to suppress all such as adhered to him. *Cromwell* was sent into *Ireland*, where the Royal Party was as yet pretty strong, which Island was reduced in the space of one year by *Cromwells* good Fortune and Valour. In the mean while the *Scots* had proclaimed *Charles* II. tho' under very hard Conditions, their King, who also arriving there safely out of *France*, whither he was gone for Shelter, was Ireland conquer'd

crowned King of *Scotland.* The Parliament thereupon recall'd *Cromwell*
out of *Ireland,* and having made him General (for they had deposed
Fairfax whom they mistrusted) sent him into *Scotland,* where he beat
the *Scots* several times, but especially gave them an entire defeat near
Leith, taking, among other places, the Castle of *Edinborough,* which
was hitherto esteemed impregnable. The King, in the mean while, having gathered a flying Army enter'd *England,* in hopes that a great many
English would join with him: But he was deceiv'd in his hopes, very
few coming to him, and *Cromwell* overtaking him with his Army near
Worcester, his Forces were routed and dispersed; so that he was forc'd
to change his Cloaths in his flight, and after a great many dangers was
miraculously saved, and escaped, by the help of a Merchant-ship, into
France.

    The King being thus driven out of the Island, the *Scots* were entirely
subdu'd under the Conduct of General *Monk,* who was sent thither by
Cromwell, who having imposed upon them very hard <161> Conditions, according to their deserts, intirely subjected them to the *English.*
This done, the Parliament began to take into consideration, how to
disband part of the Army, and to quarter the rest in the several Counties. But *Cromwell* sent away that Parliament, which had been the cause
of so much troubles, and constituted a new Parliament, consisting of
144 Members, most of them being Fanaticks and Enthusiasts; among
whom *Cromwell* had put a few cunning Fellows, who being entirely
devoted to his Service, did make the rest dance after his pipe. These
having first let these silly wretches go on in their own way, till by their
phantastical Behaviour they had made themselves ridiculous and hated
by every body, then offer'd the Supream Administration of Affairs to
Cromwell; who having accepted of the same under the Title of a *Protec-*
tour, selected a Privy Council, wherein were received the Heads of the
several Sects. Thus they who had shown so much aversion to the Royal
Power, had hatch'd out a Monarch of their own, who, without controul,
ruled the three Kingdoms of *England, Scotland* and *Ireland* at pleasure.[57]

    Cromwell, to have a fair pretence to keep on foot his Sea and Land

Charles II.
routed.

The Scots
conquered.

Cromwell
made
Protectour.

57. See note 61, p. 178, below.

Forces, which were the Foundation of his Power, began a War with the *Dutch* \A. 1652\, who seem'd to despise this new 'Monarch' [government]: But Fortune was so favourable to *Cromwell* in this War, that he took above 1700 Merchant men from the *Dutch,* and beat them in five Sea Engagements, in the last of which the *Dutch* lost *Martin Tromp,* and twenty seven Men of War.[58] The *Hollanders* then were oblig'd to beg for Peace, and to accept of such Conditions as were propos'd to them, among which, one was, *That the Province of* Holland *should exclude the Prince of* Orange *for ever, from succeeding in his Father's place.* Another was, *That they should not receive the banish'd King* Charles II. *into their Territories.*[59] Which some alledge as a reason, that he was always ready afterwards to revenge himself upon them, tho' at his return into the Kingdom \A. 1660\, they endeavoured with abundance of flattery to make amends for the former affront. It is very likely also, that the King was suspicious, that the *Dutch* <162> had fomented the Differences betwixt his Father and the Parliament.

Cromwell acquired so much Glory by this War, that most 'Princes' [potentates] sent their Ambassadours to him as if he had been a lawfull Sovereign, and desir'd his Friendship. He was no less fortunate in discovering several Plots which were made against him: For which purpose he entertained his Spies every where, even near the King's [the exiled Charles II] person; having besides this, a cunning way to draw the people over to his party, and to suppress such as envy'd his Fortune. He sent also a Fleet into the *Mediterranean,* wherewith he curb'd the Pirates on the Coast of *Barbary.* Another was sent into the *West Indies,*

---

58. Martin Harpertszoon Tromp (1597–1653) was an important Dutch admiral during mid-century. He was killed at the Battle of Scheveningen, the last naval engagement of the first Anglo-Dutch War (1652–54).

59. A reference to the so-called Act of Seclusion, a secret provision—arranged by Cromwell and Johan de Witt—of the Treaty of Westminster (1654), which ended the first Anglo-Dutch War (1652–54). The Act stipulated that William III, Prince of Orange (1650–1702), would be excluded from the office of stadtholder, thereby protecting the interests of both English and Dutch republicans. William III was the son of William II (1626–50) and Mary Henrietta Stuart, Charles II's sister. He was later married to Mary II (1662–94), Charles's niece through his brother, James II (1633–1701).

where his Designs against St. *Domingo* and *Hispaniola* miscarried, but
Jamaica he took from the *Spaniards,* notwithstanding that a great many
of his Men were taken off by Sickness; and he did considerable mischief
to the *Spaniards* by ruining their Silver Fleet.[60] He sent some Auxiliary
Troops to the *French* in *Flanders,* who, in recompence, surrender'd to
him *Dunkirk.* He died in the Year 1658, having been as great and formidable as ever any King of *England.* He was a great Master in the Art of
Dissimulation, knowing how to make his advantage of Religious Pretences; wherefore he gave liberty of Conscience to all Sectaries, whereby
he not only got their Favours, but also by dividing the people into
several Opinions, he prevented their easily joining against him.[61]

King
Charles II's
Restoration.

§30. After the death of *Cromwell* this unlawfull and violent <form
of> Government could not be of a long continuance: For tho' his Son
Richard succeeded him in the Protectorship (this was the Title used by
Cromwell, having refused the Name of King) yet was he in no ways
capable to bear such a weight. Wherefore he was soon deposed by the
Parliament, which being divided within itself, *Monk,* who was then
Governour of *Scotland,* took this opportunity, and marching with an
Army out of *Scotland* into *England,* possess'd himself of the City of
London, dissolv'd the Military Parliament, and recall'd King *Charles* II.
into his Kingdom \A. 1660\. This King did restore the ancient Form
<163> of Government in the Kingdom both in Spiritual and Temporal
Matters, for his Subjects were ready to gratify him in most respects, as
having been taught by Experience, *That the Frogs who despised to have a
Block for their King, got afterwards a Stork for their Master.*[62]

60. See note 39, p. 75, above.
61. Pufendorf regarded religious diversity as a political liability and noted the
advantages of having a state religion. See *The Present State of Germany,* VII.9, in
Pufendorf (2007), p. 204, and VIII.5–10, pp. 221–47; also *The Divine Feudal Law,*
§4, in Pufendorf (2002b), pp. 15–18, and *Of the Nature and Qualification of Religion,*
§48, in Pufendorf (2002c), pp. 102–4. See VI.21, p. 308, and note 18, p. 427, below;
also, the Editor's Introduction, p. xviii, above.
62. Pufendorf uses this allusion to one of Aesop's fables (also found in Luther's
On Secular Authority [1523], Part 2), to criticize the counterproductive discontent of
subjects vis-à-vis their rulers. See *The Present State of Germany,* VIII.3, in Pufendorf
(2007), p. 213.

This King, who judg'd, that the Greatness of *England* did chiefly depend on the Dominion of the Seas and Commerce, which was disputed by no body but the *Dutch,* did, in all probability, bend all his Thoughts that way, *viz.* How to make these proud Merchants more pliable, his hopes being grounded upon what he had seen *Cromwell* do against them. Wherefore he began a War with *Holland* \A. 1665\, which was carried on at first with equal losses on both sides: But the *English* at last taking a Resolution to tire out the *Dutch* without coming to an Engagement, they [the Dutch] ventur'd at a bold stroke, and to the great dishonour of the *English,* enter'd the River of *Thames,* firing some Ships at *Chattam.* This obliged the King to make a Peace with them by the Mediation of *Swedeland,* tho' the great success of the *French* Arms in *Flanders* may probably have contributed a great deal towards it. Yet it seems as if ever since he had kept up a Resolution of Revenging himself upon them, he being also again exasperated by the Rable in *Holland,* who affronted him afterwards. He therefore in the Year 1672 attack'd the *Dutch* at Sea, whilst the King of *France* made War against them by Land.[63] But this War did not succeed according to his expectation; for the *Dutch* did not only take from the *English* a great number of Merchant-ships, but also the *English* could not master the *Dutch* in any of these Sea-fights, partly, because the *French* {ships} would not fall on in good earnest, partly, because the *Dutch* acted very circumspectly, not giving any opportunity to the *English* to make a Descent either on *Holland* or *Zealand.* It is possible that the King's Intentions may perhaps have been frustrated by some Intrigues at home. And because the *English* Nation began to grow very jealous of the great Successes of *France,* the King was obliged to make a separate Peace with *Holland* \A. 1674\, and afterwards was receiv'd as a Mediatour betwixt the Parties then engag'd in War against one another. <164>

War with Holland.

63. The Dutch surprise attack in June 1667 on the English naval base at Chatham, up the Thames and Medway Rivers, led to the Treaty of Breda in July, which ended the second Anglo-Dutch War (1665–67). Dutch affairs during this period were under the leadership of the De Witt brothers. Resentment over the outcome of this conflict led Charles in 1670 to enact the secret Treaty of Dover (1670) with France, involving England in the third Anglo-Dutch War (1672–74). See at note 64, p. 260, and at note 34, p. 298, below.

§31. The *English* Nation is very populous and fruitfull: There are some who have reckoned, that in *England* are 9913 [9725] Parishes, in each Parish 80 Families, which make '778.183' [778.000] Families, and seven persons reckoned to each Family amounts to '6.470.800' [5.446.000] Souls, among which number it may be suppos'd to be above a Million of Men capable of bearing of Arms. This Nation is also very fit to settle Colonies in Foreign Countries, because the *English,* as soon as they are in the least settled in a place, they quickly marry, and remain there for their life time. Whereas other Nations, if they go into far distant Countries, go only with an intent to get a little Money, which they afterwards love to spend in their Native Country. The *English* are also Courageous, Brave, not fearing Death. For in former times their Land forces were much superiour to the *French,* and ever since the times of Queen *Elizabeth,* when they first began to apply themselves in earnest to the Sea, they have not been inferiour in Skill and Courage to any Nation in the World, except that the *Dutch* may be compared with them in Sea Affairs. But this is to be observ'd of the *English* Valour, that they commonly are very Furious and Brave at the beginning, yet great Hardship, Famine, and other Inconveniencies they are not so well able to endure with Patience, as being us'd to live in great Ease and Plenty in their own Country. Wherefore *Maurice* Prince of *Orange* us'd to put the *English,* that were sent to his assistance, upon desperate Enterprizes, before (as he us'd to say) they had digested the *English* Beef.[64]

They are also very dexterous in Woollen and Silk Manufacturies, |[and are generally great Improvers of other Arts and Mysteries]|[65]: Yet they are also somewhat |[Highminded, inclining themselves to Diversion]|,[66] which is the reason that they do not 'so much Work' [accomplish as much] as otherwise they might; and yet they expect to be paid for their idle Hours as well as the rest, which is the reason why they sell their Wares at a higher rate than others, and that they envy such *French* Handycrafts-men, who live among them, and are seldom

64. That is, while they were still well-nourished and energetic.
65. Rather: "many of which they have learned from the Dutch."
66. Rather: "haughty and easy-going, spending many hours each day in strolling about and puffing tobacco."

diverted from their daily Labour by any Pleasures. They being generally of <165> a melancholy temper, makes them very Ingenious, and when they apply themselves to any Science, they make great progress in the same, if they hit the right way.

But by the same rule, because there happens often to be an ill mixture of this melancholy temper, abundance of Fanaticks and Enthusiasts are to be found among them, who having form'd to themselves Opinions out of ill grounded Principles, adhere so stedfast to them, that they are not by any ways to be removed from them. Wherefore there is not any Nation 'under the Sun' [in Christendom], where more different and more absurd Opinions are to be met withall in Religion than in *England*. The 'loose sort of people' [rabble] are addicted to Thieving and Robbing upon the High-way, wherefore the Hangmen are always busie in *England*. This Nation also loves to eat and drink extreamly well; tho' there are some who will have it, that the *English* have got their way of drinking so plentifully from the *Netherlanders* in the Wars of the *Low-Countries,* and from thence have brought that ill Custom over into *England,* which before, they say, was not in use there. Their own Histories are sufficient evidences, that they have been always inclined to Rebellion and intestine Commotions. Wherefore their Kings can never be secure, except they keep a watchfull Eye over the restless Spirit of the People.

§32. The *Scots* are reported to have a share of Pride and Envy in them. They are very apt to propose to themselves great 'Matters' [hopes], and to delight in their own Inventions. They are good Land-Souldiers, and can endure more hardship than the *English,* neither are they so much addicted to their Belly, both which they have from the barrenness of their Native Country. They are very Revengefull, and intestine Broils among the Noble Families were formerly very common among them: For it was a custom, that each Family used to select one for the Head of the Family, unto whom they almost paid more respect than to the King himself, and if any one of the Family had received an Injury, he made complaint thereof to the Head of his Family: And if the Head <166> of the same Family did resolve to revenge the Injury, the whole Family, un-

Constitution of the Scotch Nation.

der the Conduct of their Head, fell upon the Family of the Aggressour
with Fire and Sword. Which abominable Custom King *James* VI. did
endeavour to abolish. Besides this, they are easily stirr'd up to Rebellion,
very obstinate in defending their Opinions to the utmost.

Their fruitfulness in Children makes them seek other Countries,
since their Country can scarce maintain them all at home. There is
another reason also to be given for this, which is the right of the First-
born, whereby the eldest Son is Heir of all the real Estate of his Father,
the rest of the Brothers being obliged to be satisfy'd with their share
in the Personal Estate.[67] These then being obliged to advance themselves as well as they can, apply themselves either to the Wars or Study:
Wherefore most Ministers in *Scotland* are said to be younger Brothers
of good Families. But in *England* it is no shame for the younger Brothers of such Families to be Merchants. In former times, before *Scotland*
and *England* were united under one King, the *Scottish* Souldiers were
in great esteem, because the *French* made constantly use of them in
their Wars, and at home they were always picquering [bickering] with
the *English:* But afterwards they grew careless of Warlike Exercises, and
especially when *Cromwell* subdu'd them, their ancient Glory was quite
obscur'd.

The *Scots* are also often very Ingenious, and well vers'd in the Latin
Tongue: And at that time, when all Liberal Sciences were suppress'd in
Europe by a long Barbarism, the same were kept up in *Scotland,* which
did furnish several other Nations with Learned Men, who instructed
them in these Sciences. But as the *Scots,* which live in the low Coun-
tries, on the South-side, are well civiliz'd, so those who inhabit the
Mountains, who are called *Highlanders,* as also the Inhabitants of the
Orkney and Western Islands, are very raw and unciviliz'd.

Of the Irish.   §33. The *Irish* are commonly esteem'd to be a fool-hardy and ill sort of
people; very lazy, yet pretty hard in undergoing the Fatigues of War.
They are very obstinate, and never to be bent from their Opi-<167>nion.

---

67. The distinction is between "unmovable goods" (*unbewegliche Güter*) and
"movable means" (*beweglichen Mitteln*).

After *Ireland* was conquer'd by King *Henry* II. abundance of *English* settled themselves in that Kingdom, whose numbers increased from time to time to that degree, that scarce the fourth part of the Island remaine in the possession of the ancient Inhabitants. And because most of the *Irish* adhere to the Popish Religion, they did not only rebel under Queen *Elizabeth*, but also under the Reign of King *Charles* I. enter'd into a most horrid Conspiracy against the *English* living among them, of whom, 'tis said, they murther'd 200.000 within the space of six Months: But when the *English* had recollected themselves, they again kill'd about 100.000 of them. *Cromwell* had once a mind to have rooted out the whole Nation, as being quite incorrigible and past hopes of any amendment. Wherefore he sent some thousands to the King of *Spain,* under condition, that none of them should return into the *English* Dominions. He used also to plague them every way, so that they are become a miserable Nation.

§34. Concerning those Countries which belong to the King of *England,* the Kingdom of *England* {itself} is a {beautiful and} Rich and Fertile Country, abounding in every thing, either for the Necessity or Pleasures of Mankind, except Oyl and Wine, and such other Commodities as do not grow in ||[the other parts of *Europe,* are of the growth of that Country.]|[68] But else they have great numbers of very fine Horses, and good Cattle, especially the best Sheep of all *Europe,* which make the best part of the native Riches of *England,* bearing so good a sort of Wooll, that an incredible quantity of the best Cloath is made in *England,* and from thence every Year transported into Foreign Parts. These Sheep feed in great Flocks in the Country without as much as a Shepherd, there being no Wolves to be met withal in *England;* the reason of which, as 'tis reported, is, that King *Edgar,* about the Year 940, did order a certain number of Wolves to be paid by the Prince of *Wales* to him as a yearly Tribute, by which means the Wolves were quite destroy'd in *England:* Tho' it is also very probable, that the great *English* Mastiffs have <168> been very instrumental in this point, it being certain, that for

The Condition of Great Britainy.

68. Rather: "[northern] European soil."

Fierceness and Strength they surpass all the rest in the World. A great quantity also of Lead, but especially of the finest Tin is to be found in *England,* which surpasses in goodness all others in that kind.

The *Sea* also is very profitable to the *English,* since it produces a great quantity of Fish, which are daily catch'd by the Inhabitants. Tho' by the Negligence and Laziness of the ancient *English,* who did not apply themselves industriously to Fishing, they have lost a great part of that advantage. But the *Netherlanders,* from ancient times, have made use of this advantage, and got vast Riches by the Fishery of Herrings and Cods, giving only a small Gratuity to the *English,* in case they have occasion to dry their Nets on their Shores; tho' oftentimes the *English,* envying the *Netherlanders,* will force them to pay more than ordinary, which has several times served as a pretext for a War betwixt both Nations. Besides this, the Sea is extreamly advantageous to *England,* for thereby the *English* being separated from their Neighbouring Nations, cannot easily be attack'd; whereas they may easily invade others: And because this Island is situated almost in the very middle of *Europe,* in a narrow Sea, where all Ships which either go East or Westward must pass by; and having, besides this, a very deep Coast and commodious Harbour[s], it lies most convenient for Commerce and Trade, which the *English* carry on in most parts of the World, and the *Dutch* hitherto have been the only obstacle that they are not become Masters of the whole Trade of the World. For it proves very disadvantageous to the *English,* that they love to eat and drink well, and that in great quantity, and by reason of their love of Ease, they are fain to employ double the number of Seamen in their Ships, of what the *Dutch* do; and besides this, they will not be contented with a small gain: Whereas the *Dutch* live very sparingly, do not refuse the Penny,[69] and therefore are easier to be dealt withall than the *English.*

They import a great deal of raw Silk into *England,* which being wrought in the Country, mightily encreases their Riches. In the same

---

69. In German: "Stübergen" (*Stüberchen*), a diminutive for *Stüber,* the German term for *stuiver,* a Dutch coin (valued between the duit and the guilder) used until the Napoleonic era.

<169> manner they do with their Woollen Manufactury now, whereas before the times of *Henry* VIII. they used to transport most of their Wooll into the *Netherlands,* where it was wrought, and turn'd to the great advantage of those Cities. But this King perceiving that his own Subjects might as well make the same benefit of it, he set up the Woollen Manufactury in his Kingdom, which increased prodigiously, afterwards, when at the time of the Troubles in the *Netherlands,* a great many of these Weavers did settle themselves in *England.* The Riches of *England* also are, as it seems, not a little increased, because it is not permitted there to any Body to carry any Gold or Silver of their own Coin out of the Land, except it be perhaps to the value of ten pound Sterling for a Traveller.[70]

But *Scotland* does not come near *England,* neither in Fertility nor Riches, having not any Commodities fit for Exportation, except Saltfish, Salt, Lead and Coals. The Western and *Orkney* Islands also produce nothing but Fish. *Ireland* abounds in Cattel, and especially in Sheep, tho' the *Irish* Wooll is not so fine as the *English,* but for the rest it is a fertile and plentifull Country. In *America* belong to the *English* Crown, the Islands of *Bermudos, Virginia* and *New England,* and some of the *Caribby Islands,* whither the *English* have sent their Colonies, and have also begun to settle themselves on the 'Continent of' [mainland in] *Guiana.* The Product of these Countries is chiefly Tobacco, Sugar, Ginger, Indigo and Cotton. They have also a Colony in the Island of *Jamaica,* from whence the *English* Buccaneers and Privateers do great mischief to the *Spanish West Indies.* For it is a custom with the *English,* That tho' they are at Peace with the *Spaniards* in *Europe,* they do them, nevertheless, all the Mischief they can in the *West Indies. Tangier* King *Charles* II. got as a Dowry with the *Infanta* of *Portugal.*[71] Lastly, The *English* also are possess'd of some places in the *Banda Islands,* and thereabouts in the *East Indies,* which are of no small consequence to them.

70. An allusion to mercantilist economic principles. See II.17, note 56, p. 87, above; and V.26, note 75, below.
71. Catherine of Braganza (1638–1705), whom Charles married in 1662. Besides Tangiers, the English also got Mumbai (Bombay) in India, a much bigger prize.

§35. The Constitution of the Government in *England* is chiefly remark-able for this, that the King cannot act at pleasure, but in 'some' [quite a few] Matters is to take <170> the Advice of the Parliament. By this Name is to be understood the Assembly of the Estates of *England*, which is divided into the Higher and the Lower House. In the first sit the Bishops and the Lords, in the latter the Deputies of the Cities, and of the 52 Counties or Shires, into which the whole Kingdom of *England* is divided. The first origin of the Parliament, as 'tis related, was this, That the former Kings of *England* did grant great Privileges to the Lords, by whose assistance they had conquer'd the Country, and kept the common people in obedience. But these in conjunction with the Bishops growing too head-strong, proved very troublesome, especially to King *John* and *Henry* III. wherefore, to suppress their Insolence, *Edward* I. took part [allied himself] with the Commons. And whereas formerly, out of each County or Shire two Knights and two Citizens only were call'd, to represent their Grievances, which having been debated by the King and the House of Lords, they used to receive an answer and to be sent home again: This King *Edward* call'd together the Commons, and consulted with them concerning the publick Affairs; tho' there are some who will have their origin to be much more ancient. This House, after it was once establish'd, did extreamly weaken the Authority of the Lords, and in process of time did not a little diminish the Regal Power; for ever since that time the Rights of the People were maintained with a high hand, the House of Commons imagining, that the Sovereignty was lodg'd among them, and if the Kings refused to gratify them in their Requests, they used to grumble at their proceedings.

And because the Power of the Parliament is not so much establish'd by any ancient Laws as Precedents and Customs, this is the reason why it is always very jealous of its Privileges, and always ready to make out of one single Precedent a right belonging to it ever after. This Parliament the King is obliged to call together as often as any extraordinary Taxes are to be levy'd (for the Parliament did assign this King, at first, for his ordinary Revenue, 1.200.000 *l. per annum,* which has been considerably augmented since) or any old Laws are to be abrogated, or new ones to be made, <171> or any alteration to be made in Religion.

For concerning these matters the King cannot decree any thing without consent of the Parliament. The Parliament [is] also used to take into consideration the state of the Kingdom, and to present their Opinion to the King, yet is the same of no force till approved of by the King. It often also calls into question the Ministers of State, concerning the Administration of publick Affairs, and inflicts Punishment upon them, with the King's approbation. And it is a common rule in *England,* that whatever is committed against the 'Constitutions' [laws] of the Realm{, or against the common good}, is done by the Ministers and Officers; for the King, they say, does never amiss, but his ill Counsellours, which is not altogether contrary to Truth. But if the Parliament should pretend to transgress its bounds, the King has power to dissolve it; yet ought the King also to be cautious in this, lest he should by an unseasonable Dissolution of the Parliament exasperate the People.

§36. If we duely consider the Condition and Power of *England,* we shall find it to be a powerfull and considerable Kingdom, which is able to keep up the Balance betwixt the Christian Princes in *Europe;* and which depending on its own Strength, is powerfull enough to defend it self. For, because it is surrounded every where by the Sea, none can make any attempt upon it, unless he be so powerfull at Sea, as to be able entirely to ruine the Naval Forces of *England.* And if it should happen, that the *English* Fleet were quite defeated, yet would it prove a very hard task, to transport thither such an Army, as could be suppos'd to be superiour to so powerfull a Force as the *English* Nation is able to raise at home. But *England* ought to take especial care, that it fall not into civil Dissentions, since it has often felt the effects of the same, and the Seeds of them are remaining yet in that Nation; which chiefly arises from the difference in Religion, and the fierce Inclinations of this Nation, which makes it very fond of Alterations.[72] Nevertheless a Wise and Courageous King may easily prevent this evil, if he does not act against the general Inclination of the People, maintains <172> a good

The Power and Strength of England.

72. This is in contrast to the Germans, as noted in *The Present State of Germany,* VII.1, in Pufendorf (2007), p. 181. Also see VIII.18, note 28, p. 348, below.

Correspondency with the Parliament; and for the rest is very watchfull, and as soon as any Commotions happen, takes off immediately the

With relation to other States.

Ringleaders. Lastly, *England* and *Scotland* being comprehended in one Island, whose chiefest Strength lies in a good Fleet, it is evident, that this King need not make any great account of such States as either are remote from the Sea, or else are not very powerfull in Shipping. Wherefore, as the King of *England* takes no great notice of *Germany* (except as far as it relates to *France* or *Spain*)[,] of *Poland* and other such like States [*Republicquen*]; so it is easie for him to curb the Pirates on the *Barbary* Coast: Which Nests of Pirates might have been easily destroyed long ago, if they had not been let alone on purpose to render the Trade in the Mediterranean difficult to the *Hamburgers,* and some others.

England has nothing to fear from *Portugal;* and this must rather

To the Northern Crowns.

hope for assistance from *England* and *Holland* against *Spain.* The Naval Strength of the Northern Crowns, *England* need not be jealous of, as long as the same is divided. Yet it cannot be for the Interest of *England,* if one of those Kings should become absolute Master of the *East* [Baltic] *Sea,* or that |[they should be fain to depend on the Discretion

To Spain.

of the *Dutch.*]|[73] Since the Naval Strength of *Spain* is mightily decay'd *England* need not fear any thing from thence: Yet does it not seem to be the Interest of *England* to fall out with that Kingdom, considering what a vast Trade the *English* have into *Spain;* for *Spain* does either consume the *English* Commodities at home, or else exchanges them for Silver, by sending of them into *America.* There are some who have computed, that in case of a War with *Spain,* the *English* would lose in effects above thirty Millions; and besides this, their Trade into the *Levant* and other places, would be greatly endangered by the Privateers of *Ostend, Biscay, Majorca* and *Minorca,* who at the time of the Wars under *Cromwell* took

To France.

1500 Merchant ships from the *English.* Tho' the Land Forces of *France* are now-a days much superiour to the *English,* this Island both for its bigness and strength making up not above a third part of *France;* yet the Naval Strength of *France* has hitherto not been able to <173> come in competition with the *English.*

73. Rather: "the Dutch should trade there at will."

It is the chiefest Interest of *England,* to keep up the Balance betwixt *France* and *Spain,* and to take a special care that the King of *France* do not become Master of all the *Netherlands;* for it is visible, that thereby his Power at Sea would be encreas'd to that degree, that he might enter on a Design of being [getting] even with *England,* for what they have formerly done to *France. Holland* seems to be the only obstacle that the **To Holland.** *English* cannot be sole Masters of the Sea and Trade, tho' for the rest they have no reason to fear the *Dutch* by Land, but only at Sea, because the *Dutch* Land Forces are not so considerable, as to be able to undertake any thing of great moment. Nevertheless, how desirous soever the *English* are to be sole Masters at Sea, yet does it not seem to be the Interest of *England,* frequently to engage it self in Wars with *Holland,* it having been observ'd, that the *Dutch,* since the Wars with *England* are rather increased in Valour, Experience, and Power at Sea. And because other Nations are not likely to suffer that *Holland* should be swallow'd up by the *English,* or that one Nation should have the {commercial} Monopoly of *Europe;* it seems therefore the best method for the *English,* to let the *Dutch* trade as well as themselves, and to set some others upon their Backs, which may give them so much work as thereby to give a check to their growing Greatness, and in the mean while, take care to establish their own Power at Sea, and Commerce abroad. But least of all it would be for the Interest of *England,* if *Holland* should be brought under the Yoak of the *French* King, who, without question, by the additional Sea Forces of *Holland,* and the advantage of the *East India* Trade, would be superiour in Power to any in *Europe.* <174>

⚒ CHAPTER V ⚒

Of France.

§1. As far as we can search into the most ancient Histories, it is evident from thence, That *Gaul*, now call'd *France*, has been a very powerfull and populous Country. For the *Gauls* [*die Gallische* nation] in ancient times had conquer'd a great part of *Italy*, where they settled themselves; who also, when they had over run *Greece* and some other <neighbouring> Countries [*Oerter*], inhabited a part of the *Lesser Asia*, which was called from them *Galatia* or *Gallo-graecia:* Yet formerly this so powerfull Country did never either rightly understand or exert its own Strength against other Nations [*die fremden*], because it was not then under the Government of one 'Prince' [lord], but divided into a great many petty States [*Staaten*], which were always at variance with one another. This much facilitated the Conquest of the *Romans* over them, who else stood not in fear of any Nation [*sic*] so much as the *Gauls*. And tho' the incomparable Valour of *Julius Caesar* was chiefly instrumental in subduing this Nation, yet with ten Legions he had work enough to effect it [only] in ten Years time. But as soon as the *Romans* had brought this fair Country [*Land*] under their Subjection, they employ'd all means to suppress the Martial Spirit of this Nation [*Volck*], in which they succeeded as well in this as in 'other Nations' [their other provinces], it being their Custom to civilize and refine the Manners of these Nations [*Leute*], thereby to render them soft and effeminate.[1]

The most ancient State of France.

Gaul subdued by the Romans.

---

1. This paragraph offers a good example of the imprecision of Crull's terminology, which cannot be used to gauge Pufendorf's own usage and consistency.

After *France* had been near 500 Years under the Dominion of the
Romans, it fell, under the Reign of the Emperour *Honorius*, into the
Hands of the Barbarous Nations.[2] For the *Goths*, after they had over-
run *Italy*, settled themselves in *Gallia Narbonensis*,[3] and the *Burgundians*, conquer'd a considerable part of the rest. But the *Franks* entring this Kingdom, settled and maintained themselves in it, giving
it the Name of *France*, after their own Name. These *Franks*, were for
certain, *Germans*, tho' some of our Modern *French* Writers pretend
to <175> demonstrate, That this Nation was a Colony of the ancient
Gauls, who being overstock'd with People at home, passed over the
Rhine, and having settled a Colony in *Germany*, after several hundred
Years, return'd into their Native Country.[4] But it is more probable,
That the *Franks* are the same 'Nations' [peoples] which were formerly
encompass'd by the Rivers of the *Mayn*, the *Rhine*, the *Weser*, and the
Sea; and which in *Tacitus*'s time were call'd *Salii, Bructeri, Frisii, An-
grivarii, Chamari, Sigambri* and *Chatti*, and who having enter'd into
a mutual Confederacy against the *Romans*, called themselves, in spite
of their Power, *Franks*, or *a free People*, as not doubting but to be able
to defend their Liberty against them. And it is certain, that they did
transplant the *German* Tongue into *France*, which was for a great
while after in fashion among persons of the best Quality, till at last
they used themselves, by degrees, to the Latin Tongue, formerly introduced by the *Romans*, which being corrupted by the *German* Tongue
produced the modern *French* Language. It is also evident, that the
Race of the ancient *Gauls* was not quite extinguish'd, but that both
Nations were by degrees united in one, yet with this difference, that
the *Frankish* Families made up the 'Body' [most distinguished part] of
the Nation.

By the Barbarous Nations.

That the Franks came out of Germany.

The origin of the French Language.

2. After the death of Theodosius the Great in 395, the Roman Empire was again
divided into eastern and western halves. Honorius (384–423) ruled in the West
while his brother Arcadius (377–408) ruled the East. Rome was sacked in 410 under
Honorius.

3. The region south of the Alps and east of the Pyrenees, along the Mediterranean, which was also called Transalpine Gaul. The in-text designation reflects the
province's capital city of Narbonne.

4. See *The Present State of Germany*, I.3–5, in Pufendorf (2007), pp. 28–31.

§2. But howsoever this be, all Historians agree in this, That the *Franks* did choose for their King, about the Year 424, *Pharamond,* who estab-lished among them wholsome Laws and 'Constitutions' [order]; yet most are of Opinion that not this *Pharamond,* but his Son *Clodion,* sirnamed *Long-hair,* invaded *Gaul;* who, after he had been several times repulsed by *Aetius* the *Roman* General, at last took *Artois, Cambray, Tournay,* and some other places as far as the River *Somme,* making *Amiens* his place of Residence. He died in the Year 447; but his Succes-sour and Kinsman *Merovaeus,* in conjunction with the *Roman* General *Aetius* and *Theodorick* the King of the *West Goths,* having beaten *Attila,* the King of the *Huns* out of *France,* extended his Dominions as far as *Mentz* [Meyntz] on one side, and on the other side conquer'd *Picardy, Normandy,* <176> and the greatest part of the Isle of *France.* The *Ro-mans* themselves contributed to this loss, for that not only in the Battel fought against *Attila,* they had lost a great many of their best Forces, but *Aetius* also being fallen into disgrace with the Emperour *Valentinian,* was by him murthered; which *Aetius* may be justly said to have been the last great Captain the *Romans* had; there being after his death no body left who could resist *Merovaeus.*

From this King sprang the first Race of the *French* Kings, which is called the *Merovi[n]gian* Family. He died in the Year 458. His Son *Childerick,* for his Lasciviousness, was banish'd; in whose stead one *Ae-gidius* of the ancient Race of the *Gauls* was set up for King. But *Child-erick,* through the faithfulness of his Friend *Guyeman,* was after an Exile of eight Years, recall'd out of *Thuringia,* whither he fled, and restor'd to his Throne; who drove back the *Britains* and *Saxons,* that made at that time great havock in *France.* He also conquer'd that part which is now call'd *Lorrain,* and took *Beauvais, Paris,* and some other places near the Rivers of the *Oise* and the *Seyne.* He died in the Year 481.

His Son *Clouis* or *Lewis,* having kill'd *Syagrius,* the Son of *Aegidius,* establish'd the *French* Monarchy, and added great Territories to the Kingdom. This King fell in love with *Clotildis,* of the Royal Race of *Burgundy,* who promised to marry him; if he would turn Christian. Which, however, he afterwards delayed to perform, till the *Alemans,* who would have got a footing in *France,* enter'd that Kingdom, whom

Pharamond the first King.

Clodion.

Merovaeus.

Childerick.

Clouis I.

he meeting with his Army near *Zulick* [Zulch], a bloody Battel was fought, where, when he saw the *French* began to fall in disorder, he vow'd, *That if he obtain'd the Victory, he would be baptiz'd;* which Vow, after the Victory he perform'd, being baptiz'd at *Reims* \A. 496\ by St. *Reim* [*Remigo*], whose example the whole Nation of the *French* followed. This King also overturn'd the Kingdom of the *Goths,* which they had establish'd in *Languedock;* uniting that Country with his Kingdom: He also conquer'd several petty Principalities, and a part of the *Higher* [southern] *Germany.* He died in the Year 511. <177>

France is divided.

§3. After the death of *Clouis, France* received a signal blow, the Kingdom being divided among his four Sons; who, tho' they annexed the Kingdom of *Burgundy* to it, yet this division weaken'd this Kingdom, and administred Fuel to the following intestine Dissentions. Nay, this impolitick dividing the Kingdom went further still, for they subdivided the Kingdom again among their Sons, which occasioned most horrible civil Commotions in *France,* these Kings endeavouring, as it were, to out-do one another in Iniquity: And among the rest, the two Queens *Brunechildis* and *Fredegundis* are infamous for their monstrous Crimes.

Clotarius II. At last, after a great many intestine Divisions *Clotarius* II. re-uniting the divided Kingdom \A. 614\, did somewhat restore its ancient State. He

Dagobert. died in the Year 628. But his Son *Dagobert* fell into the same Madness; for he not only gave part of the Kingdom to his Brother *Albert,* but also divided his own share among his two Sons; neither did he do any thing for the Benefit of the Publick during his Reign.

From this time the *French* Kings quite degenerated from their ancient Valour, giving themselves over to Laziness and Debauchery. Wherefore the Grand Mareschals of the Kingdom did by degrees assume the Power and Administration of Publick Affairs. Among these *Pipin* was famous, descended of a Noble Family in *Austrasia,* who had the Administration

Charles of Affairs during the space of twenty eight Years {until the Year 714},

Martell. under several Kings.[5] His Son *Charles Martell* succeeded his Father in

5. Austrasia referred to the region of northeastern France and Western Germany during the time of the Merovingians. Pippin was "mayor of the palace" (majordomo, *Hofmeister*) of Austrasia, that is, the king's chief administrative officer.

his Power and Office, which he rather augmented, after he was grown
famous by his Martial Exploits, having chas'd away the *Saracens,* who
about that time, conquering *Spain,* fell also into *France,* of whom he
kill'd a vast number.[6] This Man took upon himself the Title of a Prince
and Duke of *France* \A. 732\, so that nothing remain'd with the Kings
but the bare Title and an empty Name, they being kept in the Country
[on a rural estate], and once a Year carried for a Show through the City,
to expose them to the view of the People like strange Creatures. At last,
Pipin the Younger, Son of this *Charles Martell* (who died in the Year
741) having brought the great Men of the Kingdom over <178> to his
Party, depos'd King *Childerick* II. and having sent him into a Convent,
got himself proclaim'd King of *France.* This was approv'd easily enough
by Pope *Zachary,* because he being in fear of the growing Power of the
Longobards in *Italy,* did endeavour by all means to oblige the King of
France to come to his Assistance. And thus the *Merovingian* Family loses
[lost] the Crown of *France* \A. 751\. Pipin
proclaim'd
King.

The Merovin-
gian Family
loses the
Crown.

§4. *Pipin,* to convince the World that he was not unworthy of the
Crown, or else to furnish the People with other Matters than to talk of
the deposing of *Childerick,* undertook an Expedition against the *Saxons,* whom he vanquish'd in a great Battel. And he had likewise, under
the Reign of the former Kings, undertaken several Expeditions into
Germany with great Success, and subdu'd some of the Nations bordering upon the *Rhine.* Not long after an Opportunity presented itself to
make himself famous in *Italy,* For *Aistulphus,* the King of the *Lombards*
[*Langobards*], had propos'd to himself the Conquest of all *Italy;* after he
had chas'd the Governours of the *Grecian* Emperours, which were then
call'd *Exarches,* out of *Ravenna,* and all other places which were under
their Jurisdiction, and was ready to march directly against *Rome:* The
Pope *Stephen* III. being in great fear of this Enemy, and not knowing
where to find Assistance, crav'd Aid of *Pipin,* whom he at last persuaded
to take his part against *Aistulphus.* In this War *Pipin* recover'd from
Aistulphus all what he had before taken from the *Grecian* Emperours
in *Italy,* the 'Revenue' [use] of which, he, as 'tis pretended, gave to the

Pipin's
Expeditions.

He assists the
Pope against
the Lombards.

6. The Battle of Tours, or Poitiers, in 732.

Roman See, reserving to himself, as it is very probable, the Sovereignty over these places. He gained, by this Action, the Reputation of being very Zealous; and by bestowing these Revenues upon the Holy Chair, got a firm footing in *Italy,* and the advantage of swaying Matters there according to his Pleasure. He made also *Tassilo,* Duke of *Bavaria,* his Vassal, and beat the Duke of *Aquitain.*

This *Pipin,* died in the Year 768, leaving behind him two Sons, *Charles* and *Carolomannus,* who divided the Kingdom betwixt <179> them. But *Carolomannus* dying quickly after, the whole Kingdom fell to *Charles.* This *Charles* was justly sirnam'd *the Great,* he having carried the *French* Monarchy to the highest pitch of its Greatness, none of his Successours having been able to attain to the like, tho' some of 'em have aim'd at it. For having routed *Desiderius,* the last King of the *Lombards* [*Langobards*], who endeavour'd \A. 774\ to recover what was formerly taken from *Aistulphus,* he conquer'd the Kingdom, and brought it under his Subjection. He also subdu'd *Germany,* having routed *Tassilo,* who had taken upon him the Title of King of *Bavaria.* He also waged War against the *Saxons,* for the space of 32 Years, whom he at last brought under his Obedience, obliging them to embrace the Christian Faith. For which purpose he erected several Episcopal Sees and Monasteries, by the help of the Priests, to reform the barbarous Manners of this Savage People. He also beat the *Sclavonians* [Slavs], *Danes* and *Huns,* and took from the *Saracens* a part of *Spain,* as far as to the River *Iberus;* tho' his Forces, in their return home, were overthrown near *Ronceval,* where was also slain the famous *Rowland.*[7] This *Charles* was in the Year 800, at *Christmas,* being then at *Rome,* proclaim'd {Roman} Emperour by the People, by the Instigation of the Pope, in St. *Peter's* Church. Tho' he gain'd nothing by this Title, except it was the Sovereignty or Protection of |[the *Roman* Church, and the Patrimony of St. *Peter*]|,[8] if both did not belong to him before, for all the rest {which then belonged to his empire} he enjoy'd before under other Titles. He died in the Year 814.

Charles the Great.

He is proclaimed Emperour of the Romans.

7. See II.3, note 4, p. 44, above.
8. Rather: "the church at Rome, and its patrimony." Pufendorf emphasizes the restricted significance of Charlemagne's crowning and refuses to see any universal or religious significance in the event.

§5. After the death of *Charles the Great*, the *French* Monarchy began to decline again, because his Son *Lewis* sirnamed *the Pious*, was more fit to be a Priest, than a Souldier: And it is certain, that so vast a Kingdom, where the new Conquests were not yet well settled, did require a Prince of a Military Spirit. And notwithstanding he had the good Fortune to force some of the Rebellious Nations to return to their Duty, yet he committed, afterwards, two fatal Oversights; when in his life time he gave to his Sons the <180> Titles of Kings, and divided the Kingdom betwixt them. The first of which proved pernicious to himself, the second to the Monarchy. For these impious and ungratefull Sons were not for staying [waiting] for their Father's Death, but Rebelling against him, and made him, after he was deserted by every body, their Prisoner. The Bishops, who were by him kept under strict Discipline, after they had condemn'd him, forc'd him to resign the Government \A. 833\. But the great Men of the Kingdom quickly repenting, restor'd him to his Throne, and he also pardon'd his Sons.

He died in the Year 840, having before his Death made a new Division of the Kingdom betwixt his Sons; the Effects of which appear'd soon after to the World, when *Lotharius*, the elder Brother, who also had the Title of Emperour, undertook to take from his Brothers their Portion; against whom, the two other Brothers, *Lewis* and *Charles* entring into a Confederacy, forced him to divide the Monarchy with them, having first obtain'd a bloody Victory near *Fountenay unfar* [not far from] *Auxerre,* in which Battel were slain above 100.000 Men, and among them the Flower of the *French* Nation. In this Division *Germany* fell to *Lewis*'s share, which ever since has continued separate from *France,* and has made a distinct Empire. But the younger Brother, *Charles* sirnamed *the Bald,* got for his Portion the greatest part of *France, viz.* all that part which lies betwixt the *Western Ocean* and the *Meuse;* but the eldest Brother obtain'd *Italy, Provence,* and all those Counties which are situated betwixt the *Meuse, Rhine,* and the *Some [Somme].* Under the Reign of this *Charles the Bald,* the *Normans* (so they call'd the *Danes* and *Norwegians*) fell, with a considerable Force, into *France,* making great Havock where ever they came: And the Kingdom was weakned to that degree, by the last bloody Battel, and its being divided into so many

Marginal notes:

Lewis the Pious.

He divides his Kingdom.

His Sons Rebell.

Germany divided from France.

Charles the Bald.

The Normans make an Irruption into France.

Principalities (for the Sons of *Lotharius* had also shared their Father's Provinces among themselves) that it was not strong enough to chase out of its Dominions these Robbers, but was oblig'd \A. 912\, under *Charles* sirnamed *the Simple*, to give into their possession the Province of *Neustria*, which they cal-<181>led after their Name, *Normandy*.

The Sons of *Lotharius* dying without Issue, *Charles the Bald* and the Sons of *Lewis* shared their Part betwixt them, out of which *Charles* got *Provence*. At last *Charles* obtain'd the Title of Emperour, and died in the

Ludovicus Balbus. Year 877. His Son *Lewis* sirnamed *Balbus*, succeeded him, who dying soon after, left the Kingdom to his two Sons, who were very young, *viz.*

Ludov. III. and Carolomannus. to *Lewis* III. and *Carolomannus;* from whom *Lewis* King of *Germany* took *Lorrain*. *Lewis* [III.] dying in the Year 882, as did *Carolomannus* in the Year 884, none was left but a Brother of theirs by the Father's side, *viz.* the Son of *Lewis* sirnamed *Balbus*, who being then a Child of five

Charles the Simple. Years of Age, was afterwards called *Charles the Simple*. For at that time the Authority of the Kings of *France* was decay'd to that degree, that it was a common custom to give them Sirnames according to the several defects of Body or Mind, as were obvious in them. He was, during his Minority, committed to the Tuition of his Cousin *Carolus Crassus*,[9] who also had the Title of Emperour, who not long after, because he was very infirm both in Body and Mind, was deposed, and died in the Year

The decay of the Royal Authority.

The Excessive Power of the Nobles. 888. The Royal Authority being thus decay'd, and nothing but Divisions found in the Kingdom, the great Men of the Kingdom mightily increased their own Power, so that, whereas they used formerly to be Governours of their Provinces under the King's Command, they now began to claim them as a Propriety belonging to themselves, independent of the King. It is related by some, That the Kings at that time had nothing left but *Rheims* and *Laon* which they could really call their own; which Evil could not be totally suppress'd by the following Kings, till several hundred Years after.

Eudo Count of Paris crown'd King of France. After the Death of *Carolus Crassus*, *Eudo* Count of Paris got himself to be crowned King, and waged War with *Charles the Simple*, but died in the Year 898: Yet *Charles the Simple*, quickly found another Rival for

9. Charles the Fat (Carolus Pinguis), 839–88.

the Crown. For *Rudolf* King of *Burgundy*, got himself to be crowned King of *France*, making *Charles the Simple* his Prisoner, who died during his Imprisonment \A. 929\. After the Death of *Rudolf* (which <182> happen'd in the Year 936) reign'd *Lewis* IV. sirnam'd *Outremer* ["from overseas"], because he had, during the Imprisonment of his Father, shelter'd himself in *England*. This King's Reign was full of intestine Commotions; he died in the Year 954, leaving for his Successour his Son *Lotharius*, who likewise reign'd in continual troubles till the Year 985, leaving behind him his Son *Lewis* sirnamed *the Faint-hearted*, of whom the *French* Historians only say this, that he did nothing. He had for his Tutor and Administrator of the Kingdom, *Hugh Capet* Earl of *Paris*. After this King's Death \A. 987\, his Uncle, *viz. Lewis* sirnamed *Outremer's* Son, laid claim to the Crown, but was disappointed in his Pretensions by the great Power of *Hugh Capet*. He afterwards endeavour'd to maintain his Right by force of Arms, but was made a Prisoner, and dying in Prison, put an end to the *Carolinian* Race, or at least, to its Inheritance of the Crown of *France*, which had been in its possession for at least 236 Years. It is very remarkable, that this Family lost the Kingdom through the same Errour which the former lost it. For tho' this Family, by prodigious Conquests, had rais'd the Power of *France*, yet were the Conquests soon after, by the Divisions made of the Kingdom again dis-united, and even a considerable part quite separated from that Kingdom, and annexed to the *German* Empire. Besides this, by the Negligence of these Kings, and the excessive Power of the great Men in the Kingdom, *France* was reduced to a very low Condition.

§6. As *Hugh Capet*, the first Founder of the present Royal Family, obtain'd the Crown, not so much by right of Succession as by the assistance of the chief Men of the Kingdom, who excluded the right Heir; so (as it is very probable) he was obliged ||[to remit a great many of the ancient Royal Prerogatives]|,[10] and to confirm to the great Men of the Kingdom the Power of governing their Provinces, with the Titles of Dukes and Earls, under condition that they should acknowledge them-

Marginal notes:

Rudolf of Burgundy crown'd King.

Lewis Outremer.

Lotharius.

Lewis the Fainthearted.

The Carolinian Family extinguish'd.

Hugh Capet, the first of the present Race.

---

10. Rather: "to defer in many things."

selves Vassals of the Kingdom, yet not be obliged to depend absolutely on the King's Commands; so that *France* at that time was like a <183> mishapen and weak Body.[11] *Hugh,* in the mean time, re-united to the Crown (which at that time had scarce any thing left which could be call'd her own) the County of *Paris,* the Dutchy of *France,* wherein was comprehended all that lies betwixt the Rivers of *Seine* and the *Loire,* and the County of *Orleans.* Among the great Men of the Kingdom, the chief were the Dukes of *Normandy* (on whom also depended *Britainy*)[,] of *Burgundy, Aquitain* and *Gascoigne;* the Earls of *Flanders, Champaign* and *Tolouse,* the latter of which was also Duke of *Languedock:* But the Counties of *Vienne, Provence, Savoy* and *Dauphine* belong'd to the Kingdom of *Arelat,* which was a part of the *German Empire.* Yet these Kings had at last the good Fortune to see all these Demi-Sovereign Princes extinguish'd, and their Countries re-united to the Crown of *France.*

Robert.

Hugh died in the Year 996, whose Son *Robert,* a good natur'd Prince, reign'd very peaceably, he having reduc'd the Dukedom of *Burgundy,* to which, he, after the Death of his Uncle, was the next Heir, under the entire Jurisdiction of the Crown. The Tyranny exercis'd by the Pope against this King ought to be mention'd here. For, the King having an Intention of marrying *Bertha,* of the House of *Burgundy,* which Match was esteemed very beneficial to his State, and the said *Bertha* standing with him in the fourth degree of Consanguinity; besides that, he had been Godfather to a Child of hers in her former Husband's time: He desir'd and obtain'd the Consent of his Bishops, the said Marriage being otherwise against the Canon Law. But the Pope took hence an occasion to Excommunicate the King and the whole Kingdom, which proved so mischievous, that the King was deserted by all his Servants, except three or four, and no Body would touch the Victuals that came from his Table, which was therefore thrown to the Dogs. He died in the Year 1033.

The Pope ex-communicates him and his Kingdom.

11. See *The Present State of Germany,* VI.8–9, in Pufendorf (2007), pp. 173 and 176, for Pufendorf's controversial use of 'monstrous' in reference to irregular states; also see VI.21, note 43, p. 305.

The Reign of his Son *Henry* was also not very famous, except that he   Henry I.
waged some inconsiderable Wars against his Vassals. He presented his
Brother *Robert* with the Dukedom of *Burgundy,* from whence comes
the Race of the Dukes of *Burgundy* descended from the Royal Blood.
He <184> died in the Year 1060. His Son *Philip* did nothing memo-   Philip I.
rable; he was also for his Marriage excommunicated by the Pope, but at
last obtained a Dispensation. Under the Reign of this King *Philip, Wil-*   Will. Duke
liam Duke of *Normandy* conquer'd *England,* which prov'd to be the oc-   of Normandy
casion of unspeakable Miseries to *France;* for these two Kingdoms were   conquers
  England.
ever after in continual Wars, till the *English* were driven out of *France.*[12]

About the same time the first Expedition was undertaken into the   Expedition
Holy Land, which Extravagancy continued for near 200 Years after.   into the Holy
The Popes drew the most Benefit from these Expeditions, assuming   Land.
to themselves, an Authority, not only to command, but also to protect
all such as had listed themselves under the Cross. Under this pretext
also[,] frequent Indulgences were sent abroad into the World, and what
was given towards the use of this War, was collected and distributed by
their Legates. The King of *France,* and other Kings, receiv'd thereby this
Benefit, That these Wars carried off a great many turbulent Spirits: And
a great many of the Nobility used either to sell or else to mortgage their
Estates; and if any of them happened to die in the Expedition, leaving
no Heirs behind them, their Estates fell to the King. By this means also,
that prodigious number of People, wherewith *France* was overstock'd at
that time, was much diminish'd, whereby the Kings got an Opportunity
to deal more easily with the rest. Nevertheless, when afterwards the
Kings, either by Instigation of the Popes, or out of their own Inclinations, undertook these Expeditions in their own Persons, they found
the dismal effects of it. For, by so doing, the best of their Subjects
were led to the Slaughter; and yet it was impossible to maintain these
Conquests as long as they were not Masters of *Egypt:* Whereas, if this
Kingdom had been made the Seat of the intended Empire, and the
Store-house of the War, a Kingdom might have been establish'd, which
would have been able to support it self by its own Strength.

12. See IV.5, pp. 120–23, above.

Lewis the Fat. This King [Philip I] died in the Year 1108. His Son *Lewis* sirnamed
the Fat was always at variance with *Henry* I. King of *England,* and
in continual Troubles with the petty <185> Lords in *France,* who did
considerable Mischiefs from their strong Castles; yet he was too hard
Lewis VII. for them at last, and died in the Year 1137. His Son *Lewis* VII. sirnamed *the Younger,* undertook, upon the Persuasion of St. *Bernhard* [of
His unfortu- Clairveaux], an Expedition into the *Holy Land,*[13] but this prov'd a fatal
nate Expedi- Expedition, for by the Defeat which he receiv'd at *Pamphylia,* and the
tion to the
Holy Land. Siege of *Damascus,* which he was forc'd to quit, and the Fatigues of so
great a Journey, as well as the perfidiousness of some of the Commanders, after he had ruin'd a great Army, he returned with the miserable
Remainders into *France,* without having done any thing answerable
to such an Undertaking: But he committed the greatest Error, when
he divorced himself from his Lady *Eleonora,* whether out of Jealousie
or tenderness of Conscience is uncertain, she being his Cousin in the
third or fourth degree. This *Eleonora* being also the only Heiress of
Aquitain and *Poictou,* was immediately after married to *Henry* Duke of
Normandy, afterwards King of *England,* the second of that Name, who,
by this Match annexed these fair Countries to the Crown of *England.*
In fine, having been kept in a continual alarm by his petty Vassals, but
especially by *Henry* II. King of *England,* he died in the Year 1180.

Philip II. the §7. His Son *Philip* II. sirnamed *Augustus,* or *the Conquerour,* was at first
Conquerour. engaged in a War against *Henry* II. King of *England,* from whom he
took several considerable places; which, however he restored afterwards
Another Expe- to his Son *Richard,* with whom he enter'd into a League to retake *Jerusa-*
dition to the *lem* from the *Saracens,* pursuant to which, both the Kings went thither
Holy Land.
in Person with a considerable Force. But a Jealousie arising betwixt these
two Kings, nothing was done worth mentioning; for *Richard* accused
Philip, that he had an ill design against him in *Sicily,* in their Voyage;
besides that, he had refused to consummate the before intended Match
betwixt his Sister and *Richard:* Wherefore, as soon as *Ptolemais* [Acre]
had been taken by their joint Forces, *Philip,* under pretence of Sick-

13. The Second Crusade (1147–49).

ness returned into *France,* leaving only with *Ri-*<186>*chard, Hugh* III.
Duke of *Burgundy,* with some Troops; who envying *Richard,* hinder'd
the taking of the City of *Jerusalem.* After his return from that unfortunate Expedition to the *Holy Land,* he undertook a War against *Richard,*   War betwixt
which he also carried on against his Brother *John,* wherein *Philip* had   France and
                                                                               England.
much the better of the *English,* for he took from them *Normandy,* the
Counties of *Anjou, Maine, Touraine, Berry* and *Poictou.* He was very
instrumental in deposing the Earl of *Tholouse,* who, because he had
taken into his Protection the *Albigenses,* was excommunicated by the
Pope. *Philip* also obtained a great Victory near *Bouvines,* betwixt *Lisle*
and *Tournay,* against the Emperour *Otho* IV. who being joined with the
Earl of *Flanders,* attack'd him with an Army of 150.000 Men, whilst the
King of *England* was to fall into *France* on the side of *Aquitain.* This
King was so successfull in his Wars against *England,* that his Son *Lewis*
was very near obtaining the Crown of *England.* And tho' he was chased
again out of *England,* yet did he, after his Father's Death \A. 1223\, pursue his Victories against the *English* in *France,* taking from them among
others, the City of *Rochelle.*

   But this *Lewis* VIII. did not reign long, for he died in the Year 1226,   Lewis VIII.
leaving for Successour his Son *Lewis* IX. sirnamed *the Holy,* during   Lewis IX.
whose Minority, his Mother *Blanch* of *Castile* had the Supream Administration of Affairs; and tho' some of the Nobility raised great Troubles
against her, she subdued them all by her singular Prudence. In the Year
1244, the City of *Jerusalem* was ransack'd by some *Persians,* who called
themselves *Chorasmii, Lewis* being about the same time dangerously
ill, made a Vow, *That if he recovered he would undertake an Expedition*   A third
against those Infidels; which he afterwards perform'd. But before his de-   Expedition
                                                                               to the Holy
parture he issued out his Proclamation throughout the Kingdom, inti-   Land without
mating, that whoever had received any damage by his Souldiers, should   Success.
have Restitution made him, which was performed accordingly. In this
Expedition he took the strong City of *Damiata* [Dumyat] {A. 1249};
but the overflowing of the River *Nile,* hindered him from taking
Grand Cairo. After the River was returned to its usual <187> Bounds,
he vanquish'd the Enemy in two Battels; but they having receiv'd new
Reinforcements, cut off the Provisions from the *French,* who were also

extreamly pester'd with the Scurvy. The King then resolv'd to retreat towards *Damiata,* but in his March thither they attack'd him, gave him a terrible overthrow, and took him Prisoner, yet released him again for a Ransom of 400.000 Livres, he being obliged to restore also to them the City of *Damiata.* Thus he marched with the Remainders of his Army, which from 30.000 Men was moulder'd away to 6000, to *Ptolemais,* where, after he had given what Assistance he could to the Christians, he at last returned home \A. 1254\.

The first Pretensions of the French upon the Kingdom of Naples. Under the Reign of this King, *France* got first an Opportunity to intermeddle in the Affairs of *Italy,* from whence, yet this Kingdom never reapt any great Benefit. *Manfred,* natural Son of the Emperour *Frederick* II. having first kill'd King *Conrad* his Brother, made himself King of *Naples* and *Sicily.* But the Pope [Urban IV], on whom this Kingdom depended as a Fief, being dissatisfy'd with *Manfred,* offer'd the same to *Charles* Earl of *Anjou,* Brother of *Lewis* IV. [IX] King of *France,* which he having accepted of, was crowned at *Rome* \A. 1261\, with Condit[i]on, that he should pay to the Pope 8000 Ounces of Gold, make a yearly Present of a White Horse [palfrey]<, as an acknowledgment>; and |[if he was chosen Emperour, that he should not unite]|[14] that Kingdom with the Empire; the Pope being unwilling to have any one more powerfull than himself in *Italy. Charles* thereupon vanquish'd *Manfred,* and having murthered him and his Children, took possession of the Kingdom. The young *Conradin,* Duke of *Swabia,* came with an Army to recover the Kingdom, which was his Inheritance, from his Grandfather, but having been overthrown in a Battel near the Lake of *Celano* \A. 1268\, was made a Prisoner, and in the Year next following, had his Head cut off at *Naples,* upon the Instigation of the Pope, who being ask'd by *Charles, What he had best to do with his Prisoner?* answer'd, *Vita Conradini, mors Caroli; Mors Conradini, vita Caroli;* i.e. *The Life of* Conradin *is the Death of* Charles; *The Death of* Conradin *the Life* <188> *of* Charles. And as by the Death of this young Prince was extinguish'd

14. Rather: "neither permit himself to be elected emperor, nor allow the unification of."

the Noble Race of the Dukes of *Swabia,* so this *Charles* laid the first Pretensions of *France* to the Kingdom of *Naples.*

In the mean while, King *Lewis* being not satisfy'd with his former unfortunate Expedition against the Infidels, resolved to try again his Fortune against *Tunis,* either because he found, that this place lay very convenient for his Brother's Kingdom of *Sicily,* or because he hoped thereby to open a way for the Conquest of *Egypt,* without which, all the Expeditions into the *Holy Land,* were likely to prove ineffectual. But in this Siege he lost a great part of his Army by Sickness, and he died himself there in the Year 1270. From a younger Son of this *Lewis* IV. [IX] *viz.* from *Robert* Earl of *Clairmont,* sprang the *Bourbon* Family, which now sways the Scepter of *France.* An un-
fortunate
Expedition of
S. Lewis.

§8. His Son *Philip* sirnamed *the Hardy* [*Audax*] succeeded him, under whose Reign that considerable Earldom of *Tholouse* was united to the Crown of *France. Alfonsus* Son of *Lewis* IX. who had married the only Heiress of this 'Country' [earldom], happening to die without Issue, in an Expedition into *Africa.* Under the Reign also of this King fell out the so much celebrated *Sicilian Vespers,* whereby all the *French* were at one blow extirpated out of *Sicily.*[15] The Business was thus; Some *Frenchmen* had ravish'd the Wife of *John* of *Porchyta* [*Prochyta*], born at *Salerno,* who, enflam'd with Revenge, did seek for Aid of *Pieter* King of *Arragon,* hoping, by his Assistance, to drive *Charles* [Earl of Anjou] out of *Sicily;* the *Sicilians* also being very averse to the *French,* who had committed great Outrages in that Kingdom. Pope *Nicholus* V. lent a helping hand, who stood in fear of the Power of *Charles;* as did also *Michael* [VIII] *Paleologus* the *Constantinopolitan* Emperour, because *Charles* had made some Pretensions to that Empire. *John* therefore, disguis'd in a Monks Habit, travell'd about from place to place, till he had brought his Design to Perfection. It was next to a Miracle that the Design was not betray'd in three years time, it having been so long a forming in several places. At last it was <189> put in Execution \A. 1282\, it being agreed upon, that Philip the
Hardy. The Sicilian
Vespers.

15. See II.7, note 12, p. 52, above.

in the second Holyday in *Easter*, at that very time when the Bells rung in to the *Vespers*, all the *French* throughout the whole Kingdom of *Sicily* should be massacred at once, which was done accordingly, within two Hours time with great Barbarity, no person having been spared in the Massacre. Which being done, *Pieter* King of *Arragon* possess'd himself of the Kingdom of *Sicily*. And, tho' the Pope order'd the *Croisade* to be preached up against *Pieter*, and declared *Charles*, the second Son of *Philip* [of France] King of *Arragon*, and this *Philip* marched with a great Army to put his Son into possession, yet it did prove labour in vain, and *Philip* died in the Year 1285.

Philip the Handsom. His Son and Successour *Philip* sirnamed *the Handsom*, upon some frivolous Pretences, began a War with the *English* \A. 1292\, taking from them the City of *Bourdeaux*, and the greatest part of *Aquitain*, which however they soon after recover'd by vertue of a Peace concluded be-

He has ill Success in Flanders. twixt them. Not long after he attack'd the Earl of *Flanders*, who, by the Instigation of the *English* had enter'd into a Confederacy with a great many neighbouring Lords against him, from whom he took most of his strong Holds. But the *Flemings*, being soon tired with the Insolencies committed by the *French*, {revolted and} cut in pieces the *French* Garrisons; whereupon the King sent an Army under the Command of *Robert* Earl of *Artois*, to reduce them to Obedience; but he was defeated near *Courtray*, there being 20.000 *French* slain upon the Spot, which happened chiefly by a 'Misfortune' [carelessness], that the Cavalry was misled into a moorish Ground. It is related, that the *Flemings* got above 8000 gilt Spurs as a Booty from the *French* \A. 1302\. And tho' afterwards \A. 1304\ there were 25.000 killed of the *Flemings*, yet they quickly recollecting themselves, raised another Army of 60.000 Men, and obliged the King, by a Peace made betwixt them, to restore them to their 'ancient State' [previous status].

He suppress'd the Templers. This King *Philip* also, with consent of the Pope, suppress'd the rich Order of the Knights Templers, and died in the Year 1314. Whom succeeded his three Sons, each in his turn, who all died without Issue,

Lewis X. and without doing any thing of moment. The eldest, *Lewis* X. <190> sirnamed *Hutin* [headstrong], died in the Year 1316; whose Brother

Philip the Tall. *Philip* sirnamed *the Tall*, had a Contest for the Crown with his deceased

Brother's Daughter *Joan,* she being supported by her Mother's Brother, the Duke of *Burgundy,* but it was determined in favour of *Philip* by vertue of the *Salick Law.*[16] Under this King the *Jews* were banish'd out of *France,* they having been accused of poisoning the Fountains. He died in the Year 1322. Him succeeded the third Brother *Charles* IV. sirnamed *the Handsom,* under whose Reign all the *Italians* and *Lombards,* who being Usurers, did exact upon the People, were banished {from} the Kingdom. A War also was begun in *Aquitain* against the *English,* but these Differences were quickly composed by the Intercession of Queen *Isabella,* Sister of *Charles.* He died in the Year 1328.

§9. After the Death of this King, *France* was for a great many years together torn in pieces by very unfortunate and bloody Wars, which had almost prov'd fatal to this Kingdom: For a Contest arose about the Succession, betwixt *Philip* of *Valois, Philip the Handsom's* Brother's Son, and *Edward* III. King of *England,* the above-mention'd *Philip the Handsom's* Daughter's Son. The former pretended a right by vertue of the *Salick Law,* which excludes the Females from the Succession: But the latter, tho' he did not deny the *Salick Law,* yet did he alledge, That this Law did not barr from the Succession the Sons born of the King's Daughters. And it was certain, that he was nearer a kin to the deceased King than *Philip,* neither could any Precedent be brought where a Son of the King's Daughter had been excluded from the Succession to admit his Brother's Son: Yet the Estates of *France* declared for *Philip,* partly upon the persuasion of *Robert* Earl of *Artois,* partly because they were unwilling to depend on *England.* And tho' King *Edward* did dissemble at first, this Affront, and came in person to do homage to *Philip* for his Provinces which he was possess'd of in *France;* yet not long after he began to show his Resentment, the *French* having obliged him at the time when he performed the <191> Ceremony of Homage, to lay aside his Crown, Scepter and Spurs. Besides, the States of *England* did persuade him not so easily to let fall his Pretensions, and *Robert* Earl of *Artois,* being fallen out with *Philip* about some Pretensions concerning the County of *Ar-*

Charles IV.

Philip of Valois.

His Title contested by Edward III. of England, and on what ground.

16. On Salic Law, see IV.11, note 20, p. 133, above; and V.9, p. 207, below.

tois, did stir up King *Edward* to undertake a War against *France.* In the
mean time while *Philip* had defeated the *Flemings,* who were risen in
Rebellion against that Earl, to that degree, that of 16.000 Men not one
escaped the Sword {in a great battle near Mont Cassel, A. 1328}.

War with England.   In the Year 1336 the *English* began to make War against *France,*[17]
which was carried on for some Years with equal Advantage on both sides,
and was interrupted by several Truces; till at last *Edward* landed with
an Army in *Normandy,* and outbraving the *French,* approach'd to the
very Gates of *Paris.* But *Edward* making soon after his Retreat through

Battel near Crecy. *Picardy* towards *Flanders,* was overtaken by *Philip* near *Albeville,* where
a bloody Battel was fought betwixt them.[18] The *French* Forces being
extreamly tir'd by a long March gave the *English* an easier Victory. Besides this, some *Genoese* Foot retreated immediately, their Bows[19] having
been render'd useless by the rainy Weather; which the Duke *d'Alanzon*
[Alençon] perceiving, and thinking it to have been done by Treachery,
fell with a Body of Horse in among them, which caused the first Confusion. The *English* also made use of four or five pieces of great Cannon
against the *French,* which being never seen before in *France,* caused a
great terrour in the *French* Army. Several *French* Lords also being not
well satisfy'd with the King, were glad to see him defeated. This Victory
is the more remarkable, because (according to the *French* Historians) the
English were not above 24.000 strong, whereas the *French* were above
100.000. Out of which number 30.000 Foot Souldiers were slain, and
1200 Horsemen, among whom was the King of *Bohemia.* This King,
tho' he was blind, yet charg'd the Enemy on Horseback betwixt two of
his Friends, who had ty'd his Horse to theirs, and they were all three
found dead together. The next day there was a great slaughter made
among some *French* Troops, who not knowing what had pass'd the day

The English take Calais. before, <192> were on their March to join the *French* Camp.
   After this Battel the *English* took *Calais, Philip* having in vain attempted its relief with 15.000 Men \A. 1347\. This unfortunate King,

---

17. This was the start of the Hundred Years' War (1336–1453). See IV.11, p. 133.
18. The Battle of Crécy (1346).
19. The Genovese mercenaries used crossbows, while the English used longbows,
which could be strung more easily and loaded more quickly.

however, received this one Comfort, That the Dukedom of *Dauphine*   Dauphine
was annexed to the Crown of *France* by a Gift of *Hubert* the last Duke,   annexed to France.
with Condition, that the eldest Son of the Kings of *France* should bear
the Title of *Dauphin*. This *Hubert* having conceived a mortal hatred
against the then Earl of *Savoy* had before put himself under the Protection of *France;* but when afterwards by an unfortunate Accident he
kill'd his only Son, he retir'd into a Monastery, giving to the King of
France the Possession of his Country \A. 1349\. This King *Philip* also
bought *Roussilion* and *Montpelier,* and was the first who imposed that so
much abominated Tax in *France* upon Salt, called the *Gabell,* whereby   Philip
the Subjects are obliged to pay for the Sun and Sea Water at so dear a   introduced the Gabell.
rate. Wherefore King *Edward* used to call him in jest, *The Author of the*
Salick Law. He died in the Year '1356' [1350].

§10. His Son and Successour *John* was more unfortunate in his Wars   John. Unfor-
against the *English* than his Father. For the Truce being expir'd, the War   tunate in his Wars against the English.
began afresh, wherein Prince *Edward*[20] made an Inrode with 12.000
Men out of *Aquitain,* destroying all round about him; King *John* intending to cut off his Retreat, overtook him with all his Forces near
Maupertuis, two Leagues from *Poictiers.* The Prince offered the King   Battel near Poictiers.
Satisfaction for the Damage sustained, which he refusing to accept of,
attack'd Prince *Edward* in his advantageous Post, he being surrounded
with Hedges and Vineyards; but the *English,* by the help of their Bows,
soon broke through his Van-guard, and afterwards the whole Army,
which consisted of 50.000 Men, put them in Disorder, killing upon
the Spot (as it is related by the *French* Historians) 6000 *French,* among
whom were 1200 Gentlemen, the King and his youngest Son were both
made Prisoners: The three eldest had the good Fortune to escape {as
the situation began to decline, by the assistance of their majordomo
[*Hofmeister*]} \A. 1356\.

During the Father's Imprisonment *Charles* the *Dauphin* took <193>
upon him the Administration of Affairs, but the People which had

20. Not King Edward III, but his son Edward (1330–76), called the Black Prince,
who was father of Richard II.

been sorely oppress'd hitherto, being unwilling to obey it, caused great Disorders in the Kingdom. The Peasants rose up against the Nobility, and the Citizens of *Paris* made heavy Complaints. The Souldiers for want of Pay lived at Discretion, and made a miserable havock in the Country; *Charles* of *Navarre* added Fuel to the Fire, in hopes to make his own Advantage by these Troublesome times, and did not stick to make Pretensions to the Crown; yet Matters were composed with him at last. And the Estates of France refusing to accept of such Conditions as were proposed by the *English,* the King of *England* enter'd *France* with a great Army, and over-ran the greatest part of it, yet could not make himself Master of any fortify'd place. Then a Peace was concluded at *Bretigny,* a League from *Chartres;* by vertue of which the *French* were to surrender to the *English,* besides what they were possess'd of before, *Poictou, Xaintonge, Rochelle, Pais d' Aulnis, Angoumois, Perigord, Limosin, Quercy, Agenois,* and *Bigorre,* with the Sovereignty over them; besides this, *Calais,* and the Counties *d'Oye, Guisnes* and *Ponthieu,* and three Millions of Livres, as a Ransom for the King's person. This Peace \A. 1360\ was very hard for *France,* and continued not long.

A dishonourable Peace to France.

King *John,* forced by Necessity, was oblig'd to do another thing little becoming his Grandeur, for he sold his Daughter to *Galeas* Viscount of *Milan,* for 600.000 Crowns, giving her in Marriage to the said Viscount. This King presented his youngest Son *Philip* sirnamed *the 'Handy'* [Bold], with the Dukedom of *Burgundy,* it being vacant by the Death of the last Duke. From this *Philip* descended the famous Dukes of *Burgundy,* whose Territories, <at last,> devolved to the House of *Austria.* This King died in *England* \A. 1364\, whither he was gone to make satisfaction for his Son, who being a Hostage there had made his escape. Some say, that he went to see a Lady there, with whom he was much in love.

Charles the Wise.

§11. King *John* was succeeded by his Son *Charles* V. sirnamed *the Wise,* who prudently made <194> amends for the Rashness of his Grandfather and Father, never engaging himself in Battels with the *English,* but by protracting the War and secret Intrigues, endeavoured to tire out their Courage. The disbanded [French] Souldiers had mutineer'd, and were become so Insolent, that no body durst oppose them. These he sent into *Spain,* where *Pieter* sirnamed *the Cruel* and *Henry* I. fought for the Crown of *Castile.* These Forces had put the Pope in such a fear, that in their March he presented them with 200.000 Livres and a good store of Indulgences, to divert them thereby from taking their way near *Avignon.*[21] Prince *Edward* {of Wallis} also engaged himself in this War, but got nothing by it but a sickly Body and great want of Money. Wherefore he pretending to lay a Tax upon his Subjects in *Guienne,* to pay off his Souldiers, they complained thereof to the King of *France;* who having well prepared himself, and being informed that the Prince languished under a mortal Disease, summon'd him to appear in *Paris,* pretending, that the Peace made at *Bretigny* was of no force, since the *English* had not performed the Conditions, and had since that time committed Hostilities, wherefore he insisted upon his former right of Sovereignty over *Aquitain.* And Prince *Edward* having sent him a disdainful Answer, King *Charles* denounced War against the *English.*

A great many Fast-days and Processions were kept by the King's Order in *France;* and the Priests made it their business to represent the Justice of the King's Cause, and the Injustice of the *English* to the People. By this way he insinuated himself into the Favour of the *French* that lived under the *English* Jurisdiction, and persuaded his own Subjects to be more free in paying their Taxes. The Archbishop of *Tholouse* alone, did, by his cunning Persuasions, bring over to his Party above fifty Cities and strong Castles. The Constable *Bertrand du Guesolin* did also great mischief to the *English* with small Parties, and worsted them not only in several Rencounters, but also beat them out of *Perigord* and *Limosin:* But in *Guienne,* especially, the *English* Affairs were in a bad condition, after the *Spanish* Fleet, which was sent to the Assistance of the <195> *French* by *Henry* King of *Castile,* had ruin'd the *English* near *Rochelle.* After which exploit *Poictiers* was taken from them, and *Rochelle* upon very advantageous Conditions, surrender'd it self to the King of *France.* And King *Edward* being detained by contrary Winds, not being able to bring over timely Relief, *Xaintonge, Angoumois,* and some other places,

He declares War against the English.

---

21. The papal court was situated in Avignon from 1305 to 1378.

followed the Example of the former. The *English,* not long after, with an Army of 30.000 Men, marched from *Calais* cross the Country as far as *Guienne,* ravaging and plundering by the way where ever they came, yet would *Charles* never hazard a Battel with them, but contented himself to annoy them with Skirmishes, whereby he did them considerable Mischief. The Pope, in the mean while, labour'd hard to make Peace betwixt these two Crowns, but King *Edward* happening to die about that time [1377], King *Charles* took hold of this Opportunity, and attacking the *English* with five several Armies at one time, took all from them but *Calais, Bourdeaux* and *Bayonne* in *Guienne,* and *Cherbury* in *Normandy.* The *English,* during the Minority of their King,[22] being also pester'd with the Plague and the War with the Scots, were not in a Capacity to send sufficient Relief: Yet this King miscarried in his Enterprize against *Britainy.*

After the Death of Edward, Charles attacks the English with Advantage.

In the Year 1379, the Emperour *Charles* IV. came to visit him in *Paris,* where he constituted the *Dauphin* a perpetual Vicar of the Empire in *Dauphine:* And ever since, say the *French,* the *German* Emperours never did pretend to any thing in *Dauphine,* and in the Kingdom of *Arelat.* He died in the Year 1380.

Charles VI. §12. Now we are come to that most unfortunate Reign of *Charles* VI. at the very beginning of which, one of the main occasions of Mischief to *France* was, That *Joan* Queen of *Naples* standing in fear of *Charles de Duraz* [Durazzo], did adopt *Lewis* Duke of *Anjou,* declaring him Heir of that Kingdom. The Duke willingly accepting of her Offer, raised, in her behalf, an Army of 30.000 Horse, having employed thereunto the Treasure left by *Charles* V. which he had got clandestinely into his possession. With this Army he made <196> himself Master of *Provence,* which then belong'd to *Joan.* And tho' in the mean time *Charles de Duraz* having kill'd *Joan,* had made himself Master of the Kingdom, the Duke of *Anjou,* nevertheless, pursued his intended Expedition; but was, by continual Marches, and the Cunning of *Charles,* led about and

---

22. Richard II (1367–99), son of Edward the Black Prince (d. 1376) and grandson of Edward III.

tir'd to that degree, that he died in great Misery \A. 1384\, very few of so great an Army having had the good fortune to return into *France*.

The People also were generally much dissatisfy'd at the beginning, because those who had the Tuition of the King, to curry-favour with the People, had promised an abatement of the heavy Taxes. But the same being not long after again introduc'd, augmented and devoured by the Courtiers, great Troubles and Insurrections arose both in *Paris* and other places. In the mean while the *Flemings* had carried themselves insolently towards their Lord, who calling to his Assistance, the *French*, they killed 40.000 *Flemings*, together with their General *Arteville* \A. 1382\. The general Dissatisfaction of the People was much increased afterward, when a great Summ of Money was employed upon an Expedition against *England*, which proving fruitless, both the Money and Men were lost. *Lewis* Duke of *Orleans*, Brother of this King *Charles*, married *Valentina* the Daughter of *John Galeacius* Viscount of *Milan* \A. 1389\, with this Condition, That he should receive immediately, as a Dowry, not only a great Treasure of Money and Jewels, but also the County of *Ast*[*e*]; and in case her Father should die without Issue, the whole Country should be devolved on *Valentina* and her Children. Which Contract has not only furnished *France* with a Pretension to *Milan*, but also has been the occasion of great Calamities.

The first rise of the French Pretensions upon Milan.

After this another Misfortune happened to *France*, for the King, whose Brains were mightily weakened by Debaucheries in his younger Years, as he was travelling in *Britainy*, fell upon a sudden Distraction, caused, partly by the great Heat, which was then in the Month of *August*; partly, because, as 'tis reported, a tall black Man appear'd to him, who, stopping his Horse by the Bridle, said, *Stop King, whither will you go? you are betray'd.* <197> Soon after a Page being faln asleep {on a horse}, let the point of his Lance drop upon the Headpiece of him who rid [rode] just before the King, which the King being extreamly surpriz'd at, interpreted it as directed against him. And tho' this Madness did cease afterwards, yet was his Understanding much impair'd, and the Fits would return by intervals.

The King falls under an alienation of Mind.

This unhappy Accident was the occasion of that fatal Contest concerning the Administration of the Kingdom (which the King was incapable of) betwixt *Lewis* Duke of *Orleans,* the King's Brother, and *Philip* Duke of *Burgundy,* his Uncle. The first claim'd it on the account of proximity of Blood, the latter on account of his Age and Experience. The latter was most approv'd of by the Estates, who declar'd him Regent; yet the Duke of *Orleans,* by making new Intrigues, still endeavour'd to make himself the Head of the Kingdom, which caused pernicious Factions in the Court. And tho' the Duke of *Burgundy* died \A. 1404\, his Son *John* pursuing his Father's Pretensions, the Hatred so increased betwixt both Parties, that notwithstanding the Reconcilia-

The Duke of Orleans assassinated by the Duke of Burgundy. tion made betwixt them, the Duke of *Burgundy* caus'd the Duke of *Orleans* to be murther'd by some Ruffians, at Night, in the Streets of *Paris* \A. 1407\. And tho' the Duke of *Burgundy,* after having made away his Rival, and forc'd a Pardon from the King, was now the only Man in the Court, yet were the Animosities betwixt the Duke of *Burgundy,* and the Sons of the murther'd Duke of *Orleans,* not extinguish'd thereby, which divided the whole Kingdom into two Factions, one siding with the *Burgundian,* the other with the Family of *Orleans,* and occasion'd barbarous Murthers, Devastations, and such other Calamities, which are the common products of Civil Commotions. At last the *Burgundian* Faction was brought very low by the King and his Party.

The English take advantage of these Troubles. But the *English* having observ'd the intestine Divisions in *France,* landed in *Normandy* \A. 1415\ with a great Army, and took *Harfleur:* But being extremly weaken'd both in the Siege and by Sickness, they resolv'd to retreat towards *Calais.* In the mean while the *French* had got together an Army which was four times stronger than the *English,*

Battel of Agincourt. which met them <198> near *Agincourt,* a Village in the County of St. *Poll* [*Poldesperat*], where a Battel being fought betwixt them, 6000 *French* were kill'd upon the Spot, and a great number taken Prisoners, among whom were a great many persons of Quality. (The *English* Historians make this Defeat much greater, it being rarely to be observ'd, that the Historians of two Nations, who are at Enmity, agree in their Relations.)[23] Yet the *English* being extremly tir'd, could not pursue the Victory.

---

23. Pufendorf maintained that a historian's account, though written from a point of view, differed from the special pleading of a lawyer. See Seidler (1997), especially section III, pp. 210–15; and Piirimäe (2008).

In the mean time the Invasion made by a Foreign Enemy did in no ways diminish the intestine Divisions, but rather augmented them: For the Duke of *Burgundy* perceiving his Party in *France* to decline, began to favour the *English,* who, in the Year next following, landed again in *Normandy,* and had great Success. At last the Queen, who had hitherto had a share in the Government, added Fuel to the Fire: For the Constable *d' Armagnac* having now the sole Administration of Affairs, and being only balanc'd by the Authority of the Queen, took an opportunity, by the 'free Conversation' [overly loose living] of the Queen, to put such a Jealousie in the King's Head, that with the Consent of *Charles* the Dauphin she was banish'd [from] the Court. Which so incensed the Queen, that she having conceiv'd an implacable Hatred against her Son, sided with the Duke of *Burgundy,* whose Party was thereby greatly strengthen'd. Thus commenced the intestine Wars, wherein both Parties were so exasperated against one another, that they had little regard to the great Success of the *English,* who, in the mean time \A. 1419\ conquer'd all *Normandy* and *Roan* it self.

The Dauphin intending at one blow to root out the Evil of these intestine Commotions, cunningly invited the Duke of *Burgundy* to come to an Agreement with him, when at their second meeting at *Monterau,* he caused him to be kill'd. But this stroke had a quite contrary effect: For the generality of the Nation abominated the fact, and the Queen took from hence an Opportunity totally to ruin her Son, and to exclude him from the Succession. Wherefore, entring into a League with the murther'd Duke's Son *Philip,* a Peace was concluded with *Henry* V. King of *England,* by vertue of <199> which he was to marry *Catharine,* the Daughter of *Charles* VI. and during his Life to be Regent of *France,* and after his Death to be put into the full possession of the Crown of *France:* That both the Crowns of *France* and *England* should be united, yet that each Kingdom should be ruled according to its own Laws. Besides this, a Sentence was pronounc'd against the Dauphin in *Paris,* That by reason of the Murther committed by him upon the Duke of *Burgundy,* he was declared incapable of the Crown, and that he for ever should be banish'd the Kingdom. He appeal'd from this Sentence to God and his Sword, and set his Court up at *Poictiers,* so that at that time there was in *France* two Governments and two Courts. But the

The Duke of Burgundy assassinated.

Affairs of the Dauphin were in a very ill condition, very few of the
Provinces siding with him; those that did, were *Anjou, Poictou, Tours,
Auvergne, Berry* and *Languedock,* but all of them mightily exhausted of
Money. But it was happy for him, that the brave King *Henry* V. died in
the very Flower of his Age and good Fortune, as likewise did, not long
after, *Charles* VI. \A. 1422\ whose Life (by the Infirmities of his Mind,
being incapable of governing the Kingdom) had greatly obstructed the
Welfare of the Kingdom.

Charles VII.   §13. *Charles* VII. whom we hitherto have call'd *the Dauphin,* caused
himself, immediately after his Father's Death, to be proclaim'd King,
with the Assistance of the Bravest among the *French,* nevertheless his
Affairs at the beginning were under very ill Circumstances: For the
Duke of *Bedford,* who was constituted Regent in *France,* having caused
Henry VI.   young *Henry* VI. of *England* to be proclaimed King of *France* in *Paris,* in
of England   conjunction with the Dukes of *Burgundy* and *Britainy,* try'd all ways to
proclaim'd
King of   expell him quite out of *France.* His Forces were several times miserably
France.   beaten by the *English,* the greatest part of the Cities abandon'd him,
so that the *English* used to call him, in derision, *the King of* Bourges,
because he used commonly to reside there. He was at last become so
poor that he rarely could dine in Publick, and it was ob-<200>serv'd,
that one time he had nothing for his Dinner but a piece of roasted Mut-
ton and a couple of Fowls. Besides this, most of the great Men about
him being dissatisfy'd with the ambitious Proceedings of the Constable
Richmond, had left the Court, and were driving on their own Intrigues.
Misunder-   The only Comfort left to *Charles* was, that there was a misunderstand-
standings   ing betwixt the *English* and the Duke of *Burgundy;* else, if they had with
betwixt the
English and   their joint Forces vigorously attack'd *Charles,* he, in all probability could
the Duke of   not have held out long against them.
Burgundy
the only   The occasion happen'd thus; *Jaqueline* Countess of *Hennegau, Hol-*
Advantage   *land, Zealand* and *Friesland,* being divorced from her Husband, *John*
Charles had
left.   Duke of *Brabant,* a Cousin of the Duke of *Burgundy,* was married again
to the Duke of *Gloucester,* Brother of *Henry* V. The Duke of *Burgundy*
taking his Cousin's part, it caused great Heart-burning betwixt him
and the Duke of *Gloucester.* The Duke of *Bedford* endeavour'd to ap-

pease them, yet did the Duke of *Burgundy* from that time entertain a Grudge against the *English;* which encreased afterwards, when the *English* refused to put the City of *Orleans* into the Hands of the Duke of *Burgundy.* This City being besieged by the *English* was reduc'd to the utmost Extremity; the *French,* which attack'd a Convoy which was going to the *English* Camp, having been entirely beaten: Which Engagement is called *la journée des Haranes,* or, *the Battel of the Herrings.*[24] *Charles's* Affairs were then become so desperate that he had resolv'd to retire into *Dauphine,* when upon a sudden an unlook'd for help was sent him: For a Country Maid born in *Lorraine,* whose Name was *Joan,* did pretend that she was sent from God to relieve *Orleans,* and to see the King crowned at *Rheims.* Both which she effected, striking thereby great terrour into the *English;* whereas, on the other side, the *French* being greatly encouraged by this Success, saw their Affairs from henceforward mend every day. But this poor Wench following the Wars longer, as it seems, than she had in Commission,[25] was taken Prisoner making a Sally out of *Compeigne,* and being deliver'd to the *English,* was with great dishonour <201> burnt as a Witch at *Roan* \A. 1431\. The *English,* perceiving their Affairs not to go so forward as formerly, resolv'd to give them new Life and Vigour, by bringing over the young King *Henry,* and having him crowned in *Paris:* And to keep fair with the Duke of *Burgundy* they gave him the Counties of *Brie* and *Champaigne;* yet all this proved insufficient.

> The Maid of Orleans.

> The English Power declines in France.

The War therefore having been thus carried on for several Years only with light Skirmishes, both Parties being tir'd out, a Treaty was at last propos'd by Mediation of the Pope at *Arras;* but the *English* rigorously insisting upon their Pretensions, which were very hard, they were deserted by the Duke of *Burgundy,* who made a separate Peace with *Charles* \A. 1435\ upon very advantageous Conditions. There {soon} befell also the *English* another Misfortune by the Death of the Duke of *Bedford,* who hitherto had administered the Affairs in *France* with great

24. See above IV.15, at note 22, p. 140.

25. Pufendorf's language is more playful and condescending than Crull's: "das gute Mägdlein, da sie länger im Krieg verharrete, als ihre Commission [from God] gewesen war." On Joan of Arc (ca. 1412–31), also see IV.15, p. 140, above.

Prudence. After this the Cities of *France* surrender'd themselves one after another to *Charles;* among which was *Paris,* which submitted it self
to its natural Lord \A. 1436\. But because the *English* had made miserable havock throughout *France,* and the *French* Souldiers themselves
being ill paid, had committed great Depredations, without any Order
or Discipline, a great Famine ensu'd, and afterwards a great Plague. It is
related that the Wolves did snatch the Children out of the Streets of the
Suburbs of St. *Anthony* in *Paris.* The War having been thus protracted
for a considerable time, a Truce was concluded for some Years. The
King, to be rid of the Souldiers, sent them into *Alsace,* under pretence
to disturb the Council at *Basil* [Basel].[26] They killed at once 4000 *Swiss,*
but having lost double the number soon after, returned home again.

In the mean time the *English* were degenerated from their former
Valour, their Forces were extreamly diminish'd in *France,* and the Souldiers for want of Pay had given themselves over to Plunder. They wanted
good Officers, their Places were not well provided, and their Subjects
weary of the Government. *England,* at home, was divided within it self,
and the *English* weakened by two Overthrows, which they had received
from the *Scots.* <202> *Charles* therefore having met with this Opportunity, resolv'd to beat the *English* at once out of *France.* He took, for
a Pretence of the War, that they had broken the Truce in *Britainy* and
with the *Scots;* and attacking them with great Vigour in several places

He drives the   at once \A. 1449\, he drove them, within the space of thirteen Months,
English out of   {completely} out of *Normandy.* The next Year after he took from them
France.   *Aquitain, Bayonne* being the last which surrender'd it self \A. 1451\;
so that the *English* had nothing left on the Continent of *France* but
Calais and the County of *Guines: Bourdeaux* soon after revolted from
the *French,* and sought for Aid of the *English,* but the brave *Talbot*[27]
having been kill'd in an Engagement, it was retaken \A. 1453\ and {per-
manently} re-united to the *French* Crown, after it had been 300 Years in

26. The Council of Basel (1431–49) discussed, among other things, the relative authority of councils and pope and the reunion of the Western and Eastern
churches.

27. John Talbot, Earl of Shrewsbury (ca. 1388–1453)—an ancestor of Crull's
dedicatee. See p. 3, above.

the possession of the *English*. Thus did this King re-unite the mangled Kingdom, having expell'd the *English* out of its Bowels. Nevertheless he did not entirely enjoy the Fruits of his good Fortune, living at variance with his Son, who for the space of thirteen Years came not to Court. And being at last persuaded, that a Design was formed against his Life, it so disturb'd him, that for fear of being poisoned, he starved himself \A. 1461\.

§14. Him succeeded his Son *Lewis* XI. a cunning, resolute and malicious Prince, who laid the first Foundation of the absolute Power since exercised by the Kings of *France,* whereas formerly the Royal Power was kept under by the Authority of the great Men of the Kingdom. He began with reforming his Court and Ministers according to his Pleasure: Of which the great Men of the Kingdom foreseeing the Consequence, they enter'd into a League, which they called, *La Ligue du bien public, the League for the publick good;* wherewith they pretended to defend the Publick against the King's arbitrary Proceedings. Among these were the Dukes of *Burgundy* and *Britainy,* who were willing [eager] to keep the King within bounds.

    In the Year 1465, *Charles,* the young Duke of *Burgundy,* enter'd *France* with an Army, and fought a Battel with the King near *Montlehery,* wherein the Advantage was <203> near equal; but, because the King retreated a little backwards the Night following, the Duke of *Burgundy* pretended to have gained the Victory, which put him upon those Enterprizes which afterwards cost him his Life. The King extricated himself with a great deal of Cunning out of this danger, for he released the Taxes, and with great Promises and fine Words appeased the People, all which, as soon as the danger was pass'd, he revok'd at pleasure. To dissolve the knot of this Faction, he made Divisions betwixt the most powerfull, the bravest he brought over to his side by giving them particular Advantages, the rest he ruined by his Policy, especially by bribing their Friends and Servants. And being in great want of Money, he borrow'd great Summs of his Servants, and such as refused to lend, were put out of their Employments: Which, 'tis said, gave the first occasion, that the Offices were afterwards sold in *France.* But the Duke

Lewis XI.

He reduces the excessive Power of the Nobility.

A League against him.

The King's Politick Methods.

The Original of selling the Offices of France.

{Charles} of *Burgundy* persisted in his Opposition, who had in the Year
1468 hem'd him in at *Peronne,* which danger he however escaped. At
last *Lewis* was rid of this his troublesome Enemy, who had laid so many
Designs against him, he being kill'd by the *Swiss* near *Nancy* \A. 1477\.

Duke of
Burgundy
slain.

Lewis taking advantage of the great Confusion, which was occasioned
by the Death of the Duke in that Country, took possession of the Dukedom of *Burgundy,* under pretext that the same was an Appanage,[28] and
brought over to his side the Cities situated on the River *Some,* which
had been under the Jurisdiction of *Charles.* It was generally believ'd,
That *Lewis,* by way of Marriage, might easily have annexed the whole
Inheritance of this Duke unto *France,* if he had not conceived such an
implacable hatred against this House, that he was resolved to ruin it.
Two Years before the Death of the Duke of *Burgundy* King *Edward* IV.
landed with a great Army in *France,* whom *Lewis* with Presents and fair
Promises persuaded to return home again. He united to the Crown
Provence, Anjou and *Muns* [Maine], having obtained the same by the
last Will and Testament of *Charles d'Anjou,* Count *de Maine,* who was
the last Male Heir of the House of *Anjou;* notwithstanding that *Rene*
Duke of *Lorraine,* <204> Son of *Ygland d' Anjou* pretended a Right to
the same by his Mother's side. In his latter days he [Lewis] lived miserably, and grew {sometimes} ridiculous, being in continual fear of death.
He died in the Year 1483.

Charles VIII.

§15. His Son *Charles* VIII. had at the beginning of his Reign his Hands
full with the Duke of *Britainy,* and was marching with an Army to unite
that Province by main [Fr. 'hand'] force to the Crown. But understanding that *Maximilian* of *Austria* had concluded a Match betwixt *Anna,*
the only Heiress of this Dukedom and himself, the *French* King did
think it no ways adviseable to let such a delicious Morsel fall to the
share of the House of *Austria,* but obliged the Bride, partly by force,

Britainy united
to France.

partly by fair words, to renounce *Maximilian,* and to be married to
himself \A. 1491\, whereby this Country was united to *France.* And

28. An *appanage* was a grant of land, title, or office given to younger sons of
royalty in place of the right to inherit.

tho' *Henry* VII. King of *England,* did not look with a good Eye upon the growing Power of *France,* and therefore with a great Army besieged *Boulogne,* yet in consideration of a good Summ of Money he was prevailed upon to return home again; especially, since *Maximilian* (who had received a double affront from *Charles,* who had not only taken his Bride from him, but also had sent back his Daughter *Margaret,* which was promised to him in Marriage)[29] did not join his Forces with him according to Agreement. *Maximilian* took *Arras* and St. *Omer,* but being not able to go further he consented, that his Son *Philip,* Lord of the *Netherlands,* might make a Truce with *Charles.* On the other side, *Charles* gave to *Ferdinand the Catholick,* the Counties of *Russilion* [Roussillon] and *Cerdagne,* some say, to engage him thereby not to oppose his intended Expedition against *Naples.* Others say, that *Ferdinand* corrupted *Charles'*s Confessour, to persuade him, that he should restore that Country to its lawfull Sovereign.

France being thus by the Union with *Britainy* become an entire Kingdom, it began to contrive how to obtain the Sovereignty over *Italy. Charles* had a Pretension, because the Right and Title of the Family of *Anjou* and *Naples* was by the Death of the last Duke of *Anjou* and Earl of *Provence* devolv'd to <205> *Lewis* XI. and consequently to himself. But this young King received the greatest Encouragement from *Lewis* sirnamed *Morus,* or *the Black,* Duke of *Milan,* who, having Tuition of his Nephew *John Galeas,* the true Heir of this Dukedom, but a weak Prince, had under that Pretence made himself Master of the same. This Duke fearing that he might be put out of possession by *Ferdinand* King of *Naples,* whose Son *Alfonsus'*s Daughter *Isabella* was married to *John Galeas,* endeavour'd to give *Ferdinand* his Hands full of Work, that he might not be at leisure to think of him; knowing also, that *Ferdinand* and his Son *Alfonsus* were much hated by their Subjects for their Tyranny and Impiety. An Expedition was therefore undertaken against *Naples* \A. 1494\, which proved the occasion of continual Miseries to

An Expedition to Naples, and the Pretensions of it.

29. Charles had been engaged to Maximilian's daughter, Margaret of Austria (1480–1530). According to the Treaty of Arras (1482), she had been educated in France in preparation for this marriage.

Italy for the space of forty Years; for so long it was the Cock-pit for the *French, Germans* and *Spaniards,* and at last lost a great part of its \<ancient\> Liberty.

Charles conquer'd Naples. It seem'd to be ||[fatal to *Italy,*]|[30] that the wise *Italians* either could or would not prevent this Expedition, which was design'd two Years before. *Charles* had at the beginning all the Success imaginable, for the *Italian* Troops were in a very ill condition, and there being no body who durst oppose him, *Florence* and the Pope sided with him, the latter declaring *Charles* King of *Naples.* King *Alfonsus* stirr'd up by his own Conscience, abdicated himself, transferring all his Right and Title upon his Son *Ferdinand:* But his Forces being soon beaten and dispers'd, *Charles* made his solemn Entry into *Naples* with loud Acclamations \A. 1495\. Immediately the whole Kingdom submitted to him, except the Isle of *Iseria* [Ischia], and the Cities of *Brundisi* and *Gallipoli.* The Conquest of so fair a Kingdom, and that within five Months time, struck a Terrour into the *Turkish* Emperour himself, being in fear at *Constantinople,* and *Greece* being ready to rebell as soon as the *French* should land on that side.

But the Face of Affairs was quickly changed; for the *French,* by their ill behaviour quickly lost the Favour of the *Neapolitans;* the King minded nothing but Gaming, and the rest following his Example, were careless in maintaining \<206\> their Conquest. Besides this, it was look'd upon as a thing of such Consequence by the rest of the Princes of *Europe,* that the Emperour, the Pope, King *Ferdinand* of *Arragon, Venice* and *Milan* enter'd into a Confederacy, to drive the *French* out of *Italy; Charles* therefore fearing lest his Retreat might be cut off, took his Way by Land into *France,* having left things but in an indifferent state of Defence in *Naples.* In his March he was met by the Confederate Army near the River of *Taro,* where a Battel was fought, in which, tho' there were more kill'd on the Confederate side than of the *French,* yet he marched forward with such Precipitation, as if he had lost the Battel. *Charles* was no sooner returned into *France,* but *Ferdinand* soon retook, without great trouble, the Kingdom of *Naples,* to the great Dishonour

The League of Italy against the French.

He loseth Naples.

30. Rather: "a strange punishment of God."

of the *French*, who were not able to maintain themselves there a whole Year, of whom very few return'd alive into *France*. Not long after *Charles* died without Issue \A. 1498\.

§16. Him succeeded *Lewis* XII. formerly Duke of *Orleans*, who, not to lose *Britainy*, married *Anna* Widow of the late King. He made {a new} War soon after on *Milan*, pretending a Right to that Dukedom by his Grandmother's {Valentina's} side, and having conquer'd the same within '21' [twenty] days \A. 1499\. *Lewis the Black* was forc'd to fly with his Children and all his Treasure into *Germany*. But the Inhabitants of *Milan* grew quickly weary of the *French*, their 'free Conversation' [liberties] with the Women being especially intolerable to them, and therefore recall'd their Duke, who having got together an Army of *Swiss* was joyfully receiv'd, and regain'd the whole Country, except the Castle of *Milan* and the City of *Novara*. But *Lewis* sending timely Relief, the Duke's *Swiss* Souldiers refused to fight against the *French*, so that the Duke endeavouring to save himself by flight in a common Souldiers Habit, was taken Prisoner, and kept ten Years in Prison at *Loches*, where he died. Thus the *French* got *Milan* and the City of *Genoua* again.

After so great Success *Lewis* began to think of the Kingdom of *Naples:* To obtain which, <207> he made a League with *Ferdinand the Catholick*, wherein it was agreed, that they should divide the Kingdom betwixt them, so that the *French* should have for their share *Naples*, *Terre de Labour* and *Abruzze;* and the *Spaniards*, *Poville* and *Calabria*. Each of them got his share without any great trouble, *Frederick* King of *Naples* surrendring himself to King *Lewis* \A. 1501\, who allowed him a yearly Pension of 30.000 Crowns [escus].[31] But soon after new Differences arose betwixt these two haughty Nations, concerning the Limits; for the *French* pretended that the Country of *Capitanate* (which is very considerable for its Taxes paid for Sheep, which are there in great numbers) did belong to *Abruzze*, whereas the *Spaniards* would have it belong

Marginal notes: Lewis XII. · He conquers Milan. · He conquers Naples.

---

31. The *escu* (*écu*), a French gold coin worth about three pounds and bearing the imprint of a shield, circulated between the fourteenth and seventeenth centuries, when it was replaced by the Louis d'or.

to *Poville;* and from Words they came to Blows. The *French,* at first, had somewhat the better; but as soon as *Gonsalvus de Cordoua,* that cunning *Spaniard* had broke their first Fury, and *Lewis* did not send suf-

Loses it again. ficient Relief, they were as shamefully beaten again out of the Kingdom \A. 1503\, as they had been before.[32] *Lewis* endeavoured to revenge himself upon the *Spaniards* in the Year next following, but tho' he attack'd them with four several Armies, yet could he not gain any thing upon them: Wherefore he made a Peace with *Ferdinand,* and enter'd into an Alliance with him against *Philip* Son-in-law to *Ferdinand,* who having, after the death of *Isabella,* taken from him the Kingdom of *Castile,* was upheld by his Father *Maximilian,* and back'd by *Henry* [VII] King of *England,* whose Son had married his Wife's Sister.

In the Year 1507, the City of *Genoua* rebell'd against *Lewis,* but was

The Venetian War. soon reduced to her former Obedience. Then the War began afresh in *Italy,* with the *Venetians,* who being too much addicted to self-interest, had drawn upon themselves the hatred of all their Neighbours, having encroached upon every one of them; and *Lewis* especially attributed to

Lewis joins in the League against them. them his loss of the Kingdom of *Naples.* To humble this proud State a League was concluded at *Cambray* \A. 1508\, betwixt the Emperour, the Pope, the Kings of *France* and *Spain. Lewis,* by entring into a Confederacy with his mortal Enemies, had more regard to his <208> Passion than his Interest, it being certain that he might upon all occasions have trusted to the Friendship of the *Venetians.* But now he was the first that fell upon them, and defeated them in a great Battel near *Giera d'Addua* \A. 1509\, which caused such a Terror among them, that they left all what they had on the Continent, within twenty days, and if *Lewis* had pursued his Victory whilst they were under this first Consternation, he might doubtless have put a period to their Greatness. But in the mean time that he marched back towards *Milan,* not making the best of his Victory, they got leisure to recover themselves; especially since the Em-

A League against Lewis. perour *Maximilian* was not in earnest against them, and Pope *Julius* II. was reconciled to them. Nay, in the Year 1510, the Pope, *Ferdinand, Henry* VIII. and the *Swiss Cantons,* denounced War against *Lewis.* For

32. See above at II.9, note 20, p. 58.

the Pope could not look with a good Eye upon the growing Power of *France* in *Italy, Ferdinand* feared lest *Lewis* might attack *Naples,* and *Henry* being come lately to the Crown, was for making himself famous by so great an Undertaking; the *Swiss* were set against *France,* because *Lewis* had not paid them their old Arrears, and had refused to encrease their Pension, not because their Demands were extravagant, but because he would not be out brav'd [importuned] by them. In this War the *French* General *Gasto de Foix* behaved himself very gallantly; for he relieved *Bononia,* beat the *Venetian* Army, killed 8000 of them in *Brescia,* and obtained a glorious Victory against the Confederate Army near *Ravenna* \A. 1512\; in which Battel, nevertheless, this brave General, being too hot in pursuing the Enemy, was slain.

With his death the *French* Affairs began to decline, and they were again forced to leave *Italy. Maximilian,* Son of *Lewis the Black* was restored to his Dutchy of *Milan* by the help of the *Swiss:* The *Genouese* revolted, and made *Janus Fregosus* their Duke. *Ferdinand the Catholick* took from King *John* the Kingdom of *Navarre,* which the *French* in vain endeavoured to regain from the *Spaniards.* But *Lewis* being extreamly desirous to regain *Milan* enter'd into a League with *Venice,* and retook most places of <209> that Dukedom and the City of *Genoua.* He besieg'd Duke *Maximilian* in the Castle of *Novara,* but the *Swiss* coming to the Assistance of the Duke, attack'd the *French* with incredible Fury in their Camp, and drove them quite out of the whole Dukedom, which was twice taken in one Month {A. 1513}. Then *Lewis* was at one time attack'd by the Emperour, *England,* and the *Swiss;* and if the *English* and the *Swiss* had join'd, *France* would have run a great Risque: But King *Henry,* in lieu of entring into the Heart of *France,* lost his Time at the Siege of *Terouene* [Terouanne], where he defeated the *French,* that were come to its Relief, near *Guinegast;* this Battel was call'd *La journée des esperons,* or *The Battel of the Spurs,* because the *French* made better use of their Spurs than their Swords;[33] and after he had taken *Tournay,* he return'd into *England.* The *Swiss,* who kept the Duke of *Tremoville* besieg'd, were bought off with 600.000 Crowns [escus], which were

He conquers Milan again.

He is attack'd by several Princes at once.

33. That is, they spurred their horses to accelerate their retreat.

promised to them by the Duke without the King's Order, as likewise, that he should renounce the Council of *Pisa* and his Pretensions to the Dukedom of *Milan*. Which shamefull Agreement the King refus'd to ratify; and if the *Swiss* had not been more fond of the Ransom offer'd for the Hostages {given them by Tremouille} than their Blood, they [the hostages] had pay'd with their Lives for it. In the Year next following *Lewis* made a Peace with the King of *England,* who gave him his Sister *Mary* in Marriage; which young Lady, 'tis thought, did hasten the Death of the old King, which ensu'd in the beginning of the Year 1515. This King was so well belov'd by his People, that he was generally call'd, *Le Pere du Peuple,* or *The Father of the People.*

Francis I. §17. His Nephew *Francis* I. succeeded him, who having made a League with *England,* the Archduke *Charles* and *Venice,* enter'd upon a sudden into *Italy,* and took *Genoua* and some other Places without great Opposition; but being encamp'd near *Marignano,* within a League of *Milan,* the *Swiss* unexpectedly fell upon him, where a bloody Fight ensu'd [in 1515]. The *Swiss* were at last repuls'd, and found that they cou'd be beaten, having lost above 10.000; but the *French* <210> also left 4000 of their best Men upon the Spot. After this *Maximilian*[34] surrender'd himself and the whole Country to the King, on the Condition of an annual Pension of 30.000 Ducats to be paid him.

Soon after the King agreed with the *Swiss,* whom in Consideration of a good Summ, he brought again into an Alliance with *France.* He made also an Agreement with Pope *Leo* X. by vertue of which the King was to have the Right of naming Bishops and Abbots, but the Pope to keep certain Benefits out of the chiefest Church Benefices. In the Year 1518, he redeem'd *Tournay* from the *English* for a good Summ of Money. He aspires to In the Year next following, after the Death of the Emperor *Maximilian,* the Empire. *Francis* employ'd all his Engines to be exalted to the Imperial Dignity; but the *German* Princes fearing lest the *French* should endeavour to humble them, and for some other Considerations, preferr'd before him *Charles* V. This proved the Occasion of great Jealousies betwixt these

34. Maximilian Sforza, Duke of Milan, 1493–1530.

two Princes; for *Francis* being very sensible what great Advantages he [Charles] had gained by the Imperial Dignity, put himself into a good posture, to prevent his becoming Master of him and all the rest of the Princes in *Europe*. This Jealousie broke at last out into an open War, *Francis* endeavouring to re-take *Navarre* from the *Spaniards*, as thinking to have met with a fair Opportunity, whilst the Divisions in *Spain* were on Foot. The *French* conquer'd that Kingdom in a few days time, but being not carefull enough to preserve it, as easily lost it again \A. 1521\. *In a few Days he takes and loses the Kingdom of Navarre.*

Soon after the War was kindled in the *Netherlands,* occasion'd by *Robert Van de Marck,* Lord of *Sedan,* whom *Francis* took into his Protection. This *Robert* was so puft up with the *French* Protection, that he writ a Letter of Defiance to the Emperour, and fell into the Country of *Luxemburgh.* But *Charles* quickly chastis'd this petty Enemy; and being persuaded that *Francis* had encourag'd him thereunto, he took from him St. *Amand* and *Tournay.* The Business nevertheless might have been compos'd at the beginning, if the *French* had not insisted upon keeping *Fonterabia,* which in the mean time had been surpris'd by them. But the hardest task was in *Italy,* both the <211> Emperour and Pope being willing to drive *Francis* out of *Milan,* and to restore *Francis Sforza.* They effected both with good Success, for the *French* Army was not timely supply'd with Money, and being, besides this, beaten near *Bicoque,* the *French* were again driven out of *Milan* and *Genoua* \A. 1521\. And on the other side they also lost *Fonterabia.* *A War kendled in Italy.* *The French driven out of Milan.*

But what happen'd very ill to *Francis,* was, That the Constable *Charles* of *Bourbon* went over to the Emperour; the Reason of which was, That he had been for a while mightily kept under by the Queen Mother, the Chancellour *Duprat,* and Admiral *Bonnivet.* The first had commenc'd a Suit at Law against him about the Dukedom of *Bourbon,* which he despair'd to be able to maintain against so strong a Party, as believing [since he believed] that the King was underhand concern'd in the Matter. 'Tis said, that the first Cause of this Difference was, because the Duke of *Bourbon* had {not reciprocated her love for him, and had} refus'd to marry her. The Duke of *Bourbon* therefore had agreed with the Emperor and the King of *England,* That they should divide the Kingdom of *France* betwixt them; the Kingdom of *Arelat* and the Em- *The Duke of Bourbon revolts to the Emperour.*

perour's Sister having been promis'd to the Duke of *Bourbon*. But the Design being discover'd, the Duke of *Bourbon* was forc'd to fly into *Italy*. Notwithstanding the *English* had made an Inrode into *Picardy* \A. 1524\, *Francis* sent again an Army into the *Milaneze*, under the Command of the Admiral *Bonnivet*, which was beaten back with considerable loss by the Duke of *Bourbon*. This *Bonnivet* persuaded the King to go in Person into *Italy*, with this prospect, that if Things succeeded well, he [Bonnivet] should have the Glory of having been the 'Adviser' [initiator], but if they succeeded ill, the Misfortune would be cover'd by the King's Person. *Francis* therefore went with a good Resolution into *Italy*, because he saw the Duke of *Bourbon*, who in the mean time having enter'd *Provence*, had besieged *Marseilles*, did retreat before him, and having laid Siege to *Pavia*, he for two Months together harrass'd his Army in that Siege. In the mean while the Imperialists drew their Forces together, and march'd against him (who was encamp'd in the Parks [*Thiergarten*]) with an Intention either to <212> fight him or to relieve *Pavia*. *Francis* engaged with them in a Battel, but was defeated and taken Prisoner \A. 1525\. And thus the *French* were again driven {completely} out of *Italy*.

Francis defeated at the Battel of Pavia, and taken Prisoner.

Francis was carry'd into *Spain*, and kept very hardly, so that he fell sick for Grief; which hastened his Liberty, it being fear'd that he might die through Vexation. Besides that, *England* and the *Italian* Princes enter'd into a Confederacy to hinder the growing Power of *Charles*. The Conditions upon which he obtain'd his Liberty we have touch'd upon in another place;[35] but besides this, *Francis* gave his Parole of Honour, if the said Conditions were not fulfill'd, That he would return a Prisoner. But the wiser Sort did sufficiently foresee, that *Francis* would not perform the Agreement, wherefore *Gattinara* the Chancellour [of Charles V] refused to sign the Treaty, alledging, That *Charles* could get nothing else by this Treaty but the implacable Hatred of the *French*, and to be ridicul'd by every Body; that |[he had been bubbl'd and disappointed in his covetous Designs.]|[36] And *Francis* having obtain'd his

35. See above at II.10, pp. 61–62.
36. Rather: "his mind had been confused."

Liberty after thirteen Months Imprisonment, pretended, That what had been done was done {under constraint} in Prison, and contrary to his Coronation Oath which he had taken at *Rheims;* That the Kingdom was not in his disposal, he having only the use of the same for Life. The same was alledged by the Estates, and especially, by the *Burgundians,* who would in no ways consent to be separated from the Crown of *France.* If *Charles* was so much for having *Burgundy,* he ought to have taken care to have been put into possession of the same, before he set *Francis* at liberty.

As soon as *Francis* had got his Liberty, he made it his first Business to renew the League with *England* and the *Italian* States. And the new Treaty having proved fruitless which was set on foot with the Emperour, both Kings [Henry and Francis] denounced War against him. *Charles* afterwards accusing *Francis* of not having kept his Parole, the latter gave the first the Lye [accused the former of lying], sending him also a Challenge {to a duel}, which Matters were look'd upon by the World as very unbecomming the Grandeur of such 'Princes' [potentates]. *Francis* sent, after this, an Army into *Italy* under the Command of *Odet de Foix Lautree,* which <213> having made considerable progresses in the *Milaneze,* enter'd the Kingdom of *Naples,* and having taken a great many places there, laid Siege before the Capital City it self. But the *French* Affairs receiv'd the first Shock there, when *Andrew Doria,* the Admiral, leaving the *French* side, went over to the Emperour, he being dissatisfy'd that the King had refus'd to conferr upon him the Government of his Native City *Genoua,* and to restore to the *Genouese, Savona.* This *Doria* is deservedly praised, for that, when he might have been Lord of his Native Country, he chose rather to procure its Liberty, which it enjoys to this Day. But *Doria* leaving the *French* side, was the occasion that the City of *Naples* could not be cut off of their Communication by Sea. And the Plague began to reign in the Army during this long Siege, which devoured the greatest part of it, and the General himself. The Remnants of the Army were miserably treated, the Officers being made Prisoners, and the common Souldiers disarmed; the *French* were also oblig'd to quit *Milan* and *Genoua.* At last, the Emperour having obtained his Aim, and *Francis* being very desirous to see his Children at Liberty

He with the King of England declare War against the Emperour.

He sends an Army into Italy.

Peace made at
Cambray. again, a Peace was concluded betwixt them at *Cambray* \A. 1529\, by vertue of which, *Francis* pay'd two Millions of Ducats as a Ransom for his Sons, and renounced the Sovereignty over *Flanders, Artois, Milan* and *Naples.* And this was all the Benefit which this King and his Predecessours had reapt from the *Italian* Wars.

The War
breaks out
afresh. Nevertheless, some Years after \A. 1535\, the War began afresh, at which time *Francis* found a new way to make himself Master of the *Milaneze,* by first securing to himself the Dukedom of *Savoy.* Wherefore he made Pretensions upon *Charles* Duke of *Savoy* concerning the Inheritance of his Mother, descended out of the House of *Savoy,* and for some other Reasons he fell upon him, and took most of his strong Holds. In the mean time died *Francis Sforza* Duke of *Milan,* wherefore the Emperour was resolv'd to annex this Country to his House, but *Francis* could by no means digest the loss of it. *Charles* therefore entered *Provence* in person with an Army of 40.000 Foot and 16.000 Horse, ransack'd *Aix* and be-<214>sieged *Marseilles,* which however he could not take[,] his Army being in a Month's time greatly diminish'd by Sickness. An Army of 30.000 Men also enter'd *Picardy* from the *Netherlands,* which took *Guise,* but was beaten from before *Peronne;* yet afterwards took St. *Pol* and *Monstrevil. Francis* summoned the Emperour before him as his Vassal concerning *Flanders* and *Artois,* alledging, that the Sovereignty of these Provinces was inseparable from the Crown, and made an Alliance with the *Turks.* The first seemed to be very ridiculous to most People, the last very unbecoming a Christian Prince. The *French* however [did] reply, That this Alliance was eagerly sought for by

The Truce
prolong'd for
nine Years. the Emperour himself. At last {A. 1538}, by the Mediation of the Pope, the Truce which was the Year before made at *Nissa* [Nice] in *Provence* was prolong'd for nine Years, and these two great Rivals gave afterwards one another a Visit at *Aigues Mortes.* And when in the Year next following the City of *Ghent* rebell'd, *Charles* had such a Confidence in *Francis,* that he took his Journey through *France,* tho' *Charles* in the mean while had cunningly given *Francis* some Hopes of the Recovery of *Milan;* which however afterwards he would not acknowledge, because upon the Persuasions of the Constable *Montmorency,* the King had not

taken from him any Security under his Hand[37] during his stay in *Paris;* which some alledge to be one reason why *Montmorency* afterwards fell into Disgrace.

But the Truce was broke again \A. 1542\, under pretence, That the Governour of *Milan* had caused to be kill'd *Caesar Fregosus* and *Anthony Rinco* the Ambassadours of *Francis,* as they were going along the River *Po* in their Way to *Venice,* the first of whom was to have gone from thence to *Constantinople. Francis* thought to have met now with a fair Opportunity, because *Charles* had suffered a considerable loss before *Algier.* He therefore attack'd the Emperour with five several Armies at once. But the strongest of all, which lay before *Perpignan* did nothing, the Second took some Places in the Country of *Luxemburgh.* The Emperour *Salyman*[38] also made a great Diversion in *Hungary,* taking *Gran* and 'some other Places' [*Stulweissenburg*]. The great Pyrate *Barbarossa* <215> arriv'd in *Provence* with his Fleet, but did more mischief than good to *France.* But *Charles,* on the other hand, made an Alliance with *Henry* VIII. who was dissatisfy'd with *Francis,* because he had taken part with the *Scots,* and would not renounce his Obedience to the Pope. He, after he had beat the Duke of *Cleves,* who depended on the *French,* besieged *Landrecy* with a great Army, but to no purpose. In the mean time the *French* had obtain'd a most signal Victory over the Imperial Forces near *Cerisolles* in *Piedmont.* But the King could not prosecute his Victory, being obliged to recall his Troops, because the Emperour and *Henry* King of *England* had made an Agreement with an Army of 80.000 Foot and 22.000 Horse, to fall into *France;* the first by the Way of *Champagne,* the second by the Way of *Picardy,* to join their Forces near *Paris,* to ransack the City and all the adjacent Countries as far as to the River *Loire.* The Emperour took by the Way *Luxemburgh,* lay six Weeks before *Disier,* got abundance of Provision in *Espernay* and *Chasteau Thierry,* which put the whole City of *Paris* into a great Consternation; and no small Danger seemed to threaten that City, if

Francis breaks the Truce.

37. That is, in writing.
38. Suleiman the Magnificent (1494–1566).

King *Henry* had joined his Forces in time, according to his Promise: But he losing his Time in the Sieges of *Boulogne* and *Monstrevil, Charles* hearkened to a Peace, which was concluded at *Crespy* \A. 1544\. By vertue of this Peace all the Places were restored, and the Emperour promised to the Duke of *Orleans,* the second Son of the King, either his or his Brother's Daughter in Marriage, and to give for her Dowry either *Milan* or the *Netherlands;* which was not performed, because the said Duke died in the Year next following. *Francis* also made a Peace with *England* \A. 1546\, under Condition that he should have liberty to redeem *Boulogne* for a certain Summ of Money. He died in the Year 1547.

§18. Him succeeded his Son *Henry* II. to whom fell the Marquisate of *Saluzze* \A. 1548\, as a Fief of *Dauphine,* the last Marquiss *Gabriel* dying without Issue. He severely chastiz'd the City of *Bourdeaux* \A. 1549\, which had rebelled against him. In the Year next following \A. 1550\ he <216> redeemed *Boulogne* for a certain Summ of Money from the *English.* In the Year 1551, the Emperour being engaged in a War against the *Turks,* and the *German* Princes being very jealous of his Greatness, *Henry* thought to have met with a fit Opportunity to break with him. He began therefore in the *Netherlands* and *Piedmont;* and having made an Alliance with *Maurice* Elector of *Saxony,* he marched with his Army towards the *Rhine* \A. 1552\, and surpriz'd by the Way the Cities of *Metz, Toul* and *Verdun,* and would have done the same with *Strasbourgh,* if they had not been upon their Guard there. But the Elector of *Saxony* having made a Peace with the Emperour without including the King, and some Princes intreating him not to advance farther into the Empire he marched back into the Country of *Luxembourgh,* where he took some Places. The Emperour then besieged *Metz* with an Army of 100.000 Men, but the Duke of *Guise* defended himself so bravely, that the Emperour was obliged to raise the Siege with great loss. To revenge this Affront, he attack'd *Terouanne* in *Artois* with great Fury, and rased to the Ground this Fortress, which had proved hitherto so troublesome to the *Netherlands.* The same he did to *Hesdin,* both the Garrisons being put to the Sword. On the other side the *French* took

A Peace concluded at Crespy.

Henry II.

His Expedition into Germany.

Siena in *Italy*, and several Places in the Island of *Corsica*, but were again beaten out of *Siena* \A. 1555\, after they had been maul'd near *Marciano*.

In the Year 1556, a Truce was concluded at *Vaucelles* near *Cambray*, the Emperour being desirous to leave the Kingdom to his Son (to whom he had surrender'd the same) in Peace.[39] But the Truce was scarce confirm'd by Oath, when the *French*, upon the Instigation of Pope *Paul* IV. broke the same again, who having some Differences with *Spain* persuaded *Henry* to take his part. The Duke of *Guise* was therefore sent into *Italy* with an Army, but did nothing worth mentioning. In the meantime King *Philip* had gathered an Army of 50.000 Men, hoping thereby to establish his Reputation in the beginning of his Reign, and having also drawn *England* into the War, he besieged St. *Quintin*, into which place the Admiral *Gaspar Coligny* had thrown <217> himself. The Constable *Montmorency* advanced with an Army to the Relief of the Place, but retreating again in sight of the Enemies, they fell upon him, and gave him a terrible Defeat \A. 1557\. *France* had been then in the utmost danger, if this Victorious Army had march'd directly towards *Paris,* and if the Enemies Design upon *Lyons* had not miscarry'd. But King *Philip* feared least the Duke of *Savoy*, who commanded his Army, might take this Opportunity to reconcile himself to *France* upon some advantageous Conditions; wherefore he would not let him march on far into the Country, but took St. *Quintin* by Storm, and lost his Time in the taking of *Han, Chastelet* and *Noyon*. This gave leisure to the *French* to recollect themselves, and having recall'd the Duke of *Guise* out of *Italy*, they retook *Calais,* and those few other places which remained under the *English* thereabouts, as likewise *Thionville* in the Year 1559.

In the same Year a Project was set on foot, to unite the Kingdom of *Scotland* with *France,* by a Marriage betwixt Queen *Mary* and the Dauphine *Francis;*[40] but the same miscarried, no Children being born of them. The Mareschal *de Fermes,* who made an Inrode into *Flanders* was soundly beaten near *Gravelingen*. At last a Peace was concluded at

A Truce between Charles V. and Henry II.

A Project to unite Scotland with France miscarried.

39. Charles V (1500–1558) abdicated in 1556, leaving his Spanish possessions to his son, Philip II (1527–98). His brother, Ferdinand I (1503–64) inherited the Austrian possessions and the title of Holy Roman Emperor.

40. Mary Stuart, Queen of Scots (1542–87), was married to Francis II (1544–60).

Chasteau en Cambresis, which prov'd very pernicious for *France;* because, for <the Castle of *Cambray,*> the {three} Cities of *Han, Chastelet*
and *St. Quintin,* there were not only 198 Places redeliver'd to *Spain* {and
others}, and the Duke of *Savoy* restor'd, but also this Peace was partly
the Occasion of those intestine Wars, which afterwards miserably tore
in pieces the Kingdom of *France.* It was also resolv'd in *France* not to
intermeddle any more in the *Italian* Affairs, and to dissolve the Alliance with the *Turks.* After this Peace was concluded *Henry* was kill'd
in a Turnament, a Splinter of a broken Lance having got into his Eye;
for the King had challeng'd the Earl of *Montgomery* to run against him
with an open Vizier, and as soon as he was wounded he lost both his
Senses and Speech, and died within eleven days. By this Accident, the
Wedding which he celebrated for his Sister *Margaret,* which was married to *Chilibert* [Philibert] *E-<218> manuel* Duke of *Savoy,* was very
mournfully consummated.

Francis II.   §19. Him succeeded his Son *Francis* II. under whose Reign the *French*
Divisions began to break out with Fury in their own Bowels, which
continued near 40 Years, whereas formerly the violent Heat of this Nation had been quell'd, partly by the Wars with the *English,* partly by the
The Causes of   several Expeditions undertaken against *Italy.* Concerning the Causes
the intestine   of these Intestine Wars, it is to be observ'd, That after the House of
Wars of
France.   *Valois* came to the Crown, the next in Blood were those of the House
of *Bourbon,* which House was grown so Potent, by its Riches, Power
and Authority of a great many brave Persons, which descended from
it, that the preceding Kings were grown extreamly jealous of it. And,
tho' *Francis* I. at the beginning of his Reign did constitute {Charles} the
Duke of *Bourbon* Constable; yet being soon convinced afterwards, of
the Reasons which had induc'd his Ancestors to keep under this House,
he us'd all his Endeavours to humble the said *Charles* of *Bourbon.* For
this Reason he enter'd into a Conspiracy against *Francis,* which having
been discover'd, he went over to *Charles* V. and commanded as General
in the Battel near *Pavia,* where *Francis* was taken Prisoner, and was slain
in the storming of *Rome* \A. 1527\. By his Death the House of *Bourbon*
receiv'd a great blow, those who were left being look'd upon with a very

ill Eye, tho' they kept themselves very quiet to extinguish the Suspicion and Hatred conceiv'd against them.

The House of *Bourbon* being thus brought very low, the two Houses of *Montmorency* and *Guise* held up their Heads under the Reign of *Francis* I. The first was one of the most ancient in *France;* the latter was a Branch of the House of *Lorrain.* The Head of the first was *Annas Montmorency,* Constable of *France;* of the latter *Claude* Duke of *Guise.* Both of them were in great Favour and Authority with *Francis* I. but both fell into Disgrace at the latter end of his Reign, being banish'd [from] the Court. It is related of *Francis* I. that just before his Death he advised his Son *Henry* to con-<219>sult with neither of them in his Affairs, since too great and too able Ministers proved often dangerous. Yet notwithstanding this, *Henry* II. did receive both *Annas Montmorency* and *Francis de Guise,* the Son of *Claude,* into his particular Favour; who quickly grew jealous of one another, the first taking much upon him[41] because of his Experience in State Affairs, and Gravity, the latter being puff'd up with the Glory of Martial Exploits, and the Applause of the People; the Authority of the Duke of *Guise* was greatly encreas'd after he had repuls'd *Charles* V. from before *Metz,* and taken *Calais;* whereas the unfortunate Battel fought near St. *Quintin,* and the ensuing dishonourable Peace were very prejudicial to *Montmorency.* But the House of *Guise* got the greatest Advantage, after *Francis* II. had marry'd *Mary* Queen of *Scotland,* whose Mother was Sister to the Duke of *Guise:* So that during the Reign of *Francis* II. the Duke of *Guise* and the Cardinal his Brother, were the Men that bore the greatest Sway in the Kingdom; which extreamly exasperated *Montmorency* and the two Brothers of *Bourbon, Anthony* King of *Navarre,* and the Prince of *Conde,* seeing themselves thus neglected. And tho' *Anthony* was of a very modest Behaviour, watching only an Opportunity to regain his Kingdom of *Navarre* from the *Spaniards,* and having a sufficient Revenue out of his Country of *Bearn,* wherewithal to maintain himself; yet the Prince of *Conde* was Ambitious, Poor, and of a turbulent Spirit, who was not able to maintain his ||[Grandeur without some consider-

The House of Guise rises, and that of Bourbon declines.

41. That is, "thinking much of himself."

able Employment]|.[42] Besides this, he was continually stirr'd up by the Admiral *Gaspar Coligny,* an ambitious, cunning and sly Man; who, as his Enemies will have it, was very forward to fish in troubled Waters; his Brother *d' Andelot* also being of a very wild and turbulent Spirit. These three only watch'd an Opportunity to raise Commotions in the Kingdom.

Thus the great Men of the Kingdom were divided into these several Factions, at the Time when *Francis* II. began his Reign, a Prince scarce sixteen Years old, weak both in Body and Mind, and therefore inca-
Divisions about the Administra-tion of the Government. pable to rule the Kingdom by himself. Several therefore pretended to have <220> a right to the Administration of the Government, these of *Bourbon,* as being the next Princes of the Blood; the House of *Guise,* as being nearly related to the Queen, and the Queen Mother *Catharine de Medicis,* the very pattern of an aspiring and cunning Woman, hoped, That whilst the Princes were in contest about the Administration of the Government, it would fall to her share, wherefore she always fomented the Divisions, by keeping up the Balance betwixt them. This *Catherine* first sided with the House of *Guise,* dividing the Administration of Affairs with them, so that she was to have the Supream Administra-tion, the Duke of *Guise* was to manage the Military Affairs, and his Brother the Cardinal the Finances. This Agreement being made betwixt them, the Constable, under pretence of his old Age was dismiss'd from Court, and the Prince of *Conde* sent as Ambassadour into *Spain.* These, who were thus excluded, had a meeting, to consider which way they might free themselves from these Oppressions, where it was resolv'd that the King of *Navarre* should intercede for them at Court; who being put off with fair words and empty Promises, set himself at rest. *Conde* was resolv'd to try his Fortune by force; but having not a sufficient 'Interest' [strength], *Coligny* advised him, he should side with the *Hu-guenots* (for so they call'd in *France* those who profess'd the Protestant Religion) who labour'd then under a severe Persecution and wanted a Head, under whose 'Conduct' [leadership] they might obtain the free

---

42. Rather: "state without great offices" (*Staat ohne grosse Aempter nicht führen kunte*).

Exercise of their Religion: Besides that, they mortally hated those of *Guise,* whom they supposed to be the Authors of their Persecution.

The Business was thus concerted [orchestrated]; That the *Huguenots* should assemble in private, and some of them by a humble Petition to request the free Exercise of their Religion at Court; which, if it should be refus'd, the rest should be at hand, to kill those of *Guise,* and to force the King to receive the Prince of *Conde* for his chief Minister of State. The Execution of this Design was undertaken by a certain Gentleman call'd *Renaudie;* but the Enterprize being deferr'd for some time, because the Court went from *Blois* to *Amboise,* it was discover'd, and thereby render'd impracti-<221>cable, above twelve hundred that were taken paying with their Lives for it; *Conde* was also sent to Prison, and was just upon the point of receiving Sentence of Death, when *Francis* II. after a very short Reign, died suddenly \A. 1560\ of an Ulcer in the Head, which caused great Alterations in the Affairs of the Kingdom.

§20. Him succeeded his Brother *Charles* IX. then scarce eleven Years old, whose Tuition his Mother *Catharine* took immediately upon her self, hoping to enjoy it quietly, whilst the Houses of *Bourbon* and *Guise* were engag'd in mutual Quarrels; wherefore she was very carefull to uphold these Jealousies betwixt them. To find an Opportunity to set up [elevate] the Prince of *Conde* and his Party, thereby to balance those of *Guise,* she pretended to be no Enemy to the Protestant Religion, under which Pretence the same was much in request at Court. To suppress the reformed Religion, *Montmorency,* the House of *Guise,* and the Mareschal of St. *Andrew,* join'd in a Confederacy, who calling themselves *the Triumvirate,* drew also the King of *Navarre* in to their Party. After this a Conference and Disputation was held betwixt some Divines of both Religions at *Poissy,* after which, the Royal Protection was by a publick Edict, promis'd to the Protestant Religion \A. 1562\; which from the Month is call'd *the Edict of* January.[43]

This extreamly exasperated the Triumvirate, so that in the very same Year the War commenc'd. The first occasion of it was given by some

Charles IX.

The Conference of Poissy.

The first Huguenot War.

43. It was also called the Edict of Saint-Germain.

belonging to those of *Guise,* who in a small Town call'd *Vassy,* disturb'd the Protestants in the Exercise of their Religion; and a Quarrel arising thereupon, kill'd near threescore of them: Which was the first Blood shed in this Civil War; and from this time Things went very strangely [turbulently] in *France.* It is not our purpose to enumerate all the Cities that were taken, neither to speak of all the small Skirmishes which are innumerable, nor the Cruelties committed on both sides, and the 'Barbarities' [frenzy] of the Rabble; it will be sufficient for us to touch upon some of the main points. In this first War the King of *Navarre* died of a Wound, which he receiv'd in the Siege of *Roan.* Near *Dreux* <222> a bloody Battel was fought, where *Conde* at first had the Advantage, but his Souldiers falling to plundring, he was beat back again, he himself being made a Prisoner, and the Mareschal St. *Andrew* being kill'd by a Shot. 8000 Men were slain upon the Spot, and the Loss [was] near equal on both sides; [still,] the Duke of *Guise* kept the Field, but was afterwards, at the Siege of *Orleans,* treacherously murther'd by one *Poltrot,* with a Pistol shot, who was supposed to have committed the Fact by instigation of *Coligny.* Soon after \A. 1563\ a Peace was made. It is related, that above 50.000 *Huguenots* were slain in this War; on the other side, they [Huguenots] took the Church-plate and Ornaments, which they having turn'd into Money, Silver was after this War more currant in *France* than before. But *Catharine* had persuaded her self, that both Parties were reduc'd to that Condition, that she could now handle them at pleasure.

After the Peace was concluded the *English* were again beaten out of *Havre de Grace,* which the *Huguenots* had given them as an Acknowledgment for their Assistance. This Peace lasted no longer than till the Year '1576' [1567], when the *Huguenots* were persuaded, that at the interview betwixt *Catharine* and the Duke of *Alba* at *Bayonne,* a League was set on foot for rooting out the Hereticks: And in effect, they were immediately after more severely dealt with, and, as it was reported, the Prince of *Conde* and *Coligny* were to be secur'd. The *Huguenots* therefore began the Second War, during which, the Constable *Annas Montmorency* being mortally wounded in an Engagement {near St. Denys}, he told a Monk, who at his last Hour was very troublesome to him; *He*

The Second
War.

should let him be at quiet, since during the Time of 80 *Years that he had liv'd, he had learn'd how to employ one quarter of an Hour in dying.* The *Huguenots* got great Reputation for Valour in this Engagement, they being much Inferiour to the others in Number. About the same time the City of *Rochelle* declar'd for the *Huguenots,* which afterwards for 60 Years together serv'd them for a secure Retreat. Then a second Peace was concluded \A. 1568\, not with an Intention to keep it, but that each Party might find a better Opportunity to take Advantage of one another; nor were the Conditions ever fulfill'd. <223>

The War therefore was renewed in the same Year, during which the Prince of *Conde* was kill'd by a Shot, in a Battel near *Jarnack* \A. 1569\. After his Death the *Huguenots* declar'd *Henry* King of *Navarre,* the Son of *Anthony,* who afterwards was King of *France,* their Head, tho' in effect *Coligny* had the chief management of Affairs. He in vain besieged *Poictiers,* in the Defence of which Place the young Duke of *Guise* gave the first proofs of his Valour; he was also soundly beaten near *Montcontour,* where he lost 9000 Foot. He lost nevertheless nothing of his former Reputation, for he quickly recollected his broken Troops, and got together a great Army, being assisted by Queen *Elizabeth* with Money, and by the *Paltzgrave*[44] with Souldiers, he directed his March towards *Paris,* whereupon a Peace was concluded \A. 1570\ to the great Advantage of the *Huguenots,* the four strong Cities of *Rochelle, Montauban, Cagnac* and *Charité* being given them for their Security:

But the main design of this Peace was, that the King perceiving, that the *Huguenots* could not be suppress'd by Force, hop'd he might win them by Policy, therefore endeavour'd by fair Words and great Promises to make them secure. The Admiral was caress'd at Court, he being consulted withall concerning an Expedition to be undertaken against the *Spaniards* in the *Netherlands.* A Marriage also was concluded betwixt *Henry* King of *Navarre* and *Margaret* the King's Sister,[45] to which Wedding they invited the chief of the *Huguenots,* with a Design to cut

The Third War.

The Prince of Conde being slain, the King of Navarre is declar'd Head of the Huguenots.

44. That is, *Pfalzgraf* or Count Palatine, in this instance Frederick III the Pious (1515–76), the Calvinist Elector of Palatine and leader of the Protestant party in Germany.
45. Margaret of Valois (Queen Margot), 1553–1615.

The Parisian
Massacre.

their Throats in *Paris*. And first of all the Admiral *Coligny*, as he was going home from Court, was by some Villains, who were suborn'd by the Duke of *Guise*, shot with two Bullets through the Arm. Then it was agreed, That in the Year '1571' [1572], on the 24th Day of *August*, early in the Morning, when the Bells were ringing to Prayers, all the *Huguenots* should be massacred, except the King of *Navarre* and the young Prince of *Conde:* The Execution of this Enterprize the Duke of *Guise* had taken upon himself. The beginning of whose Massacre was made with *Coligny*, who was ill of his Wounds; then it fell promiscuously upon the rest, the Fury of the Mob not ceasing till after seven Days <224> slaughter. A great many other Cities of *France* follow'd the Example of *Paris*, so that within 'few' [those same] Days near 30.000 were miserably massacred. The King of *Navarre* and Prince of *Conde* were forc'd to abjure the Reformed Religion. This was the so much celebrated *Parisian* Wedding, which *Gabriel Naude* would fain represent us a State's Trick [*coup d'état*], but this is, in my Opinion, a very gross [*grob*] way of arguing.[46]

The Fourth
War.

Nevertheless the *Huguenots* did quickly recollect themselves, after the first Consternation was over, renewing the War with great Animosity and Revenge. During this War the King's Army {under the command of the Duke of Anjou} besieged *Rochelle* near eight Months together, and having lost 12.000 Men before it, News was brought, That the Duke *d'Anjou*[47] was elected King of *Poland*. Hence an Opportunity was taken to raise the Siege with some Reputation, and to make a Peace the fourth time with the *Huguenots* \A. 1573\; by vertue of which, the Cities of *Rochelle*, *Montauban* and *Nismes* were given them for their Security.

The Fifth War.

But immediately, in the Year next following, the fifth War commenc'd; at which time also a third Faction arose in *France*, which was call'd, *that*

46. In his *Considerations politiques sur les coups d'estat* (Amsterdam, 1667), Gabriel Naudé (1600–1653), librarian to Cardinal Mazarin, vindicated the "Paris wedding"—as the St. Bartholomew's Massacre was sometimes called (as it came several days after the ceremony)—as a masterpiece of state policy.

47. Henry III of Valois (1551–89) was elected king of Poland in 1573 but returned to France in 1574 upon the death of his brother, Charles IX (1550–74). He was known as the Duke of Anjou until 1574.

of the Politicians [*Politicos*]; they pretended, without having any regard to the Religious Differences, to seek the publick Welfare, to have the Queen remov'd from the Administration of the Government, and the *Italians* and those of *Guise* to be banish'd [from] the Kingdom of *France*. The Heads of this Faction were those of the House of *Montmorency*, who intended, during these Troubles, to play their own Game. These were afterwards very instrumental in helping *Henry* IV. to the Crown. During these Troubles *Charles* IX. died, leaving no legitimate {male} Issue behind him.

§21. After the Death of *Charles* IX. the Crown fell to *Henry* III. who   Henry III. was at that time in *Poland*, during whose absence his Mother *Catharine* govern'd the Kingdom, which was in a very confus'd Estate. He left *Poland* privately, and taking his Way by *Vienna* and *Venice*, arriv'd safely in *France*. But after he had taken upon him the Administration of Affairs, he deceiv'd every body in those Hopes which were conceiv'd <225> of him before. For he being addicted only to his Pleasures and Idleness, was led away by his Favourites, leaving the chief Administration of the Kingdom to his Mother. The *Huguenots* Power encreas'd remarkably after the Duke of *Alenson*, the Kings Brother, sided with them, and *Conde* and the *Pfaltzgrave, John Casimir*,[48] led an Army out of *Germany* into *France;* besides that, the King of *Navarre* found means to make his escape out of Prison. The fifth Peace was therefore concluded with the *Huguenots*, whereby they obtain'd very advantageous Conditions.

    About the same time a new Faction was set up, which was compos'd   The Holy of a great many small ones, this was call'd, *The holy Union*, or *League*,   League. which reduc'd *France* to the most miserable Condition that could be. The chief promoter of it was *Henry* Duke of *Guise*, who, perceiving, that the great Authority which he had among the People, made him to be hated by the King, endeavour'd to make a Party of his own. He made use especially of the Priests and common People of *Paris;* among whom

48. Johann Casimir (1543–92) of Pfalz-Simmern inherited Pfalz-Lautern in 1576, after the death of Frederick III, and administered the Electoral Palatinate during 1583–92. He sought to promote Calvinism and, in 1576, led an army into France to assist the Huguenots.

the Name of the *Guises* was in great Veneration. He was encouraged to undertake this Design, because the King was despis'd by all, and the Women by their Intrigues, rul'd at Court. Besides this, he pretended to be descended from the Race of *Charles the Great,* which was excluded unjustly from the Crown by *Hugh Capet.* The Pretence of [pretext for] this League was the Catholick Religion; and there was a Draught made of this League, which contain'd chiefly three things, *viz. The Defence of the Catholick Religion; the Establishment of* Henry III. *in the Throne, and the maintaining the Liberty of the Kingdom, and the Assembly of the States.* Those who enter'd into this League promis'd to be obedient to such Head or General as should be chosen for the Defence of this League, all which was confirm'd by {a terrible} Oath. At the first setting up of this League the King conniv'd at it, hoping thereby the sooner to subdue the *Huguenots;* nay, he himself subscrib'd [to] the same at the Dyet at *Blois,* declaring himself the Head of this League \A. 1577\.

The Sixth War.   Then the sixth War was begun against the *Huguenots,* but the King made Peace with them the <226> same Year, notwithstanding that they were in a very ill Condition, neither was any thing done worth mentioning in this War. The War being ended, the King returning to his Pleasures, confounded great Summs of Money, and therefore laid new and heavy Impositions upon the People, and his Favourites grew very Insolent; which increas'd the Hatred against him, and at the same time the Respect and Love of the People to those of *Guise.* Besides this, the Duke of *Alenson,* the King's Brother, declaring himself Lord of the

Spain enters the League.   *Netherlands, Philip* King of *Spain* was provoked to revenge himself of the *French,* and upheld the League. In the Year 1579 the Seventh War

The Seventh War.   was begun against the *Huguenots,* wherein also they succeeded very ill. Notwithstanding this the King made a Peace with them in the Year next following he being unwilling that they should be quite rooted out, for fear that the League might prove too strong for himself. The *German* Horse were also much fear'd, and the Duke of *Alenson* was very forward to have the Peace concluded, that he might be at leisure to employ his Forces in the *Netherlands.* This Peace lasted five Years, during which time the Hatred against the King increas'd daily, because of the heavy Taxes which were devour'd by his Favourites. He made himself also the more despis'd by playing too much the Hypocrite, and by transforming himself almost into a Monk. The *French* Glory was also much eclips'd, when the Duke of *Alenson* behav'd himself so ill in the *Netherlands*,[49] and the *French* Fleet which was sent to the Assistance of *Anthony* the Bastard, was totally ruin'd near *Tercera.*

But the League grew very strong after the Death of the Duke of *Alenson,* the King's younger Brother, the King having no hopes of any Issue of his Body: Then it was that the Duke of *Guise* propos'd to himself no less than the Crown, tho' he for a colour [pretense] set up the Cardinal of *Bourbon,* thereby to exclude the King of *Navarre.* And because it was suspected that the King favour'd the King of *Navarre,* the Priests began to thunder in the Pulpits, and to make horrid Exclamations, that the Catholick Religion was lost; the Duke of *Guise* en-<227>ter'd into a Confederacy with *Philip,* who was to furnish great Summs of Money under pretext of maintaining the Catholick Religion, and to assist the Cardinal of *Bourbon* in obtaining the Crown; but in effect, this Intention was to uphold the Divisions in *France,* thereby to disenable it to take part with the *Netherlands.* Then \A. 1585\ the Leaguers began to break out into an open War; and having taken a great many Towns oblig'd the King, according to their Demands, to forbid the Exercise of the Protestant Religion in *France.*

And so began the Eighth War against the *Huguenots,* and if the King had been in earnest to ruin them, they would have been in a very ill Condition: For tho' the King of *Navarre* beat the Duke *de Joyeuse* near *Coutras* \A. 1587\, yet did he not prosecute his Victory. And about the same time the Duke of *Guise* dispers'd the *German* and *Swiss* Forces, which under the Command of *Fabian de Dona*[50] were marching to the Assistance of the *Huguenots.* This Army, being destitute of a good Commander was miserably maul'd, and the rest sent home in a very shamefull Condition. This Victory acquir'd the Duke of *Guise* great Applause and Favour among the People, and still [further] lessen'd the Value of the

The Eighth War.

49. The Duke had lost almost a whole army during an attempt to take Antwerp in 1583.

50. Fabian I (1550–1622) of the Prussian Dohna family was then a representative of Johann Casimir and led an army into France in 1587.

King's Person; so that the Priests now did not stick to exclaim against the
King in their Sermons, calling him *a Tyrant*. The King therefore having
resolv'd with himself to punish the Heads of the League in *Paris*, they
broke out into open Rebellion, and having sent for the Duke of *Guise*
as their Protector, the King was oblig'd to leave *Paris* by Night \A. 1588\.

The League force the King from Paris.

But the King perceiving that more Cities sided daily with the League,
and despairing to overcome them by Force, took another Course to
obtain his Ends, and made an Agreement with the Duke of *Guise*, with
great Advantages on his and the Leaguers side: He pretended also to
have forgotten all past Injuries, on purpose to inveigle the Duke of
Guise. And under these specious pretences he got him to appear at the
Assembly of the Estates at *Blois*. (In the mean time the Duke of *Savoy*
had taken from the *French* the Marquisate of *Saluzze*, the only Province left them in *Italy*.) But the Estates, who were most of them Crea-
<228>tures of the Duke of *Guise*, being very urgent in their Demands,
to have the King of *Navarre* declar'd incapable of the Crown, and the
Duke of *Guise* to be made Constable, the King caus'd the Duke of
Guise and his Brother the Cardinal to be murther'd. This put those of
the League into a Rage, and with the Assistance of the Priests, the King
was in *Paris* publickly declar'd to have forfeited the Crown. Most of the
great Cities of *France* being stirr'd up by the Example of the *Parisians*
did the same, declaring the Duke *de Maine*, Brother to the Duke of
Guise, Lieutenant-General of the State and Crown of *France*, and Supream Head of the League; who endeavour'd, but in vain, to surprize
the King in *Tours*.

The Duke and Cardinal of Guise assas-sinated by the King's Order at Blois.

The King then being overpower'd by the League, and besides this,
excommunicated by the Pope, was oblig'd to make an Agreement with
the King of *Navarre* and to make use of the *Huguenots*. And having got
together a great Army, he march'd towards *Paris*, with a Resolution to
reduce that City to Obedience by Force of Arms: But the day before
the general Attack was to be made, one *James Clement*, a *Jacobin* Monk,
brought a Letter out of the City directed to the King, which whilst he
deliver'd, pretending to whisper [to] the King, thrust a Knife into his
Bowels, of which Wound he died the day following \on 2. August 1589\:
The last of the House of *Valois*.

The King makes use of the Huguenots against the League.

§22. *Henry* IV. whom we hitherto have call'd *the King of* Navarre, and, His Religion.
who was the first of the House of *Bourbon,* did at the beginning of his
Reign, meet with no less Difficulties than he had met with before. For
tho' he was lawfull Heir to the Crown, yet the 'Protestant' [Huguenot]
Religion, which he profess'd, was no small obstacle, for as long as he
was addicted to that, the League, the Pope, and *Spain,* would questionless oppose him with all their might: But if he chang'd his Religion
he was in danger of losing the Assistance of the *Huguenots* which had
been steady to him, and so {perhaps} set himself betwixt two Stools.
And it would have been very unbecoming, to have so publickly accommodated his Religion to his {worldly} Interest. Notwithstanding this,
immediately after the Death of *Hen-*<229>*ry* III. all the great Men
of the Army assembled together, promis'd him Obedience after 'several Contests' [a long debate, *disput*], under Condition, that within
six Months he would suffer himself to be instructed in the Catholick
Religion. But because *Henry* would not be bound to any certain time,
but only gave them some Hopes in general terms, it was agreed, That
the *Huguenots* should enjoy the free Exercise of their Religion, yet that
the Catholick Religion should be re-establish'd in all Cities, and the
Revenues restor'd to the Clergy. But, those of the League, because the
Duke of *Maine* at that time durst not take upon him the Title of King,
proclaim'd the Cardinal of *Bourbon,* an ancient decrepid Man, Uncle
to King *Henry,* and who was then in Custody, their King, declaring
the Duke *de Maine* Lieutenant-General of the Crown. The Leaguers
made the strongest Party, having on their side the Common People,
most of the great Cities, all the Parliaments except that of *Rennes* and
Bourdeaux, almost all the Clergy, *Spain,* the Pope, and the rest of the
Catholick Princes, except *Venice* and *Florence.* But the Heads were not
very unanimous, and the Duke *de Maine* had not Authority enough to
keep them in Unity. But on the King's side were almost all the Nobility, the whole Court of the deceas'd King, all the Protestant Princes and
States, the old *Huguenot* Troops, who had done great Service to *Henry,*
and would still have done more, if they had not mistrusted him, that
he would change his Religion.

Each Party watch'd an Opportunity of surprizing one another. The

In right margin:
Henry IV.

His Difficulties
on the account
of his Religion.

Duke of *Maine* endeavouring to surprize the King near *Diep,* was bravely repuls'd, which seem'd {to the wise} to be ominous to the League. On the other Hand, the King could not get *Paris* tho' he had taken the Suburbs. But *Henry* was not only pester'd by the League, but also for want of Money, was oblig'd to keep up his Party with fair Words and Promises. The *Spaniards* also began to intermeddle publickly in the Affairs of *France,* in hopes in this Juncture either to conquer the Kingdom, or to divide it, or at least to weaken it. But the Duke *de Maine* did underhand oppose these Designs, being unwilling, that in <230> case he could not be King himself, *France* should fall under the Subjection of *Spain.* In the Year 1590, *Henry* obtain'd a glorious Victory over the Duke *de Maine,* who had double the Number, near *Ivry.* Then he block'd up *Paris,* which was reduc'd to the greatest Extremity by Famine, but reliev'd by the Duke of *Parma* Governour of the *Netherlands.* In the Year 1591, there arose a third Faction, the young Cardinal of *Bourbon* making Pretensions to the Crown, but was very fortunately disappointed in his

The Pope Excommunicates Henry. Aim by the King. Then Pope *Gregory* XIV. excommunicated *Henry,* exhorting all his Subjects to withdraw themselves from their Obedience, which Difficulty *Henry* did not surmount without great troubles.

The *Spaniards* also declar'd themselves more freely, *Philip* offering his Daughter *Isabella Clara Eugenia* to be made Queen of *France;* which Proposal was mightily encouraged by the young Duke of *Guise,* he being then just escap'd out of his Custody, as 'tis suppos'd, by connivance of the King, who supposed, that thereby that Party might be divided, since he would certainly endeavour to oppose the Designs of the Duke

Proposals about setting up another King. *de Maine* his Uncle. After the Duke of *Parma* had rais'd the Siege of *Roan,* the *Spaniards* urg'd more and more, that the *French* would take a Resolution concerning the setting up of another King. And in the Assembling of the Estates in *Paris* \A. 1593\, which was held for that purpose, it was propos'd, That *Isabella* the Daughter of *Philip,* being born of a *French* Mother, should be declar'd Queen of *France,* and that she should have for her Husband *Ernest* Arch-Duke of *Austria.* But the *French* refusing to accept of a Foreigner for their King, *Charles* Duke of *Guise* was proposed as a Husband to *Isabella.* This Proposition relish'd very ill with the Duke of *Maine,* who thought himself so well deserving, that no body ought to be preferr'd before him; wherefore, if he could not have the Crown, he was resolv'd no body else should have it, and so employ'd all his Cunning, that there was nothing determined in the Assembly concerning this Proposition.

The King, however, plainly perceiv'd, That if he did not change his Religion, his Affairs must needs grow <231> worse, especially, since these Catholicks, who hitherto had been of his Party did threaten to leave him, if he did not perform his Promise. He called therefore the {most eminent} Bishops together, who instructed him in the Catholick Faith, and having receiv'd Absolution, he went, to St. *Denys's* Chapel to Mass \A. 1593\. And that the People might tast the sweetness of Peace, and desire it, he made a Truce of three Months, which prov'd very successfull, especially, since the fundamental Pretence, namely, *Henry's* being a Heretick, was now remov'd. *Vitry* and the City of *Meaux* were the first that surrender'd themselves to the King in the same Year, upon very advantageous Conditions; *Aix, Lyons, Orleans, Bourges* and other Cities soon followed their Example. And to encourage the rest to do the same, the King caused himself to be Crowned and Annointed in *Chartres, Rheims* being as yet in the hands of the League. Not long after *Paris* was also Surrendred by the Governour *Brissac;* and here the King was received with such joyfull Acclamations of the People, as if they had never been his Enemies, the *Spanish* Garrison being turn'd out with Ignominy, and the hissing of the Common people. Then all the rest of the Cities and Governours surrendred themselves to the King on very advantageous Conditions, which the King was willing to grant them, that he might once be put in quiet possession of the Crown, and drive the *Spaniards* out of *France.* The young Duke of *Guise* submitted himself, being made Governour of *Provence.* Then *Henry* denounced War against *Spain,* not only to revenge himself for what Troubles they had created to him before, but also to please the *Huguenots,* and to root out of the People their affection for the *Spaniards.* These were the Fruits *Philip* reapt for so many Millions, which he had bestowed in supporting the League.

|[In the beginning of the same Year]|,[51] a Knife was by a certain desperate 'Ruffian' [boy, *Buben*], called *John Castel,* thrust into the King's

The King changes his Religion.

Several Cities surrender to him.

The King assaulted and wounded by a Ruffian.

51. Rather: "At the beginning of the same war, in the Year 1594."

Mouth, whereby he lost one of his Teeth. It was the King's good fortune that he [had] just bowed himself, this Villain's aim having been at his *The Jesuits* Throat: And because it was found out, that the Jesuits had been tam- *banish'd.* pering with him, whose Principles <232> also were thought very dangerous, they were banish'd out of *France*, but some years after restored again.[52] Afterwards the Duke of *Nevers* being sent to *Rome* to obtain Absolution for King *Henry*, the same was granted by the Pope, who had been very averse hitherto to *Henry;* but perceiving that he would maintain his Crown in spite of him, was now for ingratiating himself with the King. Then the Dukes of *Maine*, and *Espernon*, and *Marseilles* were received again into the King's favour. But the War against *Spain* did not succeed according to wish. For tho' the King had got some advantages over them in the *Franche Comte*, and had beat the *Spaniards* out of *Han* in *Picardy;* yet on the other side, these took *Dourlans* and *Cambray*, the latter of which had been hitherto in the Possession of *Balagny* under *French* protection; and in the Year 1596, next following, they took *Calais* and *Ardres*. And tho' the King took from the *Spaniards Fere*, yet was that a very slender compensation of his Losses. But there happened another great Misfortune; For the *Spaniards* in the Year next following took the City of *Amiens* by surprize, which was not re-taken without great pains. In the Year 1598, the Duke of *Mercœur*, who hitherto had stood out resolutely in *Bretany*, did at last submit himself, hoping thereby to *The Edict* obtain the said Dukedom. And to set the *Huguenots* at rest, he [Henry] *at Nants.* publish'd for their security that famous Edict of *Nants* [Nantes],[53] as it is called, by virtue of which they have hitherto enjoyed the free Exercise *The Peace of* of Religion. At last a Peace was concluded betwixt *Henry* and the *Span-* *Vervins.* *iards* at *Vervins*, with Conditions, that such Places as were taken since the Year 1559, should be restored on both sides.

　　　A Peace being thus concluded, and *Henry* resolved to be {reconciled}

---

52. They were recalled by Henry himself, before his assassination in 1610.

53. The Edict of Nantes (1598) remained in effect until 1685, when it was revoked by Louis XIV through the Edict of Fontainebleau. Pufendorf criticized its revocation in *Of the Nature and Qualification of Religion* (1687); see note 17, p. 56, above. This work on church-state relations was dedicated to the Calvinist "Great Elector" of Brandenburg, Frederick William (1620–88), who invited the persecuted Huguenots to settle in his territories.

even with the Duke of *Savoy,* who under his Predecessour's Reign had taken *Saluzze,* and during the intestine Wars had raised great Troubles in *Dauphine* and *Provence,* in hopes to snatch away a piece of the dismembred Kingdom; and tho' the Duke came in Person into *France,* and promised to the King to give him some other Places in exchange of the former; yet was he not in earnest, in hopes to be upheld by *Spain,* or that the Marshal *de Biron,* with whom he kept pri-<233>vate Intelligence, should renew the civil Commotions. But the King fell upon him, and took from the Duke all what he was possess'd of on this side of the *Alpes.* At last, by Mediation of the Pope, an agreement was made \A. 1600\, that the Duke should give to *France,* in exchange for *Saluzze, La Bresse, Bugey, Valromay et* [and] *Gex.* The *Italian* Princes were very ill satisfied with this Peace, since there being no door left for *France* to enter *Italy, Italy* was left to the discretion of the *Spaniard.* But *Henry* being tired with so long and tedious War, was resolved at last to enjoy the sweet Fruits of Peace after so many years Troubles. But soon after a dangerous Conspiracy was discovered, contrived by the Mareschal *de Biron,* who intended with the Assistance of the *Spaniards* to depose the King, and to dismember the Kingdom, by setting up a great many petty Principalities; having agreed with the rest, to have for his share the Dukedom of *Burgundy.* And he refusing to accept of the King's Mercy, which he was willing to grant him in consideration of his great Deserts, was condemn'd, and his Head cut off \A. 1602\.

The King being now at Peace, did employ all his Thoughts, how *France* might recover itself after such tedious Wars, and that good Ordinances might be establish'd, but especially that his Revenues might be encreased. He establish'd for this purpose all sorts of Manufactories, and especially that of Silk, (which afterwards drew great Riches into that Kingdom.) But even in the midst of Peace he was continually troubled with his Queen,[54] who was jealous about his Mistrisses; and the *Spaniards* were always plotting both against his Person and Crown. On the other hand, *Henry* had a design to oppose the growing Power

He takes from the Duke of Savoy, all that he possessed on this side the Alpes.

The Conspiracy of the Marshal de Biron.

He introduces Manufacturies.

---

54. Henry's marriage to Margaret of Valois was annulled in 1599, and in 1600 he married Marie de Medici (1573–1642), mother of Louis XIII and Henrietta Maria, wife of the future Charles I of England.

His Design
to put a stop
to the growth
of the House
of Austria.

He is
Assassinated
by Ravillac.

Lewis XIII.

of the House of *Austria,* by keeping it within the Bounds of *Spain,* and the Hereditary Countries in *Germany.* And 'tis said, that for that purpose he concerted Measures with the *Northern* Crown[s], with *Holland,* with the Protestant Princes of *Germany,* with the Elector of *Bavaria,* the Duke of *Savoy,* the *Swiss,* and even the Pope himself. To put this design in execution, he took the opportunity of those Differences which were then on foot concerning the Succession in the Country of *Juliers,* which, that it might not be <234> devoured by the House of *Austria,* he was resolved to prevent with all his Might. This is certain, that his Preparations were greater, than seem'd to be requisite only for the business of *Juliers;* for he and his Allies had got 120.000 Men together, and prodigious Summs of Money.

The House of *Austria* on the other hand did not make the least Preparations, just as if it had fore known the fatal Blow, which happened soon after: The Army was marching towards the *Netherlands,* and the King ready to follow in a few days, having caused the Queen to be Crowned, and constituted her Regent during his absence; When the King going along the Street in *Paris* in his Coach, which was fain to stop by reason of the great Croud of the People, was by a desperate 'Ruffian' [boy, *Buben*], whose Name was *Francis Ravillac,* stabb'd with a Knife in his Belly, so that he without uttering one word died immediately \on 14. May 1610\. There are some, who make no question of it, but that this Villain was set on to commit this fact [deed], and that it was not done without the knowledge of the *Spaniards* and the Queen herself. And so fell this great Hero by the hands of a profligate Wretch, after he had surmounted great Difficulties in ascending the Throne, and had avoided above fifty several Conspiracies; which being most contrived by the Priests against his Life, were all timely discovered. His Death proved very pernicious to the Kingdom, because, during the Minority of his Son, the Power of the Great Men, and also of the *Huguenots,* did extreamly encrease.

§23. His Son *Lewis* XIII. succeeded him, being scarce nine Years of Age, and under the Tuition of his Mother *Mary de Medicis,* she endeavour'd to preserve Peace abroad by Alliance, and at home by Clemency and Liberality towards the great Men of the Kingdom, who never-theless several times raised Disturbances, whereby they made their own advantage, the Queen-Regent being not Powerfull enough to keep them in Obedience by force. As soon as the King had taken upon himself the Management of Affairs, he caused *Concini,* Marshal *d'Ancre,* who was born a *Florentine,* to be killed \A. 1617\, he having been in great Power during the <235> Queen's Regency, and by his Pride, Riches and Power, [had] drawn upon himself the Hatred of the Subjects; by his Death he hoped to appease the dissatisfied Multitude. The Queen Mother was sent away from Court to *Blois,* from whence she was 'car-ried away' [freed] by the Duke *d'Espernon* \A. 1619\. And these Com-motions were at last appeased by bestowing liberal Presents among the Great Men.

About the same time *Richlieu,* afterwards made a Cardinal, began to be in great Esteem in Court, who advised the King to establish his Authority, and to take up by the Roots the intestine Evils of *France.* He laid this down as a fundamental Principle, That he should take from the *Huguenots* the power of doing him any mischief, considering that such as were dissatisfied at any time, or that were of a turbulent Spirit, took always refuge, and were assisted by them. The first begin-ning was made in the King's Patrimonial Province of *Bearn,* where he caused the Catholick Religion to be re-establish'd. The *Huguenots* being greatly dissatisfied thereat, began to break out into Violence, whence the King took an opportunity to recover several Places from them, but sustained a considerable Loss in the Siege of *Montauban,* till at last Peace was made with the *Huguenots,* under condition that they should demolish all their new Fortifications, except those of *Montauban* and *Rochelle.* In the Year 1625, Cardinal *Richlieu* was made Chief Minister of *France,* about which time also the second War with the *Huguenots* was ended. But this Peace did not last long, because those of *Rochelle* would not bear, that the Fortress called *Fort-Lewis,* should be built just under their Noses. *Richlieu* therefore having taken a resolution at once to put an end to this War by the taking of *Rochell*[e], besieg'd it so close both by Sea and Land, that the *English,* who had had very ill Success in the Isle of *Rhée,* where they Landed, could bring no Succours into the

Richlieu comes in play.

Made chief Minister of State.

Rochelle   place.[55] Their Obstinacy was at last over-come by Famine, of 18.000
taken.   Citizens, there having been not above 5000 left, for they had lived
without Bread for thirteen Weeks. With this stroke the Strength of
the *Huguenots* was broken, *Montauban* upon the persuasion of the
Cardinal having demolished its Works [bulwarks]. <236> The cunning
Duke of *Roan* also at last made his peace, after he had been sufficiently
troublesome to the King in *Languedoc,* under condition, that the Cities
of *Nismes* and *Montpelier* should demolish their Fortifications; but for
the rest, enjoy the free Exercise of their Religion. And thus the Ulcer,
which had settled it self in the very Entrails of *France,* was happily
The Effects of   healed up.[56] It is related by some, that these Civil Wars have devoured
the Civil Wars.   above a Million of People; that 150 Millions were employed in paying of the Souldiers {alone}; that nine Cities, 400 Villages, 20.000
Churches, 2000 Monasteries, and 100.000 [10.000] Houses were burnt
or laid level with the ground.

A War in Italy.   Then *France* applied all their care towards Foreign Affairs. The King
assisted {Charles} the Duke of *Nevers* \A. 1628\, in obtaining the Dukedom of *Mantua,* which belonged to him by Right of Succession, but
whom the *Spaniards* endeavour'd to exclude from the same, as being a
French-man. In this War the Siege of *Casal* is most famous, in the de-
fence of which place, the *French* gave incredible proofs of their Bravery.
At last the business was, through the wise Management of the Popish
The first   Nuncio *Mazarini* (who then laid the first Foundation of his future
Occasion of   Greatness in *France*) composed, and the Duke of *Nevers* afterwards by
Mazarini's
Greatness.   the Treaty made at *Chierasco,* establish'd in the Dukedoms of *Mantua*
How Pignerol   and *Montferrat.* The King also bought *Pignerol* of the Duke of *Savoy,*
came into the   that so the *French* might not want a door into *Italy. France* had also
hands of the
French.   before taken part with the *Grisons* against the Inhabitants of the *Valte-*
line, who had revolted being assisted by the *Spaniards,* whereby he prevented this Country from falling into the Hands of the *Spaniards,* and
so Matters were restored to their former State.

55. The English (Charles I) sent a fleet to relieve the Huguenots at La Rochelle
in 1628.
56. See note 61, p. 178 above, on Pufendorf's view of religious diversity and its
risks.

In the Year 1631, *France* made an Alliance with *Sweden,* allowing to that King a yearly Pension, to assist him in opposing the Greatness of the House of *Austria.* But when King *Gustavus Adolphus* began to be formidable on the *Rhine,* he [France] took the Elector of *Treves* [Trier] into his [its] protection, putting a Garrison into *Hermanstein,* (which nevertheless in the Year 1636, was forced to a Surrender by Famine). In the mean time the Queen-Mother and the Kings Brother <237> the Duke of *Orleans* envying the Greatness of *Richelieu* had raised some tumults. With them also sided *Montmorency,* who paid for it with his Head, and put an inglorious end to his noble Family, which boasted to have been the first noble Family that embrac'd the Christian Religion in *France.* And tho' this business was afterwards Composed, the Queen Mother being received into Favour again, yet was she so dissatisfied, because she could not Act according to her own Will; that she retired into *Flanders,* and from thence into *England,* where she made some stay, and at last died in a very low Condition in *Cologne* \A. 1642\. In the Year 1633 the King took from the Duke of *Lorrain* his Countrey, because he had declared himself for the Emperour. And when afterwards, *viz.* after the Battel fought near *Nordlingen* \A. 1634\ the *Swedish* Affairs were in a very low Condition, and the House of *Austria* began to hold up its Head again, *France* broke out into open War with *Spain,* to balance the growing Power of the House of *Austria.* He [France] took for a pretence that the *Spaniards* had surprized the City of *Treves,* and taken the Elector of *Treves* Prisoner, who was under *French* protection.

The Queen Mother raises Troubles.

The King takes Lorrain from that Duke.

And then the War began in *Italy, Germany,* the *Netherlands* and *Roussilion,* which was carried on with various Fortune; yet so, that the *French* got the better of it at last. To touch upon some of the most remarkable Actions: The first Attack which the *French* made in the *Netherlands* {A. 1635} did not succeed very well, they having been forced to raise the Siege of *Lovain* with great Loss. In the Year 1636, *Piccolomini* marched into *Picardy,* and *Galias* into *Burgundy,* but did nothing of moment. On the other hand the *French* beat up [broke] the Siege of *Leucate* in *Roussilion* \A. 1638\, and the brave Duke *Bernhard* of *Saxen-Weimar* took the Fortress of *Brisac,* he carrying on the War with *French* Money. And after the Death of this Duke, which happened not long after, the King of *France* brought both that Fortress and his Army over to its side with Money. Yet the *French* miscarried in the same Year before St. *Omer* and *Fontarabia*, before the last of which Places the Prince of *Conde* sustained a considerable Loss. In the same Year, *viz.* on the 5th. of <238> *September, Lewis* XIV. was, almost by a Miracle, born of a Marriage, which had proved unfruitfull for twenty Years before. In the Year 1639, the *French* were beaten before *Thionville.* In the Year 1640, they took *Arras,* and in the same Year *Catalonia,* revolting from *Spain,* threw itself under the *French* Protection.

In the Year 1641, a great Misfortune hung over *Richlieu's* Head, the Count the *Soissons* having raised a dangerous Rebellion; but, he being killed in an Engagement, wherein otherwise his Party had the better, establish'd, by his Death, the Cardinal's Authority, and the Quiet of *France.* In the Year 1642, *Perpignan* was taken, at which Siege the King and *Richlieu* were both present. Monsieur *Cinqmats* did about that time first insinuate himself into the King's favour, hoping thereby to undermine *Richlieu.* And the better to balance the Cardinal, he had made some under-hand Intrigues with *Spain.* But the Cardinal having discovered the business, caused his Head to be cut off; as also *de Thou* the younger's, because he had been privy to the business; tho' he had advised against it, yet had he not discover'd it. From the Duke of *Bouillon,* who had been also of the Cabal, he took for a Punishment his strong Hold, *Sedan.* In the same Year *Richlieu* died, to his great good fortune, the King being grown quite weary of him, notwithstanding he had laid the first Foundation of the Greatness of *France,* which is now so formidable to *Europe.* The King also died not long after \14. May 1643\.

Lewis XIV. §24. *Lewis* XIV. was but Five years of Age when he came to the Crown,
Mazarini's his Mother 'tis true bore the name of *Regent* of *France,* but in effect the
Ministry. Cardinal *Julius Mazarini*[57] had the chief Management of the Kingdom; which was then in a very flourishing Condition; but every Body

57. Jules Mazarin (1602–61) was born in Italy and became a protege of Cardinal Richelieu, who recommended him to Louis XIII. Louis's wife, Anne of Austria (1601–66), relied heavily on him during her regency (1643–61).

was for enriching himself out of the Kings Purse during his Minority; and *Mazarini* was very liberal, thereby endeavouring to make them in love with his Government. But the Treasury being become empty, new Taxes were of necessity to be imposed upon the People which caused a great dissatisfaction against the Government. Neverthe-<239>less for the first Five years every thing was pretty quiet at home, and War carried on abroad.

At the very first beginning of this new Government the Duke *'d' Austria'* [d'Anguin] obtained a signal Victory against the *Spaniards* near *Rocroy;* after which he took *Thionville,* and *Gaston* the Kings Uncle *Graveling;* \A. 1644\ *Anguin* revenged the loss which the *French* had sustainded the Year before near *Dutlingen,* and, having first beaten the *Bavarian* Forces near *Friburg* in *Brisgaw* [Breißgau], he took *Philipsburg;* in the Year 1646. he beat the *Bavarian* Troops near *Norlingen,* and afterwards took *Dunkirk.* But in the Year next following he in vain besieged the City of *Lerida.* In the Year 1648. a Peace was concluded at *Munster* in *Westphalia,* betwixt the Emperour and *France,*[58] by Vertue of which the latter got the two Fortresses of *Brisac* and *Philipsburg,* the Countrey of *Puntgau* [Sundgau], and part of the upper *Alsatia.*

Peace of Munster.

But as *France* by this Peace was freed from one Enemy, so on the other hand the intestine Commotions put a stop to its great Progresses. The chief reason of these Troubles was, that some envying *Mazarini,* as being a Foreigner, they would by all means have him removed from the Helm, and this they sought with the greater Importunity, because they were not in awe of the King, who was but a Child, neither of his Mother, she being an outlandish [foreign] Woman. Some of the great Men also were for fishing in 'troubled' [murky] Waters: but above all the rest, the Prince of *Conde* would fain have been Master, and have made the Cardinal dance after his Pipe. The Cardinal was for bringing of him over to his Party by a Marriage propos'd to him; but the Prince of *Conde* perceiving that the Cardinal was for maintaining his old Post, nor would 'depend on' [be subservient to] him, rejected the

The intestine Commotions.

58. The so-called Peace of Westphalia which ended the Thirty Years' War (1618–48).

Offer as unbecoming the Grandeur of his House. There were also some Women of a restless Spirit concern'd in these Intrigues, among whom was Mad. *de Longueville,* Sister of the Prince of *Conde,* Mad. *Chevreuse, Mombazon,* and others. The first beginning was by slanderous Papers and Libels which were daily dispers'd in *Paris.* There was also a certain

The Slingers.   Faction set up {in Paris} \A. 1648\, who called themselves *the Slingers,* because they openly under-<240>took to knock down the Cardinal, as *David* struck down the Giant *Goliah* by the help of his Sling.[59] The Heads of this Faction were the Duke of *Beaufort,* and *Guadi* [Gondi] the Archbishop of *Paris,* afterwards call'd the Cardinal *de Rez.*[60] With this Party also sided the Parliament of *Paris,* which did pretend to have a great Authority against the Government at that time.

The first Insurrection was made in *Paris,* occasion'd by the taking into Custody of one *Braussel* [Broussel] a Member of the Parliament, whereupon the King left the City. Yet the Business was compos'd for that time, some things having been granted to the mutinous Party. But

The King forc'd to leave Paris.   the Faction of the Slingers renewing their former Disturbances, the King left the City a second time \A. 1649\. The Parliament having then publickly condemn'd the Cardinal, grew every day stronger, *Turenne,* who then commanded the *French* Army in *Germany,* having declar'd for that side; but he was fain to leave the Army, which was kept 'in Duty' [loyal to the king] by the help of a good Summ of Money. And tho' Matters were afterwards reconcil'd a second time at St. *Germains,* yet the Design against *Mazarin* was not laid aside; the Prince of *Conde,* who had brought over the Slingers to his Party, not ceasing to stir them up against him. But because they had a different Aim, for the Slingers were for totally pulling down of the Cardinal, but the Prince of *Conde* would only have humbled him, the Cardinal cunningly rais'd a misunderstanding betwixt them, by setting the Prince of *Conde* against the Slingers. Whereupon the Slingers were reconcil'd with the Cardinal. The Cardinal taking hold of this Opportunity, caused the Prince of

59. The French word for "sling" is *fronde;* thus, the standard reference to these troubles as *les Frondes* (1648–49, 1650–53).
60. Jean François Paul de Gondi, Cardinal de Retz (1614–79).

Conde and his Brother the Prince of *Conti,* and their Brother-in-law the Duke of *Longueville* to be taken into Custody {A. 1650}. This was putting Fuel into the Fire, every body being dissatisfy'd at the Imprisonment of the Princes. The City of *Bourdeaux* openly rebell'd. The *Spaniards* upon this Occasion took from the *French, Piombino* and *Porto Longone* in *Italy.* The Archduke *Leopold* struck Terrour into the City of *Paris* it self, on the side of the *Netherlands.* And tho' the Cardinal beat *Turenne* near *Rethel,* he being gone over to the *Spaniards,* yet <241> the Hatred against him encreas'd daily, and the Faction of the Slingers, the Parliament, and the Duke of *Orleans* were absolutely for having the Princes set at Liberty. The Cardinal therefore perceiving that nothing was to be done by open Violence, resolv'd to avoid the Storm, by setting the Princes at Liberty: And he himself retir'd to *Bruel,* the Court of the then Elector of *Collen* [Cologne] \A. 1651\. Then he was by a Decree of the Parliament for ever banish'd [from] the Kingdom of *France.*

Mazarini being thus remov'd, the Prince of *Conde* began to disturb the publick Quiet with more freedom, having engag'd himself with the *Spaniards,* and being gone to *Bourdeaux,* he began to make open War against the Government. And the *Spaniards* taking hold of this Opportunity, recover'd *Barcellona,* and with it all *Catalonia.* Then the Queen recall'd the Cardinal, who having strengthen'd the King's Army by such Troops as he had got together, fought several times very briskly with the Prince of *Conde.* But seeing that the Hatred which the Faction of the Slingers and the Parliament had conceiv'd against him, did not diminish, he took this Course, that he publickly declar'd, he was willing to leave the Kingdom, to re-establish the publick Quiet. He hoped by so doing, to lay the Blame of the Intestine Divisions upon the Prince of *Conde* alone; which Design prov'd successfull; for thereby the Eyes of the People were opened, who now plainly perceiv'd, that the Cardinal sought the Good of the King and Kingdom, but the Prince of *Conde* his own Interest, *Dunkirk* and *Graveling* being lost in the Fray. The Prince of *Conde* therefore perceiving that he had lost the Favour of the People, retir'd with his Troops into the *Spanish Netherlands.* Then the Cardinal return'd to Court, and ever after had the Administration of the chiefest Affairs of the Kingdom till his Death, without any further Opposition.

The Imprisonment of the Princes.

The Cardinal banish'd [from] France.

The Queen recalls him.

The City of *Paris* return'd to its due Obedience, the Faction of the Slingers was dissolv'd, the Duke of *Orleans* left the Court; *Rez* was taken into Custody, and *Bourdeaux* forc'd to submit \A. 1653\.

In the Year next following the *French* began again to make War on the *Spaniards;* they took *Mom-*<242>*medy* [Montmédy] with great difficulty, and fortunately reliev'd *Arras:* But they were beaten from before *Valenciennes* and *Cambray.* *France* having just made an Alliance with *Cromwell,* the joint Forces of *France* and *England* besieged *Dunkirk* under the Command of *Turenne* \A. 1658\: And the Duke *John d' Austria* and Prince *de Conde,* who came with an Army to relieve it, being repuls'd with great loss, the City was taken and deliver'd to the *English,* from whom the King afterwards \A. 1662\ redeem'd it for four Millions. About the same time *Graveling* was also retaken. At last \A. 1659\ a Peace was concluded between *France* and *Spain* near the *Pyrenaean* Mountains by the two chief Ministers of State, on both sides, *viz.* by *Mazarini* and *Don Lewis de Haro,* by vertue of which, *France* was to keep *Roussilion* and the greatest part of the places which were taken in the *Netherlands; Mary Theresa,* the Daughter of *Philip* IV. was to be married to the King, and the Prince of *Conde* to be receiv'd into Favour again. This last point met with great Opposition for a considerable time. In the Year next following died *Mazarini,* who, as 'tis said, left the King among others, this Lesson, *That he should govern himself, and not trust entirely to any Favourite.*

The first thing of moment, which the King undertook \A. 1661\, was, to settle his Revenues in a good order. He began with the Lord High Treasurer *Fouquet,* whom he took into Custody, and made a strict Inquisition against all such as having had hitherto the management of his Revenues, had enrich'd themselves therewith: The Sponges which were swell'd up with Riches, being soundly squeez'd out, brought an incredible Treasure into the King's Coffers. In the Year 1661 a Difference arose betwixt the *French* and *Spanish* Embassadours in *London,* about the Precedency at the solemn Entry made by Count *Nils Brahe* the *Swedish* Embassadour, where the *French* Embassadour's Coach was put back by Violence. This might easily have prov'd the Occasion of a War, if the *Spaniards* had not given Satisfaction to the *French,* and

The Pyrenaean Peace.

The Death of Mazarini.

A Dispute about Precedency between the French and Spanish Embassadours.

agreed, *That where-ever there were any* French *Embassadours resident, the* Spanish *should not appear upon any publick Occasions:* Which <243> the *French* do interpret, as if *Spain* had thereby declar'd, That {at all places and times} the *Spanish* Ministers were always to give place to the *French* of the same Character.

In the Year 1662, the King made an Agreement with the Duke of *Lorrain,* according to which, he was to exchange his Dukedom for an Equivalent in *France,* and his Family to be the next in right of *Succession,* if the Family of *Bourbon* should happen to fail: Which Agreement the Duke would fain have annull'd afterwards, but the King, who did not understand jesting in such a point, forc'd him to surrender to him *Marsal.* In the same Year the Duke *de Crequy* the *French* Embassadour at *Rome,* was grossly affronted there by the *Corsi* Guards, which the King resented so ill, that he took from the Pope the City of *Avignon:* But the Difference was compos'd by the Mediation of the Grand Duke of *Tuscany* at *Pisa,* and the Pope was fain to send a splendid Embassy to give Satisfaction to the King. About the same time the *French* would have got footing at *Gigeri* on the Coast of *Barbary,* but were repuls'd with considerable loss by the *Moors.* The King also sent some Troops \A. 1664\ to the Assistance of the Emperour against the *Turks,* who behav'd themselves bravely in the Battel fought near St. *Gothard,* and contributed much to the Victory. Notwithstanding which the Emperour clapt up a Peace with the *Turks,* fearing lest the King of *France* might make use of this Opportunity to fall into the *Netherlands.* Yet those Forces, which were sent to the Assistance of the *Venetians* into *Candie,*[61] did not acquire so much Glory, they being too forward and hot in the first Onset, where they lost the Duke of *Beaufort.*

In the Year 1665, the King of *France* kindled a War betwixt the *En-*

A Treaty with the Duke of Lorrain.

A Difference with the Pope.

---

61. Venetian Candia (modern Herakleion), in Crete, fell to the Ottomans in 1669 after a twenty-year siege and after the departure of French forces sent to relieve it. The Pope's efforts to relieve Candia led him to issue a bull dissolving two religious orders, so that he could use their resources for the defense of Candia against the Turks. Pufendorf's cynical take on the pope's action is found in his "Brevis commentatio super ordinum religiosorum suppressione ad bullam Clementis IX. P.M.," which is included in Pufendorf (1675) and (1995). Also see note 26, p. 346, below; and the Editor's Introduction, p. xxx.

glish and '*Dutch*' [Hollanders], thereby to weaken their Naval Force, which was so formidable to him, and in the mean while to get leisure to conquer the *Netherlands.* In the Year 1667, he enter'd the '*Nether-lands*' [Flanders] in person, and took *Charleroy, Lisle, Tournay, Doway, Courtray, Oudenarde,* and some other places, pretending, that the *Netherlands* did belong to him in right of his Queen, by vertue of the *jus devolutionis* or *right of devolution,* {as it was called} in *Bra-*<244>*bant,* notwithstanding that in the Marriage Contract she had renounc'd all her Title to it.[62] He also conquer'd the County of *Burgundy,* but after having demolish'd the Fortifications he restor'd it again, but kept those places which he had taken in the *Netherlands,* by vertue of the Peace concluded at *Aix la Chapelle* \A. 1668\. The tripple Alliance, as it is call'd, made betwixt *Sweden, England* and *Holland,* which was intended for the Preservation of the {Spanish} *Netherlands,* did greatly hasten this Peace; tho' *France* afterwards found out a way to draw the *English* Court from this Alliance and to join with him [it] in humbling the *Holland-ers* who 'he' [it was] said were too proud. For tho' *France* all along had been in the Interest of *Holland,* yet the King took it very ill, that the '*Dutch*' [Hollanders] had made a Peace at *Munster,*[63] without includ-ing *France,* and that they had been so bold \A. 1667\ as to undertake the Preservation of the {Spanish} *Netherlands;* and when afterwards the King put strong Garrisons into the conquer'd 'places' [cities], they sent a Fleet on these Coasts, as it were to brave him. The tripple Alliance also was displeasing to him, and some are of Opinion, that the King of *England,* who had not forgot the Business at *Chatam,*[64] and that the Peace concluded at *Breda* was not according to his wish, had engag'd himself in this Alliance, only to draw in the *Dutch* thereby, and so to exasperate the King of *France* against them.

At last, *France* in conjunction with *England,* made War on *Holland,* with prodigious Success at first {on land} \A. 1672\; for he took three

He attacks Flanders.

Peace made at Aix la Chapelle.

He invades Flanders.

---

62. Thus, the so-called War of Devolution (1667–68). Maria Theresa of Spain (1638–83) was a daughter of Philip IV (1605–65). On the right of devolution, see II.14, p. 80, above.

63. In 1648, as part of the Westphalian settlement.

64. See note 63, p. 179, above, and note 34, p. 298, below.

Provinces, *viz. Gueldres, Over-yssel* and *Utrecht;* besides that he had already possess'd himself of some Passes leading into *Holland:* But his
Confederate the Bishop of *Munster*[65] had not the same Success in the
Siege of *Groningen,* and afterwards lost *Coeverden* again. And the *Dutch*
had better Success at Sea, where they behaved themselves bravely in
four several Engagements, whereas the *French* Fleet, as the *English* say,
did not engage heartily: Besides, *England* grew Jealous of the great Success of the *French,* which was one reason, why the Parliament did in a
manner oblige the King [Charles II], to make a separate Peace with *Holland,* fearing, that *France,* after *England* and *Holland* had destroy'd one
another <245> at Sea, might also, at last, fall upon them. The Emperour
and Elector of *Brandenburgh* endeavour'd, immediately at the beginning of the War, to give a Diversion to *France* but to no great purpose,
since they did nothing but ruin several Provinces in *Germany,* and drew
Turenne with his Army thither, who ravag'd the Country, but especially
Westphalia. The Elector of *Brandenburgh* made a Peace with *France* at
Vossem \A. 1673\, whereby he got the Restitution of his strong Holds in
the Dutchy of *Cleves,* but as soon as he got them into his possession, he
made no great account of the Peace. In the Year next following, *France*
took the strong City of *Mastricht,* where the *French* both shew'd their
Bravery and Dexterity in attacking of places. On the other hand, the
Imperialists had good Success against *Turenne* {in Franconia}, who 'pretended' [sought] to oppose their March; for they trick'd him, and having march'd to the *lower Rhine,* in conjunction with the *Spaniard* and
Prince of *Orange,* took *Bon*[n]: This, and the loss of *Na*[e]*rden,* which
the '*Dutch*' [Hollanders] took, caus'd the *French* to leave *Utrecht* and all
the other places in the United Provinces, except *Grave* and *Mastricht:*
For it seem'd very difficult to maintain so many Garrisons, and at the
same time to have a sufficient Army in the Field to oppose the Enemy;
since it might easily have happen'd, that all Correspondency with these
places in the United Provinces might have been cut off by the Enemy.

Afterwards *Spain* and the whole *German* Empire declar'd against
France, and a great many were of Opinion, That the joint Power of

Mastricht taken by the French.

65. Christoph Bernhard von Galen (1606–78).

Spain, Holland and *Germany*,[66] would be sufficient to curb the *French,* and to carry the Seat of the War into *France* itself; but this could not be effected. 'Tis true, the *Germans* did take from the *French, Philipsburgh,* and beat them out of *Treves* [Trier], where Mareschal *de Crequi* receiv'd a Defeat. But on the other hand, the *Germans* were several times also, especially near *Sintsheim* and in *Alsace,* worsted by the *French* {A. 1674}, and oblig'd to repass [pull back quickly over] the *Rhine.* And in the Year 1675, there was a great probability that it would not have gone very well

The Death of Turenne. with them on this side of the *Rhine,* if the brave *Turenne* had not been kill'd by an <246> accidental Shot, which oblig'd the *French,* who were ignorant of his Design, after a sharp Engagement, to retire on the other

The Losses of the Spaniards in this War. [west] side of the *Rhine.* For the rest, *Spain* lost most by this War: for the *Franche Compte* was taken from them, *Messina* receiv'd voluntarily a *French* Garrison, and the *Dutch* Fleet which was sent to the Assistance of the *Spaniards* into *Sicily,* got nothing but Blows, the brave Admiral *de Ruyter* being there slain; tho' afterwards the *French* quitted *Messina* on their own accord. Besides this the *French* took from them these strong holds; *Limburgh, Conde, Valenciennes, Cambray, Yper, St. Omer, Aire* and several others. The Prince of *Orange* retook *Graves,* but in the Battel of *Seneffe* and *St. Omer,* he was worsted, and sustained a considerable

Peace at Nimmegen. loss before *Mastricht.* At last *France* ended this War very gloriously for it self, restoring to *Holland* what it had taken from those *Provinces,* but kept *Burgundy* and a great many strong places in the *Spanish Nether-lands.* In *Germany* in lieu of *Philipsburgh* it got *Friburgh,* and for the rest the *Westphalian* and *Copenhagen* Treaties were renewed, by Virtue of which *Sweden* was restored to its own again.[67]

The French Nation. §25. To consider the *French* Nation, whose History we have briefly re-lated, it must be observ'd, That it is swarming (if I may so speak) with

66. Pufendorf's order is Germany, Spain, and Holland.

67. The Treaty of Copenhagen (1660) ended the Second Northern War, between Sweden, Denmark, and Poland. France's support of Sweden at both Westphalia and Copenhagen was critical to the terms it received in both treaties. This and continued French financial support assured Sweden's pro-French foreign policy until the early 1680s.

People, and sow'd thick with Cities and Towns. Under the Reign of *Charles* IX.[68] it is related, That above twenty Millions of People paid the Poll Tax. Some say, That *Richlieu* affirm'd, that by Computation, *France* could bring into the Field 600.000 Foot, and 150.000 Horse, provided every Man that was able to bear Arms, did go into the Field. This Nation also has been always warlike: nevertheless in former times, it has been objected to them, That they were very brave at the first Onset, but after their first Fury was a little cool'd, their Courage us'd to slacken, if they met with a stout and brave Resistance: wherefore they us'd to make great Conquests, but seldom kept them very long. And after they had good Success, they us'd to grow careless, insult over the conquer'd, and put them to great <247> Hardships under their Government. But in our last Wars they have shewn sufficiently, that they as little want Constancy at last, as Heat and Fury at first. There is a great number of Nobles in *France,* who make Profession of the Sword, and make no difficulty to expose themselves to any Hazards to gain Glory. In former times, the *French* Infantry was good for nothing, wherefore they always us'd to employ *Swiss* and *Scotch:* but now a-days, their Foot are very good, and in attacking of a 'place' [fortification], they are to be preferr'd before all other Nations.

Fall of Nobility.

This Nation always hath a great Veneration and Love for their King; and as long as he is able to maintain his Authority, is ready to sacrifice Life and Estate for his Glory. The *French* are also brisk, forward, and of a merry Constitution: as to their outward appearance in their Apparel and Behaviour, they are generally very comely; and some other Nations, whose temper is more inclined to gravity, and do attempt to imitate them, appear often very ridiculous, there being a vast difference in these matters, betwixt what is natural and what is affected.[69] They are of a Genius fit to undertake {almost} any thing, whether it be in Learning, Trade, or Manufactures; especially in those things which depend more

Their Natural Qualities.

68. Charles IX (1550–74).

69. On imitating the French, see *The Present State of Germany,* VII.2, in Pufendorf (2007), p. 183. Pufendorf's younger friend, Christian Thomasius (1655–1728), wrote a *Discourse on Imitating the French* (*Diskurs von der Nachahmung der Franzosen*) in 1687.

on ingenuity and dexterity than hard labour. On the other side, the levity and inconstancy of the *French* is generally blam'd, |[which is easily to be perceiv'd by such of them as are raw and unpolish'd]|[70]; and a great many of them glory in amorous Intrigues [*Unzucht*], 'oftentimes' [now and then] more than is true; and under Pretence of Freedom, they commit great Debaucheries.

The Nature of the Country. §26. The 'Country' [land] which is possess'd [occupied] by this potent Nation, is very conveniently situated, almost in the very midst of the 'Christian World' [European Christendom]; wherefore this King may conveniently keep Correspondence with them all, and prevent *Europe* from falling into the hands of any one Prince. On the one side, it has the *Mediterranean,* on the other the Ocean, and on both sides a great many pretty good Harbours; and is well water'd with Rivers; besides that great Channel with twelve Sluces, by which the present King has joyn'd <248> the Rivers of *Garonne* and the *Aude,* and consequently the *Mediterranean* with the Ocean; which proves very beneficial for Trade.[71] It is also very near of a circular Figure, and well compacted, so that one

Its Situation. Province may easily assist another. On the side of *Spain,* the *Pyrenaean* Mountains; and on the *Italian* side, the *Alpes* are like a Bullwark to the Kingdom: but on the side towards *Germany* and the *Netherlands,* it lies somewhat open: For out of the *Netherlands, Paris* it self has often been |[hard put to it.]|[72] And this is the reason why the *French* have been so eager in getting a good part of these into their Possession, in which they have been successful in the last War, and thereby have mightily strengthen'd their Frontiers:[73] and for the same reason, they have

70. Rather: "especially as exhibited by young and inexperienced persons—to the great annoyance of other nations," as when young Frenchmen travel and make a scene.

71. The Languedoc Canal (Canal du Midi) built by Louis XIV from 1666 to 1681. Besides facilitating internal trade, the canal also allowed French shipping to avoid the long journey around Spain and exposure to the Barbary pirates.

72. Rather: "put into a state of fear [*mit Schrecken angeblasen*]."

73. The Franco-Dutch War (1672–78), which ended with the Treaty of Nijmegen, whereby France acquired the Franche-Comté and other areas of the Spanish Netherlands. See note 219, p. 520, below.

made themselves Masters of *Lorrain,* to fortify themselves on the side of *Germany;* and by degrees to become Masters of the *Rhine,* the ancient boundary of *Gaul,* which seems {to them}[74] the only thing wanting to the Perfection of *France.*

Next to this, *France* 'may be' [must be considered] one of the most **Its Fertility.** happy and most fruitfull Countries, not only for the equal Temperature of its Climate betwixt an immoderate Heat and an excessive Cold; but also, because it produces every thing, which seems to be requisite for the Sustenance and Conveniency of Mankind; so that scarce a spot of Ground is to be found in *France,* but what produces something or other for the benefit of Man. And its Product is not only sufficient for its Inhabitants, but also plentifull enough to be exported into foreign parts. The Commodities exported out of *France,* are chiefly; Wine, Brandy, Vinegar, Salt, innumerable sorts of Silk, and Woollen Stuffs, and Manufactures, Hemp, Canvas, Linen, Paper, Glass, Saffran, Almonds, Olives, Capers, Prunello's, Chesnuts, Soap, and the like. Yet in *Normandy* and *Picardy,* grow no Vines, but the common people drink Cyder. Scarce any Metals are to be found in *France,* and no Gold or Silver Mines. But this want is supplied by the ingenuity of the *French,* and the folly of Foreigners.[75] For the *French* Commodities have drawn 'Fleets' [streams] of their Money into *France,* especially since *Henry* IV. set up the Silk Manufactury there. There are some who have com-<249>puted that *France* sells Stuffs *A-la-mode* yearly to Foreigners 'only' [alone], to the value of 40 millions of *Livres,* Wine 15 millions, Brandy 5 millions, Salt 10, and so proportionably of other Commodities. Mr. *Forcy* [Fortry] an *Englishman,*[76] says, that about the year 1669, the Commodities which

74. Such qualifications tend to disappear in Crull, though they are important insofar as Pufendorf bases his accounts on each nation's own historians (see the Editor's Introduction, p. xiv, above), and because they allow him another layer of (implicit—by presentation and innuendo) commentary.

75. This is a standard complaint of Pufendorf, given his mercantilist assumptions. See *The Present State of Germany,* VII.3, in Pufendorf (2007), p. 185, and above at II.17, at note 56, p. 87; and IV.34, note 70, p. 185.

76. Samuel Fortrey [1622–82], *Englands interest and improvement: consisting in the increase of the store, and trade of this kingdom* (Cambridge: John Field, 1663; with subsequent editions in 1673, 1713, and 1744). This work advocates immigration

were brought from *France* into *England* exceeded what were carried from *England* to *France,* in value 1.600.000 *lib. Sterl.* And it is notorious that by help of such Commodities as they send into *Spain,* they get a great part of their '*West-India* Plate-Fleet' [American silver].

Yet Navigation does not flourish so much in *France* as it might. The reason seems to be, that the *French* Nation is not so much addicted to the Sea [interested in sea travel], and that other Nations have been before-hand with them in the *East* and *West-Indies.* Which is the reason, that the King, tho' he has above 100 'Capital' [war] Ships, yet cannot set out so great a Fleet hitherto, as the *English* and *Dutch,* as some think, wanting able Seamen. For it is not sufficient to Man out a Fleet once, but in time of War, Recruits must also be had. Nevertheless it may be this King will first settle his Maritime Affairs, and afterwards take his opportunity to surprize his Neighbours. *France* has very few 'Plantations' [colonies] abroad, except what is in the *Caribby Islands,* the Isles called *Tartuges,* and on the North side of *Hispaniola.*[77] They apply themselves also to fishing upon the great Sand Bank before *Newfoundland,* and catch in *Canada* and *New France* good store of Be[a]vers. They have set several Projects on foot for the *East-India* Trade, but without any great success hitherto, the *Dutch,* who are so powerfull there, opposing them with all their might.

Its Plantations.

Lastly the great strength of *France* may {also} be judged of by this, that the Revenue of the Clergy, which is possess'd of two fifth parts {and thus more than half}, as 'tis said, of the Kingdom, amounts to 104 millions and 500.000 Crowns [*Reichs-Thaler*] yearly. The King's Revenues are computed to amount now to 150 millions of Livres [*Frantzösische*

---

and enclosure; Fortrey worried—like Pufendorf—that (English) imports greatly exceeded exports. The 1673 version was reprinted in John Ramsay McCulloch, [ed.,] *A Select Collection of Early English Tracts on Commerce from the Originals of Mun, Roberts, North, and Others, with a Preface and Index* (London: Printed for the Political Economy Club, 1856), available at The Online Library of Liberty: http://oll .libertyfund.org (last consulted on January 2, 2010).

77. Hispaniola was the name for the island now occupied by Haiti (St. Dominique) and the Dominican Republic. Tortuga (Turtle) Island is off the northwestern coast of Haiti. See note 53, p. 85, above.

Gulden], whereas in the last Age [century] it did not amount to above 9 or 10 millions. At the time of *Henry* IV. to 16 millions, and in the year 1639 to 77 millions; which vast difference is in part to be ascribed to the different value of Money since those times, and the great Taxes which are im-<250>posed upon the Subjects: but without question the chief reason is, that *France* since that time has found out new ways to draw Money out of other Countries.

§27. As to the Form of Government of *France*, it is to be observ'd, That anciently there were very potent Dukes, Earls and Lords in *France*, who, tho' they were Vassals of the King,[78] yet they us'd to pay no further Obedience to him, than was consistent with their own Interest, except [when] the Kings were in a Condition to oblige them to it: But all these in process of Time were extinguish'd, and their 'Countries' [lands] {re}united to the Crown. Now a days the Dukes and Earls in *France* are nothing else but bare Titles annex'd to some considerable Estate without any Sovereignty or Jurisdiction. And whereas formerly certain 'Countries' [regions] used to be assign'd to the King's Sons, whereof they bore the Title, now-a-days only a certain yearly Revenue is allotted them, with the Title of a certain Dukedom or County, wherein perhaps they have not a Foot of Ground. And after the ancient Sovereign Dukedoms and Earldoms were abolish'd, some of the great Men of the Kingdom had taken upon themselves great Authority in the Kingdom, but by the Policy of *Richlieu* and *Mazarini* they were reduc'd to such a Condition, that they dare not utter a Word against the King.

> The Government of France.

The Assembly of the Estates (there being three of them, *viz.* The Clergy, Nobility, and the Citizens [*Bürgerschafft*], they making up the third Estate {or order}) |[were also formerly in great Veneration]|,[79] whereby the King's Power was much limited. But they having not been conven'd since the Year 1614, their Authority 'is quite suppress'd' [has died out long ago]. Those of the Reform'd Religion did prove also very

78. They held their lands as fiefs (*Lehen*).
79. Rather: "formerly had much to say."

troublesome to the Kings of *France* as long as they were in a Condition
to 'take up Arms' [defend themselves], but with the loss of *Rochelle*[80]
they lost the Power of giving their Kings any 'Disturbance' [damage]
for the future. And tho' the King hitherto does not {desire to} force
their Consciences,[81] yet he draws off a great many from that Party, by
hopes of his Royal Favour and Preferments. Heretofore the Parliament
of *Paris* us'd {also often} to oppose the King's Designs, <251> under
pretence, <that it had a right,> that the King could not do any thing of
great moment {even in state affairs} without its consent; but this King
hath taught it only to intermeddle with Judicial Business, and some
other Concerns, which the King now and then is pleas'd to leave to its
Decision. The *Gallick* Church also boasts of a particular 'Prerogative'
[freedom] in regard of the 'Court' [chair] of *Rome,* she always having
|[disputed with the Pope some part of his Authority over her]|[82]; and
the King has the Nomination of the Bishops and Abbots, all which
contributes much to the Strength <and Increase> of this Kingdom, if
{only} a wise and good King sits upon the Throne.

The Strength
of France
with regard
to England.
§28. When we duely weigh the Power of *France* in comparison with its
Neighbours, it is easily perceiv'd, that there is not any State in Christendom which *France* doth not equal if not exceed in Power: 'Tis true, in
former Ages the *English* reduc'd the *French,* but at that time they were
possess'd of a great part of it themselves; there were then several Demi-
Sovereign Princes; the *French* Infantry was then inconsiderable, and the
English Bows were terrible to them: All which is quite otherwise now,
and the *English* Landforces are now not to be compar'd with the *French*
neither in Number nor Goodness, since the *English* are unexercis'd,
and their Civil Wars have rather been carried on by Armies rais'd on
a sudden, than [by] well disciplin'd Troops, and these Wars have not a

80. See §20, p. 239, and §23, pp. 251–52, above.
81. Louis XIV revoked the Edict of Nantes in 1685, three years after the initial
publication of the *Introduction.* This passage suggests either that the action was un-
anticipated by Pufendorf or that he was hopeful of a different outcome. See note 53,
p. 248, above; and note 213, p. 518, below.
82. Rather: "refused to grant the Pope all the authority to which he pretends."

little weaken'd this Nation. On the other hand, the *English* have chiefly apply'd themselves to Sea Affairs, and in this the *French* cannot hitherto be compared with the *English;* yet *England* can scarce reap any great Advantages from *France* at Sea. For, suppose they should beat the *French* Fleet, yet they would scarce venture to make a Descent upon *France,* as having not any footing there; and the *French* Privateers would certainly do great mischief to them. But if the *English* should once miscarry at Sea, and that the *French* should once get footing in *England,* it might perhaps prove fatal to that Kingdom, since the fate of the War must be then decided by the Issue of one <252> Battel, *England* having no Inland strong Holds.

In the last 'Age' [century] *Spain* prov'd very troublesome to *France,*   To Spain. the *French* scarce being able to defend themselves against it, and having several times been oblig'd to make Peace upon disadvantageous Conditions: But besides, that at that time the *French* Infantry was good for little, and the *Spanish* Nation was then at its heighth, whereas now the *Spanish* Nobility is more for Debauchery, Gaming, and such like Intrigues, than for acquiring Glory in War; they [the Spanish] were then in full possession of all the *Netherlands,* and *Charles* V. had a great Advantage by being Emperour. But now-a-days the *Netherlands* are miserably torn to pieces, they being scarce able to Garrison the 'places' [fortresses] that remain. *Naples* and *Milan* are almost in the same condition; and *France* may easily secure the Coast of *Provence* against the *Spaniards,* who may be well satisfy'd if the *French* don't by the way of *Roussilion, Navarre,* or *Bayonne* enter *Spain. Italy* is neither willing nor   To Italy. powerfull enough {openly} to hurt *France,* but these Princes ||[are well satisfy'd]|[83] if *France* does not {desire to} pass the *Alpes* and disturb their Repose. The *French* are not powerfull enough for the '*Dutch*' [Hol-   To Holland. landers] at Sea, if they have an Opportunity to make use of all their Naval Strength, yet the *French* Privateers may do them considerable Mischief, wherefore I cannot see what benefit *Holland* can reap from a War with *France* without an absolute necessity: For the '*Dutch*' [Hollander] Land-forces gather'd out of all Nations, are not likely to do any

83. Rather: "thank God."

To the Swiss. great Feats against it. The *Swiss* also neither can nor will [wish to] hurt *France,* they being well satisfy'd if they can get Money {from it}: Wherefore the *French* need not fear any thing from them, except they should {wilfully} make them desperate, when in Confederacy with others they might prove very troublesome.

To Germany. *Germany* seems to be the only Country, which alone might be able to balance *France;* for, if |[these Princes]|[84] were well united, they are able to bring more numerous Armies into the Field, and that in no ways inferiour in Goodness to the *French;* and perhaps they might be able to hold it out with *France.* But considering the present State of *Germany,* it seems next to an impossibility, that all the Members of the Empire <253> should unanimously and resolutely engage themselves in a long War, and prosecute the same with Vigour. For it is not to be imagined, that all of them should have an equal Interest in the War, and some of them must {at length} expect to be {internally} ruin'd {and suppressed}, tho' the War in the main should prove successfull; |[but if it should succeed otherwise, they must be great losers by it without reprieve.]|[85]

The Strength of France in regard of a Confederacy. §29. But if it should be suppos'd, that *France* may be attack'd by a great many at once; it is to be consider'd, that it is absolutely against the Interest of some States, to join themselves against *France.* For, as Affairs now stand, *Portugal* is not likely to join with *Spain, Sweden* with *Denmark, Poland* with the House of *Austria,* against *France.* Neither is it probable that the *Italian* Princes will be desirous to assist the Emperour and *Spain* in [the] subduing of *France,* except we must suppose them to be willing to promote their own {slavery and} Ruin. Neither is it likely that *England* and *Holland* will agree in a War against *France,* for whilst one of them is engag'd in a War against *France,* it seems to be the Interest of the other to stand Neuter, and to promote its own Trade and Navigation {with the other's demise}. It is also not very probable, that the Princes of *Germany,* especially those of the Protestant Religion,

84. Rather: "it." See I.5, note 3, p. 17, above, on the importance of unity for both external and internal security.
85. Rather: "for when things go badly, they must expect to lose some hair."

should be willing to see *France* fall before the House of *Austria;* since both their Power and Religion would stand upon slippery Ground, if not supported by a Foreign Power. Wherefore it seems to be no difficult task to persuade some of the 'Protestant' [German] Princes, at least to sit still {in any war against France}. The *Swiss* also are not likely to co-operate |[with *Spain* and the House of *Austria* in the Conquest of *France*]|,[86] and therefore it would not be so difficult for *France* to defend [maintain] it self against the House of *Austria* and all its Confederates. Not to mention here, that in such a case, *Sweden* and {perhaps also} *Poland* would not leave *France,* if they were in a Condition to assist it. But it is not probable, that *France* should make any account upon [consider] an Alliance with the *Turks,* except in the greatest Extremity; for the *Mahometan* Princes have learn'd by Experience, that where ever they have in-<254>termedled with the Christians in their Wars, these commonly have clapt up a Peace, without including them, or having any regard to their Interest. On the other hand, *France* seems not to be strong enough to overturn all the States of *Europe* by his [its] Conquests {and to bring them all under its sway}: For *France* may be the most potent Kingdom in Christendom, but not the only one; and by extending its Conquests too far it would be weaken'd within: In the mean time, those lesser States bordering upon *France* are in great danger to be devour'd by so flourishing a Kingdom.

86. Rather: "in the raising up of Austria and Spain, and the lowering of France."

ᖆᖆ CHAPTER VI ᖆᖆ

Of the United 'Provinces' [Netherlands].

§1. 'That Country' [Those regions] which is commonly call'd the *Neth-* erlands or the *Lower Germany*, was anciently comprehended, partly un- der *Gaul*, partly under *Germany*, according as they were situated either on this or the other side of the *Rhine*, which was the ancient Boundary of these two vast Countries. That part which was situated on this side of the *Rhine*, was by *Julius Caesar*, together with the rest of *Gaul*, reduc'd under the Obedience of the *Roman* Empire. Afterwards the *Batavi* and the *Zealanders* did also submit to the *Romans*, yet so, that they were rather esteem'd {unequal} Allies than Subjects. And when in the Fifth Century, after the Birth of Christ, the *Francks* establish'd a new King- dom in *France*, these Provinces were also at first united to it: But at the same time when *Germany* was separated from *France*, most of them fell to *Germany*, few remaining with *France*.

The ancient state of the United Provinces.

The Governours of these 'Provinces' [regions] did, in process of time, under the Names of Dukes and Earls, make themselves Demi- Sovereigns, as did also other Princes of *Germany* and *France;* yet so, that it was a general Maxim among them, *To rule the People* [*Volk*] *with Mildness.* And for the |[Security of their Liberty]|,[1] they us'd <255> to grant them {many} great Privileges, in the maintaining of which this Nation [*Völcker*] was always very forward [*jaloux*]. The Estates also, which consisted of the Clergy, Nobility [knighthood, *Ritterschaft*], and Cities, were always in great Authority, and would not easily suffer

---

1. Rather: "securing of this sovereigny."

273

that any new Impositions should be laid upon 'the People' [themselves] without their consent.

The Division of the 17 Provinces. These Provinces, according to the common computation, are Seventeen in number: *viz.* Four Dukedoms of *Brabant, Limburgh, Luxemburgh,* and *Gueldres:* Seven Earldoms of *Flanders, Artois, Hainault, Holland, Zealand, Namur* and *Zutphen:* Five Lordships of *Friesland, Malines, Utrecht, Over-yssel* and *Groningen. Antwerp* has the title of a Marquisate of the {Holy} *Roman* Empire. These Provinces were anciently {almost all} ruled each by its <Prince or> Lord; but afterwards several of them were either by Inheritance, Marriages, or Contracts united together, till most of them fell to the share of the House of *Burgundy,* from whence they came to the House of *Austria* by the Marriage of *Maximilian* I. who had marry'd *Mary* the only Daugh-

The Union of the 17 Provinces. ter of *Charles* surnamed *The Hardy.* And [they] were afterwards all united under *Charles* V. who govern'd them in Peace and Prosperity. 'Tis related, that he had once taken a Resolution to make them one Kingdom, which however he could not effect, their Laws and Privileges being so different, and they so jealous of one another, that none of them would remit any thing of their Pretences in favour of the rest. {Yet he made a constitution, that the provinces should always remain together.}

Their Condition under Charles V. But the Reign of *Charles* V. over the *Netherlands,* proved so very fortunate, because he bore an extraordinary Affection to them, and they to him: For *Charles* was born in *Ghent,* educated amongst them, and liv'd a considerable time there. His Humour suited very well with theirs, he conversed with them in a friendly manner without haughtiness, employing the *Netherlanders* frequently in his Affairs, whereby this Nation was in great esteem at his Court. But under the Reign of his Son *Philip* II. these Provinces were torn to Pieces by {terrible} intestine Commotions and 'civil' [protracted] Wars, which {finally} occasion'd the Rise of a {new and} potent Commonwealth [*Republicq*] in *Europe.* This <Government> having prov'd the occasion of great Alterations, it is worth our while to search both into the cause of these <256> Commotions and the Origin of this new Government [*Republicq*].

§2. *Philip* II. therefore was not a little to be blam'd, as being partly himself the cause of these civil Troubles; for he being born in *Spain*, and educated after the *Spanish* Fashion, did favour only the *Spaniards*, representing in all his Behaviour a perfect haughty *Spaniard;* which did mightily alienate the Minds of the *Netherlanders*, especially after he resided altogether in *Spain,* and did not so much as honour the *Netherlands* with his Presence; thinking it perhaps below his Grandeur, that he who was Master of so great a Kingdom, and had such great Projects in his Head, should trouble himself much about the 'Affairs' [complaints] of the *Netherlanders*. Tho' in all Probability these might have been kept in Obedience by his Presence; for [so] his Father, the sooner to appease a Tumult which was only risen in the City of *Ghent,* did venture to take his journey through *France,* and the Territories of *Francis,* who was but lately reconcil'd to him.[2]

The cause of the Wars in the Netherlands under Philip II.

Moreover, *William,* Prince of *Orange,*[3] a crafty, thoroughpac'd [sly], and ambitious Man, did not a little foment these Divisions. For when *Philip* had taken a Resolution to go into *Spain,* and to commit the Administration of the *Netherlands* to a Governour, this Prince was contriving how *Christina,* Dutchess of *Lorrain,* might be constituted Regent of the *Netherlands,* and how he, by marrying her Daughter, might bear the greatest sway in the Government: But he miscarrying in both, because *Philip* constituted *Margaret* of *Parma,* natural Daughter of *Charles* V. Regent of the *Netherlands,* and refus'd to give his consent to the Match, was so dissatisfy'd thereat, that by doing of Mischief, he resolv'd to show his own Strength. The Earls of *Egmont* and *Hoorn* were also very much dissatisfy'd, as also a great many others, who being in great esteem with the People, were all very 'jealous of' [opposed to] the *Spaniards*. A great many also of the Nobility were for a Change, partly out of a hatred to the *Spaniards,* partly because they were naturally of a turbulent Spirit, and were become poor and over Head and Ears in Debt, as ha-<257>ving endeavour'd to outvie the *Spaniards* in Splendour at Court,

William Prince of Orange.

Discontents of the Nobility and Clergy.

2. See II.10, p. 64, and V.17, p. 230, above.
3. William I (the Silent), 1533–84.

and thereby spent more than their Incomes would allow of. The Clergy besides this, was somewhat discontented, because *Philip*, having created several new Episcopal Sees, would have employ'd the Revenues of several Abbies for the Maintenance of them, which did not only dissatisfie such as were in present Possession of these Abbies, but others also, who were in hopes of them for the future: for the Abbots were chosen by a free Election of the Monks in each Monastery, but the Bishops were nominated by the King.

Change of Religion.

But all this could not have furnish'd sufficient Fuel for so great a Flame, if Religion had not been joyn'd to them, which proves most efficacious in disturbing the Minds of the Common People, and always serves for a specious Pretence to such as are for alterations in a State.[4] There were great numbers in the *Netherlands*, who had relinquish'd the *Roman* Catholick Religion, some of them professing the *Augsburgh* Confession, some the Doctrine of the *Huguenots*, others fell into the 'Errors' [phantasies] of the *Anabaptists*.[5] *Charles* V. had by severe Proclamations and Punishments been very hard upon them, which had serv'd for nothing else than to exasperate the Minds of the People, and to promote the new Religion{s}. Wherefore it was the Opinion of *Mary* Queen of *Hungary*, the Sister of *Charles* V. and then Regent of the *Netherlands*,[6] *That they ought rather to be treated more mildly:* But *Philip* had taken a Resolution to root out by force this Heresie, either out of a Zeal for the *Roman* Catholick Religion, or because he hoped thereby to oblige the Pope, whose Favour he stood in need of at that time {for his plans}. He renewed therefore his Father's Proclamation[s], and that with more Severity against these Hereticks; and to put them in Execution, he was for setting up a {spiritual} Court of Judicature, according

Spanish Inquisition.

to the Model of the *Spanish* Inquisition; the very Name of which was terrible to every body: And in effect, this Inquisition is a very cruel Constitution [*grausam Werck*], whereby the Life, Estate, and good Name of

4. See IV.29, pp. 176–78, above.
5. See XII.27, pp. 474–77, and §41, pp. 521–23, below; *On the Nature and Qualification of Religion*, §49, in Pufendorf (2002c), p. 106; and *The Divine Feudal Law*, §14, in Pufendorf (2002b), p. 57.
6. Mary of Austria (1505–58) was regent from 1531 to 1555.

every Subject is put into the Hands of unmercifull Priests [*Pfaffen*],[7] whose chief Glory is to be Inhuman and Rigorous[8] in their proceedings; and who have a power to take up and punish any person upon <258> Suspicion only; and tho' a Man is wrongfully accus'd, he is not to know either his Accuser or Crime, and tho' he makes his Innocence appear, yet he seldom escapes without some punishment. The *Netherlanders* were the more frightned, not only because in this Court, no Privileges, no Favour of the King, nor Intercessions, did avail; but also, because they knew the *Netherlanders* to be free in their Speech, carrying, as it were, their Hearts upon their Tongues, and that by way of Trade they were obliged to be conversant with those of other Religions. Whereas on the other hand, it was natural and easie for an *Italian* or *Spaniard* to keep his Thoughts within himself.

Some are of Opinion, That the *Spaniards* were glad to see that the *Netherlanders* did begin the Fray, hoping thereby to get an Opportunity to force them to Obedience, and by suppressing their Liberty and Privileges to rule over them at pleasure. They hoped {also} that this Country might serve them one day for a Magazine [armoury], from whence they might <conveniently> attack *France, England,* {Germany,} and the Northern Kingdoms. Yet it is also most certain, that some foreign Princes did administer Fuel to nourish and augment the Flame; especially *Elizabeth* Queen of *England,* whose Intention was, by this means to cut out so much Work for the *Spaniard,* that he might not be at leisure to think of Conquering others, his great Power being at that time become terrible to all *Europe.*

Queen Elizabeth fomented their Revolt.

§3. Thus the Seeds of Civil Commotions were sown in the Minds of the *Netherlanders,* about which time \A. 1559\ *Philip* II. went into *Spain*; having so constituted the Government, that the supream Administration of Affairs should be in the Hands of the Regent[9] and the Council of State, of which Council, besides the Prince of *Orange,* were the Earl

7. *Pfaffen* is a derogatory German term for Catholic clergy.
8. Pufendorf speaks of "inhuman strictness" (*unmenschliche Strenge*). His criticism of the Inquisition is also in line with his general, consequentialist view of punishment.
9. Margaret of Parma (1522–86), regent from 1559 to 1567.

The Cardinal of *Egmont* and others, the Cardinal *Granville*, a *Burgundian*,[10] a wise
Granville. Man, and much rely'd on by the King, who had given secret Instructions to the Regent to rule according to his Advice: But the *Netherlandish* Lords quickly perceiving, that the whole Government was manag'd
according to the Counsels of the Cardinal, did sufficiently shew their
Discontent in opposing themselves a-<259>gainst it; especially when
the Cardinal press'd hard to execute the King's Commands concerning
the Establishment of the Bishops, and rooting out of the new Religion; the *Netherlandish* Lords advis'd a Toleration of the same, and to
deal more gently with the People. This {soon} rais'd a general Hatred
against the Cardinal, whereupon the Prince of *Orange,* and the Earls
of *Egmont* and *Hoorn*[11] writ to the King, *That if he* [Granvelle] *was not
remov'd, it would be impossible to preserve the Peace of the* Netherlands;
neither did they rest satisfy'd till *Philip* did consent to their Demands
\A. 1564\. But because the Regent was, after the removal of the Cardinal, sway'd by the President *Vigilites* and the Earl of *Barlemont*,[12] who in
every respect follow'd the footsteps of the Cardinal, this Joy did not last
long, but the old Discontents being renew'd, it was said, *That the Body
of the Cardinal was remov'd from the Council, but his Spirit remain'd in it.*

    Thus the Divisions continu'd in the Council of State, nor could the
Proclamations against the new Religion be put in Execution, because
Count Egmont the People began more and more to oppose them. It was therefore with
sent into consent of the Regent and Senate agreed upon, to send the Earl of
Spain. *Egmont* into *Spain,* who was to give an account to the King, of the
whole state of Affairs, and to see whether the King could find out another Remedy. The King receiv'd him very courteously as to his person,
but would not remit any thing from his Severity as to Religion. And
imagining that the cause why this Evil had taken so deep root, was
the Mildness of the Regent, he caus'd his Proclamation to be renew'd,
commanding withall, That the Counsel [*Concilium*] of *Trent* should be
introduc'd in the *Netherlands.* Besides these Severities a Rumour was

    10. Antoine Perrenot de Granvelle (1517–86).
    11. Egmont, Count of Lamoral (1522–68), the subject of Beethoven's Egmont
Overture; and Philip de Montmorency, Count of Horn (1524–68).
    12. Viglius van Aytta (1507–77); and Charles, Earl of Berlaymont (1510–78).

spread abroad, That *Philip* had agreed with *Charles* IX. at *Bayonne,* by all Means and Ways to root out the Hereticks, which was the cause why it was resolv'd to oppose the King's Intentions.

Some of the Nobility made the first beginning, who enter'd into an Association (which they called *the Compromise*) whereby they engag'd themselves, to oppose the Inquisition, and to stand by one another, if any one should be molested for his Religion; but solemnly protested, That they had no other Aim by so do-<260>ing, but the Glory of God, the Grandeur of the King, and the Peace of their native Country. This Association was drawn up by *Philip Marnix* Lord of *Aldegonde,* and subscrib'd by 400 Persons of Quality, among whom the chiefest were *Henry* of *Brederode, Lewis* Earl of *Nassau,* Brother of the Prince of *Orange,* the Earls of *Culenburgh* and *Bergh.* These met at *Brussels* \A. 1566\, and deliver'd a Petition to the Regent, wherein they desir'd, That the Proclamations issu'd forth touching Religion might be annull'd. The Regent answer'd them in courteous but general terms, telling them, *That she would know the King's Pleasure in the Matter.* 'Tis said, That the Earl of *Barlemont,* who stood then near the Regent, did tell her, *That they were no ways to be fear'd, because they were only* Geusen *or* Beggars;[13] which has render'd the Name of the *Geusen* very famous afterwards, they having had a Beggars Pouch [as] the Coat of Arms of that Confederacy.

An Association of the Nobility.

In the mean while abundance of Pamphlets were spread abroad, which did more and more exasperate the People. And because *Philip* had given but a very indifferent Reception to those Deputies, which were sent into *Spain,* to pray for a Mitigation of these Proclamations, and had refus'd to comply in the least with the Sentiments of the People, it came to an open Insurrection. So that the new Religion was not only publickly profess'd and taught in a great concourse of People, but the Rabble also fell to plundering of [Catholic] Churches and pulling down of Images. And tho' the Prince of *Orange* and the Earl of *Egmont,* did what they could to 'appease' [quiet] this Tumult, yet had the King conceiv'd a shrewd Suspicion as if they had been in the bottom of it;

Breaking of Images.

13. From the French *geux* or *geuse.*

wherefore they were consulting {in various ways about} their own safety, but could, as yet, not come to any {proper} Resolution. In the mean time, the Regent <having> rais'd some Troops, and endeavour'd either by Fear or fair Words, or any other ways to reduce the dissatisfy'd Party to Obedience, some of whom did by Submission and other Services endeavour to be reconcil'd to the King. And this Design succeeded so well, that without any great trouble and the punishment of a very few, the Country was restor'd to its Tranquility: Nevertheless, because it was <261> rumour'd abroad, that a great Army was marching out of *Spain* against them, a great many of the 'Inhabitants' [citizens], and especially of the Handycrafts Trade, did retire into the neighbouring Countries. The Prince of *Orange* himself disliking this calm retir'd into *Germany*.

§4. It was then the Advice of the Regent, that the King should come in person, without any great Force, into the *Netherlands,* and by his Presence and Clemency endeavour entirely to heal the ulcerated Minds

The Duke of Alva. of the People. But he follow'd the Advice of the Duke of *Alva* [Alba],[14] who advis'd to make use of this Opportunity to bring the *Netherlands* under the Yoak, and to strike Terrour into the rest. He march'd \A. 1568\ with a 'brave' [considerable] Army through *Savoy* and *Burgundy* into the *Netherlands,* and having immediately taken into Custody the Earls of *Egmont* and *Hoorn,* whom he pretended to have been underhand the Authors of these Troubles, declar'd all those guilty of High Treason that had had any hand in the Association, the Petition, and pulling down of the Images. And a Court was erected of twelve Judges, from which no Appeal was to be allow'd, where Judgment was to be given concerning these Matters, [and] this Court was commonly call'd *The bloody Council.* Before this Court, the Prince of *Orange* and some other Lords, who were fled, were summon'd to appear, and upon non-appearance they were declar'd guilty of High Treason, and their Estates Confiscated. The same Severity was us'd against others of less note. This caus'd such a Terror among the Inhabitants, that they left their Habitations in Troops

14. Fernando Álvarez de Toledo y Pimentel, Third Duke of Alba (1507–82), governor of the Netherlands from 1567 to 1573.

[great numbers]. He caus'd also Citadels to be built in several great Cities, among which one of the chiefest was that of *Antwerp*.

In the mean time the Prince of *Orange* had brought together considerable Forces in *Germany*, some of which, under the Command of *Lewis* his Brother, falling into *Friesland*, beat the Count of *Arembergh*, the Governour of that Province. But soon after the Duke of *Alva*, having first caus'd the Earls of *Egmont* and *Hoorn* to be beheaded, march'd against him in person. Not long after the Prince of *Orange* fell with a great Army into <262> *Brabant*, but was beaten back by the Duke of *Alva*, and his Forces dispers'd. The Duke of *Alva* puff'd up with this great Success, did not only cause a most magnificent Statue to be erected at *Antwerp;* but having also form'd a Design to conquer the *Netherlands* with their own Money, he impos'd a Tax upon them, of the hundredth Penny, to be paid of the whole value of all Estates; and besides this, the twentieth Penny to be paid of all Moveables, but the tenth of all Immoveables, as often as they were sold.[15] This did exasperate the *Netherlanders* to the utmost degree. And whilst the Duke of *Alva*, being in great want of Money, was busie in squeezing out these Taxes, and was upon the point of forcing the Inhabitants of *Brussels*, who refus'd to pay it, News was brought, That the banish'd *Netherlanders*, who were turn'd Privateers [*Wasser-Geusen*], and had about 24 Ships of 'indifferent' [modest] Strength, had \on April 1, 1571\ under the Conduct of the Earl of *March* taken the City of *Briel* in *Holland*. Then most Cities of *Holland*, out of a Hatred to the *Spaniards*, and the tenth Penny, revolted from the *Spaniards*, except *Amsterdam* and *Schonhoven*, which remain'd for some time under the Obedience of *Spain*.

It was a grand mistake in the Duke of *Alva*, that during his Regency of four Years, he had not secur'd the Sea Coasts. The revolted Places chose for their Governour the Prince of *Orange*, swearing to him Allegiance as the King's Stadtholder, as if they had only revolted from the Duke of *Alva* and not the King. A great many Privateers then join'd from *France* and *England*, who within the space of four Months made

The Earls of Egmont and Hoorn beheaded.

Briel taken.

---

15. The latter corresponded to a traditional Spanish sales tax called the *alcabala* or *alcavala*.

up a Fleet of 150 Ships, who had their Rendezvouz at *Flushing*, and afterwards did great Mischiefs to the *Spaniards*. The Duke of *Alva* was not in a condition to resist this Storm, because the Earl of *Bergh* had not only at the same time taken a great many places in *Gueldres, Friesland* and *Over-yssel*, but also *Lewis* Earl of *Nassau*, had with the Assistance of the *French*, surpris'd *Mons:* Which City the Duke of *Alva* endeavour'd {first} to recover by force of Arms, and the Prince of *Orange*, who with an Army newly rais'd in *Germany*, had made prodigious havock in *Brabant*, <had> in vain endeavour'd to relieve <it>, [and] was [then] retir'd into *Holland.* Wherefore this <263> City was surrender'd upon Articles to the Duke of *Alva.* He then try'd all ways to reduce the revolted places to Obedience by force, having among others, pillag'd *Malines* and *Zutphen*, quite destroy'd *Naerden*, and taken *Haerlem* after a tedious Siege, the Inhabitants of which City were most barbarously treated.

§5. The Affairs of the *Spaniards* in the *Netherlands* being by the rigorous proceedings of the Duke of *Alva* (who us'd to bragg, that during his Regency of six Years he had caus'd 18.000 to be executed by the Hangman) put into Confusion, he was recall'd in the Year 1573. *Lewis Requesenes* succeeded him, a Man of somewhat a milder Temper, but who had a very ill beginning of his Regency, the Fleet which he had sent out to relieve *Middleburgh* being destroy'd before his Eyes, and the City surrender'd to the Prince of *Orange:* Yet the Prince also receiv'd a great Blow; for his Brother *Lewis*, who led an Army to his Assistance out of *Germany*, was routed near *Grave* upon the *Mockerhyde*, where he and his Brother *Henry* were slain in the Field. After this Victory the *Spanish* Souldiers mutiny'd for want of Pay, and liv'd <upon free Quarters> in *Antwerp* till all was paid. Then the Siege of *Leyden* was undertaken, which was reduc'd to the utmost extremity by Famine, till a Dyke of the *Maese* was cut through, by which means, and the help of a *North West* Wind at Spring tide, the Country round about being put under Water, the *Spaniards*, after a great loss sustain'd, were forc'd to leave it. In the Year next following \A. 1574\ the Emperour endeavour'd by his Mediation to compose these Troubles, and a Meeting was held for that purpose betwixt the Deputies of both Parties at *Breda*, which prov'd fruitless. Then the *Spaniards* took *Ziricuzea* [Zirickzee] after a

Siege of nine Months; but before the place was taken *Lewis Requesenes* died \A. 1576\. After his Death the Council of State took the Administration of the Government into their Hands, which was approved by the King.

§6. In the mean time the Hatred of the *Netherlanders* against the *Spaniards* was more and more en-<264>creas'd, especially after the Souldiers, who were grown mutinous for want of Pay, <and> had committed great Outrages, [so] that the Council of State had declared them Enemies, giving leave to the Inhabitants to take up Arms against them. During which Disturbances *Maestricht* and *Antwerp* were plunder'd: Which disposed the rest, to enter upon a Treaty with the Prince of *Orange* at *Ghent*, which contained, That the Provinces had made a Peace betwixt themselves, That the Proclamations issued forth during the Regency of the Duke of *Alva* should be annull'd, and the *Spaniards* sent out of the Country: Which Contract, tho' it was ratify'd by the King, yet he had {secretly} taken a Resolution quickly to disunite them again. For this purpose he constituted *Don John d'Austria,* his natural Brother, Governour of the *Netherlands.* The Prince of *Orange* forewarn'd the *Netherlanders,* That he ought not to be trusted; notwithstanding this, he was receiv'd by [a] plurality of Voices, they having oblig'd him to subscribe the Contract made at *Ghent,* and to send away the *Spanish* Souldiers. But the Prince of *Orange* and the Provinces of *Holland* and *Zealand* were not well satisfy'd with this Agreement, and the rest also quickly began to mistrust him. He gave them sufficient occasion to believe that their Jealousie was not ill grounded, when he by Surprize made himself Master of the Castle of *Namur,* under pretence to secure his person against any Attempts, which so disturb'd the *Netherlanders,* that they took up Arms to drive him out of *Namur.* They also took all the strong Holds, where any *German* Garrison was left, and demolish'd the Castles. And sending for the Prince of *Orange* to come to *Brussels,* they constituted him Grand Bayliff[16] of *Brabant.*

This encrease of the House of *Orange* made some great Men envi-

The Treaty of Ghent.

Don John d'Austria made Governour.

16. That is, Ruart (from *rewaard* or *ruwsard*) or Stadholder, meaning governor of a province.

ous, who made a Party to balance it; among whom, one of the chiefest

Archduke Matthew. was the Duke of *Arshot.* These called in *Matthew,* Archduke of *Austria,* whom they made Governour of the *Netherlands,* who coming with all speed \A. 1577\ was also receiv'd by the Party of the Prince of *Orange,* under condition that the Prince should be his Lieutenant, and he not do any thing without the consent of the Estates. On <265> the other

Alexander Duke of Parma. hand, *Alexander* Duke of *Parma* came with an Army out of *Italy* to the Assistance of *Don John d' Austria,* who bringing with him a good number of old *Spanish* Troops, beat the Army of the Estates near *Gemblours,* and took *Louvain, Philipville, Limbourgh,* and several other places. The Estates then finding themselves alone not strong enough, offer'd to put themselves under the Protection of *Henry* III. King of *France,* and he having refus'd to accept it, the same offer was made to the Duke of *Alenson* his Brother, who having accepted of it, came into the *Netherlands:* But [he] could do nothing of moment, the Provinces and great Men being so divided among themselves, that no body knew who was Master.[17]

There arose also a new Division among the Estates, when upon Request of those of the Reformed Religion, Liberty of Conscience was allow'd in the *Netherlands;* which was willingly consented to by those of *Ghent* and others; but *Artois, Haynault,* and some other *Walloon* Cities, that were very zealous for the Catholick Religion, did oppose it with great violence; and having by degrees separated themselves from

Malecontents. the rest, set up a new Faction, who were call'd *the Malecontents.* During these Troubles *Don John d' Austria* died, leaving the Government

The Duke of Parma. to the Duke of *Parma,* who was confirmed in his place by *Philip.* He began his Regency with the taking of *Maestricht,* and bringing over the *Walloon* Provinces, *viz. Artois, Haynault,* and the *Walloon Flanders,* to the King's Party by accord.

The Union of Utrecht the Foundation of the Commonwealth. §7. The Prince of *Orange* therefore perceiving that the Contract of *Ghent* was quite broke, and that the Great Men who envied one another, and the several Provinces, that were of a different Religion, were

---

17. Literally, cook or waiter (*Koch oder Kell[n]er*).

scarce ever to be United: And yet being desirous to secure himself, and to establish the Protestant Religion, \A. 1579\ he got the Estates of the Provinces of *Gueldres, Holland, Zealand, Friesland* and *Utrecht*, to meet. Here it was agreed, that they would defend one another as one Body; that they would consult concerning Peace and War, Taxes, and the like, with common Consent; and that they would maintain 'Liberty of Con-<266>science' [freedom of religion].[18] This Union, made at *Utrecht*, (wherein also afterwards *Over-Yssel* and *Groningen* were included) is the Foundation of the Common-wealth of the United *Netherlands*. At that time their Affairs were in so low a Condition, that they coined a Medal, wherein their State was represented by a Ship without Sails, 'or' [and] Rudder, left to the Mercy of the Waves, with this Inscription, *Incertum quo fata ferant* ["it is uncertain where the fates may lead (us)"].

The Fortune of the Prince of *Orange* absolutely depending now on this Union, he made it his business to hinder the Conclusion of the Treaty of a general Peace, which by the Mediation of the Emperour was set on foot at *Collen* [Cologne], because a general Peace might easily have dissolved this Union. And, because the Affairs of the *Netherlands* grew worse and worse every day, the *Spaniards* having taken one after another, the Cities of *Bois le Duc, Breda, Tournay, Valenciennes, Malines,* and Others, and a great many of the Great Men being gone over to the *Spanish* Party: The Prince of *Orange* on the other hand being well assured, that the *Spaniards* one time or another would revenge them-selves upon him and his friends; and finding himself not in a capacity to maintain the Cause against them, he persuaded the Estates of the *Netherlands* that they should renounce all Obedience to *Philip*, who had violated their Privileges confirmed to them by Oath, and make the Duke of *Alenson*[19] their Soveraign, with whom he had underhand made an agreement, That the United Provinces should fall to his [own] share. And the Estates of *Holland, Zealand* and *Utrecht*, were then for mak-

18. An example of how the translator renders Pufendorf's German in terms of his own language and intellectual context. "Freedom of religion," which includes exter-nal actions, is not the same as internal "liberty of conscience." See Saunders (2003).

19. Hercule François, Duke of Anjou and Alençon, 1555–84, was the youngest son of Henry II and Catherine de Medici of France.

ing him their Soveraign, except the Cities of *Amsterdam* and *Gouda;* and questionless it would have been done afterwards, if his unexpected Death [in 1584] had not prevented it.

§8. The Duke of *Alenson* having obtained the Soveraignty \A. 1581\, raised the Siege of *Cambray,* which was besieged by the *Spaniards,* and in the year next following was at *Antwerp* proclaimed Duke of *Brabant,* and at *Ghent* Earl of *Flanders.* But his Power being confined within very narrow Bounds by the Estates, he, by the advice of his Friends, re-solved to make himself Absolute. He proposed to the Estates, That if he should die without Issue, these Countries might be United <267> with the Crown of *France;* which being denied him, he took a strange Reso-lution; *viz.* By surprize to make himself absolute Master of *Antwerp,* and some other Cities. For this purpose several Thousands of *French* were already got privately into *Antwerp,* which were beaten out by the Citizens with considerable Loss. They made the like Attempts upon several other Places on the same day, which every-where miscarried, except at *Dendermond, Dunkirk,* and *Dixmuide.* And thus the *French* having lost at once all their credit, and the affection of the *Netherland-ers,* the Duke of *Alenson,* full of shame and confusion, returned into *France,* where he died soon after [in 1684].

The *French* intermedling with the Affairs of the *Netherlands,* had drawn with it another Evil; which was, That Foreign Souldiers were again brought into the *Netherlands,* which was against the Agreement made with the *Walloons.* Then \A. 1583\ the Duke of *Parma* re-took *Dunkirk, Newport, Winoxbergen, Menin, Alost,* and some other Places in *Flanders. Ypres* and *Bruges* did also submit \A. 1584\. And in the same Year the Affairs of the Estates received a great Blow by the Death of *William* Prince of *Orange,* who was stabb'd in his Palace at *Delft* by a *Burgundian,* whose Name was *Balthasar Gerhard.* By whose Death the *Netherlands* being without a Head, were left in great confusion.[20]

20. William I (the Silent) of Orange (see note 3, p. 275, above) was assassinated (with pistols) on July 10, 1584. The assassin himself did not collect the 25,000 gold crowns that Philip II had placed upon William's head, but they were actually paid to his mother.

§9. After the Death of Prince *William*, the Estates did make *Maurice*,[21] His Son Prince Maurice made Stadtholder. Son of the deceased, Stadtholder of *Holland, Zealand*, and *Utrecht;* and he being but eighteen Years of Age, they constituted the Earl of *Hohenloe* his Lieutenant. But the Soveraignty they proffered to the King of *France*, who being at that time distracted with intestine Wars, was not at leisure to accept of it. The Duke of *Parma* in the mean while taking advantage of this juncture of Affairs, reduced *Antwerp* by Famine within a Twelve month's time; as also *Dendermond, Ghent, Brussels, Malines* and *Nimeguen* by Force. After the Loss of *Antwerp*, the Estates, who were for submitting Themselves to any body but the *Spaniards*, offered the The English Confederacy. Soveraignty over them to Queen *Elizabeth*, which she refused to accept of: Yet she entred with them into a more strict <268> Alliance, by virtue of which she obliged her self to maintain a certain number of Souldiers at her own Charge in the *Netherlands*, which, with all the other Forces of the Estates, were to be Commanded by an *English* General. And the Estates did Surrender to the Queen, as a Security for the Charges she was to be at, the Cities of *Flushing, Briel* and *Rammakens*, or *Seeburgh* upon *Walchorn*, which were afterwards \A. 1616\ restored to the Estates for the Summ of One Million of Crowns.

The Queen sent *Robert Dudley*, Earl of *Leicester*, as General into *Holland;* who being arrived there \A. 1586\, was made by the Estates their The Regency of the Earl of Leicester. Governour-General, and that with a greater Power than was acceptable to the Queen; but he did no great Feats. For the Duke of *Parma* not only took *Grave* and *Venlo*, and forced him from before *Zutphen;* but he also administer'd the publick Affairs at a strange 'rate' [manner], to the great dissatisfaction of the Estates, to whom he had rendred himself suspected. Their Discontents were much augmented, after *William Stanley*, who was by the Earl of *Leicester* made Commander in Chief in *Deventer*, had betray'd that City to the *Spaniards*. The Year next following, the Earl of *Leicester* attempted the Relief of *Sluice* [Sluys] in *Flanders*, but to no purpose; and being returned into *Holland*, where he

---

21. Maurice of Nassau (1567–1625) became stadholder in 1585 but did not succeed as Prince of Orange until 1618, after the death of his older brother Philip William (1554–1618), who was in Spanish custody until 1596. See §13, p. 293, below.

by several suspicious Undertakings augmented the Differences betwixt him and the Estates, he returned very ill satisfied into *England;* where, by Command of the Queen, he resign'd his Office of Governour.

The State of Affairs in Holland begins to mend. §10. Hitherto the Affairs of the United *Netherlands* (whom henceforward we will call *Hollanders*) had been in a very ill Condition; but from this time forwards they began to mend a-pace, and became more settled. This was partly occasioned by the Ruin of the two Provinces of *Brabant* and *Flanders,* which were reconciled to the King, upon condition, That such as would not profess themselves *Roman Catholicks,* should leave the Country within a prefixed time: A great many of these flocking into *Holland,* made its Cities very populous. Especially all the Traffick of *Antwerp* was transplanted to *Amsterdam,* which rendred that City very Rich and Potent at Sea. Besides this[,] <269> *Philip,* like those, who will hunt two Hares with one Dog, did not only attempt to Invade *England* with a great Fleet \A. 1588\, but also sent in the Year next following the Duke of *Parma* with an Army to the Assistance of the League in *France;* both which proving fruitless, the *Hollanders* had in the mean while leisure given them, to put themselves into a good posture. Whereas the Duke of *Parma* had wisely advised the King, that he should with all his Power first subdue the *Hollanders,* before he engaged in another War. For *Maurice,* whom they had, after the Departure of the Earl of *Leicester,* made their Generalissimo both by Sea and Land, had restored their lost Reputation.

His first Attempt was upon *Breda,* which he took by a Stratagem \A. 1590\. In the Year next following he took *Zutphen, Deventer, Hulst* and *Nimeguen.* And in the Year 1592, *Steenwyck* and *Coeverden.* In the same Year the Death of the brave Duke of *Parma* proved a great Loss to the *Spaniards.* For the *Spanish* Souldiers growing Mutinous every-where, did not a little advance the Progresses of the *Hollanders. Gertrudenbergh* was taken \A. 1593\ in the sight of the *Spanish* Army. In the Year next following *Groningen* was reduced, whereby the United Provinces were made entire, and secured on this side of the *Rhine.* In the Year 1596, *Albert,* Arch Duke of *Austria,* arrived as Governour of the *Netherlands,* who began his Regency with the Taking of *Hulst.* And, because *Philip,*

Arch Duke Albert, Governour of the Spanish Netherlands.

being oppressed with Debts, was fain to shut up his Exchequer, *Albert,* for want of Money, was not in a capacity to undertake any thing of moment in the Year next following, but was soundly beaten near *Tougenhout* [Tournout]. And after the Trade of the *Hollanders* with *Spain* and *Portugal,* whither they used to send their Ships under Foreign Flags, had been quite cut off; whereby the *Spaniards* hoped the sooner to reduce them to Obedience, Necessity, and the desire of Lucre, taught them another way to obtain vast Riches. For by this means the *Hollanders* were forced to try whether they could Sail themselves into the *East-Indies,* and to attempt to find out a nearer Way thither round about the *North.* But this Design not succeeding, they took the common Course about *Africa;* and having with incredible Pains, in <270> spite of all the Resistance made by the *Portuguese,* settled a Trade there, a great many Merchants and others, who knew no better way to employ their Ready-money, erected several Societies to Trade into the *East-Indies:* All which were by virtue of a Patent granted by the Estates, formed into one Company \A. 1602\, which did afterwards prodigiously encrease its Power in the *East-Indies,* and has conveyed unconceivable Riches into *Holland.*[22] In the Year 1597, *Maurice* took *Rhinebergh, Meurs,* and all the rest of those Places of *Over-Yssel,* which were as yet in the possession of *Spain.*

The East-India Company.

§11. In the Year 1598, ||[they found out another Decoy]||[23] for the *Hollanders.* For because it was generally pretended, that they would not live under *Spanish* subjection, *Philip* found out this artifice: He Married his daughter *Isabella Clara Eugenia* to *Albert,* Arch-Duke of *Austria,* giving unto her as a Dowry *Burgundy* and the *Netherlands;* yet, with this Condition, That the same should return to *Spain,* if no Heirs proceeded from this Match, which the *Spaniards* were very well assured of, the Princess being pretty well in Age; and besides this, having been spoiled before by means of some Medicaments administred to her to prevent Conception. The *Netherlands* being then by this means, according to

Isabella Clara Eugenia.

22. The Dutch East India Company, whose capture of a Portugese carrack Hugo Grotius defended in the twelfth chapter of *De Jure Praedae* (*On the Law of Booty*), which was published separately in 1609 as *Mare Liberum* (*The Free Sea*).

23. Rather: "[the Spaniards] devised another trial."

outward appearances freed from a Foreign Subjection, as having got their own Prince, it was hoped the *Hollanders* would the easier re-unite themselves with the other Provinces; because a Peace being lately concluded betwixt *France* and *Spain* at *Nervin,* the *Hollanders* had thereby lost their chief Confederate. But the *Hollanders* remained stedfast in their former Resolution, rejecting all Propositions of Peace made by the Emperour and the Arch Duke *Albert.*

Battel near Newport.   In the Year 1600, *Maurice* fell into *Flanders,* with an intention to besiege *Newport,* but was met by *Albert,* where a bloody Battel ensued, and *Maurice* obtained a most glorious Victory, who was otherways always averse to Field-fights, and would never have resolved at that time to have ventured the whole Fortune of *Holland* upon the Issue of a Battel, if he had not been forced to it; wherefore, without **Siege of Ostend.** attempting any thing farther, he return-<271>ed into *Holland. Albert* then undertook the Siege of *Ostend* \A. 1601\, during which both sides did their utmost, till *Ambrose Spinola* forc'd the place {A. 1604}, the **The Conquests on both sides.** besieg'd having no more room left to make any Retrenchments. 'Tis said, that the *Hollanders* lost within the Town above 70.000 Men, and the *Spaniards* without a great many more. But in the mean time the *Spanish* Fleet under the Command of *Frederick Spinola* was destroy'd, and *Rhinebergh, Grave* and *Sluce* taken by *Maurice.* In the Year 1605, *Spinola* retook from the *Hollanders, Lingen, Groll* and *Rhinebergh,* and *Maurice* sustain'd some loss before *Antwerp.* The last glorious Action in this War was, that of *James Heemskirke,* who burned the *Spanish* Fleet in the Harbour of *Gibraltar,* where he himself was kill'd.

The *Spaniards* therefore finding it impossible to reduce *Holland* by force, which they found encreas'd in Strength by the War; and being besides this, 'jealous of' [apprehensive about] *Henry* IV. and quite out of breath by this tedious War, they resolv'd to make an end of it at any rate [cost]. How desirous the *Spaniards* were of the Peace may easily be conjectur'd from hence, That *Albert* himself propos'd the Treaty to be at the *Hague,* and first sent *Spinola* himself thither as Embassadour, whereas the *Hollanders* |[carry'd it very high]|,[24] and were very resolute.

24. Rather: "acted very haughty and irritable."

The Business met with great difficulty, before it could be brought to the conclusion of a Truce of twelve Years: The greatest obstacle was, that the *Hollanders* urg'd it closely [insisted], That *Spain* without any Exception should declare them a free People, which the *Spanish* Embassadours {unable and} refusing to do, at last this Medium was found out; That *Spain* and the Archduke *Albert* did declare, they would treat with the {united} *Netherlanders*, As {with} a free 'Nation' [people]. And they being not satisfy'd also with this, the President *Janin*, who was sent thither in behalf of *France*, answer'd, That the word *As* could not add much to the Strength of *Spain*, nor diminish theirs; and that it was their Business to secure themselves and their State by Arms and not by Words. Both Parties kept what they were possess'd of, and the *Hollanders* maintain'd their Navigation into the *East Indies*, which the *Spaniards* would fain have got from them; but the chief cause, why the *Hollanders* at that time when their Affairs were in so <272> good a Condition, consented to a Truce, seems to be, that they began to be 'jealous' [suspicious] of *France*, for fear, lest that King should snatch *Flanders* away upon a sudden, which must needs have prov'd their Ruin. Besides this, *Maurice* being grown very Powerfull during this War, was likely to be troublesome to their Liberty. And this was the first step which *Holland* made \A. 1609\ towards the Establishment of a ||[free Common-wealth.]|[25]

A Truce of 12
Years.

§12. Soon after the Truce was concluded, the *Hollanders* were engaged in the Business concerning the Succession of the Country of *Juliers;* for the Emperour, after the death of the last Duke, being very desirous to annex these Countries unto his House, had sent the Archduke *Leopold,* to make a Sequestration, who took the strong City of *Juliers,* but was beaten out again by the *Hollanders,* with the Assistance of the *French.* But a difference arising afterwards betwixt the Elector of *Brandenburgh* and the Duke of *Newburgh* [Pfalz-Neuburg], who had 'at first' [temporarily] made an Agreement betwixt themselves {about those lands}; and the Duke of *Newburgh* having called to his Assistance

A Quarrel
about the
Dutchy of
Juliers.

25. Rather: "proper [or rightful, *rechtmässigen*] republic." See IV.1, note 1, p. 115, above.

Spinola, who took the City of *Wesel:* The *Hollanders* on the other hand
sided with the Elector of *Brandenburgh,* and put Garrisons into *Rees*
and *Emeric,* whereby the Country of *Cleves* was involved in the War of
the *Netherlands.*

The Differences between the Remonstrants and Contra-Remonstrants.

§13. But there arose a more dangerous intestine Division in *Holland*
betwixt the *Arminians* or *Remonstrants* (as they are termed) and others;
which Division was partly occasioned by a 'State' [political] jealousie,
partly by Disputes among the Divines.[26] We have said before,[27] that
Prince *William* did endeavour under-hand to be Soveraign over the
United Provinces, which was prevented only by a very few Voices. Then
after his Death his Son *Maurice* pursued the same Design, but was opposed by the chief Men among them; who alledged, That their Labour
was very ill bestowed, if in place of a great One, they should be brought
under subjection to a little 'Prince' [lord, *Herrn*]. Among these, one of
the chiefest was *John* of *Olden Barneveldt,* Pensionary of *Holland,* who
had been always for upholding the publick Liberty. But because the

Afterwards manag'd by State Policy.

Authority of the Captain-General was <273> more conspicuous during the War, *Maurice* endeavoured to set aside the Treaty with *Spain;*
but *Barnevelt* did, as much as he could, promote the Truce with *Spain,*
knowing that in time of Peace, the Authority of the Captain General
would be diminish'd, which *Maurice* kept in good remembrance.

In the mean time *Arminius,* a professour of Divinity in the University of *Leyden,* had defended several Propositions concerning Predesti-
nation, and some other Articles relating to the same, with less rigour
than the rest of the Reform'd Churchs had hitherto generally taught.
His Opinion was after his death oppos'd by one *Francis Gomarus.* This
Dissension being spread abroad, most of the Clergy sided with *Gomarus,* but the chief States men with *Arminius.* But because the generality

26. On the role of quibbling theologians (divines) in fomenting religious dis-
cord, see *On the Nature and Qualification of Religion,* §46, in Pufendorf (2002c),
p. 99; and *The Divine Feudal Law,* §94, in Pufendorf (2002b), p. 225. Also see notes
36 and 37, at p. 354, below.

27. See §7, p. 285, above.

of the People |[followed]|[28] the footsteps of the Clergy, *Maurice*, who after the Death of his elder Brother, was become Prince of *Orange*,[29] declared himself for the *Gomarists*. And there happening great Tumults in several places; *viz.* at *Alckmaer, Leyden* and *Utrecht*, the Prince took this opportunity to displace up and down such Magistrates as adhered to the *Arminians*. *Barnevelts, Hugo Grotius*, and some others, were, under the same pretext, taken into Custody; the first by a Sentence of the States General lost his Head in the 72d. Year of his Age; *Grotius* was condemned to a perpetual Imprisonment; out of which he afterwards made his escape by means of his Wife, who had enclosed him in a Chest. And tho' at the Synod of *Dort* \A. 1619\ the Doctrine of *Arminius* was condemned as erroneous, yet this Violence of the Prince against a Man, who had deserved so well, was very ill resented by a great many: And these two Factions have ever since taken so firm root there, that it is not improbable, but at last they may occasion the ruin or change of the State.

§14. But Dangers from abroad did afterwards appease these inward Dissensions. For the time of the Truce being expired \A. 1621\, the War began a-fresh with *Spain*. In the Year 1622, *Spinola* took *Juliers*, but was obliged to raise the Siege from before *Bergen op Zoom;* because the Count of *Mansfeld* and *Christian* Duke of *Bruns-*<274>*wick*, having defeated the *Spanish* Army near *Fleury*, march'd to the Assistance of the *Hollanders*. To revenge this Affront, *Spinola* besieged *Breda* {A. 1624}; and Prince *Maurice* having in vain endeavour'd to raise the Siege; and besides this, his Attempt upon the Castle of *Antwerp* having proved unsuccessfull, he fell into a deep Melancholy, and died \A. 1625\, *Breda* being not long after forc'd by Famine to surrender it self.

To Prince *Maurice*, succeeded in the Stadtholdership and all other Offices, which had been in his possession, his Brother *Frederick Henry*, who took *Groll* \A. 1627\. In the Year 1628, *Pieter Heyn* took the *Spanish*

The Spanish War renew'd,

Prince Maurice dies.

Prince Frederick Henry I.

28. Rather: "always [*durchgehends*] follows."
29. See §9, note 21, p. 287, above.

Silver fleet; and in the Year next following the Prince took *Bois le Duc* [*Hertzogenbusch*]. During this Siege, the *Spaniards* made an Inrode into the *Velaw* [Velau], hoping thereby to give the *Hollanders* a diversion, who were put into a great Consternation. But the *Hollanders* on that very day surprized the City of *Wesel*, which oblig'd the *Spaniards* to repass the River *Yssel* as fast as they could: And from that time forwards the *Spaniards* despair'd of ever reducing *Holland* under their Obedience.

In the Year 1630, the *Hollanders* got first footing in *Brasile*. In the Year 1631, they surprized some Thousands of *Spaniards* near *Bergen op Zoom*, who were gone out in Shallops[30] upon some secret Enterprize. In the Year next following the Prince took *Venlo, Ruremond, Limburgh* and *Maestricht*, and *Pappenheim* endeavouring to relieve the last, was soundly beaten. In the Year 1638 the Prince took *Rhinebergh*, but in the

A League Offensive between France and Holland. Year next following the *Spaniards, Limburgh*. An Offensive Alliance was made betwixt *France* and *Holland* \A. 1635\, wherein they had shar'd the *Netherlands* betwixt them: But this Alliance prov'd fruitless, the *Hollanders* being very well satisfy'd, that this Design did not succeed, being glad not to have the *French* for their Neighbours on the Landside: But the *Spaniards* surpriz'd *Shenkenshantz*, which the *Hollanders* retook not without great trouble \A. 1636\. In the Year 1637 the Prince retook *Breda*, but the *Spaniards, Venlo* and *Ruremond*. In the Year 1638, the *Hollanders* were 'bravely' [thoroughly] beaten near *Callo;* but in the Year 1639, *Martin Tromp* entirely destroy'd the *Spanish* Fleet, which lay in the <275> *Downs*,[31] and was intended to attack *Sweden*, in conjunc-

Prince William II. tion with the *Danes*. In the Year 1644, *Ghent*, and in the Year next following *Hulst* was taken by *William* II. who had succeeded his Father: It is thought, that he might also have taken *Antwerp*, if the Province of *Zealand* and *Amsterdam* had not oppos'd it, they being grown powerfull out of its Ruins.

Peace concluded at Munster. At last, a Peace was concluded at *Munster* \A. 1648\, betwixt *Spain* and *Holland*, wherein it was declar'd a free 'Common-wealth' [people],

---

30. Cf. *Chaluppen* (German) and *chaloupes* (French), small boats used to maneuver and service larger ships.
31. A sheltered area off the coast of England just north of Dover.

to which *Spain* should for the future make no Pretensions whatsoever. And tho' *France* and the Prince did oppose this Peace with their utmost Endeavours, yet the *Hollanders* did consider, that the *Spaniards* having granted all that they could desire, the Cause of the War ceas'd: They fear'd, besides this, that *Spain* might be brought too low, and *France* grow too powerfull; and the Province of *Holland* was considerably indebted. Thus *Holland* ended this tedious War with great Reputation, but the *Spaniards* with great Dishonour, having besides this, quite enervated themselves. Tho' this is observable, that as long as the *Hollanders* were engag'd in the War against *Spain,* they were favour'd by every body except the *Spanish* Party; but immediately after the Peace was concluded, both *France* and *England,* by whom they had been hitherto upheld, gave manifest proofs of their Jealousie of them.

§15. But the *Hollanders* could not enjoy Peace very long; for soon after *Brasile* rebell'd against them, submitting it self to the *Portuguese,* which prov'd very disadvantageous for the *West-India* Company; but the *East-India* Company drew great Advantage from it; for this having occasion'd a War with *Portugal,* which lasted till the Year 1661, the *Hollanders* took from the *Portuguese* almost all the places, which they were possess'd of in the *East-Indies.* War with Portugal.

In the Year 1650, a remarkable Dissension arose in *Holland,* which might have prov'd the cause of great Calamities. For the War with *Spain* being now at an end, some of the States, and especially the Province of *Holland,* were of <276> Opinion, That to ease the Publick, their Forces should be diminish'd; which the Prince oppos'd, under pretence, that it would not be adviseable to be without an Army, as long as *France* and *Spain* were engag'd in a War. And the Opinion being divided concerning this Business, it was agreed upon by the Majority of the States-General, who were great Friends of the Prince, that the Prince should visit in person these Cities, to try, whether he could convince the Magistrates in this point: Against this petition'd some of the Cities in *Holland,* and especially *Amsterdam,* fearing, that if the Prince should come in person to them, he might, by changing the Magistrates and other Alterations, do something which might prove prejudicial to their Lib- Divisions in Holland.

erty. The Prince being dissatisfy'd at these proceedings, reply'd, That this was done to affront him and his Office, and therefore desir'd, that Reparation should be made him; but the Cities insisted upon their former Resolution, alledging, that it was according to their 'Privileges' [right and freedom]. Then the Prince took into Custody six {lords} of the States of *Holland,* whom he suppos'd to be chiefly against him, among whom the chiefest were the Sieur the *Witt,* Burghermaster of *Dort,* whom he sent all together Prisoners to the Castle of *Louvesteyn.* He also privately order'd some Troops to march towards *Amsterdam,* to surprize that City; but some of these Troops having lost their way in the Night-time, the Design was discover'd by the *Hamburgher* Post-boy: And the *Amsterdamers* perceiving that the Prince intended to force them to a Complyance, open'd their Sluces, and put the Country round about it under Water: At last the Business was agreed, and the Prince had this Satisfaction given him, that the Sieur *Bicker* Burghermaster of *Amsterdam* was depos'd, and the Prisoners in the Castle of *Louvestein* were set at liberty, under condition that they should be discharg'd from their 'places' [offices]. But this Business was likely to have been the occasion of more troubles, if the Prince had not died soon after. Soon after his death, *viz.* in the Year 1650, on the 13th day of *November,* his Princess was brought to Bed of *William* III. the present Prince of *Orange.* <277> In the Year 1651, the United Provinces held a grand Assembly, where they renew'd the Union, being now destitute of a Governour.

The Witt and others made Prisoners by the Prince.

The Birth of Prince William III.

War with the English Parliament.

§16. Not long after the *Hollanders* were engag'd in a heavy War with the *English* Parliament, which at the beginning being very ambitious [desirous] of their Friendship, sent one *Dorislaw* to the *Hague,* who before he had his publick Audience, was murther'd by some *Scots* who were all mask'd. And the Parliament having receiv'd no Satisfaction upon this account, began to look with an ill Eye upon them [the Hollanders], which they little regarded, till *Cromwell* had reduc'd the *Scots.* And, tho' the Parliament sent other Embassadours to the *Hague,* yet the *Dutch* were not very forward, but were for protracting the Treaty, till the Embassadours having been affronted by the Rabble, departed dissatisfy'd: Whereupon the Parliament gave out Reprisals against them, declaring withal, That no Merchandises should be transported into *England*, except in *English* Bottoms, and the *English* Privateers began to fall every where upon the *Dutch* Merchant ships. The *Hollanders*, who were not very unanimous among themselves, did resolve at last, to try first whether the Business might be compounded by fair means, and if that did not succeed, to begin the War in good earnest, and for this purpose Embassadours were sent into *England*. *Tromp* in the mean while was sent out with a Fleet, to secure their Commerce, and meeting with the *English* Admiral *Blake*, and refusing to strike,[32] a bloody Engagement ensu'd, which ended with equal loss on both sides. The *Hollanders* pretended, that this had happen'd by accident; both Parties however made great Preparations for War, and fought twice, the Advantage remaining on the *English* side, notwithstanding they were beaten near *Leghorn*. But in the last Engagement the *Hollanders* having lost their Admiral *Tromp*, and seven and twenty Men of War, they were oblig'd \A. 1654\ to conclude a Peace with *Cromwell*, which was very advantageous and glorious on his side, they being among other Articles oblig'd, for the future, never <278> to make any one of the House of *Orange* their Stadtholder. It was observ'd, that the *Dutch* Ships were not large enough, which Error the *Hollanders* corrected afterwards. A Peace.

    In the Year next following the *Hollanders* were grown jealous of the great Success of the *Swedes* against *Poland*, and being desirous to prevent the *Swedes* from becoming Masters of *Prussia*, they stirr'd up the King of *Denmark* against them. But the *Danes* having been worsted in this War, the *Hollanders* sent a Fleet to relieve *Copenhagen*, which was besieg'd by the *Swedes* {A. 1658}: A bloody Battel was fought in the *Oresound*,[33] betwixt the *Swedish* and *Dutch* Fleets, wherein the *Hollanders* lost two Admirals, but nevertheless gain'd their point in relieving of *Copenhagen*. And in the Year next following they also bore their share in the Battel of *Funen*, till at last a Peace was concluded \A. 1660\ before *Copenhagen*, to the small Satisfaction of the *Danes*, who accused the *Hollanders*, that Differences with Swedeland.

---

32. That is, to strike or lower one's flag, in acknowledgment of the other's superiority.

33. The strait between the Danish Zeeland and the Swedish Scania.

they had not been zealous enough in their Assistance against the *Swedes;* but the *Hollanders* were afraid, that *England* and *France* might declare for *Sweden,* and under that pretence fall upon them; besides that, they thought it their Interest, not to let *Denmark* grow too powerfull.

The Second War with England.

§17. *Holland* was then for a few Years at Peace, till {A. 1665} a bloody War broke out betwixt them and the *English,* who could not but think the flourishing Trade and great Power of the *Hollanders* at Sea, to be very prejudicial to them. *France* blew up the Coals, being desirous to see these two mighty States weaken one another's Power. In this War the *English* had the Advantage in the first and third Engagements, but the *Hollanders* in the second: But the *English,* at last, 'being willing to save Charges' [wishing to avoid costs], did resolve only to infest [harass] the *Hollanders* by their Privateers, and not to equipp a Fleet, which the *Hollanders* taking an advantage of, ventur'd to enter the River of *Thames;* and having landed near Chattam, they burn'd several Ships in the Harbour. This oblig'd *England* to make a Peace with them, which was by <279> mediation of the Crown of *Sweden* concluded at *Breda.* In this War *Holland* recover'd its Reputation, which it had lost in *Cromwell's* time, and shew'd it self not to be inferiour in Strength at Sea to *England;* but they discover'd their Weakness on Land, the Bishop of *Munster* having been very troublesome to them.[34]

England and France declare War with Holland.

§18. At last, in the Year 1672, a prodigious Storm fell upon *Holland,* which at first threaten'd its ruin; *France* attacking it by Land, and *England* by Sea. It was surprising to see how the *French* in a few days time took the Provinces of *Gueldres, Over-yssel* and *Utrecht,* which occasion'd so general a Consternation, that some are of Opinion, they might have taken *Amsterdam* it self, if they had immediately gone towards it, whilst the first Consternation lasted. Some lay the fault upon *Rochford,* who having receiv'd Orders to make an attempt upon that City, tarry'd two

34. On the raid up the Thames, also see note 63, p. 179, and note 64, p. 260, above. On Christoph Bernhard Freiherr von Gallen (1606–78), prince-bishop of Münster, see V.24, at note 65, p. 261, above.

days at *Utrecht*, which he 'bestow'd' [spent] in receiving of Complements, the *Amsterdamers* getting thereby time to take a Resolution for
their Defence. It serv'd also for a great Encouragement to the *Hollanders*, that the Bishop of *Munster* was forc'd to go away from before *Groningen*, he having, together with the Elector of *Collen* [Cologne], taken
the *French* side.

In the Year next following the *French* took *Maestricht* from the *Hollanders*. But the *Hollanders* having behav'd themselves bravely in four
Sea Engagements, and the Parliament of *England* being become very
jealous of *France*, a separate Peace, was by the Mediation of *Spain*, concluded betwixt *Holland* and *England*. The Emperour and *Spain* having
then declar'd for *Holland*, the *French* King took his Garrisons out of
all the conquer'd Places {A. 1674}, having first exacted from them great
Contributions,[35] except *Naerden* and *Grave*, which were retaken by
force. Thus the *Hollanders* got all their places again except *Maestricht;*
Rhinebergh which belong'd to the Elector of *Collen* being restor'd to
him, and the 'Country' [cities] of *Cleves* to the Elector of *Brandenburgh*.

This War also restor'd the Prince of *Orange* to the same Dignity,
and that under better <280> Conditions than they had been in the
possession of his Ancestors. For the Common People, which already
favour'd the House of *Orange*, being put quite into a Consternation
by the prodigious Success of the *French*, and being persuaded, that this
Misfortune was occasion'd by the Treachery of some who sat at the
Helm, and that no body but the Prince could restore the decay'd State,
did raise Tumults in most Cities, which the Prince was forc'd to appease, by deposing the former Magistrates, and putting in their room
such as he knew were favourers of himself. In one of these Tumults
Cornelius and *John du Witt*, two Brothers, were miserably murther'd by   The Du Witts
the Rabble in the *Hague;* though a great many are of Opinion, That   murther'd.
especially the last of these, who had so long sat at the Helm, had better deserv'd of his native Country. Tho the Prince had been not a little
instrumental in appeasing the Commotions, whereby *Holland* was put
in a condition to recover it self, yet he was not so successfull in his War

35. That is, they were looted and burned.

against *France:* For he receiv'd a considerable loss near *Seneffe* \A. 1674\, he was repuls'd before *Maestricht* \A. 1676\, and endeavouring to relieve St. *Omer,* he was defeated \A. 1677\ by the *French;* and the *Dutch* Fleet which was sent to the Relief of *Sicily* had no great Success. At last their Fear, that through long War their Liberty might be endanger'd by the Prince, influenc'd them to make a separate Peace with *France,* by virtue of which *Maestricht* was restor'd to the *Hollanders.*[36]

The Constitution.
§19. The Seven Provinces[37] of the *United Netherlands* are fill'd with a prodigious number of People, there being some, who have computed, that in the Province of *Holland,* the Number amounts to two millions and 500.000. And unto this vast Number of People is to be attributed their Industry, increase of Trade and great Riches; for in a Country which is not the most fruitfull, and where every thing is very dear, they must else of necessity perish by Famine: But most of the Inhabitants were transplanted thither out of other Countries; out of *France* during the times <281> of the Civil Commotions; out of *England* under the Reign of Queen *Mary;* out of *Germany* during those long Wars there; but chiefly, out of the other Provinces of the *Netherlands,* at the time of their revolting from *Spain.* These Strangers were invited into this Country by its convenient Situation, the Liberty of Religion and the Government [*Regiment*]; by its extraordinary Constitutions [*Policey*] and Conveniencies for Trade and Correspondency in all Parts; and at last, by the great Reputation which the States have gain'd abroad, by their wise Management [*Regierung*] at home, and Success of their Arms abroad. And because every body, who either brings some Means along with him, or has learn'd something to maintain himself withall, finds a good Reception in *Holland;* even those who are 'prosecuted' [persecuted] in other places find a 'certain' [secure] Refuge in this Country.

Their Genius.
The *Netherlanders* are commonly very open-hearted, down-right and honest, very free in Words and Conversation, not easily to be mov'd or

36. The war ended in 1678 with the Treaty of Nijmegen.
37. Friesland, Gelre, Groningen, Holland, Overijssel, Utrecht, Zealand.

stirr'd up; but if once made soundly angry, not easily to be appeas'd.[38] If you Converse with them without Haughtiness and with 'Discretion' [modesty], so as to accommodate your self a little to their Inclinations, you may do with them what you please. *Charles* V. us'd to say of them, *That there was not a Nation under the Sun, that did detest more the Name of Slavery, and yet if you did manage them Mildly and with Discretion, did bear it more patiently.* But the Rabble here is very bad, it being a common Custom to speak ill and despicably of their Magistrates, as often as things do not answer Expectation.

The *Hollanders* are very unfit for Land-service, and the *Dutch* Horsemen are 'strange' [wretched] Creatures, yet those who live in *Gueldres,* and upon the Borders of *Westphalia,* are tolerably good. But at Sea they have done such Exploits that they may be compar'd with any Nation in the World. And the *Zealanders* are esteem'd more Hardy [*kecker*] and Venturous [*wilder*] than the *Hollanders.* They are also generally very parsimonious, not much addicted to the Belly, it being not the Custom here to spend their yearly Income, but to save every Year an overplus. This saving <282> way of living upholds their Credit, and enables them to bear such heavy Taxes without being ruin'd by them. They are very fit for all sorts of Manufactury, and very much addicted to Commerce, not refusing to undergo any Labour or Danger, where something is to be got, and those that understand Trade deal very easily with them. They are very punctual in every respect, pondering and ordering a thing very well before they begin it. And there is scarce any Nation in the World so fit for Trade as the *Dutch,* this being very praise-worthy in them, that they always choose rather to get somewhat by their own Industry, than by Violence or Fraud. But especially, the great<est> Liberty which they enjoy, is a great Encouragement for Trade. The chiefest Vice among them is Covetousness, which however is not so pernicious among them, because it produces in them Industry and good Husbandry. There is a great many who have been amaz'd at the great 'Conduct' [wisdom]

38. Pufendorf spent almost two years, from late 1659 to late 1661, in the Netherlands after he had been released from a Danish prison and before he moved to Heidelberg. See the Editor's Introduction, pp. x–xi.

which has appear'd in the management [*conduite*] of their Affairs, not-withstanding that the *Hollanders* in general are rarely of extraordinary Wit [*esprit*] or Merits: Some alledge this for a Reason, That a cold Temper [*Kälte*] and Moderation of Passions are the fundamental Qualifications of such as intend to manage State Affairs.[39]

The Nature of the Country.
§20. The Seven *United Provinces* are not very large in Extent, they being to be reckon'd but for one {small} Corner of *Germany;*[40] but they are fill'd up with so considerable a Number of beautiful, large and populous Cities, that no other place of the same bigness is to be compar'd to it. Besides the Seven Provinces, they are possess'd of some Cities in *Flanders* and *Brabant*, viz. *Hulst, Sluce, Ardenburgh, Bois le Duc, Maestricht, Breda, Bergen op Zoom, Grave*, and some others. They also keep a Garrison in *Embden*, thereby to secure the River of *Embs*. The Country in general is more fit for Pasture than Tilling, it producing scarce so much Corn as is sufficient for the fifth part of its Inhabitants. But this want is made up by the Industry of the Inhabitants, and the great conveni-<283>ency of so many Rivers and the Seas, fit for Fishing and Navigation. The Herring Fishery and that of Codds brings in vast Riches to them; and some *English* have computed, That the *Hollanders* sell every Year 79.200 Lasts (which makes 138.400 Tuns) of Herrings,[41] which amount to the value of 1.372.000 *l.* {sterling} not including what is transported into *Spain, Italy* and *France* {excluding Roan[ne]}, and what is consum'd at home.

Of their Shipping and Commerce.
But their Shipping and Commerce is of much greater Advantage to them, which does flourish there to that degree, that some are of Opinion, That in *Holland* are more Ships than in all other parts of

39. This statement, and Pufendorf's characterization of the Dutch in general, appears to be based on Sir William Temple's *Observations upon the United Provinces of the Netherlands* (1673), especially chap. 4 ("Of Their People and Dispositions") and chap. 5 ("Of Their Religion"). See Temple (1814), especially pp. 115, 138–39, 141–42, and 147. Also see note 50, p. 308, below.

40. The United Provinces belonged to the Burgundian Circle of the Holy Roman Empire. See II.20, p. 95, above.

41. In German: "jährlich bis 79200. Last Hering." A "Last" [load] was a technical term for measuring the volume of ships in terms of tons.

Europe. Besides, *Holland*'s Situation in the midst of *Europe* makes it very fit for Trade, so that it sends its Ships with great Conveniency into the *East* and *Western* Seas; and through the Commodiousness of those vast Rivers of the *Rhine, Meuse, Elbe, Weser,* and *Embs,* draw the Commodities out of *Germany;* and in exchange for these vends its Manufacturies there: For *Holland* has in regard, especially of the *Rhine* and the *Meuse,* a great Advantage in its Trade before *England,* tho' this on the other hand, has better Harbours and a deeper Coast: And because *Holland* is at the latter end of the Year commonly overflown with Waters, which makes the Air very thick and foggy, Nature has been kind to this Country, in that about that time the Wind blows much *Easterly,* which disperses the Vapours, refreshes the Air, and renders it wholsome; but from hence it is that their Harbours are often shut up with Ice for three Months together, whereas they are always open in *England.*

The *Hollanders* trade almost into every Corner of the World, they having been very carefull to erect Fortresses and Colonies in far distant Countries. But the *East-India* Company, especially, has vastly encreas'd her Trade and Riches; for this Company has extended her Trade from *Besora* [Basra], which is situated near the great Bay of *Persia,* at the very Mouth of the River *Tigris,* all along a prodigious Tract of rich Ground near the Sea side as far as to the utmost parts of *Japan;* she stands there in Confederacy with many Kings, and with many of them has <284> made Treaties of Monopolies, and is possess'd of a great many strong Holds in those parts. The Capital City there is *Batavia* [Jakarta], in *Java Major,* where the Governour General keeps a Court like a King, under whose Jurisdiction are the other places. The Company is Sovereign Mistress over all these Countries, the chiefest of which are the Isles of *Molucca* and *Banda, Amboina, Malacca,* the Coast of the Island of *Zeilon, Patiacatta, Musulapatan, Negapatan* upon the Coast of *Cormandel, Cochin, Cananor* and *Cranganor* upon the Coast of *Malabar,* and several more; whether they have a free Trade in the *East-Indies* with *China,* I cannot affirm, tho' it is certain that the *Chineses* drive a great Trade with them in *Batavia;* but in *Japan* they have the whole Trade alone, no *Portuguese* being permitted to come there. This Company is able to set out a Fleet of betwixt 40 and 50 'Capital' [war] Ships, and

East-India Company.

to raise an Army of 30.000 Men. The first Funds of this Company did amount to sixty Tuns of Gold, which in the space of six Years, deducting all the Charges and Dividends made to the Owners, was encreas'd to three hundred Tuns of Gold.

The West-India Company. The Funds of the *West-India* Company was of fourscore Tuns of Gold, and flourish'd extreamly at the beginning, but [it] ruin'd it self by making too great Dividends, and not keeping a Fund sufficient for the carrying on of the War against *Spain.* Besides, those concern'd in this Company were more eager after Conquests than Trade, and when *Brasile* revolted they receiv'd a capital blow: Yet they are possess'd in *Guinea,* of the Castle *de Mina* and if I am not mistaken of *Loanda* in *Angola,* and some other places, as also some of the *Caribby Islands,* and of *New Holland,* in the *Northern* parts of *America.* They have also lately begun to erect some Colonies in *Guiana,* and on the great River of *Orenoque.*

Some of the most 'curious' [knowledgeable] have observ'd, that a great many things concurr in *Holland* for the promoting of Trade, which are not to be met withall all at once in any other Country: As for example, the great quantity of People, the Conveniency [opportune location, *Gelegenheit*] and Security of the Country, the small Interest which is paid <285> for Money, which shews the great Superfluity of ready Money [cash]; the Severity us'd against Thieves, Cheats, and Banquerooteers; the Bank of *Amsterdam,* great number of Convoys, and moderate Customs, that they are so exact and regular in their way of Trading, that the Magistrates are generally Merchants, or at least, such as have an Interest in Commerce; That they are Masters in the *East-Indies,* and that by reason of the Frugality and Industry of the Inhabitants, far more Commodities are exported than imported. And it is observable, that tho' the *Hollanders* are Masters of the Spice in the *Indies,* yet they use them least of all themselves. They have also the greatest share in the Silk-trade in *Persia,* and yet they cloath themselves in Woollen Cloath, generally speaking. Nay, they sell their fine Cloaths abroad, and send for courser out of *England* for their own use. They sell their delicious Butter, and send for other out of the *North* of *England* and *Ireland* for their use. *French* Wines and Brandies are the chiefest Commodities which are consumed here, yet even when they make {such} a Debauch, they ||[are not overlavishing.]|[42]

§21. From what has been said, it is manifest that the Strength of this Common-wealth [*Republic*] is founded upon Trade and its Naval Force, which is absolutely necessary to maintain the former; nor is there any Country so stock'd with good Seamen, for the setting out [manning] of a great Fleet. But on the Land-side, where the Country cannot be under Water, it is not near so strong. For tho' they do not want Money to raise an Army of Foreigners, yet is it not always adviseable, for a Common-wealth to rely only upon such as have no other tye but their Pay, since they may easily prove unfaithfull, or else, mis-led by the General, assist him in over-turning the Liberty of the State. And it has been in regard of this that some have advised, that the Provinces of *Holland* and *Zealand* should separate themselves from the rest, and only endeavour to strengthen themselves betwixt the *Meuse*, the *Rhine*, and *South-sea* [*Zuiderzee*]; and in case of Necessity, by opening of <286> their Sluces, put the Country under-water; but for the rest, only endeavour to strengthen themselves at Sea: But to examine this Proposition, is not now my business.

Strength and Weakness of this Common-wealth.

There are {also} several {considerable} Inconveniences that proceed from the very Form of the Government [*Regierung*] of this State. For, to speak properly, these seven Provinces do not make up one entire Common-wealth [republic], but there are seven Common-wealths [*Republicquen*], which by the Union at *Utrecht* are joined into one Confederacy [*Systema*];[43] they have their Deputies constantly residing at the *Hague*, whose business it is to take care of such Affairs as concern the

Form of Government.

42. Literally: "do not allow much to drip on their shirts."
43. "System" is a technical term for Pufendorf. See *On the Law of Nature and of Nations*, VII.5.16–22, and the dissertation "On Systems of States" (*De systematibus civitatum*, 1667), which is also contained in Pufendorf (1675), pp. 264–330. In *The Present State of Germany*, VI.9, in Pufendorf (2007), pp. 176–78, Pufendorf characterizes the German Empire as an irregular (monstrous) state somewhere between a limited monarchy and a system of states. Also see V.6, note 11, p. 200, above. The whole of §21 is important for understanding Pufendorf's views on different forms of state, as well as the related question of interstate frameworks. See Seidler (2011).

whole Union; and if any thing of moment is to be decreed, they send
to the several Provinces, and according to the Approbation of these
they make their Decrees: these Deputies are called the States-General.
Nay, it seems {also} that each Province is rather a Confederacy, than
one <City or> Common-wealth [*civitas*], because the several Members
of each Province do treat with one another like Confederates, and not
like one Body, where one is superiour to the other, or |[the majority of
Votes determines a business]|.[44] For even in the Provincial Assemblies a
great many things cannot be determined by the Plurality of Votes, but
every {single} Member's consent is required. Which shows, that these
Provinces and Cities [are] not united by so strong a Tye, as those who
are govern'd by one Soveraign, except as far as {common} Necessity {and
interest} obliges them to keep together.

   And the great Cities are {also} fill'd with {much terrible} Rabble;
which if once put in motion, uses to make strange work [*lose Händel*] among them. It is therefore the great Care of the Magistrates, that
they are kept in constant Employment to get Bread, for Famine would
quickly be the occasion of great Tumults here. There is also a {secret}
Jealousie betwixt *Holland* and the other Provinces; the former pretending to some Prerogative, as being the most Powerfull, and contribut-
ing most to the Publick; whereas the others are for maintaining their
Liberty and Equality. All the rest of the Cities are especially jealous of
Amsterdam, because this City draws abundance of Trade from the rest,
and puts them in apprehension, as if She were ambitious to domineer
over them.

   But the greatest <287> Irregularity [*Irregularität*] happens in their
Prince of Constitution, by means of the Prince of *Orange,* who having the Fa-
Orange.   vour of the Common people, of the Land-Souldiers and the Clergy (for
the Clergy hate the *Arminians,* who being of the *Barnefelt* Faction, are
Enemies of the Prince) seems to endanger their Liberty.[45] Wherefore
the chief Men [*Optimates*] in the Cities, to whom belongs {by right}

----

44. Rather: "the majority lords it over the minority [*die meisten über die wenigsten
herrschen wolten*]."
45. See VI.13, pp. 292–93, above.

the Magistracy [*höchste Gewalt*] there, possess their 'places' [might, *Macht*] in continual fear, except they will be pliable to the Prince of *Orange;* Whose interest is also inconsistent with that of the 'State' [common good], because no Land war can be advantageous for *Holland;* whereas in time of War, his Authority {in its reliance on foreign soldiery} is much greater than otherwise. And therefore according to this Form of the Government, scarce a firm {and constant} Peace can be establish'd at home. It may easily happen that the Prince may aspire to be their Soveraign. And when the Province of *Gueldres* did offer to him the Soveraignty \A. 1675\, he did give them to understand, That if all the rest were of the same Opinion, they should have no occasion to look for him behind the Wine-pipes [*Fässer*], as the *Jews* did for *Saul;*[46] yet the wiser sort are of opinion, that he would reap no great benefit [*Profit*] from this Soveraignty, since it would be scarce possible to keep so many great Cities in Obedience against their Will. For Cittadels and Garrisons would prove the Ruin of Trade [*Commercien*], which never flourishes where |[absolute Power controuls the Subject.]|[47] Wherefore it seems 'more' [most] adviseable for the Prince to be satisfied with what Power he has, it being certain, that if he knows how to manage the Humour of the People, he is almost able to do what he pleases.

It has been a great Dispute, whether it be for the advantage of these *Netherlands,* to have a Governour General. Those who are for the Affirmative, alledge, That this Country having been from ancient Time under the Jurisdiction of a limited Soveraignty [*limitirte Herren*], has been used to that Form of Government; That it conduces to the outward Splendour of the Commonwealth, and to uphold the Authority [*Ansehen*] of the Magistrates in the Cities; That thereby {popular} Factions and Tumults are kept under and suppressed. That thereby are prevented a great many Inconveniences in execu-<288>ting any designs of moment, which 'were' [are] incident to an Aristocratical and Democratical State [*Staat*]; *viz.* Slow and divided Counsels in Consultations, delays

Whether it is their advantage to have a Sovereignty.

46. I Samuel 10:22.
47. Rather: "it is constrained [*Zwang leiden*]."

in Executions, and the divulging of secret Designs [*Heimlichkeiten*]; all which we will leave undetermin'd here.

Other Defects of this Common-wealth.   This is also to be esteemed one of the Weaknesses of this Common-wealth, that so great a number of Inhabitants cannot be maintained by the Product of the Land, but must get their Bread from abroad, and by the help of Foreigners. Wherefore the certain Ruin of this Common-wealth is at hand, when ever its Trade and Navigation should be stopt; which however is not altogether impossible to happen.

The difference of Religion is commonly reckoned among the weakness[es] of a State.[48] But some make this one of the main Pillars of the {currently} flourishing Condition of *Holland*, because it ||[contributes greatly to the Strength and Encrease of this]|[49] State. The Reformed Religion is here the Establish'd Religion [*die Oberhand hat*], all the rest being only tolerated [*geduldet*]. The *Papists* are connived at, but also they keep over them a strict Eye, for fear the Priests, who all depend on the Pope, should enter into a Correspondency with *Spain*. Yet it is rarely seen in *Holland*, that one Subject hates the other, or 'prosecutes' [persecutes] him upon the Score of Religion. It has been the Saying of some, that in other Countries Religion doth more good, but in *Holland* less harm.[50]

It is also very inconvenient for the Inhabitants, that all sorts of Victuals are sold at so excessive a Rate: The reason of which is, That the greatest Revenues of *Holland*, are raised by way of Excise upon these Commodities;[51] and it is a common Saying, That before you can get a Dish of Fish ready dress'd upon your Table at *Amsterdam*, you have paid above Thirty several Taxes for it. And notwithstanding all these heavy Impositions, the State is much in debt. There are some also who pretend, that the Traffick [*Commercien*] of the *Dutch* does {on its own}

48. See note 61, p. 178, above, and note 18, p. 427, below; also see the Editor's Introduction, p. xviii.

49. Rather: "greatly increases the number of inhabitants, which contributes most to the strength and size of their."

50. See Sir William Temple, *Observations upon the United Provinces of the Netherlands* (1673), chap. 5, in Temple (1814), p. 162. See note 39, p. 302, above.

51. That is, "imposten auf die consumtion" or a consumption tax.

grow less and less; for which they alledge several Reasons; *viz.* That since the Peace concluded at *Munster,* other Nations have also applied themselves to Trade. That the Price [value] of the *East-India* Commodities does fall every Year, and yet the Char-<289>ges of the Company increases daily. For whereas formerly five or six *East-India* Ships coming home yearly, were reckon'd very considerable, now eighteen or twenty do return; which so over-stocks them with these Commodities, that they are obliged to lay them up in their Ware-houses for a considerable time, before they can vent [sell] them without Loss. They alledge also, that Corn has been of late years so abundant in *France, Spain, Italy* and *England,* that the *Hollanders* have not sent much of it into these Parts, it being their custom to fetch Corn from off the *East* [Baltic] *Sea,* where they vent, in exchange of it, most of their Spices: That the great Addition of Fortifications and sumptuous Buildings to the City of *Amsterdam,* have taken up a great quantity of Ready-money [*Capitalien*], which might have been better employed in way of Trade; and that |[Luxury and Debauchery]|[52] does encrease daily in that City.

But the Reason why the *Hollanders* had such ill Success {on land} at the beginning of this {latest} War,[53] seems to be, that by the great Eagerness of Gain and Trade, their Martial Heat [spirit] was almost extinguish'd; and that after the Peace concluded at *Munster,* they being not apprehensive of any Invasion by Land, they only applied themselves to strengthen their Power at Sea, and having dismissed their best Officers, they had supplied their place with their own Relations; whose Motto [*Symbolum*] was, *Peace and a good Government.* For at the time of the War with *England* \A. 1665\ they had dismissed the Old *English* Bands [soldiers]; and in the Year 1668, the *French* Troops, both which were the 'flower' [core] of their Armies, which 'of necessity' [in any case] must have been reduced into a very ill condition, since the Prince of *Orange* had no more 'concern' [to do] with them. Besides this, they thought themselves very secure, not imagining that *France* would

---

52. Rather: "excess" (*Überfluß*) and "magnificence" (*Pracht*). Debauchery was for Pufendorf a French vice. See V.25, p. 264, above.
53. The Third Anglo-Dutch War, 1672–74.

either dare, or be able to attempt a Conquest over them, as long as they were sure, that the Emperour and *Spain* would side with them; neither did they imagine that the *English* would join with the *French* against them. And at last they hoped, they would beat the *English* out of the Sea, before *France* should be able to take three or four Places. <290> They {still} relied upon the old Way of making of War, when a whole Company was taken up with the Taking of one Place, and when whole Books were composed of the Taking of *Groll*, or the Sar[54] of *Ghent*. It is also believed, that some of the *Hollanders* were not sorry, that they had no great Success by Land, hoping thereby to bring into discredit the Conduct, and to diminish the Authority of the Prince, whom they had been obliged to make their Captain-General against their Will.

The Neighbours of Holland.

§22. As for the Neighbours of *Holland*, and what it has to fear or to hope from them; it seems that the *English* are the most dangerous <Neighbours to the *Hollanders*>, they being the only Nation that have been formidable to them hitherto, against their Pretensions to the Dominion of the Seas and Trade; who are extreamly dissatisfied, that this new Common-wealth, which, when it was in a very tottering condition, was strongly upheld by them, has now been before-hand with them[55] in the *East-Indies,* and daily spoil their Markets almost every-where {else}.

England.

For, because an *English-man* is naturally proud, and loves to live well; whereas a *Hollander* minds nothing so much as his Gain, being satisfied with an indifferent share, nor spends any thing idly; a *Hollander* can sell cheaper than an *English-man,* and Strangers will always rather deal with the first than the last. It is therefore in all probability the chief Interest of *Holland,* not to irritate *England,* and rather to allow them some Ceremonial Prerogatives at Sea, such as striking, and the like; but withall to strengthen their Power at Sea, that, in case *England* should really contest with them for the Trade and Fishing, it may be able to make

54. The Sassevaart or Sasse canal, built by Charles V in 1547 to connect Ghent to the sea.
55. The German expression "vor dem Hamen fischen" (to fish in front of the net)—meaning to exploit someone else's efforts, or to take advantage of them—was a favorite of Martin Luther.

head against them. The *Hollanders* must also, as much as is possible, endeavour to encourage the same sort of Manufacture, as is in *England,* and either to make these Commodities better, or at least to sell them cheaper, thereby to get the advantage from them.

The *Hollanders* ought to stand in great fear of *France* on the Land- France. side, especially since that <291> King[56] is their great Enemy, having opposed for a considerable time all their Designs. It is therefore very necessary to be in a good posture on the Land-side, and to keep fair with the Princes of *Germany,* who else would permit the *French{man}* to march through their Territories, or else perhaps join with him. They must endeavour the Preservation of the *Spanish Netherlands* which they ought to consider as their Frontiers, and whereby *Spain* is obliged always to Side with *Holland* against *France.*[57] They must {also} take {better} care {than before} to be provided with good Officers, and {above all} to put the Province of *Holland* into a better Posture of Defence on the side of *Gueldres.* It is not easie to be supposed, that *England* and *France* will join again against *Holland,* which may be prevented by the *Hollanders.* It is also the Interest of *Holland* to take care, that the Naval Strength of *France* do not increase too much, and to prevent, as much as in them lies, that they do not settle a Trade in the *East-Indies.* And because *France* draws the Riches of all *Europe* to itself by its Manufacturies, the *Hollanders* must try to imitate them, and furnish other Nations with the like.

From *Spain, Holland* need fear nothing {any longer} either by Sea or Spain. Land, since that time, that ||[this Kingdom has lost all its labour against them.]||[58] Nay, it is their Common Interest now that they cultivate a mutual good Understanding, to stop the Progresses of the *French* in the *Netherlands.* And the *Spaniards* have scarce any thing left them, from which the *Dutch* could have any prospect of Benefit, they being not in a Capacity to conquer or to maintain the *West-Indies.* And though the

56. Louis XIV.

57. The southern provinces remained under Spanish control until the War of the Spanish Succession (1701–14), after which they went to Austria.

58. Literally: "the former has thoroughly blunted its teeth on the latter [*jenes an diesem seine Zähne recht stumpff gebissen*]."

Hollanders may be very troublesome to the *Spanish* Silver Fleets, yet the

Portugal. *Spanish* Privateers may also do them considerable mischief. *Portugal* has no Pretensions against *Holland,* and it ought most to stand in fear of the *Hollanders,* because these would be glad of an opportunity to take from the *Portuguese Brosile* [Brazil], and what they have left in the *East-Indies,* which |[however they would not so easily be able to execute.]|[59] Because the *Hollanders* <292> are obliged to fetch their Bread out of the

The Northern *East-Sea;* they have always taken care that neither of the *Northern* Kings
Crowns. should be Master alone of the *East-Sea;* which Balance is the easier kept now, since the *Sound* is divided betwixt *Sweden* and *Denmark.* And it is notorious enough what Game they have play'd with these two Kings.

For the rest, it is the general Interest of *Holland,* to |[keep fair with all other Princes]|,[60] thereby to maintain a free Commerce everywhere. And in these Places where they cannot Trade alone, it is the Interest of the *Hollanders* either by goodness or cheapness of their Commodities, and an easie Deportment to endeavour to draw the chief Benefit of Trade to themselves. For this is the easier and less odious Way to heap up Riches, than if they should attempt publickly to 'mix' [ruin] the 'Foreign' [sea] Trade of all other Nations; since it would prove impossible for them alone to maintain a general Monopoly. <r273>

59. Rather: "they [the Hollanders] still seem capable of taking from them."
60. Rather: "to live in friendship with the rest of the world."

CHAPTER VII

Of the Switzers.

§1. |[These Countries which are possess'd now by the *Switzers*]|[1] be- First Original
longed formerly to the *German* Empire; but that they were united in of this
one Commonwealth [into a special republic] was occasioned thus; the wealth.
three small Counties [*Landschafften*] of *Ury, Switz,* and *Under-Walden,*
which commonly are call'd the three *Forest Towns,* enjoy'd very antient
{freedom and} Privileges, which they pretended to have been granted
them by the Emperor *Lewis,* Surnamed the *Pious,* yet so, that the Emperor used to send thither an Imperial Judge or Vicar [*Reichsvogt*], who
had the supreme Jurisdiction in criminal Affairs [*Capital-Sachen*]. There
were also some Monasteries in those Countries which, tho they enjoy'd
particular 'Privileges' [rights], yet did they not interfere with the Liberty
of the People. But there lived a great many Noblemen among them
also, who by degrees getting the ascendant over the Common People
[*das Volck*], did oppress their Liberty, especially during the differences
which were betwixt the Emperors and the Popes, when the Nobility
us'd to side with the Popes, but the Commonalty with the Emperor.
These divisions betwixt the Nobility and the People grew very high
at the time of the great Interregnum, which happen'd after the death
of the Emperor *Frederick the Second,* which breaking out into an open
War {A. 1260}, the whole Nobility was driven out of the Country; but
by the Emperor *Rodolfus's* Authority, a reconciliation having been made
betwixt them, the Nobles were restored to their Estates.

1. Rather: "Those peoples [*Völcker*] which are now called Swiss."

Thus these Countries did enjoy their <former> Liberty {unimpeded},
till the Reign of *Albert* I. who having conceived a hatred against them,
because they had sided with his Rival *Adolph* of *Nassau,* {and because
he} was very desirous to annex them {along with many other things} to
his Hereditary Countries; the Monasteries therefore, and a great many
of the Nobility, having, upon his desire, submitted themselves to the
Jurisdiction of the House of *Au-*<r274>*stria:* The same was also proposed to the three abovementioned places, who refusing his proposition, he set over them Imperial Judges or Vicars, who, contrary to the
antient Custom, began to reside in strong Castles, and having first try'd
by perswasions to bring them over to the House of *Austria,* afterwards,
when they found their labour lost that way, grew very burthensom to
the People by their oppressions; neither were the Petitions made against
them by the Commonalty in any ways regarded by the Emperor; nay
the Judge of *Under-Walden,* who's name was *Geisler,* was become so
extravagant, that he set his Hat upon a Pole in the Market-Place of
Altorf, commanding that every body should pay the same respect to
his Hat as to himself; thereby to make a tryal of their Obedience. And
among others one *William Tell* having often pass'd by without paying
his Respect, he forced him to shoot with an Arrow through an Apple,
which was placed upon his own Sons Head; but this man whilst he was
'carrying' [being led] to prison, making his escape, stirr'd up the hatred
of the People against the Judges.

The first §2. There were at that time three Men of great Authority [*ansehnliche*]
Union of among them, *viz. Werner Stouffacher,* born in *Switz, Walter Furst* born in
the Switz. *Ury,* and *Arnold* of *Melchtale* born in *Under-Walden:* These entred into
an Association, whereby it was agreed among them, to rid themselves
of this Tyranny, and to restore their antient Liberty. A great many more
having entred afterwards into this Association an agreement was made
betwixt them; that in the year 1308. on the first day of *January,* they
would surprize these Judges in their strong Castles, and drive them
out of the Country. This Confederacy was made in the year 1307. on
the 17. of *October;* and having afterwards been put in execution in the
abovementioned year, on the first day of *January,* these three places

entred into a Confederacy for ten years for the mutual Defence of their antient Liberties. In the year 1315. *Leopold* Arch-Duke of *Austria,* Son of *Albert* I. marched with an Army of 20.000 Men to force them to Obedience; against whom they marched out with 1300 men, and whilst the *Austrian* Forces were <r275> marching betwixt the Lake [Aegeri] and inaccessible mountains, some of the *Switzers* by rowling down upon them, and throwing great heaps of stones among them, put the Enemy in confusion, whilst the rest fell upon them and entirely defeated them near *Morgarten.* Then these three places renewed their Confederacy, and having confirmed it by solemn Oaths, they agreed it should continue for ever. This was done at *Brun,* in the year 1320. on the *7th.* of *December.* And this is the first beginning of that Commonwealth [*Republic*], whose Confederates us'd to call themselves *Edytsgenossen* (which signifies Ally'd by Oath) but strangers call them in general *Switzers,* from that one place called *Switz.* The Battel near Morgarten.

§3. Nevertheless the first intention of this Confederacy was not to separate themselves from the *German* Empire, but only to maintain their antient Privileges; tho by degrees they began to Administer their own Affairs at home without sending their Deputies to the Dyets of the Empire: and the *Switzers* were not till in the year 1648. *viz* in the *Westphalian* Peace declared quite Independent from the *Roman* Empire; for the Emperor *Lewis* IV. had confirmed the former Confederacy, and in '1320' [1323] had sent them a new Imperial Vicar or Judge, unto whom, after having received new assurances to be maintained in their Privileges, they did Homage, in the name of the Emperor. But the following Emperors gave them full power to choose Judges among themselves, granting them the supreme Jurisdiction both in Civil and Criminal Affairs.[2] The first design of this Confederacy.

In the year 1332. *Lucern,* and in the year 1351. *Zurick.* entred into this Confederacy. *Lucern* was formerly under the Jurisdiction of the House of *Austria. Zurick,* which is the chiefest of the Confederacy, was formerly a free Imperial City. Immediately after *Glaris,* and in the year 1352. *Zug* and *Bern* were United with the former. The *Switzers* after

2. In German: "in Blut- und Bürgerlichen Sachen."

this time had great Wars with the House of *Austria,* and in 1386 slew

Battel near
Sempach.

Leopold Arch-Duke of *Austria,* with a great many Nobles, in the battel near *Sempach.* In the year 1444. the *Switzers* did give another proof of their Valour; for the *Dauphin* of *France,* afterward, call'd *Lewis* XI. march-<r276>ing with a great Army to disturb the Council then held at *Basil,* was attack'd by 1900 *Switzers* with such fury, that tho they all fell in the enterprize, yet did they strike such a terror into the *French,* that they quickly retreated homewards.

Wars with
Charles Duke
of Burgundy.

§4. In the year 1476 the *Switzers* were engaged in a war against *Charles* Duke of *Burgundy,* who was stirr'd up by *Lewis* XI. who was for setting the Duke at [to] work. Against him *Rene* Duke of *Lorain,* and the Bishops of *Strasburgh,* and *Basil,* made an Alliance with the *Switzers:* The Emperor *Frederick* III. also being desirous to revenge the quarrel of his House, commanded them to fall upon the Duke of *Burgundy,* who then was an Enemy of the Empire. And having afterwards made a Peace with the Duke without including the *Switzers,* he hop'd they would be severely chastized by this brave Prince; but things happen'd quite contrary to his expectation; for the *Switzers* defeated the Duke in three great Battels; the first near *Granson,* afterwards near *Murten,* where the Duke had an Army of one hundred thousand Men, and at last near *Nancy* in *Lorain,* where the Duke himself was killed. By these Victories the *Switzers* gained great Reputation. In the year 1481. *Fribourgh* and *Solothurn;* in the year 1501. *Basil* and *Shafshausen,* and last of all *Appen-Zell* were united with this Confederacy.

The whole body then of the *Swisse* Confederacy [*Systema*] is composed of 13 Commonwealths [*Republicquen*], which they call Places [*Oerter*]; but the *Italians* and *French* call them *Cantons;* among these

Their Allies.

Zuric, Bern, Lucern, Zug, Basil, Fribourgh, Solothurn, and *Shafshausen,* are Cities; *Ury, Switz, Underwalden, Glariss* and *Appen-Zell,* are Countries [*Landschafften*], where are a good number of Towns and Villages to be met withal. The *Switzers* have also some other Confederates, *viz.* the Abby and City of S. *Gall,* the *Grisons,*[3] the *Vallesins,* the Cities of

3. Graubünden, the easternmost of the Swiss cantons. Pufendorf says "die Rhaetos oder Pündter," from the Roman province of Rhaetia.

Rot[t]weil, Mülhausen, Bienne, the *Biel, Geneva,* and *Newburgh* on the Lake: There are also among them several Cities and some Countries, which are either subject to the whole Confederacy or to some particular Commonwealths [*Oertern*]. <r277>

§5. The *Switzers* were also obliged to fight against the Emperor *Maximilian* I. for their Liberty; he having stirr'd up the *Swabian* League against them \A. 1499\, hoping by this way to chastise them. But the *Switzers* for the most part got the better of their Enemies, till through the mediation of *Lewis* Duke of *Milan* a peace was made betwixt them. Not to relate here some intestine Commotions among them, scarce worth mentioning, they have done great Actions abroad, under the Conduct of other Nations [*Voelcker*], and more especially under the *French:* For *Lewis* XI. having, whilst he was *Dauphin,* sufficiently tryed their Valour in the engagement near *Basil,* sought by all ways after he was King, to make use of the *Switz* {especially their infantry} in his Wars; wherefore he allowed them a certain yearly Pension: And his Son *Charles* VIII. made use of the *Switzers* with good success in his Expedition against *Naples;* for the *Italians,* when they saw the *Switzers* make such a prodigious havock among them by the help of their Battel-Axes and large Back-Swords; they were so surprized at it, that they counted the former Wars but like Childrens play in comparison of this, and |[look'd upon the *Switzers* more like some Monsters than Soldiers.]|[4] *Lewis* XII. also employ'd the *Switzers* in his Service in his *Italian* Wars, tho they lost great part of their Reputation there. For these *Switzers* which were listed in the Service of *Lewis Menis*[5] Duke of *Milan,* refusing to fight against their Countrymen that were in the *French* Army, thereby betray'd this Prince into the hands of the *French.*

Some other Wars of the Switzers.

4. Rather: "the Italian gentlemen considered the Swiss to be almost without honor, since they struck down without ceremony whoever appeared in front of them [. . . *und wolten die Italienischen Cavallieri die Schweitzer fast nicht für ehrliche Kerle halten, weil sie ohne Ceremonie niederschlugen, wer ihnen vorkahm*]." This remark refers to the tendency of the Swiss to disregard the conventions of chivalric combat, as happened also in earlier battles such as Morgarten (see §2, p. 210, above).

5. Ludovico Sforza (il Moro, "the Moor," a reference to his dark complexion), 1451–1508. Crull's "Lewis Menis" refers to the half-moon or crescent (*menis*), which was a symbol of the Ottoman Empire.

Their Wars §6. But in the year 1510. the *Switzers* left the *French* Service; for the
with France. time of agreement with *France* being expired, they demanded a larger
Pension, and which *Lewis* XII. refused to pay them, thinking it unbecoming the grandeur of a King to be imposed upon by these Highland
Peasants (as he used to call them). He having therefore dismissed them,
took into his Service some of the *Grisons* and *Germans* in their stead.
But this proved very disadvantageous to *France;* for they [the Swiss]
listed themselves under Pope *Julius* II. and did great Service against
France. They attack'd the *French* who <r278> were much more numerous, with such fury \A. 1513\, near *Novara,* that after a bloody Fight they
not only routed them, but also quite beat them out of *Italy.* Afterwards
they fell into *Burgundy* and besieged the City of *Dijon,* where the Duke
of *Tremoville* was obliged to make a very dishonorable agreement with
them, and was glad to send them home with fair promises of great sums
of Money; and if he had not stop'd their progress they would certainly
have put *France* into the utmost danger, the King of *England* being at
the same time faln into *France* on the other side. The *Switzers* attack'd
Francis I. in his Camp near *Marignano* \A. 1515\; the fight lasted two
days, and after a great deal of bloodshed on both sides the *Switzers*
retired in good order. Wherefore *Francis* I. in the year next following
gained their Friendship by a great sum of Money, whose example the
succeeding Kings have followed ever since. Their antient Reputation is
much diminished of late years, partly because they are not altogether
so furious now, partly because other Nations have found out a way to
bring their Infantry into a better condition. And besides this, those
great Back-Swords which the *Switz* used to handle with so much dexterity by the extraordinary strength of their Arms, are quite out of use
in *Europe.*

The Nature §7. As to the 'qualifications of these Countries' [nature of the lands],
of the Soil. which are Inhabited by the *Switzers,* they are very different; for in the
mountainous parts scarce any thing else but Pasture Grounds are to
be met withal; but tho the Valley and flat Country produce Corn and
Wine in considerable quantities, yet among so vast a number of Inhabitants there appears no great plenty here, since Foreign Commodi-

ties cannot be imported without great difficulty, and what is deficient in the native Soil, is not repaired by Traffick and Manufactories. 'Tis therefore accounted a common calamity among the *Switzers* if once in some years the Plague does not come among them, to rid them of so many superfluous Mouths. Yet they enjoy this benefit by the situation of their Country, that, by reason of the high Mountains and narrow Passages, it is almost inaccessi-<r279>ble, especially on the *Italian* side, and in the midst of the Country; for some of the outward parts are of a very easie access.

§8. The *Switzers* pretend to be downright honest and true to their word; and indeed, they are generally Simple and Plain-Dealing, without any great Cunning or By-Designs; but they are couragious and soon provoked to wrath. They are steadfast in their Resolutions, from whence they don't easily recede; their valour, constancy, talness and strength of Body, has so recommended them to a great many Princes, that they choose their Guards among them; and the King of *France* maintains a considerable number of *Switz* Foot Souldiers. They are very forward to fight, but not to undergo any other hardship or labour; they expect to have duely their pay, if that fail, they return home as fast as they can; from whence comes the Proverb, No *Money no* Swisse. They do not love to bear hunger or hardship in other Countries because they have enough of that at home. It is one of the Articles of Agreement made with *France,* that that Crown shall never have less than 6000 at a time in pay, and that these are not to be separated: That in case these Articles should not be perform'd, they may be in capacity to assist one another: They also never will be imploy'd in any Sea service. *The Genius of this Nation.*

§9. The main strength of this Confederate Commonwealth consists in the number of its 'Inhabitants' [available soldiery]: For <in> the City of *Bern,* which has the greatest Territories, pretends alone to be able to send into the Field 100.000 fighting Men {within three days}. And it is not to be questioned, but that, if they had been ambitious of making Conquests, at that time when their Glory was at the highest pitch, or had not wanted 'Conduct' [leadership], they might easily have brought *Their strength and weakness.*

under their Subjection the *Franche Comte,* and a great part of *Lombardy;* but the reason why they did not aim at Conquests was partly their 'Inclination' [contented disposition], which did not prompt them to encroach upon their Neighbours; partly the 'constitution' [form] of their Government, which seems to be <r280> unfit for great and suddain Enterprises: For each Canton by itself considered is a Democracy, the highest Power being lodged in the *Guildes;* and it is certain, that such as are of little Understanding <and Experience>, are always very positive in their opinions, and suspicious of 'all mankind' [others' advice]. And the whole Confederacy is altogether adapted {only} for their common Defence, and for the |[maintaining of a firm Union]|[6] betwixt themselves. The difference of Religion is also a main obstacle among them, some of them being Roman Catholicks but most 'Protestants' [Reformed], and both Parties great Zealots in their Religion: Wherefore it seems a hard task to make them all truly unanimous, except forc'd by the necessity of a common Danger. And in this 'Democratical Government' [popular equality] it is not to be supposed, that |[one man can have sufficient Authority to sway the rest]|,[7] and to stir them up to any great and sudden Enterprise. And this slowness of their publick Counsels[8] is such a check upon their natural Valour [*kriegerisch Blut*] at home, that they can employ it no better than to sell it for a little money to other Nations.

Their neighbours. §10. This is the very reason why the *Switzers* are the best Neighbours in the World; as being never to be feared, and always ready to assist you in case of necessity, if you pay them for it. On the other hand, they need not stand in great fear of their Neighbours. The States of *Italy* are not in a capacity to do them any harm, and *Germany* is not willing to hurt them. If the House of *Austria* should attack them, they are able

6. Rather: "resolution of differences that may arise."
7. Rather: "any distinguished citizen [*grosser Bürger*] can so far surpass the rest [*eminiren*] that he can guide the entire nation [*sic*] as he wishes."
8. Pufendorf considered this a weakness of both democracies and systems (confederacies) of states. See *On the Law of Nature and of Nations,* VII.5 (on the forms of states), and Seidler (2011).

to defend themselves, and besides this, they may in such a case be sure to be back'd by *France*. *France* alone seems to be their most dangerous Neighbour; and it has been the wonder of many, why the *Switzers* rely 'altogether' [only] upon the *French* Alliance and Promises, and do not in the least endeavour {better} to secure their Country against the growing Power of *France;* and that in the last war they left the *Franche Comtè* to the mercy of the *French,* which opens the Passage into their Country, and enables the *French* to levy Souldiers on their Frontiers at pleasure.

It seems therefore to be the present Interest of *Switzerland,* not <r281> to irritate the *French*, and nevertheless to take care, that they do not make themselves Masters of their Frontier Places, *viz.* of *Geneva, Newburgh* on the Lake, the Four Forest Towns, and *Constance.* That they do not send too great a number of their Men into the *French* Service, whereby they may exhaust their own Stock of Souldiers; and that such as are sent into the *French* Service, may be engaged not to be forgetful of their Duty to their native Country, so as to be ready to return home in case of necessity. On the other hand, *France* seems to have no great reason to attack the *Switzers,* as long as they are quiet and do not <pretend to> oppose the *French* Designs; it being evident, that if *France* had once obtained its aim, the *Switzers* would |[be obliged to submit themselves]|.[9] And it seems at this time more Advantageous for the *French* to make use of the *Switzers* as their {willing} Allies, than by 'conquering them' [suppressing their liberty], to make them refractory Subjects, who, by reason of their natural stubborness, must be bridled by strong Garisons, which would scarce be maintained out of the Revenues of so poor a Country. <r282>

9. More sarcastically: "have few reasons to compliment them"; that is, would not be treated [as] well by them.

Of the German Empire.

§1. *Germany* was not antiently one Commonwealth [*Republic*], but di-   The antient
vided into a great many {moderately sized} States [*Staaten*], {sovereign   condition of
Germany.
to themselves} and independent of each other, most of them being Democracies: And tho some of them had their Kings, yet these had more
Authority to Advise than to Command. These several States [*Völcker*]
were at last united under the Government of the *Francks:* The Kings
of the *Merovingean* Family having undertaken several Expeditions into
Germany, did reduce several of these States under their Subjection: And   Charles the
Charles the Great reduced all *Germany* under his Jurisdiction, he being   Great.
at the same time Master of *France, Italy, Rome,* and a part of *Spain;* all
which Provinces he committed to the care of certain Governours, who
were called *Graves* [*Grafen*] or *Marc-Graves* [*Marggrafen*]. The *Saxons*
retained more of their antient Liberty than the rest; wherefore the better to keep this, then barbarous Nation [*Volck*] in obedience, he erected
several Episcopal Sees in *Saxony,* hoping, by the influence of the Christian Doctrine, to civilize this barbarous People. *Lewis* Surnamed the   Lewis the
Pious, Son of *Charles* the Great, had three Sons, *viz. Lotharius, Lewis,*   Pious.
and *Charles* [the Bald], who divided the Empire of the *Francks* among
them. In this Division *Lewis* got for his share all *Germany,* as far as it
extends on this side of the *Rhine,* and also some Countries on the other
side of that River, by reason of the Vineyards, as 'tis said, which are on
both sides. All which he was possess'd of as Sovereign, without being in   Lewis K. of
any ways dependent on his elder Brother, much less the younger, who   Germany.
had *France* for his share: And at that time *Germany* was first made a
Kingdom independent of any other. <r283>

§2. *Carolomannus*, the Son of this *Lewis*, did, after the death of *Charles the Bald*, who was King of *France*, and had born[e] the Title of *Roman* Emperour, conquer *Italy*, and took upon him the Imperial Dignity, notwithstanding that *Lewis*, Son of *Charles the Bald* and King of *France*, had, upon instigation of the Pope, assumed the same Title. After him

C. Crassus. succeeded his younger Brother *Carolus Crassus*, who maintained both the Kingdom of *Italy* and the Imperial Title. But the great Men in *Germany* having deposed the said *Charles* \A. 887\, they made *Arnolph*, the Son of the abovementioned *Carolomannus*, King of *Germany*, who went into *Italy* \A. 894\ and took upon him the Title of *Roman* Emperour, for which had contended for a good while *Berengarius* Duke of *Frioul*, and *Guido* Duke of *Spoleto*. But after the death of *Arnulph* \A. 899\,

Lewis the his Son *Lewis*, Surnamed the *Child*, obtained the Crown of *Germany*,
Child.   under whose Reign the Affairs of *Germany* were in so ill a condition, that he had no leisure to look into those of *Italy:* For *Arnulph* had called to his assistance the *Hungarians* against *Zwentepold*, King of *Bohemia* and *Moravia*, who had Rebell'd against him, with whose assistance he reduced *Zwentepold* to obedience; but the *Hungarians*, who were at that time a most barbarous Nation, having got a taste of *Germany*, made an inroad into that Country, ravaging every where with an inhuman Cruelty. They also defeated *Lewis* near *Augsburgh* \A. 905\, obliging him to pay them a yearly Tribute<; notwithstanding which, they ravag'd and plundered wherever they came>. This overthrow was chiefly occasioned by the Kings tender Age, and the Divisions of the great Men among themselves, who aimed at nothing more than to establish their own Authority.

Cunrad.   After the death of *Lewis* \A. 911\, *Cunrad*, Duke of *Franconia*, was elected King [of] *Germany*, under whose Reign the Potent Dukes of *Lorain*, *Swabia*, *Bavaria*, and *Saxony*, did pretend to maintain the Sovereignty over their own Countries, and a Hereditary Possession; which *Cunrad* was not able to prevent; and because *Henry* Duke of *Saxony* was the most Potent, and *Cunrad* feared, that at last he might quite withdraw himself from the *German* <r284> Empire, he upon his Death-bed advised the rest of the Princes of *Germany* to make him their King, which was done accordingly. And thus the Empire was transferred from the *Carolingian* Family to the *Saxons* {A. 919}.

§3. *Henry* Surnamed the *Birdcatcher,* did bridle the Fury of the *Hungar-* Henry the
ians: For they having made a great inroad into *Germany,* and demanded Faulconer.
the Yearly Tribute from him, he sent them a Mungeril-Dog, and afterwards Defeated them in a bloody Battle near *Merseburgh,* where he slew
80.000 of them. Under the Reign of this King, the greatest part of the
Cities which are situated on |[the sides]|[1] of the *Rhine,* were either Built,
or else Fortified with Walls. This *Henry,* also did Conquer the *Serbes*
and *Wendes,* a *Sarmatick* or *Sclavonian* Nation, who being possessed of
a large Tract of Land in *Germany,* on the River *Elbe,* he drove out of
Misnia, Lusatia and the Marquisate of *Brandenburgh.* After he had re-
established the Affairs of *Germany,* he died in the Year 936.

After him succeeded his Son *Otto,* Surnamed the *Great,* who at first Otto the
was engaged in heavy Civil Wars against several Princes, but especially Great.
against those who pretended to be of the Race [*Stamm*] of *Charles* the
Great, and were extremely dissatisfied that the Royal Dignity was transferred to the *Saxons.* He was also very Fortunate in his Wars against the
Danes. To the *Hungarians,* who ventured to make another Incursion
into *Germany,* he gave a capital overthrow near *Augsburgh,* since which
time, they never have dared to shew themselves in *Germany.* In *Italy*
there had been great Confusions for a long time, the Soveraignty having been usurped sometimes by one, sometimes by another, till at last
Otto being called thither, possessed himself both of the Kingdom of
Italy and the Imperial Dignity {of Rome}, it having been then agreed,
that both the Imperial and Royal Dignity of *Italy,* should be insepa-
rably annexed, without any further Election, to the Royal Dignity of
Germany, and that no Pope should be chosen without the Approbation
of the King of the *Germans,* and *Otto* was Crowned at *Rome* {A. 962}:
tho' this Conquest has proved not very beneficial to *Germany,* the succeeding Popes having made it their Business to <r285> raise continual

1. Rather: "this side."

Disturbances, which was not easy to be prevented, because these Places were not kept in 'awe' [check] by strong Castles or Garisons. Wherefore as often as the Popes were pleased to raise new Commotions, the *Germans* were obliged to send great Armies thither, which continual Alarms consumed {in vain} great quantities of Men and Money: In lieu of which, their Kings had scarce any Revenues out of *Italy,* except that they had Free Quarters and Entertainment [maintenance] given them during their stay there.

Otto II.   This *Otto* died in the Year 974 leaving for his Successour his Son *Otto* II. who also at first met with great Disturbances from some of the Princes of *Germany.* Afterwards *Lotharius* King of *France* would have made himself Master of *Loraine,* and had very near surprised the Emperour at *Aix la Chapelle:* But *Otto* marched with an Army through *Champaigne* to the very Gates of *Paris;* but in his return home received a considerable Loss. At last a Peace was concluded at *Rheims,* by Vertue of which, *Loraine* was left to the Emperour. He then undertook an Expedition into *Italy* against the *Greeks,* who had made themselves Masters of that Country; these he overthrew at first, but received afterwards a grand Defeat, because the *Romans* and those of *Benevento* 'immediatly turned their Backs' [foolishly fled]; he himself fell into the Hands of the Enemy, but found means to make his Escape from them, and revenged himself against the former for their Infidelity. He died not long after of Vexation {A. 983}.

Otto III.   His Son *Otto* III. {also} did employ a great part of his Reign in appeasing these Tumults, which were raised in *Rome* by the 'Consul' [mayor] *Crescentius,* who aiming at the Sovereignty, was hanged for his pains by Order of *Otto,* who was afterwards \A. 1001\ poysoned by the Widdow of the said *Crescentius* with a pair of Gloves made up with a certain sort of Poyson. *Otto* having left no Children behind him, the Crown was conferred upon *Henry* II. surnamed the *Lame,* Duke of *Bavaria,* who sprang from the *Saxon* Race; with whom *Ecbart* Landgrave of *Hesse,* did contend for the Crown, but lost his Life in the Quarrel. This Emperour was entangled in continual Troubles in *Italy,* and chastised *Boleslaus* King of *Po-*<r286>*land.* Because he was a great Benefactor to the Clergy, he was made a Saint after his Death \A. 1024\.

§4. *Henry* II. having left no Children behind him, the Princes elected   Conrad II.
Conrad Sali Duke of *Franconia,* Emperour <in his room>, which occasioned great Jealousie in the *Saxons,* and great Wars in *Germany.* This
Emperour met with great Disturbances both in *Germany* and *Italy,*
which were at last all {happily} composed. *Rudolf* the last King of *Burgundy* and *Arles* dying without Issue, left him that Kingdom by his last
Will, which he took Possession of and united the same with *Germany,*
having forced *Eudo* the Earl of *Champaigne* who made a pretension
upon it, to resign his Title \A. 1034\. He was also very Fortunate in his
Wars against the *Poles* and *Sclavonians,* and died in the Year 1035.

Him succeeded his Son *Henry,* Surnamed the *Black,* who was con-   Henry III.
tinually allarm'd by the *Hungarians* and the Popes Intrigues, against
whom he maintained the Imperial Dignity with great bravery. He died
in the Year 1056. His Son *Henry* IV. his Reign was very long, but also   Henry IV.
very Troublesome and Unfortunate. Among other Reasons, this may be
counted one of the Chiefest, that he being but Six Years of Age when his
Father died, was left to the Tuition of such as had no true Care of his
Education; and besides this, by selling the 'Church' [spiritual] Benefices
{for money} without having any Regard to Deserts, had done considerable Mischief to the Empire [*Regiment*]. Wherefore *Henry* coming to
his riper Years, and perceiving how the Ecclesiasticks had got all the best
Possessions of the Empire into their Hands, he resolved to dispossess
them again, whereby he drew upon himself the hatred of the Clergy.
The *Saxons* were also his great Enemies, because he had by Building up
of some Fortresses endeavoured to restrain their Insolencies; and tho'
he often kept his Court in *Saxony,* yet he seldom preferred the *Saxons*
to any Offices. Most of the Princes were also dissatisfied with him,
because he rarely advised with them concerning the publick State of Affairs, but either followed the Advice of his Counsellors, who were most
of them Men of mean Birth, or else his own Head. These and <r287>
some other Reasons, set the *Saxons* against him in an open Rebellion,
with whom he waged long and bloody Wars, till he vanquished them
at last.

But Pope *Hildebrand* or *Gregory* VII. and his Successours, did raise a   The Pope
more dreadful Storm against him; for the Popes having long since been   gives him great
trouble.

vexed to the Heart, that they and the rest of the Clergy should be subject to the Emperour, *Hildebrand* thought to have now met with a fair Opportunity to set the Clergy at Liberty, at a time when the Emperour was entangled in a War with the *Saxons,* and hated by most Princes of the Empire. The Emperour had lived somewhat too Free [dissolute] in his younger Years, and the {many} Church Benefices having been rather bestowed upon Favourites or such as payed well for them, than such as deserved them, furnished the Pope with a specious Pretence to make a Decree, that |[it was not the Emperour's right to bestow Bishopricks or other Church Benefices upon any Body]|,[2] but that it did belong to the Pope. The Emperour was also summoned to appear at *Rome,* and to give an Account concerning his Mis-behaviour, and in case of failure, he was threatened with an Excommunication. On the other Hand, the Emperour having declared the Pope unworthy of his Office, would have deposed him. So the Pope excommunicated the Emperour, discharging all his Subjects from their Allegiance due to him, which proved of such Consequence in those Times, that all his Authority fell to the Ground at once among most of his Subjects, whereby he was reduced to the greatest Extremity. For most Princes assembled at *Trebes* {A. 1076}, where they deposed *Henry:* which Sentence, however, was so far mitigated afterwards, that the same should be left to the Pope's decision. *Henry* therefore accompanied by a few, was obliged to undertake a Journey in the midst of the Winter into *Italy,* and being arrived at *Canusio* [Canossa], was fain to stay three Days barefooted in a coarse Woollen Habit in the outward Court, and in an humble posture, to beg the Pope's Absolution, which he at last granted him.

But⁺ the Emperour received no great Advantage by it, for the *Italians* were quite disgusted at this Demeanour of his, which obliged the Emperour to make use of his \<r288\> former Authority to reduce them to Obedience. In the mean while the Princes of *Germany* by instigation of the Pope, did elect *Rudolph* Duke of *Swabia* their King {A. 1077}; but the *Bavarians, Franconians,* and the Countries next adjacent to the *Rhine* did remain in obedience of the Emperour *Henry.* Thus a bloody

2. Rather: "the Emperor should not appoint bishops or other clergy."

War ensued, wherein *Rudolph,* and the *Saxons* were vanquish'd in two battels, and in the third he lost his right hand and life. Then *Henry* call'd together an Assembly of the Bishops, and having deposed *Hildebrand,* he caused another to be chosen in his room [place]: |[He also return'd home himself, and banish'd]|[3] *Hildebrand* \A. 1084\. But the *Saxons* {nonetheless} persisted in their Rebellion against the Emperour, who was again Excommunicated by the Pope, and having first set up *Herman* Duke of *Luxemburgh,* and after his death, *Ecbert* Marquess of *Saxony* for their Kings, but to no purpose; they at last stirr'd up the Emperors Son against the Father. Against him the Emperour raised a great Army, whom the Son met, and in a deceitful manner begg'd his pardon: Upon his perswasions the Father having abandon'd his Forces, and being upon his Journey to the Dyet at *Mayence,* accompanied by a few, this antient Prince was made a Prisoner and Deposed \A. 1106\. He died soon after in great misery, who, in sixty two battels which he had fought in his life time, generally obtained the Victory.

His Son Rebels.

§5. As soon as *Henry* V. was made Emperour he followed his Fathers example in maintaining the Imperial Dignity: For as soon as he had settled the Affairs of *Germany,* he marched with an Army towards *Rome,* to renew the antient Right of the Emperours in nominating of Bishops, and to be Crowned there. The Pope, *Paschel* II. having got notice of the Emperours design, raised a great Tumult at *Rome,* where the Emperour was so close beset, that he was fain to fight in Person for his safety: But the Emperour having got the upper hand, made the Pope a Prisoner, and forced him to give his consent to his demands. And this their Agreement was confirmed by solemn Oaths and Execrations; yet no sooner had the Emperour turn'd his back, but the Pope having declared the Agreement <r289> void, stirr'd up the *Saxons* and the Bishops in *Germany* against the Emperour. With these *Henry* was engag'd in a very tedious War; and perceiving at last, that there was no other way left to compose these differences, he granted the Popes demands, by renouncing his Right to nominate Bishops, at the Dyet held at *Worms* \A. 1122\:

Henry V.

3. Rather: "Thereafter he conquered Rome and chased away."

which resignation, as it greatly diminish'd the Emperour's Authority, so on the other hand, it strengthened the power of the Pope.[4]

Lotharius the Saxon.   This Emperour died without issue \A. 1125\. Him succeeded *Lotharius* Duke of *Saxony*, who had for a Rival in the Empire *Cunrad* Duke of *Franconia*, whom he quickly oblig'd to beg fair Quarters. This Emperour having twice undertaken an Expedition into *Italy*, did with great Glory restore Tranquility to that Country; and, because he used to flatter the Pope, he was in great esteem among the Clergy. He died in

Cunrad III.   the year 1138. After his death *Cunrad* III. {duke in Franconia} obtained the Imperial Dignity, who was opposed by *Henry* Duke of *Saxony* and *Bavaria,* and his Brother *Wolff,* which occasioned bloody Wars against him. But peace being restored among them, he undertook an Expedition into the Holy Land, where he underwent great Calamities; for, tho he fought his way through the *Saracens,* and arriv'd safely at *Jerusalem,* yet after he had lost the greatest part of his Army, without doing any thing of moment, he was fain to return home. But whilst he was busie in making preparations for another Expedition into *Italy* {to compose the tumults there} he died, in the year 1152.

Frederick I.   §6. *Frederick* I. succeeded him, who by the *Italians* was Surnamed *Barbarossa,*[5] Duke of *Swabia,* who immediately at the beginning of his Reign, having setled the affairs of *Germany,* did afterwards reduce *Italy* under his obedience; which however was not of long continuance; for the *Milaneses* quickly Rebell'd, but were severely chastis'd, their City having been laid level with the ground. He was also in continual broils with the Pope, against whom, and his Associates, he obtained several Victories; yet being at last tired out with so many wars, he made peace with him, especially since his Son *Otto* had been taken Prisoner by the *Venetians.* At the concluding of this Peace, 'tis said, that <r290> Pope *Alexander* III. did set his foot upon the Emperours neck, which

---

4. The Concordat of Worms (1122), agreed to by Henry V and Pope Callixtus II, ended the so-called investiture controversy and allowed the emperor to invest bishops with secular authority (symbolized by a lance), while their spiritual authority (symbolized by ring and crosier) was henceforth bestowed by the pope.
5. Barbarossa means "red-beard."

by a great many is taken for a fable. This Emperour was the last who maintained the Authority of the *German* Emperours in *Italy.* Last of all he undertook an Expedition into the Holy Land against *Saladin* the Sultan of *Egypt,* who had taken the City of *Jerusalem:* He beat the *Saracens* several times, but endeavouring to pass over a River in *Cilicia* on Horseback, or as some will have it, intending to wash himself in the River, he was drowned \A. 1189\.

And tho his Son *Frederick,* after his Fathers death, did take a great many Cities in *Syria,* yet the whole Expedition had a very bad end, the greatest part of the Army, together with the Duke *Frederick* having been consumed by the Plague, or Famin. *Frederick* [I.] was succeeded by his Son *Henry* VI. in the Empire, who, with his Lady *Constantia,* got the Kingdoms of *Sicily, Calabria* and *Apulia.* This Emperour went to *Rome* to receive the Crown from Pope *Celestin,* when the Pope sitting in his Chair, and the Emperour on his knees, put first the Crown upon his head, but immediately struck the same off again with his foot, intimating thereby, as if it was in the power of the Popes to give and to take away the Imperial Crown. He died in the year 1198, having just then made great preparations for an Expedition into the Holy Land, and sent his Army before, he being ready to follow. Henry VI.

§7. After the death of *Henry* VI. the *Germans* were miserably divided among themselves; for *Frederick* II. his Son, being then but five years old, his Uncle *Philip* pretended to have the Tuition of his Nephew, and the Administration of the Empire, according to the last Will of the deceas'd Emperour; but this being opposed by the Pope, he perswaded some of the Princes to elect *Otto* Duke of *Saxony. Germany* was thus miserably torn in pieces, most siding with *Philip,* the rest with *Otto.* After a long war an agreement was made betwixt them, that *Otto* should Marry the Daughter of *Philip,* but lay down the Royal Title, till the death of *Philip,* when the same was to be restored to him. Not long after \A. 1208\ *Philip* was murthered at *Bamberg* by *Otto* the *Palatin* [Count Palatine] of *Wittel*[*s*]*bach.* Philip.

After his death {the aforementioned} *Otto* obtained <r291> the Imperial Dignity, and having been Crowned at *Rome,* he resolved to reunite Otto VI.

such places as were unjustly possess'd by the Popes to the Empire, which
so exasperated the Pope, that he Excommunicated him, exhorting the
Princes to elect another Emperour. Most of them were for *Frederick* II.

Frederick II.

Son of *Henry* VI. which made *Otto* to hasten into *Germany;* but having
in vain endeavour'd to maintain himself in the Empire, he was forc'd
{A. 1212} to surrender the Imperial Crown to *Frederick* the Second, King
of *Sicily* and *Naples,* and Duke of *Suabia;* who, after he had bestowed
a considerable time in setling the Affairs of *Germany,* went into *Italy,*
where he was Crowned by the Pope. In the year 1228, he undertook an
Expedition into the Holy Land, and retook *Jerusalem* from the *Saracens.* He was continually allarm'd by the intrigues of the Popes, who
were for playing the Masters in *Italy;* against whom he bravely [*männiglich*] maintained his Right. This occasioned several Excommunica-
tions to be thundred out against him by the Popes, who ||[raised great
disturbances.]||[6]

From hence had their rise the two 'famous' [terrible] Factions in *Italy,*

The Guelfs
and Gibellins.

whereof those who sided with the Pope, called themselves *Guelfs,* but
these who were for the Emperour, *Gibellins;*[7] which two factions, for a
considerable time after, occasioned great Commotions in *Italy:* And tho
Frederick behav'd himself bravely against the Pope and his Associates,
yet the Popes Excommunication, had such powerful Influence in that
Superstitious Age, that, after the Pope had solemnly deposed him in the
Council held at *Lyons* \A. 1245\, some Princes of *Germany* did choose
Henry, Landgrave of *Thuringia* their King, who was commonly call'd
the King of the Priests [*Pfaffen König*]; but he dying in the year next
following, some Princes declared *William* Earl of *Holland* their King;
who was not able to Establish himself, being opposed by *Cunrad,* Son
of *Frederick* II. who was appointed to succeed his Father in the Empire.
In the mean time his Father had been very unsuccessful in *Italy,* who at
last died in the year 1250. *Cunrad* having left *Germany,* retired into his

6. Rather: "incited against him whomever they could."
7. Guelf comes from the German *Welf,* referring to the Welfen dynasty of Bavaria
and Saxony, while Ghibelline comes from *Waiblingen* (near Stuttgart), a stronghold
of the Hohenstaufen dukes of Swabia. See p. 42, note 3, above, and Editor's Introduction, p. xxv, note 59.

Hereditary Kingdoms of *Naples* and *Sicily,* where he died \A. 1254\. *William* Earl of *Holland* was {also} slain in a battel against the *Frizolanders* [Frisians], in the year 1256. <r292>

§8. With the death of *Frederick* II. the Authority of the *German* Emperours in *Italy* was quite extinguish'd: And that it might not be revived again, the Pope gave the Kingdom of *Naples* to *Charles* Duke of *Anjou,* who, by the Instigation of the Pope, caused the young *Cunradin* (who being the Son of *Cunrad,* was come to recover his Hereditary Kingdom, and taken Prisoner in a battel fought betwixt them) to be executed by the hands of the Hangman; with whom was extinguish'd the Race of the Dukes of *Swabia.* A long Interregnum.

In the mean time there were great divisions among the *German* Princes, concerning the election of a new Emperour; some of them had chosen *Richard* Duke of *Cornwal,* Son of *John* King of *England,* and the rest were for *Alfonsus* X. King of *Castile;* both were elected in the year 1257. *Richard* came on his Journey as far as the *Rhine,* to take possession of the Empire, but, for want of Money, was forc'd {to his disgrace} to return home again: And *Alfonsus* came not {even} within the sight of *Germany.* Then there was a complete 'and long vacancy of the Throne' [*interregnum*] in *Germany:* during which time there was nothing to be seen but confusion, every body pretending to be Master. These Civil Disorders were of the worse consequence, because that about the same time the three great Families of the Dukes of *Swabia,* the Marquesses of *Austria,* and *Landgraves* of *Thuringia* being extinct, a great many aspired to possess themselves of these Countries.[8] To be short, the longest Sword was then the best Title [*das Faustrecht*], and he that could master another kept him under subjection; and robbing and plundering was an allow'd exercise [*eine freye Kunst*] at that time. Against these outrageous Proceedings several of the Cities upon the *Rhine* enter'd into a Confederacy \A. 1255\, with whom a great many other Princes {and

8. More literally: ". . . many were licking their lips for these derelict lands [*nach dero verlassenen Ländern vielen das Maul wässerte*]." Cf. p. 92, note 63, above. Pufendorf wrote a dissertation *De interregnis* (1668) which was included in his *Dissertationes academicae selectiores* (Lund, 1675).

lords} afterwards joyning their Forces, they demolish'd the strong Holds of these Robbers, and clear'd the Highways.

Rodolph Earl of Habsburgh. §9. At last \A. 1273\ *Rodolph* Earl of *Habsburgh* and *Landgrave* of *Alsace* (from whom are descended the present Arch-Dukes of *Austria*) was unanimously chosen Emperour; who, the better to establish himself in the Throne, <293> Marry'd his three Daughters to three of the great Princes of *Germany, viz.* to *Lewis Palatin* of the *Rhine,* to *Albert* Duke of *Saxony,* and to *Otto* Marquess of *Brandenburgh.* After the death of *Frederick* Marquess of *Austria,* who had his Head cut off at *Naples,* together with *Cunradin, Ottocar* the King of *Bohemia* had possess'd himself of *Austria, Stiria, Crain,* the *Windishmarck* and *Portenau.* But *Rodolph,* who thought that his Family had more Right to it[,] having retaken these Countries, from *Ottocar,* gave them in Fief to his Son *Albert;* and to the second, whose name was *Rodolph,* the Dukedom of *Swabia:* Besides this, the Grandson of *Albert* got *Crain* and *Tyrol.* Thus *Rodolph* did by obtaining the Imperial Dignity, raise his House from a moderate State to great Power and vast Riches. But tho he was often invited to come into *Italy,* yet he could never be perswaded to it, alledging that old and notorious saying of the Fox, *Quia me vestigia terrent;* because the footsteps deter me.[9] Nay he declar'd a great many Cities there Free, for Sums of money; by which the Kingdom of *Italy,* being first torn into a great many pieces, was quite lost: But *Germany* he took into his particular Care, and destroy'd a great many Castles there which serv'd for a retreat for Robbers. He was the first that introduc'd the use of the *German* Tongue in all Publick Courts and Private Transactions, whereas formerly the *Latin* Tongue had been made use of in the like cases. He dyed in the year 1291.

His[+] Son *Albert* did lay claim to the Empire, but by the 'Interest' [in-
Adolph. tervention] of the Archbishop of *Mayence, Adolph* Earl of *Nassau,* who was his kinsman, was chosen Emperour; the Archbishop being in hopes

---

9. Horace, *Epistles* I.1.74, referring to Aesop's fable about a fox who will not enter an aged lion's den because "the footprints frighten me" (that is, all go in and none come out).

|[to have, under him, the supreme Management of the Affairs]|[10]; but *Adolph* not being willing to depend on the Archbishop, he [the latter] conceived a hatred against him. Some did {also} think it unbecoming the grandure of the Emperour, that he engaged in a League with *England* against *France* for a Sum of Mony paid to him by the *English;* but this might admit of a very good excuse, since besides this, the *English* had promiss'd the Emperour to assist him in the recovery of the Kingdom of *Arelat,* a great part of which *France* had, during the Troubles in *Germany,* <294> taken into its possession. On the other hand *France* sided with *Albert,* who being advanced near the *Rhine,* the Archbishop   Albert I. of *Mayence* did assemble some of the Electors, who being dissatisfied with *Adolph,* depos'd him, and chose *Albert* Emperour in his stead. A bloody Battel was fought betwixt these two near *Spires* {A. 1298}, wherein *Adolph* being slain, the Imperial Crown remain'd to *Albert:* But because he aim'd at nothing more than to enrich himself, his Reign was both very unglorious and unfortunate. His Covetousness was at last the occasion of his death; for his Nephew *John* Duke of *Swabia,* whom he had dispossess'd of his Country, murder'd him near *Rhinefeld* \A. 1308\.

§10. After his death, *Philip* King of *France* endeavour'd to obtain the Imperial Crown, but was prevented by the Electors, who, upon the perswasion of the Pope, chose *Henry* VII. Earl of *Luxemburgh.* This   Henry VII. Emperour, after he had setled *Germany,* undertook a journey into *Italy,* with a resolution to suppress the <Civil> Commotions there, and to reestablish the Imperial Authority. The beginning of this undertaking proved so prosperous, that every body hoped for great success from it: But in the midst of this prosperity he was murther'd by a Monk, who   Poisoned by a had given him a poison'd Host, he having been hired by the *Florentines,*   Monk. the Emperours Enemies, to commit this fact.

In[+] the year 1313, the Electors were again divided in the Election of a new Emperour, some having given their Votes for *Lewis* Duke of   Lewis the *Bavaria,* the rest for *Frederick* Duke of *Austria.* The first was Crown'd at   Bavarian.

---

10. Rather: "that the latter would rule the Empire as he himself advised and preferred."

Aix la Chapelle, the latter at *Bonn.* These two carry'd on a War against each other for the Imperial Crown during the space of nine years, to the great detriment of the whole Empire: At last *Frederick* being made a Prisoner in a battel fought in the year 1323. *Lewis* became sole Master of the Empire, and restored its Tranquility. But he afterwards went into *Italy,* to back the *Gibellines,* who were of his side, and tho at first he was very prosperous, yet could he not settle his Affairs to any purpose, because the Pope had Excommunicated him. Wherefore also the Popes Associates in <295> *Germany,* malgre [despite] all his resistance, were always too hard for him; and at last, by the perswasions of the Pope, stirr'd up the Electors against him, who chose *Charles* IV. Marquess of *Moravia,* Son of *John* King of *Bohemia,* Emperour in his stead; who nevertheless, as long as *Lewis* lived, was not much taken notice of. He died {finally} in the year 1347. It is to be observed, that the preceding Emperours used generally to make their Progress thro' the Empire, and to maintain their Court out of the Revenues belonging to the Empire: But this *Lewis* IV was the first who kept his constant Court in his Hereditary Country, and maintain'd it out of his own Revenue; whose example the succeeding Emperours follow'd, the Revenues belonging to the Empire having been by degrees extremely diminish'd.

Charles IV. §11. After the death of *Lewis,* there were some who would have made void the former Election of *Charles,* and had chosen in his stead *Edward* King of *England* who did not think fit to accept of the Imperial Dignity: The same was also refused by *Frederick* Marquess of *Misnia:* At last *Gunther* Earl of *Swartzburgh* was elected; whom *Charles* caused to be poison'd, and by his Liberality establish'd himself in the Empire. During his Reign he gave away a considerable part of the 'Dependencies' [means, *Mitteln*] of the Empire, and among the rest he granted to *France* the perpetual Vicarship of the Kingdom of *Arelat;* and in *Italy* he sold what he could to the fairest bidder: But he was not so careless of his Kingdom of *Bohemia,* unto which he annex'd, among other Countries, that of *Silesia.* He was a great favourer of the Cities which he dignified with such Privileges, that they might the better be able to maintain themselves against the Power of the Princes: The best thing that ever he

Margin notes:

Excommunicated by the Pope.

did, was, that he caused first to be compiled the *Golden Bull*,[11] wherein **The Golden Bull.**
were set down the Rules to be observed in the elections of the ensuing
Emperours, and Divisions among the Electors, prevented for the future.
He died in the year 1378. having not long before by great Presents made
to the Electors, prevailed with them, to chose his Son *Wenceslaus* King **Wenceslaus.**
of the *Romans:*[12] But he being very brutish and careless of the Affairs
of the Empire, was deposed by the <296> Electors \A. 1400\, which he
little regarded, but retired into his Hereditary Kingdom of *Bohemia,*
where he lived for a considerable time. After *Wenceslaus* was deposed,
Jodocus Marquess of *Moravia* was chosen Emperour, but he happening to die within a few months after, before he could take possession
of the Empire, *Frederick* Duke of *Brunswick* was elected in his stead, **Fredrick of Brunswick.**
who, in his Journey to *Francfort* was, by instigation of the Archbishop
of *Mayence,* murthered by the Earl of *Waldeck.* At last *Rupert, Palatin* **Rupert.**
of the *Rhine* was chosen Emperour; who Reigned with great applause
in *Germany;* but his Expedition into *Italy* proved fruitless. He died in
the year 1410.

§12. After the death of *Rupert, Sigismund* King of *Hungary,* Brother to **Sigismund.**
Wenceslaus, was made Emperour; a Prince endow'd with great Quali-
ties, but very unfortunate in his wars, having, before he obtained the
Imperial Crown, received a great defeat from the *Turks* near *Cogrelis*
[*Nicopoli*] \A. 1395\; which was occasioned by the too much heat and
forwardness of the *French* Auxiliaries. He caused *John Huss,* notwithstanding the safe Conduct granted him, to be burnt at the Council of
Constance; whose death his adherents, who called themselves *Hussites,*
did revenge with great fury upon *Bohemia* and *Germany;* this War having taken up the greatest part of his Reign. He died in the year 1437.

After[+] him succeeded his Son-in-Law *Albert* II. Duke of *Austria,* and **Albert II.**
King of *Hungary* and *Bohemia,* who did not Reign a whole year. He
died in the year 1439. whilst he was very busie in making preparations

11. At the Diet of Nuremberg in 1356.
12. See note 23, p. 60, above, and *The Present State of Germany,* IV.9, in Pufendorf
(2007), pp. 109–10.

Fredrick III.   against the *Turks*. Him succeeded his kinsman *Frederick* III. Duke of *Austria;* since which time all the succeeding Emperours have been of this House. During his Reign several disturbances were raised in *Germany,* which were neglected by the Emperour. He also had some differences with *Ladislaus,* Son of *Albert* II. concerning *Austria,* and was attack'd by *Matthias Hunniades* King of *Hungary;* which war he prosecuted with more patience than vigour. He died in the year 1493. Him

Maximilian I.   succeeded his Son *Maximilian* I. who had the good <297> fortune by his Marriage with *Mary* the Daughter of *Charles* the *Hardy* Duke of *Burgundy,* to annex the *Netherlands* to the House of *Austria.* As he was very fickle in his undertakings, so the[ir] success was generally answerable to it and various; and his Wars with the *Switzers,* and those in *Italy* against the *Venetians* had but a very 'indifferent' [bad] end: The chiefest thing of moment done by him, is, that whereas formerly all differences in *Germany* were decided by the Sword [*Faustrecht*], he reestablished the Peace of the Empire [*Landfrieden*]. He died in the year 1519.

Charles V.   §13. Him succeeded his Grandson *Charles* V. King of *Spain* and Sovereign of the *Netherlands;* under whose Reign the face of Affairs in *Germany* was remarkably changed; which was occasioned by the Religious Differences set on foot about that time: For the Pope had caused Indulgences to be sold here in so scandalous a manner, that the wiser sort began to be asham'd of it. Wherefore *Martin Luther* Doctor of

The Reformation.   Divinity and Professor in the University of *Wittenbergh,* held a publick Disputation against it \A. 1517\; who being opposed by others, |[all the neighbouring Countries were alarm'd at it.]|[13] *Luther* at first did submit himself to the decision of the Pope, but finding that he [the latter] favour'd the Indulgence Merchants, and that he was condemn'd by him, he appealed to a free <General> Council, and then began to go farther, to 'examine' [challenge] the Popes Authority; and having laid open some Errours and Abuses which were crept in <among them>, his Doctrine was so approved of by some of the Princes and free Imperial Cities, that they began to banish the Priests and Monks out of

13. Rather: "a great alarm soon ensued therefrom."

several places, and to 'reduce their Revenues' [appropriate their posses-sions]. And tho the Emperour did declare *Luther,* at the Dyet of *Worms* \A. 1521\, an Out-Law, and endeavour'd by several Proclamations to put a stop to these Proceedings and Innovations; nevertheless, the Em-perour being then engag'd in a war with *France,* and therefore not in a capacity to apply himself in good earnest to the suppressing of this Division, *Luthers* Party grew daily stronger.

Perhaps+ he [Charles] was afterwards not very sorry, to see the 'wound' [sickness] encrease, that he might make the better benefit <298> of the Cure.[14] There having been a Proclamation publish'd {afterwards} \A. 1529\, at the Dyet of *Spiers,* which was in no ways agreeable to the *Lutheran* Princes, they protested against the same, from whence they are called Protestants. In the year next following \A. 1530\ they delivered a Confession of their Faith to the Emperour at *Augsburgh,* and entered into a Defensive Alliance at *Smalkald;* which League was renewed in the year 1535 when a great many Princes and Free Imperial Cities were received into it. This League made at *Smalkald* was a great eye-sore to the Emperour, who used all means to dissolve the same: But the Protestants, who now began to trust to their own strength, standing by one another, the Hostilities began on both sides, and the Protestants did bring into the Field \A. 1546\ an Army of 100.000 Men, under the Conduct of *John Frederick* Elector of *Saxony,* and *Philip* Landgrave of *Hesse.* If they had fal'n immediately upon the Emperour, whose Forces were then not joined, they might in all probability have worsted him; but having lost the first opportunity, the Emperour strengthen'd him-self, that he forced the Protestants to quit the Field and to disband their Forces. He also caused a diversion to be given the Elector at home by his Kinsman *Maurice,* which had such influence upon the Free Imperial Cities, that they were oblig'd to submit themselves and to pay consider-able Fines.

In the year next following the Emperour fell into *Saxony,* and hav-ing defeated the Elector near *Michlbergh,* took him prisoner; against whom he pronounced sentence of Death, which however he chang'd

The Rise of the Name of Protestants.

The League at Smalkald.

---

14. That is, to exploit the situation for his own advantage.

into an Imprisonment. *Philip* Landgrave of *Hesse* having also submitted himself, was, contrary to agreement, made a Prisoner; whereby the Protestant Religion in *Germany* was reduc'd to great extremity. The Electorat of *Saxony* was given to *Maurice* Duke of *Saxony,* who at last being resolved not to permit any longer that both the Religion and Liberty should be quite destroy'd, neither that his Wifes Father the Landgrave of *Hesse,* who upon his Parole had surrendred himself to the Emperour, should be {longer} detain'd a Prisoner, fell so suddenly with his Forces upon the Emperour, that he was very near having surprised his Person at *Inspruck* \A. 1552\. *Henry* II. King of *France* having also made an Inroad on the o-<299>ther side of *Germany,* surprized *Metz, Tullie,* and *Verdun.* King *Ferdinand* therefore the Emperours Brother interposing his Authority, a Peace was {finally} concluded at *Passau* \A. 1552\; where their Religion was secured to the Protestants, till matters could be better setled at the next ensuing Dyet. The Landgrave was released; as likewise *John Frederick* the Elector, who was dismissed out of prison a little before by the Emperour. At last the Religious Peace in *Germany* was establish'd, at the Dyet at *Augsburgh* \A. 1555\, where it was provided, that neither Party should annoy one another under the pretext of Religion, and that such of the Church Lands and Revenues, as the Protestants had been possess'd of before the Peace concluded at *Passau,* should remain in their possession.

The Boors [peasants] also in *Germany* raised a most dangerous Rebellion under the Reign of *Charles* V: of whom there were kill'd above 100.000 \A. 1525\. In the year 1529, the City of *Vienna* was besieg'd by *Solyman* the *Turkish* Emperour, but to no purpose, he being oblig'd to raise the Siege, not without considerable loss: And afterwards \A. 1532\ the *Turks* who were marching with a great Army into *Austria,* were beaten back again. In the year 1534 the Anabaptists were for erecting a new Kingdom in *Munster* in *Westphalia,* under the Conduct [leadership] of *John,* a Taylor of *Leiden,* and one *Knipperdolling;* who receiv'd the 'dire' [deserved] Reward of their madness.

At last this great Prince *Charles* V. surrender'd the Imperial Dignity to his Brother *Ferdinand* I. King of *Hungary* and *Bohemia,* who united these two Kingdoms to the House of *Austria,* he having Married *Anna*

(marginal notes)

A Peace concluded.

An Insurrection of the Boors.

He Resigns.

Ferdinand I.

Sister of *Lewis* King of *Hungary* and *Bohemia,* who was slain in the battel fought against the *Turks* near *Mohatz.* He Reign'd very peaceably in *Germany,* and died in the year 1564. Him succeeded his Son *Maximil-* Maximilian II. *ian* II. who also Reign'd in peace, except that a Tumult happen'd at that time in *Germany,* raised by one *William Grumpach* and his Associates, who having first murther'd *Melchior Zobel* the Archbishop of *Wurtzburgh,* had plunder'd that City; they also endeavour'd to stir up the Nobility and to raise disturbances in other places. This man having been declar'd an Outlaw, was protected by *John Frederick* Duke of *Saxony,* who paid dearly for it, *Gotha,* one of his best strong Holds having been demolish'd, and he himself taken Prisoner \A. 1567\. *Ma-*<300>*ximilian* died in the year 1576. Him succeded his Son *Rudolph* II. who Reign'd Rudolph II. also very peaceably in *Germany,* except that the *Hungarian* Wars did now and then keep the *Germans* a little in exercise; and that in the year 1609, the right of Succession in the Country of *Juliers* was brought in question. At last his Brother *Mathias,* Arch-Duke of *Austria* grew impatient to possess his Brothers Inheritance before his death, to him *Rudolphus* surrender'd *Hungary* and *Bohemia,* and at his death \A. 1612\ he left him his other Countries and the Imperial Crown.

§14. Under the Reign of *Matthias,* the ill Humours did so encrease by Matthias. degrees in *Germany,* that towards his latter days they caused violent Convulsions.[15] The origin of this war, which lasted thirty years, was this: In the Religious Peace formerly concluded at *Passau,* two Parties Origin of the were only included, *viz.* the *Roman Catholicks,* and those who adher'd German Wars. to the *Augsburgh* Confession [that is, Lutherans], the free exercise of Religion being forbidden to all others. But some of the States [estates] of the Empire, among whom the chiefest were the Elector *Palatin* and the Landgrave of *Hesse Cassel,* having since that time receiv'd the Reform'd Religion, commonly call'd the *Calvinian,* the *Roman Catholicks* were against their enjoying the benefit of the Religious Peace. These on the

15. The "ill humours" (*bösen Feuchtigkeiten*) gave rise to the "violent convulsions" (*schrecklich Fieber*) of the Thirty Years' War. Pufendorf often used sickness metaphors for social and political conditions. See *The Present State of Germany,* VII: "Of the Strength and Diseases of the German Empire."

other hand alledged, that they did belong, as well as the rest, to the *Augsburgh* Confession, and that the whole difference did only consist in some few passages: But the rest of the Protestants who strictly adher'd to the Words of the *Augsburgh* Confession, were not for receiving them into the same Communion, yet it was their opinion, that they ought not to be prosecuted for the differences that were betwixt them.

But afterwards these controverted Articles were by the heat of the Priests[16] explain'd in so different a manner, that the name of a *Calvinist* became as odious to some Protestants, as that of a *Roman Catholick*. The *Roman Catholicks* taking hold of this opportunity, caressed the old Protestants, especially those in the Electorate of *Saxony,* unto whom they represented the *Calvinists* as ||[a Generation equally destructive]||[17] to both Parties; whereby they hop'd to disjoyn them from the rest, and after they had destroy'd them, to make the easier work with <301> the rest of the Protestants. These therefore of the Reformed Religion, entered into a Confederacy for their common security; into which there having been receiv'd a great many other Protestant Princes, it was call'd

The Evangelical Union. the *Evangelical Union.* In opposition to this Confederacy, the *Roman Catholicks* made an Alliance among themselves, which they call'd the *Catholick League,* whose Head was the Duke of *Bavaria,* constant Rival of the Elector *Palatin.* There happened also some other matters which had exasperated both Parties, *viz.* that the Protestants had ||[reduced a great many Church Revenues]||,[18] after the Peace at *Passau;* that the Cities of *Aix la Chapelle,* and *Donawerth,* had been very hardly dealt withal, and some other matters, which were manifest proofs of the Animosities of both Parties against one another.

The Bohemian Tumults. §15. Both Parties being thus exasperated and prepared for War, did administer fuel to that flame which quickly after broke out in the Kingdom of *Bohemia.* The *Bohemians* pretended, that the Emperour *Matthias* had taken from them their Privileges, and having raised a Tumult,

16. VI.13, at note 26, p. 292, above.
17. Rather: "equally inimical."
18. Rather: "acquired many church possessions [*geistliche Güter*]."

did throw three Persons of Quality, who spoke in the Emperours behalf, out of the Castle Windows \A. 1618\; and immediatly after entered with an Army into *Austria:* In the mean while *Matthias* dy'd, whose Nephew *Ferdinand* (who also succeeded him in the Empire) the *Bohemians* had before his death received for their King; but now, under pretence that he had broken the Contract [*conditiones*] made betwixt him and the Estates, had renounc'd *Ferdinand,* and offer'd the Crown to *Frederick* Elector *Palatin.* This young Prince[19] was perswaded by some of his Friends [*seine Leute*], who were of an unsettled Spirit, and not diving deep enough into a business of such Consequence, to accept of this offer, before he had laid a foundation for such an undertaking: For the *Bohemians* themselves were fickle and unfaithful, *Bethlem Gabor* Inconstant. *England* was not for medling in the matter; *Holland* was very backward in giving assistance. The Union which they chiefly rely'd upon, was a Body with a great many Heads, without vigour, or <302> any constant Resolution.[20] Besides this, *France* did endeavour to dissolve this League, as being not willing that the Elector *Palatin* and the rest of the Reform'd Religion, should grow too potent; for fear, that in time they might afford their assistance to the *Hugonots,* whose destruction 'was then in agitation at' [then preoccupied] the *French* Court.

 In the beginning of this War the Affairs of *Ferdinand* look'd with an ill Aspect; because *Bethlem Gabor,* Duke of *Transilvania,* fell into *Hungary,* in hopes to become Master of that Kingdom;[21] and there were also great discontents among his Subjects in *Austria:* but he having recovered himself by the Alliance made with the Duke of *Bavaria,* the Elector *Palatin* lost, with that unfortunate Battel fought on the white Hill [White Mountain] near *Prague* \A. 1620\, at once all his former advan-

Ferdinand I.

The Crown of Bohemia offer'd to the Elector Palatin.

The ill success of the Elector Palatin.

19. Frederick V (1596–1632) was only twenty-three when he accepted the crown of Bohemia in 1619.

20. On this constant theme in Pufendorf, see *On the Law of Nature and of Nations,* VII.4.11; *The Present State of Germany,* VII.9, in Pufendorf (2007), p. 205; and XII.6, note 11, p. 422, below. The Protestant Union headed by Frederick was a defensive military alliance founded by his father Frederick IV (1574–1610) in 1608.

21. Gabriel Bethlen (1580–1629), Calvinist prince of Transylvania, was brother-in-law to Gustavus Adolphus of Sweden. His troops arrived late at the decisive Battle of White Mountain.

tages: For *Ferdinand* soon after reduc'd *Bohemia, Moravia,* and *Silesia* to obedience {with little effort}. *Spinola* made an inroad into the *Lower Palatinat,* which was deserted by the Forces of the 'League' [Union]. The Duke of *Bavaria* got the *Upper Palatinat* and the Electoral Dignity. The Elector of *Saxony,* who had been very instrumental in reducing of *Silesia,* had for his reward *Lusatia,* in Fief of the Kingdom of *Bohemia.*

The War spread in Germany.

In+ the mean time the Marquess of *Durlach, Christian* Duke of *Brunswick,* the Earl of *Mansfield,* and some others who were of the Elector *Palatins* Party, march'd with their Armies up and down the Country, and the Emperour, under pretence of pursuing them, sent his Forces into all parts of the Empire. Against these the Circle of the *Lower Saxony* arm'd itself, having made *Christian* IV. King of *Denmark,* General of that Circle: But he having receiv'd a great overthrow near *Kings Lutter* \A. 1626\, from *Tilly* the Imperial General, the Emperour over-ran all the *Lower Saxony;* and having oblig'd King *Christian* to make Peace with him at *Lubeck* \A. 1629\, he began to get footing near the Coast of the *Baltick.*

The Proclamation concerning Church Lands.

§16. The Emperour by this success being arrived to such a pitch of Greatness, that he did not question but for the future to be absolute [*zu seinem Willen zu haben*] in *Germany;* <303> did publish a Proclamation \A. 1629\, enjoining the *Protestants* to restore to the *Catholicks* all such Church Lands or Revenues, as were taken from them since the Peace made at *Passau.*[22] Under this pretence he hop'd quickly to subdue the rest of the Protestant Princes, not questioning but that the Catholick Estates would easily be forc'd to submit themselves to his pleasure.

Gustavus Adolphus.

The+ Protestants, 'tis true, enter'd into a Defensive Alliance at *Leipsick,* but without any great prospect of success, if *Gustavus Adolphus,* King of *Sweedland* had not come to their assistance. This King was induc'd to enter *Germany,* partly because the preservation of his own State seem'd to depend on the Emperours not getting firm footing on the *Baltick,*

22. Ferdinand II's so-called Edict of Restitution (1629) attempted to enforce the "ecclesiastical reservation," which had been widely ignored since the Treaty of Passau (1552). The reservation had stipulated that henceforth no Catholic possessions could be lost through their holder's conversion to Protestantism.

partly because several of the *German* Princes had crav'd his assistance, partly also because the Emperour had assisted the *Poles* against him in *Prussia,* and he stood in a good corespondency with *France* and *Holland,* who were very jealous at the Greatness of the House of *Austria.* This King came with an Army into *Germany* \A. 1630\, and drove the Imperial Forces [*Völcker*] out of *Pomerania* and the neighbouring 'Countries' [provinces]. In the mean time the Imperial General *Tilly* had quite destroy'd the {wretched} City of *Magdeburgh,* and was upon his march against the Elector of *Saxony,* whom he did not question but to rout quickly: But King *Gustavus* having join'd his Forces with those of the Elector of *Saxony,* defeated *Tilly,* in that eminent Battel near *Leipsick;* where the Emperour at one stroke lost all his hopes which he had conceiv'd from the happy success of his Arms during the space of twelve years before. From thence he march'd on to the *Rhine,* where he made almost miraculous progresses; but because the Elector of *Saxony* had not so vigorously attack'd the Hereditary Countries of the Emperour, he had thereby leisure given him to raise another Army, under the Conduct of *Wallenstein;* against whom the King lay encamp'd for a considerable time near *Nurenbergh* \A. 1632\; and afterwards in the battel of *Lutzen,* tho his side gain'd the Victory, he lost his life. <304> Gustavus's Death.

After[+] his death his Generals and Confederates carry'd on the war, under the Conduct of *Axel Oxenstern,* Chancellour of *Sweden,* with indifferent good success [*glücklich genug*]; but having receiv'd an entire defeat in the battel near *Norlingen* \A. 1634\, which they fought without necessity, they lost 'all' [most of] their Conquests. The Elector of *Saxony* having also concluded a peace with the Emperour at *Prague* \A. 1635\, which was extremely disliked by the Protestant Party; the Emperour was now again in hopes to drive the *Swedes* by force out of *Germany:* But by the valour and conduct of their Generals the *Swedish* Affairs began to look with a better face, who carry'd the War again into the very Hereditary Countries of the Emperour. At last all parties began to incline to a peace; for the Emperour and the 'Princes' [estates] of *Germany* were tired out with the war; *France* began to be divided at home by Commotions; *Holland* had made a separate peace with *Spain;* and the *Swedes* feared that the *Germans,* of whom was compos'd the greatest The War continued.

part of their Army, might at last grow weary of being instrumental in the Ruin of their native Country [*Vaterland*], or that one unfortunate blow might chance to rob them of the Fruits of their former Victories; a Peace was therefore concluded \A. 1648\ at Osnabrugge with *Sweden,* and at *Munster* with *France;* by virtue of which the *Swedes* got |[a part of]|[23] *Pomerania, Bremen,* and *Wismar,* and five Millions of Crowns for the payment of their Forces. *France* kept *Brisac, Suntgaw,* |[a part of *Alsace* and *Philipsbourg.*]|[24] By this Peace the Authority [*Hoheit*] of the States [estates] of *Germany* and the Protestant Religion were Established at once; and the Emperours Power confin'd within such Bounds, that he could not easily hereafter attempt any thing against either of them; especially since both *Sweden* and *France* had a free passage left them, from whence they might easily oppose him, if he design'd to transgress these Limits. During this war \A. 1637\ dy'd *Ferdinand* II. whom succeeded his Son *Ferdinand* III. who died in the year 1657. In whose stead was, in the year next following, elected Emperour his Son *Leopold.* <305>

§17. After the *Westphalian* Peace *Germany* remained {more or less} in peace for a considerable time, except that \A. 1659\ the Emperour and Elector of *Brandenburgh* (at which time the *Swedes* were engag'd in a War with *Denmark*) fell into *Pomerania;* but these differences were compos'd by the peace made at *Oliva.*[25] In the year 1663. a war began with the *Turks;* when the *Turks* took *Newheusel;* but were also, especially near St. *Godhart,* soundly beaten. Some are of opinion, that if the Emperour had at that time vigorously pursued his Victory, he might have beaten them out of *Hungary;* since the *Turks* were put into a great consternation by the *Persians,* and some Rebellious *Bassa's,* and the *Venetians* did so vigorously push on the Siege of *Canea:*[26] But the

Peace of Osnabrugge and France.

Ferdinand the Third.

Leopold.

War with the Turks.

23. Rather: "upper" or western.
24. Rather: "the province [*Landvogtey*] of Alsace and the garrison in Philipsburg."
25. The Peace of Oliva (May 1660) ended the First Northern War of 1655–60.
26. Canea (Chania), in Crete, was taken by the Ottomans in 1645 after a two-month siege. Their campaign continued until the fall of Candia in 1669, which ended several centuries of Venetian control over the island. See note 61, p. 259, above, and the Editor's Introduction, p. xxx.

Emperour was so forward in making peace with them, because, as it is supposed, he was 'jealous' [suspicious] of *France*.

And in the year 1672. *Germany* was again entangled in a war with *France;* which was occasioned by the great progresses of the *French* against the *Hollanders,* who were reliev'd by the Emperour and the Elector of *Brandenburgh:* For tho in the year before the Emperour had made an Alliance with *France,* whereby he had promised, not to meddle in the War if *France* should attack one of the Triple Alliance;[27] nevertheless he sent his Forces towards the *Rhine,* under pretence that it belong'd to him as being Emperour, to take effectual care, that the flame which was burning in the neighbouring Countries, might not prove destructive to *Germany:* And the Elector of *Brandenburgh* made heavy complaints, that the *French* had made great havock in his Territories of *Cleves.* The *French* on the other side sent an Army towards *Germany,* in hopes to oblige the Emperour not to concern himself in this War; but the *French* having not only committed great outrages in the Empire, but also taken into possession the City of *Treves* [Trier], and made great havock in the *Palatinat,* the Emperor perswaded the States of the Empire to declare war against *France. Sweden* was also afterwards engag'd in the same war; which was ended by the peace made at *Nimwegen* \A. 1679\; whereby *France* got *Friburgh* in *Brisgau,* in lieu of *Philipsburgh;* and *Sweden* was resto-<306>red to those Provinces which it had lost during the war.

§18. If we duly consider <the Genius of> this Nation, which inhabits this great Empire, it is most evident, that this Nation ever since the memory of Men has been very brave, and addicted to War; and that *Germany* has been an inexhaustible Source of Souldiers, since there is scarce ever any want of Men, who are ready to serve for Money: and if they are once well Disciplined, they are not only good at the first onset, but are very fit to endure the hardships and inconveniences of a long war. There are not in any other Nation so many to be met withal, that are ready to list themselves in Foreign Service for Money; neither is

War with France.

Peace of Nimwegen.

The Genius of this Nation.

27. The Triple Alliance was a defensive pact (against France) formed in 1668 by the Dutch, the English, and the Swedes.

there any Country in Christendom where greater Forces both of Horse and Foot may be raised, than in *Germany.* But besides this, the *Germans* are much addicted and very fit for Commerce, and all sorts of Handycrafts Trade; and not only the inhabitants of the Cities do apply themselves with great industry to the same; but also if a Countryman [peasant] gets a little beforehand in the World [has some means], he puts his Son to some Handycraft's Trade or another, tho a great many of them afterwards run into the Wars. They are generally very free [frank] and honest, very ambitious to maintain the so much praised Fidelity [*Glauben*] of the ancient *Germans;* they are not easily stirr'd up to raise Tumults, but commonly are willing to remain under the same Government ||[where they are Educated.]||[28]

Nature of §19. Tho the *German* Empire has no Possessions abroad, except you
the Soil. would account *Hungary* to be such; which is under subjection to the House of *Austria;* nevertheless it is a Country of a vast extent by it self, which is full of great and small Cities, Towns and Villages: The Ground is very Fertile in general, there being very few spots to be met withal of any large extent, which do not produce something or another for the sustenance of Mankind; so that there is every where great plenty of all sorts of Provisions. *Germany* also abounds in all sorts of Minerals,
Its especially in Mines <307> of Silver, Copper, Tin, Lead, Iron, Mercury,
Commodities. and other sorts. It has abundance of Springs that furnish waters for the boyling of Salt: and those several great Navigable Rivers where with it is adorn'd, make it very commodious to transport its Commodities from one place to another. The Commodities of *Germany* are these: viz. Iron, and all sorts of Instruments made of it, Lead, Mercury, Wine, Corn, Beer, Wooll, course Cloth, all sorts of Linnen and Woollen Manufactories, Horses, Sheep, &c. If therefore the *Germans* would apply themselves to imitate these Manufactories at home, which are now Imported [into Germany] by Foreigners, or else wou'd be contented with their own, and not make use of Foreign Manufactories, those Commodi-

28. Rather: "to which they have been accustomed." Cf. IV.36, at note 72, p. 187, above.

ties which are Exported out of *Germany*, wou'd much surpass these which are Imported; and therefore it would of necessity grow very Rich, especially since a considerable quantity of Silver is digged out of the Mines there.

§20. As for the 'Form' [mode, *Art*] of Government in *Germany*, it is to be considered, that it is not like some Kingdoms, where the Kings have the whole Power in their hands, and according to whose commands the Subjects are obliged to comport themselves; neither is the 'Sovereign' [regal] Power here circumscribed within certain bounds, as it is in some Kingdoms of *Europe*, where the Kings cannot exercise {certain acts of} an 'absolute' [supreme, *höchsten*] Sovereignty without the consent of the Estates: But *Germany* has its particular Form of Government, the like is not to be met withal in any Kingdom of *Europe*, except that the antient Form of Government in *France* came pretty near it. *Germany* acknowledges but one <Supreme> Head, under the Title of the *Roman Emperour*; which Title did at first imply no more than the Sovereignty over the City of *Rome*, and the Protection of the Church of *Rome* and her Patrimony. This Dignity was 'first' [permanently] annexed to the *German* Empire by *Otto* I. but it is long ago since the Popes have 'robb'd' [deprived] the Kings of *Germany* of {the reality of} this Power, and only have left them the bare Name.

> Form of Government.

But besides this, the {so-called} Estates of *Germany*, some of which have great and potent Countries [*Landschafften*] in their possession; have a considerable share of the Sovereignty over their {land and} <308> Subjects; and tho they are Vassals of the Emperour and Empire, nevertheless they ought not to be consider'd as Subjects {in a literal sense}, or <only> as |[potent or rich Citizens in a Government]|[29]; for they are actually possess'd of the supreme Jurisdiction [*Lands-Obrigkeit*] |[in Criminal Affairs]|[30]; they have power to make Laws and to regulate Church Affairs (which however is only to be understood of the Protes-

29. Rather: "noble [*vornehme*] citizens in a republic"; that is, it is not an aristocracy. See note 1, p. 115, above.
30. Rather: "as they call it, over their subjects' life and limbs."

tants), to dispose of the Revenues arising out of their own Territories; to make Alliances, as well among themselves as with Foreign States, provided the same are not intended against the Emperour and Empire; they may build and maintain Fortresses and Armies of their own, Coin Mony, and the like. This grandeur [*Hoheit*] of the Estates, 'tis true, is a main obstacle that the Emperour cannot make himself absolute [*en souverain*] in the Empire, except it be in his Hereditary Countries; yet this has been always observ'd, the more potent {and esteemed} the Emperour is, the more <he has exercised his Authority, and> the Estates have been forced to comply with his commands: and it is {also} certain, that the grandure of the Estates, except what is {explicitly} contained in the *Golden Bull* concerning the Electoral Dignity,[31] was more founded upon antient Customs and Precedents, than any 'real' [explicit] Constitutions; till in the *Westphalian* Peace their Rights and Authority have been expresly and particularly confirm'd and establish'd.

Strength and weakness of this Empire. §21. Tho it is certain that *Germany* within itself is so Potent, that it might be formidable to all its Neighbours, if its strength was well united and rightly employ'd; nevertheless this strong Body has also its {considerable} infirmities, which weaken its strength, and slacken its vigour: its irregular 'Constitution' [form] of Government is one of the chief causes of its Distemper; it being neither one entire Kingdom, neither properly a Confederacy [*Systema*], but participating of both kinds: For the Emperour has not the 'entire' [perfect] Sovereignty over the whole Empire, nor each Estate in particular over 'his' [its own] Territories; and the former is more than a bare Administrator [*Director*], yet the latter have a greater share in the Sovereignty than can be attributed to any {mere noble} Subjects or Citizens <whatever, tho never so great>. And this seems to be the reason why at last the Emperours did quit their

31. The Golden Bull, issued by Charles IV at the diet of Nuremberg in 1356, designated seven Electors (*Kurfürsten*) to choose a King of the Romans, who would later be crowned Holy Roman Emperor. It also established other features of the electoral process that continued to be observed over the coming centuries. See note 23, p. 60, above.

<309> pretensions upon *Italy*, and the Kingdom of *Arelat*;[32] because these potent Princes of *Germany*, and the turbulent Bishops, who were continually stirr'd up by the Popes, used to give them so much work, that they had enough to do to take care of *Germany* as the main Stake, without being able to concern themselves much about other {remote} parts. Yet do I not find any instances in History, that any of the antient Emperours did endeavour to subdue the Princes, and to make himself absolute Master of *Germany*.

Why the Emperour quitted the Kingdom of Arelat.

But this ambitious {and for Germany so harmful} Design *Charles* V. as it seems, was first put upon by the *Spaniards*, or, as some will have it, by *Nicolas Perenot Granvel*.[33] And truly the Electors had the same reasons not to have admitted him to the Imperial Dignity, as they had not to admit *Francis* I. King of *France:* And common Reason tells us, that no Nation [*Volck*] that has the Power of Electing [*freye Wahl*] a Prince, ought to choose such a one as is possess'd before of a considerable Hereditary Estate, that he may think it his Interest to take more care of that than the Elective Kingdom: For he either will certainly be very careless of the Interest of the Elective Kingdom, or else he will make the Interest of the Elective Kingdom subservient to that of his Hereditary Countries, and make use of the Strength of the first to maintain the latter, and render it more Powerful; or else he will endeavour, by making himself Sovereign over the Elective Kingdom, to make it dependent on his Hereditary Estate.

What is the Interest of the Electors.

Germany found all these three inconveniencies by experience, under the Reign of this Emperour; for he came very seldom into *Germany*, and that only *en passant:* He never made the true Interest of *Germany* the Rule of his Designs, but all was carried on for the grandeur and increase of his House; and at last, under pretence of Religion, he attempted to suppress entirely the antient Liberty of the Estates. On the contrary, if

The Conduct of Charles.

32. The kingdom of Arelat (Arles) was created in 933 by the joining of upper and lower Burgundy. It was ruled by independent kings until 1032 and absorbed into France in 1378.

33. Nicolas Perrenot de Granvelle (1486–1550) became advisor to Charles V in 1530.

Germany had an Emperour at that time who had not been possess'd of any Countries, or at least an inconsiderable part without the Empire, the true Interest of the Empire would have been his Rule; and it would have been his business not to side with either of these two Potent and couragious Nations of the *French* and *Spa-*<310>*niards,* but to have look'd upon them like an Arbitrator [*arbiter*], and whilst they had been fighting together to have, according to the circumstances of Affairs, sometimes ballanc'd one, sometimes another, so that one might not become Master of the other; and thereby gain such advantages, as might prove prejudicial to *Germany:* For it is a far different case, whether I come in betwixt two Parties as a Mediator [*Drittmann*], or whether I am 'engaged' [bound] to one certain Party: For in the first Case, I can engage my self as deep as I think fit, and at least take care to come off harmless; but in the latter case I must needs be a loser, let things go how they will, and at last another shall reap the Fruits of my Labour.

Of the Guaranties of the Circle of Burgundy.　And⁺ to give a specious Colour to these Consequences, so prejudicial to *Germany, Charles* V. did gain this Point, at the Dyet of *Augsburgh* \A. 1548\, upon the Estates, at that time, when having brought the Protestants very low, no body durst oppose it, that they should take upon them the Guarantie of the Circle of *Burgundy;* whereby *Germany* was obliged to be always engaged in the Wars betwixt *Spain* and *France,* and with its Treasure and Men to assist the *Spaniards* in the defence of the *Netherlands.* I must confess, that it is not the Interest of *Germany,* to see these Countries fall altogether into the hands of *France;* nevertheless it is not absolutely necessary that the Estates in *Germany* should Ruin themselves for their sake; since there are others also, who are better able, and have the same Interest that *Germany* has, to preserve these Provinces.

The attempt which *Charles* V. made against the Protestant Religion in *Germany,* was a true *Spanish* Design: For not to mention here the notorious Falsities in the *Roman Catholick* Religion, I cannot for my life see, what could move the Emperour, if his aim had been for the sole Interest of the Empire, to act contrary to the general Inclination of the Nation, and not rather to take hold of this so favourable opportunity, to free himself from the Tyranny of the Popes, who for several

Ages together had trampled upon the *German* Empire; and with the superfluous Church-Lands, to encrease his own, and the Revenues of the Empire, or at least to give liberty to the Bishops to Marry without quitting their Church <311> Benefices.[34] If the Emperour would have given a helping hand, the Reformation would have been as easily setled in *Germany*, as it was in *Sweden, England* and *Denmark.*

After⁺ these *Spanish* <States> Maxims had lain a while dormant {after the time of Charles V.}, they were at last revived, and that with {almost} more vigour, under the Reign of *Ferdinand* II, besides a great deal of misery which did from thence accrue to *Germany:* this was the cause that the Estates of *Germany*, to preserve their Liberty, were obliged to seek for Foreign Aid, by which means they {admittedly} maintain'd their Liberty; but it had been questionless more advantageous to *Germany*, not to have wanted the assistance of Foreigners, who were not forgetful to make their own advantage by it. Now if it may be supposed, that there are some remnants of the *Spanish* Leaven, it may easily be conjectur'd, what jealousie and distrusts must be betwixt the Members of the Empire, and how contrary and different their Counsels and Actions must needs be: and tho perhaps by setling a good understanding betwixt the Supreme Head and Estates, a medium might be found out to obviate this and some other 'inconveniencies' [illnesses, *Unheil*], yet there reign various and great 'Distempers' [weaknesses] amongst the Estates themselves, which seem to render the best Remedies and |[Counsels]|[35] either 'ineffectual' [impossible], or at least very difficult:

    Among these must be counted the Religious Differences betwixt the Catholicks and the Protestants in general; which Differences do not only depend on the several Opinions in Matters of Faith, but also on a Worldly Interest; the Catholicks endeavouring upon all occasions to recover such Possessions as were taken from them since the Reformation; and the Protestants being resolved to maintain themselves in the Possession of them. Wherefore it has been observ'd, that sometimes the *Roman* Catholicks have been more guided by |[their particular Inter-

Marginal note: Ferdinand pursues the Spanish Maxims.

---

34. A reference to the "ecclesiastical reservation"; see note 22, p. 344, above.
35. Rather: "those useful for the common good."

est, and by their Clergy, than by that of the Publick.]|[36] Nay, it is to be fear'd, that if *Germany* should be vigorously attack'd by a potent Foreign Enemy, that some of the Popish Bigots [*Pfäffisch gesinnte*] would not be so 'backward in' [opposed to] submitting themselves under the yoke, and be willing to lose one Eye, provided the Protestants might lose both. <312>

The difference between the Protestants. Beside,[+] the Protestants are again sub-divided into two Parties; there being among them some differences concerning several Articles of Faith; which, by the heat of the Clergy, were widen'd to that degree, that both Parties were brought to the very brink of Ruin.[37] The great number of Estates |[augments the Distemper]|,[38] it being next to an impossibility, that among so many, there should not be some, who either prompted by their passions, obstinacy, or for want of Understanding, may not deviate from the[ir] true Interest, or be misled by |[ill Counsellours to act against the same]|[39]; so that it would be a miracle to see so many Heads <not> well united. The Estates are also very unequal in Power; from whence it often happens, that some of the most Potent are for being {almost} like Sovereigns, and therefore being inclin'd rather to act according to their particular Interest [*ihre eigene raison d'Etat*] and Grandeur than for the 'Publick' [common freedom], they make little account how they Ruin |[the less powerful.]|[40] These therefore, when they see that the Laws cannot protect them, are at last oblig'd to take more care of their own preservation, than of the 'Publick Liberty' [common good], as thinking it indifferent by whom they are oppress'd. Not to mention here, the jealousie which is betwixt the three Colleges of the

---

36. Rather: "the interests and passions of the clergy, than by the common [*gemeine*] freedom." Pufendorf often distinguishes the divisive interests of the clergy from those of the faithful and the political community. See note 26, p. 292, above, and XII.14, pp. 438–40, below.

37. On religious conflict among Protestants see *The Present State of Germany*, VIII.7, in Pufendorf (2007), pp. 228–29. Pufendorf wrote his late work on religion, *The Divine Feudal Law* (*Jus Feciale Divinum*, 1695), to bridge the doctrinal differences between Lutherans and Calvinists.

38. Rather: "also contributes to their weakness."

39. Rather: "others to engage in damaging ventures [*schlimmen Anschlägen*]."

40. Rather: "their smaller fellow-estates [*Mit-Stände*]."

Empire,[41] and the 'several pretensions and differences' [strange quarrels] which are among 'some' [most] of the Estates: I could wish that I could find out as easie a {practical} remedy against these and some other the like Diseases, as I have enumerated them, and demonstrated their pernicious Consequences.

§22. As to the Neighbours of *Germany,* the *Turks* border upon *Stiria,* *Croatia,* and *Hungary:* The two last do not properly belong to *Germany,* but yet belong to the House of *Austria,* and are like a Bulwork to it; so that *Germany* is much concern'd in the preservation of them. The *Turkish* Emperour has greater Revenues out of his vast Territories, and perhaps is able to raise a greater number of Men than the *Germans* can do; nevertheless he is not so formidable to them: for the *Hungarian* Wars are very troublesome to the *Turks;* because the *Asiatick* Forces, and other supplies of Provision and Ammunition, are not without <313> great difficulty carried so far; neither can these Forces be put into Winter Quarters there, as being not used to so cold a Climate, the neighbouring depopulated Provinces being also not able to maintain them. The *Turks* also are in continual fear, that, as soon as they have bent their whole Force against *Hungary,* the *Persians* may fall upon them on the other side, or some of the Bassa's towards the East Revolt from them. And a well Disciplin'd Army of *Germans,* will scarce shrink before all the *Turkish* Forces; and when *Germany* is resolv'd to stand the brunt, the *Turks* will, I believe, quickly be weary of attacking it.

Italy is in no ways to be compared with *Germany* either for its strength or number of Men, besides that it is divided into several States, by which it is disabled to attack any Foreign State, much less so Potent an Empire, which being possess'd of some Passes leading into *Italy,* might in time take an opportunity to renew its pretensions upon that Country.

The[+] *Switzers* are very good Neighbours to *Germany,* as having neither will nor power to attack it, especially since they are destitute of

The Neighbours of Germany.

The Turks.

Italy.

The Swisse.

---

41. A reference to the three chambers at an imperial diet: the electors, the secular and ecclesiastical princes, and the imperial cities. On the makeup and procedures of the diet, see *The Present State of Germany,* V.24–26, in Pufendorf (2007), pp. 150–54.

Poland. good Horsemen: Neither can *Poland* compare its strength with *Germany;* for tho the *Poles* can bring a great number of Horse into the Field, yet they are not to be compared with the *German* Horse, much less their Foot, to the *German* Infantry: wherefore the *Poles* cannot undertake any considerable {sieges of cities;} and if the *Poles* should enter into an Alliance with another <Prince>, and make a diversion to the *Germans,* by falling upon the back of them, it would not be difficult for the *Germans* to be even with them; since they are not well provided with Frontier Places, or any strong Holds within the Country which are able to withstand an Enemy; whereas in *Germany* they would meet with Places which would give them sufficient work: And in such a case perhaps the *Muscovites* might easily be prevailed withal to fall upon the back of them: but it is not to be supposed, that such a Commonwealth as this [*sothane Republicquen*] will easily attempt an offensive War <against its Neighbours>; yet it is of great consequence to *Germany,* that *Poland* may not be brought under subjection to the *Turks,* or any other Power. And these two Nations are able to do one another considerable <314> Services, if they would with their Joint-Forces attack the *Turks.*

Denmark. *Denmark*[+] has no pretensions upon *Germany,* and the best Land-Forces of the *Danes* being Listed [recruited] in *Germany,* their Army may be Ruin'd, only [merely] by the Emperours recalling the *Germans* out of that Service, if they should attempt any thing against the Empire. Neither do I believe that *Germany,* but especially the Circles of the *Higher* and *Lower Saxony,* will be so careless of their own Interest, as to let *Denmark* become master of *Hamborough* and *Lubeck.*

England. *England*[+] cannot do any harm to *Germany,* except by disturbing the {maritime} Trade of *Hamburgh;* tho it seems to be the Interest of the *English,* rather to enjoy the benefit of their Free Trade there. On the other hand, the *Germans* may do a service to the *English* against the *Hollanders,* by Land, whilst these are engag'd with them in a War at Sea.

Holland. *Holland*[+] has neither power nor inclination to attack *Germany:* For if the *Germans* should be recall'd out of the Service of the *Dutch,* their Land-Forces would make but a very indifferent show: Neither can they reap any benefit by making new {land} Conquests; but it seems rather to be for their purpose to keep fair with the *Germans,* that in case of a War with their Neighbours, they may make use of their assistance.

Spain⁺ cannot pretend to do any considerable mischief to *Germany,*   Spain. if the Head and Members [of Germany] are well united; but if it should joyn with the Head against the Members it may prove mischievous, especially by the assistance of <their> Money {and provocations [*Anschlägen*]}: but in such a case there would questionless not be wanting some that would oppose its designs.

Swedeland⁺ alone is not so powerful as to be in any ways formi-   Sweden. dable to *Germany* {as a whole}; neither is this Kingdom for making any more Conquests on that side, since |[thereby it would lose more of its own strength, than it can gain by them]|[42]: but on the other hand, it is of great Consequence to *Sweden,* that the state of Religion and of the Government, remain in the same condition as it was setled in the *Westphalian* Peace; and that *Germany* {not} be subjected or ruled by any absolute Power [*keinen souveränen Herrn bekomme*]. <315>

France⁺ has of late made itself so Powerful, that this Kingdom alone   France. may do more mischief to the *Germans,* than any of the rest of their Neighbours. *France,* in consideration of its {well-composed} Form of Government, has a considerable advantage over *Germany;* for the King there has all the best Men, and the Purses of his Subjects at command, and employs them as he thinks fit: But however such is the strength of *Germany,* that if well united, it need not much dread *France;* for *Germany* is capable of raising as numerous, if not more numerous Armies, than *France,* and may as 'easily' [long] recruit them: Besides this, the *German* Souldiers (every thing duly consider'd) will scarce 'turn their backs' [be inferior] to the *French.* There might also be a way found out, for *Germany* to keep always a sufficient Army on foot against *France;* at least it is not easily to be suppos'd, that if *France* should attack *Ger-*

---

42. Rather: "additional provinces would burden rather than fortify it, and fragment its inner strength." The reference is to the Continental possessions of Sweden, particularly upper or western Pomerania, which had been ceded to it by the Westphalian settlement.

many in good earnest, all the rest of *Europe* would be lookers on: but if *Germany* be divided within itself, so that either one Party should join with *France,* whilst some others stand Neuters, till *France* has devour'd some of the Neighbouring States, then nothing but fatal Consequences can attend it.[43] <316>

43. This concern about German disunity, especially vis-à-vis an aggressive France, still preoccupied Pufendorf as he prepared the second (posthumous) edition of *The Present State of Germany* in the late 1680s and early 1690s. See there at VII.6, in Pufendorf (2007), p. 197.

Of Denmark.

§1. *Denmark* is one of the most antient Kingdoms in *Europe,* which was Established a great many years before the Birth of our Saviour, but for want of 'good' [accurate] Histories it cannot be precisely determin'd at what time it had its beginning, nor how long each of its antient Kings Reign'd, or what were their great Deeds. We will not therefore detain the Reader by inserting here their bare Names, but only to touch upon such matters as are with some certainty transmitted to Posterity. {.sidenote: Denmark a very antient Kingdom.}

Among the most antient Kings, *Frotho* III. is most famous, who, 'tis said, did Reign just before the Birth of Christ, and was a most Potent Monarch, who Rul'd over *Denmark, Sweden, Norway, England, Ireland,* and other Neighbouring States. The Borders of his Territories were on the East-side *Russia,* and on the West-side the *Rhine.* 'Tis also related, that he Conquer'd the *Vandals,* which lived then in these Countries that now are call'd *Pomerania* and *Mecklenburgh,* and that he was the first King that stiled himself King of the *Vandals.* {.sidenote: Frotho III.}

Gotrick 'tis said, did {greatly} assist *Wittekind,* the King of the *Saxons,* against *Charles* the Great.

Erick⁺ {who began to reign A. 846} is commonly reckon'd to have been the first Christian King of *Denmark* (tho some pretend, that his Brother *Harald,* who Reign'd before him, was the first). Under this Kings Reign the Christian Religion was propagated in *Denmark* by the help of *Ansgarius,* then Bishop of *Bremen;* which afterwards King *Gormo* II. endeavouring to root out again, was forc'd by the Emperour *Henry,* surnamed the *Bird Ketcher,* to grant the free Exercise of the Christian Religion throughout his Kingdom. His Son *Harald* was attack'd by {.sidenote: Erick I.}

the Em-<317>perour *Otto* I. from whom the Sea betwixt *Jutland* and *Holland* has got the Name of *Otten Sound;* because the Emperour there threw in his Lance to mark the utmost Limits of his Expedition. His

Suen Otto. Son *Suen Otto*[1] came to the Crown in the year 980. who being taken Prisoner by the *Jutins,* was redeem'd by the Women, who gave their Gold and Silver Ornaments for his Ransom: In recompence of which he granted them this Privilege, that whereas they used only to have a small Portion in Mony out of their Fathers Inheritance, they for the future should have an equal share with the Males. He also Conquer'd a part of *England,* and died in the year 1012.

Canut II. His[+] Son *Canut,* or *Cnut* II. [I.] surnamed the Great,[2] was King of *Denmark, Norway* and *England,* having Conquer'd the latter of these three by force of Arms, tho *England* did not remain long under the subjection of the *Danes;* for after his death, *Harald* and only *Hardiknut* Reign'd in *England;* after whose death the *Danes* were again chased out of *England.* Besides this, *Magnus,* Son of *S. Olaus* King of *Norway,* made himself Master of *Denmark;* which Kingdom however, after his death, *Sueno* II. obtain'd, but he was forc'd to fight for it against *Harald Hardrode,* then King of *Norway.* He died in the year 1074. Him succeeded his Sons *Harald* VII. (who Reign'd but two years) and *Canute* IV. This King did give great Power to the Bishops in *Denmark* and granted the Tenths of all the Revenues of the Country to the Clergy. At which the *Jutes* being exasperated, slew him at *Oden Sea* \A. 1087\; but the Clergy as an acknowledgement of his Favours bestowed upon them, placed him in the number of Saints, and his memory was afterwards celebrated with full Cups at their Feasts, by those who call'd themselves the *Knutgylden,*[3] from him. His Brother *Olaus* IV. succeeded him, who

---

1. Harald's son, Sweyn [Sven, Svend] I Forkbeard (ca. 960–1014), was named after Otto I at his baptism.

2. He was Canute II of Denmark and Canute I of England.

3. The term *Knutgylden* is unclear, though probably associated with the "cult of Canute" that arose after the canonization of Knud IV (the Holy) in 1101. Knud's (r. 1080–86) so-called martyrdom on July 10, 1086, at St. Alban's church in Odense, which he had built and staffed with Benedictine monks from England, was as much due to his vigorous assertion of royal prerogative as it was to his many temporal favors to the Catholic clergy in Denmark. The only canonized Danish king, he is still considered (by Catholics) as that nation's patron saint.

died in the year 1095. and after him Reigned his Brother *Erick* II. who took *Julin,* at that time a great City in *Pomerania.* He died in the Isle of *Cyprus* {A. 1105} in his Pilgrimage to *Jerusalem.* <318>

§2. After his death the whole Kingdom was in great Confusion, especially when three at once fought for the Crown, *viz. Sueno* III, *Canute* VI, and *Waldemar* I. These, after they had waged wars together for many years, did at last agree to divide the Kingdom into three parts: but *Canute* having been assassinated by *Sueno,* and *Sueno* again having been slain in a Battel against *Waldemar,* he got the whole Kingdom into his {sole} possession \A. 1157\. He subdued the *Rugians* and *Vandals,* who had hitherto proved very mischievous to *Denmark;* he also destroyed the City of *Julin.* 'Tis related that he laid the first Foundation of the City of *Dantzwick* \A. 1164\ and under the Reign of this King *Absalom* Bishop of *Roshild* first began to build the City of *Copenhagen. Waldemar* died in the year 1182. Him succeeded his Son *Canute* VI. who waged great Wars against the *Vandals,* and at last forced their Princes to be his Vassals; taking upon himself the Title of King of the *Vandals* or *Slaves.* He took from *Adolf* Earl of *Holstein,* among other places, the City of *Hamburgh* {A. 1200}, which however twenty seven years after did {again} shake off the *Danish* Yoke. He having also conquered *Esthonia* and *Livonia,* the Christian Faith was established in these Countries by his means. He died in the Year 1202.

    After⁺ him reigned his Brother *Waldemar* II. who at the beginning was a very fortunate and potent Prince, and had under his Subjection, besides *Denmark,* the Countries of *Esthonia, Livonia, Curland, Prussia, Pomerania, Rugen, Mecklenburgh, Holstein, Stormar, Ditmarsen* and *Wagern,* as also the Cities of *Lubeck* and *Lauenburgh.* But he lost a great part of them again by the following occasion: *Henry* Earl of Swerin having undertaken a journey to the Holy Land, had committed, during his absence, his Lady and Country to the care of *Waldemar:* but having been informed, after his return, that the King had lived in Adultery with his Lady; he, to revenge this Affront, took him Prisoner by stratagem, and after he had kept him three years in prison dismist him, making him pay for his ransom the sum of 45.000 marks of fine Silver. The Countries of *Mecklenburgh* and *Pomerania,* and the

Marginal notes: Waldemar I.   Canute VI.

Cities of *Lubeck* and *Duntzwick* [Dantzig] <319> taking hold of this opportunity, revolted from *Waldemar; Adolf* Earl of *Shaumnburgh* took from him *Holstein* and *Stormar;* the Knights of the Cross took *Esthonia* and *Livonia.* And endeavouring to recover these 'Countries' [places] \A. 1227\, he was vanquished in a Battel fought near *Bornhove,* by the Earl of *Shaumburgh.* Yet he recovered *Reval* and *Esthonia;* and died in the year 1241.

Erick V. §3. His Son *Erick* V. succeeded him in the Kingdom, tho he had also given some parts of it to his other Sons; *viz.* to *Abel, Sleswick;* to *Canute, Bleckingen;* and to *Christopher, Laland* and *Falster.* These were each of them for being Sovereigns in these Countries; but *Erick* pretending that they ought to be his Vassals, there were great Commotions in *Denmark,*

Abel. till *Erick* was miserably murthered by his Brother *Abel* \A. 1250\; and *Abel* after he had reigned two years was slain by the *Friselanders* and *Dit-*

Christoph. I. *marsians* \A. 1252\. Whom succeeded his Brother *Christopher* I. Against this King the Archbishop of *Lunden* raised abundance of Troubles, and the King having imprisoned him, he was by the rest of the Bishops and Clergy excommunicated, and with him the whole Kingdom. And at last the King was by them poisoned \A. 1259\, as 'tis thought, with the Host.

Erick VI. After[+] him reigned his Son *Erick* VI. who was at Variance with the Bishops, and engaged in Wars against *Sweden* and *Norway;* at last he was taken Prisoner in a Battel by *Erick* Duke of *Holstein,* and was barbarously murthered by some of the great Men of the Kingdom \A. 1286\.

Erick VII. He left the Crown to his Son *Erick* VII, who immediately, in the first year of his Reign, had great contests with the King of *Norway,* who had given protection to the Murtherers of his Father. He also had some other Differences with some of the neighbouring States, and died in the year 1319.

Christoph. II. Him succeeded his Brother *Christopher* II, who got his Son crowned in his Life time. This King was banished [from] the Kingdom by his Subjects, who, under pretence of being oppressed with Taxes, elected in his stead *Waldemar* Duke of *Sleswick* their King. But they grew also quickly weary of him, and recalled *Christopher,* who afterwards in a

battel fought against this *Waldemar* lost his Son *Erick* \A. 1332\. Under
<320> the Reign of this King, *Schonen* [Scania] being sorely oppressed
by the *Holsteiners,* who were in Possession of it, surrendred itself to
Magnus King of *Sweden:* And *John* Duke of *Holstein,* perceiving that
he could not maintain it by force, sold all his Right and Title to it, for
70.000 Marks. fine silver. Under the Reign of this King, *Denmark* was
torn into so many pieces, that very few places were left to the King. He
died in the year 1333. After his death there was an Interregnum in *Denmark* during the space of seven years: In the mean time the *Holsteiners*
had brought the greatest part of *Denmark* under their Subjection; till
the *Danes* making an Insurrection against them, endeavour'd to chase
them out of *Denmark* and for this purpose call'd *Waldemar* the Son of
Christopher II (who had been Educated at the Court of the Emperour
Lewis the *Bavarian*) into the Kingdom.

§4. *Waldemar* III. did somwhat restore the decay'd State of the King-   Wald. III.
dom, having partly forc'd and partly bought the *Holsteiners* out of
Denmark: He sold *Hisponia* and *Reval*,[4] to the Knights of the Cross
{A. 1346}, for 28.000 Marks, fine silver; which sum he bestow'd most
upon a Journey which he undertook into the *Holy Land.* But he got
Schonen again from *Magnus Sameck* [*Schmeeck*][5] the then King of *Sweden* {A. 1360}, by fair promises; and by an agreement made betwixt him
and *Albert,* King of *Swedeland*[6] {A. 1366}, *Gotland* was also surrendred
to him, and some other places belonging at that time to *Sweden.* He
was frequently at Wars with the *Hanse* Towns, and died in the year 1375.

After[+] him Reign'd his Grandson *Olaus* VI. born of his Daughter *Mar-*   Olaus VI.
garet and *Hacquin,* King of *Norway.* During his Minority the Mother
had the supreme Administration of Affairs. Having after his Fathers
death {A. 1380} obtained the Crown of *Norway* {as well}, he laid also

---

4. "Hisponia" is a mistake for Estonia (Pufendorf has "Estland"). "Reval" (Revel)
was the Danish name for Tallinn (in Estonia, or Estland), named after its surround-
ing province of Rävala.
5. Magnus Eriksson (1316–74), also called Magnus Smek (Pet-Magnus).
6. Crull uses "Sweden" or "Swedeland" interchangeably (for Pufendorf's
"Schweden").

claim to the Kingdom of *Sweden,* because his Father was Son of *Magnus Sameck* [*Schmeeck*], King of *Sweden;* but he died young {A. 1387}.

In⁺ his stead the *Danes* and *Norwegians* received for their Queen *Margaret,* his Mother; and she having declar'd *Erick Pomeran,* her Sisters Daughters Son, her Associate in the Government, enter'd into a War against <321> *Albert* King of *Sweden.* But the *Swedes* being in general dissatisfied with their King, deserted him, acknowledging *Margaret* for their Queen. *Albert* fought a Battel against *Margaret,* but was defeated and taken Prisoner with his Son; whom *Margaret* did not release till after seven years Imprisonment, under condition that he should either pay 60.000 Marks, fine silver, for his Ransom, or else resign his Pretensions to the Kingdom of *Sweden;* and he having perform'd the last, *Margaret* caused *Eric Pomeran* to be Crowned King of *Sweden* \A. 1396\. In the year next following the Estates of all the three Northern Kingdoms assembled at *Calmar,* where *Erick* having been declared their King, an agreement was made among them, that these three Kingdoms for the future should be Rul'd by one King.⁷ *Margaret,* who had been an extraordinary good Queen to *Denmark,* died in the year 1412.

After whose death *Erick* was sole King over these three Kingdoms; but he was in continual broils with the *Holsteiners* (who were assisted by the *Hanse* Towns) concerning the Dutchy of *Sleswick;* which differ-
Eric Pomeran. ences were at last composed. He surrendred to his Cousins, the Dukes of *Pomerania,* \A. 1348\ the Island of *Rugen,* which had been a considerable time under *Danish* Subjection. In the mean time the *Swedes* were grown very discontented, because *Erick* did not Govern them according to his Coronation Oath, and oppress'd them by his Foreign Officers [*Bediente*]; which oblig'd them to stand up for the Defence of their Liberty. The *Danes* also, seeing that he was very careless of the Affairs of the Kingdom, and did always live in *Gotland,* did withdraw themselves from his Obedience, alledging, among other matters, that because he had been endeavouring to Establish his Cousin *Bogislaus* Duke of *Pomerania* in his Throne, in his life time, he had thereby violated their
Christopher. Right of a Free Election: And having chosen in his stead *Christopher*

7. The so-called Union of Kalmar (1397–1423). See note 10, p. 542, below.

Duke of *Bavaria, Erick*'s Sisters Son, he was Deposed \A. 1439\, and retired into *Pomerania*, where he ended his life {in complete obscurity}. *Christopher* Reigned till the year 1448. with whose Reign the *Danes* were very well satisfied. <322>

§5. After his Death the *Danes* made an offer of that Crown to *Adolf* Christian I. Duke of *Sleswick* and Earl of *Holstein;* But he being very antient and infirm refused to accept of it, and recommended to them *Christian* Earl of *Oldenburgh,* his Sisters Son, whom both the *Danes* and *Norwegians* declared their King; and in this Family these two Crowns have remained ever since, by a continual succession. This King, soon after, began a War with the *Swedes* (who had made one *Charles Cnutson* their King) because they would have driven the deposed King *Erick* out of *Gotland;* but King *Christian,* coming to his assistance, made himself Master of that Island. Besides this, some of the *Swedish* Nobility, who were dissatisfied with *Charles Cnutson,* having sided with *Christian,* the War began to be carried on very vigorously betwixt these two Nations. In this War the Archbishop of *Upsal* did attack *Charles* with such Success, that he obliged him to retire into *Prussia,* and *Christian* was crowned King of *Sweden* \A. 1458\. But the *Swedes* being again dissatisfied with *Christian,* recalled *Charles Cnutson* \A. 1463\ when the War began afresh: and notwithstanding *Charles Cnutson* died in the year 1470, and *Christian* came with a great Army into *Swedeland,* yet cou'd he not maintain himself in the Throne, his Forces having been defeated near *Stockholm.* In the year 1471[8] the Emperor *Frederick* III. gave to him in *Fief, Ditmarsen,* as also to the Country of *Holstein* the Title of a Dukedom. He married his Daughter *Margaret* to *James* III. King of *Scotland,* giving her for a Dowry the *Orkney Islands* and *Hetland,* which had hitherto been dependent on the Kingdom of *Norway.* He died in the year 1481.

In whose stead the *Danes* and *Norwegians* chose his Son *John*[9] their John. King, who divided the Dukedom of *Holstein* with his Brother *Frederick.*

8. In Pufendorf's text, this date is actually associated with Christian's defeat in the previous sentence.
9. Johannes (Hans) of Denmark (1455–1513).

This King *John* after he had reigned in peace for a considerable time, did at last enter into a War against *Sweden,* and having defeated the *Dalekarls,*[10] forced *Steenure* [Steen Sture][11] the Governour to surrender himself and the City of *Stockholm,* and was crowned King of *Sweden* \A. 1497\. But in the year 1501, he was miserably and shamefully beaten by the *Ditmarsians,* whom he would have brought under <323> his Subjection, and afterwards *Steen Sture* also drove him out of *Sweden.* He was in continual broils with him and his Successor *Suane Sture,*[12] who were assisted by the *Lubeckers,* till these Differences were at last composed; soon after which he died {A. 1513}.

Christian II. §6. Him succeeded his Son *Christian* II \A. 1513\, who drew upon him the Hatred of the *Danes,* partly because he entertained a Woman of mean birth [*Dirne*] in the *Netherlands,* whose name was *Duivecke,* to be his Mistress, and was strangely led by the Nose by her Mother *Sigibirta,* a crafty old Woman; partly because he had caused *Torber Oxe,* the Governour of the Castle of *Copenhagen,* to be, as 'tis thought, unjustly executed. In the mean time great Differences were arisen in *Sweden* betwixt *Steen Sture* the younger and *Gustave Trolle* the Archbishop of *Upsal,* the first having destroyed the Castle of *Steka,* which belonged to the latter. King *Christian* coming to the Assistance of the Archbishop took him along with him into *Denmark,* where they laid the Design against *Swedeland.* A Decree therefore was obtained from the Pope, wherein he having condemned the *Swedes* to undergo great Penalties for the violence offered to *Gustave Trolle.* King *Christian,* to put this Decree in execution, sent his Forces into *Sweden,* where *Steen Sture* being slain in an Engagement, the whole Kingdom was put into Confusion by his Death: And King *Christian,* coming at last in person, forced *Christina,* the Widow of *Steen Sture,* to surrender the City of *Stockholm.* At last

10. Inhabitants of Dalarna, a region in central Sweden. See note 13, p. 549, below.
11. Sten Sture the Elder (1440–1503).
12. The regent, Svante Nilsson (1460–1512), had no direct relation to Sten Sture the Elder. However, Svante's son, Sten Sture the Younger (1493–1520), adopted the Sture name for political reasons.

a general Amnesty having been published first, he was crowned King of *Sweden*. But when the *Swedes* thought themselves most secure, he caused some of the chief Men, under pretence of the former Violences committed upon *Gustavus Trolle,* to be executed by the Hangman, and committed besides great Cruelties \A. 1520\.[13] In the mean time, *Gustavus Erickson,*[14] who had been a Prisoner in *Denmark,* having made his Escape arrived in *Sweden;* and with the assistance of the *Dalekarls,* whom he had stirred up, entirely drove the *Danes* out of *Sweden,* which ever since has maintained its Liberty against the *Danes.*

By this time the Hatred of the *Danes* against *Christian* was mightily encreased; and <324> the *Jutes* having first of all withdrawn themselves from their Obedience to him {A. 1523}, it put him into such a Consternation, that he retreated with his Wife and Children into the *Nether-* *lands.* The *Danes* chose in his stead his Uncle *Frederick* Duke of *Holstein* for their King. *Christian,* having raised some Land-forces, did endeav- our to regain the Throne, but they were dispersed again. *Charles* V. also, his Brother in law,[15] was so intangled in the War with *France,* that he could not send him sufficient Succours. At last he came with a Fleet into *Norway,* where he surrendred himself[16] to *Cnut Gyldenstern,* who promised him security. But King *Frederick,* alleging that he was not obliged to keep that promise, made him a Prisoner \A. 1532\, and sent him to the Castle of *Sunderburgh.* But having resigned his Title to the Kingdom \A. 1546\, he was removed to the Castle of *Callenburgh,* where he died \A. 1559\.

§7. *Frederick* I. entred into an Alliance with *Gustavus* King of *Swe-* *den,* and the Hanse Towns, against the deposed King *Christian;* and forced the Cities of *Copenhagen* and *Malmoe,* which adhered to *Christian,* to surrender themselves to him. He also granted great Privileges to the Nobility, and died in the year 1533, the year after he had made

13. The so-called Stockholm Bloodbath, ca. November 7, 1520.
14. Gustavus Eriksson (1496–1560), whose father died in the Stockholm Bloodbath (1520), initiated the Vasa dynasty of Sweden as Gustav I (1523–60).
15. Christian's wife, Isabella of Austria, was a sister of Charles V of Spain.
16. His fleet had been wrecked offshore.

Christian III.   *Christian* II. his Prisoner. Him succeeded his Son *Christian* III. who
met with great Opposition at first from *Christopher* Earl of *Oldenburgh*
and the *Lubeckers,* who pretended to restore the imprisoned *Christian*
to the Throne, and had brought several Provinces over to their side; but
he at last surmounted these Difficulties, with the Assistance of *Gustavus*
King of *Sweden,* and made himself Master of *Copenhagen* \A. 1556\.
And because the Bishops had been all along against him, they were
excluded from the general Agreement; and having been deposed in the
same year, the Protestant Religion was at the same time established in
Denmark and *Norway.* He reigned very peaceably after that time, and
died in the year 1558.

Frederick II.   §8. His Son and Successor *Frederick* II. subdued the *Ditmarsians*
\A. 1560\: then he entred into a War against *Erick* King of *Sweden,*
which was carried on with great <325> losses on both sides for the space
of nine years: at last a Peace was concluded at *Stetin* \A. 1570\, by the
mediation of the Emperour, and the Kings of *France* and *Poland.* He
Reign'd afterwards very peaceably in *Denmark,* till the year 1588 when
he died.

Christian IV.   Under⁺ the Reign also of his Son *Christian* IV. the Kingdom was in
great Tranquility, till the year 1611, when he attack'd the *Swedish* King
Charles IX. and took from him *Calmar* and *Elfsburgh.* But \A. 1613\
he made Peace with *Gustavus Adolph,* the Son of *Charles;* by virtue of
which he restor'd these places unto him, in consideration of a good Sum
of Money. He was entangled in the Civil Wars of *Germany* \A. 1625\;
for he having been made General of the Circle of the *Lower Saxony,* he
thereby came to be engag'd in a War against the Emperour: But this
War proved very disadvantageous to him, he having receiv'd a great
overthrow near *King-Luttern,* and being oblig'd not only to quit *Germany,* but the Imperialists also enter'd *Holstein* and *Jutland* itself: Yet he
recover'd all again by virtue of a Peace made at *Lubeck* \A. 1629\, except
that he lost the advantage of some Ecclesiastical Possessions in *Germany,* which he intended for his Sons. When *Swedeland* was afterwards
engag'd in the *German* Wars, he offer'd his mediation betwixt them and
the Emperour; in hopes thereby to recover his losses of the Ecclesiastical

Possessions, and to prevent that the *Swedes* might not get a firm footing in *Germany.* In the mean while he was very vexatious to the *Swedes,* endeavouring by all ways and means to stop the career of their Victories in *Germany,* and to spoil their Trade at home; till at last the *Swedes* being sorely vex'd that their Ships were continually detain'd and confiscated in the Sound, did resolve to put an end to these inconveniencies; and after they had let the *Danes* know, that they would no longer suffer these Injuries, fell with an Army into *Holstein* and *Jutland* \A. 1643\, and at last also into *Schonen.* In this War the *Danes* were great losers both by Sea and Land, but by the extraordinary Valour of their King they maintain'd themselves, till by the mediation of *France,* a Peace was concluded at *Bromsebroo* \A. 1645\; by virtue of which the <326> *Swedes* got *Gothland, Osel,* and *Junperland* [*Jempteland*], and *Holland* [*Halland*][17] was given them as a Pledge for the space of thirty years. The *Hollanders* [*sic*] also taking hold of this opportunity, did regulate the Toll of the Sound, which hitherto having been raised at pleasure, had been very troublesome to them. He died in the year 1648.

§9. Him succeeded his Son *Frederick* III. who upon the perswasions of the *Hollanders,* attack'd the *Swedes* \A. 1657\, promising himself great success against them, at that time when he supposed that then King *Charles Gustavus* had quite weaken'd his strength against the *Poles;* but the *Swedish* King came upon a sudden with an Army into *Holstein* and *Jutland,* and among others, took the Fortress of *Fredericksudde* by storm; and there happening an extraordinary hard Frost at the beginning of the year 1658. he march'd over the Ice, first into *Funen,* where he surprised the *Danish* Troops; from thence taking his way over *Langeland, Laland* and *Falster,* into *Zealand.* This prodigious success obliged King *Frederick* to conclude a Peace with him at *Roshild,*[18] by virtue of which, besides some other advantages, he surrendered to the *Swedes, Halland, Bleckingen, Schonen, Bornholm, Babus,* and *Drontheim* in *Norway.*

Frederick III.
War with
Sweden.

17. Not the Dutch province, but a coastal province in southwestern Sweden situated just above Scania.
18. The Treaty of Roskilde (1658).

But⁺ King *Charles Gustavus* being inform'd, that by the perswasions of the Emperour, the Elector of *Brandenburgh,* and the *Hollanders,* the *Danes* had resolv'd to renew the War, as soon as the *Swedes* had left the Country, or should be again engaged in a War with *Germany* or *Poland,* he resolv'd to be beforehand with them, and returning into the Isle of *Zealand,* took *Cronenburgh,* and Besieg'd *Copenhagen* by Sea and Land. In the mean while the *Dutch* sent a Fleet to Relieve *Copenhagen,* against whom the *Swedes* fought with great bravery: But in the year next fol-
The Siege of Copenhagen. lowing \A. 1659\, the *Swedes* did in vain storm *Copenhagen,* and besides this, lost the Battel in *Funen: Bornholm* revolted, and *Druntheim* was retaken. And tho the *Danes* endeavour'd to carry on the War against the *Swedes,* hoping to have now after the death of their King *Charles Gustavus,* met with an opportunity to revenge themselves for their former losses; <327> yet acccording to a Project concluded upon by *France,*
A Peace concluded. *England* and *Holland,* a Peace was made near *Copenhagen,* almost upon the same Conditions with that concluded formerly at *Roshild,* except that *Bornholm* and *Druntheim* remained in the possession of the *Danes;* in lieu of which some Lands were assigned to the *Swedes* in *Schonen.*[19]
The King declared absolute and the Crown hereditary. A⁺ Peace being thus concluded, the King, at the Dyet held at *Copenhagen,* was declared an absolute Sovereign, and the Crown Hereditary; whereby the great Privileges of the Nobility were abolished, and a new Form of Government introduced, where the whole Management of Affairs depends absolutely on the King's pleasure.[20]
Christian V. This⁺ King died in the year 1670. Him succeeded his Son *Christian* V. who after he had put his Affairs into a good Posture, entred into an Alliance with the Emperor, *Holland* and their Confederates. And seeing that the *Swedes* had been worsted in the Country of *Brandenburgh,* he hoped to have met with a good opportunity to break with *Sweden.* He began therefore \A. 1675\ with the Duke of *Holstein:* who, not foresee-

19. This assignation of Scania (Schonen) to Sweden led in 1666 to the founding of the University of Lund (named Carolina after Charles Gustav), to which Pufendorf relocated from Heidelberg in 1668.
20. Danish royal absolutism and hereditary monarchy were formally established in 1661 in the Hereditary Monarchy Act, and more fully in the Royal Law (*Kongeloven*) of 1665.

ing the Design, came to him at *Rensburgh,* whom he forced to quit all his Advantages which he had obtained by the Peace of *Roshild,* and to surrender into his hands the Fortress of *Tonningen,* which he caused to be demolished, and afterwards took *Wismar* <from the *Swedes*>.

In⁺ the year next following he entred *Schonen,* where he took *Helsingburgh, Landscrone* and *Christianstad,* as also the Isle of *Gotland,* with little Resistance. But he having detach'd some Troops to invest *Halmstad,* they were surprized by the King of *Sweden,* who routed them and such as were not slain were all made Prisoners. Not long after, the whole *Danish* Army was beaten out of the field in a bloody Battel fought near *Lunden.* In the year 1677. King *Christian* besieged *Malmoe,* but having miscarried in a Storm which he made upon the place, he was forced to raise the Siege; and soon after received another Overthrow in a Battel fought near *Landscrone* betwixt him and *Charles* [XI] King of *Sweden.* In the Year next following the *Danes* were obliged to raise the Siege of *Babus,* and to surrender *Christianstadt,* <328> which [was] reduced to Extremity by Famine: but at Sea they had better Success; yet, by virtue of a Peace made betwixt them,²¹ they restored all such places as they had taken from the *Swedes.*

He maketh War upon Sweden.

A Peace.

§10. It is evident, out of {their} antient History, That this Nation has been formerly very warlike: but in our age [century] the *Danes* have lost much of their antient Glory, because the Nobility have been rather for enjoying their Revenues in Plenty and Quietness, than for undergoing the fatigues of War, and the Commonalty have followed their Example. This may also perhaps be alleged for a reason, that they having seldom been engaged in any Wars, but with *Sweden,* (except that *Christian* IV. made war in *Germany,* which however was carried on chiefly by *German* Souldiers) which could not be of any long Continuance, the *Danes* often wanted opportunity to keep themselves in exercise; especially since they had the conveniency of making use of the *Germans,* whom they [en]listed for money: and the number of Inhabitants seem'd to be but proportionable to the Country, which is of no great extent. Since the

The Genius of this Nation.

21. The Treaty of Nijmegen (1679).

King has been declared Soveraign, all means have been employed to improve the Military force of the Nation; but it seems that the National Forces, without the help of the *Germans,* will not be of any great Consequence, as to Land-service. Neither is it the King's interest to put his Nobility upon Martial Exploits, or that they should grow famous in War, for fear they should make an Effort to recover their former Privileges.

The Norwegians.

The⁺ *Norwegians* undergo all sorts of hardship with more Courage and Vigour, whereunto they are inured by their Climate and Air. But the *Danes,* since they have been Masters of *Norway,* have always endeavoured to keep under this Nation, by taking from them all opportunities of exerting their vigour, and there are very few left of the antient Nobility in *Norway.* Yet the *Norwegians* are now adays very good Seamen, and the *Dutch* make good use of them in Sea-service: and a great many of the Inhabitants of *North-holland,* where they are addicted to Fishing, were originally of *Norway.* <329>

Nature of the Soil.

§11. The country of *Denmark* is of no great extent, yet it is generally very Fertile, and fit both for Tillage and Pasturage; for a great number of Oxen and Horses are yearly Transported out of *Denmark* to other places. And a considerable quantity of Corn is sent out of *Denmark* into *Norway* and *Island* [Iceland]. The Seas near *Denmark* are pretty well stock'd with Fish, which however are rather for the benefit of the Inhabitants, than for exportation. There are little or no Manufactories there, the Inhabitants being not fitted for such works; neither is [are] there any Commodities fit for Exportation in great quantities. On the other hand, the *Danes* are oblig'd to Import Wine, Salt, good Beer, and Woollen Manufactury for Cloaths. They have begun to bring Spices themselves out of the *East-Indies,* where they have a small Fort upon the Coast of *Cormandel.*²² The Toll, which is paid by Foreigners in the Sound in ready money, is a very good Revenue in *Denmark.* Which is the reason why the *Danes* can scarce forgive the *Swedes,* that they do not pay this Tributary Toll to *Denmark.*

22. The southeastern coast of India, across from modern Sri Lanka.

Norway is for the most part a very raw Country, yet it produces several Commodities fit for exportation, *viz.* dry'd and salted Fish in great quantity, Timber, Board, Masts, Tar, Pitch, and the like. There are also in *Norway,* Silver, Copper, and Iron Mines. But it produces not Corn sufficient in quantity for the maintenance of its Inhabitants, nor to brew Beer; besides it wants also the same Commodities which are wanting in *Denmark.* As for its situation its [it is] very commodious, to Export and Import Merchandises to and from other Sea-Coasts in *Europe. Island* [Iceland] is stock'd with Fish, some salted Flesh, and very good Down Feathers, which the Inhabitants are fain to exchange for such Commodities as are, besides Fish and Flesh, requisite for the sustenence and convenience of Life. The *Fenock Islands* do for the most part live on their Sheep and Fish. Besides that, *Denmark* cannot raise   Its defects. a considerable Army of its Natives, this is also a great weakness to this Kingdom, that not only *Norway* and *Denmark* are separated by the Sea, and cannot keep correspondency together but by that way; but also that this Kingdom is divided into so many Islands; <330> so that if an Enemy once becomes Master at Sea, he must needs prove very troublesom to *Denmark.*

§12. As to the Neighbours of *Denmark,* it Borders on one side upon   Neighbours of *Germany;* for *Holstein,* which belongs to the present Royal Family, is a   Denmark. Fief of the Empire. And tho the Land Forces of *Denmark* do not come to any comparison with those of *Germany,* and *Jutland* lies quite open   Germany. on that side; yet the Islands are very secure from the *Germans,* who are not provided with Shipping, except it should happen that the great and lesser *Belt*[23] should both be frozen, which happens very rarely. Neither is there any great probability that these two States should differ, except [if] the pretensions upon *Hamborough,* which the King of *Denmark* will not easily let fall, should furnish an occasion for War. And to speak truly, it is so delicious a morsel, that it may easily provoke an Appetite. But it will be a very difficult task for the King of *Denmark* to attain his

23. The Great Belt separates the Danish islands of Funen and Zealand; the Little Belt lies between Jutland Peninsula and Funen.

aim by open force, except there should happen a 'very strange' [special] juncture of Affairs, or that the inward Divisions, or else by treachery, this City should give an occasion for its Ruin. In the mean while it is not easily to be supposed, that the Neighbouring *German* Princes should suffer that a City of so great Consequence should fall into the hands of a Foreign Prince. In fine, it is of vast Consequence to *Denmark,* to hold a good understanding with *Germany,* since from thence it must draw the greatest part of its Land-Forces, wherewith to defend itself against *Swedeland.*

Sweden.   With[+] the *Swedes Denmark* has been in continual Broils for a considerable time; and it seems that there is an old grudge and animosity betwixt these two Nations, arising chiefly hence, that the *Danes* have formerly always endeavour'd to make themselves Masters of *Sweden,* and to reduce this Kingdom into the same condition as they had done *Norway.* Besides, that afterwards they have made it their business, by ruining their Shipping and Trade, to prevent the growing Greatness of *Sweden:* But *Sweden* has always vigorously defended itself, and in latter times has gain'd great advantages upon *Denmark;* for the *Swedes* have not <331> only recover'd *Schonen,* and secured *West Gothland,* by the Fortress of *Babus;* but they have also a way open into *Jutland,* out of their Provinces in *Germany.* On the other hand, the *Danes* have made it their business hitherto, by making Alliances with the Enemies of *Sweden,* to get [back] from them these Advantages. But if we consider, that these two Kingdoms are now divided by their natural Bounds[,] to preserve which, *France, England* and *Holland* seem to be mutually concern'd; and that as in human probability *Denmark* cannot conquer or maintain itself in *Swedeland;* so the other States of *Europe,* are not likely to suffer, that *Sweden* should become Master of *Denmark:* It seems therefore most convenient, that these two Kingdoms should maintain a good understanding, and be a mutual security to one another against their Enemies.

Holland.   From[+] *Holland Denmark* may expect real assistance, in case it should be in danger of being Conquered; since the prosperity of *Holland* depends partly on the free Trade of the *Baltic;* and if one should become Master both of *Sweden* and *Denmark,* he would questionless keep

these Passages closer than they are now. But the *Danes* also are sensible
enough, that the *Hollanders* will not engage themselves any further in
their behalf, than to keep the ballance even, for fear they should with
an increase of Power, attempt hereafter, to raise the Toll in the *Sound* at
pleasure. But as long as *Holland* sides with *Denmark England* will not
be fond of the *Danish* Party, but rather declare for the other side; for the
preservation of *Denmark,* and the Trade in the *Baltic,* is not of so great
consequence to *England,* as it is to *Holland.* England.

The+ *Muscovites* may prove very serviceable to *Denmark* against *Swe-*
den: yet cannot the *Danes* make any great account upon an Alliance
with them; because it is very difficult to maintain a Correspondency
with them, especially if the *Poles* should declare for *Sweden:* Besides
that, the *Muscovites,* as soon as they have obtained their aim, commonly
have but little regard to Alliances, or the Interest of their Allies. *Den-*
mark can have no great reliance upon *Poland,* except that Crown should
be engag'd in a War against *Sweden. France* has <332> hitherto shewn
no great concern for *Denmark,* because it has always been in Alliance
with its Enemies; yet *France* would not willingly see it ruin'd, because
no State of *Europe* would desire the two Northern Kingdoms should be
under the Subjection of one Prince: But I cannot see any reason, why an
offensive Alliance with *Denmark,* should be profitable to *France. Spain*
is more likely to wish well to *Denmark,* than assist it, except it should
happen, that *Swedeland* was engaged in a War against the House of
Austria, or any other Allie of *Spain.* <333>

The
Muscovites.

Poland.
France.

Of Poland.

§1. The *Poles,* who anciently were called *Samartians,* and afterwards   Origins of
Slavonians, derived their Name from the Nature of the Country [*Land*]   the Kingd.
                                                                          of Poland.
which they possess; which lies most upon a Plain, for *Pole* signifies in
their language a *Plain;* tho some are of opinion that the Word *Polacki,*
is as much as to say, the Posterity of *Lechus.* This Nation [*Volck*] formerly did inhabit nearer to the Country of the *Tartars;* but after vast
Numbers out of *Germany* 'entred' [invaded] the *Roman* Provinces, their
places were supplied [taken] by the nations living behind them. And
it seems that *Poland* being in the same manner left by its Inhabitants,
which were then *Venedi* or *Wends,* they made room for the next that
took their Place. These [Poles] then, as 'tis said, having taken possession
of this Country about the year 550, did, under the Conduct of *Lechus,*   Lechus.
lay there the Foundation of a new State. *Lechus* resided at *Gniesen,* being encouraged thereunto by an Eagles Nest which he found there, and
taking it as a good *Omen,* put an Eagle into the Arms [*Wappen*] of the
new Commonwealth, giving to that City the name of *Gniesen,* which
in the *Polish* Language signifies a Nest. This Nation first setled it self in
that part of the Country, which now goes by the name of the great[er]
and lesser *Poland;*[1] neither did their Limits [borders] extend any further,
tho since that time they are mightily encreased.

---

1. Greater Poland designated the western and central areas, while lesser Poland
referred to the southeastern tip of the country.

Twelve §2. The first Governours [*Regenten*] of this Nation did not assume to
Vayvods or themselves the Title of Kings, but only that of Dukes; and the first
Governours. form of Government was very inconstant: for after the Race [*Stamm*] of
Lechus was extinguished (tho it is uncertain how many of them, and for
<334> how long a time they Ruled, or what were their Atchievments)
twelve Governours [*Obristen*], which in their Language are called *Vay-vods*, did administer the Government, who having at first regulated and
refined this barbarous People [*rohe Volck*] by good Laws <and Constitu-
tions>, at last were divided among themselves.

Cracus. Wherefore {around the Year 700} the *Poles* elected for their Prince
one *Cracus*, who having restored the Commonwealth to its former {or-derly} State, built the City of *Cracovia*, so called after his own Name,
Lechus II. which he made his place of residence. Whose youngest Son *Lechus* II.
to obtain the Principality, murthered his elder Brother; but as soon as
the Fact was discovered, he was banished [from] the Country. After him
Venda. \A. 750\ ruled a Virgin, whose Name was *Venda*, the only |[Daughter
left of the Children]|[2] of *Cracus*, who having vanquished one *Ritiger* a
German Prince that pretended [sought] Mariage to her[,] out of a blind
Superstition, drowned herself in the River of *Weixel*.

After her death the administration of the Government returned again
to the Governours or *Vayvods*, which continued for some time, till the
Poles elected <again> for their Prince a Goldsmith called *Premislus*, who
Lescus I. is also called *Lescus* I. because he had by a Stratagem defeated the *Mora-vians*, who had made an Irruption into *Poland*. But he leaving no Issue
behind him a Horse Race was instituted, with condition that the Victor
should succeed in the Government. One of the Competitours had laid
Iron Hooks in the Ground, by which means the others Horses having
been lamed he was the first that came to the Goal, but the Fraud being
discovered he was killed upon the spot. In the mean while a certain
poor Fellow on foot had run the Race and was the next 'to' [after] the
Impostor, whom the *Poles* declared their Prince \A. 776\. His name
Lescus II. was *Lescus* II. and as some say, was slain in the Wars against *Charles* the
Lescus III. Great \A. 804\. Him succeeded his Son *Lescus* III. who having appeased

2. Rather: "remaining child."

Charles the Great, with Presents, made Peace with him, either {it seems}
as an unequal Allie, or else |[by acknowledging himself his Vassal.]|[3] He
left *Poland* to his Son *Popiel,* whom he had begot in Wedlock; but to his   Popiel I.
natural Sons he gave the neighbouring Countries of *Pomerania, Marck,*
Cassubia, with some others. Him succeeded his Son *Popiel* II. an 'ill'   Popiel II.
[bad] man, who upon the perswasion of his Lady mur-<335>thered his
Father's Brothers, [and] 'tis reported that out of their dead Bodies came
forth Mice, which devoured *Popiel* with his Wife and Children.

§3. After his Death there was an *Interregnum* full of troubles, till \A. 820\   Piastus.
the *Poles* declared *Piastus,* a 'Country-fellow' [mean peasant] born at
Crusswitz, their Prince, from whom ever since such of the Natives as
obtained the Royal Dignity, were called *Piasti.* His Posterity has reigned
for a long time in *Poland,* from whom also descended the race of the
Dukes of *Lignitz* and *Brieg* in *Silesia,* which is but lately extinguished.
'Tis said that he was 120 Years old before he died. His Son *Ziemovitus*   Ziemovitus.
began his Reign in the Year 895. a Warlike and brave Prince; whom succeeded \A. 902\ his Son *Lescus* IV. a 'good' [calm] and peaceable Prince.   Lescus IV.
Much of the same temper was his Son *Ziemovistus* [*Ziemomislus*], who   Ziemovistus.
began to Reign in the Year 921.

This Prince had but one Son, who being blind was in the seventh
Year of his Age (in which Year, according to the Custom of those times,
his Head was to be shaved, and he to receive his Name) restored to his
Sight, which was then taken for an Omen, that he should be enlightened with the Christian Faith. His Name was *Micislaus* I. and began   Micislaus I.
his Reign in the Year 962. He having a great many Wives and no Children, occasioned in him a desire to turn Christian, for some *Germans*
representing to him, that if he left the Heathenish Superstitions he
would certainly beget Children; he was perswaded by them to remove
his Heathenish Wives, which he did, and married *Dambrateca* [*Dam-
brawcam*], the Daughter of *Bogislaus* Duke of *Bohemia.* Before he married her, he was baptized himself \A. 965\, and <first> introduced the
Christian Religion into *Poland,* as also that custom which has obtained

3. In German: ". . . daß er Carolo beständigen Respect zu erweisen sich verplichtet."

since there, that at the time when the Gospel is read in the Mass, the Men half draw their Cymetars to signify that they were ready to fight for the Christian Faith.

Boleslaus Chrobry, the first King of Poland. §4. Him succeeded \A. 999\ his Son *Boleslaus Chrobry,* who was by the Emperour *Otto* III. dignified with the Title of King, who also remitted unto him all the Pretensions [right, *Recht*] which the former Emperours had upon *Poland;* and this in consideration for the kind entertainment which <336> he had received from *Boleslaus* in his Pilgrimage to the Grave of *Albart* [*Adalbert*] Bishop of *Gniesen,* which being then very famous for some Miracles, was visited by the Emperour to fulfil his Vow which he had made during a precedent Sickness. This first King of *Poland* behaved himself very bravely in his Wars against the *Red Russians,* the *Bohemians, Saxons* and *Prussians.* He also instituted twelve Senators as his Assistants in the administration of the Government.[4]

Miccislaus II. But his Son *Miccislaus* [*Miecislaus*] lost for the most part his Father's Conquests, *Moravia* having among the rest been taken from him by the '*Bohemians*' [duke of Bohemia]. He began his Reign in the Year 1025. and died in the Year 1034. leaving but one Son behind him, whose **Casimir I.** Name was *Casimir,* who being an Infant, his Mother *Rixa* administred the Government for a while. But the *Poles* being dissatisfied with her, she fled with her Son into *Germany,* who in his Journey in *France,* 'assumed the Order and Habit of' [became] a Monk. During his absence, there were great Disturbances in *Poland, Maslaus* having about that time made himself Master of *Masuria,* which for a long time after, remained independent of the Kingdom of *Poland.* At last the *Poles* prevailed upon *Casimir,* to leave his Monastery and accept the Crown. And to perswade the Pope to absolve him from his Vow, they promised, that for each Head, except those of the Nobility and Clergy, they would contribute yearly a Farthing towards the maintaining of a perpetual burning Lamp in the Church of St. *Peter* in *Rome,* and cause their Heads to be shaved above their Ears like Monks. After he came to the Crown he beat {the aforementioned} *Maslaus* and the *Prussians,* and restored the Kingdom to its former tranquility.

4. In German: "als Gehülfen des Reichs."

His⁺ Son *Boleslaus* Surnamed the *Hardy*, {who assumed the crown
A. 1058,} did at first wage War against his Neighbours the *Prussians, Bo-*
hemians and *Russians* with great Success; but afterwards giving himself
over to all manner of Debauchery, and having been 'checked' [warned]
for that reason by *Stanislaus* the Bishop of *Cracau*, who also at last excommunicated him, he cut him to pieces before the Altar. Then he
was excommunicated by the Pope, and perceiving himself to be hated
by every body, left the Kingdom, and at last {supposedly} murthered
himself. <337>

Boleslaus the Hardy.

§5. Him succeeded \A. 1082\ his Brother *Vladislaus*, who standing in
fear of the Pope, would not at first take upon him the Title of King. He
met with great Troubles both at home and abroad, which however he
overcame at last. Him succeeded \A. 1103\ his Son *Boleslaus* III. a brave
Souldier, who obtained a signal Victory over the Emperour *Henry* V. in
a Battle fought in the *Dogsfield* near *Breslau*. There was never a Prince in
Poland more Famous for Military Atchievements than himself; it being
related of him, that he fought forty five Battles all with good Success,
except the last of all, fought against the *Red Russians*, which was lost by
the Cowardise of the *Vayvod* of *Cracovia*, unto whom the King for a
recompence sent a Hare-skin and Spinning-Wheel, which so troubled
him, that he hanged himself: But the King also was so troubled at this
Defeat, that he died of grief \A. 1139\, leaving four Sons behind him.

Vladislaus I.

Boleslaus III.

Among whom *Vladislaus* II. obtained a great part of the Kingdom
with the Name of a Prince, yet the other Brothers also shared several
great Provinces among themselves, according to their Father's last Will.
This occasioned great Divisions and Civil Wars betwixt these Brothers; and *Vladislaus*, who pretended to dispossess the rest, was himself
obliged to quit the Country. After him *Boleslaus Crispus* {or IV.} his
Brother was made Prince of *Poland* \A. 1146\, who was forced to wage
War against the Emperour *Conrade* III. and *Frederick* I. who would
have restored *Vladislaus*. At last a Peace was concluded betwixt them,
by Vertue of which, *Poland* remained to *Boleslaus*, but he was obliged to
surrender *Silesia*, which was then dependent on *Poland*, to *Vladislaus*,
which being afterwards {through his descendants} divided into a great
many Dukedoms, at last fell to the Crown of *Bohemia*. This *Boleslaus*

Vladislaus II.

Boleslaus IV.

also received a great overthrow from the *Prussians,* his Army having by the treachery of a 'Guide' [traitor] been misled into the Moors and Boggs.

Miccislaus III.   Him succeeded \A. 1174\ his Brother *Miccislaus* Senior, but he was
Casimir. deposed for Male-administration. Him succeeded his Brother *Casimir* \A. 1178\, who is 'only' [most] famous for that he chastised [drove out]
Lescus IV. the *Prussians.* He died in the year 1194. His Son *Lescus* {IV.} Surnamed the *White,* was fain [compelled] to contend with the banished *Miccislaus* for the Kingdom with various Success, <338> till *Miccislaus* died \A. 1213\. Whose Son *Vladislaus* also raised some Disturbances against him for a while, till at last he was forced to leave him in the quiet possession of *Poland.*

The first   Under the Reign of this *Lescus* the *Tartars* made the first In-road into
In-roads of *Russia,* and have ever since proved very troublesome and mischievous
the Tartars. to *Poland.* This *Lescus* was forced to wage War with *Sventopolek,* whom he had constituted Governour of *Pomerania.* He having made himself Duke of *Pomerania* did dismember it from the Kingdom of *Poland.* *Conrade,* also the Brother of *Lescus* had got the possession of *Masovia* and *Cusavia,* who being not strong enough to defend himself against the *Prussians,* who were fallen into his Country, he called in the Knights of the Cross,[5] who were then by the *Saracens* driven out of *Syria.* Unto these he surrendred the Country of *Culm* [Chelmno] under condition, that such places as by their help should be conquered in *Prussia,* should be divided betwixt them; which afterwards proved to be the occasion of great Wars betwixt them and *Poland.*

Boleslaus V.   To[+] *Lescus* succeeded \A. 1226\ his Son *Boleslaus,* Surnamed the *Chast*[e], under whose Reign the *Tartars* committed prodigious Barbarities in *Poland,* and from thence made an In-road into *Silesia,* where in a Battel fought near *Lignitz,* they slew so many of the Inhabitants, that they filled nine great Sacks with the Ears which they had cut off. His Reign was besides this full of intestine Troubles. Him succeeded \A. 1279\
Lescus VI. his Cousin *Lescus,* Surnamed the *Black,* who was very Fortunate in his

---

5. That is, the Teutonic Order, an order of German knights founded during the Crusades.

Wars with the *Russians* and *Lithuanians:* he also quite rooted out the *Jazygians,* which then inhabited *Podolia,* but the Civil Commotions and frequent Incursions of the *Tartars,* occasioned great Disturbances in the Kingdom. He died in the year 1289.

§6. After the Death of *Lescus,* there were {for a good while} great Con- tests in *Poland* concerning the Regency; till at last \A. 1295\ *Premislus,* Lord of Great *Poland* got the upper hand; who also reassumed the Title of King, which the Regents of *Poland* had not used during the space of 200 years; ever since that the Pope, after the banishment of *Boleslaus* the *Hardy,* had forbid them to choose a King of *Poland.* And <339> the succeeding Princes were not very ambitious of that Title, because the Country was divided among several Persons. But *Premislus* did think himself powerful enough[6] to make use of it. He was murthered by some *Brandenburgh* Emissaries, after he had reigned but seven Months.

    After him was elected *Vladislaus Locticus,* or *Cubitalis,* who did not stile himself King, but only Heir of *Poland.* But he having been deposed \A. 1300\ for Male-administration, *Wenceslaus* King of *Bohemia* was elected in his stead. But after his Death, which happened in the Year 1309. *Locticus* was restored, who waged great Wars against the Knights of the Cross, whom he at last vanquished in a great Battel. Under his Reign the Dukes of *Silesia* who were Vassals of *Poland,* submitted themselves to the Crown of *Bohemia.* He died in the Year 1333. Him succeeded his Son *Casimir* the *Great,* who having subdued all *Russia,* united it to the Kingdom of *Poland,* so that it should enjoy the same Laws and Liberties. He also first introduced the *Magdeburgh* Laws and Constitutions[7] into *Poland,* and the Duke of *Masuria* did then first submit himself as a Vassal to the Crown of *Poland.* He died in the Year 1370. leaving no Issue behind him; and by his Death the Male-Race of *Piastus* lost the Crown of *Poland.*

Premislus.

Vladisl. III.

Casimir III.

6. Literally: "thought that he had enough land [*vermeinte . . . gnug Land zu haben*]."
7. The so-called *Magdeburger Recht,* the law of the quasi-autonomous city of Magdeburg, became after 1284 a model for many other municipalities in eastern Europe. It addressed a wide range of affairs including commerce, marriage, inheri- tance, punishment, and judicial procedure.

Lewis. §7. After *Casimir* the Crown of *Poland* was devolved to *Lewis* King of *Hungary,* the Sister's Son of *Casimir:* The *Poles* were not well satisfied with him, because he favoured the *Hungarians* too much. He died in the Year 1382. *Sigismund* King of *Hungary* would fain have succeed[ed] him in *Poland,* but the *Poles* refused him. Some proposed *Zicmovitus* the Duke of *Masuria,* but *Hedwig* the Daughter of King *Lewis,* for whom the *Poles* would by all means reserve the Crown of *Poland,* would not accept of him for her Husband. At last the *Poles* Crowned Jagello, or the above-mentioned *Hedwig,* and married her to *Jagello* Duke of *Lith-* Vladisl. IV. *uania,* under Condition that he and his Subjects [*Volck*] should turn How Lithuania Christians, and *Lithuania* should be united to *Poland* in one body. was united The first Condition was performed immediately, for he was baptized, to Poland. and called *Vladislaus* IV. But the performance of the second Article was delayed by the Kings <of *Poland*> <340> for a considerable time after, under pretence that the *Lithuanians* were not well satisfied in this Point, but in effect, because they were unwilling to surrender their right of Succession to the Dukedom of *Lithuania;* till at last this Union was perfected under the Reign of King *Sigismundus Augustus.* This *Jagello* defeated the Knights of the Cross in a memorable Battel, where 50.000 Men having been slain, he took from them a great many Cities in *Prussia,* but they afterwards recovered themselves. He died in the Year 1434.

Vladisl. V.   Him succeeded his Son *Vladislaus* V. who also afterwards was made King of *Hungary,* where he was engaged in a War against the *Turks.* In this War *John Huniades* first defeated the *Turks* near the River *Morava,* and *Vladislaus* so beat them upon the Frontiers of *Macedonia,* that they were forced to make a Truce for Ten Years. But upon the perswasions of the Pope, who sent the Cardinal *Julian,* to absolve the King from his Oath, this Truce was broken; and not long after that memorable Battel was fought near *Varna,* where the King himself was kill'd. This Defeat \A. 1445\ was very shameful and prejudicial to the Christians.

Casimir IV. §8. In his stead *Casimir* {IV.} was made King of *Poland:* A great part of *Prussia,* which was weary of the Government of the Knights of the Cross, did surrender it self under his Protection: This occasioned a heavy War betwixt them and the *Poles,* which having been carried on a great while with dubious Success, a Peace was at last concluded by the mediation of the Pope; by Vertue of which, the *Poles* got *Pomerellia, Culm, Marienburgh, Stum* and *Elbing,* the rest remaining under the jurisdiction of the Knights of the Cross, under Condition, that the Master of that Order should be a Vassal of *Poland,* and a Duke and Senator of that Kingdom. Much about the same time, the Duke of *Vallachia,* did submit himself as a Vassal to the Crown of *Poland.* Under the Reign of this King, the Deputies of the Provinces [*die Landboten*] first appeared at the Dyets of the Kingdom. *Vladislaus* the Son of this *Casimir* was made King of *Bohemia,* and afterwards also of *Hungary,* tho' his own Brother *John Albert* did contend with him for the latter, but being soundly beaten, was obliged to desist from his Preten-<341>sions. *Casimir* died in the Year 1492.

Him succeeded his Son *John Albert,* who received a signal overthrow in *Vallachia* from the *Turks* and rebellious *Vallachians.* The *Turks* also fell into *Poland,* but by a sudden great Frost a great many Thousands of them were 'starved' [frozen] to Death. Under the Reign of this King, the Dukedom of *Plotzko* in the Country of *Masovia* was united to {the crown of} *Poland.* He died in the Year 1501. Whom succeeded his Brother *Alexander,* but he did not Reign longer than till the Year 1506.

Whom succeeded *Sigismund* one of the most Famous Princes of his time. This King was engaged in three several Wars against the *Muscovites,* wherein the *Poles* always were Victorious in the Field, but the *Muscovites* who had got *Smolensko* by Treachery, kept the possession of that place. The War which he waged with the Knights of the Cross in *Prussia,* [was] at last composed under these Conditions; that *Albert* Marquess of *Brandenburgh,* who was then Master of that Order, should receive the Eastern parts of *Prussia* as a hereditary Fief from the King, and should acknowledge himself hereafter a Vassal of the Crown of *Poland.* Under his Reign also the whole Country of *Masovia* was reunited to the Crown of *Poland.* He also fought very successfully against the *Vallachians,* and died in the Year 1548. leaving for his Successour his Son *Sigismundus Augustus.*

Under his Reign *Livonia* submitted it self to *Poland,* as being not able

John Albert.

Alexander.

Sigismund.

Sigismundus
Augustus.

to defend it self against the *Muscovites,* who already had taken *Dorpt, Felin,* and several other places. In this publick Consternation *Estland* and *Reval* did surrender themselves to *Erick* King of *Swedeland.* But the Archbishop of *Riga,* and the Master of the Teutonick Order, did seek for Protection of the King of *Poland,* which he would not grant them upon any other terms, than that they should submit themselves to the Crown of *Poland.* Whereupon the Master of the Order {*Gotfried Ketler*} having abdicated himself, surrendred the Castle of *Riga* and some other places to the *Poles.* And he in recompence of his Loss was made Duke of *Curland* and *Semigall.* This occasioned a War betwixt the *Poles* and *Muscovites,* wherein these took from the former *Plotzka.* This King died \A. 1552\ without Children, and by his Death the Male Race of the *Jagellonick* Family was quite extinguished. <342>

§9. After his Death there were great Contentions in *Poland* concerning the Election of a new King, and at last by the majority of Votes, *Henry* Duke of *Anjou,* Brother of *Charles* IX. King of *France,* was declared King of *Poland,* who arriving there \A. 1574\ was crowned in the same Year. But he had scarce been four Months in *Poland,* when having Notice that his Brother the King of *France* was dead, he in the Night time, and in a thick Fog, for fear the *Poles* should detain him, relinquished *Poland,* and taking his way through *Austria* and *Italy* into *France,* took Possession of that Kingdom.[8]

The *Poles* being extreamly vexed at this Affront, were for electing a new King. A great many were for *Maximilian* of *Austria,* but *Stephen Batori* Prince of *Transylvania* having been declared King by the plurality of Votes, quickly came into *Poland,* and excluded *Maximilian* by marrying *Anna* the Sister of *Sigismundus Augustus.* This King reduced the City of *Dantzick,* which had sided with *Maximilian*[,] to obedience. Afterwards he fell upon the *Muscovites,* taking from them *Plotzko* and the {adjoining district, and many} neighbouring Countries [places]. At last he made Peace with the *Muscovites,* under this Condition, that they should resign to him the whole Country of *Livonia,* in lieu of which

(margin: Henry of Valois Duke of Anjou.)

(margin: Steph. Batori.)

8. See V.20–21, pp. 237–44, above.

he would restore to them such places as he had taken from them in *Muscovy.*

This King adorned the Kingdom with wholesome Constitutions [*Justiz*], and established the Militia of Horse, which Souldiers being paid out of the fourth part of the Royal Revenues, are commonly called the *Quartians;* these he disposed upon the Frontiers to defend the same against the Incursions of the *Tartars.* By this means that Tract of Land which from *Bar, Bracklavia* and *Kiovia,* extends it self betwixt the two Rivers of the *Dniester* and the *Borysthenes* [*Dnieper*], as far as to the *Black Sea,* was filled with populous Cities and Towns, which is now called the *Ukraine,* it having been formerly a desolate Country. He also put into a good Order and Discipline the *Cosacks,* who served for Foot Souldiers, giving to them *Techtimorovia,* situated on the River *Borysthenes,* which they made afterwards their Magazine [*Zeughaus*], and the place of Residence of their Governours. Before this time the *Cosacks* were only a wild and barbarous <343> sort of Rabble who were gathered out of the *Polish Russia,* and having settled themselves {mostly} in the Island{s} of the River *Borysthenes* beneath *Kiovia,* lived upon Robbing and Plunder. These *Cosacks,* after they were brought into good Discipline [*die Form einer rechten Armee*] by this King *Stephen,* have been for a considerable time serviceable to the Crown of *Poland,* not only against the Incursions of the *Tartars,* but also by their cruising into the *Black Sea,* have done great Mischief to the *Turks.* For they have had Courage enough to ransack the Cities of *Trebisond* and *Sinope,* nay, even the Suburbs of *Constantinople* with other places. This brave King, whilst he was making Preparations against the *Turks,* died in the Year 1586.

The Cosacks.

§10. After his Death, *Sigismund* Son to *John* King of *Swedeland* was made King of *Poland,* who had this Advantage, that his Mother *Catherine* had been Sister of *Sigismundus Augustus,* and so consequently was descended from the *Jagellonick* Race. Some of the *Poles* proclaimed *Maximilian* their King, but he coming with some Forces to take Possession of the Kingdom, was beaten and taken Prisoner, and before he obtained his Liberty, was obliged to renounce his Title to that Crown. After the Death of *John* King of *Sweden* \A. 1592\, *Sigismund* went in

Sigism. III.

the Year next following into *Swedeland,* where he was Crowned King
of *Sweden.* But having afterwards lost that Crown, it occasioned a War
betwixt *Poland* and *Sweden.* In the beginning of this War, *Charles* IX.
King of *Sweden* took a great many places from the *Poles* in *Livonia,*
which were however most of them afterwards retaken by the *Polish*
General and Chancellour *Zamoiski:* Besides this, the King of *Sweden*
was vanquished in a great Battel fought \A. 1605\ |[near *Kirckholm* and
Riga]|,⁹ where he narrowly escaped himself. But some intestine Divi-
sions being arisen betwixt the King and the Nobility of *Poland,* King
Charles got an opportunity to recover himself.

The occasion   In⁺ the mean time there was a War kindled betwixt the *Muscovites* and
of the War   *Poles* by the following occasion: There was a certain Person in *Poland*
between
Poland and   who pretended that he was *Demetrius* the Son of *John Basilowitz,* Grand
Muscovy.   Duke of *Muscovy,* and that he was to have been mur-<344>thered by
the Order of *Boris Gudenow,* who hoped thereby to obtain the Succession in 'the Empire' [Muscovy] after the Death of *Theodore* the eldest
Son of the said *John Basilowitz,* but that another {youth} had been killed
in his stead. This Man |[having found great Encouragement from]|¹⁰
George Mniszeck the *Vayvod* of *Sendemir,* promised to marry his Daughter. Wherefore this *Vayvod* with the Assistance of some other *Polish*
Lords <having> gathered an Army that marched with *Demetrius* into
Muscovy \A. 1605\: And the Grand Duke *Boris Gudenow* happening to
die suddenly soon after, *Demetrius* was well received by the *Russians;*
and having vanquished such as pretended to oppose him, he came up
to the City of *Muscovy,* where he was proclaimed Grand Duke: But he
quickly made himself odious to the *Muscovites,* they suspecting him to
be an Impostor, but did however hide their resentments till the arrival
of the *Polish* Bride. In the mean while the *Muscovites* (under the Conduct of those of *Suski,* who were by their Mother's side descended from
the Family of the Grand Dukes) had under-hand got together about
20.000 Men. These at the time when the Nuptials [*das Beylager*] were
celebrating with great Pomp \A. 1606\, raised a Tumult, attacked the

9. Rather: "at Kirchholm near Riga."
10. Rather: "being greatly esteemed by."

Castle, and cut to pieces *Demetrius* and a great many *Poles* who were come along with the Bride, tho' some of the chiefest defended themselves bravely and escaped their Fury.

Then+ *Basilius Suski* was proclaimed Great Duke in the publick Market place, who caused there the Body of *Demetrius* to be exposed to publick view, but he being extreamly defaced by his Wounds, his Face could not be discerned by the multitude. Immediately after, a rumor was spread abroad, that *Demetrius* was escaped, and another appeared soon after, who pretended to be the same *Demetrius*. Whether it was the same or not, is not yet determined; this is certain that the *Poles* did acknowledge him as such, they being very desirous to revenge the former Affront and the Death of their Friends. This Old or New *Demetrius* did march \A. 1608\ with a great Army composed of *Poles* and *Cosacks* into *Muscovy*, where he several times beat *Suski*, whom he obliged to set at Liberty the captive Bride, and to beg the King of *Poland* [that is, Sigismund] to recal his Subjects. But the Bride having acknow-<345>ledged this *Demetrius* for her Husband, he got a great 'part' [following] both in *Muscovy* and *Poland* that sided with him, and would quickly have ruined *Suski*, if he had not been succoured by the King of *Sweden* who sent *Pontus de la Gardie* with some Forces to his Assistance.

{King} *Sigismund*+ also took hold of this Opportunity, to try whether he could at least recover *Smolensko* and *Severia* from the *Muscovites*. Wherefore he besieged *Smolensko* in the Year 1609. which however he could not make himself Master of till the Year 1611. when he took it by Storm. In the mean time, the *Poles* which had hitherto sided with *Demetrius*, were recalled by *Sigismund*, who did think it not convenient that so considerable a part of his Forces should be under the Command of another. By the removal of these Forces, *Suski* had leisure given him to recollect himself, and with the Auxilaries sent him out of *Swedeland*, he marched \A. 1610\ against the *Poles* who had besieged *Smolensko*, but was defeated by the *Poles* near *Clusin*.

By this overthrow the Affairs of the *Muscovites* were again put into a very dangerous Condition. Wherefore they took this 'Resolution' [stratagem] to avoid the Danger which threatened them from the *Polish* side. They deposed *Suski*, who by his Misfortunes was become odious

Basil. great Duke of Muscovy.

Sigismund makes his advantage of these Troubles in Muscovy.

to them, and offered the Crown of *Muscovy* to *Vladislaus*[11] the Prince
The Policy of *Poland*. By this means they hoped at one stroak to ruin *Demetrius*,
of the and to be reconciled to the *Poles*, in hopes, that they might easily meet
Muscovites. with an Opportunity hereafter, when they had once rid themselves of
the present Danger, to rid themselves also of the Prince of *Poland*. And
this 'Project' [trick] succeeded very well, for the *Polish* Troops immediatly left the Party of *Demetrius; Suski* was surrendred to the *Poles*,
||[who promised to the *Muscovites*, what had sworn before Allegiance
to *Vladislaus*, that he]||[12] should appear {as soon as possible} in Person
in *Muscovy* in the Year 1610. But King *Sigismund* by the perswasions of
some of his Friends refused this offer, thinking it more for his purpose
to Conquer *Muscovy* by Force of Arms; which Opportunity, however,
he missed of, since he did not immediatly march towards the City of
Muscovy, which he might have taken at the first Assault.

The Oversight   But the *Muscovites* having discovered the Design of the *Poles*, did
of Sigismund. 'unanimously' [the more readily] revolt from *Vladislaus*, <346> especially since they had in the mean while been rid of *Demetrius*, who
had been murthered by the *Tartars* that were his {body-}Guards. They
therefore attacked the *Polish Garrison* in the City of *Muscovy*, which
consisted of Seven Thousand Men, but these defended themselves
bravely; and besides this, set Fire to the whole City, which before had
180.000 Houses, where abundance of People were burned. Nevertheless
the *Muscovites* recovered themselves and besieged the *Polish* Garrison in
the Castle of *Muscovy*. If King *Sigismund* immediatly after the taking of
Smolensko, had sent them Relief, as he easily might have done, he questionless might have established his Affairs in *Muscovy*. But he marching
back with his Army into *Poland*, and sending to their Relief neither
Men nor Money, the Garrison who had before plundered the Treasury
of the Great Duke, to the number of [numbering] 7000. leaving some
to Guard the Castle, <fought their way through the *Muscovites*, and>
came to King *Sigismund* to demand their Pay. And tho' *Sigismund* be-

---

11. Vladislav IV (1595–1648), eldest son of Sigismund III (1566–1632).
12. Rather: "and the Russians swore allegiance to Vladislaus. In turn, the Poles
then in Moscow promised that Vladislaus."

gan {finally} to apply himself in good earnest to re-establish his Affairs in *Muscovy,* yet all his Designs were by the jealousie which reigned betwixt the Generals so long delayed, till the *Poles* who had the Guard of the Castle of the City of *Muscovy,* were forced by Famine to surrender it. Thus all was lost {for Poland} in *Muscovy;* {and} for *Sigismund,* who was the more troubled at it, because he had made an account [planned] by the Conquest of *Muscovy,* to open his way into *Swedeland.*

Besides⁺ this, the *Poles* sustained in the same Year a considerable Loss in *Moldavia.* Prince *Vladislaus* did undertake \A. 1617\ an{other} Expedition into *Muscovy,* but to no great purpose, wherefore he made a Truce with them for fourteen Years, wherein it was agreed, that the *Poles* in the mean time should keep in their Possession the Dukedom of *Severia, Zernigo* [Czernigo] and *Novogrod,* which they had taken during these Troubles in *Muscovy.* In the mean time *George Farensbach* did surrender several places in *Livonia* to the King of *Sweden, Gustavus Adolphus,* but it was suspected that he intended to betray the King; for soon after, the same *Farensbach* was reconciled to King *Sigismund,* unto whom he restored all the places, except *Pernau.* <347>

The Poles defeated in Moldavia.

In⁺ the Year 1620. the *Poles* were engaged in a War against the *Turks,* that were as 'tis supposed, stirred up by *Betlem Gabor* Prince of *Transylvania;*¹³ for *Sigismund* having assisted the Emperour¹⁴ against him, *Betlem Gabor* was for making them a Diversion by the help of the *Turks.* The *Turks* therefore entred Moldavia with an Intention to banish that Duke, who sided with the *Poles.* The *Polish* General Zolkieuski coming to the Assistance of the Duke of *Moldavia* advanced too far into the Country, and as he was marching back, was totally routed {by the Turks} and himself slain upon the place. In the Year next following the *Turks* marched with their whole Forces against *Poland,* who were met by the *Poles* near *Chocim* under the Command of Prince *Vladislaus.* The *Polish* Army was about 65.000 strong, but the *Turks* {and Tartars} 392.000 Men, commanded by the *Turkish* Emperour *Osman* in Person. The *Turks* did attempt three times to take the *Polish* Camp by Storm,

A War betwixt the Poles and Turks.

13. That is, Siebenbürgen, in modern Romania.
14. Ferdinand II (1578–1637) of Austria, Holy Roman Emperor from 1619 to 1637.

but were as often repulsed with great Loss. But the *Poles* in the mean while suffered extreamly for want of Ammunition and Provisions, and were mightily weakened by Sicknesses and the Mortality among their Horses. Nevertheless the *Turkish* Emperour {finally} made a very honourable Peace with them, after he had left [lost] 60.000 Men, in these several Storms made upon their Camp, and a greater Number in his march back to *Constantinople.*

The Invasion of Gustavus Adolphus.

In⁺ the mean time King *Gustavus* <*Adolphus*> falling into *Livonia,* took the City of *Riga* \A. 1621\ without any great Resistance. And the rest of *Livonia,* except Dunneburgh was Conquered by the *Swedes* in the Year 1625. King *Gustavus* entred *Prussia* with an Army in the Year 1626. where he took the Cities of *Marienburgh* and *Elbing,* besides some other Places: This War was thus carried on without any 'General' [major] Engagement till the Year 1629. when *Hans Wrangel* the *Swedish* General {quite} defeated the *Poles* near *Gorzno.* Then the Emperour sent 'some Forces' [several thousand men] to the Assistance of the *Poles,* who in a Battel fought near *Stum,* were very near having made King *Gustavus* their Prisoner. But the *Polish* Affairs being after this Battel fallen into great Confusion, a Truce was concluded by the mediation of *France* and *England* till the {month of June in the} Year 1634. the *Swedes* being in the mean while to keep <348> in their Possession *Elbing, Memel, Braunsberg, Pillau,* and what else they had taken in *Livonia. Sigismund* died in the Year 1632.

Vladis. IV.

§11. After his Death his Son *Vladislaus* IV. was declared King, who in the Year next following, obtained a signal Victory over the *Muscovites* that had besieged *Smolensko;* for he not only forced them to raise the Siege, but also brought the *Muscovite* Army into such streights, that they were forced to surrender themselves. And the *Turks* who would have made a Diversion to him, were also bravely repulsed. At last \A. 1634\ *Vladislaus* made a very advantageous Peace on his side with the *Muscovites,* by vertue of which these renounced all their Pretensions upon the two large Dukedoms of *Smolensko* and *Czernichow.* This |[begot such a Terrour]|[15] among the *Turks,* that they freely made him Restitution

15. Rather: "brought him such renown."

for the Damages sustained in their last In-road, having also caused the *Bashaw* [pasha] who commanded these Forces, to be strangled. The Truce with *Sweden* was prolonged \A. 1635\ at *Stumsdorf* in *Prussia,* for 26 Years, where the places possessed before by the *Swedes* in *Prussia* were restored to the *Poles,* because the *Swedish* Affairs in *Germany* were then after the Battel of *Norlingen* [1634] in a very ill Condition, and besides this, the *English* and *Dutch* were extreamly dissatisfied with the Tolls that were paid in *Prussia.*

In⁺ the Year 1637. the Foundation was laid of the War with the *Co-sacks,* which has brought unspeakable Mischiefs upon the *Poles.* The business happened thus: As the number of the *Cosacks* was greatly en-creased by the great number of {dispersed} Boors, which frequently ran into [joined] them, so 'the' [many] great Men in *Poland* had 'purchased' [acquired] great Estates in the *Ukraine,* who were of Opinion, that their Revenues would be considerably encreased, if the Liberty of the *Cosacks* were reduced into more narrow bounds. Wherefore they having advised the King, that they ought to be more restrained for the future; the *Polish* General *Koniecpolski,* did cause the Fortress of *Hudack* to be built {for that purpose}, just at a point where the River of *Zwamer* falls into the *Dnieper* or *Borysthenes.* The *Cosacks* endeavoured to prevent the perfecting of this Work by force, but being routed by the *Poles,* were obliged to surrender <349> their General *Pauluck* and some of their Chief Men among them, who were all, notwithstanding a Pardon was promised them before hand, beheaded. Besides this, it was decreed in the Dyet, that all their former Priviledges [*alle Freyheit*] and the Fortress of *Techtimorovia* should be taken from them, and that in their stead, a new body of Militia should be settled there. To put this Decree in execution, the *Polish* Army marched into the *Ukraine,* against which, the *Cosacks* fought with great bravery, promising nevertheless that they would be faithful to the Crown of *Poland,* if their ancient Priviledges were confirmed to them, which the *Poles* did promise them, but did not perform; nay, did even treat some of them very ill. For among other oppressive Methods, they took also from them some of their *Greek* Churches.[16] Their General Chmielinski was also grosly Affronted, for

The Cause of the War with the Cosacks.

16. Ukrainian Cossacks generally adhered to the Greek Orthodox religion.

which he could obtain no Satisfaction [*Justitz*]. For the King having granted him a Priviledge to build some Mills, a certain Gentleman [nobleman] whose Name was *Jarinski,* burnt the same, having also ravished his Wife, and afterwards killed both her and her Son.

§12. In the mean time *Vladislaus* died \A. 1647\, whom succeeded his

John Casimir.   Brother *John Casimir.* Then *Chmielinski* to revenge himself, stirred up the *Cosacks* against the *Poles,* who with Burning, Plundering and Ravishing, did what Mischief they could to the *Polish* Nobility. And the Senators having desired the King to march out into the Field against them, they were answered by him, That they ought not to have burnt down their [Chmielinski's] Mills. Whereat the *Poles* being extreamly

The Poles   dissatisfied brought together an Army of 50.000 Men, which being
defeated by   defeated by the *Cosacks,* there were killed 10.000 upon the Spot, and be-
the Cosacks.   sides this, they took the City of *Kiovia* [Kiev]. To revenge this Affront, the *Poles* summoned the seventh Man throughout the whole Kingdom, and marched against the *Cosacks* without the Consent of the King, but were again miserably beaten by them. But *Chmielinski* celebrating the Nuptials of his Son {in Kiev} with the Daughter of the Prince of *Vallachia,* the *Poles* surprised the *Cosacks* thereabouts, plundered the City, and took the *Grecian* Patriarch prisoner. The *Cosacks* then sent to the King to know whe-<350>ther this had been done by his Authority; and the King having answered. No, but that it had been done by the Nobility to take revenge of the *Cosacks;* these joined with the *Tartars* and fell into *Poland;* against these the King went in Person into the Field at the Head of the Nobility, and defeated them in a Battel, but the King having afterwards made an Agreement with them, the Nobility was greatly discontented with the King's proceedings, alledging, that the King had granted too much to the *Cosacks.*

The   Whilst[+] the Jealousies reigned in *Poland,* the *Muscovites* fell into
Muscovites   *Poland* \A. 1653\, and having brought the *Cosacks* over to their Party,
join with   besieged *Smolensko,* which they took in the Year next following; and
the Cosacks.   having ravaged every where in *Lithuania,* they took *Wilea* [Vilnius] and some other Cities, where they committed great Barbarities.

In[+] the Year 1655. another Storm threatened the *Poles.* For *Charles*

Gustavus King of *Swedeland* having with an Army of chosen Men en-
tred that Kingdom, first Conquered great *Poland* and *Masovia* [Ma-
suria], and afterwards the lesser *Poland,* with the capital City *Craconia*
[Cracow], from whence he marched into *Prussia,* where almost all the
Cities surrendred themselves, except *Dantzick* where were at first a great
many Citizens that favoured the *Swedes,* but by the perswasions of some
'Ministers' [preachers], were kept in Obedience [*Devotion*] to *Poland.*
The Resistance which was made by this one City, was the main Reason
why all the Advantages got by the *Swedes* proved fruitless at last, and
that they could not maintain themselves in *Prussia,* notwithstanding
that not only the whole Militia of *Poland,* and that part of *Lithuania*
which was not under the subjection of the *Muscovites,* had submitted
themselves to the *Swedish* Protection, but also, that King *John Casimir*
himself fled into *Silesia.* For the *Poles* having recollected themselves
after the first Consternation was over, and being joined by the *Tartars,*
fell upon such of the *Swedish* Forces as were dispersed up and down the
Country. The *Lithuanians* also revolted, and killed all the *Swedes* that
were in Winter Quarters with them. King *Charles Gustavus* also had
greatly weakened his Army, not only by the great March towards *Jero-
slavia* [Jaroslaw], but also *Czarneski,* the *Polish* General did often with
his Light-Horse fall up-<351>on the Rear of the Army, and did considerable Mischief. In the mean while the *Poles* also had retaken *Warsovia,*
where they had made the *Swedish* Governour *Wittenbergh* and some
other great Officers Prisoners, contrary to the Articles made at the surrendry of the Place. And tho' King *Charles Gustavus* having been joined
before by the Elector of *Brandenburgh's* Forces did vanquish the *Poles*
and *Tartars* in a memorable Battel which lasted three Days, and was
fought near *Warsovia,* yet all the Princes of *Europe* began to look about
them, and to consult about a *Diversion* to be made *Sweden.* The *Muscovites* fell into *Livonia,* where they besieged *Riga,* but to no purpose. The
Hollanders did give plainly to understand, that they were not willing
that *Prussia* should come under the subjection of *Swedeland.* And the
Danes also began to be in motion.

On the other hand, *Ragozi* Prince of *Transylvania* entred *Poland* with
an Army, to try whether perhaps he could obtain that Crown for him-

Ragozi
Prince of
Transylvania
invades
Poland.
self. But the King of *Sweden* being obliged to march out of *Poland* against the *Danes, Ragozi* made a bad Market [mess] of it; for before he could reach his own Country, he was totally routed, and oliged to make a shameful accord with the *Poles*. Which misfortune however he might have avoided, if he, according to the advice of the King of *Sweden,* who promised to keep the *Poles* so long in play, till he was out of danger, would have taken his march directly over *Brescie, Pinsk,* and so further towards his own Frontiers. But *Ragozi* would by all means take his way near *Cracaw.* Then the *Poles* retook *Cracaw* and *Thorn,* and chased the *Swedes* out of *Curland,* who had before taken the Duke of that name Prisoner. The *Poles* also besieged *Riga,* but were beaten from thence by the *Swedish* General *Helmfeld.* And tho the *Poles* by the Peace made at *Oliva* \A. 1660\ recovered all *Prussia* again, yet were they obliged to renounce all their pretensions upon *Livonia,* and to leave the *Muscovites* in the possession of *Smolensko, Severia* and *Kiovia.* Neither could they appease the *Cosacks,* some of them having put themselves under the protection of the *Muscovites,* some under the *Turks,* whereby they shewed the way to the *Turks* into *Poland.* Neither could the King put an end <352> to the intestine divisions and jealousies, wherefore at last tired with these troubles *John Casimir* resigned the Crown, and living a retired life in *France* in the Abby of St. *Germain,* he there dyed a few years after.

§13. There being now left none of the Royal Family in *Poland,* several Foreigners pretended to the Crown. But at last \A. 1670\ a *Piastus,* Michael
Wiesnowizki. whose name was *Michael Wiesnowizki,* was declared King, chiefly by the Votes of the lesser Nobility. His short Reign was full of intestine commotions, and the *Turks* in the mean while did not cease to do considerable mischief in *Poland;* having in the year 1672. taken *Caminieck* in *Podolia,* which Fortress having been formerly thought impregnable, serves them now for a door, through which they may enter *Poland* at pleasure. A Peace was then concluded with the *Turks,* by vertue of which the said Fortress remained in the possession of the *Turks,* the *Poles* also having promised to pay to the *Turks* a yearly Tribute. This King dyed in the year 1673. In whose stead in the year next following

the *Polish* General *John Sobieski* was 'made' [elected] King of *Poland*,   John Sobieski.
he having in the year before attack'd the *Turks* in their Camp with such
success, that of 32.000 Men scarce 1500 escaped alive.[17] He renewed the
War with the *Turks,* but concluded a Peace with them in the year 1676.
by vertue of which the *Turks* kept the Fortress of *Caminieck,* but remitted the yearly Tribute to the *Poles.* He being a Man of great capacity, it
is hoped that he may prove a good King of *Poland*.[18]

§14. It is to be considered concerning the *Polish* Nation, that whoso-   The Genius of
ever is not a Nobleman in *Poland,* is esteemed a Boor [*Bauer*]. For the   this Nation.
Inhabitants of the Cities are very little regarded, and the Tradesmen
are most[ly] Foreigners. But the Boors are esteemed nor used no better than Slaves [*Leibeigene*], being also very raw and barbarous, both
in their Life and Conversation [*Sitten*], wherefore when we talk of the
Poles, thereby ought 'only' [mostly] to be understood the Nobility. They
are therefore commonly downright and honest, |[very seldom given to
the art of dissembling]|[19]; they are of a very generous spirit, and expect
a great deal of re-<353>spect. And if you give them as much respect
as they pretend to, they are no less courteous, and will willingly pay a
respect again to you; and their words and behaviour are full of Pomp
and Ceremony. They are very liberal, or rather profuse; and not given
to be parsimonious, tho they should want the next day. This Nation
also is very 'fierce' [forward, *frech*] and 'extravagant' [unbridled, *unben-
dig*], much inclined to an uncontroled liberty, or rather licentiousness
and petulancy. Wherefore 'Plots' [*Confoederationes*] and Conspiracies
against their Kings are frequent among them, whose Actions they can-
vase [canvass, *syndiciren*] with a great deal of freedom, being always
jealous of the least point of their Liberty. They do not want courage,
but they are more fit to act with a sudden heat, than to endure long the
fatigues of War. And because the Nobles only apply themselves to the

17. At the battle of Chocim [Khotyn], in 1673.
18. John III Sobieski (1629–96) ruled Poland for twenty-two years (1674–96)
and defeated the Turks again at the decisive Battle of Vienna (1683), where the Ottoman advance into Europe was finally halted.
19. Rather: "and know little of the subtle arts of simulation and dissimulation."

War, who never serve but on Horseback, and the rest of the Inhabitants [*Volcks*] are ||[of no great spirit]|,[20] their infantry gathered out of the Natives is not worth much, wherefore they are obliged in their stead to make use of Foreigners listed into their Service, or of the *Cosacks,* who are courageous and active [*hurtig*].

The Nature
of the Soil,
&c. Its
Commodities. §15. This Country [*Land*] is of a vast extent, and very Fertile in general, fit both for Tillage and Pasture, or breeding of Cattel. For *Holland* draws most of its 'Corn' [grain] out of *Poland,* and the *Polish* Oxen are sent in great numbers into *Germany.* The *Polish* Wool also is in good esteem abroad. *Poland* abounds with good Horses. *Lithuania* produces abundance of Hon[e]y, which is most consumed by the Inhabitants, who make Mead of it; the rest is exported, as likewise abundance of Wax, Hemp, Flax, Leather, Pot-ashes, Salt, Wood, and the like. But on the contrary the Commodities which are imported here are Silk, woollen Stuffs and Cloaths, Tapestries, Sables, *Hungarian* and *Spanish* Wines, abundance of Spice, which they use in great quantity in their Dyet. If the *Poles* were addicted in the least to good Husbandry, and would apply themselves a little to Manufactures, the Commodities fit for exportation here, would much surpass those which need be imported. <354>

Poland[+] is very populous and full of Towns and Villages. Some have computed that the King and the Nobility have in their possession 90.000 Cities and Villages, the Bishops and Canons 100.000, the rest of the Clergy, *Monks* and *Nuns,* 60.950. Which in all amounts to the number of 250.950 Towns and Villages. Yet I will not be answerable for this account.

The strength
of the
Kingdom. §16. The chief strength of this Kingdom {when it prospers} consists {mostly} in the Nobility. The *Poles* have formerly given out that they could raise 150.000 Horse, some say 200.000, out of the Nobility. Which seems to be a little largely spoken, except you would reckon among them their {accompanying} Servants. This is certain that in no

---

20. Rather: "maintained very badly [*sehr schlecht gehalten wird*]."

Kingdom of *Europe* there is so great a number of Nobles. They also may find a way to raise a proportionable [considerable] Infantry out of the *Cosacks*. And if they will stretch a little their Purses, they are able enough to raise [sums] sufficient for the maintaining of a great Army. But here is the mischief, that the King cannot levy any extraordinary Taxes, without the consent of the Nobility, and both the Clergy and the Nobility are very backward [disinclined] in paying of any Taxes, or at least grow quickly aweary of them, except it be in case of the highest necessity. And this is the reason why the King of *Poland* cannot carry on a War long with vigour. Besides this when the Nobles are summoned to appear in Arms, they come slowly into the Field, and are not easily kept under Discipline. The *Polish* Armies have also this inconveniency in them, that where 10.000 fighting Men are, at least five times the number of Servants and 'idle Fellows' [*Trotz*]²¹ follow the Camp, which proves a destruction to their own Country, and occasions scarcity of Provisions both for Men and Horse.

Their weakness.

§17. Concerning their Form of Government; it is to be observed that the *Poles* live under one Head, who bears the Title, and lives in the Splendour becoming a King; but if you consider his Power, which is circumscribed within very narrow bounds, he is in effect no more than the Prime [*Princeps*] or Chief Regent in a Free Commonwealth [*Republic*]. This King is always chosen by <355> a free Election, where every Noble Man there present has his Vote; and tho the *Poles* have been always inclined to keep to the Royal Race, yet have they never been for declaring a Successour during the life of the present King; but have always |[expected the vacancy of the Throne]|,²² as being of opinion, that this time is the most proper to abolish such Abuses as perhaps are crept in under the former Reign, and to prevent all means which may prove prejudicial afterwards to their Liberties. But, that, during this Vacancy, all disorders may be prevented, Justice is then exercised with

Their form of Government.

21. The German term suggests willful resistance, and thus idleness due to lack of cooperation or disagreement.
22. Rather: "been willing to allow an interregnum to occur."

more severity than at other times: the Archbishop of *Gniesen,* who is the Primate of *Poland* [*Primas Regni*], being in the mean while the Regent [*Director*], or as it were Interrex of the Kingdom.

The *Poles* have had for a considerable time this Maxim, that they would rather choose a King out of a Foreign Princely Family, than out of their own Nobility; as being of Opinion that thereby the equality among the Nobility may be better preserved; for a Foreigner is no more engaged to one than to another; whereas a Native always prefers his Kindred and Relations [*Schwäger*] before the rest: and this Rule they have observed ever since the time of *Jagello,* who being a *Lithuanian,* united *Lithuania* with *Poland.*[23] But they had not the same good fortune with *Sigismund* King of *Sweden,*[24] partly because the situation of these two Kingdoms is such: that both cannot well be governed by one King; partly because they were thereby engaged in a heavy War against *Swedeland,* which else might easily have been avoided; but they have been always very careful not to take their Kings out of the House of *Austria,* fearing lest they should be treated like the *Hungarians* and *Bohemians.* In the two last Elections they have chosen two Kings[25] out of their own Nobility, and whether thereby these Factions which have hitherto been predominant in that Kingdom, can be suppressed, time will shew.

The Revenues of the King. This Elective King has a great Revenue out of the Lands belonging to the Crown, and has the sole power to dispose of all vacant Offices, Dignities and Benefices; but he cannot make new Laws, begin a War, impose new Taxes, or undertake any other Matters of great moment, **The Estates of the Kingdom.** without the consent of the Estates. The E-<356>states in *Poland* are composed of the Bishops and some Abbots, of the Palatins or Vaywods, which are Governours of the Provinces [*Landschafften*], of the Castellans or Governours of Castles, and of the chief Officers [*vornehmsten Bedienten*] of the Kingdom; these compose the Senate, which consisted formerly of 150 Persons; besides these there are {the *Landbotten* or} the

23. Vladislaus II Jagiello (1362–1443); see §7 above.
24. Sigismund III Vasa (1556–1632); see §10 above.
25. Michael Wiesnowizki (1640–73) and John Sobieski (1629–96); see §13 above.

Deputies of the Nobility out of each District, who have almost the same power which the Tribunes of the People had at *Rome;* since one single person among them by entring his Protest may annul a Decree at the Dyet; and these Deputies use their Tongues [*Maul*] very freely at the Dyet, both against the King and his Ministers; from whence it often happens that Matters are debated here with great confusion, since by the capricious humour of one Deputy the benefit of the whole Dyet is lost at once; especially since a certain time of six weeks is prefixed by the Laws for the holding of the Dyet, which they rarely suffer to be Prorogued, and that not but for a very few days; but they call this right of contradicting, the Soul of the *Polish* Liberty.

The King is also obliged to bestow all the vacant Benefices upon the Nobility, and cannot reserve any for his own use, or bestow them upon his Children without consent of the Estates, neither can he buy or take possession of any Noblemens Lands. The King also is not Master of the Judicial Courts; but there is a certain High Court of Justice, the Judges whereof are Nobles: first Instituted by King *Stephen Batori.*[26] These Judges are changed every twelve months, and keep their Session six months in the year at *Petricovia,* and six months again at *Lublin,* and from these no Appeal lies to the King; except that some Cases of the greatest Consequence are determined at the Dyet; but Cases belonging to the King's Exchequer, or to his Revenues, are determined by the King. The *Poles* are extreamly fond of this form of Government, as being very suitable to their natural fierce inclinations [*Frechheit*]; yet the same is very improper for any sudden and 'great' [prolonged] undertaking, and contributes not a little to the weakness of this vast Kingdom, especially when the Nobility is {especially} refractory, and jealous of the King. <357>

Of the Administration of Justice.

§18. The Neighbours of *Poland* are on one side the *Germans,* where there is an open Country [space] upon the {respective} Frontiers; and particularly *Poland* borders upon {the emperor's hereditary lands in} *Silesia,* and in one corner upon *Hungary.* 'Tis true that the *German*

Neighbours of Poland.

Germany.

26. See §9, pp. 386–87, above.

Empire is much superiour in strength to *Poland*, but the interest of both these Kingdoms [*Reiche*] is such, as not to have any great occasion to differ with one another, except *Poland* should perhaps join with such Estates in *Germany* as would upon an occasion oppose the setting up of an Absolute 'Sovereignty' [monarchy] in the Empire; and in such a case the *Poles* would not want [lack] assistance |[either from the *German*, or

The House foreign Princes]|,[27] that must concur in the same Interest. The House of
of Austria in *Austria* alone is not powerful enough to conquer *Poland*, or to maintain
particular. a Country which is of so vast an extent and very populous, and lying all upon a level is not secured by [m]any fortified places. If no body else should side with *Poland*, the *Turks* themselves would not easily suffer that the House of *Austria* should acquire such an advantage, and the *Turks* are the fittest instruments to prevent it. But the House of *Austria* has often endeavoured, tho the wisest among the *Poles* have always opposed it, to unite the Kingdom of *Poland* to their Family by an Election; but the *Poles* are conscious of the danger which might accrue from this Union to their Liberty; and besides this they are no great admirers of the *Germans*, whose modesty and 'good Husbandry' [frugality] they commonly despise.

The Interest But it is of great consequence to *Poland*, that the *Turks* may not
of Poland and become quite Masters of the *Upper Hungary*, and much more that they
Germany,
with reference do not get footing in *Moravia;* since thereby they would open their way
to the Turk. into the very Heart of *Poland*. And on the other hand it is the common Interest both of the House *Austria*, and of all *Germany*, that the *Turks* may not become Masters of *Poland*, since thereby they would open their way into *Germany*. For the old saying of *Philip Melanchton, Si Turca in Germaniam veniet, veniet per Poloniam,* if the *Turks* come into *Germany* they will certainly come by the way of *Poland*, did not arise from a Prophetick Spirit, but has its good Reason in Geography. And it seems to be the common In-<358>terest of *Poland*, and the House of *Austria*, to keep up a mutual good understanding, since they both cover {a large part of} one anothers Frontiers, and *Poland* draws a great

27. Rather: "both in Germany itself [from those also opposed to such absolutism], and from others."

advantage from its Oxen and Salt which are sent into *Germany.* And if *Poland* should engage it self 'in good earnest' [too much] against the House of *Austria;* it ought to be 'jealous' [apprehensive] of the *Moscovites,* who may attack it [from] behind, except *Moscovy* were otherwise employed before {against someone else}. *Poland* also may be troublesome to the House of *Austria,* when that House is engaged in Wars against *France, Sweden,* or the *Turks.* Wherefore for a considerable time the House of *Austria* has endeavoured by Marriages to Allie *Poland* with their Family, and to gain a considerable party in the [Polish] Senat. And *France* has followed the same methods to draw *Poland* from the Interest of the House of *Austria;* and the *Poles* having been caressed by both parties have got no small advantage by this Rivalship.

    Brandenburgh[28] also borders 'on one side' [for a good distance] upon *Poland,* and tho he alone cannot hurt it much, yet experience has taught us that in conjunction with others he has been able to create great troubles to the *Poles.* Tho on the other hand it is to be feared, that perhaps upon a good occasion offered to the *Poles* they may attempt to unite all *Prussia* to their Kingdom, [just] as the Elector of *Brandenburgh* knew how to time it, when he obtained the Sovereignty over it.[29] As long as the differences betwixt *Poland* and *Sweden* were on foot, *Denmark* by making a diversion could be very serviceable to *Poland;* but since the causes of these differences are taken away, *Poland* need not make any particular reflection upon *Denmark.* *Swedeland* and *Poland* have all the reason in the world to cultivate a mutual good understanding, since they may be very serviceable to one another against the *Moscovites.* *Poland* borders upon *Moscovy* by a great tract of Land, where the Frontiers are common to both: These two Kingdoms seem to be very near equal in strength; and tho the *Poles* are better Soldiers than the *Moscovites,* yet has the Great Duke of *Moscovy* this advantage over them, that he is absolute {monarch} in his Dominions. And it is of great consequence to either of them, which of these two is in the pos-

(margin notes: Brandenburgh. Denmark and Sweden. Moscovy.)

28. That is, "the Brandenburger" (personified); hence the use of "he."
29. See §12 above. By taking advantage of the conflict between Sweden and Poland, Brandenburg obtained sovereignty over Prussia through the Treaty of Wehlau (1657) and the Treaty of Oliva (1660).

session of *Smolensko,* to recover which <359> the *Poles* ought to employ all their strength. For the rest, these two States being both obliged to have a watchful Eye over the *Turks,* can assist one another against them in case of necessity.

The Tartars. The⁺ *Tartars* are the most pernicious Neighbours of *Poland,* for they are a Nation living by depredations [*ein flüchtig räuberisch Gesindel*], who surprise their Neighbours, and when they have loaded themselves with {human and other} Spoils return Home again {to their nests}, where you cannot be revenged of them, they being so nimble, and having nothing worth taking from them. Wherefore what ever mischief they do must be taken as if you were bit by a Dog, except you can catch them in the fact, and make them pay for it with their Heads.

Moldavia. Against these the Country of *Moldavia* used to be a Bulwark to *Poland.* For through that Country the *Tartars* have a direct passage into the Provinces of *Poland,* which may be shut up against them by the help of that Prince. Wherefore the *Poles* do much lament the loss of this Dukedom, which having been formerly a Fief of that Crown, tho that Duke payd also some Tribute to the *Turks,* was brought in the year

The Cosacks. 1612. entirely under the *Turkish* subjection. The *Cosacks* also used to be very serviceable against the *Tartars,* as living near the Isthmus of the *Taurick* Chersonese,[30] and therefore were conveniently situated to cut of[f] their retreat in their return Home. But the *Poles* by their ill entertainment have so exasperated the *Cosacks,* that since they have done as much mischief to them, as formerly they used to do good. And if the *Poles* should not be able by fair means to bring over the *Cosacks* again to their side, and these should either submit themselves to the *Moscovites* or the *Turks,* or that these should quite root them out, then *Poland* has got an incurable Ulcer on that side, which may prove fatal to all the Neighbouring Provinces of the *Ukrain.*

Lastly,⁺ the *Turk* is a dangerous Neighbour to *Poland,* whose strength is much superior to that of *Poland,* especially if the *Poles* are not assisted by the *Cosacks,* or by some Foreign State [*frembder Hilfe*]. For, tho the *Polish* Cavalry may not be inferiour to the *Turks,* yet cannot I see

30. That is, Crimea.

which way they can bring into the Field such Forces as may be equal to the *Janisaries.* Tho the negligence and <360> domestick divisions of the *Poles* have lately been the chief inducements, which have drawn the *Turks* so deep into *Poland.* There is not any thing which would more conveniently secure the *Poles* against the *Turks,* than if the Princes of *Moldavia, Wallachia* and *Transylvania,* did belong to *Poland,* they being able to hinder the passage of the *Turks* into *Poland.* But, because the *Poles* have long ago lost this advantage, or rather neglected it, it is their business now, to take care that ||[the *Turks* do not advance deeper into the Country.]||[31] And to take away all pretensions of a War from the *Turks,* it seems very necessary that the *Poles,* as much as in them lies, do take care that the *Cosacks* do not in time of Peace commit depredations upon the *Turkish* Subjects. For else the *Turks* are not to be blamed, if endeavouring to root out these rapacious Birds they destroy their Nest, and make the *Ukrain* a vast Wilderness. When *Poland* is engaged in a War with the *Turks,* it may expect some Subsid[i]es from the *Pope.* The House of *Austria,* is able, by making a diversion to the *Turks,* to give relief to *Poland;* but this House hitherto has not been forward to attack the *Turks,* if these have not been the first aggressors. The *Moscovites* also might contribute something this way, if there were any hopes of a 'true' [constant] understanding betwixt these two Nations; but as the case now stands, the *Poles* must chiefly rely upon their own strength, and by the circumstances of their own affairs be able to judg how far they ought to engage themselves against the *Turk.* <361>

31. Literally: "they [the Poles] don't let the dog come any farther into the kitchen."

CHAPTER XI

Of Moscovy.

§1. The first origin of this Empire, and the atchievements of their anti-ent Princes [*Regenten*] are very uncertain and obscure, since what is to be found of this nature among an ignorant people, is all very {meager and} confused: So much is certain, that this great Empire was formerly divided into a great many petty Lordships, which afterwards were united in one body. We will only relate in a few words, that the *Russians* in the year 989. first embraced the Christian Religion, at which time their Prince, *Wolodomir* married *Anne,* the Sister of the *Grecian* Emperour *Basilius Porphyrogenitus.* In the year 1237. their Prince *George,* was slain by *Battus* the King of the *Tartars;* whereby the *Russians* being brought under the subjection of the *Tartars,* their Princes were dependent on them. After a long time they at last freed themselves from this slavery under their Prince *John,* Son of *Basilius* the Blind, who began his Reign in the year 1450. Under his Reign *Russia* was first united into one considerable Body, he having subdued most of these petty Princes, which had divided *Russia* among them; especially the Dukes of *Tiver* [Tver] and of *Great Novogrod* [Novgorod], in which City 'tis said he got a booty of three hundred Cart loads of Gold and Silver. This Prince built *Juanogrod* [Ivangorod], a Castle near *Narva.*

§2. Him succeeded his Son *Basilius* who {A. 1509} took *Pleskeu* [Pskov], which was formerly a free City. From the *Poles* he also took *Smolensko,* but was soundly beaten by the *Astracan* [Casan] *Tartars,* who at the same time ransack'd the City of *Moscovy.* Him succeeded \A. 1533\ his

The antient State of Russia.

John.

Basilius.

John
Basilowitz.

Son *John Basilowitz*,[1] a cruel Tyrant, who conquer'd the two Kingdoms of the *Tartars* of *Casan* and *Astracan,* and <362> united them to *Muscovy.* He used the *Livonians* very barbarously, having killed one *Furstenbergh* the Master of the Order of [Teutonic] Knighthood there, which was the occasion that the City of *Reval* and whole *Tethland* [Estland] surrender'd themselves to *Swedeland,* and all the rest of *Livonia* to *Poland.* He was at first victorious against the *Poles,* but afterwards *Stephen Batori* took from him *Plotzko* and several other places. He died in the Year 1584. and unto him succeeded his Son *Theodore* {or *Faedor*} *Ivanowitz,* a very simple Prince, against whom the *Swedes* waged War about *Ingermanland.*

Theodore
Ivanowitz.

Boris
Guidenow.

§3. This *Theodore* dying without Issue,[2] his Brother in Law *Boris Guidenow* [Gudenov] did by his Intrigues obtain the Empire, but with very indifferent Success, especially after the supposed [false] *Demetrius* began to contend with him for it; during which Troubles he {suddenly} died \A. 1605\. His Son *Theodore* {or *Faedor*} *Borissowitz* was proclaimed Great Duke of *Muscovy,* but the *Muscovites* having afterwards for the most part sided with the supposed [false] *Demetrius,* he was taken Prisoner and murthered, after he had but Six Months enjoyed the Title of Grand Duke. What became of the supposed *Demetrius,* and how *Basilius Zuski* took upon him the Imperial Dignity \A. 1606\, we have related before.[3] To this *Zuski, Charles* IX. King of *Swedeland* offered his Assistance against the second supposed *Demetrius,* which he at first refused to accept of. But afterwards, when the other began to be too strong for him, he earnestly desired the same, promising to surrender to *Charles* as an acknowledgement, *Kexholm.* The King sent to his Assistance *Pontus de la Gardie* with some Thousand Men, who were very serviceable to the *Muscovites;* nevertheless they [the latter] made a great many Evasions, refusing to deliver up these places which they

1. Ivan IV Vasilyevich (1530–84), also known as Ivan the Terrible.
2. The interregnum of 1598–1613, between the death of Theodore (Feodor) Ivanovich, the last Rurik ruler of Russia, and the ascendancy of Mikhail I Feodorovich, the first Romanov, was known as the "time of troubles."
3. See X.10, pp. 388–89, above.

had promised before; wherefore the *Swedes* took them by Force, and thereby united *Carelia* and the rest of *Ingermanland* with the Kingdom of *Sweden*. How this *Basilius Zuski* was delivered up to the *Poles*, how the supposed [false] *Demetrius* was slain, and *Vladislaus* Prince of *Poland* made Duke of *Muscovy*, has been related before. <363>

§4. At last \A. 1613\ *Michael Fadorowitz* Son of the Patriarch *Theodore Mikitowitz* [Nikitich], [and] born of the Daughter of *John Basilowitz*[4] maintained himself in the Empire, who having concluded a Peace with *Sweden* and *Poland* restored tranquillity to the *Muscovites*. Him succeeded \A. 1645\ his Son *Alexius Michaelowitz*, who in the Year 1653, falling upon the *Poles*, took from them *Smolensko* and *Kiovia*, and committed great depredations in *Lithuania*. And having entred *Livonia* \A. 1656\ took *Dorpt*, *Kokenhusen* and several other places of less Note, but was obliged to raise the Siege of *Riga* with great Loss. And by vertue of a Peace made with *Swedeland*, was obliged to relinquish them all again. In the Year 1669, one *Stephen Ratzin* raised a Rebellion against him, and having brought under him *Casan* and *Astracan*, commited great depredations all over the Country, but being taken Prisoner, received his due reward, and the rest were reduced to their former obedience. And because some of the *Cosacks* had submitted themselves to his [Michaelowitz's] Protection, he was thereby engaged in a War with the *Turks*, wherein he got but little Advantage. He died in the [year] 1675. Him succeeded his Son *Theodore Alexowitz* a young and sickly Prince, of whom we can say nothing as yet.[5]

§5. Of the Qualifications [qualities] of the *Muscovites*, nothing very praise-worthy can be said. For among them there is no such Education [*Cultur*] as among most other *European* Nations [*Völckern*], Reading

Michael
Fadorowitz.

Alexius
Michaelowitz.

Theodore
Alexowitz.

The Genius of
this Nation.

---

4. Nikitich's wife, Xenia Shestova (d. 1631), was also known as Martha (Marfa) the nun, because she had been forced into a convent by Boris Godunov. Her relation to Ivan the Terrible is disputed.

5. Feodor (Theodore) III Alexeevich died in 1682 and was succeeded by his younger brother, Peter I the Great (1672–1725). Peter initially ruled together with his half-brother, Ivan, and assumed sole rule in 1696.

and Writing being the highest Degree of Learning among them, and the Learning of their Priests themselves does not go further than to be able to read a Chapter out of the Bible, or to read a piece of a Sermon [*Postille*]. They are also 'jealous' [mistrustful], cruel and bloody-minded; unsupportably proud in prosperity, and dejected and cowardly in adversity. Nevertheless they have such an Opinion of their own Abilities and Merits, that you can scarce ever pay them sufficient Respect. They are very fit for and cunning in 'the Trade of Usury' [haggling, *Schacherey*], but are of a servile Temper, and must be kept under by severity. At all sorts of Games and Sports their end is with blows and fighting; so Sticks and Whips are the usual instruments among them. They are of a strong <364> Constitution, able to undergo all sorts of |[Fatigues, even Famine and Thirst.]|[6] In Field-Fights and Sieges they are worth nothing, because they are soon brought into Confusion, and are themselves of Opinion, that other Nations are their Masters in this Point. But they defend a Fortress to the utmost, not only because they are very fit to undergo hardships and all sorts of misery, but also because they know it is present death to them if they return home after they have surrendred a Fortress by accord. Nevertheless, they do endeavour {daily} to bring their Soldiers under better Discipline, for which purpose, they make use of a great many *Scotch* and *German* Officers, who are to instruct them in all manner of Exercises as practiced among other *European* Nations. But they do not allow that the *Muscovites* should serve abroad and |[learn themselves the perfection of Military Arts and Exercises]|,[7] because the Grand Duke stands in fear, that if they should grow too knowing, they might be for making Innovations at home.

The Nature of the Country and Commodities. §6. The Territories of the present Grand Duke of *Muscovy* are of a very large extent, yet so, that a great many parts are meer Wildernesses scarce inhabited at all. The *Muscovites* have at home great plenty of 'Corn' [grain], 'Cattel' [livestock], all sorts of Game, Fish, Salt, Furrs and all other Necessaries. They have a great many Commodities fit

6. Rather: "hardship and labor, including cold and hunger."
7. Rather: "thereby improve themselves [*dadurch sich zu perfectioniren*]."

for exportation, especially, Furrs and their precious Sables, which are esteemed at a high Rate among their Neighbours, Salt-Fish, Cafiarr [caviar], Hides, Tallow, Wax, Honey, Pot-ashes, Soap, Hemp, and the like. But the Commodities which are imported to them are Silk Stuffs, Gold, Silver and Woollen Cloths [*Lacken*], Tapestry, Pearls and Precious Stones, Spices and Wines, but the latter not in any great Quantities; Tobaco is now a prohibited Commodity there. They keep it for a constant Custom in their way of Trade {with strangers}, not to buy with ready Money, but to exchange Commodities for Commodities, and it is against the Constitutions of [*verbotten ist*] *Muscovy,* to export any 'Coin' [money]. Their greatest Trade is at *Archangel* [Arkhangelsk], which way the *English* first found out in the Year 1553. But since that time the *Hollanders* and *Hamburgers* have followed their Example. Before that time, this Trade was car-<365>ried on by the way of *Narva* and *Reval* [Tallinn], but tho' this was the shorter way, yet did the foreign Merchants not care to be so much in subjection to the *Swedes* and *Danes.* There is also a considerable Trade carried on with the *Persians* {and Armenians} upon the River of *Wolga* by the way of *Astracan.*

§7. The Form of Government here is an absolute Monarchy; the Grand Duke, whom they call in their Native Language *Czar,* ||[being not tied up to any Laws or Rules]||,[8] unto whom his Subjects are obliged to pay Obedience without reserve [*ohne Maß und Ziel*], so that they are no more than Slaves, which also su[i]tes best with their natural Constitution. And ||[therefore this absolute Power of the Prince is a great addition to his Strength]||,[9] since he cannot only raise some Hundred Thousands of Men at the first Command, but also has vast Riches and prodigious Revenues. These do accrue to him, not only out of the Taxes and income of so vast a Country, but also because the Grand Duke himself has the monopoly of Sables, and if I am not much mistaken, also Farms out all publick Inns, Taverns and Ale-houses himself, which amounts to

Form of Government.

Strength of the Country.

8. Rather: "ruling according to his own discretion."
   9. Rather: "this absolute obedience of the subjects contributes much to the strength of the prince, which is great in any case."

a prodigious Revenue in a Country where the Nation is much addicted to drinking. He makes also his Presents to Foreign Princes and Ambassadours in Sables, but receives in lieu of them Gold and Silver. Besides this, it is a common Custom with him, to set a new Stamp upon Crown Pieces, and to oblige his Subjects to take them for double the value: From whence it cannot be supposed but that this Prince must lay up vast Treasures. *Muscovy* also enjoys this Advantage before other States, that it is not to be attack'd on the backside, because its Territories are on the {north-west, north, and} North-East side surrounded by a vast unnavigable Sea, and vast Wildernesses.

Neighbours of Muscovy. The Persians. §8. The Neighbours of *Muscovy* are on the Eastside, the *Persians*. These two States cannot hurt one another much, the *Caspian* Sea, 'unaccessible Countries' [inconvenient roads] and vast Wildernesses being their common Borders; wherefore it is not worth their while to extend their <366> Conquests upon one another {in these places}. But they may be

Tartars. serviceable to one another by making a Diversion to the *Turks*. The *Tartars* are troublesome Neighbours to the *Muscovites,* who make no account of Faith or Alliances, but make a Trade of Robbing and Plundering, against whom there is no Remedy, but to kill them as fast as one can; and this is not so easily to be done, because they are very nimble. The *Crim[ean]-Tartars* are the most mischievous to *Muscovy,* [and] to hinder their Incursions, the *Muscovites* are obliged to keep a considerable number of Horse upon the Frontiers, and they give them sometimes a Diversion, with the help of the *Donisque*[10] *Cosacks,* and the *Nagage* [Nağaybäk-] and *Calmuck-* [*Kalmyk-*] *Tartars*. If the *Muscovites* could maintain themselves in *Kiovia,* and a part of the *Ukraine,* it would serve them at once to bridle these Robbers, and for a Bulwark against the *Turks*. For the *Turks* do not immediately border upon *Muscovy,* but by the Country of the *Crim-Tartars,* who being Vassals of the *Turks,* they make use of them like their hunting Dogs. Wherefore it is of great consequence to *Muscovy,* that the *Turks* do not become Masters of

10. *Donischen,* referring to the Danube (Donau).

the whole *Ukraine,* since thereby they would be enabled with the help of the *Cosacks* and *Tartars* to do great mischief to *Muscovy.*

The[+] *Muscovites* ought to have a watchful Eye over the *Poles,* they being so situated, that they may do the greatest mischief to *Muscovy,* especially since the *Poles* are much better Souldiers than the *Muscovites* in the Field. But the *Muscovites* have at present a great Advantage against *Poland,* since they are possessed of *Smolensko, Severia* and *Kiovia,* which cover their Frontiers on that side. *Muscovy* need not fear any thing much from that side where it borders on *Sweden,* not only because it is able enough to defend it self there, if every thing is quiet at home, but also because the *Swedes* are not ambitious to make any more Conquests on that side, since to maintain such large and far distant Countries, would be more hurtful than profitable to their State. And the Kings of *Sweden* have of late shewed no great inclination to fight with the *Muscovites.* But, if the *Swedes* in conjunction with the *Poles* should attack the *Musco-*<367>*vites,* they would put them very hard to it; whereas also the *Muscovites* may prove very troublesome to *Swedeland* if they should join in conjunction with the Enemies of *Swedeland.* Nevertheless, the *Muscovites* ought not to make any great account upon an Alliance with *Denmark,* because they are far distant from one another, and therefore cannot revenge themselves upon one another; if one of them should put a Trick upon the other, and as soon as he has obtained his aim, leave the other in the lurch: Neither have the *Muscovites* hitherto appeared at any general Treaties. <368>

Poland.

Sweden.

Of the Spiritual Monarchy of Rome: *or, of the* Pope.[1]

§1. The 'Pope' [papacy, *Pabstthum*] may be considered two different ways: First, As far as the Articles which are taught by him and differ from [those of] other Christians, are agreeable or disagreeable with the Holy Scriptures, and consequently useful or prejudicial to Salvation, which Consideration we leave to Divines [*Theologis*]. Secondly, As far as the Pope is not only possess'd of a considerable Principality [*Staat*] in *Italy,* but also pretends to be the Sovereign and Supreme Head of Christendom, at least in Spiritual Matters, and in effect, exercises the said Power [*Gewalt*] in those States of *Europe* which profess themselves of the same Communion with him.

Politick Reflections upon Popedom.

This⁺ second Consideration 'belongs' [is very relevant] to the Politicians, for this spiritual Sovereignty does introduce great alterations, and interferes with the Supreme Civil Power [*hohe Bürgerliche Gewalt*]; nay, circumscribes and maims it. Wherefore since Religion has been so interwoven with the 'Civil' [political] Interest, it belongs to the perfection of an understanding Politician [*weltverständigen Mannes*], to be well instructed whence this Spiritual Monarchy had its Original, and by what means it hath so mightily increased and is preserved. From whence also will appear, of what nature are the chiefest Controversies now in vogue

1. Rather: "Of the Spiritual Monarchy of the [Papal] Chair at Rome." This phrasing makes clearer that Pufendorf's is a structural critique focusing on an institution rather than on a person.

among Christians in the Western Parts of the World, how far they are owing either to the various Interpretations of the Holy Scripture, or to worldly Interest [*zeitlichem Absehen*]; so that from thence a Wise Man may easily judge, whether at any time these Controversies are likely to be composed or not.[2] <369>

§2. Now to look back to the first beginning of things, we find, that before the Nativity of our Saviour the Inhabitants of the whole Universe, except the *Jews,* lived in gross Ignorance as to 'Spiritual' [divine] Affairs. For what was commonly taught concerning the Gods, was for

The Blindness of Heathens in Matters of Religion.

the most part involved in Fables and most extravagant absurdities. 'Tis true, some of the learned among them, have pretended to give some rational Account concerning the 'Nature of the Gods' [divine essence] and the State of the Soul; but all this in so imperfect and dubious {and unfounded} a manner, that they themselves remained very uncertain in the whole matter. They agreed almost all of them in this Point, that mankind ought to apply it self to the practice of Vertue, but they did not propose any other Fruits, but the Honour and Benefit which from thence did accrue to Civil Society. For what the Poets did give out concerning the rewards of Vertue and punishments of Vice after Death, was by these who pretended to be the wisest among them, look'd upon as Fables, invented to terrify and keep in awe the common People. The rest of the People lived at random, and what the Heathens called Religion, did not contain any Doctrine or certain Articles concerning the knowledge of Divine Matters. But the greatest part of their Religious

2. Pufendorf's consistent view was that differences among Protestants (particularly Lutherans and Calvinists) could be resolved through biblical interpretation, while those between Protestants and Catholics could not, because the latter supposedly cared more about worldly interests than truth. See *The Present State of Germany,* VIII.7–8, in Pufendorf (2007), pp. 224–37, and *The Divine Feudal Law,* §§8–10, in Pufendorf (2002b), pp. 24–31. Thomasius adds in *Politische Betrachtung,* in Pufendorf (1714), p. 4, that the "greatest utility" of Pufendorf's essay lay in its ability to reveal whether Lutheranism itself retained any remnants of papal "political tricks" (*Staatsstreichen*), and whether, and how, these could be eliminated or altered without disturbing the body politic [*das gemeine Wesen*]. All further references to Thomasius's commentary on Pufendorf will be to this work. Also see the Editor's Introduction above, p. xxxi.

Worship consisted in Sacrifices and Ceremonies {and certain holidays}, which tended more to Sports [*Spiel*] and Voluptuousness, than to the Contemplation of Divine Things. Wherefore the Heathen Religion did neither Edify in this Life, nor afford any Hopes or Comfort at the time of Death.

§3. At that time the *Jews* were the only Nation unto whom God had revealed the true Religion, which could lead Mankind in the way of Salvation {of souls}. Nevertheless, there was a vast difference betwixt that and the Christian Religion, not only because the Jewish Religion represented the Saviour of the World and the Fountain of Salvation in Types [*Fürbilde*] and Promises; whereas the Christian Religion comprehends the reality and accomplishment of the same; but also because the Jewish Religion was cloathed with a great many and those very burthensome Ceremonies: And 'some' [many] of them being ac-<370>commodated to the {regulation [*Polizey*] and} natural inclination of that Nation, they proved an obstacle to the general reception of that Religion by all Nations: This ceremonial part being like a Wall, whereby the *Jews* were separated from other Nations. The Constitution of the Jewish Religion.

'Tis true, all other Nations were not excluded from receiving Salvation through the Belief [*Vertrauen*] in the Saviour of the World who was to come. There were also some among the *Jews,* who were very careful, and applied themselves to the conversion of such {heathens} as they kept Correspondence withal. But it was not decreed by God Almighty to send all over the Earth at that time his Delegates or Apostles, instructed with peculiar Gifts to call all Nations to unite themselves with the Jewish 'Church' [religion]: And what was done by some 'private' [particular] Persons in converting of Infidels, was of no great consequence in comparison of the whole World.

Besides this, the Jewish Nation being at that time the selected People of God, adorned with great Prerogatives, and having the possession of the only Temple of God, was grown so proud, that the *Jews* despised all other Nations besides themselves. They being also obliged by the Institution of their Ceremonies, not to converse too familiarly upon several accounts [in many respects] with other Nations; this occasioned a mutual hatred betwixt the *Jews* and them, which was a main obstacle to the propagation of the Jewish Religion. Neither could other Nations easily digest this, that as often as they were to attend the solemn and publick divine Service, they were first to travel to *Jerusalem,* as if it were not in their power to build a Temple equal to the other near home. Besides this, such as received the Jewish Religion, were esteemed among them one degree below the Natives, which was the reason why very few could resolve for the Jewish Religion's sake, to be despised among them as Foreigners.

The Christian Religion is proper for all the world. §4. But the Christian Religion is not only much clearer, and also has other great Prerogatives above the Jewish, which Consideration we will leave to the Divines: But it is also freed from those Circumstances which were particular to the Jewish Religion, and endowed with all Qualifications requisite for an universal <371> Religion; wherefore every one is obliged [*schuldig sind*] to receive and embrace it, which deserves particularly to be remarked, that hereby we may investigate and penetrate to the very bottom, the propriety [*Eigenschafft*] and genius of the Christian Religion. For here is no particular place appointed by God Almighty for performing in publick the Divine Service, nor can any place claim a Prerogative before another, so that no Nation henceforward has any occasion to make exception [complain] about the remoteness of the Temple; but in all places you may lift up holy Hands unto him, no Temple in the World having any particular promise appertaining to it that God will sooner hear your Prayers in that than in another. No Nation has according to the Christian Religion, a precedency before another, whereby one may claim a Prerogative above the other. Here is no *Jew,* no *Greek,* no Bond nor Freeman, but they are all one in Jesus Christ.[3] Here is no particular Family or Tribe appointed by God for the publick administration of Divine Service as it was among the *Jews;* but none is excluded here, provided he be endowed with the necessary Qualifications. There is no Article in the Christian Religion, which

3. Galatians 3:28 and Colossians 3:11.

forbids us |[to cultivate with others either familiarity]|,[4] or to render to one another the Duties required from us by the Law of Nature.[5]

It[+] is purely and by it self considered, quite separated from all worldly Ends and Interests; yet is her Doctrine not in the least repugnant to, or alters Civil Society or Laws, as far as they are consonant to the Law of Nature [natürlichen Rechten], but it rather (tho' that is not her main intention) confirms the same. There is nothing to be found in the Christian Religion, which is destructive to the Ends of Civil Society, or which hinders us from living honestly, quietly and securely under the protection of Civil Magistrates, or from executing in every respect the highest Civil Power according to the Law of Nature, 'true' [sound, gesunden] Reason and the Necessities of the State, or from administring all Offices and performing such Duties without offending against the Rules of Christianity, as are requisite for the maintaining a State established according to the Law [Recht] of Nature.[6] The Christian Religion rather promotes all these things, expres[s]ly commanding us strictly to observe every Commandement <372> of the Law [Gesetz] of Nature, and especially those where no temporal punishment could be conveniently inflicted by the Civil 'Constitutions' [laws], and to perform our Duty with all Faithfulness and Zeal, as far as the same is consonant with Honesty [Erbarkeit] and the Law of Nature.

Wherefore[+] not any Philosophy or Religion whatsoever is in this point to be compared with the Christian Religion, which may be evident enough to all who will make a true comparison betwixt this and

Not contrary to Civil Government.

No other Religion or Philosophy comparable to it.

4. Rather: "to live with all humans as good friends."

5. Pufendorf thought that Christianity embodied the sociality principle central to his notion of natural law. See On the Law of Nature and of Nations, II.3.15.

6. Thomasius, pp. 16–17, says that this applies in both peace and war, and he refers to his father's dissertation against Machiavelli (Jacob Thomasius, Religione Christiana non minui fortitudinem bellicam, contra Nicolaum Machiavellum [Lipsiae: Wittigau, 1670]), which maintained that "the Christian religion does not make people incapable of martial courage" (Religionem Christianam non ineptos reddere ad fortitudinem bellicam). The same claim occurs in Pufendorf's dissertation "On the Agreement of True Politics with the Christian Religion" (De concordia verae politicae cum religione Christiana, Lund, 1673), §9, in Pufendorf (1675), pp. 561–68.

all the rest. And every body is therefore obliged [*verpflichtet*] as he hopes to answer for his Soul before God, not only to receive the Christian Religion, but also all Sovereigns and Magistrates [*jeder Regent*] ought for the above-mentioned reasons, and out of a Duty belonging to their Office, to introduce and maintain it. If it is objected, that the Effects of the Christian Religion are not so visible, 'nor' [and] that the Life and Conversation of a great many Christians is not different from that of the Heathens and *Turks;* it is to be observed, that this Fault is not to be imputed to the Christian 'Doctrine' [religion], but to the 'Inclinations' [wickedness, *Boßhaftigkeit*] of such as profess the name of Christians, but will not in earnest apply themselves to alter their evil Inclinations, and to live according to the wholesome Precepts of this Religion.

Concerning the outward Government of Religion.

§5. As what we have hitherto said, can scarce be denied by the more understanding sort, so there arises now a Question, *viz.* Whether, according to the Doctrine of the Christian Religion it is absolutely requisite, that the outward Direction <or Government> of the same be committed to another, besides him who has the supreme Civil Power in a State? or, which is much the same, Whether according to the Christian Doctrine, it be necessary that the outward Government of it be lodged with the whole Body, or one of the Clergy in particular[, who is] {completely} independent of the Supreme Magistrate? Or, whether there ought to be but one Sovereign Administrator [*Director*] of the Christian Religion, on whom all other Christian States ought to depend in this Point? Or, which some take for the same thing, whether every State ought to be governed according to its own 'Constitutions' [affairs, *Angelegenheit*] and Interest? Or whether all other States are obliged to be <373> Slaves to one, and to promote the Interest of that one, with the Detriment and Ruin of their own.[7]

What is meant by the external Government of Religion.

By⁺ the outward Direction or Government of the Christian Religion, we understand the Power of constituting certain Persons for the exercising of the publick Divine Service, and the supreme {supervision

7. Thus, the relevance of this essay to the *Introduction* as a whole, which articulates the interests of states.

and} Jurisdiction over their Persons; the supreme Administration and Direction [*Inspection*] of such Possessions as are dedicated to Religious Services. The Power of making Laws for the outward 'maintenance' [welfare, *Wohlstand*] of Religion, and the 'determining' [supreme adjudication] of such Differences as may arise among the Clergy under what pretext soever it may be, and such like.[8] We make a 'great difference' [distinction] betwixt the outward Direction of Religious Affairs and betwixt the Ministry of the Church, which consists in teaching, preaching and administring of the Sacraments, all which, doubtless belong only unto the Clergy.[9]

This Question also is to be understood of a Church already planted and established {*de Ecclesia jam plantata & constituta, non de adhuc constituenda & plantanda*}, not of a Church that is {still} to be planted and established. For since the Christian 'Religion' [doctrine] owed its Original to Divine {special} Revelation, no humane Power could pretend to have any Direction in the same, before this Doctrine was thoroughly proposed and taught by such as had an immediate Authority for so doing from God Almighty. For when our Saviour after his Resurrection did send his Disciples as Delegates and Apostles throughout the whole World, to publish and introduce the Christian Religion, they received their Commission for Preaching every where not from the supreme Civil Magistrates, but from God himself: wherefore Kings as well as the common People were obliged to acknowledge them as immediate Messengers of God, and obediently to submit themselves to their Doctrine; and it would be next to an absurdity if any one should pretend to a Direction in such Matters, as he was not instructed in before. From whence arises {also} this Consequence, that what has been said is to be understood of such Sovereigns or supreme Magistrates as themselves profess the true Christian Religion, but not of those who are Infidels or erroneous in the chief Articles of the Christian 'Faith' [doctrine]. For to

8. See *Of the Nature and Qualification of Religion*, §§6–7, in Pufendorf (2002c), pp. 18–21.

9. Thomasius, p. 21, qualifies by noting that this is only "according to rules of decorum" (*ex regulis decori*), which make it inappropriate (*es nicht wohl schicket*) to mix the personae of ruler and teacher.

commit the Direction of Religion to the latter, would be to make the
Wolf a Shepherd.[10] <374>

The Consideration of this Question according to the nature of Religion in general.

§6. This Question may be considered in three several ways: First,
Whether this Necessity arises from the Nature of each Religion in
general? Or, Secondly, Whether it arises from the Genius of the Christian Religion in particular? Or, Thirdly, Whether the same is imposed
upon us by Divine Institution or the 'particular' [positive] Command
of God? That it should proceed from the natural Constitution of Religion in general, I am in no ways able to find out. For Reason does
not tell me, that if I intend to serve God, I must of necessity make a
division in the State, and thereby introduce two different Powers independent of one another. The dismembring of the supreme Power,
or such a double-headed Sovereignty in a State, administers continual
Fuel, which at last breaks out into Jealousies, Divisions, and intestine
Commotions.[11] On the other hand, it is in no ways contrary to Reason
to serve God, and at the same time leave the supreme Direction of
the outward Matters belonging to Divine Service, to such as have the
supreme Power in the State; if we suppose that those who have the
supreme Power in their Hands, will not impose any thing upon their
Subjects which is false or erroneous.

It cannot be denied, that as every one is bound [*schuldig ist*] by the
Law of Nature to serve God; {so} also is it at the same time in his Power
[*Macht*] to perform the outward Ceremonies[12] in such a manner as he
believes they are most pleasing to God. But after Civil Societies [*Gesell-
schaften*] were instituted, that same Power is thereby devolved to those
who have the supreme Administration of Affairs in a Civil Society. And

10. Thomasius, pp. 24–25, disagrees with this restriction and makes fewer religious demands of a civil ruler. See note 29, p. 431, below.
11. On double-headed sovereignty in a state, see note 20, p. 343, above. Thomasius, p. 27, notes how the distinction between governance of worldly and of spiritual
matters played into the hands of the pope, who knew how to turn the former into
the latter and thus wielded both kinds of authority. Supposedly, this mistake was
retained in Protestantism.
12. Literally: "to arrange the outward symbols [*Zeichen*] of divine service."

the most antient Fathers [*Haußvätter*] who did not live under any 'regulated Government' [*Republic*], exercised this Power in their Families, which used to be transferred to the Eldest Son, as *hereditas eximia* (or a hereditary Prerogative) if the Brothers, after the Father's death, did resolve {still} to live together in one Community [*Gemeinschaft*]. But when afterwards 'Civil Societies' [*Republicquen*] were instituted, the same Power was transferred to the Heads of these Societies, and that out of a weighty Consideration: For if every one had been left to his free Choice in this Point, the various and different Ceremonies in the Divine Service[13] must needs have introduced Confusions, {contempt, hatred,} Divisions and <375> intestine Commotions.[14] And tho' by the *Jews* the publick Ministry was hereditary to one particular Family, yet the inspection and supreme Direction {of priests} was among them reserved to those who had the supreme Civil Power in their Hands, as the same is practiced among most other Nations.

§7. Neither can any Reason be given why the Christian Religion is particularly so qualified, as to imply a necessity, that the abovementioned Direction should be committed to any other than the supreme Magistrates [*Obrigkeit*], tho' it contains something more {about the service of God} than is taught us by the Light of Nature; since we suppose that by vertue of this {external} directive Power, they ought not to impose any thing upon us contrary to the Word of God, nor be a hinderance to the Priests in performing 'the Ministry' [their divinely established office] according to the Ordinances of God in the Holy Scriptures. Neither can I find out any Reason, why the supreme Magistrates should want means duly to qualify themselves for this Administration or Direction. At least, they may let this Direction be exercised under their Author-

According to the Nature of the Christian Religion in particular.

13. Pufendorf speaks throughout not of "ceremonies" but of the inner and outer "service" (*Dienst*) of God.

14. Thomasius, pp. 29–30, grants that this may result if individuals devise their own religious forms, but he denies that such inconveniences necessarily arise from there being a diversity of religious groups in society, as long as they are not allowed (by the civil authority) to vilify and persecute one another.

ity by such as have acquired 'sufficient' [special] abilities for the same: In like manner as Sovereigns exercise their Power by others in Civil Affairs,[15] so the Power of making Laws was never denied to appertain to Sovereigns, tho' it is certain that a {proper} Doctor or Professor of the Law, ought to be better instructed in them than is required from a King. For both in these and other Matters, Sovereigns ought to act with the Advice of such as have applied themselves th[o]roughly to such Affairs. And as it is against the Interest of a Good and Wise King, if this 'Power' [*Direction*] be not well exercised, so it is both his Duty and Interest to see the administration of Religious Matters well performed. For the more zealous and earnest he is in maintaining the Christian Religion, the 'more obedient and better qualified' [better and more pliant] his Subjects are likely to be, and he may the better hope for the Blessing of God Almighty. Neither can any thing be alledged why God Almighty should not as well afford his Assistance to a Christian and Orthodox [*rechtgläubigen*] Sovereign as to any other, to perform this Government {well and} praise worthily.

Lastly, because the Christian Religion does not in any other <376> way derogate from Civil Ordinances and Laws, or from the Power of Civil Magistrates [*hohen Obrigkeit*] as far as they are founded upon the Law of Nature; so it is not to be supposed that it disagrees from this in this one Point {alone}, except a positive Command of God can be alledged for the proof of this Assertion. Whether there be such a Command in the Holy Scriptures, which expresly forbids Sovereigns to intermeddle with this Direction, and allows the same to others in the highest degree of Sovereignty without any dependency [on civil author-ity] at all, those are obliged to prove, who endeavour to maintain this Assertion. In the mean while we will inquire into the first Occasion, and by what 'degrees' [steps] this 'Ecclesiastical Monarchy' [spiritual sovereignty] was established in the Western Churches.

15. More literally: ". . . just as they allow other parts of the supreme sovereignty to be administered under their direction and supervision." On the parts of supreme sovereignty and the need to keep them unified, see *On the Law of Nature and of Nations*, VII.4, especially §§10–12.

§8. The Apostles therefore having after the Ascension of our Saviour, according to the Instructions received from his own Mouth, begun to spread the Doctrine of the Christian Religion in far distant Countries, met with great approbation in a short time, both among the *Jews* and other Nations [*sic*]; but more especially among the Common People, which having hitherto lived in gross Ignorance and in a miserable Estate, very joyfully received this Doctrine, which enlightened and comforted them in the miseries of this Life. The Apostles also themselves, who were of mean Extraction and of no great Authority [standing, *Stand*], used to converse most among this sort of People, as having the most easie access to them as their equals. But Men of Quality and Learning {and statesmen} did scarce at first think it worth their while to apply themselves diligently to search into the bottom of this Religion, and very few of them would profess it.

If⁺ we may inquire into the Reasons why it was the pleasure of the Wise God to choose this way of planting the Christian Religion, it seems very probable, that God was not pleased to introduce the Christian Religion by the Power and Authority [esteem, *Ansehen*] of Civil Magistrates, nor by the Assistance of Learned Men, 'because' [so that] it might not be deemed hereafter a 'State Trick' [political invention], or a Philosophical Speculation; but that whenever a due comparison might be made betwixt the slender beginnings and prodigious encrease of this Religion, the World might from <377> thence conclude, that the whole was something above humane Power. And because the Learned had proved unsuccessful with all their subtilties in their Discoveries concerning Divine Matters;[16] and that *Socrates* and some others who were sensible of the vanity of the commonly received Superstitions, and had condemned them as such, had not been able to abolish those, and in lieu thereof, to introduce a better Religion;[17] God Almighty was willing to convince the World of the Vanity of worldly Wisdom, and to

Side notes:

First propagation of the Christian Religion.

The Methods of God in Establishing the Christian Religion.

16. They had found out "little that is worthwhile" in this respect. Thomasius, p. 35, speaks here of *praejudicium autoritatis:* their interest in maintaining their authority, which conflicts with the search for truth.

17. Plato's Socrates criticizes poetic representations of the gods in *Republic,* Book II.

shew, how easie it was for him to effect this great Work by the means, even of poor Fishermen.

Besides this, the Doctrine of the Apostles seemed to be full of absurdity to the Philosophers and Politicians [*weltklugen Leuten*], the same being founded upon, and begun with Jesus who was crucified. For it appeared very strange to them that the Apostles should acknowledge him for the Son of God and their Saviour, who was of a hated and despised Nation, who having lived without any great 'Splendour' [esteem], or performed any great Heroic Actions; had besides this, not made himself Famous throughout the World by long 'Study' [teaching] or Preaching, but had in his younger years suffered a most infamous Death. And this is [also] the reason why the Jesuites, when they teach the 'Christian Religion' [Gospel] among the refined *Chineses,* do not begin with the <Doctrine of the> Passion of Christ; but argue first with them out of the Principles of natural Religion, and so at last come about to this Article of the Christian Faith. But whether these Fathers by this method are likely to be more successful than the Apostles I will not determine here. It may also be alledged, that God was pleased to deliver the common People among the Heathens, before great Men, out of their misery and darkness; because the first were 'seduced' [misled] by the latter, and upheld in their Superstition; for these, tho' they were sensible of the {deception and} Vanity of the Pagan Religion, yet did not do their utmost endeavours to search after a better. Wherefore God Almighty by first drawing away the 'common People' [rabble, *Pöbel*] from Paganism, did undermine the whole Structure [*dieser Machine*], which was {then} forced to fall of it self. Since the simplicity and credulity of the common People were the Foundation Stones of the Pagan Religion. <378>

Why the meanest first converted.

§9. 'The Christian Doctrine' [Christendom] therefore having been most of all, at first, spread abroad among the common People, as I have said before, it was grievously oppressed and persecuted afterwards by the *Roman* Emperours; for in the Territories of the *Roman* Empire it had its first beginning and chief increase. One of the main occasions of these Persecutions was their Ignorance of the true nature {and foundation} of this new Religion, or what was the main end of it; since they

Persecution of the first Church.

saw the number of the Christians daily encrease, who all despised the Pagan Religion. The Emperours thought it below their high Station to make a due enquiry into <the Foundation of> this Doctrine, and there were very few among the first Christians that were fitly qualified to represent their Doctrine in 'due' [plausible, *scheinbarer*] form to People of Quality. These therefore used to be led away by the false sugges- The tions of the Enemies of the Christians, who insinuated to them, that Calumnies the Christians in their nocturnal Assemblies, did practise all sorts of Primitive against the Debaucheries much after the manner as formerly used to be practiced Christians. at the Festivals of *Bacchus,* or else that they were then Plotting against the State.

There[+] were also not a few among the *Romans,* who being averse to The Politick any Innovation whatsoever, were of Opinion, that since the *Roman* Em- Reasons of the Romans pire had stood in a flourishing Condition several Ages past under the against it. antient Religion, the same ought not to be abrogated; especially, they did think it in no ways becoming [for] the 'common People' [rabble] to pretend to an Innovation and to more Wisdom than their Sovereigns.[18] The Christians also having {made} among themselves |[a certain Form of Ecclesiastical Government]|,[19] this rendred them suspected to the *Roman*[s], who looked upon them as such that were for setting up a Faction against the State, and erecting a new Society [state, *Staat*] in it, and so to divide the Empire, and at last make themselves Masters of it: Some also there were, who perceiving, that the more the numbers of the Christians increased, the less frequented were the Temples of the Heathens, and that the *Roman* Empire began to decline and received great shocks; they perswaded themselves that these Misfortunes befel them, because those Gods through whose Assistance the *Roman* Em-

18. Pufendorf defended innovation (*novatio*) in philosophy but opposed it in religion—except in this instance. He was especially wary of innovation by the rabble and of religious innovations that produced political instability. See IV.26–28, pp. 169–75, above, on the English religious wars, and passim below. Moreover, he responded to charges of being an innovator himself, in his autobiographical *Apologia pro se et suo libro* (1674), §4, p. 13, and in *Specimen controversiarum circa ius naturale ipsi nuper motarum* (1677), chap. 2: "De novitatibus philosophicis," pp. 128–33, both in Pufendorf (2002a).

19. Rather: "some rules [*Verfassung*] concerning the practice of their religion."

pire arrived to <379> the Pinacle of its Grandeur, were now despised among them, and therefore looked upon the Christians as an {evil} Atheistical Generation, endeavouring to over-turn the very Foundations of Religion.

And because the Christians refused to adore the Idols, notwithstanding the Emperours Commands, and suffered the most prodigious Tortures and Death with constancy and even Joy; they were treated like a perverse and obstinate[20] sort of People by the *Romans,* who encreased their Cruelties to maintain their Authority [*Ansehen*] against them. But no sufficient Reasons can be alledged for the justification of these Persecutions against the Christians, which ought to be considered no otherwise than unlawful [*unrechtmässige*] Tyrannies, and pernicious Abuses of the supreme Civil Power. For their Subjects had received this Religion according to the express Command of God, which could nor ought not to be opposed by the Civil Power; the Magistrates as well as the Subjects being obliged [*schuldig*] to receive it, except they would grosly sin <against God Almighty>. Neither could their Ignorance serve them for an excuse, since this being a new 'Doctrine' [matter, *Sache*], it was their Duty to take due information concerning the same, before they had sent the Innocent 'Christians' [people] to Execution, only, because they refused to obey the Commands of their Sovereigns, which 'ought' [could] not to oblige them to Obedience in this Point. For no body ought to give Sentence of Death against any one before he is duly informed concerning the nature of the Crime, he is accused of.[21]

20. Thomasius, pp. 43–44, notes that obstinacy (*Halsstarrigkeit, pertinacia*) became part of later heresy (*Ketzerey*) accusations that sought to make heresy a punishable (civil) crime—a practice which he himself opposed in his disputation "Is Heresy a Punishable Crime?" (*An haeresis sit crimen?* 1697), in Thomasius (2007), pp. 148–206.

21. There is a general tension in Pufendorf between the claims of civil authority and, as here, the claims of conscience or religion. He is ultimately forced to prefer the claims of conscience, but given the duty of civil authorities to maintain social order, he seeks to confine it as narrowly as possible by means of other assumptions and requirements, for both rulers and subjects. See *On the Law of Nature and of Nations,* VIII.1.6; and *Of the Nature and Qualification of Religion,* §6, in Pufendorf (2002c), pp. 18–19; §48, p. 104; §52, pp. 112–14; and "Animadversions . . . upon . . . Adrian Houtuyn" (the *Anhang* or Appendix to the previous work), pp. 123–40.

§10. And because the Sovereigns [*Obrigkeit*] did at first not concern themselves for the welfare of the Christian Religion, the Christians therefore did without their assistance constitute |[a Ministry and the outward Church Government]|[22] among themselves, which was maintained among them as well as it could. For this is common to all Societies [*Gesellschaften*] which are instituted {in a state} without the {knowledge or} consent of the Supream Magistrate, that the Members thereof are forced to agree among themselves, which way to order {and regulate} their Affairs best, and to Constitute certain Rules [*Ordnungnen*], and Governours [*Directores*] for the management of the Societies: Else, according to the Rules of Policy [*Politic*], founded upon the Law [*Recht*] of Nature, the outward Government of Reli-<380>gion belongs to the Sovereigns.[23] But because the Magistrates would not perform their 'duty' [office] at that time, the Christians were obliged to Constitute Ministers [*Kirchen-Diener*] of their own accord, who received their maintainance from the Charity of good 'Christians' [people].

And if any Errors did arise, or other matters happened of such consequence, that the same could not be decided by one assembly [*Gemeine*],[24] several of these Assemblies used to consult among themselves concerning the matter in question, or leave the determination to an Assembly [meeting, *Zusammenkunft*] of such Ministers as were next at hand [nearby]. Tho it is certainly else not to be allowed in a State, that private persons should Constitute a Society among themselves, consisting especially of a considerable number; yet the Assemblies [*Gemeinen*] and Synods of the antient Christians are not therefore to be deemed unlawful Meetings [*Collegia* und *Conventicula illicita*]; since their only aim was the exercise of their Religion, which being commanded them

The first Church Government.

22. Rather: "the divine service [*Gottesdienst*] and the external direction of churches [*der Kirchen*]." Pufendorf is thinking of separate churches or religious communities, not of the church in general.

23. See *On the Law of Nature and of Nations*, VII.4.8; *Of the Nature and Qualification of Religion*, §7, in Pufendorf (2002c), pp. 20–21, and §48, pp. 102–4. In contrast to Pufendorf, Thomasius, p. 47, insists that in this regard the law of nature does not distinguish rulers according to their belief or unbelief.

24. *Gemein[d]e*: a commune, community, or congregation; a "meeting" in the sense of nonconformist and Quaker congregations.

by God {himself}, ought not to have been opposed by any human 'Power' [statutes, *Satzungen*].

Neither is it reasonable, that because the Magistrates were careless both of their 'Duty' [office] and their own Salvation, the rest also who had knowledge of the 'true Religion' [right path], should lose the benefit of their Salvation; against which no Civil Power {can and} ought to extend its Jurisdiction [power, *Gewalt*]. And, as it is allowable for every body to defend himself with his own Strength and Weapons, if Magistrates either can or will not protect him: so, if a Sovereign will not do his Office [*das Ihrige*] as to the preservation of my Soul, I have as much more right [*Fug*] to take care of it without him, as the Soul is dearer to me than the Body; and as by the exercise of the True Religion [*rechten Gottesdienst*] my Fellow Subjects are less endangered, than by a violent defense of my own person; for no body by becoming a Subject in a Civil Society, does thereby renounce the priviledge of taking care for his Soul and Body.

Otherwise no doubt is to be made, that if it had been the Will of God to introduce the Christian Religion by the Conversion of the Emperours and Kings, these would with their Commands [*Edicta*] have |[assisted the Apostles in their Office]|,[25] thrown down the Temples of the Idols, abolished the Pagan 'Idolatry' [religious services], and would according to the instruction of the Apostles, have Constituted the outward |[Church Government]|,[26] and <381> maintained it afterwards. For it is evident enough, that this has been the manner of proceeding, as to this point[,] in 'other Countries' [several places], where the Christian Religion |[has been first introduced into the State, by the authority of their Sovereigns.]|[27]

What persuasions arise thence.

§11. Nevertheless because the first Christians were obliged, when the Magistrates failed in their Duty, |[to regulate and Constitute a Church

---

25. Rather: "seconded the sermons of the apostles."

26. Rather: "direction of the Christian religion."

27. Rather: "was accepted first by the state's rulers [rather than by the common people]." Thomasius, pp. 50–51, says that such examples prove nothing, and he opposes the suggested use of force by Christian rulers toward pagan religions.

Government]]²⁸ among themselves, this has occasioned the rise of several Errors, which are of no small consequence. For, some have from thence, endeavoured to make this inference, that the people {or the community [*Gemeine*]}, as they stand in opposition to Sovereignty, has an original and inherent Right to Elect Church Ministers [*Kirchen-Diener*]. Tis true a 'Minister' [priest] ought not to be obtruded upon an Assembly against their will, especially if they have a 'lawful exception' [substantial cause] against him; because he would edifie but little in his Station; nevertheless, it is not from hence to be concluded, that, because some Assemblies have been obliged to provide themselves with Ministers when the Magistrates did neglect their 'Duty' [office], therefore the same Right is ever since Originally in the People. For <without this supposition> an Assembly has as little right to call and Constitute a Church Minister, as to dispose of Publick Offices and Employments in the State. And if in some places the Common People or some others have such a Right, it is enjoyed either by connivance, or a concession from the Supreme Magistrate, whom we {always} suppose to be a Christian and Orthodox.²⁹

Some also have been endeavouring to draw from thence this Conclusion, *viz.* That the outward Church Government is {necessarily} separate and distinct from the Supreme Civil Power, and that it ought to be administred either by the whole Clergy, or else to depend absolutely [*souverainement*] on one single person of the Clergy; so that, according to this supposition, there must be in each Christian State two distinct Bodies independent of one another, one of which must be called the Ecclesiastick (*Ecclesia*) the other the Politick State (*Civitas*), and each of them to be Sovereign in its Government [*Direction*]. But, tho this has been made use of sometimes [*provisionaliter*], when Magistrates were quite negligent of their Duty, this <382> ought not to be drawn into Consequence, when Magistrates are ready, duely to execute their Office.

Neither does it follow, that the same power [*Macht*] which belonged

28. Rather: "to arrange religious services [*Gottesdienst*]."
29. Thomasius, p. 54, again disputes this final condition, noting that an unorthodox or nonbelieving ruler may appoint orthodox church officials. See note 10, p. 422, above.

to the Apostles at that time when the Church was first to be Established, is now devolved to such Church Ministers as have not an immediate Vocation from God in the Established Church. For the Office of the Apostles was 'particular' [special], and very different from the {ordinary} Church Ministry [*Kirchen-Bedienung*]<, as it is exercised now adays>; in like manner as the outward Church Government [*Direction*] is very different from the Ministry. And as every 'lawful' [ordinary] Church Minister is therefore not immediately an Apostle, so the King is therefore not immediately a Priest. And tho the Christian Religion ows its Original to God, and is above human reason; nevertheless the Supreme Magistrate may be capable of having {supervision and} the outward direction over it, with the assistance of such persons as are best versed in such Affairs.

And, from what has been said, this Conclusion may be made: *viz.* That the practice of the Primitive Church as to this Point of the outward Church Government, is not to be made a perpetual and universal Rule of the Church Government in a State, which is under the Jurisdiction of a Christian and Orthodox Magistrate. For that practice was accommodated to the Circumstances of their Affairs then: But, where both the whole People and the Sovereign have received the Christian Religion, the case is quite different, and implies not any necessity that the State should thereby become a Body with two Heads.

Constantine could not quite alter the former State of the Church. §12. After *Constantine* the *Great* had embraced the Christian Faith, the Church began to get another 'Face' [form, *Gestalt*], the Sovereign being then fitly qualified to take upon him the outward Church Government. Nevertheless the said outward Church Government could not be so immediately and regularly ordered, as if from the first beginning the Sovereigns [*souveräne Herren*] had received the Christian Religion; For, there were a great many remnants left of the former provisional Church Government, which afterwards occasioned great abuses in the Western or Latin Church. For, it was scarce possible for these Emperours, who passed then but for Novices in the <383> Christian Religion, to make use at first of their Power in Ecclesiastical Matters, and to bridle the Authority of the Bishops and Clergy, that were very backward [loath] to part with it.[30] They were rather obliged to keep fair with them, and to make use of their assistance to Establish themselves in the Throne, since most of their Subjects being then become Christians paid a profound Veneration to their Priests. The first Christian Emperors also made use of 'several' [many] Ministers and Officers in their Courts, who were as yet Pagans; wherefore it seem'd not just [proper], that Matters concerning the outward Church Government,[31] should be determined by a Council [*Concessibus*], whereof some Members were Heathens.

This[+] was the reason why the 'Vocation' [nomination and appointment] of Bishops and other Ecclesiasticks [*Geistlichen*] was performed for the most part according to the Customs introduced before. And not only such Controversies as arose concerning certain Articles of Faith, but also <of> such as had a relation to {laws about} the outward 'Order and Government' [*Wohlstand und Ordnung*] of the Church, and all other differences of moment among the Clergy of the higher Rank [*vornehmen Geistlichen*] were brought before the Councils, or the Assemblies of the Clergy where these did pretend alone to have the right to Preside and to give their Votes; Tho it is certain that not only the right of calling them together belongs to the Sovereigns, who also for a considerable time have exercised that power; but also the direction and Presidentship of such Assemblies: whatever matter is to be debated there, <does at least belong to the Prince,> [and] if their Decrees shall pass afterwards for, and have the power of a Law or a definitive Sentence [*sententiae judicalis*] in the State.

'Indeed' [Of course,] the Supreme Magistrates, no more than the Clergy {as a whole} can pretend to a right of introducing new Articles of Faith, or of explaining the Scripture according to their own pleasure: Nevertheless, the whole Duty of a Christian[32] being contained in the

Of making Bishops.

Of Presiding in Councils.

---

30. Thomasius, p. 61, attributes this situation to Constantine's individual failures and political intentions, and he generally disputes Pufendorf's claim that non-Christian sovereigns are either unable or unsuited to govern church affairs.

31. Thomasius, p. 62, asserts that all government (*Direction, Regiment*) is external and rejects the distinction between external and internal church affairs, noting the pernicious consequences of Constantine's allowance of the latter to the bishops. See note 11, p. 422, above.

32. Rather: "all that a Christian is to believe and do."

<whole> Scriptures, which God has |[commanded to be published for the benefit of]|[33] Mankind, and not <to be> committed, like Sibylline Oracles, to the custody of certain Priests; and since others as well as the Clergy |[have the opportunity]|[34] to comprehend the Sense of the Holy Scripture, it seems not at all contrary to reason, that the Civil Magistrates should have <384> at least the Supreme direction [*Directorium*] of these Assemblies, where matters concerning the different interpretations of the Scripture are to be debated.[35]

From hence also this benefit will accrue to the Publick, that thereby the extravagant Heats and immoderate Passions, which are commonly obvious in these Disputes, may be moderated, matters may be debated with prudence [*vernünftig überwogen*], and not stretched too high out of a fondness of contradicting, nor that any one by malicious interpretation of his Words and Opinion may fall under Slanders and Censures, or the Excommunication be thundred out without necessity against the innocent. And because the first Christian Emperours did either neglect this their Right, or had no 'opportunity' [ability] of {appropriately} exercising it, this occasioned great confusion in some Councils: From hence also the Pope took an opportunity, after he had set himself above the Western Bishops and Councils themselves, to take upon him an Authority to decide Controversies <even> concerning Articles of Faith, to introduce such Canons or 'Ecclesiastical' [spiritual] Laws in the Church[es], as he thought most proper for his Interest and State, and by pretending to the highest Jurisdiction to exempt the Church from the Jurisdiction [*Gewalt*] of the Civil Magistrates: For when once this Opinion was established, that all these Matters did belong of right to the Clergy only, without having any respect to the Civil Power, the Pope did pretend to the same |[by the same Right, by which]|[36] he had set himself above the Clergy and the whole Church.

Abuses in the Councils. (margin note)

33. Rather: "promulgated to all."
34. Rather: "can and should use the means."
35. Thomasius, p. 68, notes that the settling of such controversies at a council by a plurality of votes is, precisely, to have the articles of faith, and the interpretation of Scripture, decided by human beings. Moreover, p. 69, the secular power does not exercise *Directorium* over such meetings if it merely enacts what the clergy alone has decided there.
36. Rather: "after."

§13. Besides this it was the Custom among the Antient Christians, that they very seldom pleaded their Causes, according to the admonition of *S. Paul*,[37] before the Pagan Judges: But, in case of differences among themselves, they used to refer the same to the decision of a Bishop, that by their Contests they might not give any occasion of Scandal to the Heathens, since it might seem unbecoming, that those who made profession of despising 'worldly Riches' [temporal things], should quarrel among themselves about the same. This Custom as it was very useful and praiseworthy at that time; so because it was not Abrogated, but rather confirmed afterwards by the <385> Christian Emperors, tho the Courts of Justice were then Governed by Christian Judges, the Bishops afterwards pretended to a formal [*ordentliche*] Jurisdiction, which did not only derogate from the Authority of Temporal Judges, but also the Bishops were thereby diverted from performing such Duties as properly belonged to their Office.

There was also another Custom among the first Christians, that if a scruple arose concerning nearness of Blood in Marriages, they used to take the Opinion of the Priests in this Case, and if any differences did arise betwixt married People, it used to be referred to the Arbitration of the Priests; who at the time also when the Nuptials were Celebrated, used to give them their Benediction and Pray with them. This, if in itself considered, very good beginning, furnish'd an occasion of great Abuses afterwards, the Pope having from hence taken a pretext to subject all Matrimonial Affairs, concerning Divorces, Nullities of Marriages, Successions, Inheritances, and the like, of the greatest Consequence, under his Jurisdiction [*Forum*], who, to render his pretensions the more plausible, did make Marriage a Sacrament.

Besides+ this, the first Christians were |[very desirous]|[38] to recommend their Religion to the Heathens by a Holy and Innocent Life, especially since some sort of Vices were not punishable according to the Pagan Laws. Wherefore in the Primitive Church, if any one had given a Publick Scandal by his vicious Life, a certain Church Penance was laid upon him, which at the utmost did amount to this, that he

Of the Episcopal Jurisdiction.

Concerning Marriages.

Concerning Excommunication.

37. 1 Corinthians 6:1–8.
38. Rather: "obliged and eager" (*solten und wolten*).

was excluded from the Communion of the Christians. Which Custom as it is not unreasonable, so it may be of good use in a Christian State,[39] provided the Civil Magistrate have the Supreme direction, and take care that such a Censure [*censura sacra*] be not abused out of obstinacy or private 'ends' [interest] and passion. Especially since these Censures have had such an {notable} influence upon Civil Societies, that in the Eighth Age [century] no body would Converse with any one that was Excommunicated. And this Power ought not to be given to the absolute disposal of any one {in a state}, |[except to the Sovereign]|,[40] if you will not divide the Sovereignty. But in what manner the Popes have afterwards abused this {ecclesiastical} <386> Censure, and extended it even to the Excommunication of Emperors, Kings, and whole Commonwealths [*Republiquen*] {who would not dance to their pipe}, and by forbidding the Publick Exercise of Divine Service, Absolving the Subjects from their Allegiance, and bestowing their Kingdoms upon others, have forced them to a compliance {much} against their own Interest, is sufficiently known out of History. Yet in the Eastern Empire these Abuses did not grow up to the same height, for the Emperors at *Constantinople* did at least so far maintain their Authority against the Clergy, that they [the latter] durst not pretend to dominere over them. Besides that the Eastern Bishops wanted [lacked] an opportunity to set themselves one above the other, because the Bishop at *Constantinople* had no other Prerogative allowed him, but Precedency of Rank above the others without [outside] his Diocess, but not any Jurisdiction.

The Origin of the Authority of the Popes. §14. But in the Western parts the Church afterwards took quite another Face, since the Bishop of *Rome* had 'projected' [concocted] a peculiar sort of a 'Monarchy' [sovereignty], which 'by degrees' [over time] he brought to perfection, and [which] has not had its parallel ever since the memory of mankind, it being founded upon quite other Principles, and upheld by very different means from other States.

39. In German: "unter Christlicher Obrigkeit."
40. Rather: "without the sovereign's direction."

The more influence this 'Monarchy' [sovereignty] has had for several hundred years together upon the States and Affairs of *Europe,* and has been maintained with great Zeal by one, and opposed by the other party, the more it will be worth our while, to dive into the first Origin and Constitution of it, and to alledge some reason, why in the last Age [century] this 'Monarchy' [sovereignty] was reduced to a tottering condition, but has recollected its vigour in ours. From whence a 'wise' [reasonable] Man also may be able to judge what success may be hoped for from the Projects of those, who are for reconciling the differences betwixt the Protestants and Papists.[41] Wherefore, it may be said, that towards the increase of this 'Monarchy' [sovereignty] {in the Occident}, so pernicious to the Supreme Civil Power, has not a little contributed, tho afar off, the Barbarity and ignorance,[42] which, after the decay of the *Roman* Empire, did spread itself over the Western parts. For 'bad' [counterfeit] Wares are best vented in the dark, or at least by a dim light: And an ignorant person is sooner pre-<387>vailed upon to believe ridiculous Stories than a <wise> Man versed in all sorts of {rational} Sciences.

Barbarity and Ignorance contributed to it.

There[+] were several causes, which promoted this barbarity, which did degenerate afterwards into the worst sort of pedantry, (whereas the former Age had been 'sufficiently instructed with learned Men' [fairly learned].) One of the principal ones was the Invasion made upon the Western Provinces of the *Roman* Empire by those Nations [*Völcker*], who tho sufficiently Brave, were ignorant of Learning; which occasioned for one or two Ages after great {ruin and constant} Changes in the Government, bloody Wars, horrible disorders, and all sorts of mis-

The Causes of this ignorance.

41. The Catholic bishop Christopher Royas de Spinola (1626–95), Gottfried Wilhelm Leibniz (1646–1716), and the Lutheran Georg Calixt (1586–1656) and his Helmstedt syncretism, which Pufendorf considered naive. In the Preface to *Basilii Hyperetae,* in Pufendorf (1679), Pufendorf referred to the "simplistic" and "harmful" thoughts of "untimely peacemakers" in religion, who only undermined the Protestant cause against Catholics. His critique of syncretism was also expressed in a letter to Adam Rechenberg (December 16, 1690), in Pufendorf (1996), #197, p. 300, which refers to the "crazy proposal" of Calixt, who does not see that reconciliation with Catholics is "not practicable" at that time. See §40, pp. 514–16, below.
42. In German: "Verdunckelung der guten Wissenschaften."

eries in the Empire. And Learning being the product of Peace and Prosperity, it is little regarded in times of War, or during the Distractions
of a State; since then there is but little leisure time given for the use of
Books. The Schools are commonly destroyed, and the Teachers obliged
to make shift, where best they can, a 'Musquet' [holster] being at such
times of more use than a School Satchel. The {poor} School-Masters
especially are forced to shut up Shop at such times, if the victorious
Enemy is ignorant of Learning, and makes no account of Books.

There are also some who affirm that the Clergy was accessary to
this barbarism. For, because the Philosophers had under the Reigns of
the Pagan Emperours proved very mischievous to them, and afterward
under the Christian Emperours continued to oppose themselves against
the Clergymen <especially>, these had conceived such a hatred against
Philosophy, and against all such as professed it, that they not only in-
fused the same into their Auditors, but also removed out of the Schools
and took from the young Students, who were committed to their care,
the Pagan Authors, under pretence that they might otherwise be again
infected with the erroneous Principles of the Pagans, and that it could
not but be sinful for Christians to read such Books as were filled every where with the names of the Pagan-Idols, which they would not

S. Hierom's   have as much as named by Christians. They related a Story concerning
Dream.   S. *Hierom*[43] how that he was whipped in a Vision with Rods {by Satan},
because he used frequently to Read the Works of *Cicero;* and about the
year 400. after the Birth of our Saviour, the Council of *Carthage* forbid
[forbade] the Bishops <388> the reading of Pagan Authors. And Learning [*studia*] being in those miserable times become almost useless except
to those who intended to profess Divinity, and the remnants of Learning being lodged therefore {only} among the Clergy, the main Institution in the Schools {which were ruined in any case} was only directed
for that Purpose, and the rest of the young Disciples [*studiosi*] were not
very forward to dive much into the secrets of Antient Learning. And
that Ignorance and Barbarism have greatly promoted the establishment
of 'Popery' [the papacy] is evident enough to those, who will consider

43. St. Jerome (ca. 342–410).

that in a learned Age those Decretals [*Epistolas Decretales*]⁴⁴ which are ascribed to the first Popes, could never have passed Muster [been considered genuine]; which nevertheless have been made use of to persuade the People that the Bishops of *Rome* have exercised an Authority from the very beginning of Christianity, to prescribe Laws 'of' [to] the {whole} Christian World.

But⁺ when afterwards the times proved more favourable in *Europe*, and the Popes perceived that some [*die* Ingenia] among the most considerable Nations [*sic*] of *Europe* could not be longer kept in a gross Ignorance, they introduced into the Schools, over which they had assumed the Supreme Direction, the most miserable sort of Pedantry, which is also maintained by their Creatures with great earnestness in their Schools to this very day. But above all the rest, it seems that the ignorance of the true Principles of Policy [*der rechten gründlichen Politic*], has had a main stroke in laying the Foundation of Popery, for want of which they [the people] were not then duely instructed concerning the |[Foundation, Nature, and Perfection]|⁴⁵ of the Supreme Civil Power, and {among other things} that no State could be esteemed 'well Established' [perfect], where the Supreme Civil Power was either divided or diminished. And the *Grecian* and *Roman* Politicians themselves had divulged most pernicious Doctrines concerning the division and mixture of the Supreme Power, whereby they had enamoured the People with an Aristocratical or Democratical sort of Government, but infused into them such a hatred against Monarchy, that it was a common Maxim among them, that the more they could 'incroach upon the Authority' [tie the hands] of the 'Prince' [monarch], the more it must turn to the advantage of the State. In this pernicious Opinion a great many were confirmed by the 'Tyrannical proceedings' [violent rule] of the <389> Emperours, who were mortally hated by most of their Subjects. It was

The Pedantry introduced into the Schools.

The Greek and Roman Politicians prejudicial to Monarchy.

---

44. Decretals were pontifical letters issued in response to specific inquiries, and distinguished from the canons issued by church councils. They were collected in the Middle Ages and constituted an important part of canon law. See §22, note 83, p. 458, below.

45. Rather: "origin, characteristics, and perfection of the power and rights [*Macht und Rechte*]."

therefore no great wonder, that at the time of this general 'Ignorance' [barbarism] the knowledge of true 'Policy' [politics] was not taught among the Christian Clergy, since it seem'd to them to be repugnant to their Profession.[46] From hence it was, that, when by degrees the Foundation of the 'Ecclesiastical' [spiritual] Sovereignty was laid, few did th[o]roughly understand {at the beginning, when it could have been interrupted} of what Consequence this undertaking was, and how prejudicial it would prove to the Supreme Civil Power, when ever it could be brought to perfection. And we see even to this day, that in those Schools, which are under the care of the Popish Clergy, the Principles of <true> 'Policy' [politics] are either {entirely} neglected, or at least so disfigured that they may not be hurtful to the Authority [*Herrschaft*] of the Popes, but rather serve to support it.

Why Rome was made the place of Residence of the Ecclesiastical Monarchy. §15. But the chief reason, why *Rome* was chosen for the place of Residence of the 'Ecclesiastical Monarchy' [spiritual sovereignty], seems to be, that this City had a particular Prerogative of being the Capital City of the *Roman* Empire, where the Christian Religion at first had its rise and increase. For what is related concerning S. *Peter's* Chair is nothing but a vain pretence, which may be easily seen from thence, that afterwards the Bishop of *Constantinople* had the next place assigned him after the Bishop of *Rome,* only because that City was then the {new} place of Residence of the Emperour, and new *Rome.* And when afterwards the Western *Roman* Empire was come to decay, and the City of *Rome* had lost its former lustre, the Bishop of *Constantinople* disputed the precedency with the *Roman* Bishop.

After the Persecutions, which the Christians had endured under the Pagan Emperours, were ceased, and they afterwards enjoyed their full Liberty, the Clergy began, under pretence of introducing a wholesome Order in the Church, to Establish {openly in the state [*Republic*]} a particular sort of 'Government' [state, *Staat*] or Hierarchy, the Bishops

---

46. It is only false religion and false politics that create problems. See Pufendorf's "On the Agreement of True Politics with the Christian Religion" (*De concordia verae politicae cum religione Christiana,* Lund, 1673), §1, which was also included in Pufendorf (1675), pp. 543–82; and *On the Law of Nature and of Nations,* VII.4.8.

having then {to this end} begun to claim a great Prerogative above the Priests. The Bishops also were made subordinate to one another, so that commonly the inspection over the Bishops in a certain Province was committed to the Bishop of the Capital [*vornehmsten*] City of the <390> same Province, who being then called Metropolitans,[47] did afterwards, *viz.* about the Eighth Century[,] most of them assume the name of Archbishops. Four of them were most eminent above all the rest, *viz.* The Archbishops of *Rome, Constantinople, Antioch* and *Alexandria,* these being then the four principal Cities of the *Roman* Empire; and the Archbishop of *Jerusalem* was added to their number, because of the Antient Holiness of that City. And tho the Emperor *Phocas,* out of a spite against the Patriarch of *Constantinople,* who would not approve of the Murther committed upon *Mauritius,* did grant the precedency to *Boniface* III. the then Bishop of *Rome,* who did thereupon take upon him the Title of Oecumenical Bishop;[48] yet this Prerogative did not extend any further than to bare Precedency, nor did imply any Power or Jurisdiction over the rest, which the other Patriarchs never acknowledged. And a considerable time before, when the Bishop of *Rome* pretended to put his Commands upon the Bishops of *Africa,* and for that purpose alledged a Canon of the Council of *Oliva* [*Nicea*], which was falsified, they sent him back a very smart Answer.

And+ in the whole business there is [are] no footsteps [traces] of a Divine Institution to be met withal, the same being purely Human, nor can any reason be alledged, why the Bishop of *Rome* possesses the first Rank, 'other than' [or] why he of *Antioch* has the third among them. And because one State cannot prescribe Laws to another, therefore if any Prerogatives have been granted to the Bishop of *Rome* by the *Roman* Emperors, or the Antient Councils, (which were nothing formerly but an Assembly of the Clergy of the *Roman* Empire,) the same do

Margin notes: Metropolitans. Patriarchs. Of the Popes Power.

---

47. That is, prefects of the "mother-city" (*metropolis*).

48. Flavius Phocas was Byzantine emperor during 602–10, after toppling Flavius Mauricius Tiberius (r. 582–602). He was close to Boniface III (pope from February to November 607) while the latter was nuntio at Constantinople, and later issued for him a decree that the Roman pope, rather than the patriarch of Constantinople, was to be regarded as "universal bishop" of the Catholic church.

not oblige any other State, nor can they extend beyond the Bounds and Jurisdiction of the antient *Roman* Empire. But if we put the Case that some Christian <Princes or> States have afterwards allowed to the Pope a certain power over the Church in their Dominions, this was either done because they either understood not ||[the true nature of this Power]|,[49] or because they were deceived by the Popes. In the first Case the same is to be deemed nothing else but a <Treaty or> Alliance {of one or other state} with the Pope, the better to Administer the 'Church' [spiritual] Affairs with the <391> Pope's Direction. Such a Treaty or Alliance [*foedus*] as it Originally proceeds from the Consent of that State; so the same may be Annulled again, in the same manner as other Alliances are, whenever it proves prejudicial to the State, or the Pope begins to abuse the Authority [*Gewalt*] granted him by the State. But if the Pope has either by Fraud or 'Imposition' [error, *Irrthum*] obtained his Power [*Gewalt*] over other States, these so ||[misguided and thus surprised]|[50] States, have a right [*befugt*], as soon as they have discovered the Fraud, and are convinced of their Error, to shake off such an unjust Usurpation, and besides may demand satisfaction for the dammages sustained by these impostures.

Further Increase of the Ecclesiastical Sovereignty. §16. Neither could the Bishops of *Rome* extend their Power over the Western parts all at once, but it was introduced from time to time, by degrees[51] and by various Artifices, and under several pretences. For, when they had once fastened their 'Paws' [claws], they did not retreat till they had obtained their pretensions, tho they were several times denied admittance. They did very wisely take hold of that opportunity which presented itself, and was the chiefest of all in my judgment, What contributed to it. when the Emperors began to choose other places of Residence besides *Rome,* since by their constant presence there they might easily have kept under the ambitious designs of the Bishops. For the Bishops of *Constantinople,* who questionless were no less proud and 'ambitious'

49. Rather: "on what foundation his pretended power actually rested."
50. Rather: "deceived and erring."
51. According to Thomasius, pp. 94–95, the two most important steps were the ascendancy of clerics over the laity and the ascendancy of bishops over other clergy.

[conceited] than those of *Rome,* could never gain this Point. The next thing which mainly contributed to this Power, was, that afterwards the Western Empire was divided into several new Kingdoms, erected by barbarous and Pagan Nations [*Völckern*]; and these having been converted to the Christian Faith with the assistance of the *Romish* Church, thought themselves obliged to pay to her a profound respect, and to honor her as the most antient and the principal of the Western parts.

To⁺ recite all the particulars here is not for our purpose, it will be sufficient to touch upon some of the main Points: it is therefore to be remarked, that since the Fifth Century the Bishops which lived on this side of the *Alpes* used to go to *Rome* to visit the Sepulchres of S. *Peter* and S. *Paul* out of a Superstition or a Devo-<392>tion {that became} very common in those days, or because they thereby intended to testifie their firm adherency to the Christian Faith. This voluntary Devotion was afterwards by degrees changed into a necessity, and such as neglected it, used to receive severe rebukes. From hence it was easie for the Popes afterwards to pretend that the Bishops ought to 'receive' [request] their Confirmation from *Rome.* Some other Bishops and Churches also, that were Novices in comparison of the antient *Roman* Church used to refer themselves to, and ask the advice of the Church of *Rome* concerning some Matters of great Consequence, and the true use and interpretation of the Canons.[52] And when they once perceived at *Rome* that their answers were taken as decisions, they began to send their Decrees before they were demanded, under pretence that *Rome* being the first Seat of 'the Christian Bishops' [Christianity] it ought to take effectual care that the Canons and Ecclesiastical Laws were duely put in Execution. Under the same pretence they made themselves immediate Judges over the Differences arisen betwixt the Bishops, and incroaching upon the Right and Jurisdiction of the Metropolitans, used to depose such Bishops, as according to their Opinion had not a right Ordination; or such as were accused of some enormous Crimes, they obliged to appear before them at *Rome* to defend their Cause. And if there were

The Popes Confirmation of Bishops.

52. Canons were regulations and decrees issued by church councils. See note 44, p. 439, above.

some that pretended to a Prerogative, or to obtain an Exemption from the {usual} Canons, they did Travel to *Rome,* where they were kindly received and incouraged in their demands, whereby the Staple [market] of Dispensations and Favours to be granted, was establish'd at *Rome.* And if any one had lost his Cause before the ordinary Judge, he used to Appeal to *Rome,* where he was kindly received and 'incouraged' [well advised]. The *French* Historians relate, that, because the Emperor *Henry* [Honorio] had made the City of *Arles* the Capital City over seven Provinces, the Pope Constituted the Archbishop of the said City his Vicar in *France,* for fear lest the said Archbishop might by degrees attempt to make himself Patriarch of {all} *France.* And this Archbishop chose rather to have the inspection, tho precariously [at another's pleasure], over seventeen Provinces, into which *France* was divided at that time, than to be the Head only of <393> seven in his own right. This Man to add the more Authority to his Commision, did as much as in him was, endeavour to 'Establish' [expand] the Popes Authority there.[53]

Afterwards[+] in the Eighth Century, when great Disorders and Debaucheries were become frequent among the Monks and Clergy, an
Of the Monk Winifred. *English* Frier, whose name was *Winifred,* and who afterwards called himself *Boniface,*[54] did out of a particular Zeal take upon himself the Reformation of the Manners and Lives of the Clergy; and did endeavour to Establish the Christian Religion in several parts of *Germany,* but especially in *Thuringia* and *Friezland.* This Man, to acquire the greater Authority to himself, had entirely Devoted himself to the Interest of the *Roman* Chair, from whence he received the Episcopal Pall,[55] and the Title of Archbishop of *Mayence,* having also been Constituted by Pope *Gregory* III. [as] his Vicar, with full Power to call Councils, and to Constitute Bishops in those places which were by his assistance Converted to the Christian Faith, and with ample recommendations to those Nations, and to *Charles Martel,* the then Grand Master [*Groß-*

53. Pope Zosimus made Patroclus, bishop of Arles, the vicar of all Gaul. This happened in 417, during the reign of Flavius Honorius, Western Roman Emperor from 395 to 423.

54. St. Boniface (680–754), the so-called apostle of Germany.

55. The *pallium* was a white sash worn over the shoulders, representing the office and authority of a bishop.

Hofmeister] of *France,* that he should take him into his protection, which he very willingly did. And when afterwards his Son *Carlomannus* shewed a great forwardness to have the Church Discipline 'regulated' [instituted], *Boniface* was very willing to take upon him this Office to the great advantage of the *Roman* Chair. He also at the request of *Carlomannus* call'd a Council in *Germany,* and at the request of *Pepin* several Synods in *France,*[56] where *Boniface* always was President in the quality [capacity] of Legat of the *Roman* Chair. In the first Council the Clergy signed a certain Confession of Faith, whereby they obliged themselves, not only to maintain the Catholick Faith, but also to remain in constant Union with the *Roman* Church, and to be obedient to the Successours of S. *Peter.* This *Boniface* also was the first, who put it upon the Bishops of *Germany* to 'receive' [request] the Episcopal Pall from the Pope, [and] who sent it to the Bishops of *France* without their request, thereby to unite them with the *Roman* Chair. And when once these Ornaments were become customary amongst them, they were put <394> upon them afterwards as of absolute Necessity, and the Episcopal Function was forbidden to be exercised by them before they had received these Ornaments.

Besides+ this, the Popes assumed to themselves an Authority of giv- Annals.
ing leave to the Bishops to remove from one Episcopal See to another, and obliged all the Western Bishops to receive their Confirmation from *Rome,* for which they were obliged to pay a certain Summ of Money as an acknowledgement, which was since converted to Annals [*annates*].[57] The Popes also by making void the Decisions of the provincial Synods or Assemblies, overthrew their Authority; wherefore when every body plainly perceived that the Decrees of these Assemblies could produce no other Effects but to be continually annulled by the Popes, without as much as hearkening to any Reasons, they were by degrees quite abolished. Pope *Gregory* VII.[58] also forced the Bishops to swear an Oath of Fealty to the Pope, and by a Decree forbid [forbade] that none should

56. The Concilium Germanicum (742), and Pippin the Short (d. 768), brother of Carloman.

57. Annates were a tax on the first year's income from a new bishopric or benefice.

58. Gregory VII (ca. 1020–85) excommunicated Henry IV (1050–1106), who had deposed him at the Diet of Worms (1076).

dare to condemn any one that had appealed to the Pope. They were also not forgetful in sending Legates or Nuncios to all places, whose business was, to exercise in the name of the Pope the same Authority which had formerly belonged to the Bishops, Metropolitans and Provincial Assemblies.

Riches of the Church. §17. This growing 'Ecclesiastical' [spiritual] Sovereignty was the more prejudicial to the supreme Civil Power, the more the Church <daily> increased both in Numbers and Riches. The first Foundation of the Wealth of the Church was laid by the Liberality and Charity of 'Princes' [potentates] and other great Men, who were of Opinion, that they did a very agreeable Service to God Almighty if they were liberal and bounteous towards his Church and the Clergy. And after they [the latter] had once perswaded the People, that by doing good Works, among which the Gifts and Donations for Pious uses had the first place[,] they could and must deserve [earn] Heaven from God Almighty; this Liberality was increased to a high degree. Yet the voluntary Contributions of the People not being able to satisfy the avarice of the Clergy, which increased together with their Riches, other ways and artifices were found out to empty the Peoples Purses, and a great many unne-<395>cessary Institutions [*Actus*] introduced which were to be purchased for Money. Then it was that the saying of Masses for the living and the dead, Purgatory, Indulgences, Dispensations, Pilgrimages, Jubilees, and the like, were introduced without {end or} measure. They had besides this, always a watchful Eye over such as were at the point of death, since they knew that Men were commonly not so addicted at that time to their worldly Riches, which they were else to leave to their Heirs who often rejoiced at their Death: Nay, they were not ashamed to make a profession of begging.

The Policies of the Popes in the Croisade. Among[+] other Tricks, the Popes did in the Eleventh and the following Century turn the Croisadoes [Crusades] to their great Advantage [*Profit*]. For in these expeditions after the People had once received the Sign of the Cross to assist in the recovery of the Holy Land, the Popes pretended to the supreme Command and Direction {over them}; they took the Persons and Estates of such as had received the Cross under their particular Protection, exempting them thereby {until their return} from the Civil Jurisdiction both in Civil and criminal Causes, and rendring their Dispensations and Indulgences more frequent and flourishing than before; the Pope's Legates did dispose of such Alms, Collections and Legacies as were given for that purpose, and under the same pretext received the Tenths from the Clergy;[59] nay, even pretended to put their Commands upon 'Princes' [kings and lords] to receive the Cross themselves. These {crusades} they imployed afterwards against such as were declared by them Scismaticks or Hereticks, whose possessions they used to confiscate and bestow upon those who had proved serviceable to them, without asking the Advice of the Sovereign [*Obersten Lehen-Herrn*], who durst not but invest these with those 'Countries' [possessions] that were presented to them by so high a Hand.

§18. No less did the number of Ecclesiasticks increase proportionably to the increase of the Riches of the Church, because there were not wanting such as were willing to have a share of them without taking much pains. For it was not thought sufficient to have an ordinary Minister, Chaplain and others necessary for the exercising of Divine Service belonging to each <396> Church, but also each Cathedral had {to have} a Chapter of Canons,[60] and there were great numbers of Persons of high and low Quality that were forward [eager] in taking upon them these profitable and in no ways burthensome Functions, because the inconveniency of Celibacy[,] which the Pope in the Eleventh and the following Century forced upon the Ecclesiasticks not without great trouble and reluctancy[,] was sufficiently recompenced by the Honours and Revenues which they enjoyed quietly in their several Stations.

Multitude of Ecclesiasticks.

59. A tenth part of the income from an ecclesiastical holding, which was to be paid to the papacy.
60. Literally: "ein Collegium Canonicorum oder Thum-Herrn." Regarding the latter term (which is related to *Kaiserthum, Fürstenthum,* and—collectively—to *Heidenthum* and *Christenthum*), Thomasius, p. 109, questions whether such abuse had been eliminated by Protestants, and refers to his own annotations to *Severini de Monzambano de statu imperii germanici ad Laelium fratrem, dominum Trezoliani, liber unus, accesserunt scholia continua . . . in usum auditorum conscripta a Christiano Thomasio* (Halle: Salfeld, 1695; repr. 1714), particularly II.14 and VIII.9.

Fryars and
Nuns.

Besides,⁺ an innumerable 'multitude' [swarm] of Fryars and Nuns settled themselves all over Christendom. This sort of People began first to appear in the World at the time of the great Persecutions, but in the Fourth and following Centuries did multiply their numbers to a prodigious degree. In the beginning they lived upon what they could get by their Handy-work; a great many used to give their Goods to the Poor, tho' voluntarily,⁶¹ and lived under the Direction of the Bishops, according to a Discipline prescribed in the Canons. In the Seventh Century especially, Fryars and Nuns were much in vogue in those Western Parts, which were every where filled up with Monasteries and Nunneries built by the encouragement of Princes and other great Men that endowed them with great Revenues. But when the Charity and Liberality of the People seemed almost to be exhausted by the great Charges bestowed upon so many {old} rich Monasteries, and yet there were not enough {places therein} to contain all such as were desirous to enter into this sort of Life; at last in the Thirteenth Century the Order of the

Mendicants.

Mendicant-Fryars⁶² was erected: These made a great shew of Holiness, because they would not be taken for such as were forward [eager] to choose a Monastick Life to live in plenty, but for such as had taken a resolution to bid farewel to all the Pleasures of this World, and at the best, maintain themselves by Alms.⁶³

The Motives
to embrace
this manner
of Life.

A great many have embraced this severe 'Order' [lifestyle], out of an Opinion of a particular Holiness and Merit, which they believed did belong to this Order, or rather an 'Ecclesiastick' [spiritual] Ambition; the {inborn} Pride of Mankind being so great <and natural to some>, that they did not think the Commands of God sufficient{ly burdensome}, but rather would receive Hea-<397>ven from God Almighty as a desert than as a gift, and were ambitious of having a preference before others, even in the other Life. Some there are who embrace a Monastick

---

61. That is, even though they were not obliged to.

62. Thomasius, p. 111, mentions four orders: Augustinians, Carmelites, Dominicans, and Franciscans.

63. Thomasius, p. 112, accuses the mendicants of falling prey to the ancient error of taking sensuality (*Wollust*) as the only vice, and thereby overlooking ambition and greed.

Life out of desperation,[64] some out of laziness. A great many are by their Parents and 'Relations' [friends] sent into a Monastery out of Superstition or Poverty, 'and' [or] to prevent the ruin of a Family by the division of the Estate among a great many Children. And out of these Fryars the Pope has chosen his Regiment of Guards [*militem Praetorianum*],[65] which he lays in Garrison not only to plague the Laiety, but also to curb the Bishops and the rest of the Clergy. It was for this reason that the Pope did uphold the Fryars with so much zeal against the Bishops, ‖[in the Tenth Century, especially, when]‖[66] they withdrawing themselves from the Jurisdictions of the Bishops, did submit themselves to the immediate Authority of the Pope. And the Popes know so well how to handle them, that tho' there are great Jealousies on foot betwixt their several Orders, as for example, betwixt the Franciscans and Dominicans, they nevertheless keep so even a ballance betwixt them, and so equally dispose of their Favours towards them, that one Order may not oppress another, or that any of them may have any reason to complain of the Pope's partiality.

These[+] Fryars also used to interfere often with the regular Clergy, as pretending to a great share in {the alms and} the Legacies and Burials of the richer sort, [and] to the direction of Consciences and the administration of the Sacraments. From hence did arise a continual envy and hatred from the Bishops and regular Clergy against these Fryars, who being upheld by the Pope's Favour, were not concerned at their anger.[67] And therefore whenever any Bishop attempted any thing against the Pope's Authority, these Fryars with their clamour and noise pursued him every where like so many Hounds, and rendred him odious to the common People, amongst whom they were in great veneration, through their outward appearance of Holiness; and from thence it came

Prejudicial to the regular Clergy.

---

64. Thomasius, p. 113, quotes the common saying: "Desperation makes either monks or soldiers" (*desperatio facit aut monachum aut militem*).

65. *Praetorian guards* were originally protectors of a Roman general's tent and person. During imperial times they became the bodyguard of the emperor.

66. Rather: "as gradually, and especially in the thirteenth century[,]."

67. Literally, the passage speaks of "die Feigen weisen" (an obscene gesture equivalent to "give them the finger").

to pass, that the Bishops who opposed the Pope's Authority never could make a great Party among the 'common People' [rabble]. Besides this, the Fryars always kept a watchful Eye over the actions of the Bishops, giving continual advices concerning them to their Generals residing at *Rome*, where-<398>by the Popes were enabled to oppose timely any design intended against their Authority. And these Fryars proved the main obstacle, why the Bishops could not so effectually oppose the Pope's Authority [*Gewalt*] which he assumed over them, so that being destitute of means to |[help themselves]|,[68] they were forced to follow the current. Tho' it is also certain, that 'some' [many] of them were very well satisfied with it, as believing that they did participate of the Grandeur of their supreme Head, and that thereby they should be exempted from the Jurisdiction of the Civil Magistrates [*Weltlichen Fürsten*], which was more dreadful to them than a foreign Jurisdiction exercised by those of their own 'Order' [guild, *Handwercks*], |[from whom they had all the reason to expect more Favour.]|[69]

Nevertheless it is also undeniable, that a great many Bishops, especially among those on this side the *Alps* bear a {secret} grudge to[ward] the Pope's Authority to this very day, which evidently appeared at the Council of *Trent,* where the *French* and *Spanish* Bishops did insist very closely upon this Point, that it might be decided, 'whether' [that] Bishops are <not> obliged to Residence {in their own respective churches} by the Law of God, which is also the Opinion of the *Jansenists* (as they are called) in *France* and the *Netherlands*.[70] The more refined sort did easily perceive what their Intention was by making this Proposition. For if God had commanded them this, it must also be a consequence that he had given them means and instructed them with sufficient Power (*qui dat jus ad finem, dat jus ad media*) and that therefore they were not obliged to go to *Rome* first, and to purchase an Authority to exercise their 'Function' [office]. The Pope met with great Difficulties [*war* . . .

68. Rather: "justify rejecting it [the pope's power]."
69. Literally: "since crows are typically loath to peck out one another's eyes."
70. The Council of Trent (1545–63). Jansenists were neo-Augustinian followers of bishop Cornelius Jansenius (1585–1638), who emphasized original sin, weakness of the will, and the need for divine grace.

angst und bange] before he could surmount this obstacle at the Council of *Trent,* wherefore it is very likely that this will be the last Council,[71] since the Pope will scarce hereafter put his Grandeur to the hazard and the decision of such an Assembly; which also seems now to be of no further use, since the Jesuits and some others have taught that the Pope is infallible and above Councils, ‖[from whom they ought to receive a confirmation, and a binding or obliging Power.]‖[72] But let it be as it will, the Bishops are for their own sakes obliged not to withdraw themselves from the Popes subjection, since thereby they would fall under the jurisdiction [*Gewalt*] of the Civil Power, and would {in that case} be obliged to seek <399> for Protection from their Sovereigns [*Landes-Herrn*] {in order to maintain themselves}, who must be 'Potent Princes' [mighty potentates], <if they should protect them against the Pope>; wherefore they are now forced to choose the least of two Evils.

§19. Tho' the Church was never so abounding in Riches and in great numbers of Ecclesiasticks, yet was it absolutely necessary, that the Pope if he intended to establish an 'Ecclesiastical Monarchy' [spiritual sovereignty], should not be in any ways dependent on any Temporal Prince; and that he should reside in a place which was free from all subjection to any Civil Power but himself; that he also should be possessed of such an 'Estate' [state, *Staat*], as might be sufficient to maintain his Grandeur, and ‖[not to be liable to be taken away from him upon any pretence whatsoever]‖[73]; where also his adherents might find a safe retreat whenever they should be pursued by the Civil Power {for this reason}. To establish this was a business of a considerable time and labour, neither could it be effected without great opposition, and 'that by' [without] a great many Artifices and knavish Tricks.

How the Church was freed from all Power over it.

And it is certain that as long as there was an Emperour in the Western Empire, and as long as the Empire of the *Goths* lasted in *Italy,* the Bishops of *Rome* could not so much as think of this Greatness. But this

71. In fact, the next major council was Vatican I, convened in 1869. See note 92, p. 464, below.
72. Rather: "and that the latters' power to obligate must be confirmed by him."
73. Rather: "allow him not to be compelled by a withdrawal of support."

How the Popes withdrew themselves from their subjection to the Emperours. having been destroyed under the Emperour *Justinian,* and *Rome* and *Italy* made a Province of the *Grecian* Empire, then it was that the Popes took their opportunity to exempt themselves from the Jurisdiction of these Emperours, whose Authority was mightily decayed in *Italy,* partly by the ill management of their Governours at *Ravenna,* partly by their own weakness and want of Strength; for the *Lombards* were Masters in *Italy,* and in the times of *Justinian* II. one Emperour was for ruining the other. Besides this, some of these Emperours were against the adoring of Images, and *Leo Isaurus*[74] quite ejected them out of the Churches, because this adoration was wholly degenerated into Idolatry, and |[as to the outward appearance]|,[75] the Saints were more regarded than God himself. This undertaking was very vehemently opposed by Pope *Gregory* II. who stood up for the Images, partly because the *Roman* Chair found this Superstition very advantageous; partly because the Pope took it very ill <400> that the Emperour should undertake a Reformation in Matters of Religion without his Knowledge and Consent, and that at that time when he was busie to introduce the 'Ecclesiastical Monarchy' [spiritual sovereignty] in the Western parts; partly also, because he thought to have met with an opportunity to withdraw himself {entirely} from the Jurisdiction of the *Grecian* Emperours. The better to obtain his Aim, he stirred up the *Romans* and *Italians,* who hitherto had been under the Obedience of the Emperours, to refuse to pay them Tribute; and the Governour residing at *Ravenna,* endeavouring to maintain the Emperour's Right, was slain in a Tumult. Whereby the Jurisdiction and Power of the *Grecian* Emperours was abolished in those parts of *Italy,* and these Countries [*Länder*] began to be free and independent 'on' [of] any Foreign Jurisdiction.

The Pope seeks for Protection in France. §20. By these means the Pope had freed himself from the Jurisdiction of the Emperours of *Constantinople,* but not long after he was threatened by another Enemy, who being nearer at hand, was likely to prove more troublesome to him than formerly the Emperours who lived at so

74. Leo Isaurus (717–41).
75. That is, "it seemed that [*dem Ansehen nach*]."

considerable a distance. For the Kings of the *Longobards* endeavoured first to make themselves Masters of those parts which were fallen off from the Emperour, and afterwards of all *Italy.* They had already taken *Ravenna,* and there was none left in *Italy* who was able to stop their Victories. The Popes were then hard put to it, and knew not where to seek for Protection except of the Kings of *France,* who at first endeavoured to finish these Differences by an amicable Composition, but the *Longobards* not being willing to rest satisfied therewith, they resolved by force of Arms to maintain the *Italian* Affairs. They were easily prevailed upon to undertake this Business, not only because Pope *Zachary* had approved of the Proceedings of *Pepin,* who having 'abdicated' [deposed] the lawful King, was from a Grand-Marshal become King of *France;*[76] but also they had thereby an opportunity offered them to make Conquests in *Italy,* whereof the *French* Nation has been always very ambitious.

Pepin and afterwards *Charles* the Great, having been so Fortunate in their Wars against <401> the *Longobards,* as to Conquer their whole Kingdom; they gave to the Papal Chair all that Tract of Land which had been formerly under the Jurisdiction [*Exarchat*] of the *Grecian* Governours. There are some who are of Opinion, that to obtain this {extravagant [*allzufette*]} Gift [*Donation*], the Pope made use of the fictitious Donation of *Constantine* the Great, which in those barbarous times was easily imposed upon the ignorant World.[77] Besides this, the *French* Kings had great Obligations to the Pope for the above-mentioned reason, and were also fond of acquiring the name of pious Princes, by bestowing liberal Presents [on the clergy] out of other Mens Possessions. For it was in those Days a common Custom, that Men of all degrees made it their Business to out-do one another in Liberality towards the Clergy. Nay, the 'Princes' [kings] used to grant them these Possessions without any incumbrances, that thereby the Ecclesiasticks might be

76. See V.3–4, pp. 194–96, above.
77. The Donation [from *donum,* gift] of Constantine was a document actually dating from around 750–800, but supposedly going back to Constantine (ca. 272–337), which granted the pope extensive privileges and possessions. It was later shown to be a forgery by Lorenzo Valla (1405–57). See Valla (2008).

sure to enjoy free possession of what they had bestowed upon them. These extravagant Donations were none of the least Causes why the Clergy afterwards did labour with so much vehemency to withdraw themselves from the Jurisdiction of the Civil Magistrates [*der Könige Herrschaft*], as fearing that these extravagant Donations and Grants might be recalled and declared void by their Successours. Wherefore it has been always a Maxim of Wise Men, that Princes by granting extravagant Priviledges and Gifts, 'made' [make] their Subjects rather Jealous [ill-disposed] than Friends {toward themselves}; since those who have obtained them, living always in fear that the same either in part or wholly, may be taken away again, imploy all means so to establish themselves as to be in a capacity to maintain themselves therein in spite of the Prince.

Those Learned Men who are of an impartial Judgment, 'take it for granted' [are of the opinion], that the Pope 'did pretend' [wanted] to exercise a Sovereign Power over these Countries [*Lande*] granted to him by the *French* Kings, but that the People refused the same, as being for maintaining their Liberty; and thinking it very odd, that the Pope who was an Ecclesiastical Person [*Geistlicher*], should pretend to be also a <Worldly> Prince [*Fürsten*]. When therefore the *Romans* mutinied against Pope *Leo* III. he was forced to seek for Assistance from *Charles* the Great, who restored the Pope. But on the other hand, the Pope and People of *Rome* proclaimed *Charles* Emperour, whereby he was <402> put into possession of the Sovereignty over that part of *Italy*, which formerly belonged to the Jurisdiction of the Governours at *Ravenna*, and the other remnants of the Western Empire; so that the Pope afterwards enjoyed these Countries under the Sovereign Jurisdiction of the Emperour, who therefore used to be called the Patron and Defender of the Church, till the Reign of the Emperour *Henry* IV.[78]

78. Henry IV (1050–1106). Also see §4 above. Thomasius, pp. 127–28, disputes the interpretation of this paragraph and, referring to Pufendorf's *The Present State of Germany*, I.12, and to the beginning of section §21, maintains that the emperor obtained only a *Schutzrecht* over the pope, who became his client. The German emperors might have kept the pope at bay if they had properly exercised this right of protection.

§21. But the Popes began at length to grow weary of the Imperial {pa- The Pope
tronage or} Protection, because the Emperour's Consent was required withdraws himself from
in the Election of a Pope, and if they were mutinous, the Emperours the Obedience
used to check them, and sometimes turn them out of the Chair. To of the Em-
exempt themselves from this Power of the Emperours over them, the perours, and establishes an
Popes have for a long time <together> imployed all their Cunning and Ecclesiastical
Labour before they could {fully} obtain their Aim. They used to make Sovereignty.
it their constant Business to raise intestine Commotions against the
Emperours, sometimes in *Germany*, sometimes in *Italy*, thereby to diminish their Power [*Kräfte*] and Authority [*Ansehen*]. The Bishops, <es-
pecially> in *Germany*, were {also} always very busie, as being dissatisfied that they were dependent on the Emperours, who 'nominated the
Bishops' [conferred bishoprics], and therefore joyned with the Pope to
assist him in setting up |[the Ecclesiastical Sovereignty.]|[79]

The Reign of the Emperour *Henry* IV. furnished them with an opportunity to put in execution their Design, this Emperour by his Debaucheries and ill management of Affairs, living in discontents and continual broils with the Estates of *Germany;* and as soon as *Gregory* VII.
who was before called *Hildebrand,* a proud, resolute and obstinate Man
got into the Chair, he began to exclaim against the Emperour, that the
granting of Church-Benefices did not belong to him, since he made
a {disgraceful} Traffick with them, and sold them to all sorts of {evil}
People whom he installed before they had taken Holy Orders. And
when the Emperour resolved to maintain his antient Right and Title,
he excommunicated him, and stirred up the Bishops and the {other} Pope Gregory
Estates of *Germany* against him, who made him so much work, that he excommuni-
was obliged to resign his Right of Constituting of Bishops. The Pope cates Hen. IV.
under this pretext, did not only in-<403> tend to exempt the Bishops from the Emperour's Jurisdiction, but the main point was to make

79. Rather: "a perfect [complete, actual] sovereignty of the clergy." Thomasius,
p. 130, identifies this as the critical move: if the clergy had not been freed from
the power of worldly authorities, the pope could not have attained this either. Accordingly, wherever clergy are not subject to civil authorities, there are remnants of
"political papism" (*politischen Pabstthums*), a notion which Thomasius used also in
reference to church-state relations in Protestant territories.

himself Sovereign over *Italy*, and to make all the other Princes submit to the Pope's Authority. And some are of Opinion, that this Design might have been put in execution, considering that *Europe* was at that time divided into so many Principalities [*Herrschaften*], and most of these Princes being not very Potent, might either out of a Devotion, or to avoid falling under the Jurisdiction of more Potent Princes, submit themselves under the Pope's protection and pay him Tribute. It is therefore not improbable, that if three or four Popes had succeeded one another, instructed with sufficient Capacity to cover their Design with the Cloak of Holiness, and in the mean while to uphold the Interest of the People against the Oppressions of their Princes, the Popes might have made themselves absolute 'Sovereigns' [monarchs] both in Temporal and Spiritual Affairs.

The Pope endeavours to subject the Emperour. Neither⁺ did the Pope only pretend to free himself from the Emperour's Jurisdiction over him, but also endeavoured to make him his Subject; for he pretended to be his Judge, he summon'd him before him to make answer to the Complaints of his Subjects, excommunicated him, and declared him to have forfeited his Right and Title to the Empire. And tho' his Son, the Emperour *Henry* V. did endeavour to recover what was forcibly taken away from his Father, and made Pope *Paschal* a Prisoner, whom he forced to restore to him the right of Constituting of Bishops, yet were the whole Clergy in *Europe* so dissatisfied hereat, and raised such Commotions, that at last \A. 1122\ he was obliged to resign the same again <into the Pope's hands>.

Disputes in England about the investiture of Bishops. Much⁺ about the same time there were great Disputes concerning this Point in *England,* which were composed in such a manner, that the King should not pretend to the Power of investing of Bishops, but that these should do Homage to him. \A. 1107\ The last of which the Pope was very unwilling to grant, who would fain have had the Bishops to be quite independent [*mit keiner Pflicht*] of the King, which was {also} the reason why he [did] expressly forbid the Bishops in *France* to follow this Example; but King *Lewis* VI. and his Successours did maintain their Right with so high a <404> Hand, that the Popes were never able to establish their pretended Right in *France*.

Neither did the Popes think it advisable to fall out at once with

the Emperour and *France,* but that it would be more secure to have
one at hand to uphold them against the other; especially {since}, the
Popes were not so much for weakening of *France,* because they were
not so nearly concerned with that Kingdom, as for humbling the Em-
perours that were Potent in *Italy,* and |[pretended to the Sovereignty
over the City of *Rome.*]|[80] Neither was *Germany* so intirely united {in
itself} as *France,* and most Princes of *Europe* being then very jealous of
the Grandeur of the Empire, were very willing to joyn with the Pope
against the Emperours, under pretence of upholding the Authority of
the Holy Church and Papal Chair. 'Tis true, the two Emperours *Frederick* I. and II. did afterwards endeavour to restore the antient Imperial
Right [*Gewalt*] {over the pope}, but were not able to attain their aim,
especially since *Italy* was divided into the two Factions of the *Guelfs*
and *Gibellines,* the first whereof were for the Pope, the latter for the
Emperour, which caused such a Confusion in *Italy,* that the Emperours
could never afterwards reduce *Italy* to an entire Obedience.[81] And because after the death of the Emperour *Frederick* II. the whole Empire
was during that long vacancy of the Throne [*interregnum*], put into
great Confusion and Disorders, the succeeding Emperours |[found so
much work in *Germany,* that they were not in a Condition to look after
Italy]|,[82] whereby the Pope had sufficient leisure given him to make
himself Sovereign both as to his own Person, and over the Possessions
belonging to the Church of *Rome.*

§22. But the Pope not being contented to have attained this degree of
Grandeur [*Hoheit*], quickly set on foot another Doctrine, which was
of far greater consequence, *viz.* That the Pope had an indirect Power
[*dominatio*] over Princes, {and} that it belonged to him in his own Right
to take Care how they governed and managed their Affairs. For tho'
they did not expresly pretend in gross terms that Princes did depend
on them in 'Civil' [worldly] Affairs, yet they believed that the supreme

The Pope pretends to a Power over Princes even to depose them.

80. Rather: "wanted Rome obedient to themselves."
81. See VIII.7, p. 332, above.
82. Rather: "thanked God that they were able to manage things in Germany [at
least], and had little further care about Italy."

'Ecclesiastical' [spiritual] Power did entitle them to an Authority to judge concerning the Actions of <405> Princes, whether the same were good or bad, to 'admonish' [remind] them, to correct them, and to command what was fitting, and to forbid what was unfitting to be done. If therefore Princes waged War against one another, the Pope pretended to have an Authority to command a Truce to be made betwixt them, to bring their Differences before him, and refer them to his Decision, not without threatnings that he would not only excommunicate them in their Persons, but also forbid the exercise of Divine Service and administration of the Sacraments throughout their whole Kingdom. They also did believe it belonged to their Office to obviate all publick Scandals, to defend such as were oppressed, and to see Justice done to all the World. It was from this pretension, that they received the Complaints of all such as pretended to be oppressed; nay, they went further, for they sometimes took information concerning the Injuries {supposedly} done by Princes to their Subjects, and concerning some Impositions laid upon the People, whereby the People thought themselves aggrieved, which they forbid [forbade] to be levied upon them under the penalty of Excommunication. Sometimes they used to declare the Possessions of such as were excommunicated, forfeited, exposing their Persons to danger, and releasing the Subjects from their Oaths of Allegiance, under pretence that the Government of a Christian People ought not to be trusted to the management of such as had rebelled against the Church. This has been attempted against a great many Crowned Heads, and put in execution against some of them.

How they colour over this Power.

This⁺ abominable pretension (as they perswade the ignorant [*ungelehrten*]) was founded upon their fictitious Decretals [*Decretal-Brieffen*][83] upon which they have built their Canon-Law, which grants to the Pope

83. A reference to the (now) so-called False Decretals emphasizing the supremacy of the pope, which were published between 847 and 852 by a pseudonymous Isidore Mercator. Decretals in general were papal pronouncements or "rescripts" responding to questions about ecclesiastical discipline. They go back as far as the fourth and fifth centuries and were later included in the great compilations of canon law, including the Decretum of Gratian (the first *corpus juris canonici*) around 1150. See §14, note 44, p. 439, above.

an unlimited Power over Christians, by vertue of which, he may as the Common Father,[84] send out his Commands to all Believers, and admonish them concerning all such Matters as belong to {the welfare of their} Religion and their Salvation, and in case of Disobedience, lay punishments upon them. For that the Predecessours of *Gregory* VII. did not make use of this Power (they say) was because the preceeding Emperours, either kept themselves within their bounds, or else the Popes lived an <406> ungodly [*schlimm*] Life. To give specious colours to these pretensions, they made use of ||[the Examples of *Ambrose* and *Theodosius*]|[85]; they used to relate how the *Spanish* Bishops had obliged King *Wamba* by way of penance to lay down the Crown: As also, how the Bishops of *France* had deposed *Lewis* Surnamed the *Pious,* who afterwards 'could' [would, *wolte*] not recover his Crown without the Consent and Authority of another Assembly of Bishops. They alledged for another Example, how *Fulco* then Archbishop of *Rheims* had threatened *Charles* Sirnamed the *Simple,* to absolve his Subjects from their Oaths of Allegiance, if he made an Alliance with the *Normans,* who were then {still} Pagans. They supposed that it was without question, that the Pope's Power did extend it self beyond that of all other Bishops, since it was not limited by any thing, except by the express Canons of Councils and Decrees of the Popes {themselves}, wherein nothing was contained against this Power of deposing of Kings; and (they say) it was not to be supposed that they could have been forgetful of this point. And because they had 'assumed' [presumed] a Power to give the Name and Title of a King to some who either prompted by their Ambition or Superstition had begged the same from them, they supposed that by the same Right, they might take away the Crown from such as they esteemed unworthy of wearing it.

84. Thomasius, pp. 143–44, notes that the ecclesiastical title of "father," which was originally a term of affection (*Liebes-Nahme*), came later to signify paternal power (*Macht-Nahme*).

85. Rather: "what Ambrose did against the Emperor Theodosius." Theodosius (347–95) was the last emperor to rule over both parts of the Roman Empire. Ambrose had excommunicated him for his severe response to an uprising in Thessalonica but then readmitted him and induced him to reverse his policy of toleration toward pagans.

They⁺ also had forbid to marry within the seventh degree of Consanguinity [*Blutfreundschaft*] and the fourth of Affinity [*Schwagerschaft*],⁸⁶
whereby they often met with an opportunity to be troublesome to
Princes: For because it seldom happened among those of so high a
Rank, but that one side or other was within one of these degrees, they
stood in continual fear lest the Pope should disturb their Negotiations,
except they humbly begged for a Dispensation; and in both cases ‖[the
Popes knew how to make their advantage of them.]‖⁸⁷ Lastly, the Popes
having abundance of Business to dispatch, did thereby draw the best
and most refined Wits [*geschicktesten Leute*] to their Courts, who used
to go thither to look for Imployment, and to perfect themselves in the
great School <of *Europe*>. These were always for promoting the Pope's
Interest and Designs, from whom they expected their promotion; besides that, the whole Clergy did adhere to him as to their supreme
Head. <407> Pope *Boniface* VIII. did clearly give us to understand 'his
meaning' [all this] at the *Jubilee* kept in the year 1300. when he appeared
sometimes in the Habit of an Emperour, sometimes in that of a Pope,
and caused two Swords to be carried before him as the Ensigns of the
'Ecclesiastical' [spiritual] and 'Civil' [worldly] Power.

The Papal   §23. But the Popes could not long enjoy this unsufferable Usurpation
Authority   [*Gewalt*] in quiet, for it was so often called in question, till they were
opposed.   obliged to draw in their horns, and to make their pretensions a little
more 'plausible' [subtle]. 'Tis true, in the Business with the Emperours,
the *Henrys* and the *Fredericks,* they got the upper hand; nevertheless,
they met betwixt while often times with very 'indifferent entertainment'
[rough treatment], and such things were sometimes publish'd against
them as were little to their Honour, and from whence it might easily
be judged by those that were impartial, that not the Glory of God, but
their own Grandeur [*Hoheit*] was the chief aim of their undertaking.
But when *Boniface* VIII. pretended to play the same Game with *Philip*

86. *Consanguinity* refers to blood (biological) relations, while *affinity* includes
one's spouse and his/her in-law relations.
87. Rather: "they had mostly to dance to his [the pope's] pipe."

Surnamed the *Handsome,* King of *France,* he [the latter] watched his opportunity so well, and gave him such a blow, that the Pope felt the smart of it. And to avoid the Scandal which the common People might take at these so severe proceedings against the Pope, use was made of this pretext, that what was done against his Person, was not intended against the Vicar of Jesus Christ, but against a pernicious Person, who by unlawful means was got into the {papal} Chair, and that a general Council ought to be called to free the Church from his Oppressions.[88]

But[+] the ensuing Schisms have proved the most pernicious to the Popes Authority, as also the double Elections which have been made <at several times>, when the Cardinals being divided, set up two Popes at once, who used by turns to excommunicate and revile one another, and to maintain themselves in the Chair, were fain [obliged] to flatter the Kings, and acknowledge that they were beholding to them. This Division was an evident sign, that the Elections of these Popes had not been guided by the Holy Spirit, but been influenced by some ill Designs and Intrigues. Wherefore it was also the Opinion of the Wiser sort, that in such a case, neither of them ought <408> to be acknowledged as Pope, but that a new one ought to be chosen, which was also put in execution at the Council of *Constance* [1414–18].

The Schisms much weakned their Power.

The first Schism arose, according to my Opinion in the year 1134. or as some will have it 1130. when after the death of *Honorius* II.[,] *Innocent* II. and *Anacletus* were both chosen Popes. And tho' the first had the greater party on his side, yet did the King of *Sicily* and Duke of *Aquitain,* vigorously uphold the latter; and his adherents did after his death choose another in his stead, who called himself *Victor,* with whom *Innocent* made an agreement, so that he voluntarily relinquished his pretension, and acknowledged him his Superiour. 'But' [Similarly] after the death of *Adrian* IV. two Popes were again elected at one time, *viz. Alexander* III. and *Victor* IV. To the first adhered *France, England,* and *Sicily;* to the latter, <the Emperour> *Frederick* I.[,] all *Germany* and

88. Philip IV the Fair (1268–1314) and Boniface VIII (1235–1303). Among other actions, in 1307 Philip violently disbanded the French Knights Templar, whose loyalty was directly to the pope.

{most of} the Clergy of *Rome*. And after his [Victor's] death, those of his party chose three successive Popes, all whom *Alexander* out-lived. These used to make a common Trade to excommunicate and revile one another, and each of them were fain [obliged] to behave themselves towards their Protectours, more like a Client than a Master.

But much greater was the Schism after the death [1378] of *Gregory* XI. when again two Popes were elected at once, whereof one resided at *Rome,* the other at *Avignon.* This Schism lasted through several successions, near the space of Forty Years; during which time, both parties excommunicated one another very frequently, and committed great Cruelties. *France, Scotland, Castile, Savoy* and *Naples,* were of the side of the Pope that resided at *Avignon,* but all the rest of Christendom declared for the other at *Rome.* Both parties took great pains to set out the |[great numbers of Saints]|[89] that were of their party, and what Miracles and Revelations were {supposedly} made concerning their approbation [in support of their claims]. And both sides knew how to produce such Reasons, that at last there was no other remedy left <them> but to force both the Anti-Popes to abdicate themselves at the Council of *Constance,* and to choose a new one in their stead.

The last Schism of all arose \A. 1433\ when the Council of *Basil* [Basel] having deposed *Eugenius* IV. did in his stead elect *Felix* V. Pope, unto whom the former would not submit. And these Dissentions were continued till after the death of <409> *Eugenius,* when *Nicholas* V. was chosen in his stead, unto whom *Felix* for quiet sake, did resign the Chair upon very advantageous terms in the year 1438.

It[+] is very easily to be imagined how these Divisions did expose to publick view the Secrets [*pudenda*] of these Fathers. Since from hence an opportunity was taken {as well} to make use of the Assistance of the Councils to bridle the Popes, and from the Popes to appeal to these[,] which were now made use of to terrify the Popes withal, whenever they pretended to transgress their bounds. The Popes could the less refuse to acknowledge the Power of the Councils <at that time>, because

Hence an occasion taken to bridle the Popes Power by general Councils.

89. Rather: "authority of great and holy persons."

Gregory VII.[90] himself after the quarrel betwixt him and the Emperour {Henry IV} was renewed, had proposed to call a Council to be held in a place of Security, where both Friends and Foes, both the Clergy and Laiety might meet, to judge whether he or the Emperour had broke the Peace, and to concert Measures how to re-establish the same. *Gelasius* II. who had Differences with *Henry* V. made the same Declaration, adding withal, that he would rest satisfied with what Judgment his Brothers the Bishops should give[,] who were constituted Judges in the Church by God Almighty, and without whom, he could not decide a Business of this nature. So *Innocent* III. had writ, that he would not undertake to decide the Marriage Controversie [in 1199] betwixt *Philip Augustus* [of France] and *Engebourgh* [Ingeborg] of *Denmark* without consulting a general Council; for if he should attempt any such thing, he might thereby forfeit his Office [*Ampt*] and Dignity [*Stand*]. Which words seemed [to] intimate, that a Pope for mismanagement {of his office} might be deposed.

And when afterwards these and the like words were made use of against the Popes, it was then too late to endeavour to make them pass for [mere] Compliments; since {in any case} it proves often dangerous to be too modest in matters of such consequence. Wherefore the Council of *Pisa* in the year 1409. did depose the two Anti-Popes, *Benedict* XII. and *Gregory* XII. in whose stead they chose another, *viz. Alexander* V. In the same manner the Council of *Constance* did not only confirm the deposition of these two Popes, but also turned out *John* XXIV.[91] who was made Pope after the death of *Alexander* V. In the same manner the Council of *Basil* [Basel, 1431–49] did with *Eugenius* IV. and <410> besides this made a Decree that neither at the Court of *Rome,* neither in other places[,] any mony should be taken for the dispatch[es] of Ecclesiastical Affairs. All which as it shook the very Foundation of the Papal 'Chair' [state], so it was not to be admired [wondered at] that the

90. See §§16 and 21 above.

91. Baldassare Cossa (1370–1419), the antipope John XXIII, who was supported by the Medici. There actually was no John XX, and that number's omission accounts for the discrepancy.

Popes were very averse afterwards to call the Council of *Trent* [1545–63], and were forced to make use of all their 'cunning' [arts], that nothing might pass there to the prejudice of their Grandeur, and that since that time they have bid farewel to Councils for ever.[92]

Concerning the Seat of the Popes being transferred to Avignon. §24. Among {these} other divisions, this {too} has proved very prejudicial <(as it seems)> to the Authority [*Ansehen*] of the Popes, that *Clement* V. did transfer the Papal Chair from *Rome* to *Avignon,* as I suppose, upon instigation of *Philip* Surnamed the Handsom, King of *France,* who having had great differences with *Boniface* VIII. was Excommunicated by him. To render this ineffectual, he thought it the most proper way if the Pope resided in *France,* and that thereby the like would be prevented for the future; since it was very probable that the greatest part of the Cardinals hereafter would be taken out of the *French* Nation. The Popes made this City their constant place of Residence for seventy years together, not to mention that some of the Anti-Popes also did Reside there {later on}. This changing of the Seat carry'd along with it 'several' [many] inconveniencies, which proved very prejudicial to the 'Ecclesiastical Monarchy' [spiritual sovereignty]. For the Pope's Authority was among other things also founded upon this belief, that S. *Peter* had been {bishop} at *Rome,* and by his {personal} presence had Communicated a particular Prerogative and Holiness to that Chair, and whether the same could be transferred to *Avignon* seemed somewhat doubtful to a great many; besides this, the Pope was then for the most part obliged to |[comply with *France*]|,[93] and to live as it were at the Discretion of the *French* Kings. Tho also the *French,* who then thought they had a great Catch, have since complained, that they got little else by the presence of the *Roman* Court than Simony, {chicanery,} and another abominable Vice not fit to be named. Besides this the Court of *Rome* being then kept among Strangers, as it were, out of its Natural Element[,] its Faults were <411> the sooner discovered, and the whole the more despised.

92. See §18, pp. 450–51, at notes 70 and 71, above.
93. Rather: "dance according to the French pipe."

This removal also of the Court of *Rome* {also} proved very prejudicial to the 'Revenue' [possessions, *Gütern*] of the Church in *Italy*. For after the Authority of the Emperors in *Italy* came to decay, each State was for living free, and being Sovereign itself, and the Factions of the *Guelfs* and *Gibellines* caused most horrid distractions [disturbances]. And the Authority of the Pope being vanish'd by his absence, they made bold with the Church Possessions. Most Cities of the Ecclesiastical State {especially} upon the persuasions of the *Florentines* had sent away the Popes Legats, and acknowledged no Sovereign. The Emperor *Lewis,* Surnamed the *Bavarian,* who was at Enmity with the Pope, but in great esteem among the Inhabitants of the Ecclesiastical State, {also} did pretend to the Sovereignty over the same, as being a Fief of the Empire, which he granted to such as upheld his Party against the Pope. The Patrimony of the Church was then but very slender, and tho the Popes recovered part of it afterwards, {meanwhile} they were obliged to leave most in Possession of what they had got.

But the City of *Rome* was nevertheless at last forced to submit to the Popes power, which it had resisted so long, when *Boniface* IX. in the year 1393. put on the Bridle, by 'building' [fortifying] the Castle of *S. Angelo*. 'And' [But] *Alexander* VI. was the chief cause that the Ecclesiastical State was reduced {again} under the Obedience of the Popes. This Pope had a Natural Son, whose name was *Caesar Borgia,* but who commonly is called Duke of *Valence,* from the Dukedom of *Valence,* which he got with his Lady *Charlotte d' Albret*. The Pope being very ambitious to make this his Son a great 'Prince' [potentate] in *Italy,* proposed this expedient to him, that he must drive out these petty Lords, which were then in Possession of the Ecclesiastical State, and when he had made himself Master of these places, he would confirm him in the Possession of them <for ever>. He [Caesar] succeeded very well in this Enterprise, having made away with most of these petty Lords, some by Force, some by Treachery; for he used to stick at nothing, alledging, that whatever he did could not be done amiss, since he had received his Commission from his Father, who was endowed with the Holy Ghost. And being reduced to the utmost want of mony, where-<412>with to pay his Soldiers, he and his Father agreed to Poison [*hinrichten*] the richest Cardinals at a Feast intended for that purpose; ||[some of whom they also knew to be averse to]|[94] their Designs. But the Servant who had the management of the business having out of carelesness fill'd the Pope and his Son a Cup out of the Poisoned Flasks, the Father died immediately, the Son narrowly escaping by the help of some Sudorificks. And not being able so to influence the next {papal} Election, as to get one chosen fit for his purpose, the whole design of *Caesar Borgia* came to nothing. 'Tho' [Thus] after the death of *Pius* III. who Sate but a few Weeks in the Papal Chair, *Julius* II. a most mortal Enemy of *Borgia*[,] was chosen in his stead, who having taken into his Possession all what he had got before, banish'd him out of the Country. Neither did this Pope rest satisfied, till {by many intrigues} he had recovered all what formerly belonged to the Church, (except *Ferrara* which was not re-united with the Papal Chair, till about the latter end of the last Age [in 1598], when the Legitimate Race of the Dukes of *d'Esté* was extinct). This Pope also prevented the *French* from becoming Masters of *Italy*.

Luther gives a great blow to the Grandeur of the Pope.

§25. But when the 'Ecclesiastical Monarchy' [papacy] seem'd to be come to the very Pinacle of its Grandeur, when all the Western parts were either in Communion with, or in Obedience to[95] the Church of *Rome*, except some few Remnants of the *Waldenses* in *France*, and of the *Hussites* in *Bohemia*, {which were of no consequence,} and when <just> the differences arisen betwixt Pope *Julius* II. and *Lewis* XII. which easily might have occasioned another Schism, were after the death of the first happily Composed by *Leo* X.[,] and all the {old} complaints against the Ambition of the Court of *Rome* were almost extinguished, there was such a Revolt made from the Chair of *Rome*, first raised upon a very indifferent [slight] occasion, that a great part of *Europe* withdrew itself from the Obedience of the Pope, who was thereby put in danger of losing all. We will in this, as we have done in all other matters, only relate how far human Counsels and helps were concerned therein.[96]

94. Rather: "who also could have opposed."
95. Actually: both . . . and. . . .
96. Thomasius, p. 169, refers here to Pufendorf's *The Present State of Germany*, VIII.5ff.

For the hidden Counsels and Works of God Almighty, ought in our judgment rather to be re-<413>ceived with admiration and a submission, than to be dived into with presumption. And what *Tacitus* says, in a certain place, may conveniently be applyed here: *Abditos numinis sensus exquirere illicitum, anceps, nec ideo assequare, i.e.* To search into the hidden designs of God is unlawful, uncertain, nor are they to be penetrated by us.[97]

Pope+ *Leo* X. of the House of *de Medicis* was an affable, and magnificent Man, very liberal towards all honest and learned Men, who might have made a very good Pope, if he had but had an indifferent [mediocre] knowledge of Religion, and an inclination to Piety, whereas he was very careless of both. He having lived very splendidly {in his flourishing state [*Staat*]}, and by his Liberality and Magnificence exhausted the <Apostolical> Chamber [treasury], and not being {personally} acquainted with the Arts of acquiring Riches, made use of the Cardinal *Laurence Puccius*, who at last, when all the other Gold Mines were emptied, proposed the way of raising mony by Indulgences.[98] These Indulgences were therefore 'sent abroad' [offered for money] all over Christendom, both for the dead and the living, |[Eggs, Milk, and the like were allowed to be eaten on fast days.]|[99]

The several sums of mony thereby to be raised, were beforehand assigned to certain uses; All what was to be Collected in *Saxony* and thereabout, as far as to the Sea side, having been granted to *Magdalen* the Pope's Sister; She to make the best of the Pope's Grant, had committed the whole management of her share to one *Arcimbold* a

The Virtues and Faults of Leo.

97. Tacitus, *Annals* VI.8.23–24. This is one of the few passages in the work where Pufendorf speaks in the first person, perhaps to dramatize the occasion. He regarded the Protestant Reformation in providential terms. See *The Present State of Germany*, V.9, in Pufendorf (2007), p. 126; and *Of the Nature and Qualification of Religion*, §54, in Pufendorf (2002c), pp. 120–21.

98. Lorenzo Pucci (1458–1531). Indulgences, which granted a sort of pro-rated relief from Purgatory, had also been issued, as well as sold, before this time.

99. Rather: "also that one might eat eggs and dairy foods on fast days, and other such things." The connection of this final remark with indulgences as a revenue-generating device is unclear, unless it suggests that compensatory indulgences could be bought for violating such rules.

Bishop by his Title and Coat; but who was most experienced in all the *Genoese* Tricks of Merchandising. He again employed such as did proffer the most, and had no other prospect [aim] than the getting of mony.[100] It had been formerly a Custom in *Saxony* that the Hermits of the Order of S. *Austin* [Augustine] used to proclaim the Indulgences. But *Arcimbold's* Commissioners, did not think fit to trust them at this time, as knowing them to be expert in that Trade, and fearing that they might not deal fairly with them, or at least that they might not bring in more mony than used to be gathered at other times. They chose therefore the *Dominicans* to Preach up the Indulgences, which the *Austin* Friers took very ill, as being thereby defrauded of their Authority [*Ansehen*], Right and Profit. The <414> *Dominicans* in the mean while, to show themselves 'well qualified' [diligent] for this new Employment, did magnifie their Ware to that extravagant degree, that their Auditors were extremely scandalized at it; especially since the Commissioners lived in continual debaucheries, and spent with great infamy, what the poor Country Fellows spared out of their Bellies, to redeem their sins.

Luther opposes Indulgences. This obliged *Luther,* a Frier of the Hermits Order of S. *Austin,* to oppose these impudent Merchants [*Krämern*] of Indulgences; and having duely weighed the matter with himself, he in the year 1517. did affix 95. Theses concerning this Point at *Wittenbergh,* and *John Tezel,* a *Dominican* Frier, published some other Theses in opposition to those, at *Franckfort* {on the Oder}. Thus the Dispute having been set on foot, each of them began to enlarge himself upon the abovementioned Theses. But *Luther* having upon his side both Reason and Scripture, his Adversary had nothing to alledge for himself, but the Authority of Afterwards the the Pope and the Church. Wherefore *Luther* was obliged to make an Popes Power. enquiry, upon what Foundation the Authority of the Pope was built, and in what condition the Church was at that time; which led him

100. Giovanni Angelo Arcimboldi (d. 1555) was one of three commissioners in charge of indulgences in Germany and Scandinavia, along with Christopher de Forli (the Franciscan General) and Albrecht, Margrave of Brandenburg and Archbishop of Magdeburg and Mainz. The Dominican, John Tetzel (1465–1519), served first under Archimbold and then under Albrecht.

by degrees unto the discovery of the Errors and Abuses, which were crept into the Church, and to an invective against the Impostures, and scandalous lives of the Monks and Priests [*Pfaffen*], and that ||[it was a duty incumbent upon the Magistrates]||[101] to abolish these Abuses. And to this purpose, as also to ||[oblige the Magistrates to uphold his Doctrine]||,[102] he spoke very magnificently concerning the Nature and Grandeur of the Civil Power, which the Priests hitherto had represented as despicable. By which means he at first got a great 'Party' [acclaim], and his Doctrine was spread abroad every where.

§26. But that we may the better understand the Reason, why a Poor Frier was able to give such a blow to the Chair of *Rome*, we must, next to the Supreme Direction of God Almighty, consider the circumstances of these times, and what disposition there was at that juncture of time in the minds of the People in General. First then, *Luther's* Propositions concerning the Indulgences were very good and reasonable, and a great <415> many Divines [*Theologi*], which afterwards opposed his Doctrine, were at first of his side, as were also some Cardinals, and *George* Duke of *Saxony* himself. His Adversaries were so perverse, that 'every body' [honest people] lamented their folly and perverseness. Neither was it at first in the least suspected, that things would go so far as they did. *Luther* himself had at first not the least thoughts of falling off from the *Pope*. The Emperor *Maximilian* had no aversion to the Doctrine of *Luther*, and it is credibly related, that, when he first heard of him, he did say; that this Frier ought to be kept safe, since good use might be made of him. Some Monks only, and these Commissioners, who were likely to be the losers by it, {foolishly} did make such a clamour, and raised such tumults by blowing up the Coals, that this small Spark broke out into a great Flame.

Whole Christendom was also in a miserable condition {at that time}, 'it' [the world] being quite overwhelmed with Ceremonies; the perverse Monks, did what they pleased {with impunity}, and had entangled ten-

The Circumstances of these times.

---

101. Rather: "magistrates [*Obrigkeit*] were authorized [*befugt*]."
102. Rather: "obtain support [*Rückenhalt*] for himself."

der Consciences in their {indissoluble} Snares. All Divinity [*Theologie*] was turned into {sheer} Sophistry. New Doctrines and Propositions were broached, without any regard, how they ought to be proved and maintained. And the whole Clergy of all degrees had rendred their Lives <and Conversations> odious and despised to the World. The late Popes *Alexander* VI. and *Julius* II. had been infamous for their {depravity,} Pride, Treachery, turbulent Spirit, and other such like Vices, as were very ill becoming Ecclesiastical [*Geistlichen*] persons. Such Bishops as were fit for something had quite entangled themselves in worldly business; a great many of them led a most scandalous Life, and were more expert in Hunting, than skilled in the Bible. The Priests [*Pfaffen*] and Monks were over Head and Ears in {the grossest} Ignorance, and scandalized the Common People by their Debaucheries [*ruchlosen Leben*], and their {insatiable} Avarice was grown unsupportable to every body.

The Ignorance of Luther's Adversaries.

Besides+ all this, those who first pretended to oppose *Luther,* were a sort of simple, miserable, and some of them debauched wretches; these, when they saw *Luther* maintain his Arguments in a manner which was not common at that time, were soon confounded and put to a *nonplus,* not knowing where to begin or to end. <416> 'Tis true, in former Ages also the Clergy had not been free from Vices, but the Ignorance of those barbarous times had served them for a Cloak. But after *Europe* began to be restored to its 'flourishing' [enlightened] condition, and all sorts of Learning began to dispel the former darkness, it was then that these abominable Spots {and their ugliness} became more conspicuous to the Eyes of the World. As the ignorant [*ungelehrten*] Priests and Monks, who could not bear the glance of this bright shining Light, were stark mad at those who had restored Learning to *Europe,* and did them all the mischief they could, and when they found themselves worsted by them, used to make a Point of Religion of their different Disputes, <and to accuse those of Heresie that were more Learned than themselves:> so these used to expose their folly, and as much as in them lay to discover their {shame and} Ignorance to the World. 'Twas upon this account, the impudent Monks pick'd a quarrel with *John Reuchlin,* whom they fain would have made a Heretick; from whence that learned {Franconian} Gentleman *Ulrick van Hutten* (if I remember right) took an opportunity to expose them most miserably in *Epistolis obscurorum virorum.*[103] Whilst the War betwixt the Lovers and the Persecutors of Learning was {still} carried on with great heat on both sides, *Luther*'s Doctrine appeared in the World. And because the Monks made it their business to bring the <most> learned Men into the same Quarrel which they had against *Luther,* in hopes to strike them both down at one blow, this proved the occasion that most of the learned Men [*Cultores bonarum literarum*] in *Germany* did actually side with *Luther:*

Erasmus favoured Luther.

It[+] is also undeniable that *Erasmus* of *Rotterdam* had a considerable share in the Reformation, for he had before already discovered, and reprehended a great many Abuses and Errors, he had rejected the 'School Divinity' [scholastic theology], and recommended the reading of the Bible and Fathers: he had ridiculed the Barbarity <and Ignorance>, which was upheld by the Monks {and priests [*Pfaffen*]}, and approved at first *Luther*'s Cause, tho he always excepted against [disliked] his violent and biting way of writing. His silence alone proved very mischievous to *Luther*'s Adversaries. For *Erasmus* being then esteemed the most learned Divine [*Theologum*] of his Age, every body took his silence for a <417> kind of an approbation of *Luther*'s Cause. And when he afterwards published his Treatise *de libero Arbitrio* [1523], it made no great impression upon the minds of the People, since it sufficiently appeared, that it was rather writ to please others, than of his own inclination. Besides that this was not the main Point in dispute, and *Luther* did refute sufficiently his Propositions.[104]

The[+] Princes and Estates of *Germany* also having been sufficiently convinced, that heavy Impositions had been laid upon them of late

103. Johann Reuchlin (1455–1522), grand-uncle of Melanchthon, fostered the study of Hebrew in Germany and opposed, in 1510, the project of Johann Pfefferkorn (1469–1523) and the Cologne Dominicans to destroy Jewish books in Germany (for being hostile to Christianity). Ulrich von Hutten (1488–1523) was the presumed author of *Epistolae obscurorum virorum* (1515–17), a satire on monastic ignorance focusing on the theologians of Cologne, which was used by Reuchlin's defenders. Reuchlin remained a Catholic, while von Hutten eventually joined with Luther.

104. Luther responded to Erasmus with *De servo arbitrio* (1525). Thomasius, pp. 180–81, has a long note on Erasmus and expresses the wish for a detailed and impartial biography.

under several pretences by the Court of *Rome*, for no other purpose
but to maintain the Grandeur of <the Ecclesiasticks at> *Rome*, were
extremely dissatisfied with the Pope. The general fear which was then
in *Germany* of an Invasion by the *Turks*, and the differences arisen betwixt *Charles* V.[,] *Francis* I. and *Henry* VIII. did greatly promote the
Reformation {as well}, since there was but little time for to think much
of these Disputes. Some are of Opinion, that [1] *Charles* V. did connive
at the spreading of the Doctrine of *Luther* throughout *Germany*, hoping
by these Divisions to get an opportunity to suppress <the antient Liberty of> the Estates, and to make himself Sovereign over *Germany*. For
else (they say) he might easily have quensh'd the Fire at first, *viz.* in the
year 1521. when he had *Luther* in his power at *Wormes* [Worms], where
he might have |[secured him, which would have passed well enough for
a State Trick.]||[105] But it is not so evident, whether, tho *Luther* had been
murthered against the Publick Faith [*parole*] granted him, thereby his
Doctrine would have been rooted out; it is more probable that [2] the
Emperor, being then but young, did not at that time foresee of what
Consequence this business might prove afterwards; and that he did not
think it advisable at that juncture of time to break with the Elector of
Saxony, who was then in great Authority. Neither could he 'pretend'
[afford] at the same time, when he was engaged in a War against *France*
and the *Turks*, to attack the Princes of *Germany* that were then courted
by *Francis*, and who began to make Alliances with them. Yet it is certain that under the pretence of Religion he afterwards made War upon
the Protestant Estates of *Germany*, and intended <418> by their ruin
to open himself the way to the <Absolute> Monarchy over *Germany*.
And tho he was very succesful in the War against the League made at
Smalkald, nevertheless he could not accomplish his projected design,
because he stood in need of the assistance of the *German* Princes against
France, and the *Turks*, and to obtain the Imperial Crown for his Son
Philip. Nay [Pope] *Paul* III. himself dreaded the 'growing greatness'
[fortune] of the Emperor, to that degree that he stirr'd up the *French*

105. There is a play on words: "seized him by the head, which could have passed
for a coup d'etat."

to oppose his prevailing Power, and to prevent the entire ruine of the Protestants, allowed them [the French] to make use of the Alliance with the *Turks* against the Emperor, who he feared intended a thorough Reformation of the Court of *Rome*.

And+ besides all this the ill Conduct of the Pope did great mischief to 'the *Roman* Catholick Party' [himself]. For it was a grand mistake in *Leo* X. that he with so much violence declared himself for these Merchants of Indulgences, and by his Bull of the 9. of *November* in the year 1518. decided the Points in Controversie betwixt them, whereby he cut off all <hopes and> means for an Accommodation {and deprived Luther of all hope for an amicable settlement}. It would questionless have been better for him to have stood Neuter, and to have imposed silence upon both Parties, and in the mean while to have found out an expedient to appease *Luther*.[106] And Cardinal *Cajetan* did {also} in the year 1519. act a very imprudent Part at *Augsburgh,* when he dealt so very rudely with *Luther,* and refused to accept of his Proposal, *viz.* that he would be silent, provided his Adversaries would do the same. For by this refusal made to so resolute a Man, whom he would have obliged to make a Recantation, he forced him to do his utmost, and to fall directly upon the Pope himself. It would have been no difficult matter to have granted him, that some corrupted Manners were crept into the Church, to keep him from meddling with the Reformation of the Doctrines. But on the contrary, the Pope making continual instances [requests] at the Elector of *Saxony's* Court, to have *Luther* delivered up to him, *Luther* was thereby obliged, to show the unreasonableness [*Unfug*] of the Pope, and to demonstrate that his own Doctrine was built upon a very solid and good Foundation {so that the elector might not listen to the pope}. And the Pope rendred his Cause very <419> suspicious, that he, when {later} *Luther* appeal'd to a Council, did by making a great many evasions protract to call one: From hence it was evident that he did not trust much to the goodness of his Cause, if it were to be debated before {free and} impartial Judges. It was also an unlucky hit for the Pope,

The ill Conduct of Leo and Cardinal Cajetan.

---

106. Thomasius, p. 188, refers to *The Present State of Germany,* V.9 and VIII.6, for further elaboration of this point.

when he fell out with *Henry* VIII. who to spite the Pope, did open the Door for the Protestant Religion to be settled in *England.* Likewise did those of the House of *Navarre* propagate and protect the Protestant Religion[107] in *France*, out of a hatred, as some say, against the Pope, who had shown the way to *Ferdinand* the Catholick into that Kingdom. Besides this there were abundance of good Men of the *Roman* Catholick Religion, who were glad to see that *Luther* did wash the scabby Heads of the Monks [*Pfaffen*] with so strong a Lye, as he did. So that every thing seemed to concur to promote the Decree of God Almighty.

Why the Doctrine of Luther was not spread farther.

§27. But, why the Doctrine of *Luther* was not spread farther, and the 'Ecclesiastical Monarchy' [papacy] was not quite overturned, several Reasons may be alledged. First it is to be considered, that, |[in those States, where *Luther's* Doctrine was received]|,[108] the Supreme {supervision and} Direction in 'Ecclesiastical' [spiritual] Affairs became necessarily to be devolved on the Civil Magistrates {in each of them}. For if any one of these States would have pretended to this Direction over the others of the same Communion, these, who would have thought themselves no less capable, would never have acknowledged the same. Which did not a little weaken their Union and Strength, and was the main occasion [reason], that they could not act so unanimously and vigorously against the Pope, as he against them.

It is also to be considered, that this Reformation was not undertaken after mature deliberation {about all things}, and as it were on purpose to form or set up a new State; but this great Revolution [*Veränderung*] happened upon a sudden and unexpectedly, so that the whole Work was carried on as occasion offer'd and by degrees. And tho *Luther* was the first, that gave the Alarm,[109] yet the rest did not think themselves obliged to follow precisely his Opinion, but were also ambitious of having contributed something towards the Reformation. This occasioned Disputes among <420> themselves, and because no body had an Au-

Divisions among the Protestants.

---

107. That is, the Calvinism of the Huguenots.

108. Rather: "after various states had renounced the papacy."

109. Literally: "that hung a bell around the cat's neck." Thomasius, pp. 192–93, explicitly rejects a *ius prioritatis* here.

thority among them, to decide these Controversies, each Party persisted obstinately in their Opinion; from whence arose such a Schism, that they became neglectful of the Common Enemy, and fell upon one another. This furnished the Popish Party with a very probable Argument, who cry'd out aloud the Hereticks were faln into Confusion among themselves, as not knowing what to believe; and since they had left the Church of *Rome,* they were brought into an endless Labyrinth.

There were also a great many of the Protestants, who under pretext of the Gospel did lead an impious and scandalous life, as if by the Liberty of the Gospel they had obtained a License to abandon themselves to all sorts of Vices. This gave also occasion to the Papists to defame the Doctrine of *Luther;* especially since he had with great severity reproved the licenciousness of the Clergy, and had been generally applauded for it. It also proved very mischievous to *Luther's* Doctrine, that immediately after {its promulgation} whole swarms of {detestable} Fanaticks, Anabaptists and the like appear'd in the World, and that the Boors in *Germany* ran as it were mad, and made a most dangerous Insurrection.[110] When some 'Princes' [potentates] took this Point into Consideration, the Doctrine of *Luther* began to become suspicious to them, as if thereby the {lawless} licenciousness of the 'Common People' [mob, *Pöbels*] was Taught and Authorised; which they looking upon as a greater Evil, than what oppression they were likely to suffer from the Clergy, did {begin} with all their Power {to} oppose the Doctrine of *Luther.* | The Licenciousness of some Protestants.

There+ are some who will have it, that the University of *Paris* also had a share in this. For *Luther* having persuaded himself, that this University was dissatisfied at *Leo* X. because he had abolished the Pragmatick Sanction, concerning the Elections of Bishops;[111] and that therefore the | The University of Paris.

110. The Peasants' Revolt (1525), which Luther condemned. Thomasius, p. 196, attributes the event to the fact that inner inclinations and visions replaced reason in the explication of Scripture. He contrasts this irrational extreme to that of an extreme [*spitzigen*, 'pointy,' detail-oriented] rationalism.

111. The so-called Pragmatic Sanction of Bourges (1438), issued by Charles VII, limited the pope's role with respect to the Gallican church, particularly in the appointment of bishops. It was superseded by the Concordat of Bologna (1516), agreed to by Francis I and Pope Leo X.

Members thereof would be glad of an opportunity to revenge themselves, he submitted his Disputation with *Eckius* to their Judgment; but
these gave their Judgment against him, and that in very hard words.
The Kings of *Spain* also did afterwards consider that it was for their
purpose [*Vorhaben*] to 'take upon them' [allege] the protection of the
Roman Chair; wherefore they opposed <421> the Protestant Doctrine
with all their might, and so powerfully assisted the League in *France*,
that *Henry* IV. if he would maintain his Crown, was obliged to leave
the Protestant Religion.[112]

Zwinglius   Some+ also have observed; that when *Zwinglius,* and afterwards *Cal-*
and Calvin.   *vin,* began all upon a sudden to introduce too great a Reformation, not
only as to the |[inferiour but also the Essential parts of the Church]|,[113]
and thereby fell from one extreme to another: this proved a main obstacle to the increase of the Protestant Religion. For *Luther* had hitherto
made very little alteration in |[outward Matters.]|[114] He had left in the
Churches the Ornaments, 'Clocks' [bells], Organs, Candles, and such
like, he had {initially} retained the greatest part of the Mass, but had
added some Prayers in the Native Tongue[,] so that he was looked upon
by most as a Reformer of the Abuses {in the Church} only: But when it
seem'd that this Revolution was likely to become Universal, *Zwinglius*
appear'd in *Switzerland,* as did *Calvin* afterwards in *France;* these, instead of following the footsteps of *Luther,* began to Preach against the
Presence of the Body of Christ in the <Sacrament of the> Lord's Supper,
abolish'd all sorts of Ceremonies and Ornaments, destroyed all Reliques, broke the Altars and Images, abolish'd all order of the Hierarchy,
and despoiled Religion of all such things as did most 'affect' [attract]
the Eyes and exteriour Senses <of the People>. This caused an aversion

112. The Catholic (or Holy) League was formed by Henry Duke of Guise in 1584
in order to contest Henry III's conciliatory policies toward the Huguenots. It was
effectively neutralized in 1594 when the Huguenot Henry of Navarre assumed the
French throne as Henry IV, after officially converting to Catholicism.
    113. Rather: "external form of the church, but also the essential elements of the
faith." See *The Present State of Germany,* VIII.7.
    114. Rather: "matters to which people were accustomed."

<and animosity> in the Common People against them, and increased its Zeal for that Religion, which it had received from its Ancestors.[115]

The Riches of the Church did partly promote *Luther's* Doctrine, a great many having thereby taken an opportunity to possess themselves of these ample 'Revenues' [goods, *Güter*]; nevertheless the same kept a great many Prelates under the obedience of the *Roman* Chair, who, if they had not been afraid of losing their Rich Benefices, would not have been so backward [reluctant] to side with *Luther's* Party. This was manifestly to be seen in *France,* where both the Prelates and Common People [*der gemeine Mann*] had made no great account of the Popes Authority before the Reformation, but when they saw that those of the Reformed Religion were for |[breaking into their Quarters]|,[116] they agreed better afterwards with <422> the Court of *Rome,* and the Commonalty [*das Volk*] was {also} very Zealous against the Reformed Religion.

§28. But besides this the Pope, as soon as his adherents had recovered themselves from their first consternation and his Enemies were faln out among themselves, has since settled his Affairs in such a manner, that the Protestants in all likelyhood will not only not be able to hurt him for the future, but he also by degrees gets ground of them {again}. For those things wherewith *Luther* did upbraid them, and did the most mischief to them, they have either quite abolish'd, or at least they are transacted in a more decent manner; *Si non castè, tamen cautè.*[117] They have also made use of the same Weapons, wherewith *Luther* did attack them. For the Popes now a days do not insult with so much haughtiness over

The Popish Sovereignty recovered.

115. Pufendorf consistently regarded Zwingli and Calvin as spoilers of Luther's enterprise, a sentiment for which he is criticized by Thomasius, pp. 198–99. In his final work, *The Divine Feudal Law* (*Jus feciale divinum*, Lübeck, 1695), Pufendorf sought explicitly to reconcile the two Protestant (Lutheran and Reformed) confessions, mainly by refuting the latter on scriptural grounds.

116. Rather: "making an end of them [*den Garaus spielen*]."

117. This Latin phrase occurs in Boccaccio's *Decameron* (ninth day, second novel), where an abbess, herself discovered in a sexually compromising position (with a "lusty priest"), advises a young nun detected in a similar indiscretion: "If not chaste, then at least careful."

Princes, but treat them with more Civility and Lenity. It is true, in the last Age [century] *Paul* IV. behaved himself very impudently towards *Spain,* and in our Age *Paul* V. did the same with *Venice.* But by the mediation of wiser Heads, these Differences were {soon} Composed, before they could draw after them any further ill Consequences; and the Popes ever since have been sufficiently convinced, that these hot-headed proceedings are in no ways suitable to their 'present condition' [state, *Staat*]. For *Paul* V. did quickly 'give fair words' [listen to reason], when the *French* Ambassadour made him believe, that the *Venetians* had sent for some Ministers from *Geneva,* ||[to be instructed in the Principles of the Reformed Religion.]||[118] Neither have of late years sate such Debauchees in the Papal Chair as *Alexander* VI. or such Martial Popes as *Julius* II. was, but of late they have endeavoured to carry on their Intreagues under hand, whilst they in outward appearance pretend to be the Promoters and Mediatours of Peace. That most scandalous Trade of Indulgences, and that gross sort of Simony they have set aside, whilst they make it their business to cajole the People out of their mony, in a 'more handsome' [better] manner.

The Bishops, Priests, and Monks, more Regular and Learn'd than heretofore.
The+ Bishops are now of another {noticeably improved} Stamp, and 'carry it on' [bear themselves] with much more gravity than before the times of *Luther,* nay, there are now among the Prelats eccellent <423> and well qualified Men. The Ordinary Priests and Monks also have been much 'Reformed' [refined] in their Manners, and {commonly} been obliged to lay aside their former brutish Ignorance [*die alte* brutalität]. *Luther* and his adherents did at first gain mightily upon the People[119] by their most excellent and learned Sermons, and {edified much} by their Books which they publish'd {in the common language,} thereby to excite the People to Piety, {fear of God}, Prayers, godly Meditations and Exercises. Both which the Papists have imitated since, for among them now adays are to be found most excellent Preachers, and very good Prayer-Books; so that the Protestant Clergy has now not much to object against them, as to their ability or outward behaviour. They

118. Rather: "and would soon declare themselves well reformed [*gut reformirt*]."
119. That is, they attracted many listeners.

have also got a very good insight into all the Controverted Points, and have a dosen or more Distinctions at hand against any Objection. For example: whereas nothing seems more ridiculous, than that the Pope should grant his Indulgences for twenty or thirty thousands years <to come>, they know how to give this a fine colour by these Distinctions of *Intensive* and *Extensive, Potentialiter* and *Actualiter*,[120] which 'relish strangely' [resonate greatly] with young Students, and the 'ignorant' [unlearned] suppose them to be terms full of Mysteries. And because {in Luther's time} the Ignorance of the Clergy, and the hatred conceived against Learning and learned Men, had proved very prejudicial to the 'Popish Monarchy' [papacy], the Popish Clergy, and especially the Jesuits, have since altered their Course, and {instead,} having taken upon them the Education of Youth, have pretended {almost} to the Monopoly of Learning |[among the *Roman* Catholicks]|[121]; so that <since that time> Learning [*Studia*] has not only not been prejudicial but very profitable to them.

Lastly,[+] they now adays do not {any longer} make use of Fire and Sword to 'propagate the *Roman* Catholick Religion' [expand the papacy], but the chief Men [*Häupter*] among the Protestants are inticed to come over to their Party with fair Words, great Promises, and actual Recompenses [*Gutthaten*]. If any one who is well qualified will go over to their Party he may be sure to make his Fortune, since the Wealth of their Church[es] furnishes them with sufficient Means to maintain such a Person, |[tho his Merits were not extraordinary.]|[122] Whereas on the contrary, if any one goes over from them to the Protestants <Religion>, and either has <424> not wherewithal to live, or else is endowed with extraordinary qualifications [*Capacität*], he must expect nothing but 'want' [hunger].

Last of all, those of the House of *Austria* have greatly promoted the

How they make Converts.

---

120. For instance, mere external performance could not guarantee remission of punishment associated with a sin, since a proper internal disposition was required as well; the grant of indulgences was conditional or qualified in certain ways.

121. Rather: "in their territories [*an ihren Orten*]."

122. Rather: "and easily allows them to fill a useless belly." See *The Divine Feudal Law*, §8, in Pufendorf (2002b), pp. 24–25, and §10, p. 28.

The House of Austria most Zealous for Popery. 'Popish Interest' [papacy], when they drove the Protestants out of the Hereditary Countries in *Germany*,[123] out of the Kingdom of *Bohemia* and the 'Countries' [provinces] belonging thereunto, and lately have done the same to the Protestants in *Hungary*, except to a very few; or else have forced them to 'profess themselves *Roman* Catholicks' [accept the popish religion].

The Temporal State of the Pope. §29. From what has been said {so far} it may easily be understood, 'in what manner' [to what extent] this 'Ecclesiastical' [spiritual] Sovereignty has extended her Power over the Western parts of Christendom. But throughly to understand the 'whole' [inner] Structure, and Composure of this Engine, and by what means it is sustained, it will not be improper to consider the Pope in two different ways; first as a Prince in *Italy*, and secondly as the spiritual 'Monarch' [sovereign] over the Western Church. As to the first it is to be observed, that the Pope may be reckoned a 'Potent Prince' [great lord] in *Italy*, but is in no ways to be Compared with {most of} the other 'Princes' [potentates] in His *Europe*. The 'Countries' [lands] under his Jurisdiction are the City of Dominions. *Rome*, with her Territories situated on both sides of the River *Tyber;* the Dukedom of *Benevento* in the Kingdom of *Naples*, the Dukedoms of *Spoleto, Urbino* and *Ferrara*, the Marquisate of *Ancona*, several places in *Tuscany* [Etruria], {as also in} *Romaniola* or *Flaminia*, where are situated *Bologna* and *Ravenna*. In *France* the 'Country' [earldom] of *Avignon* belongs to him. *Parma* is a Fief of the Church, which *Paul* III. granted to his Son {Peter} *Lewis Farnese*. But since that time a 'Constitution' [rule, *Verordnung*] has been made, that it shall not be in the power of any Pope to Alienate any {vacant} Fief, or to grant any of the 'Countries' [properties] belonging to the Church in Fief to any person whatsoever, to prevent the 'ruin' [weakening] of the 'Ecclesiastick' [papal] State, and, that, in case the Revenues from abroad should fail, the Pope nevertheless might not want means to maintain himself and his Court. The Kingdom of *Naples* is also a Fief of the Church, in acknowledgment

123. As distinguished from those regions of the German (Holy Roman) Empire subject to the Hapsburgs because of their (elective) imperial status only.

of which the King of *Spain* every year presents the Pope with a white Horse, and some thousands of Ducats. What other <425> Pretensions the Court of *Rome* makes are out of date. For the rest, these 'Countries' [lands] are 'indifferently' [sufficiently] Populous and Fertile, having several Cities of Note, out of which the Pope {supposedly} receives a Revenue of two Millions {of gold} *per annum.* And the Popes Ministers take effectual care, that their Subjects may not be overgrown in riches.

Perhaps[+] there might be a considerable number of good Soldiers maintained out of the Ecclesiastick Estate, but his [the pope's] Military strength is scarce worth taking notice of, since he makes use of quite other means to preserve 'his State' [himself] than other 'Princes' [potentates] do. He maintains about twenty Gallies, which have their Station at *Civita Vecchia.*[124] The chief State maxim of the Pope, as a Temporal Prince is, that Peace may be preserved in *Italy,* and that *Italy* may remain 'in the same State' [divided], as it is now, and especially, that there may not be introduced any 'other' [new] Sovereign Power, which might prove so formidable as to |[domineer over]|[125] the rest. He must take great care that the *Turks* may not get footing in *Italy,* and [that] in case of an Invasion from the *Turks,* not only *Italy* would be obliged to join against them, but also whole Christendom must be called in to help to chase out these Barbarians, since no Christian Prince would be contented that this 'delicious Country' [noble land] should fall into their hands.

His Forces.

The[+] Pope has nothing to fear more from the *German* Empire, as long as it |[remains upon the same Foundation.]|[126] But if it should fall under the Government of an Absolute Monarch [*souveränen Herrn*], it is likely he might attempt to renew the Antient Pretensions [*Recht*].[127] *Spain* and *France* are the two Kingdoms, which are most formidable to the Pope. Against them the Pope makes use of this Maxim, that he either sets them together by the Ears, or at least keeps up the Ballance

How he stands with relation to Germany, Spain and France.

124. A port city northwest of Rome, on the Tyrrhenian Sea.
125. Rather: "prescribe laws to all."
126. Rather: "retains the same form of government [*Regierungsform*]."
127. On the emperor's highly qualified (nonsovereign) position in the empire, see *The Present State of Germany,* chap. V, in Pufendorf (2007), pp. 111–58.

betwixt them, that one may not become quite Master of the other. I am apt to believe that the Pope would be glad with all his heart, that the *Spaniards* were driven out of *Italy,* especially out of the Kingdom of *Naples.* But it is scarce to be supposed, that he should be able to do it by his own strength, and to make use of the *French* in this case, would be to fall out of the Frying-Pan into the Fire. Therefore all what the Pope can do, is, to take care, <426> that *Spain* may not encroach upon others in *Italy;* and <there is no question but> if the *Spaniards* should attempt any such thing, *France* and all the other *Italian* States would be ready to oppose their design. Neither can it be pleasing to the Pope, if <the King of> *France* should get so much footing in *Italy,* as to be able to sway Matters there according to his [its] pleasure, which the Pope ought {also} to prevent <with all his might>.

The Pope need not fear much from the other States of *Italy.* For tho' some of them are under hand his Enemies, 'and' [because they] dread his Spiritual Power, [and] some of them also have been chastised [badly treated] by the 'Court of *Rome*' [papal chair], nevertheless, they must at least in outward appearance pay to the Pope a due Veneration, neither dare they as much as devise [intend] to make any Conquests upon the Pope. Notwithstanding this, they ‖[would not look with a good Eye upon the Pope, if he should pretend to make any Conquests upon his Neighbours]‖[128] and [thereby to] enlarge his Dominions; ‖[this refined Nation being extreamly jealous, and desirous to keep up the ballance betwixt the States of *Italy.*]‖[129]

Particular Constitution of the Popish Monarchy as Spiritual.

§30. But if we consider the Pope, secondly, as the Spiritual 'Monarch' [sovereign] of Christendom and the Vicar of Jesus Christ upon Earth, we meet in this Spiritual State with such <surprising and> subtile pieces, that it must be confessed, that since the beginning of the World, there has not been set up a more artificial 'Fabrick' [body] than the 'Popish Monarchy' [papacy]. It has required the more 'sagacity' [craftiness]

128. Rather: "should also not suffer the pope to overthrow one of them."

129. Rather: "because this same nation [Italy as a whole] will, if it is wise, be very jealous [careful] to maintain a good balance among its internal powers [*weil selbige kluge Nation sehr jaloux ist ihre inwendige Kräffte wohl zu balanciren*]."

to erect and sustain this Structure, the more the ends of this Sovereignty are quite different from the ends of all other States in the World, and the more feeble the Title appears upon which it is founded. For it is the <main> end of other Commonwealths [*Republiquen*], to {be able to} live in Security and Peace; for the maintaining of which, the 'Subjects' [members] contribute a share out of their Goods and Possessions; nay, venture their |[lives that they may sufficiently provide against the attempts of malicious People, and live in security and without danger from their Enemies.]|[130] And besides this, it is the Duty of 'every Subject' [everyone therein] to take care that he may be able to maintain himself out of his own |[Revenues, or by his Labour]|[131] and Industry. But the Popish 'Monarch's' [empire's] <chief> design is, that the Popes and 'the' [their] <427> Clergy may live in {might,} Plenty and Splendour in this World, |[all which is to be maintained at the Cost and Charge of other People, who must be perswaded to part with their Money by several shining Arguments and artificial Persuasions.]|[132] And whereas other States are fain [obliged] to maintain their {military} Forces and Garrisons with great Expences, the Pope on the contrary entertains his Militia{, however large it may be,} without any 'Charge' [trouble], but rather with Profit to himself. And whereas it is also a State Maxim [*Rath*] among the wiser 'Princes' [rulers], not to extend |[their Conquests]|[133] too far, the Pope has no 'occasion' [need] to imitate them in this point, since it is neither dangerous nor troublesome to him, tho' he extends his Jurisdiction over {territories in} the *East* and *West Indies*.

The Rights [*Rechmässigkeit*] of Sovereignty are founded upon evident and undeniable Principles [*Raison*] and divine Institution, since without it, it is impossible that mankind should live honestly, securely,

130. Rather: "very bodies and lives, so that they have at hand such power [*Macht*] as allows them to enjoy external and internal security, and to live free from the malice and injuries of other people." See *On the Law of Nature and of Nations*, VII.1, VII.2.1, VII.4.3, and VII.4.5.

131. Rather: "means [*Mitteln*], labor."

132. Rather: "though in such a way that they provide for their security and upkeep with other people's means, who are gotten to make these available through all kinds of fancy arguments and devices [*Künsten*]."

133. Rather: "the boundaries of one's realm [*Reich*]."

commodiously and decently [orderly]. But to find out ‖[the same necessity and foundation of]‖[134] the Pope's Sovereign Authority, 'and' [or] to
demonstrate that as the Peace and Welfare of Mankind, cannot subsist
without a supreme Civil Power [*hohe Obrigkeit*]; so the Christian World
cannot be without a 'supreme Ecclesiastical Power' [sovereign spiritual
head], is <in my mind> impossible to be done. He that is unwilling to
believe this, let him find out a demonstrative proof and he will ‖[be the
miracle of the World.]‖[135]

But if the Pope's Champions pretend to a positive Command from
God Almighty, they are obliged to prove by clear and 'evident' [dis-
tinct] proofs, and that in all its clauses and determinations out of the
Holy Scripture; that our Saviour when he sent his Disciples all over
the World to preach 'the Christian Faith' [his doctrine], did give them
full Power, not only to propagate the Christian Doctrine among all
Nations [*Völckern*], and not to be dependent on any humane Power in
their Office, so as thereby to be hindered from preaching or forced to
add or retrench any thing from their Doctrine (which Power is unques-
tionable)[,] but also that they had a Power granted them, to put into
the {public} Ministry [*Lehrampt*] of the Gospel, and that without the
Consent of the Magistrates (tho' the same professed the true [*in ihrem
rechten Verstand*] Christian Religion) as many and whom they pleased;
that they also might grant to these again full Power to increase their
Order ‖[to such a number as they should think fit <428> themselves]‖,[136]
without ‖[having any regard to the Civil Power or Magistrates, whose
Right and Title is thereby empaired.]‖[137] And because they cannot live
upon the Air, they must also have a Power granted them to seek out all
ways and means not only for their subsistance, but also for carrying on
their pride and extravagancies [*zur Pracht und Überfluß*]. They must
also have a prerogative granted them of being exempted from {obedi-
ence to} the Civil Jurisdiction[,] both in their persons and [in] such

134. Rather: "such a clear and well-founded title for."
135. Rather: "amaze us with his subtlety [hair-splitting, *Spitzfindigkeit*]."
136. Rather: "without measure and purpose [*ohne Maß und Ziel*]."
137. Rather: "being contradicted by anyone, including those whose rightful
power is thereby diminished."

possessions as ||[they have acquired to themselves]||,[138] tho' the same appertain to [derive from] the Revenues [*Güter*] of the Commonwealth [*Republicq*], are situated in 'the' [its] Territories, and enjoy the protection of the Sovereign, who is to have no power to lay Taxes upon them, to prescribe them limits or imploy them to any other uses. They must also prove that the supreme Direction over this Order[,] as well concerning {the performance of} their Office as [well as] their Possessions[,] does belong to one of the same Order on whom the rest depend as their Sovereign, and that the Civil Magistrates cannot pretend to any superiour Jurisdiction [*Recht*] over them, tho' the 'Ecclesiastical' [spiritual] Order either by its number[s] or misbehaviour should prove pernicious to the State, and tho' the State could not be maintained {or made to prosper} without the Revenues of the Ecclesiasticks, ||[which must not be imployed for the benefit of the publick without the Consent of him who has the supreme Direction over this Order.]||[139]

Besides this, they are obliged also to prove {clearly} some other *Hypotheses* of theirs, which are [asserted as] Matter of Fact. As for example, that our Saviour Christ did grant the Spiritual Sovereignty over the Church to 'St.' [the apostle] *Peter* only, without allowing the least share to the rest of the Apostles. That he did grant this Prerogative, not only to <St.> *Peter* for his own person, but also that the same should be a perpetual Inheritance {with the same right} to such as should succeed him in that place where he resided as Bishop. Besides this, they must prove that <St.> *Peter* was actually Bishop of *Rome,* that he exercised 'the same Power' [such sovereignty] there, and {irrevocably} granted the said Prerogative to no other place where he used to preach besides *Rome.*

And because these Points {with all their determinations} are so very hard to be proved, the Popish Doctors are obliged to be very cautious in proposing these Questions distinctly to 'the World' [their own people],

138. Rather: "their order has somehow acquired." Pufendorf's first point pertains to the juridical accountability of individual clerics, while the second refers to the clergy's collective holdings.

139. Rather: "unless the director of their order should generously approve of such use." The original contains a hint of mockery. See II.19, at note 61, p. 91, above.

but rather [must] treat of the same confusedly and 'superficialy' [deceptively]. It is rather their business to fill <429> the Peoples Heads with far-fetch'd Arguments which do not so nearly touch the point, *viz.* concerning the great Promises, that the Gates of Hell shall not prevail against the Church, concerning the great Authority [*Ansehen*] and Prosperity of the Church, her Antiquity, the Succession of the Popes, the Holy Fathers and Councils, the Authority of so many Ages and 'Nations' [peoples], Miracles and such like stuff, fit for a {well-sounding} Declamation. They also make use of another expedient, *viz.* that if any one dares to contradict these things, he is immediately[,] without hearing his reasons, branded with the Name of a Heretick and esteemed as one that being a 'novice' [pretender] and ignorant in his Trade, {because he has not honestly learned it,} |[ought not to be so bold as to contradict his Master]|,[140] but deserves to be burnt.

Why the Popish Sovereignty was to be exercised in the Form of a Monarchy. §31. It is easily to be imagined, that this spiritual Sovereignty was of necessity to be established in the form of a Monarchy, since it |[was in no ways suitable to]|[141] a Democratical or Aristocratical Government, not only by reason of several inconveniences which would have attended it, but more especially, because that so many different Heads as sway a Democratical and Aristocratical Government, would even by the most {precise and} severe Laws never have been kept in such a Union, but that by raising of Factions{, parties,} and Dissensions they would have easily overturned a Work which was {in any case} built upon so slight a Foundation. But among the several sorts of Monarchical Governments, they have chosen such a one as that <by all the Art of Men>, there could not have been invented one more suitable to their purpose; it being most certain that all the speculative Inventions of the most refined 'Politicians' [political writers], are not in the least to be compared to what may {in fact} be met withal in this Popish Monarchy.

140. Rather: "does not have the honor [*Ehre*] of speaking as a master or a journeyman." In the guild system, a distinction between those whose practice of a trade was warranted by proper apprenticeship, and those who performed such actions unlicensed and on their own (that is, without title and assurance of quality).
141. Rather: "would not have lasted long with."

'Tis true, some 'Princes' [kings] have gained |[to themselves and their Government a great Authority]|,[142] by pretending to be the Off-spring of the Gods, and that they had laid the Foundation of their Government by the express Command of the Gods and by their 'peculiar Approbation' [gracious signs]; wherefore they used to be after their death placed in the number of the Gods, and were adored as such. But the Pope has gone farther, and perswaded the People that he is the Lieutenant [*Stadthalter*] of Jesus Christ, who has all Power <430> in Heaven and Earth, and his Vicar [*Vice-Deus*] in the World, and that in a more exalted Sense than it is spoken of the Magistrates, that they are Ministers of God's Justice upon Earth. For he pretends that he has the Power of dispensing {all} the 'Merits of' [grace earned by] Jesus Christ, and that such as refuse to acknowledge this Prerogative [*Hoheit*], are not capable of obtaining Salvation. And since there is nothing more powerful in this World to induce People to a profound Veneration than the Divine Majesty, and no motive more strong to enforce from them an obedience and an entire submission to all sorts of hardship {and expense} than the fear of God's wrath and eternal damnation {of their souls}; it is evident that if this Point is once gained and the People thoroughly perswaded, there needs no further proof of the rest of their Articles of Faith, than that αὐτὸς ἔφα, the Pope has determined it so.[143]

Besides⁺ this, most Nations having esteemed an hereditary Government [*regna successiva*] the most convenient and least dangerous, have introduced that form into their States; but this form of Government could not suite with <the intention of> 'this Spiritual Monarchy' [the papacy]. For in these States where the Crown 'is hereditary' [passes from father to son], it must of necessity sometimes happen, that the same is devolved to Princes who are Minors; and it would be an odd sight, that a Child that rides the Hobby-horse, should be taken for the Vicar of Christ, and that the Protectour [*Vorsteher*] of Christendom should want a Tutor [need a guardian]. Neither is it to be supposed that

Why it must be an elective Monarchy.

142. Rather: "for their persons and kingdoms a special regard [*Ansehen*]."
143. See *On the Law of Nature and of Nations,* II.3.20 and VII.4.11, on the relative importance of worldly and spiritual sanctions.

young Princes could behave themselves so gravely and wisely, as seems to be requisite for a Person of his station; neither can it as much as be hoped, that a whole succession of 'Princes' [young lords] should be inclinable to such a Function. In a word, an hereditary succession would have made it the same with a {mere} temporal State, which could never have been maintained long upon so 'awkward and slight a Foundation' [unnatural a title]. For the great Ministers {of this state} themselves would have been for putting by [overthrowing] the Pope, that they might succeed in his stead; whereas these seeing they cannot possess themselves of the Papacy by open force are now very obedient, in hopes that either they themselves or at least their Friends [*die ihrigen*] may one time or another attain to this Dignity by Election. Besides this, it might easily have happened, that in case <431> the Royal Family should have been extinguished, such Dissensions might {easily} have arisen concerning the Succession, that the whole 'Frame of the State' [machine] would thereby have been disjointed [torn apart].

Why the Pope was to live in a State of Celibacy. It+ was also thought convenient [that] this <spiritual> Sovereign should be obliged never to marry, which seemed most suitable to the gravity of this Court, since a great train of Ladies living in great splendour and plenty would have made such a figure, as must needs appear but little suitable to excite others to a Holy Life and Devotion. |[Wherefore it was the main design, by a fained hypocrisy to impose a belief upon the People, as if the Court of *Rome* was so wholly taken up with spiritual Affairs, that there was no room left for worldly Pleasures.]|[144] It was also reasonably supposed, that a Prince who had Wife and Children might sometimes be led away to take more to heart the private Interest of his Family than the publick Good of the State, since there can scarce be any thing more prevailing upon a Man, than the consideration of the welfare, and preservation of Wife and Children. And what *Alexander* VI. and *Paul* III. did with their Bastards, have been convincing Instances of this position 'to' [at] the Court of *Rome*. It is possible that they also took this into consideration, that if a Temporal

144. Rather: "Moreover, the pretense of holiness [*Scheinheiligkeit*] required the appearance that one had no taste for fleshly delights and feelings."

<foreign> Prince should obtain 'this Dignity' [the papacy], he 'would' [might] entail it upon his House {and lineage as an inheritance}, which inconveniencies are now avoided by the Obligation which is laid upon the Pope never to marry.

The[+] Conclave is also a most admirable Invention to bridle the im-   The Conclave.
moderate Ambition, and prevent those Schisms, which used formerly miserably to <afflict the See and> weaken the Authority of the 'Popes' [papal chair]; besides that, thereby a long Vacancy of the Chair [*inter-regna*] is prevented, and by means of this Election, it is much easier to pick out one that is fitly qualified to represent the [act the part of a] great and artificial Hypocrite, and afterwards to make the People believe, that are ignorant of the Intrigues of the Conclave, that it was by the particular providence of God Almighty, that such a Person was chosen as was the most {suitable and} worthy to be God's Vicar upon Earth. Thus much at least may be obtained by an Election, that such a Person is chosen as is well versed in 'the Arts of Po-<432>licy' [worldly intrigues] and <their> ambitious Designs [*Regiersucht*], and whose Age being above the folly and extravagancies [heats] of young Men, may by his years and long experience appear more venerable in his Function.

It is also a very wise Ordinance concerning the Election of a Pope,   What
that he is to have two third parts of the Votes in the Conclave, which   Qualifications
                                                                          are necessary
seems to have been introduced, that the new Pope might not be dis-   for one that
pleasing to a {too} great number of Cardinals. Now a days it is a general is to be
                                                                          chosen Pope.
maxim in the choice of a Pope, to elect {not a *transalpinus* but} an *Ital-
ian,* which is not only done because they rather will bestow this Dignity and Advantage upon a Native of *Italy* than upon a Foreigner, but also because the security and preservation of the Papal Chair depends <in a great measure> on the ballance which is to be kept betwixt *France* and *Spain,* which is not to be expected from a *French* or *Spanish* Pope, who would quickly turn the Scale, and by granting too great Prerogatives to his Country-men, <endeavour to> exclude others from the Papal Chair. They also choose commonly a Pope who is pretty well [on] in years, but very seldom a young one, [so] that also others may be in hopes of at-taining the same Dignity, and that a young Pope during a long Regency [reign] may not undertake to alter their Customs and Maxims, or to

make his Family so Rich and Potent and set up so many Creatures of his own, as thereby to entail the Papal Chair upon 'his House' [these]. Besides that, |[in this station where the Pope need not to go into the Field, there is more occasion for a grave antient Man than a vigorous young Person.]|[145] It is also another Maxim among them, to take care that he may not be too near a Kin to the deceased Pope, that the vacant 'Church-Benefices' [*spiritual* beneficia] may not {all} fall into the Hands of one Family, and [that] the new Pope may be the sooner prevailed upon to amend the Faults of his Predecessor. Lastly, they are commonly for choosing such a one as is neither too much addicted to the *Spanish* nor the *French* Interest, yet that he 'be not hated by' [not hate] either of these two parties. Wherefore it is {also} a Custom among them, that both these Crowns {openly} give in a List of such <Cardinals> as they would have excluded from being elected Pope.

Notwithstanding all this it often so happens, that one is chosen Pope of whom no body thought be-<433>fore, when the Cardinals are tired out by so many Intrigues, and are glad to get out of the Conclave. It is also often observed, that a Pope proves quite another Man after he is come to sit in the Chair than he was before, when yet a Cardinal. The Pope at his entring upon the Government, is not tied to any certain Rules or Capitulations, since it would seem very unbecoming to controul by humane Laws and Contracts <the Power of> him who is pretended to be {so abundantly} endowed with the Holy Ghost.

College of the Cardinals.

But[+] the College of the Cardinals is as it were the standing Council [*perpetuus Senatus*] of the Ecclesiastical State, in like manner as the Chapters of the Cathedrals are to the Bishops in *Germany.* With those the Pope 'advises' [consults] concerning Matters of the greatest moment; nevertheless it often happens that the Popes and their Nephews make but little account of their Advice {and consent}, but act as they please. The chief 'Prerogative' [dignity] of the Cardinals consists chiefly in that they have the Power of choosing a Pope, and that out of their own 'Body' [midst, *Mitteln*], they being supposed to be the next to

---

145. Rather: "the vigor of youth is not required for this office [*Ambte*], since one need not be able to go into battle but only to dine with gravity."

him, and best acquainted with the Affairs of the Court of *Rome,* which is one necessary qualification of a Pope. Their ordinary number is Threescore and Ten, which is seldom complete. They now a-days are treated by the Title of your Eminency, according to a Decree of Pope *Urban* VIII. whereas they were formerly called Most Illustrious (*Illustrissimi*) which Title was grown very common in *Italy.* And because the Cardinals had got a 'new' [more elevated] Title, the Princes of *Italy* 'pretended' [wanted] also to be treated by the Title of your Highness (*Altezza*) whereas formerly they were very well satisfied with the Title of your Excellency (*Excellenza.*) The Election of the Cardinals depends <absolutely> on the Pope's pleasure who nevertheless, constantly takes notice of such as are recommended to that Dignity by *France, Spain* and other 'Princes' [potentates]. The Parasites of the Court of *Rome,* are not ashamed to 'maintain' [write], that the Cardinal's Cap is equal in Dignity to a Crowned Head, and 'to this day' [at the least] they [cardinals] pretend to have the precedency before the Electors of the Empire.

Ever[+] since the time of Pope *Sixtus* IV. *viz.* since the Year 1471. the Popes have made it their {special} Business to enrich {and elevate} their Families out of the Church Revenues, of which there are very remarkable Instances. For it is <434> related that *Sixtus* V. during his Regency [reign] of five Year, did bestow upon his Family above three Millions of Ducats; and *Gregory* XV. had in two Years and three Months, got together the value of three Millions {*Scudi*} in Lands [*Gütern*], without reckoning what he left in ready Money.[146] It is reported of the House of the Barbarini's, that at the death of *Urban* VIII. they were possessed of 227 Offices [*chargen*] and Church-Benefices, most of them reckoned at three, five, eight and ten {or more} Thousand *Scudi* a piece, whereby it is said, they got together a Treasure of 30 Millions of *Scudi.* This has been represented as a very scandalous thing by 'some' [many], but if duly considered, it is a great folly to suppose, that since the main intention of the 'Popish Sovereignty' [papacy] is to enrich {and to elevate the standing [*Ansehen*] of} the Clergy, the Popes should stifle their natural

The Popes enrich their Kindred.

---

146. *Ducats* were gold coins going back to the Middle Ages, and *scudi* were silver coins first issued by Charles V in 1551.

inclination toward their 'Kindred' [family], and not make Hay whilst the Sun shines. This is rather <to be look'd upon as a> common <Infirmity>, that Favourites and others whilst they are Fortunate are envied by others, who are vexed because Fortune is not so favourable to them. Besides that, the Revenues of the Church are so great, that the Popes[,] since they need not entertain any considerable Army, scarce know how to employ them better.

Since[+] the time of Pope *Urban* VIII.[147] a Custom has {also} been introduced, to make one of the Pope's Nephews Chief Minister <of the Ecclesiastical State>, whom they call Cardinal Patroon (*Cardinal Patrone*). Among other Reasons, why the Pope commits the management of Affairs [*das Regiment*] to one of his Nephews, this is {especially} alledged for one; that by reason of the nearness of Blood, he ought to be preferred before others, and that by so doing, the Pope's Person is better secured against any attempts which are sooner made upon his Life than [that] of <other> hereditary Princes, whose death their Successours 'are able' [tend] to revenge. How fearful the Popes are of Poyson, may be judged from thence, that as often as the Pope receives the Sacrament [Communion], his Chaplain who is to administer the Bread and Wine, is obliged to taste of both before the Pope. It is also pretended, that by the Ministry of the Nephews, this Advantage is obtained, that the other Ministers and Governours have not so much opportunity to enrich themselves, and to put one another <435> out of place, which is the common Custom in Elective States. For their Nephews are few in number, and therefore sooner to be satisfied; neither will they easily suffer that others should enrich themselves, since they are sensible that all the hatred falls upon themselves. They are also very serviceable to the Pope, {it is supposed,} in that they more freely can disclose the Interests of <the several> Princes to him, than other Ministers [*Bedienten*] who are not so nearly allied [*zugethan*] to him, and that they are fain to be more circumspect in their management of Affairs, for fear, lest |[they may one time or another be called to an account]|[148]; for which reason

Cardinal Patroon.

147. Urban VIII was pope from 1623 to 1644.
148. Rather: "others revenge themselves upon them at some time."

it is their Business, so to oblige one Prince or another, that they may upon all occasions be sure of his 'Protection' [support]. Besides, that by their Assistance, Affairs may be carried on with much more secrecy than otherwise. And if the Pope were destitute of their Counsel [services], he would be obliged to have recourse to the Cardinals, who most commonly are very partial [*parteyisch*], being most of them engaged to foreign Princes either by Pensions or Benefices.

§32. The Subjects of this 'Ecclesiastical Monarchy' [spiritual sovereignty] may commodiously be divided into two several sorts; the first comprehends the whole Clergy, the second all the rest of Christendom, as far as the same |[professes the Roman Catholick Religion]|,[149] which is commonly called the Laiety. The first may be compared to the standing Army of a 'Prince' [potentate], who thereby maintains his {great} Conquests; the rest are to be deemed as {mere} Subjects 'that are' [and] Tributaries to the Prince, and are obliged to maintain those {great} standing Forces at their {considerable} Charge.

<aside>Concerning the Celibacy of the Popish Clergy.</aside>

The first have this particular Obligation upon them, that they must {all} abstain from Marriage. This is done under pretence of a special Holiness, and that thereby they may be the more fit to perform their 'Duty' [office] without any hinderance; but the true reason is, that they should not prefer the Interest and Welfare of their Wife and Children, before that of the Church, and in consideration thereof, not side with those Princes under whose Jurisdiction they live, or that they should not 'enrich' [support] their {wife and} Children with the Revenues of the Church, but be the more ready 'upon all occasions' [in all respects] to execute the Pope's Will, especially <436> against such Princes, under whose Protection they live. For since Wife and Children are esteemed the 'dearest' [greatest] Pledges, |[not to be left to the discretion of an enraged Enemy]|,[150] they [the clergy] could the easier despise the anger of their Princes, if they had no other Care to take but for themselves {and were not bound to the commonwealth [*Republic*]}, a single Man

149. Rather: "adheres to the Roman church."
150. Rather: "by one who has them within his power [as hostages]."

not needing to fear a livelihood in any place whatever. And it has {in any case} been the main endeavour of the Popes to exempt the Clergy by all means from the {dependence and} Jurisdiction of the Civil Magistrates, and to make them only 'dependent on' [answerable to] himself. Besides this, the avaricious Clergy would not have made so good a Harvest if it had been taken for granted among the People, that the same was collected for their Wife and Children, whereas now it is pretended, that they receive not for themselves, but for the maintainance of the Church. But those who have been so busie to force Celibacy upon the Clergy, were {shamefully} forgetful in not prescribing them at the same time a {suitable} *Recipe* against Incontinency, <and> which they seem to

Their Number. stand in great need of. How vast a number there is of this sort of People, may be best judged out of what is related of Pope *Paul* IV.[151] who used {supposedly} to brag, that he had 228.000 Parishes, and 44.000 Monasteries under his Jurisdiction, if he did not mistake in his account, especially as to the Monasteries.

The Clergy may again be subdivided into two sorts, *viz.* those who are bare Priests and Ecclesiasticks [*Geistliche*], and those who have engaged themselves by a particular Vow, *viz.* the Monks and Jesuits who are to be esteemed the Pope's 'pretorian Bands' [bodyguard]. 'They' [These militias] receive for their pay {great} Honours and Dignities, 'great Revenues' [a fat income], a quiet Life, without any great Labour, and 'live always near a good Kitchin' [a guaranteed meal]; but those who have addicted themselves to a more strict Order, are fed with the <vain> belief of Holiness, great Merits and particular Prerogatives above others.

The Popish §33. The Pope makes use of this Artifice to keep the Laiety in Obedi-
Doctrine suted ence, that he persuades them to receive and consider {him and} his
to the State. 'Ecclesiastical' [spiritual] Troops, as the <Chief> Promoters of their Salvation, and Masters over their Consciences; which |[serves like a Bridle to lead and turn them about according to the Will of the Clergy.]|[152]

---

151. Paul IV was pope from 1555 to 1559.
152. Rather: "is the strongest bridle for leading someone as one wishes." See §26, pp. 469–70, above, and §34, p. 502, below.

<437> And that every thing may be accommodated to the 'Interest' [purpose] of this Spiritual 'Monarchy' [sovereignty], several Articles of the Christian Religion have been by degrees stretched or patched up with new Additions; and any one that will duly weigh these Matters wherein they differ with their Adversaries, will soon find that in those points there is generally a mixture of Interest as to the Authority, Power and Revenues of the Clergy.

Among those in the first place is to be reckoned the Doctrine concerning the Authority [*Hoheit*] and Power of the Pope, whereby they pretend to set him above Councils, and make him Infallible; which point is stretched to the utmost by the Jesuits, because, if that stands fast, all the rest is soon proved. Wherefore, what has {always} been taught formerly, and if I am not mistaken, is taught even to this Day, by the Doctors of the *Sorbon, viz.* that the Councils are equal to, or rather above the Pope, is destructive [contrary] to the 'very fundamental Constitution' [foundation] of the Popish 'Monarchy' [state], since this Doctrine smells strongly of a Democracy, which is 'directly' [entirely] contrary to a Monarchy.[153] And it is not <easily> to be reconciled how the Pope |[who pretends to have]|[154] such great Prerogatives <above all others>, should be subject to the Censure of his Creatures and Vassals. For as they will have it, whatsoever either the Holy Scripture, or the antient Fathers have attributed to the Church, ought <altogether> to be applied to the Pope {alone}, |[in like manner, as what is spoken of a whole Kingdom, is commonly to be understood of the King.]|[155]

The+ Laiety has been debarred from reading the Holy Scripture, {and this permitted only to the clergy,} by which means not only the Authority of the Clergy is maintained among the People, as if the Priests were the only 'Men' [ones] that have a privilege to approach to the Divine Oracles; but also the Laiety is thereby prevented from finding

As that of the Pope's Power.

The prohibition of the Laietys reading the Scriptures.

153. Thomasius, p. 257, notes that conciliarism (as an affair of the clergy alone) is antithetical not only to the religious authority of the pope but also to the secular sovereign's *ius circa sacra*. It merely transforms the church from a monarchical into an aristocratic institution.

154. Rather: "to whom are attributed."

155. Rather: "according to the well-known saying, that whatever a king does is attributed to the kingdom." This logic holds if the Church is in fact a monarchy—which Pufendorf disputes.

out those points in the Scripture which are repugnant to the Interest of
the Clergy: For if the People should once ||[get a true Understanding of
the Scripture]|,[156] they would not be so forward to follow so blindly the
Instructions of the Priests. They also by this means prevent the Laiety
from {bothering about and} diving too deeply into Divinity, which they
pretend belongs only to the Clergy; and for this reason it is that they
{also} attribute the Power of explaining the Scripture to the <438> Pope
only, that nothing may be brought to light, which may in any ways be
prejudicial to 'the spiritual Monarchy' [his state]. For the same reason
the Pope pretends to have the sole Authority of deciding all Controversies whatsoever.

Traditions.   It+ is also given out <among the People>, that the Holy Scripture
is 'imperfect' [incomplete], which must be 'explained' [completed] by
<antient> Traditions; whereby they gain this point, that if they invent
any Doctrine for the Interest of 'the' [their] <spiritual> State whereof
there is not the least footsteps [traces] to be found in the Holy Scripture, they without any other proof, may only have recourse to the antient Traditions.

Venial and   The+ distinction betwixt Venial and Mortal Sins, as also what is
Mortal Sins. alledged *de casibus reservatis*,[157] is barely [only] invented for the benefit of
the Clergy. That infinite number of Books of Confession,[158] enough to
fraight [freight] whole {East India} Fleets withal, is not published with
an intention to correct Vices, but that by laying a Tax upon the same,
the Clergy may the better be able to maintain their 'Grandeur' [power],
and satisfie their Avarice. The most 'comfortable' [comforting] Doctrine
of remission of Sins, has wholly been accommodated to the Interest of
Penance.   the Clergy. For, because it would not have turned to the profit of the
Clergy, if every one who truly repented should obtain remission of his

156. More literally: "wise up [*gar zu klug werden*]."
157. These are cases where forgiveness is not within the power of just any confessor but "reserved" to a higher (human) authority. Mortal and venial sins are distinguished by their gravity: mortal sins, unless absolved, entail eternal "death" or
damnation.
158. Manuals detailing various kinds of sins, interspersed with scriptural passages
and prayers.

Sins, only by Faith in the Merits of Christ; it has been the Doctrine of the Church of *Rome,* that it was an essential piece of penitence, and the means to obtain forgiveness of Sins, if a most exact and precise account of every individual Sin committed was given to the Priest. By which means, they not only keep the People under their Devotion, and make such impressions upon them as are fitting for their purpose; but they also come thereby to the knowledge of all Secrets, Counsels, Designs and Inclinations of the People, which they make good use of for their benefit; notwithstanding, that they are under an obligation not to reveal any thing that is told them by way of Confession; for, else it would be impossible for them to persuade the People to act {so uncomfortably and} against the natural Inclination of all Mankind.[159]

The Priest has also a Power to command works of satisfaction to be done, whereby he com-<439>monly has his good share. For tho' {only} certain Prayers, Pilgrimages, Fasts, Flagellations and the like, are often imposed upon them for Penances, yet they also very often condemn some, and especially the richer sort[,] in a good sum of Money, to be given <instead of a Penance> to a certain Monastery, Church, or the Poor, among whom are {also} the Mendicant-Fryars. These 'honest Fellows' [good people] call themselves *minimos fratrum,* according to the 25. Chap. of St. *Matthew,*[160] that they may have a fair shining pretence to fill their Purses. For by this Interpretation, the Christians have got this benefit, that they are obliged to feed and maintain 100.000 lazy, 'idle' [stout] Fellows. Besides this, the first sort of Penance may be redeemed with Money, if you think it too hard to be performed. And who that is wealthy, would not be 'civil' [deferential] and liberal towards his Father-Confessour, to oblige him to a mitigation of the Penance, or because he has already shewed himself favourable before?

Why[+] good Works have been made meritorious and {placed among} the means of obtaining Salvation from God Almighty, is easily to be guessed. For when they were {afterwards} to give a definition of good

Merit of good Works.

---

159. That is, people are loath to reveal their own failings and misdeeds to others.
160. Matthew 25:40: ". . . whatever you did for one of the least of these brothers of mine. . . ."

Works, they were sure to put in the first place, that the People ought to be liberal towards the Clergy, Churches and Monasteries, and to perform every thing which is commanded them by the Pope and his adherents, tho' never so full of Superstition and Hypocrisy. Neither must this be forgot, that they also have taught, that the Monks are not only able to perform good Works sufficient for themselves, but that also they have an overplus of Merits[161] which they can 'sell' [leave] to the {poor} Laiety. And out of this overplus, they have laid up an inexhaustible store very profitable to the Clergy, which costs them nothing {to acquire or preserve}, which does not grow musty nor ever decays, and which cannot be returned 'upon their hands' [in time], when the Buyer finds out the Cheat.

Ceremonies.   Their+ Religious Exercises are so full of Ceremonies, so many superfluous Feasts and Processions are instituted, so many {unnecessary churches,} Chapels and Altars erected[,] only to employ so great a number of Clergymen, who else would appear like so many idle Fellows, |[whereas now it turns all to their profit]|[162]; which is also the reason why they have encreased the number of Sacraments to seven, since they <440> know that none of them can be administered, but the Priest gets [something] by it. The Mass without Communicants[163] has been introduced and proclaimed a Sacrifice both for the dead and the living, that they might have an opportunity to put both the dead and the living under Contribution. For no body undertakes any thing of moment, but he has a Mass sung first, for the good success of the thing in hand. No body of wealth dyes, but he orders a good store of Masses to be sung for his Soul, all which brings grist to the Priest's Mill.

Half   On+ the other hand,[164] after it once was become an abuse, that the
Communion. Laiety did receive the Sacrament [the host] without partaking of the Cup, it was made into a Law. And tho' the contrary was very evident

161. The so-called treasury of merit, which could be dispensed through the sale of indulgences.

162. Rather: "and because there is always something 'left over' during such works."

163. That is, when a priest celebrates mass all by himself without anyone else present to share in the communal meal, often multiple times in a row.

164. The implied contrast is between an expansion and a contraction of a practice.

both by the Institution of Christ, and the practice of the Church for a great many Centuries, yet did they persist with great obstinacy, because it should not seem that the Clergy had committed an Errour; and also that they might have a Prerogative before the Laiety in this Sacrament.[165] And to ridicule the more impudently both God and Men, they give to the Laiety a Chalice which is not consecrated, which in very despicable Terms they call the rinsing Chalice,[166] as People when they have eaten any uncleanly thing, use to rinse their Mouths.

Marriage[+] also was to be made a Sacrament, tho' nothing is more absurd, that the Clergy might have an opportunity to draw all matrimonial Causes under their Jurisdiction, which are often very profitable, very various and of the greatest Consequence, since the 'welfare' [status, *Stand*], inheritance and succession of <most> People, nay, even of whole Kingdoms depend thereon. This obliged *Mary* Queen of *England* to endeavour the re-establishment of Popery in that Kingdom; for without the Pope's Authority, she must have passed for a Bastard.[167] And *Philip* III. King of *Spain* was among other reasons obliged to the Pope, because he had given Dispensation to his Father to marry his own Sister's Daughter, of whom *Philip*[168] was born, which Marriage would not easily have been approved by other Christians. There were also so many prohibited degrees [of proximity] introduced <on purpose>{, and a spiritual relation invented,} that the Clergy might have frequent opportunities to give Dispensations, whereby they know how to <441> feather their Nest.

Marriage made
a Sacrament.

By the Extreme Ointment [last rites] the Priest |[takes an occasion to exhort the dying people]|[169] to leave Legacies for pious uses, which they

Extreme
Unction.

165. Thomasius, p. 274, notes that Lutherans have retained many of these practices, particularly private confession and exorcism.

166. A vessel into which the priest rinses off the particles that may cling to his fingers after distributing communion.

167. Mary I (Tudor), half-sister of Elizabeth I, reigned 1553–58. Henry VIII had divorced Mary's mother, Catherine of Aragon.

168. Philip III (1578–1621).

169. Rather: "has a good opportunity to remind dying people in a friendly way." Here as elsewhere, Pufendorf's language is often more ironic and sarcastic than Crull's.

commonly know how to apply to the advantage of their own Order.

Purgatory. Purgatory was invented for no other purpose, but that the dying Man, who at that time is not so greedy of 'worldly' [his] Goods, which he is to leave to others, might be liberal towards the Clergymen, in hopes, by their intercession and a good number of Masses to get the sooner out of

Reliques, this hot place. The Veneration paid to the Reliques, has also been very
Prayers to beneficial to the Clergy; these are employed, besides other uses, to re-
Saints. ward people of Quality, that have done great services to the Pope, with a piece of an old Bone <in lieu of a better present>. The Adoration of the Saints serves for a pretext to build the more Churches, institute more Feasts and employ and feed a greater number of Priests. The power, which the Pope has assumed of Canonization, gives him a considerable authority among the People, as if it were his prerogative to bestow Dignities and Offices upon whom he thinks fit, even in Heaven, and that God Almighty cannot but accept of such Referendaries,[170] as the Pope is pleased to represent to him. By this means he ||[makes himself Master of the Inclinations of the People though living in far distant places]|,[171] unto whom he proposes this as a {great} Recompense of their Credulity and Ambition, if they stick at nothing to promote his Interest. And ever since this Superstition has taken root <in Christendom>, those who have been Canonized have 'for the most part' [only] been Clergymen, who {mostly} either by a new invented Hypocrisie, or outward appearance of Holiness had made themselves famous <in the World>. Or if by chance one Layman or another has attained to this Dignity, either he himself, or at least those that interceeded for him, have been fain [obliged] to deserve very well of the 'Papal' [Roman] Chair. Not to mention here, in what [other] manner they by {various} fictitious Miracles, several sorts of Images, Apparitions, Exorcisms, Indulgences, Jubilees, prohibition of divers sorts of Victuals, and such like tricks used to fool the People out of their mony. <442>

170. Saints were conceived as "referendaries" because they received petitions and interceded between God and humans.

171. Rather: "can also bend to his will people in other commonwealths [*Republiquen*]"; that is, by creating saints for them. This makes clearer the political and international implications of the practice. See note 1, p. 115, above.

§34. Next to what has been said, the Universities [*Academien*], which ~ The
have partly been Instituted by the Popes Authority, partly by other ~ Universities
States, yet so that most of them have been Confirmed by the Popes, ~ have promoted
who also have claimed the Supreme Direction over the same, have been ~ Sovereignty.
'mainly' [very] instrumental in maintaining the Popish Sovereignty. It is
evident enough of what Consequence this Direction must needs be <to
the Pope>. For, since in the Universities Men {who will teach or direct
others} are first imbued with such Opinions, as they {themselves} afterwards are to make use of during their whole Life, and instil them into
others, the Universities, and 'Sciences there to be taught' [studies pursued there] were to be sure to be accommodated to the Popes Interest.

Neither were the Professours of Divinity [*Theologiae*] here, who
claimed the Precedency before all others, the only Creatures of the
Pope, but also the Professours of the Canon Law, who were as busie
as any to put his Decrees{, and chicanery,} upon 'the World' [Chris-
tendom], and to maintain his Authority. For the World may thank the
Canon-Law for the first Introduction of those long Law Suits, which
the Clergy pretended to belong to their Jurisdiction, [so] that by receiving of Bribes they might the sooner satisfie their Avarice. The greatest part of the Philosophers were also the Popes Slaves, and if one or
another attempted to investigate the true causes [*Grund*] of Things,
he was sure to be kept under by all the rest. The Divinity and Philosophy which was professed in these Universities were not taught with
an intention to make the 'young Students' [people] more learned and
understanding [*klüger*], but that |[the ingenious by these confused and
idle terms might be]|[172] diverted from throughly investigating those
matters which 'would' [could] have led them to the whole discovery of
the Popish Intreagues. For their Scholastick Divinity is not employed
in searching and explaining the Holy Scripture, but for the most part
entangled in useless questions, invented chiefly by *Peter Lombard,*
Thomas Aquinas, Scotus, and the other Patriarchs of Pedantry. And what
they call Philosophy is nothing else but a 'Collection' [swill] of 'foolish

172. Rather: "well-endowed minds might be preoccupied with dark and empty
subtleties [*Grillen*] and thereby."

Chimera's' [wretched subtleties], {consisting of} empty Terms, and very bad Latin, the knowledge of which is rather hurtful than profitable {to good minds}, if you have not been better In-<443>structed otherwise. |[So that all what they pretended to, was to take care that the Sciences might not be fundamentally taught to the Students.]|[173]

With these Trumperies the Universities were not only 'over-run' [vexed] during the former barbarous times, but even continue to this very day; and tho most Sciences [*die gute Wissenschaften*] are so much improved, the old Leaven is with 'great' [strange] Industry preserved and propagated: on the contrary all the {good and} solid Sciences, especially such, as are Instrumental in |[discovering the Vulgar Errors of the World]|[174] are suppressed. Above all the rest, the most 'useful' [necessary] of all, the Doctrine of Morality is much misinterpreted {by them} and entangled in an endless Labyrinth, that the Fathers Confessours may not want means to domineer over the Laymens Consciences, and to entangle them with so many dubious and double meaning insinuations, that they are thereby rendred incapable to <examine and> rule their Actions, according to solid Principles, but are obliged to be guided <blindfold[ed]> according to the pleasure of their {interested} Fathers Confessours.

Why the Jesuits have taken upon them the Education of the Youth. §35. But, because Learning had given the main blow to the Pope, at the time of *Luther*'s Reformation, the Jesuits, who may well be called the Popes Guard *du* Corps, have afterwards |[taken upon them the management of the Youth]|[175]; for they not only teach <publickly> in the Universities [*Academien*], but they have also engrossed [monopolized] to themselves the Instruction of the Youth <in the Schools>, that they might have all the opportunity so to guide and direct them in their Studies [*literas*], that they might not only not prove prejudicial, but rather advantageous to the Kingdom of Darkness.[176] For by this way of

---

173. Rather: "So that all their knowledge [*Wissenschaft*] has been geared to preventing anyone from really knowing [*wissen*] anything."

174. Rather: "opening people's eyes in regard to human actions."

175. Rather: "devoted themselves to pedagogy."

176. See Hobbes, *Leviathan,* Part IV.

managing the Youth [*Kinder*-Information] they have not only acquired vast Riches and Authority to their Order, but also have been very instrumental in maintaining the Popish 'Monarchy' [state], which they are bound to do by a particular Vow above all the other Monks.

They make it their business to imprint into the tender minds of the Youth a Veneration for the Pope, and so to guide their inclinations as they think it most profitable [serviceable] to the[ir] State <of the Church>. |[They use]|[177] the young people from their infancy to persist obstinately in their 'conceived' [once-formed] Opinions, and that no {contrary} Reasons <444> ought to prevail against them, whereby they render them incapable of ever attaining the knowledge of Truth. They have also {thereby} an opportunity throughly to <investigate and> discover the Capacities and Inclinations of their Disciples, which they {can} make good use of to their advantage, whenever these are imployed in State Affairs. But such as they find of an extraordinary Capacity or abounding in Wealth, they endeavour by all means to draw into their Order. So that the main intention of their School Discipline which is so famous throughout the World, is, to uphold the Pope's 'Sovereignty' [state]. They boast of extraordinary methods to teach the Latin Tongue to young people [*Knaben*], but they take a particular care, that they do not let their Disciples grow too wise, except such as are to be received into their Order.

And, because, they have by this management of the Youths [*Schulmeisterey*] brought a great many able Men [*Leute*] over to their Order, and are besides this very gentile and civil in their Conversation {and manner of life} (in which point they are far above all the other Monks, who are most of them full of 'Incivility' [coarseness] and Pedantry) they have found means, under pretence of being Confessours, to creep into most Courts, and to insinuate themselves into the very 'Secrets' [intrigues] of the State; so that in a great many 'Courts' [places] they have the greatest sway in the Councils; And there <you may be sure> they will never be forgetful of the Popes and their own Interest. Nevertheless by their insatiable Avarice, and forwardness of medling in all

177. Rather: "That is to say, they habituate."

Affairs they have made themselves odious in some places; And because the Jesuits have trespassed {much} upon the Authority and 'advantages' [income] of the other Monks, who are of more antient Orders, these are grown jealous of them to the highest degree.

Licensing
of Books.

Neither⁺ ought it to be passed by in silence, that the Pope and his 'adherents' [creatures] pretend to have a right of Censuring and Licensing all Books whatsoever, whereby they may easily prevent that nothing may come to light, which might prove prejudicial to them. And in Censuring of Books they are so impudent [*leichtfertig*] as not only to strike out of the antient Authors, when the same are to be reprinted, at pleasure, such passages as they dislike, but also they do not stick to insert such new passages <445> as are suitable to their intentions. If any Book is to be published in their Territories first[,] the same is |[exactly revised and corrected.]|[178] And if it should happen by chance, that something |[should be overseen in the first Edition]|[179] which does not suit with their Interest, it is marked in an Index [*Indice expurgatorio*] <made for that purpose>, that it may be omitted in the 'next' [second] Edition.[180] But the 'Books' [writings] of their Adversaries are {summarily} prohibited, nay the reading of them is not allowed, but to some particular persons, and that not without special leave, and these are such as they know to be 'thorough-paced' [crafty] and intirely devoted to their Interest. By so doing they may lay to their Adversaries charge what they please, since their Subjects never get sight of the others Refutation.

It has {also} been a general observation, that since the scandalous life of the Monks [*Pfaffen*] had <not only> been very prejudicial to the Popish Monarchy, |[but also that the Protestants had set out their Vices

178. Rather: "carefully reviewed [*übersehen*]."

179. Rather: "has crept in."

180. Developed after the Council of Trent (1545–63), the *Index Expurgatorius* was a list of problematic passages in otherwise acceptable books that needed to be corrected (that is, censored) before Roman Catholics would be allowed to read those books. It was later included in the more general *Index Librorum Prohibitorum* (Index of Forbidden Books), which forbade entire works. The latter Index was actively maintained until after the Second Vatican Council (1966). Pufendorf's *Introduction* was placed on the Index in 1692. See Editor's Introduction, p. xxix, above.

in their natural colours]|[181]; The Papists have bespattered the Protestant 'Ministers' [teachers] with the same Vices as they were charged withal, and have not only |[represented the infirmities]|[182] of some particular persons <to the World>, but also have laid to their charge the most heinous crimes they could invent; and afterwards have challenged their Adversaries to prove the contrary; which Calumnies have such influence |[, at least upon the simple and common sort of People, that it gives them a great aversion to]|[183] the Protestants. They also do not want impudence to set out at a high rate [boast about] their Miracles, Martyrdoms and other great Feats, which generally are {supposed to have been} transacted in far distant Countries; by which means they gain a great Credit [*Ansehen*] at least by the 'inconsiderate multitude' [simple-minded]. Among others *Edwin Sandys* an *English* Knight has discovered [an] abundance of these tricks in his Treatise concerning the State [*Zustand*] of Religion.[184]

§36. The Pope also makes use of 'more violent' [harsher] means to maintain his Authority. In former Ages his Excommunication was a most terrible thing; when whole Countries [*Ländern*] were forbidden the {public} exercise of Religious Worship; by which means the Popes have often obliged Emperours and Kings to come and creep to the Cross. But now adays this Weapon is not frightful to any body <446> except to some petty States in *Italy*. Nevertheless in *Spain* and *Italy* they have set up a certain Court, which is called the Office of the Holy Inquisition, where Information is taken and all such proceeded against as have in any ways rendred themselves suspected of Heresie: And it is counted the worst sort of Heresie, if any one attempts any thing against the Pop-

Excommunication and Inquisition.

181. Rather: "after the Protestants had vividly [*männiglich*] exposed it in their public writings."

182. Rather: "cobbled together the indiscretions."

183. Rather: "among their own people [that is, Catholics], that they form the worst impressions of."

184. Edwin Sandys (1561–1629), son of Archbishop Edwin Sandys (1516–88), published *A Relation of the State of Religion in Europe* (1605). Pufendorf owned a 1646 German translation (from Italian and French) of this work. See Palladini (1999a), #1458, p. 341.

ish Law and Doctrine, or against the Pope's Authority. This serves for a {strong} Bridle to curb the People withal, and to the Inhabitants of those Countries is as terrible as the Plague, since matters are transacted with so much severity in this Court, that scarce any body, that falls under the Inquisition, escapes their hands without considerable loss.

Some Reasons why the People remain in the Communion of the Church of Rome.

§37. Though the <Supreme> Direction and Administration of the <Romish> Religion, together with their other 'rules' [means], which serve to uphold it, and have been 'alledged' [detailed] by us here, are a sufficient awe upon the People {to keep them obedient}; And besides this, the Popish Clergy know how to manage their Affairs with that dexterity as to give some satisfaction to every one; |[so that I am]|[185] apt to believe, that a great many, who live under the Popish subjection, are verily persuaded, to believe, what[ever] the Priests tell them, to be 'real' [true], since they {also} want [lack] means and opportunity of being 'better' [differently] instructed; Nevertheless it is very probable that a great many of the more learned and wiser sort [*Weltverständigen*] |[are sufficiently convinced, in what manner things are carried on among them]|,[186] and that therefore it is in respect of some particular considerations, that they do not free themselves from this Yoke. I am apt to believe, that most are kept back, because they do not see how to remedy this Evil [*Werck*]; And 'yet' [so] they are unwilling to ruin their Fortunes{, which they have under the papacy,} by going over to the Protestant side, where they are not likely to meet with so plentiful a share. These Temptations are not easily to be resisted, wherefore they think it sufficient for the obtaining of Salvation if they believe in Jesus Christ and trust upon his Merits, but for the rest think it of no great consequence if in some matters, which |[are the inventions of Priests]|,[187] they by conforming themselves play the Hypocrite, and believe as much concerning them as is suitable with their Opinions. They suppose it to be of no <447> great consequence, [besides,] that perhaps

185. Rather: "and, I am quite."
186. Rather: "see well enough how the entire business [*Sache*] hangs together."
187. Rather: "have been patched into Christianity."

the Female Sex and the vulgar sort of People [*canaille*] that are always fond of extravagancies,[188] do believe these things in good earnest.

There are also, questionless, not a few, who not having sufficient Capacity to distinguish betwixt such Points in Religion, as are commanded by God, and betwixt such as are invented by the Clergy for private Ends, and perhaps coming afterwards to the knowledge of <some of> these deceits, they take all the rest for fabulous Inventions {as well}, only covering their Atheistical Principles with an outward 'decent behaviour' [appearance, *Schein*] to save themselves the trouble of being questioned and disturbed. Every Man of Sense may without difficulty imagine how easily a sensible [*von* esprit] *Italian* or *Spaniard*, that never has read the Bible or any other Protestant Book may 'fall into this Errour' [have such thoughts], if he once has had an opportunity to 'take notice of the Intrigues' [look at the cards] of the Clergy; tho' it is certain, {as well,} that since the Reformation of *Luther*, the 'Church of *Rome*' [papacy] has changed her Habit, and |[her Garment appears far more decent]|[189] than before.

But besides this, there are a great many Persons of Quality as well as of a meaner [*mittelmässiger*] Condition, who make their advantage of the 'Romish Religion' [papacy], where they have an opportunity to provide for their 'Friends' [relatives], by putting them either into some Order or other of Knighthood, or into that of Monks, or other Ecclesiasticks [*Geistlichen*], by which means a great many Families are eased of a great Charge, and sometimes are raised by it. At least the superstitious Parents are well satisfied when they see their Children are become such Saints: And those that {ultimately} cannot make their Fortunes {in the world} otherwise, run into a Monastery, where they are sure to be provided for.

All these conveniences would be taken away if the Popish Monarchy should fall, and |[the Church Revenues were applyed to the use of]|[190] the State. The 'Popish Doctrine' [papacy] also has got so firm footing

---

188. Thomasius, p. 317, qualifies here, noting that there are many rational persons of the female gender, which should not be summarily associated with the vulgar.

189. Rather: "puts on much more of an appearance [*Schein*]."

190. Rather: "spiritual properties [*Güter*] were incorporated into."

in those 'Countries' [places] where it now rides triumphant, that if any of their 'Princes' [potentates] should endeavour to root it out, he would find it a very difficult Task, since the Priests [*Pfaffen*] would be for raising Heaven and Earth against him, and {ultimately} not stick to find out another *James Clement* or *Ravilliac* for their purpose.[191] Besides this, most of those Princes are tied by a Political Interest to the Church of *Rome,* and by intro-<448>ducing a Reformation [*Veränderung*] cannot propose any advantage to themselves, but rather cannot but fear very dangerous Divisions and Innovations.

What States are tied by a particular Interest to the Church of Rome.

Italy.

§38. *Italy* by its particular Interest is obliged to support the 'Popish Monarchy' [papal chair], it being much to the 'advantage' [grandeur, *Hoheit*] of this Country, that the Pope resides among them, especially since now a days no other but *Italians* do attain to this Dignity; so that there is scarce a great 'Family' [house] in *Italy,* but some of their 'Friends' [members] have some 'dependence on' [benefit from] the Roman Chair.

Poland.

Because the Bishops and {rich} Prebendaries in *Poland* are always chosen out of the {native} Nobility{, which derives great advantage therefrom}; the Noblemen who have the chief sway of Affairs in that Kingdom are tied to the Popish Interest, and [in turn] the Bishops who are there also Senators of the Kingdom, have a great influence in all the Transactions of any moment. The Clergy is {likewise} very Potent in

Portugal.

Portugal, and in case of any Innovation, would be {greatly} assisted by the *Spaniards;* this was the reason why the *Portugueses* of late years have been fain to comply with the Pope, notwithstanding that the Pope[,] to curry favour with *Spain,* did not many years ago treat them so ill in the matter of Collation of {new} Bishopricks,[192] which else might have served them for a fair Pretence, to withdraw themselves from the Obedience of the Roman Chair.

191. Jacques Clement (1567–89), a Dominican friar, assassinated Henry III of France in 1589. François Ravaillac (1578–1610), also a Catholic, assassinated Henry IV of France in 1610.

192. The popes refused, because of Spanish pressure, to recognize the Portuguese monarch or fill vacant Portuguese bishoprics during that country's struggle for independence against Spain (1640–68).

Some[+] of the Estates of *Germany* are to this day adhering to the Popish Interest; among the Imperial Cities that of *Cullen* [Cologne] is the
Chiefest, which City is overrun with Ecclesiasticks [*Pfaffen*]{, and also
various lesser cities}. Besides this, there are abundance of Counts and
others of the 'Nobility' [free knights], that hitherto have not thought
fit <by turning Protestants,> to exclude themselves from Ecclesiastical
Dignities and Benefices. Among the Temporal Princes, <the Elector of>
Bavaria has stuck close to the Romish Religion, because the House of
Bavaria has always had a great Appetite to the Imperial Crown, which
hope it must lay aside, if it should leave the Popish Religion.

What has induced some Protestant Princes to return 'to the Romish Communion' [under the papacy], is sufficiently known. Neither
is it much to be 'admired' [wondered] at, that the present Bishops
and Prelates stand firm to the Popish Interest in *Germany*, since they
find it more advantageous to be 'great' [rich] Princes than <449> poor
Preachers. Besides this, they have been deterr'd from undertaking any
Reformation [*Veränderung*] by the Example of two Electors of *Collen* [Cologne], which they in the last Age [century] did begin with a
very unfortunate Success in their Dominions.[193] After *Charles* V. (being
influenced by the *Spanish* Counsels) did let slip the Opportunity of
setling the Protestant Religion throughout the Empire;[194] the Emperours have ever since that time, for reasons of State, not been able to
disentangle themselves from the 'Popish Sovereignty' [papacy] if they
had been never so willing. For as the case now stands, the Ecclesiastical
Princes of the Empire are tied to the Emperour's Interest, from whom
they hope for Assistance against the Secular Princes in case of necessity.
But if the Emperour should abandon the 'Church of *Rome*' [pope], the

193. Thomasius, pp. 325–28, identifies these as Hermann of Wied, Archbishop-
Elector Cologne (1477–1552), who was excommunicated in 1547, and Elector Geb-
hard Truchsess von Waldburg (1547–1601), also of Cologne, who was deposed in
1583.

194. The passage is more general: "After good opportunities for reforming the Empire were missed during Charles V's time, due to Spanish attacks [*Anschläge*], . . ."
Charles divided and defeated the German Protestant rulers, including the Schmalkaldic League (1531–47). Any suggestion that he himself might have wanted to further the Reformation in Germany, other than for political reasons, is misleading.

whole Clergy would be against him; and he could not promise himself any certain Assistance from the Secular Princes, especially since <some of> the most ancient Houses of those Princes, that now have laid aside the hope of attaining the Imperial Crown, by reason of difference in Religion, would then pretend to have the same right to that Dignity with the House of *Austria.* The Pope also upon such an occasion would not cease to stir up Heaven and 'Earth' [hell] against him, and the King of *France* would not let slip this Opportunity, but would with all his might endeavour to obtain the Imperial Dignity, in which design he perhaps might meet with encouragement from {many of} the Clergy.

Spain.   The⁺ *Spaniards* pretend to be the greatest zealots of the 'Romish Religion' [papal chair], because they stand in need of the Pope's Favour to assist them in the {peaceful} preservation of the Kingdom of *Naples* and the State of *Milan;* and they commonly use to lay their Designs under the cover of preserving and 'maintaining' [spreading] the Roman Catholick Religion, wherein, however they have for the most part miscarried, not to mention here that the Clergy is very Potent in *Spain,* and that the common People |[thro' the false perswasions of the Priests, have got a great aversion against]|¹⁹⁵ the Protestants.

France.   *France*⁺ does outwardly shew it self not so fond of 'the Popish Interest' [Rome], nor has the *Gallick* Church ever acknowledged the Pope's absolute Power over her. And whenever the Pope 'pretends' [seeks] to encroach upon the Liberty of <450> the *French* Church, the Parliament of *Paris* is ready to take notice of it. The Doctors also of the *Sorbon* have rejected several Propositions, which were maintained by the Pope's Parasites. They also keep so watchful an Eye over the Pope's Nuncio there, that it is not easy for him to transgress his Bounds. The Nuncio's, when they go out of *Rome,* carry the Cross upright, but as soon as they enter the Territories of *France,* they let it down till such time as they have obtained leave from the King to exercise their Function, when they are fain to oblige themselves by their own Hand-writing, that they will not act otherwise in this Station, and no longer than[,] it pleases the King. They also must make use of a *French* Secretary, and at their departure,

195. Rather: "have been made to imagine horrible things about."

leave behind them a {sealed} Register concerning their Negotiation, and also are tied to several other Formalities, without which, all their Negotiations are accounted void and of no force. From hence it is that the *French* say, that the Pope's Nuncio there, has his Commission both from their King and the Pope, and that it is precarious, and may be recalled by the King at pleasure. And it is {also} to be observed that the Pope's Nuncio puts by [lowers] his Cross in any place where the King is present, thereby it is intimated that his Commission [*Jurisdiction*] ceases when the King is present.

Nay, it is credibly related, that 'under the Ministry' [during the time] of Cardinal Richlieu it was debated in *France,* whether they should not constitute a Patriarch of their own in that Kingdom; tho' as far as I can see, this design would not have proved so very advantageous to *France.* For the Clergy must needs have become very ||[jealous of the King's Power, for fear he]||[196] might take this Opportunity to retrench their ample Revenues [*Intraden*]. And if the King of *France* has not laid aside his thoughts and pretences upon the Imperial Crown, he can never suppose to obtain his aim, if he should withdraw himself from the Roman Chair. For if so Potent a Prince as the King of *France* is, should once obtain the Imperial Dignity, it is very likely he would not only revive the antient 'Pretensions' [rights] of the Emperours upon *Rome,* which have ||[for a long while been lying dormant]||[197]; but he would also under the specious pretence of protecting the Roman Chair, endeavour to recover such Possessions [rights] as had been seque-<451>stred [received in trust] from the Church of *Rome.* On the other hand, the Pope is heartily afraid of a *French* Monarchy, being well convinced that it would endeavour a thorough Reformation [*sic*] of the Court of *Rome,* and that his Wings would be clipt to that degree, that in effect he would be no more than a Patriarch. Neither ought he to exspect any better treatment if the *Spanish* Monarchy had been brought to perfection; {just} as either of them must needs have been destructive to the Protestant Religion.

196. Rather: "dissatisfied with this, for fear that the king."
197. Rather: "through silence been almost extinguished."

The main
Pillar of
the Popish
Monarchy.

It⁺ may therefore be taken for granted that <one of> the main
Pillar <s> of the Popish Monarchy is the jealousy and ballance, <which
is to be kept up> betwixt these two Crowns; and that it is the Pope's
Interest, as much as in him lies, to take care that one of these Crowns do
not ruin the other, and set up for an 'universal Monarchy' [monarchy
of Europe]. If we look into the transactions of former times, we shall
find that the Popes have long since observed this Maxim. 'Tis true, after
the death of King *Henry* II.[198] when *France* was <extreamly> weakned,
the Popes were forced to be good *Spanish* whether they would or no, the
Spaniards having then found out the way to oblige them to it by fair or
foul means. They knew how to influence the Popes by their Nephews,
who were for setling and enriching their Families, whilest their Kins-
men [the popes] were alive.[199] Those they brought over to their party by
granting to them Pensions, Church-Benefices, large Possessions, great
Offices and advantageous Matches; who in acknowledgement of the
same used often to make the Pope ‖[good *Spanish,* even against his
inclination]‖[200]; but if they resisted these temptations, they used to prosecute these Nephews with a vengeance, after the Pope's decease. And it
was their constant practice in those days, to exclude such from the Papal
Chair, as they [the Spanish] thought were bent against their Interest.
But as soon as *France* began to recover its Strength, the Popes managed
themselves with more indifferency {and freedom}, and shewed no more
favour to either side, than they thought was ‖[suiting with their present Circumstances.]‖[201] It is remarkable that the Jesuit *Guicardus* in a
Sermon preached in *Paris* in the {year} 1637. in the Month of *July,* did
say, that the War which the then King of *France* waged against <452>
the *Spaniards,* was to be deemed a Holy War, carried on for the preservation of the Holy Religion.[202] For if the King of *France* had not taken

198. Henry II died in 1559.
199. See the end of §31, pp. 491–92, above.
200. Rather: "do more for Spain than he perhaps should have."
201. Rather: "useful to their own state [*Staat*]."
202. Literally: "against [ir]religion"—presumably, against the Spanish version of
Catholicism. / "Guicardus" may refer to Nicolas Caussin, 1583–1651, a noted Jesuit
homilist who was Louis XIII's confessor from March to December 1637, when he
was relieved of his post after a sermon before the king encouraging the latter to

up Arms, the *Spaniards* designs were so laid, as to make the Pope an Almoner [chaplain] to the King of *Spain.*

§39. But as to those who have withdrawn themselves from the Pope's Obedience, it is certain the Pope would be glad, if they could be reduced to his Obedience {again}, provided it might be done by such means, that thereby one party were not so much strengthened as to become terrible to all *Europe.* For it is better to let my Enemy live, than to kill me and my Enemy at one stroke. It was for this reason, that we read that Pope *Paul* III. was vexed to the heart at the stupendous Success of the Emperour *Charles* V. against the Protestants, which made him {immediately} recall his Troops that were sent to his Assistance. And if *Philip* II. had been successful in his expedition against *England. Sixtus* V. would questionless have acknowledged his Errour of assisting him {so eagerly} in this Enterprise. So *Gregory* XV. during the Differences betwixt those of the *Valtelins* and the *Grisons* sided with the last, the Protestants[,] against *Spain.*[203] Neither was *Urban* VIII. dissatisfied at the Success of *Gustavus Adolphus* against the House of *Austria,* especially since the latter had given much about the same time an evident instance to the World, as to the business of *Mantua,* that they used to give no better treatment to Roman Catholicks than Protestants. Some have remarked, that when *Ferdinand* II. did desire some Subsidies from the Pope, which he had promised before, the Pope {instead} sent him plenary Indulgences for him and his whole Army at the point of death,

The Pope's Inclination towards the Protestants.

---

oppose Richelieu's Protestant alliances and end France's war (since 1635) against Spain—except that this is the opposite of what Pufendorf says in the passage. Also, "Guicardus" is linguistically closer to Jean Guiscard (Guignard), 1563–95, a Jesuit associated with John Chastel, the would-be assassin of Henry IV in December 1594, who had studied at the Jesuit College at Clermont. As for a speech in July, it was Richelieu who spoke then to the Council of State, equating the queen's pro-Spanish machinations with treason: the passage remains unclear. On Caussin and Guignard, see O'Neill (2001), vol. 1, pp. 724–25, and vol. 2, p. 1840.

203. Gregory XV (1554–1623, pope from 1621). Veltlin (Valtellina) was a strategic, confessionally mixed area in northern Italy; neighboring Grisons (Graubünden) was one of the Protestant Swiss cantons. Gregory helped to evict Spain from Veltlin, which it had taken over after the outbreak of the Thirty Years' War (1618) because of larger, geopolitical considerations.

that they might be prepared to dye with the more Courage. And some Years ago, the Court of *Rome* was no less concerned at the then prodigious Success of *France* in *Holland,* when this State seemed to be reduced to the utmost extremity.

But the chief aim of the Pope is, to reduce by all manner of Artifices the Protestants to his Obedience. To obtain this end, he sets the Protestants together by the Ears, flattereth the Protestant Princes, and takes care that many of them may marry Roman Catholick Ladies; the younger Brothers [*Cadets*] out of the <453> greatest Families he 'obliges' [induces] to come over to his Party, by bestowing upon them great Dignities and Church-Benefices, all that will come over to his side are kindly received and very well used, neither do they write so much against the Protestant Divines [*Theologos*], but rather |[endeavour to set up and maintain Controversies among them.]|[204] By these Artifices the Popish Clergy has got very visible advantages in this Age [century] over the Protestants, and are likely to get more every day, since they see with the greatest satisfaction that their Adversaries do weaken themselves by their intestine <Quarrels and> Divisions.

No Peace is to be expected betwixt the Roman Catholicks and Protestants.

§40. From what has been said it is easily to be judged, whether those Differences which are on foot betwixt the Roman Catholicks and the Protestants may be amicably composed, either so that both Parties should remit something of their pretensions, and, agree to one and the same {*Symbolum* or} Confession of Faith,[205] leaving some by-Questions to be ventilated in the Universities; or so that both Parties may retain their Opinions, and yet, notwithstanding this Difference [*dissensus*], might treat one another like Brethren in Christ and Members of the same 'Church' [Christian community].[206] Now if we duly weigh the

204. Rather: "[merely] allow them to bicker with one another, and the like."

205. A *symbolum* refers to a creed or set of doctrines publically subscribed to by members of the same faith. For Lutherans this was the *Book of Concord* (1580/1584), a compilation of ten foundational documents that united believers, including the final, bipartite Formula of Concord (1577), which summarized the basic tenets of the faith.

206. In *The Divine Feudal Law,* §7, in Pufendorf (2002b), p. 23, Pufendorf refers to this as "a Reconcilement mixed with a Toleration."

'Circumstances' [substance] of the matter, and the Popish Principles, such a 'Peace' [settlement] is to be esteemed absolutely impossible; since the Difference does not only consist in the Doctrine, but {also} both Interests are absolutely contrary to one another.[207]

For first the Pope is for having the Church-Possessions restored; but the Protestants are resolved to keep them in their 'possession' [current condition]. The Pope pretends [wants] to be the supreme Head of Christendom[,] but the Protestant States will not part with their Prerogative of having their Direction [*ius*] *circa Sacra,* which they look upon as a precious Jewel belonging to their Sovereignty. And to pretend to live in Communion and Amity with the Pope, and not to acknowledge his Sovereignty in Ecclesiastical Affairs, is an absolute contradiction. In the same manner, as if I would be called a Subject in a Kingdom, and yet refuse to acknowledge the King's Authority. Besides this, the infallibility of the Pope is the Foundation Stone of 'the Popish Sovereignty' [popedom], and if that is once removed, the whole Structure must needs fall, wherefore it is impossible for the Pope, and that for <454> reasons of State, to abate any {least} thing from his pretensions wherein he differs from the Protestants. For if it should be once granted that the Pope had hitherto maintained but one single erroneous point, his infallibility would then fall to the ground; since, if he has erred in one point, he may be erroneous in others also. But if the Protestants should allow the Pope's infallibility, they at the same time must 'deny their whole Doctrine' [grant him all the rest]. And it seems not probable that the Protestants can ever be brought to contradict and at once to recal |[their Doctrine concerning the vanity of the Popish Tenets.]|[208] Nay, if it might be supposed that the Laiety should do it, what must become of the Clergy? Where will they bestow [put] their Wives and Children?

Wherefore, how good soever the intention may have been of those {on both sides,} that have proposed a way of accommodation betwixt

---

207. See *The Divine Feudal Law,* §10, in Pufendorf (2002b), pp. 28–31, and §12, pp. 35–37, on the futility of trying to reconcile Catholics and Protestants, because of the worldly emoluments sought by the former.
208. Rather: "all they have taught against the pope up to now."

the Papists and Protestants, which is commonly called Syncretism,[209] they are certainly nothing else but very simple <and chimerical> Inventions, which are {only} ridiculed by the Papists; who in the mean while are well satisfied to see that the Protestant Divines bestow their labour in vain as to this point, since they (the Papists) are no losers, but, rather the gainers by it. For this Syncretism does not only raise great Animosities among the Protestants, but also does not a little weaken their Zeal against the Popish Religion: It is easy to be imagined, that some, who do not thoroughly understand the 'Differences' [matter], and hear <the Divines> talk of an accommodation betwixt both Religions, are apt to perswade themselves, that the Difference |[does not lie in the fundamental points]|[210]; and if in the mean while they meet with an advantageous proffer from the 'Roman Catholicks' [papacy], are sometimes without great {or further} difficulty prevailed upon to bid farewel to the Protestant Religion. It is {also} taken for a general Rule, that a Fortress and a Maiden-head [virginity] are in great danger, when once they begin to parly.

Strength of §41. But if the Question were put, whether the Pope with all his ad-
the Protestants herents be strong enough to reduce the Protestants under his Obedi-
and Papists. ence {again} by force; it is evident enough that the joint power of the Papists is 'much' [noticeably] superiour to the strength of the Protestants. For {all} *Italy,* <455> all *Spain* and *Portugal,* the greatest part of *France* and *Poland,* adhere to the Pope, as also the weakest part of the *Swiss Cantons.* In *Germany* those hereditary 'Countries' [provinces] which belong to the House of *Austria,* the Kingdom of *Bohemia,* and {now also} the greatest part of *Hungary,* all the Bishops and Prelates, the House of *Bavaria,* the Dukes of {*Pfaltz-*}*Neuburgh,* and [the] Marquisses of *Baden*{*-Baden*}, besides some other Princes of less note; some Counts, Lords and others of the 'Nobility' [free knights] and some {free} Imperial Cities, besides others <of the Roman Catholick Communion> that live {now and then} 'under the Jurisdiction of' [among]

209. See §14, note 41, p. 437, above.
210. Rather: "is ultimately not so great and important."

the Protestant States [estates]; all which according to my computation make up two thirds of *Germany.* There are also a great many Papists in *Holland,* neither is *England* quite free of them. But of the Protestant side are *England, Sweden, Denmark, Holland,* most of the Secular Electors and Princes, and <the> Imperial Cities in *Germany.* The *Hugonots* in *France* are 'without strength' [disarmed], and the Protestants in *Poland* being dispersed throughout the Kingdom are not to be feared. *Curland* [*Kurland*] and the Cities of *Prussia* may rest satisfied, if they are [merely] able to maintain the free exercise of their Religion; neither is *Transylvania* powerful enough to give any considerable Assistance to the Protestant Party.

The Papists also have this Advantage above the Protestants, that they all acknowledge the Pope for the supreme Head of their Church, and at least to outward appearance {and verbally}, are unanimous in their Faith; whereas on the contrary, the Protestants are not joined under one visible spiritual Head, but are miserably divided among themselves. For not to mention here those Sects of lesser note, *viz.* the *Arminians, Socinians, Anabaptists* and such like, their main Bod[y] is divided into two Parties, of very near equal Strength, *viz.* into the *Lutherans* and those of the Reformed Religion, a great many of which are so exasperated against one another, that they could not be more against the Papists themselves.

Divisions of the Protestants.

Neither⁺ are the Protestants united under one 'Church-Government' [religious constitution] <or Liturgy>, but each of these States regulate the same according as they think fit. Neither can it be denied, but that the Roman Catholick Clergy in general is more zealous and industrious in propagating their Religion than the Protestants; a great many of <456> these making no other use of the{ir} 'Church-Benefices' [spiritual offices], than to maintain themselves out of them, just as if it were a meer Trade; ||[and the propagating of the Christian Faith, is the least of their Care, or at least only their by-work.]|[211] Whereas the Monks and Jesuits gain great applause by their Missions in the '*East* and *West-Indies*'

Other Inconveniencies.

211. Rather: "while the building of God's kingdom is held in abeyance [*in der Reserve steht*]."

[Orient and America]; and tho' perhaps they brag more than is true of their great Success there, yet is this 'Institution' [beginning] in the main very praiseworthy. Besides this, there is such an {almost} implacable jealousy betwixt <some of> the {most distinguished} Protestant States, that it is not probable that they will be one and all against the Papists: not to mention others here, such a jealousy is betwixt *Sweden* and *Denmark*, as likewise betwixt *England* and *Holland.* Tho' on the other hand, there is as great a jealousy betwixt *France* and *Spain,* which will always be an obstacle to any union betwixt these two Crowns against the Protestants. So that notwithstanding the {multifaceted} unequality betwixt the Papists and Protestants, these need not fear |[the Pope's Power.]|[212]

The Hugonots of France.   Nevertheless,[+] there is a <great> difference to be made as to those Protestants, that live in a Protestant State, independent 'on' [of] any other, and those who live under the jurisdiction of a 'Roman Catholick Prince' [popish lord], the latter of which are not so very well assured of the free enjoyment of their Religion {as the former}. For the *Hugonots* in *France* have no other Security but the King's bare Word, and the Edict of *Nantes,* which would stand them but in little stead, if the King of *France* should be overcome with a Zeal like to that of the *Spaniards,* or the House of *Austria.* Yet does it not seem probable to me, that the King of *France* shou'd easily 'pretend' [attempt] to force them to another Religion, as long as they are quiet; since he ought to consider what great Services the *Hugonots* have done to *Henry* IV. without whose Assistance he would in all likelihood not have been able to obtain the Crown.[213]

The Protestants of Poland. |[It is not easily to be supposed, that the *Poles* should raise a persecution against the Protestants in *Curland* and *Prussia*]|,[214] especially as long as the City of *Dantzick* maintains her Liberty.

Of Germany.   The[+] Protestants in *Germany* are so considerable, that {if all were unified under one head,} they may be esteemed equal in strength to a

---

212. Rather: "that they will be forcibly subdued by the pope."

213. See §22, note 53, p. 248, and note 81, p. 268, above. Louis XIV's revocation of the Edict of Nantes in 1685 (three years after the current work) evoked Pufendorf's *Of the Nature and Qualification of Religion* (1687).

214. Rather: "Poland, too, should not think it easy to persecute Curland and Prussia on account of religion." Both observations seem intended as much to persuade or exhort, as to describe.

{sizeable} Kingdom. But their being divided under several Heads, and that <457> of a different Interest, {and the fact that they are fairly scattered,} much abates their strength. And the Emperours within the space of a hundred Years, have twice {already} reduced them to that extremity, that both their Religion and Liberty (which are so link'd together, that one cannot be lost without the other) seemed to be near gone, if *France* and *Sweden* had not prevented it.[215] 'Tis true, there has of late Years a new Maxim been set up, *viz* that the Protestants of *Germany* are now in a capacity to maintain themselves without the assistance of the two above-mentioned Crowns, and that <the Elector of> *Brandenburgh* is the most fitly qualified to be their Head, and to have the Direction among them: And as it is {greatly in} the Interest of the House of *Austria* to uphold them in this belief, so *Brandenburgh* and *Luneburgh* make {partial} use of this supposition to cover their designs of getting into their possession those Provinces, that were given to *Sweden* as a recompence for having been so instrumental in preserving the Religion and Liberty of |[the Protestants of *Germany*.]|[216]

But suppose they should compass [achieve] their Design, it is {first} most certain that those two Houses by the addition of those 'Countries' [provinces], would be much less formidable to the Emperour, than they were at that time when they were {still} upheld by *Sweden*. And {second} it is a great mistake if they perswade themselves that what assistance they may exspect from *Denmark* and *Holland,* can countervail what they had from *France* and *Sweden.* If {third} the Emperour should obtain his Ends and drive those two 'Nations' [crowns] {entirely} out of *Germany,* and restore the *Spanish* 'Interest' [party], and then tire out the Estates by |[sending great Armies against them]|,[217] it would

215. Sweden's intervention (in 1630) in the Thirty Years' War was critical to the Protestant cause, and it remained, along with France, a so-called guarantor power of the Westphalian accord (1648). In the previous century, France's political conflicts with Charles V had prevented the latter from pursuing his religious aims in Germany. The two interests bear upon one another.

216. Rather: "these as well as the other German estates." Lüneburg refers to the electorate of Saxony. Sweden's claims to western Pomerania (and several smaller territories) were acknowledged in the Treaty of Westphalia.

217. Rather: "having them maintain his army, and by other inconveniences of war."

be a {big} question who would be able to oblige the Emperour in such a case to 'disband' [withdraw] his victorious Forces? Or whether the Emperour might not under some pretence or another keep his Army on foot, and oblige the States [estates] to provide for them <in their Territories>? Whether *Brandenburgh* and *Luneburgh* would be able <alone> to oppose the Emperour's design? But {fourth} if the Protestant Estates should find themselves not strong enough to resist his Power, it would be the Question whether these {now alienated} Crowns would be immediately ready at their demands, or whether the circumstances of their Affairs would {then} be such, as to be able to undertake such a task? Or whether at the time <458> of {extreme} imminent danger such a one as {King} *Gustavus Adolfus,* would be sent down from Heaven, who could act with the same Fortune and Success. For he that believes, that <the> Religion is sufficiently secured by Seals and Deeds [legal documents], or that the Emperours have laid aside all thoughts of making themselves Sovereigns of *Germany,* if an {appropriate} occasion should present it self, especially since Religion, and the recovery of the Church possessions furnishes them with so specious a pretence, must needs have lost the memory of all past transactions.[218]

But the <last> Peace made at *Nimmeguen* has sufficiently convinced the World, that these designs could not be put in execution.[219] Those Protestant States therefore that are Independent <on other Princes> need not fear |[the power of the *Roman* Catholicks.]|[220] For, {just} as two States that are of the same Religion, nevertheless differ in State

218. Thomasius, p. 362, notes that Pufendorf wrote this passage while still in the employ of Sweden and that his changing views led to his transfer to Brandenburg in 1688. In 1682 Pufendorf still considered Austria the main threat to German Protestantism, and France and Sweden as its main supporters. However, by the late 1680s, as he was revising *The Present State of Germany,* France had become the main threat to the independence of the German estates. This shift is clear in chap. VIII of the posthumous (1706) edition, which Pufendorf prepared in the late 1680s.

219. Thomasius, p. 365, is unsure about Pufendorf's meaning here. The Treaty of Nijmegen ended the congerie of wars known collectively as the Franco-Dutch War (1672–78), which had pitted France, England, and the archbishoprics of Cologne and Münster against the United Provinces and its allies (Brandenburg, Austria, Spain).

220. Rather: "that they will be externally compelled to give up their religion."

Interests, and are jealous of one another, which is plainly to be seen betwixt *France* and *Spain,* and betwixt *England* and *Holland;* so, though States are of a different Religion, it is not from hence to be concluded, that if a 'Potent Prince of the *Roman* Catholick Persuasion' [a mighty popish state] should attempt to ruin a Protestant State, the other '*Roman* Catholick' [popish] States would not prevent it, if it was {at all} for their Interest to see that Protestant State preserved.

The[+] best way then to preserve the Protestant Religion is, that each of these States take effectual care, how the same may be well preserved in their several States. And this may be done without any {subtle,} crafty 'inventions' [methods], as the '*Roman* Catholicks are' [papacy is] obliged to make use of, but only by plain and simple means. One of the main Points is, that both the Churches and Schools may be 'provided' [staffed] with persons fitly qualified [*tüchtigen Personen*] for that purpose; That the Clergy by their wholesome Doctrine and a good Life, may shew the way to the rest. That the people in general, but more especially such as in all likelyhood one time or another may have a great sway in the State, be well instructed in the true and Fundamental Principles of <the Protestant> Religion, that thereby they may be 'proof against' [resistant to] the Temptations of the Court of *Rome* [papacy], especially when they are to Travel in Popish Countries. That the Clergy may 'be' [make themselves] so qualified as to be able to oppose the devises and designs [*Streichen*] of their <459> 'Enemies' [adversaries], who every day busie themselves in finding out new Projects against them{; and other similar things}.

The best way to preserve the Reformed Religion.

Some[+] are of Opinion, that the Protestant Party would be mightily strengthned, if the two Chief Factions among the Protestants, that besides the difference in their Doctrine, |[are also of a different Interest, which seems to flow from their various Opinions]|,[221] could be reconciled to one another; and they believe this not impracticable, if the |[old hatred, animosities, pride, and selfconceited Opinions]|[222] could

Whether the Lutherans and those of the Reformed Religion are likely to agree.

221. Rather: "do not otherwise collide on account of opposing interests flowing from religion."

222. Rather: "hatred, bitterness, self-love, pride, preconceived opinions, and distortions."

be laid aside. But if we duly take into consideration the general inclinations [*humeur*] of mankind, this seems to be a hard supposition.
For those who peruse the {polemical} Writings of both Parties without
partiality, cannot but 'admire' [be amazed], how their Authors are often
obliged to rack themselves, that they may maintain their Opinions[,]
whether they be consonant to the Scriptures or not: As likewise how
they bring to light again the old Arguments, which have been 'refuted'
[throttled] a thousand times before. Neither will this do the business,
if one Opinion should be supposed as good as the other; since such an
indifferency would be a <shrewd> sign, that |[the whole must needs be
very indifferent to us.]|[223] Neither can we without danger declare some
Points, in which we differ, problematical, since I do not see how we can
pretend to have a power to declare a certain Article either necessary <or
Fundamental,> or problematical {as we please}.

Some 'therefore' [also] have thought upon this expedient, to make a
tryal, whether out of the 'Articles' [points], wherein both Parties agree[,]
could be Composed a 'perfect' [complete] Systeme of Divinity, which
might be linked together like one Chain, {and formed from beginning
to end} according to {an exact} Art. If this could be effected, though
some different Opinions remained {left over}, as long as this Chain was
kept entire, we might be assured that we did not differ in the Fundamental Points{, and in the means} necessary to the obtaining of Salvation; and what remained undecided would not be of such Consequence
as to hinder us from being united into one <Body or> Church. But
before a true Judgment can be given of this Proposition [proposal], it
would be requisite that such a Systeme composed according to Art,
were proposed to the World.[224] For my part I know no better advice,
than to leave it to the direction of God Almighty, who perhaps one time
or another will <460> put us in the way of finding out a good Expedient. For untimely remedies may {merely} prove the occasion of new
Divisions. In the mean while it behoves both Parties notwithstanding

223. Rather: "one does not care much about the whole matter." Thomasius,
pp. 371–73, criticizes this as a "rather superficial" remark.
224. This was the project attempted by Pufendorf in *The Divine Feudal Law*
(Lübeck, 1695), in Pufendorf (2002b).

these differences to be mindful of their joint Interest against their Common Enemy, since they may verily believe that the Pope has no more kindness for the *Lutherans,* than for those of the Reformed Religion.

But⁺ as for the 'other Sects of less note' [smaller sects], *viz.* The Socinians, Anabaptists, and such like, it is evident that their Principles cannot possibly be reconciled with our Religion; For those who adhere to the first, do not consider the Christian Doctrine otherwise than a {nice} Moral Philosophy, and the latter scarce know what to believe themselves. Besides this, the Anabaptists have hatched out I know not what {new} rules of Policy [*Policey*], which, ||[if not suppressed in time]|,²²⁵ must prove 'destructive' [very dangerous] to the State. But whether the Socinians also have any such projects in their Heads, I am not able to determine, since hitherto they have not ||[been powerful enough to raise any disturbances in the State.]||²²⁶ <461>

Socinians and Anabaptists.

225. Rather: "wherever they may gain the ascendancy."
226. Rather: "yet had enough control in any place to be able to move the state in a certain direction." Radical Anabaptists had tried to establish a theocracy in Münster from 1534 to 1535. For Pufendorf's views on minor religious sects, also see §27, pp. 474–77, and §41, p. 517, above; *Of the Nature and Qualification of Religion,* §49, in Pufendorf (2002c), p. 106; and *The Divine Feudal Law,* §14, in Pufendorf (2002b), pp. 57–58, and §84, p. 200. Thomasius, pp. 377–80, sees no reason for not tolerating these sects and notes that this has occurred without problems in Holland and Denmark. He also defends them against the charge of heresy and refers to his own writings on that subject. See note 14, p. 423, and note 18, p. 427, above.

Of the Kingdom of Sweden.

§1. The *Swedish* Historians have out of their ancient Monuments shown the World, that the Kingdom of *Sweden* is the most an- Sweden the tient Kingdom in *Europe,* and that this Country, was, after the Del- most ancient Kingdom in uge, sooner stored with Inhabitants than the other parts of *Europe.* Europe. Nevertheless it is very uncertain who were the first Inhabitants, and at what time they first settled there, as likewise whether they were immediately governed by Kings, or whether the Fathers of Families had the chief sway among them, till the Regal was grafted on the Paternal Power. The names and deeds of their Kings, and the time of their Reigns are also not easie to be determined, for the List which has been published of these Kings, is not so Authentick, but that it may be called in question; And, as to the transactions of those times, they are most of them taken out of antient Songs and Fabulous Legends, and some of them out of the allegorical Traditions of their antient Poets or Scalders,[1] which have perhaps been wrongly interpreted by some Authors.

And *Johannes Messenius* in his *Scandinavia Illustrata,* does not stick to say, that the old *Swedish* Historiographer *Johannes Magnus* did strive to outdo in his bragging History, the *Danish* Historian *Saxo Grammaticus. Johannes Magnus* makes *Magog,* the Son of *Japhet* Grandson First Founders of *Noah,* the first Founder of the *Schytick* [Scythian] and *Gothick* Na- of the Gothick Nation. tions, and says that from his two Sons *Sweno,* and *Gethar* and [or] *Gog,*

---

1. *Scald* or *skald* is a medieval Scandinavian term for troubadour.

the *Swedish* and *Gothish* Nations had their names.[2] He relates, that after this Family was extinguished, *Sweden* was during the space of four hundred years under the Government of certain Judges, and that about eight hundred years after the Deluge, both the Kingdoms of the *Swedes* and *Gothes* were uni-<462>ted under *Bericus,* who in person planted a Colony of the *Gothes* beyond the Seas, after having Conquered the *Ulmirugii,* who then inhabited *Prussia,* from whence he extended his Conquests over the *Vandals.* A considerable time after, these Nations did settle themselves not far from the Mouth of the River *Danube* near the Black Sea, from whence having under taken several Expeditions both into *Asia* and *Europe,* at last in the third and fourth Centuries after the Birth of Christ, did enter the *Roman* Provinces on this side of the *Danube,* and carried their Conquering Arms into *Italy* and *Spain,* where they erected two Kingdoms. But the greatest part of this Relation is contradicted by *Messenius,* who also rejects the List, which *Johannes Magnus* had given us, of the Kings before our Saviour's Birth, alledging that the times before Christ's Nativity, are all involved in fabulous Narrations, as to those Northern parts, and that most of these Kings lived after the Birth of our Saviour. But, since even the Chronology of the first Centuries after Christ's Nativity, and the Genealogy of those Kings is somewhat uncertain in these Countries, it will suffice to mention here some few of the most famous among them, till the latter times furnish us with an opportunity to relate things with more certainty.

Othin or Woden. §2. Sixty years before the Birth of Christ, the famous *Othin* or *Woden,*[3] having been driven by *Pompey* out of *Asia* with a great number of people,

2. Johannes Messenius (1579–1636), *Scondia illustrata: seu chronologia de rebus Scondiae, hoc est Sueciae, Daniae, Norvegiae, . . . primum edita, et observationibus aucta à Johanne Peringskiöld,* 14 vols. (Stockholm, 1700–1705). This was the first complete edition of the work. Johannes Magnus or Johan Månsson (1488–1544), papal legate to Sweden (see §9a, p. 554, below), wrote a *Historia de omnibus gothorum sueonumque regibus* (Rome, 1554). Saxo Grammaticus (ca. 1150–1220), was author of a sixteen-volume *Gesta Danorum* on medieval Danish history that appeared in various later editions, including that by Stephan Hansen Stephanius, *Saxonis Grammatici Historiae Danicae Libri XVI* (Soroe, 1645). On the peculiar self-characterization of Nordic nations as "Gothic," see Neville (2009).

3. Odin and Wotan were also, respectively, the names of the chief Norse and Anglo-Saxon gods.

first Conquered Russia, afterwards the *Saxons* and *Danes,* and last of all *Norway* and *Sweden,* about twenty four years before Christ's Birth. *Othin* kept for himself *Sweden* only, yet so, that all the other Scandinavian Princes should own him as their Supreme Lord, from whence came that Custom which was used for several hundred years after, *viz.* That at the great and general meetings of these Nations, the King of *Denmark* used to hold the Bridle of the King of *Sweden's* Horse, whilst he mounted it, and the King of *Norway* the Stirrup. He was succeeded by *Frotho* surnamed *Jorgo,* who covered the Temple at *Upsal*[a] with Gold, and surrounded its Pinacle with a golden Chain. After him were these following <463> Kings: *Niord, Sigtrug, Asmund, Usso, Hynding, Regner, Halvard, Helgo, Attilus, Hother, Roderick* surnamed *Singabond, Hogmor,* and *Hogrin, Erick, Haldan, Sivand, Erick, Haldan, Ungrin, Regnald.*

    About the year 588. *Rodolf* was King of the *Gothes,* but being vanquished by the *English,* whom he left in the possession of that Kingdom, he himself fled into *Italy,* where he sought Sanctuary of *Dicterick* the King of the *Gothes.* In the mean while *Frotho,* either the Son, or else a Kinsman of *Regnald,* was King of *Sweden,* whom succeeded these following Kings[:] *Fiolmus, Swercher, Valander, Vislur,* who was burnt by his own Sons. *Damalder,* who was Sacrificed by his own Subjects to their Idol at *Upsal. Domar, Digner, Dager, Agnius,* who was hanged by his own Wife. *Alrick* and *Erick,* who slew one another in a single Combat. *Ingo, Hugler, Haco, Jerundar, Hacquin* surnamed *Ring,* under whose Reign that most memorable Battel at *Brovalla* was fought, betwixt the *Swedes* and *Danes,* where thirty thousand Men were killed on the *Danish,* and twelve thousand on the *Swedish* side. This King Sacrificed nine of his Sons to the Idol at *Upsal,* and would have done the same with the tenth, who was the only Heir left to the Kingdom, if he had not been prevented by the *Swedes.* Him succeeded his Son *Egillus,* whom followed in the Kingdom of *Sweden, Otbar, Adel, Ostan, Ingvard, Amund, Sivard, Hirot* or *Herolt,* who married his Daughter *Thera* to *Regnertbethen* King of *Denmark.*

    Ingellus the Son of *Amund,* succeeded *Hirot* in the Kingdom of *Sweden;* who, the night after his Coronation caused seven of those petty Princes, that were Vassals of the Crown of *Sweden* to be burnt in their Lodgings; and afterwards exercised the same Cruelty against five more of

Frotho.

Battel fought near Brovalla.

Ingellus.

the same Rank. His Daughter *Asa,* that was married to *Gudrot* a Prince of *Schonen,* exceeded her Father in Cruelty, for having murthered her Husband and his Brother, she betrayed the Country to the Enemies; which so exasperated *Ivan,* the Son of *Regner,* King of *Denmark,* that he fell with great fury upon *Ingellus,* who had taken his Daughter into his Protection, destroying all with Fire and Sword. *Ingellus* being reduced to the utmost extremity, by the advice of his Daughter <464> burnt himself, his Daughter, and the whole Family, in his own Palace, except his Son *Olaus,* who sheltered himself in *Wermeland.* After the death of *Ingellus,* a certain Nobleman, of an antient Family in *Sweden,* whose name was *Charles,* assumed the Royal Title and Power, but *Regner* King of *Denmark,* who pretended that it belonged to his Son, did send a challenge to the said *Charles,* and having killed him in the Combat, transferred the Kingdom of *Sweden* to his Son *Bero* or *Biorn,* who was *Hirots* Daughters Son.

Bero. §3. Under the Reign of this *Bero* or *Biorn, Ansgarius,* a Monk of *Corvey,* **The Christian** and afterwards Bishop of *Bremen,* was sent into *Sweden,* by the Emper- **Doctrine first** our *Lewis* the *Pious,* to Preach the Gospel in that Kingdom. \A. 829\ **taught in** But the King refusing to hearken to his Doctrine, was by the *Swedes* **Sweden.** banished [from] the Kingdom, together with his Father *Regner.* His **Amund.** Successor *Amund* did also Rule but a very few years, and having raised a most horrible Persecution against the Christians, was also banished [from] the Kingdom. The *Swedes* being quite tired out with *Amund's* **Olaus.** tyrannical Government, did call in *Olaus,* out of *Wermeland* to be their King, who to establish himself in the Throne, married the Daughter of *Regner* to his Son *Ingo,* and thereby obtained the quiet possession of the two Kingdoms of the *Swedes* and *Gothes.* \A. 853\ Not many years after[,] *Ansgarius* returned into *Sweden,* and Converted *Olaus,* (who then resided at *Birca* a most populous City) to the Christian Faith. *Olaus* then marched with a Potent Army into *Denmark,* and having committed the Administration of that Kingdom to his Son *Ennigruus,* returned into *Sweden;* where he was by his Heathen Subjects Sacrificed **Ingo.** to their Idol at *Upsal.* His Son *Ingo,* the better to Establish himself in the Throne, married the *King of Denmark's* Daughter, and afterwards was killed in the War against the *Russians.* \A. 890\

Him Succeeded his Son *Erick* surnamed *Weatherhat,* famous for   Erick.
his skill in Witchcraft, who was succeeded by his Son *Erick* surnamed   Erick
Seghersell, who Conquered *Finland, Curland, Livonia,* and *Ebestland.*   Seghersell.
From *Denmark* he retook *Halland* and *Schonen,* and at last drove the
Danish King *Swen* out of *Denmark,* who could not re-<465>cover his
Kingdom till after his [Erick's] death. His Son *Stenchill,* surnamed the   Stenchill the
Mild, was Baptized at *Sigtuna* (a great City at that time) and having   Mild.
destroyed the Idol at *Upsal,* and forbid his Subjects upon pain of death
to Sacrifice to the Idols, the Pagans were so enraged thereat, that they
slew and burnt him near *Upsal,* and with him the two Christian Priests
that were sent to him by the Bishop of *Hamburgh.* His Brother *Olaus*   Olaus.
nevertheless obtained from King *Etheldred* of *England* several Christian Priests, who not only preached the Gospel in *Sweden,* but also the
King, and a great number of People were Baptized by one of these called
Sigfried in a Fountain called *Husbye,* which is called St. *Sigfrieds Kalla
Wel* to this day. This *Olaus* was surnamed *Skotkonung,* because upon
the persuasion of the *English* Priests he granted to the Pope a yearly Tax
against the *Saracens,* which was called *Romskot.*[4] This *Olaus* took from
Olaf Tryggvason the Kingdom of *Norway,* which he however recovered
afterwards. This *Olaus Skotkonung* was also the first who made a perfect   The Swedes
union betwixt the two Kingdoms of the *Swedes* and *Gothes,* who had   and Gothes
hitherto been often at great enmity with one another.   Kingdom.
To+ *Olaus* succeeded his Son *Amund,* under whose Reign the Chris-   Amund.
tian Religion increased very succesfully in *Sweden;* after whom Reigned
his Brother *Amund,* surnamed *Slemme,* a Man very negligent both in   Amund
maintaining Religion and Justice. He was slain with the greatest part   Slemme.
of his Army by *Cnut* King of *Denmark,* near a Bridge called *Strange-
pelle.* After his death the *Gothes* and *Swedes* disagreed about the Election of a new King, the first choosing *Haquin* surnamed the *Red,* the   Haquin the
latter *Stenchill* the younger. At last it was agreed betwixt them, that   Red.
Haquin being pretty well in years should remain King during his life,
and should be succeeded by *Stenchill.* After the death of *Haquin,* who   Stenchill.
Reigned thirteen years, *Stenchill* the younger, *Olaus Skotkonung's* Sisters Son, began his Reign, who vanquished the *Danes* in three great

4. That is, a "Rome tax" (*Rome skatt*).

Ingo the Pious. Battels. Him succeeded *Ingo* surnamed the *Pious*. This King utterly destroyed the Idol at *Upsal*, which so enraged his Pagan Subjects, that they Banished him [from] the Kingdom, and afterwards murthered him in *Schonen*, he was buried <466> in a Convent called *Wamheim* in *West-Gothland*. After him reigned with great applause his Brother *Halstan*, whom succeeded his Son *Philip*. \A. 1086\ *Ingo*, *Philip*'s Son, and his Queen *Ragoild*, were also very famous for their Piety and other Vertues: she was after her death \A. 1138\ honoured as a Saint, and her Tomb frequently visited at *Talgo*. This King left no Sons, but two Daughters, *Christina* and *Margret*, the first was married to St. *Erick*, the second to *Magnus* King of *Norway*. He was poisoned by the *East Gothes*, who were grown weary of the *Swedish* Government. Under the Reign of these five last Kings there were golden times in *Sweden*, the Christian Faith was then Established and the Subjects lived in Peace and Plenty.

§4. After the death of *Ingo*, the *East Gothes*, without the consent of the other Provinces, made one *Ragwald Knaphofde*, a Man of great bodily Strength, but of no great Wisdom, their King, who was slain by the *West Gothes*. In his stead the *East Gothes* chose *Swercher* II. a very good King, who nevertheless was murthered by one of his Servants. After the death of *Swercher*, the *East Gothes* chose his Son *Charles* for their King, but the *Swedes* at their General Assembly at *Upsal* Elected *Erick* the Son [of] *Jedward*, he having married *Christina* the Daughter of *Ingo* surnamed the *Pious*. But both the *Swedes* and *Gothes* considering afterwards, how necessary it was to keep up the Union betwixt these two Kingdoms, made an agreement that *Erick* should remain King over both Kingdoms, but that *Charles* should succeed him, and that afterwards their Heirs should Rule the Kingdom in the same manner in their several turns.

This *Erick* having reduced the *Finns* to their former Obedience, obliged them to receive the Christian Doctrine. He also ordered the antient Constitutions of the Kingdom to be Collected into one Book, which was called after his name St. *Erick*'s Law. \A. 1154\ He was slain in the Meadows near *Upsal* by *Magnus* the King of *Denmark*'s Son, who

Halstan.

Philip.

Ingo.

Ragwald Knaphofde.

Swercher II.

Erick the Holy.

having first defeated his Army, was proclaimed King. \A. 1160\ But the *Swedes* and *Gothes* under the Conduct of *Charles* the Son of *Swercher,* fell again with such fury upon the *Danes,* <467> that they kill'd all the *Danes* with their King and his Son upon the spot, and out of the spoil built a Church near *Upsal* which they called *Denmark. Charles* there- fore, the Son of *Swercher*[,] became King of *Denmark,* who Reigned with a general applause; till *Cnut* the Son of *Erick* returned out of *Norway,* and under pretence that he [Charles] had abetted his Father's death, surprised and killed him. \A. 1168\ His Lady and Children fled into *Denmark,* where having got some assistance they joined with the *Gothes* under the Conduct of *Koll,* the Brother of *Charles,* to recover the Kingdom, but their General was killed upon the spot, and their Forces dispersed by *Cnut Erickson.* After which he Reigned very peaceably for the space of twenty three years.

Charles the Son of Swercher.
Cnut Erickson.

After the death of *Cnut, Swercher* the Son of *Charles* was made King of *Swedeland,* but had for his Rival *Erick,* the Son of the last deceased King. At last the difference was thus Composed, that *Swercher* should remain King during his life, but should be succeeded by *Erick.* But *Swercher,* who notwithstanding this agreement was for settling the Crown upon his Family, did barbarously murther all the Sons of *Cnut,* \A. 1207\ except *Erick,* who escaped into *Norway;* from whence he returned with some Forces, and being assisted by the *Swedes* vanquished *Swercher,* who fled into *West Gothland.* Having obtained Succours of sixteen thousand Men, from *Waldemar,* the King of *Denmark,* he attempted to recover his Kingdom, but was miserably beaten by *Erick's* Army, he himself narrowly escaping into *Denmark* \A. 1208\; from whence he not long after again fell into *West Gothland,* but was again defeated and slain in the Battel \A. 1210\, leaving *Erick Cnutson* in the quiet possession of the Throne, who renewed the former agreement made betwixt these two Families, and Constituted *John* the Son of *Swercher* his Successour in the Kingdom. \A. 1219\ He married *Ricitot* the Sister of *Waldemar* King of *Denmark,* and dyed in *Wisingsoe.* Him succeeded according to agree- ment, *John* the Son of *Swercher,* who Reigned but three years and dyed also in the Isle of *Wisingsoe,* which was the general place of residence of the *Swedish* Kings in those days. <468>

Swercher III.
Erick Cnutson.

Erick Lespe. §5. After the death of *John, Erick,* the Son of the former King *Erick,* became King of *Sweden,* who being lame, and besides this lisping, was surnamed the *Lisper.* There was about that time a very Potent Family in *Sweden* called the *Tolekungers,* who aimed at the Crown. To bring these over to his Party the King had married three of his Sisters to three of the Chiefest among them, he himself having married *Catharine* the Daughter of *Sweno Tolekunger.* But these being grown more Potent by this Alliance; *Cnut Tolekunger* rebelled against the King, and having worsted him, obliged him to fly into *Denmark;* from whence he soon returned with a strong Army and vanquished *Tolekunger,* and having caused him and *Halingar* his Son to be slain, restored the Peace of the Kingdom.

Celibacy of Clergy introduced in Sweden. Under the Reign of this King it was that *Gulielmus Sabinensis* the Pope's Legat did first forbid the Priests in *Sweden* to Marry, whereas before that time it had been a common Custom among the Priests there to Marry, as well as Laymen.[5] This *Erick* under the Conduct of his Brother in Law *Birger Yerl* forced the *Finnes* to return to Obedience, and to receive the Christian Faith, and built several Fortresses upon their Frontiers. He dyed without issue in *Wisingsoe.* \A. 1250\

Waldemar. Whilst *Birger Yerl* was absent in *Finland,* the States [estates] made *Waldemar* the eldest Son of *Birger Yerl* their King, as being the deceased King's Sisters Son: \A. 1251\ Who being Crowned in the year next following, the Administration of the Kingdom was committed during his minority to his Father *Birger,* who augmented the antient Law Book, and deserved so well of the Publick, that upon the request of the Estates he was created a Duke, whereas before he had been only an Earl, or as it is in their antient Language *Yerl.* He met with great opposition from the *Tolekungers,* who had not quite laid aside their pretensions to the Crown, so that their jealousie at last broke out into open War. But the Duke, under pretence of making an agreement with them, after having granted them a safe Conduct persuaded them to give him a meeting, where having made them all Prisoners caused them to be Executed, except *Charles Tolekunger* who fled into *Prussia,* and re-<469>mained there all his life time. Things being thus settled, he [Birger] gave to

5. Eric XI Ericsson (1216–50) was king of Sweden during 1222–29 and 1234–50.

his Son, in Marriage, *Sophia* the Daughter of *Erick* King of *Denmark*, \A. 1263\ and laid the first foundation of the Castle and City of *Stockholm;* and tho his Son was become of Age, yet did he never surrender the Government to him as long as he lived.

He died \A. 1266\ after he had been Regent fifteen years, leaving four Sons, *Waldemar* King of *Sweden, Magnus* Duke of *Sudermanland, Erick* of *Smaland,* and *Benedict* of *Finland,* who [together] afterwards raised great Disturbances: for *Waldemar* having, during his Pilgrimage to *Rome* and *Jerusalem,* left the Administration of the Kingdom to his Brother *Magnus,* at his return accused him of having aimed at the Crown. The *States* of *Sweden* held an Assembly \A. 1275\ at *Strengness* to compose these differences if possible; but met with so much difficulty that it was impossible to be effected. Wherefore *Magnus* and *Erick* being retired into *Denmark,* soon returned from thence with a considerable Force; and having routed the Vanguard of King *Waldemar,* made him their Prisoner. Whereupon *Magnus* called together the Estates of the Kingdom; who being most of them of his Party, did assign the whole Kingdom to Duke *Magnus,* except only East and West *Gothland, Smaland* and *Daht,* which the King was to have for his share. But this Agreement lasted not long; for the *Danes,* who had not received their Subsidies promised by *Magnus,* siding with *Waldemar,* the War was renewed, which was carried on with various Success; till at last the *Danes,* having received satisfaction for the Money due to them, left *Waldemar* in the lurch, who, in the presence of the Estates, resigned the Kingdom to *Magnus.*

§6. *Waldemar* having resigned the Kingdom, *Magnus* was crowned at *Upsal:* \A. 1279\ who resumed the Title of *King of the Swedes and Goths,* which had not been used by his Predecessors ever since the time of *Olaus Skotkonung,* but is since retained by the Kings of *Sweden* to this day. Under this King's reign the Family of the *Tolekungers* began to raise new Commotions, and being assisted by some of the Nobil[i]ty, murthered *Ingemar Danschkep* the King's Favourite, and took *Gerbard* the <470> E. [earl] of *Holstein* and Father-in-law to the K. [king] Prisoner, laying also close Siege to the Castle of *Joncoring;* which oblig'd the K. to ap-

Magnus.

pease them for that time by fair Promises: but not long after the E. was released, the K. accused them before the Assembly of the Nobility of High Treason, and caused them all to be executed at *Stockholm,* except *Philip* of *Runby,* who was fain to redeem his Life at a very dear Rate. And with this Stroke the Greatness of the Family of the *Tolekungers* was quite laid in the dust. Having thus settled his Affairs, he got his Lady *Hederig* crowned at *Suderasping;* and, with the advice of the Senators, made King *Waldemar* a Prisoner in the Castle of *Nicoping,* where he died four years after. \A. 1288\ *Magnus* died in *Wisignioc* \A. 1290\, but was buried at *Stockholm* in the Church of the *Grey Friars,* having left the Tuition of his Son *Birger,* who was but eleven years of age, and the Care of the Kingdom[,] to *Torckell Cnutson* the Rix-Marshal. *Torckell Cnutson* was Regent for the space of thirteen years, during which time he also imprisoned King *Waldemar's* Son; but after their decease he sent an Army into *Carelia,* and having subdued this Nation, and induced them to receive the Christian Faith, he built on their Frontiers the Fortress of *Wibourg,* and took from the *Russians Kekhelm.* \A. 1292\

Birger II.

King *Birger* being by this time come to his riper Years, married *Mereta* the Daughter of *Erick* King of *Denmark;* and having sent new forces into *Carelia* and *Ingermania,* built the Fortress of *Norburgh* on the Frontiers of *Russia* \A. 1298\, which however a few years after was retaken and demolished by the *Russians.* Soon after he declared his Son *Magnus,* who was but three years old his Successor in the Kingdom, which was confirmed by the chief Men of the Kingdom, and especially by his Brothers. \A. 1303\ But this solemn Transaction was of no long continuance, for the Brothers quickly fell into divisions among themselves, and the two younger growing mistrustful of the King, the Marshal [Cnutson] retired first into *Denmark,* and from thence into *Norway,* to make use of that King's Intercession to recover their Inheritance, which King *Birger* had seised upon; but all this proving ineffectual, they made several Inroads into *West-Gothland,* and killed and dispersed the *Swedish* Troops that were sent to oppose them. The <471> King went at last in person with an Army, and was met by his Brothers with some Forces, which they had obtained of the King of *Norway;* when by the Intercession of some Senators, the Differences betwixt the

Brothers were composed, and the two younger restored to their Estates in *Sweden*.

This Agreement cost the old *Torckell* [Cnutson] his Head \A. 1305\, who, under pretence of having upheld the Animosities betwixt the Brothers, and some other matters laid to his charge, was beheaded at *Stockholm*. But no sooner was this Wise Man dead, but the two younger Brothers began to aim again at the Crown, and having surprised the K. and Q. at their Country Seat called *Hatuna*, forced him to resign the Kingdom, and to surrender the Crown and City of *Stockholm* to his Brother *Erick*, who made the King a Prisoner in the Castle of *Nicoping*; but his Son *Magnus* was, during this Tumult, carried into *Denmark*. The King of *Denmark* undertook 3 several Expeditions to relieve his Brother-in-law and Sister, but to no great purpose, only that at last it was agreed, that the King, Queen and their Children should be set at liberty, and the matter decided in the Assembly of the Senate of the Kingdom. The Senate therefore having been called together at *Arboga*, it was there concluded, That in case King *Birger* would pardon all past Injuries, and be contented with what part of the Kingdom should be assigned to him, he should be set at liberty: which was performed accordingly, the Senate and his Brothers having again sworn fealty to him.

Thus matters seemed to be composed for the present, when not long after a greater Storm broke out. \A. 1308\ *Erick* the King of *Denmark*, having made an Alliance with *Haquin* King of *Norway*, came with an Army of 60.000 Men into *Sweden*, to assist King *Birger* in bringing his Brothers under his Subjection: their first Success was answerable to their great Preparations, having taken *Joncoping*, and forced the Duke's [Erick's] Forces to fly before them; but the *Danes*, who began to be in want of Provision, being most of them gone home, there was a Meeting appointed betwixt the Brothers to be held at *Helsinburgh*, where the former Agreement made at *Arboga* was renewed; by virtue of which Duke *Erick* was to have *West Gothland, Daht, Halland, Wermeland,* <472> and *Smaland;* Duke *Waldemar* was to have for his share *Upland, Oeland* and part of *Finland;* the rest was to remain under the King, and the Dukes to hold their Possessions in Fief from him. Thus all Animosities seemed to be laid aside, and the three Brothers lived in great splendor, striving to out-do one another in Magnificence; which occasioning some new Taxes, proved also the occasion of some Insurrections in the Kingdom, which were nevertheless happily appeased, and Peace restored to the whole Kingdom.

In⁺ the mean while Duke *Waldemar* in his journey from *Calmar* to *Stockholm,* gave a visit to the King at *Nycoping* \A. 1317\, who not only treated him with extraordinary Civility, but also desired him to return and bring his Brother along with him, *by which means he hoped that the very seeds of their former Animosities betwixt them might be rooted out. Waldemar,* being overcome by these fair Promises, over-persuaded his Brother *Erick,* who was very averse to it at first, but at last consented. Being arrived in the Castle where the King was, they were kindly received and splendidly entertained at Supper; but they had not been long in bed, and most of their Servants dispersed into several Quarters of the Town, till they were made Prisoners, beaten, abused, and half naked, loaden with Irons, thrown into a strong Tower, their Servants having been all either killed or taken Prisoners. The King marched directly for *Stockholm,* in hopes to surprise the City; but the News of this barbarous act having been already carried to *Stockholm,* they not only repulsed him, but also pursued him to *Nycoping.* The King perceiving that they intended to besiege *Nycoping,* retired to *Steckeburgh;* but before his departure, having caused the Doors of the Prison to be barricado'd up, he threw the Keys into the River, and commanded upon pain of death, not to open the Doors till his return. Soon after *Nycoping* was besieged, but before it could be forced both the Brothers died by Famine. King *Birger* having by this Treacherous fact animated the whole Kingdom against him, sought for Aid in *Denmark;* and having obtained some Forces, shifted with them from place to place, till some of them were surprized at *Sudercoping,* and the *Danish* Horse having also left *Ny-*<473>*coping,* the King, destitute of all, retired with the Queen into *Gothland,* leaving his Son *Magnus* in the Castle of *Stegeburgh.* The *Swedes* having immediately after invested the Place, forced it to *surrender* by Famine, and sent *Magnus* a Prisoner to *Stockholm.* The Senate of the Kingdom made there *Matthew Ketelmundson* Regent of *Sweden* \A. 1319\, who vigorously prosecuted the Remnants of the King's Party, which obliged King *Birger* to seek for shelter to *Christopher* King of *Denmark*.

§7. After K. *Birger* had left *Gothland,* the Estates assembled at *Upsal,* chose for their King *Magnus*[,] the Son of D. *Erick*[,] being then but 3 years old. The Year next following *Magnus* the Son of K. *Birger,* notwithstanding that the Senate and Estates of the Kingdom had sworn Fealty to him as to their future King, was villainously sentenced to death and beheaded accordingly, and King *Birger* and his Queen died soon after for Grief.

Margin note: Magnus Smeeck.

But the *Swedes,* who had conceived great hopes of their new King, found themselves extreamly deceived in their Expectation after the death of *Ketelmundson,* who at first managed affairs with great Prudence. For the King being now of age married *Blanch* the Daughter of an Earl of *Namur,* and laying aside the old Counsellors made use of the Advice of his young Favourites, among whom one *Benedict* born in *West-Gothland* had the chief place. The Inhabitants of *Schonen* being sorely oppressed by the *Holsteiners,* put themselves under his protection, which was afterwards confirmed by *Waldemar* King of *Denmark,* and the *Sound,* by common consent, made the common Borders of these two Kingdoms on that side. After he had ruled twelve years in peace, he undertook an Expedition against the *Russians,* which succeeded very ill, [he] being obliged to redeem the peace by the surrender of a part of *Carelia.* His Treasury having by this War been mightily exhausted, he not only imposed new and heavy Taxes upon the people, but also pawned a great many of the Crown Lands. Pope *Clement* VI. also had excommunicated him because he had applied the Revenues of S. *Peter,* given to the *Roman* Chair by *Olaus Skotkonung,* to the use of the *Russian* War.[6]

The People being extreamly discontented at these Pro-<474>ceedings, the Senate perswaded the King that he should cause his two Sons to be declared Kings, *viz. Erick* of *Sweden,* and *Haquin* of *Norway,* which

6. See §3, p. 529, above.

was done accordingly. The Nobility being now headed by a new King [Erick], began to withdraw from their obedience to the old King [Magnus], and killed his Favourite *Benedict*. The King who now began to see his Errors, sought for Aid from the King of *Denmark,* which so exasperated the Nobility, that they obliged the young King to take up Arms against his Father, which occasioned a bloody War, till at last \A. 1357\ the Kingdom was divided betwixt them, the Father having got *Upland, Gothland, Wermeland, Daht, North-Halland, West-Gothland* and *Oeland.* But *Schonen, Bleckingers, South-Halland, East-Gothland, Smaland* and *Finland* fell to the Son's share.

But[+] notwithstanding this agreement, the jealousie continued betwixt the Father and Son, and not long after the Father having sent for his Son [Erick] under pretence of some Business of great moment, he was there poysoned by his Mother. By his death King *Magnus* being put again into the possession of the whole Kingdom, studied nothing but revenge against the Nobility. The better to encompass his design, he made an under-hand Alliance with the King of *Denmark,* unto whom he surrendred *Schonen* again; who not only took possession of it, but also by connivance of King *Magnus* fell into *Gothland* and *Oeland* \A. 1361\, where he killed a great many Boors, plundered the whole Country, and demolished *Borgholm.* The *Swedes* being thus put to a nonplus, submitted themselves to the protection of *Haquin* King of *Denmark* [Norway], who made his Father *Magnus* a Prisoner in the Castle of *Calmar.*

The Senate of the Kingdom then perswaded King *Haquin* to marry the Daughter of *Henry* Earl of *Holstein,* which he seemingly consented to at that time. But the Bride in her Voyage into *Sweden,* having been driven on the Coast of *Denmark,* was detained by *Waldemar* King of *Denmark,* who intended to marry his Daughter to King *Haquin. Albert* Duke of *Mecklenburgh* and the Earls of *Holstein* did denounce War against the King of *Denmark* if he did not release the Bride, but King *Waldemar* had in the mean while so well managed the Affairs with *Haquin,* that he resolved to marry *Margaret* <475> his Daughter. The Bride was then set at Liberty, but being arrived in *Sweden* was so slightly received by King *Magnus,* who in the mean time had obtained his Liberty, that she retired into a Nunnery; and those Senators who urged the King[7] to perform his Marriage-Contract, were by *Magnus* banished [from] the Kingdom, who soon after married his Son to *Margaret,* that was then but eleven years old. \A. 1363\ At this Wedding which was held at *Copenhagen, Waldemar* caused the Parents of *Haquin* to be poysoned, which worked so violently upon *Blemba* [his mother], that she died immediately, but King *Magnus* was preserved by the skill of his Physicians.

§8. Those *Swedish* Lords that were banished by King *Magnus,* having for some time lived in *Gothland* did at last agree among themselves to elect *Henry* Earl of *Holstein,* King of *Sweden.* But he being a Man in years, and not willing to entangle himself in those troublesome Affairs, recommended to them *Albert* Duke of *Mecklenburgh,* King *Magnus's* Sisters Son. The banished Lords therefore having chosen his second Son, whose name also was *Albert*[,] their King,[8] carried him into *Gothland,* and from thence to *Stockholm,* which they easily took, being assisted by a strong party within the City. Having then called together such of the Nobility as they knew to be Enemies to King *Magnus,* they proclaimed *Albert* King in the City of *Stockholm.* \A. 1364\ *Magnus* and his Son [Haquin] having thereupon got together considerable Forces both in *Sweden* and *Denmark* marched against King *Albert* into *Upland,* and were met [by] him near by *Encoping,* where a bloody Battle ensued, the Victory inclined to *Albert's* side, King *Magnus* was taken Prisoner, *Haquin* wounded but escaped the Hands of his Enemies. \A. 1365\

During the imprisonment of King *Magnus, Sweden* was reduced to a most miserable estate, by the Wars that were carried on betwixt King *Albert* and *Haquin* and *Waldemar,* the two last sending continual Supplies into *Sweden* to uphold their Party, and *Haquin* was grown so strong, that he defeated King *Albert* in a Battel and besieged *Stockholm.* \A. 1371\ At last it was agreed that King *Magnus* should have his Liberty, paying a Ransom of 12.000 Marks of fine Silver, and resign the Crown

Albert Duke of Mecklenburgh.

---

7. Haquin, presumably, though Magnus seems to have regained a say in things.
8. Albert of Mecklenburg (ca. 1338–1412) was the second son of Duke Albert II of Mecklenburg and Euphemia Eriksdotter, the sister of Magnus Eriksson.

of *Sweden* and *Schonen* to <476> King *Albert,* which was performed accordingly, King *Magnus* retiring into *Norway,* where he was drowned by accident. King *Haquin* did not long survive his Father, and his Son *Olaus* dying very young, Queen *Margaret* after his decease was sole Queen of *Norway.* By the Death of this *Olaus,* the antient Race of the *Swedish* Kings was extinguished, which ever since the time of St. *Erick, viz.* for the space of 220 Years had ruled in *Sweden.* \A. 1376\

Not long after, *Waldemar* King of *Denmark* died without leaving any Male Heirs behind him. In whose stead the *Danes*[,] to unite *Norway* with *Denmark,* declared his Daughter *Margaret* their Queen. King *Albert* by the Death of his Enemies being now established in the Throne of *Sweden* began to slight the *Swedish* Nobility, and to employ the *Germans* in his Service, who grew very Rich and Potent; and his Treasury being exhausted by the war which was carried on against *Denmark,* he demanded from the States [estates] that part of the Revenues of the Clergy, and some of the Lands which belonged to the Nobility[,] should be incorporated with the Crown, which they refusing to consent to, he nevertheless pursued his Intentions by open Violence. Whilest therefore some that were no losers by it and hoped to partake of the Booty, sided with the King, the rest were consulting how to deliver themselves from these oppressions, and having renounced their obedience to King

Margaret. *Albert,* sought for Protection by *Margaret* Queen of *Denmark,* which she granted them, upon condition that if she should deliver them from King *Albert,* she was to be Queen of *Sweden.* Which the *Swedes* being forced to accept of, she was proclaimed Queen of *Sweden.*

This proved the occasion of unspeakable miseries, both Parties committing great Outrages in the Country, which was quite exhausted before, by King *Albert*[,] who also at last was forced to pawn the Isle of *Gothland* for 20.000 Nobles[9] to the *Prussian* Knights of the Cross; notwithstanding which[,] being not able to defray at length the Charges of the War, he challenged Queen *Margaret* to a Battel to be fought in

The Battel of   the Plains of *Talkoping* in *West-Gothland.* \12. Sept. 1388\ The appointed
Talkoping.   day being come, a bloody Battel was fought in the before-mentioned

---

9. *Nobles* were gold coins introduced in England during the fourteenth century.

Plain, where the Queen's Forces at last ob-<477>tained the Victory, King *Albert* and his Son being taken Prisoners. But this Victory rather encreased than diminished the miseries under which the Kingdom had groaned before, because the Dukes of *Mecklenburgh;* Earls of *Holstein* and the *Hanse* Towns sided with King *Albert's* Party, who sent constant Supplies from *Rostock* and *Wismar* by Sea to *Stockholm, Calmar* and other strongholds in their possession, from whence the *German* Garrisons made miserable havock all round the Country, and the Sea Coasts were extreamly infested by Privateers, which had quite ruined the Trade of the Kingdom. This pernicious War having thus lasted seven Years, a Treaty of Peace was set on foot at *Helsingburgh* \A. 1394\, which proving fruitless, another meeting was appointed at *Aleholm* \A. 1395\, where it was agreed that the King, his Son, and the rest of the Prisoners of note should be set at Liberty, under condition that he within the space of three Years, resign all his pretensions to the Kingdom unto Queen *Margaret,* or else return to Prison; and that in case of failure, the Cities of *Lubeck, Hamburgh, Dantzick, Thorn, Elbingen, Saralsund* [Stralsund], *Stetin* and *Campen* should oblige themselves to pay 60.000 Marks of fine Silver to the Queen.

Thus King *Albert* returned into *Mecklenburgh,* after he had reigned 23 Years in *Sweden.* He had notwithstanding this agreement, not laid aside his hope of recovering his Kingdom, for which he had made great preparations, if his Son had not died, two Years after, when he at the appointed time resigned his pretensions, and the places as yet in his possession[,] to the Queen, and at last ended his days in his native Country of *Mecklenburgh.* Thus *Margaret* became Queen over all the three Northern Kingdoms, which she governed with extraordinary Wisdom, yet so that the *Danes* were much better satisfied with her Government than the *Swedes.*

§9. Queen *Margaret* having restored Peace to the Northern Kingdoms, her next care was to unite these three Crowns for ever on [under] one Head. For which purpose she had sent for *Henry*[,] a young Duke of *Pomerania,* her Sister's Son, whose name to please the *Swedes,* she <478> changed into that of Erick. This Prince, tho' very young, was in the sec-

Erick Duke of Pomerania.

Union made
at Calmar be-
twixt Sweden,
Denmark and
Norway. ond Year after the releasing of King *Albert,* proclaimed King. In the Year
next following, the Senators and Nobility of all the three Kingdoms
being assembled at Calmar \A. 1396\, where also the young *Erick* was
crowned, the Union of the three Kingdoms was proposed, which at last
was perfected and confirmed by Oath, and by the Hands and Seals of
the States [estates] of the three Kingdoms;[10] which might have tended to
the great Advantage of these three Nations, if the *Danes* had not afterwards broke this Union, and endeavoured to make themselves Masters
of *Sweden,* which proved the occasion of bloody Wars betwixt these two
Kingdoms. But because King *Erick* was but very young, Queen *Margaret* had the administration of Affairs during his Minority, when the
Swedes and *Norwegians* soon perceived that the Articles of this Union
were likely to be but ill observed, since the Queen preferred the *Danes*
and other Strangers much before them, and what Taxes she levied in
Sweedland, were for the most part spent in *Denmark,* where she generally resided.

In the eighth Year after King *Erick* was crowned, Queen *Margaret* attempted to re-gain the Isle of *Gothland* from the *Prussian* Knights, without paying the Ransom; but having not succeeded in her Enterprise,
she redeemed it for 10.000 Nobles. King *Erick* being by this time come
to his riper Years, married \A. 1410\ *Philippa* the Daughter of *Henry* IV.
King of *England,* and having after his Aunt's Death, which happened
not long after \A. 1412\, taken upon him the sole management of Affairs, he was intangled in a tedious War with *Henry* Earl of *Holstein,* the
Hanse Towns, and the Dukes of *Mecklenburgh* and *Saxony,* about the
Dutchy of *Sleswick,* which at last cost him his three Kingdoms. For his
Subjects being over-charged with Taxes, which were employed towards
the War, that could at the best only prove beneficial to *Denmark,* and
their Commerce being interrupted with the *Hanse* Towns, it occasioned
great discontents among them; besides this, the King's Officers had
used the *Swedes* very tyrannically, and the King had upon several occasions receded from the Articles of Union made at *Calmar,* especially

10. The Treaty of Kalmar (1397) formally created a Nordic Union among Denmark, Norway, and Sweden. See note 7, p. 364, above.

<479> when he sent the most antient *Swedish* Records into *Denmark,* which at last obliged the *Swedes* to take desperate Counsels.

The first Insurrection was made by the *Dalekarls,*[11] who being headed by a certain antient Nobleman in those parts called *Engelbrecht Engelbrechtson,* besieged one of the King's Officers called *Josse Erichson,* who had exercised great Tyranny over them, in his Castle, neither could they be appeased till he was deposed from his Office, and another put in his place. But this Calm did not last long, for the Boors being again stirred up by *Engelbrecht* over-ran all the neighbouring Country, destroying with Fire and Sword, all such as would not side with them; and being joined by one *Erick Pueke,* who headed the *Northlanders,* they took a great many strongholds, killing all the Foreigners they met withal, whose seats they destroyed, and at last forced the Senate of the Kingdom assembled at *Wadstena,* to renounce their Allegiance to the King. These intestine Commotions obliged King *Erick* to make Peace with the *Holsteiners* and the Hanse Towns, and to turn all his Forces against the *Swedes.* But his Fleet being for a great part destroyed by Storms, he arrived with the rest at *Stockholm,* but not being able to cope with so great a multitude, as *Engelbrecht* had raised against him; he was fain to make a truce with them for twelve Months. In the mean while he retired into *Denmark,* leaving only a Garrison of 600 Men in the Castle of *Stockholm.* After his departure *Engelbrecht* was declared *Generalissimo* over all the Forces of the Kingdom, who, at last upon the perswasion of the Archbishop *Oluf,* agreed to a Treaty to be set on foot betwixt the King and his Subjects, where it was agreed that the *Swedes* should again acknowledge him for their King, provided he would stand to the Union, which the King at that time consented to, reserving only to his free disposal the three Castles of *Stockholm, Calmar* and *Nycoping,* all the rest being to be committed to the Government of the Natives of *Sweedland.*

Thus things seemed to be restored to the antient State, but no sooner had the King got the aforesaid Castles into his possession, but he began to recede, and having left a Garrison of 300 Men in the Castle

---

11. See note 10, p. 366, above, and note 13, p. 549, below.

of *Stockholm,* retired upon a sudden into *Denmark.* King <480> *Erick* having thus left the Kingdom a second time, the *Swedish* Senators, who feared that he might soon return with a greater Force, being assembled at *Arboka,* called together the whole Nobility, and a Burger-Master out of each City, to consult about the present exigency of Affairs; but before they could come to any steady resolution, *Engelbrecht* by the assistance of some of the Citizens of *Stockholm,* had made himself Master of that City, and besieged the King's Lieutenant in the Castle. The Treaty being thus broke off, and the flame of Rebellion rekindled, the Marshal *Charles Cnutson*[12] was declared Governour and General of the Kingdom: This was like to have occasioned great Disturbances, if *Engelbrecht,* who pretended to be injured by this Choice, had not been first appeased with great Promises, and afterwards murthered by one *Benedict Suenson,* with whom he had an old quarrel. \A. 1436\ But *Erick Pueke* the chief Companion of *Engelbrecht* taking up his Friend's Quarrel against his Murtherers that were protected by *Charles Cnutson,* it occasioned great Jealousies betwixt them. The Castles of *Stockholm* and *Calmar* being also in the King's possession, and some of the Chiefest of the Kingdom grown very jealous of the greatness of the Marshal, the Treaty was renewed with the King at *Calmar,* who came thither in Person, and promised to put into all Offices and Places of Trust, Natives of *Sweden,* and having made *Benedict Suenson* Governour of the Castle of *Calmar,* appointed an Assembly of the Senate and Nobility to be held in *September* following when he would be ready to surrender all the Strongholds into the hands of the Native Subjects of *Sweden.*

But in the mean time the King in his Voyage from *Gothland* to *Suderkoping,* was overtaken by a violent Tempest, wherein most of his Ships having been lost, he narrowly escaped drowning. As soon as the *Swedes* got notice of this Misfortune, not knowing whether the King was alive or dead, it was resolved that the last Treaty made at *Calmar* should remain in Force. Pursuant to this Decree, the Marshal having partly by great Promises, partly by Threats, got into the possession of all the Castles of the Kingdom, seemed to want nothing to accomplish

Charles Cnutson.

12. Karl Knutsson (1409–70).

his Designs, but the Title of a King, where-<481>at *Erick Pueke* being vexed to the Soul, raised a great number of Boors against him, who having defeated the Marshal and his Forces, would quickly have put an end to his Greatness, if he under pretence of reconciliation had not invited *Erick Pueke* to an interview, and notwithstanding his Faith given, sent him to *Stockholm,* where he was beheaded. \A. 1437\ In the mean while, the Senators of the Kingdom having got notice that the King was alive, appointed an Assembly to be held at *Calmar,* where the King was to fulfil the former Treaty; but the King not coming at the appointed time, Commissioners were sent into *Denmark* to treat with him about the performance of the Agreement made at *Calmar,* which he refusing to do, they made an underhand League with some of the great Men in *Denmark* against King *Erick,* the effects of which he felt soon after.

Whilst these things were transacting in *Denmark,* the Marshal had by his cunning got the whole Power of the Kingdom into his hands, and obtained from the Senate in *Sweden,* to appoint a certain day for the King to appear in *Sweden,* and put an end to those Differences that were then betwixt him and the Estates, and in case of a refusal, they renounced their Allegiance to him. But the Archbishop *Oluf,* and some of the Chief Men of the Kingdom, that were dissatisfied at the Marshal's proceedings did so far prevail by their Authority, that a General Assembly of all the Senators of the three Northern Kingdoms should be held at *Calmar,* which in all likelihood might have had better Success than before, if the Archbishop had not been poysoned in his Journey thither by the Marshal. Notwithstanding this, the rest of the Senators appeared at *Calmar,* but the King's Commissioners refusing to acknowledge and to confirm the Treaty made at *Calmar,* which the *Swedes* insisted upon, the whole meeting proved fruitless.

In the mean time King *Erick* was retired with all his Treasure out of *Denmark* into *Gothland,* and the *Danish* Senators who as well as the *Swedes* had been dissatisfied with the King for a considerable time before, agreed with the *Swedes* to renounce their Allegiance to him, and to choose one in his stead, that would maintain the Union betwixt these Kingdoms. The *Danes* therefore sent <482> to *Christopher* Duke of *Bavaria,* who being King *Erick's* Sister's Son, had for some time lived

Christopher Duke of Bavaria.

in *Denmark,* desiring him to accept of that Crown. \A. 1439\ As soon as he arrived in *Denmark,* Ambassadors were sent to the Marshal and the other Senators of *Sweden,* that were then at *Calmar,* to notifie the arrival of the Duke of *Bavaria,* and to treat with them to receive him also for their King, as the only means to maintain the Union and Peace betwixt those Kingdoms. The Marshal and his Party were not a little surprised at this Proposition; but perceiving that, at the Dyet held at *Arboga,* most of the Estates were inclined to maintain the Union, and receive *Christopher* for their King, they also agreed with the rest of the Estates, and *Christopher* was received by the Marshal and the Senators with great Pomp at *Calmar,* from whence being conducted to *Stockholm,* and from thence to *Upsal,* he was there crowned King of *Sweden,* and soon after returned into *Denmark.* After he had reigned four years, he married *Dorothee* the Daughter of *John* Marquis of *Brandenburgh;* and King *Erick,* who was yet in the possession of *Gothland,* doing considerable damage to the *Swedish* Ships, he was prevailed upon by the Senate to undertake an Expedition into *Gothland.* Whilst every body was in great expectation about the success of this Enterprise, he upon the sudden clapt up a Peace with King *Erick,* leaving him in the quiet possession of *Gothland.* \A. 1448\ He died at *Helsinburgh,* in his Journey to *Joncoping,* whither he had called together the Senate and Nobility of *Sweden,* having left great Legacies to several Churches in *Sweden;* but the *Danes,* who had all his Ships, Ammunition, rich Furniture and ready Money in their hands, would not pay one groat of it.

Charles Cnutson.

After[+] the death of K. *Christopher,* the Estates of *Sweden* that were assembled at *Stockholm* were divided into two parties, some of them being for deferring the Election of a new King, till such time as the Senators of the 3 kingdoms could, at a general Assembly chuse a King, according to the Union agreed upon betwixt them; but the Marshal and his Party, which was the strongest, were, without having any respect to the Union, for chusing immediately a King of their own: this Contest lasted for se-<483>veral days, and that with such heats that they were ready to come to blows, till at last the Marshal *Charles Cnutson's* Party prevailed, who was chosen King of *Sweden.* But the *Danes* offered the Crown of *Denmark* to *Adolf* Duke of *Holstein,* and he by reason of his old Age, having refused to accept of it, they made *Christian* Earl of *Oldenburg,* the Duke's Sister's Son, their King. *Charles,* at the very beginning of his Reign, besieged King *Erick* in the Castle of *Wisby,* who having deluded the *Swedish* Generals with a Truce, did, in the mean while provide himself with all Necessaries, and was at last relieved by *Christian* King of *Denmark;* who sent him into *Pomerania,* where, in the City of *Rugen,* he ended his days, without making any further pretension to the Crown.

In⁺ the mean while the *Norwegians,* except some of the Nobility, had made *Charles* also their King, which occasioned almost a continual War betwixt him and *Christian* King of *Denmark,* in which King *Charles* was pretty successful at first; but after the death of the brave *Thord Bonde,* his General, who was barbarously murthered; King *Christian,* with the Assistance of the Archbishop of *Sweden* and several others of the *Swedish* Nobility, who were Enemies to King *Charles,* proved too hard for him: for the Archbishop having surprised the King's Forces at *Strengness,* besieged him in the City of *Stockholm;* so that King *Charles* finding himself reduced to the utmost Extremity, resolved to embarque with all his Treasure for *Dantzick,* where he arrived safely, after a Voyage of three days, in the tenth year of his Reign. \A. 1458\

No sooner had King *Charles* left the Kingdom, but the Archbishop, having got all the Strongholds of the Kingdom into his hands, sent to *Christian* King of *Denmark,* to invite him into *Sweden,* who being arrived with a considerable Fleet at *Stockholm,* was, by the Senate and Nobility declared King of *Sweden,* and crowned at *Upsal.* He reigned at first with a general satisfaction of the *Swedes;* but some years after, by his Cruelty and heavy Impositions laid upon the People, became odious to them: for he not only caused some of the Great men, that were falsly accused of holding a Correspondency with King *Charles,* to be tortured to <484> death, but also exercised great Cruelty against a great number of *Boors,* that were risen in Arms against him; and having conceived a jealousie of the Archbishop, he caused him to be carried Prisoner to *Copenhagen.* This so exasperated *Katil* the Bishop of *Lyncoping* that he raised an Insurrection against the King, and forced him to retire into *Denmark;* and tho the King returned the year next following with a

Christian I.

548   CHAPTER XIII

considerable Army, yet being defeated by the Bishop's Forces, he was forced to leave the Kingdom a second time; \A. 1464\ and the Bishop having laid siege to the City and Castle of *Stockholm,* where King *Christian* had left a Garrison, sent for assistance to King *Charles,* who being glad of this Opportunity, came with some Forces (which he had gathered in *Poland* and *Prussia*) into *Sweden,* where he was no sooner arrived, but the City of *Stockholm* was surrendred to him, and he again received as King of *Sweden.*

But this Joy was of no long continuance; for a difference being arisen betwixt him and Bishop *Katil,* about the exchanging the Archbishop that was Prisoner at *Copenhagen,* the said Bishop did underhand agree with King *Christian* to restore him to the Kingdom of *Sweden,* under condition that he should set the Archbishop at liberty. According to this agreement, a Reconciliation being made betwixt K. *Christian* and the Archbishop; the latter was received very splendidly by the Bishop, and was no sooner arrived in *Sweden,* but having raised some Forces against King *Charles,* defeated him in a bloody Battel fought upon the Ice near *Stockholm,* and forced him to abjure his Right and Pretension to the Kingdom. After the King's Resignation, the Archbishop made himself Master of all the Strong-holds of the Kingdom, without any opposition, except that one *Nils Sture,* a particular Friend of K. *Charles's,* traversed sometimes his Designs. This *Nils Sture* and one *Erick Axelson,* Governour of *Wibourg* in *Finland,* having at last made a party against him, play'd their Game so well that *Erick Axelson,* who had married King *Charles's* Daughter, was declared Regent of the Kingdom. \A. 1486\ But the A. Bish. [archbishop] was obliged to surrender *Stockholm* and some other Strong holds into the Regent's hands. Nevertheless the hatred betwixt the two exasperated Factions, headed by *Nils Sture* and *Erick Nilson* (of which <485> party was also the Archbishop) continued with great animosity. *Erick Nilson* and his Party, under pretence of protecting the Archbishop against the Power of King *Charles* and his adherents, endeavoured the Restauration of King *Christian,* but *Nils Sture* and his Party openly declared, that they would either have King *Charles* restored, or at least maintain the Regent in his Station. These two Parties did not only commit great Insolencies and Murthers,

<aside>Erick Axelson.</aside>

making great havock all over the Country, but at last also came to an open War, wherein the Archbishop's Party being worsted, he died for grief; and the Common People in hopes to put an end to the miseries of the Kingdom once more restored *Charles* to the Crown.

But⁺ *Erick Nilson, Erick Carlson, Trolle* and some others having again raised some Forces against him, and surprised his Army during the time of the Truce, \A. 1463\ again forced him to seek for shelter in [among] the *Dalers*,[13] whither being pursued by *Erick Carlson* he with an unequal number gave him a signal overthrow, forcing him to retire into *Denmark*. King *Charles* being soon after returned to *Stockholm*, (which City and the whole Kingdom he recommended before his death to *Steen Sture* his Sister's Son) he there died in the same year, \A. 1470\ leaving the Kingdom in such a confusion, that for a twelve month after, there was a meer Anarchy in *Sweden*, some having declared for King *Christian*, some for *Steen Sture* to be made Regent of the Kingdom. At last the Government was committed to *Steen Sture*, who having vanquished King *Christian* in a memorable Battel fought near *Stockholm*, \A. 1471\ and forced him to retire with his broken Forces by Sea into *Denmark*, got into the possession of the whole Kingdom of *Sweden*. And tho' King *Christian* kept the Regent of *Sweden* in a continual alarm as long as he lived, and several meetings were held concerning his Restauration, yet there was no open War betwixt the two Kingdoms, and *Steen Sture* reigned for a considerable time with a general applause; so that King *Christian* during his Regency, never durst return into *Sweden*, but died in *Denmark* in the year 1481.

After⁺ the Death of King *Christian*, the *Danes* and *Norwegians* having made *John* the Son of *Christian* their <486> King, the *Swedes* also agreed with King *John* upon certain Articles, which the King having confirmed to them under his Seal, he was declared King of *Sweden*. But the Regent *Steen Sture*, notwithstanding this solemn Transaction remained in the possession of the Kingdom for fourteen Years after, under pretence that the *Danes* had not fulfilled their Promise accord-

---

13. *Dalekarls*, from Dalarna or Dalecarlia, an area in central Sweden. See note 10, p. 366, above.

ing to the Articles of the Treaty, during which time the Kingdom was miserably afflicted by intestine Divisions, and [by] the Wars which were carried on against *Denmark* and *Russia*. The Senators therefore of *Sweden* having in vain endeavoured to perswade *Steen Sture* to lay down his Office, at last deposed him from the Regency, and craved Assistance

John II.   from King *John*, who having defeated *Steen Sture* and his Party near *Stockholm*, was by the Senate and the Regent himself received as King of *Sweden* and his Son *Christian* declared his Successor after his death in that Kingdom. \A. 1497\ This King reigned very peaceably for a while, but after some Years by the perswasions of some Courtiers, fell into the same Errour which had been the undoing of his Predecessors: For under pretence that the Revenues of the Crown were extreamly diminished, he obliged *Steen Sture* and several others to surrender the Fiefs belonging to the Crown, which they were in possession of, some of which he bestowed upon the *Danes* and *Germans*. Besides this, his Governours had committed great Insolencies in their Provinces, which so exasperated the People, that as soon as the News of his defeat in *Ditmarsen* was spread over *Sweden*, the *Swedes* being headed by *Steen Sture*, assembled at *Wadstana*, where having renounced their Allegiance, they bid open defiance to him, alledging that he had not fulfilled the Articles of the Treaty made at *Calmar*.

The[+] King being surprised at this unexpected News sailed forthwith for *Denmark*, leaving the Queen with a good Garrison at *Stockholm*, which City was thereupon besieged by *Sture;* who being soon after again constituted Regent of the Kingdom, forced the Castle of *Stockholm* to a surrender, and got almost all the rest of the Strongholds in *Sweden* into his possession; notwithstanding which, the *Danes* burnt *Elfsburgh* and *Oresteen*, <487> and committed great Cruelties in *West-Gothland*, under the Conduct of *Christian*[,] King *John's* Son, who had done the like not long before in *Norway*, where he had rooted out almost all the Noble Families. Yet because the Queen was as yet in *Sweden*, the fury of the *Danes* was for a while appeased by the intercession of the *Lubeckers* and the Cardinal *Raimow*, who having procured Liberty for her to return into *Denmark*, she was conducted by the Regent to the Frontiers of *Smaland*. But in his return to *Joncoping*, he died suddenly, and his death having been kept secret for a while, there was a strong suspistion that he had been poysoned by *Mereta* the Widow of *Cnut Alfson,* thereby to open the way to her Bridegroom *Suante Sture,* to the Regency of the Kingdom. \A. 1503\

As soon as the news of the Regent's death was spread all over the Kingdom, the Estates convened at *Stockholm,* where it was disputed for some time, whether King *John* should be recalled, or *Suante Nilson Sture* should be made Regent, till the latter having prevailed, the said *Sture* was made Regent of the Kingdom. \A. 1504\ Then the War was renewed with King *John,* which was carried on with various Success, both Parties committing great devastations, without any other remarkable advantage. The *Danes* having at first stirred up the Emperour, the Pope and the *Russians* against the *Swedes,* did considerable mischief, but the Regent having made a Peace with the *Russians,* and set the *Lubeckers* against *Denmark,* retook *Calmar* and *Bornholm,* and would in all likelihood have made greater Progresses, if he had not soon after died at *Westekaos,* in the eighth year of his Regency. \A. 1511\

After the death of this Regent, there were again great Divisions in the Senate about the Election of a new Regent; the younger sort were for choosing *Steen Sture* the deceased Regent's Son: But the Archbishop and Bishops, and the rest of the antient Senators, would have elected *Gustavus Trolle*[,] an antient Wise and experienced Man. \A. 1512\ After several prorogations and very hot debates, at last *Steen Sture,* who was favoured by the common People, and had most of the Strongholds of the Kingdom in his hands, was declared Regent, and King *John* died in the year next following at *Ahlburgh* in *Jutland.* \A. 1513\ After his death, the *Danes* <488> and *Norwegians* had declared *Christian* his Son their King[,] but the *Swedes* who had not forgot his cruelties formerly committed in *West-Gothland* desired time to consider of a thing of such importance. King *Christian* finding himself after four years tergiversation deceived in his hopes, and that the Regent would not part with his Power by fair means, did not only stir the Pope *Leo* X, up against him, but also brought *Gustavus Trolle* the new Archbishop by great Presents over to his side, and perswaded the *Russians* to make an in-road into *Finland. Steen Sture* being soon convinced of the Archbishop's sinister

Steen Sture the younger.

Intentions, had tendered the Oath to him, which he refusing to take, was besieged by the Regent in his Castle of *Stecka*. Then it was that the Archbishop called King *Christian* to his Assistance, who having taken some Ships loaden with Amunition belonging to the Regent, and in vain endeavoured to relieve the besieged Castle, the War was begun on both sides. For the Archbishop having been forced to surrender the Castle and his Office, Pope *Leo* thereupon excommunicated the Regent, laying a Fine of 100.000 Ducats upon the *Swedes*, and enjoyning the execution thereof to King *Christian*. Pursuant to this Decree, the King of *Denmark* fell with a great Army into *Sweden*, and was met by the Regent and his Forces in *West-Gothland*, but the Regent having received a Wound there, of which he died soon after at *Strengness*, his Army first retreated, and being deprived of a Leader, afterwards dispersed. King *Christian* then having divided his Army, sent one part into *West* and *East-Gothland*, which were soon subdued, and marched with the rest to *Strengness*. \A. 1520\

The⁺ Archbishop taking hold of this opportunity, reassumed his Archi-Episcopal Dignity, and being assisted by two other Bishops and seven of the Senators of the Kingdom did declare *Christian* King of *Sweden* in the name of the Estates at *Upsal*. The King having been Crowned by the Archbishop *Trolle*, and received the City of *Stockholm* by a surrender into his hands, treated the *Swedes* at first with abundance of humanity, but soon after, found out a Weapon wherewith to destroy his Adversaries, and this was the business concerning the degradation of the Archbishop and the ruining of his Castle <489> of *Stecka*. For tho' the King by an Amnestie had pardoned all past Offences, yet no satisfaction having been given to the Pope, the Archbishop in his Name, demanded a million pounds of Silver in reparation of the damages done to the Church at *Upsal*, and his Castle of *Stecka*. And to make up the matter, it was pretended that Gunpowder had been conveyed into the King's Palace to blow him up. *Steen Sture*'s Widow, his Mother in Law, fifteen others besides the Senate and Commonalty of *Stockholm*, were accused as Actors and Abettors, who were all condemned as Hereticks, ninety four of them, all People of Note, being beheaded at *Stockholm* and their Servants hanged up with Boots and Spurs. The deceased Regent's body having been digged up, was exposed among the rest of the executed Persons, and the Quarters set up and down the Country. His Widow and Mother in Law were forced to purchase their Lives with the loss of their whole Estate, and were nevertheless with a great many other Women of Quality committed to Prison. In *Finland, Hemoning Gudde,* notwithstanding his former Services done to him, was with ten more executed by the King's Command, the Abbot of the Convent at *Nydala* was with eleven Monks drowned by his Orders, and two Gentlemen's Sons, one of nine, the other of seven years, beheaded at *Joncoping,* and after he had in this manner murthered 600 of his *Swedish* Subjects he returned into *Denmark.*

§9a.[14] But in the mean while that King *Christian* was busied in bringing the *Swedes* under the *Danish* yoke, by all manner of inhumane Barbarities, *Gustavus Erichson* (whose Father had been beheaded by the Tyrant, and his Mother thrown in Prison) had sheltered himself among the *Dale Karls,* who being made sensible of the danger which threatened them and the whole Kingdom, had made *Gustave* their Head, whose example being followed by the Estates of *Sweden,* they soon after declared him Regent of that Kingdom, except the Archbishop and his Party, that remained firm to the *Danish* Interest. King *Christian* being violently exasperated at *Gustave,* revenged himself upon his Mother and two Sisters, whom he sent from *Stockholm* to *Copenhagen,* where <490> they perished in Prison; he issued also out an Order, that no quarter should be given to any *Swedish* Nobleman, and committed great Barbarities wherever he came. The *Swedes* on the other hand, under the Conduct of their Regent *Gustave,* repaid the *Danes* with the same Coin wherever they met them, and with the Assistance of the *Lubeckers* besieged *Stockholm,* which was as yet in King *Christian's* Possession, when they received the joyful news out of *Denmark,* that the *Jutlanders* had renounced their Allegiance to King *Christian.* \A. 1523\ This so encouraged *Gustave* and his Party, that they did not only drive

Gustavus I.

---

14. Crull repeats section numeration §9. To maintain the subsequent numeration, the second occurrence has been redesignated as "§9a."

King *Christian's* Forces out of most Provinces of the Kingdom, retook *Oeland* and *Borkholm,* but also recovered the Castle and City of *Calmar,* and made *Gustave* King of *Sweden,* who thereupon immediately summoned *Stockholm* to a surrender, and the Garrison being without hopes of relief, surrendred the City and Castle to the *Lubeckers,* who restored the same to King *Gustave.*

In the mean while King *Christian* was retired with his Queen into the *Netherlands,* and the *Jutlanders* having made *Frederick* I, King *Christian's* Uncle, their King, would fain have perswaded the *Swedes* to follow their example, but these being not ambitious of continuing the Union with *Denmark,* had refused their proffer, and chosen *Gustave* their King. But King *Gustave* finding the Treasury mightily exhausted by these long intestine Wars, he not only taxed the Clergy to pay considerable Sums towards the payment of his Souldiers, but also made bold with the superfluous Ornaments of the Churches, against which, *Brask* the Bishop of *Lincoping* having protested and made complaint thereof to *Johannes Magnus* the Pope's Legate, *Peter* Bishop of *Westeraas* endeavoured to raise an Insurrection among the *Dalekerls.*

But[+] whilest these Bishops were employed in maintaining their Privileges, the Protestant Religion had begun to spread all over the Kingdom. The same was by some Merchants and *German* Souldiers first introduced into *Sweden,* and some *Swedish* Students, that had studied at *Wittenbergh,* had brought along with them into their Native Country, both the Doctrine and [the] Writings of *Luther.* Among these one *Olaus Petri* was <491> the chiefest,[15] who having been an Auditor of *Luther,* at his return into *Sweden* was made a Canon and Protonotary to the Bishop of *Strengness;* this Man after the death of the Bishop, having

15. Olaus Petri or Olof Persson (1493–1552) studied at Wittenberg from 1516 to 1518 and was seminal to Swedish Lutheranism. He was chancellor for a brief time in 1531 and later became pastor of St. Nicholas Cathedral in Stockholm. Many important Swedish Reformation documents came from him, mostly in the vernacular; they include a translation of the New Testament, a hymn book, a church manual, a prayerbook, and many sermons. Petri also wrote a history of Sweden, the *Historia de gentibus septentrionalibus* (*History of the Nordic Peoples*), published at Rome in 1555.

brought *Lars Anderson* the Archdeacon over to his Opinion, began not only to defend *Luther's* Doctrine publickly in the Schools, but also to publish the same from the Pulpit. The Bishop being absent, Dr. *Nils* Dean of that Chapter, with all his might opposed this new Doctrine, which being come to the King's Ears, he advised with *Lars Anderson,* who having instructed him in the chief Points of it, and in what manner a great many *German* Princes had taken away the superfluous riches of the Clergy, began to hearken to his Opinion, resolving nevertheless to go on cautiously in this business, and to see how some Princes in *Germany* should proceed in this Affair, as also how the Bishops in *Sweden* would relish this Doctrine. In the mean while Pope *Hadrian* IV. had sent his Legate into *Sweden* to endeavour the extirpation of this Heresie, and the Clergy of *Sweden* grew every day more refractory, refusing to pay the Taxes imposed upon them, as being contrary to their Privileges. On the other hand, *Olaus Petri* being encouraged by the King, was not silent, but defended his Cause both by Dispute and Writing, with such Success, that the King not only constituted him Minister in the great Church of *Stockholm,* and put into other vacant Church-Benefices, such Ministers as had studied at *Wittenbergh,* but also constituted over the Dominicans and Black Fryars,[16] such Priors as he knew to be faithful to him, and such of them as were Foreigners he banished [from] the Kingdom, and told unfeignedly to Bishop *Brask,* that he could not deny Protection to the *Lutherans,* as long as they were not convinced of any Crime or Errour.

Reformation begun in Sweden.

But[+] all this while one *Soren Norby,* who still adhered to King *Christian,* had *Gothland* in his Possession, and did considerable damage to the *Swedes* in their Trade; against him King *Gustavus* having sent *Bernhard van Melan* with some Forces to reduce the said *Island,* and *Norby* finding himself too weak put himself and the Island under the Protection of *Denmark,* which occasioned some differences between these two Northern Kings, <492> who had been very good Friends ever before.

16. The expression is redundant, since "black friars" refers to Dominicans, who were so designated because of the black cloaks worn over their white habits.

About this time *Olaus Petri* was publickly married in the great
Church at *Stockholm*,[17] and the King had not only demanded the
Tenths of the Clergy towards the maintenance of his Forces,[18] but also
Quartered some of his Horse in the Monasteries, which so incensed
Bishop *Brask,* that he forbid [forbade] in his whole Diocese so much as
to name the Doctrine of *Luther.* But the King having understood that

First Transla- *Olaus Petri* was busie in Translating the New Testament into the *Swed-*
tion of *ish* Tongue, commanded the Archbishop, to take care that the *Roman*
the New
Testament into Catholicks also should make a Translation, which though it relished
Swedish. very ill with the Bishops,[19] yet were they fain to comply with the King's
command, who, to mortifie them the more, also ordered a Disputation
to be held at *Upsal* betwixt Dr. *Pieter Galle* and *Olaus Petri,* concerning
the chiefest Points in question betwixt the *Roman* Catholicks and *Lu-*
therans, where *Olaus Petri* had much the better, and his Translation was
approved of before the others, which had been patched up by so many
Translators. In the mean time the *Danish* Clergy had given a considerable Subsidy to their King [Frederick I] to be employed against King
Christian, wherefore King *Gustave,* taking hold of this opportunity,
[likewise] demanded a considerable supply from the *Swedish* Clergy,
but these objecting that it was against their Privileges and Rights, the
King ordered the same to be examined in another Dispute betwixt
Olaus Petri, and Dr. *Pieter Galle,* and because they were not able to
prove their Title out of the Holy Scripture, the King concluded them
to be dependent on his pleasure, and at the Dyet held at *Westeraos* [Vas-
teras] not only demanded a supply from the Clergy, but also proposed
that the superfluous Bells should be taken out of the Churches, and be
employed towards the payment of the Debt due to the *Lubeckers.*
And because the Archbishop grew more troublesome every day, the

17. In this he followed Luther's example.

18. *Tenths* were that portion of the clergy's income which they paid every year to
the pope. They were distinguished from the annates, which were a portion of their
first year's income from benefices similarly owed. See note 57, p. 445, and note 59,
p. 447, above.

19. During the Reformation Protestants turned to the vernacular, for both doctrinal and pastoral reasons, while Catholics generally adhered to Latin and its clerical interpreters.

King first took him into Custody, and afterwards sent him [as] Ambassadour into *Poland,* from whence he never returned into *Sweden.* He
also commanded another Disputation to be held concerning the chief
Points in question betwixt the *Lutherans* and *Roman* Catholicks, which
however met with great opposition from Bishop *Brask,* and the <493>
rest of the *Roman* Catholick Clergy, who set up a Country Fellow,
against *Gustave.* \A. 1527\ This Fellow pretended to be the Son of *Steen
Sture* (notwithstanding he was dead a twelve months before) and having
got a party among the *Dalekerls,* and being upheld by Bishop *Brask* and
the Bishop of *Druntheim* in *Norway,* and encouraged in his undertaking
by King *Frederick* of *Denmark,* laid open claim to the Crown, threatning all the *Lutherans* and especially the City of *Stockholm* with Fire and
Sword, which was the most forward in settling the Protestant Religion.

About⁺ the same time the Emperour [Charles V] had besieged Pope
Clement VII. in the Castle of St. *Angelo,* wherefore King *Gustave* taking
hold of this Juncture, appointed a Dyet to be held at *Westeraos,* where in
his Declaration he professed; *that the* Roman *Catholick Clergy had made
it their business to charge him with making Innovation in Religion for no
other reason, but that he would not let them domineer over the Laymen,
and [that he] had forced them to submit to the Civil Power, and to give part
of their superfluous Riches, some of which they had got by fraud, towards
easing the Common People of those burthensome Taxes (which he hitherto
had been forced to impose upon them.) And that for the same Reason the
Emperour himself had been forced lately to teach the Pope his duty.* The
same thing was proposed by the King to the whole Dyet, where he told
them; that the superfluous Revenues of the Clergy ought to be annexed
to the Crown, and especially such Lands as since the year 1454 had been
given to the Clergy, should be restored to the right Heirs, promising
withal that the Common People should be for the future eased of their
Taxes; in case they would give their consent to the reduction of the
Revenues of the Clergy.

And the better to get the consent of the Temporal Lords and Senators he made a great Banquet, where he gave the next place to himself to
these Senators, whereas the same had belonged formerly to the Bishops,
who now were forced to be contented with the next place after them,

the third place was given to the rest of the Nobility, the fourth to the inferiour Clergy, the fifth to the Citizens, the sixth to the Boors; which so exasperated the <494> Clergy that they assembled in the Church of St. *Egidius,* and secretly took a resolution among themselves not to obey the King in this Point, nor to surrender any of their Revenues, or to recede from their antient Religion. And Bishop *Brask* freely told the King, *that the Clergy of the Kingdom had such a strict dependency on the Pope, that without his consent they could not do any thing whatsoever.* Which as it met with great approbation from all the rest of the Clergy, and from some of the Temporal Estates, so the King was so incensed thereat, that he immediately rose from his Seat, and told the Estates that he was ready to Abdicate the Kingdom, if they would repay him his Charges and Monies which he had laid out for that use, and to show them that he was in earnest, retired for several days with some of his chief Officers into the Castle. The Estates being much surprised at the King's resolution, especially when they saw the Citizens of *Stockholm* to be stedfast to the King, and that Dr. *Peter Galle* was worsted by *Olaus Petri* in a late Disputation, thought it their best way to beg the King's pardon and to intreat him not to resign the Crown. Upon their reiterated request the King having been at last prevailed upon to come out of the Castle, demanded from several Bishops to surrender into his hands their Castles, and to subscribe a Decree made at this Dyet, concerning the regulating of the Clergy, which they were fain to comply withal. As soon as the Dyet was ended he took not only from the Monasteries such Lands as had been given to them since the year 1454. but also several other Church Lands and precious moveables, all which he annexed to the Crown.

Church Lands reduced in Sweden.

In the mean while the Bishops and their party were not idle, but were contriving all manner of mischief against the King, though with small success. For the *Dalekerls,* who had made an Insurrection, were frightened by the King to comply with his commands, and to send away their Leader, the supposititious *Sture;* and *Sigismund* King of *Poland,* unto whom the dissatisfied party had proffered the Crown, did not think fit to accept of it; so that Bishop *Brask,* despairing at last of the *Roman* Catholick Cause, under pretence of a Journey retired to *Dantzick.* <495>

The⁺ King having surmounted all these difficulties, thought convenient not to defer any longer his Coronation, which having been solemnized at *Upsal* with the usual Solemnity: \A. 1528\ he summoned the Rebellious *Dalekerls* to appear before him at *Thuana,* threatning them with Fire and Sword if they did not appear at the appointed time; The Rebels being throughly frightened by the King's severity appeared without Arms at the appointed place where he caused several of the Ringleaders to be Executed, and dismissed the rest, after having promised to be obedient for the future. In *Helsingland* he appeased the tumultuous multitude with threats, and fined their Leaders, and having called together a Synod of the Clergy at *Orebro,* where the King's Chancellour was President, the chiefest Points of the Popish Doctrine were there abolished, and in their stead the Protestant Religion introduced, where it was also ordered, that a Protestant Professor of Divinity should be Constituted in each Cathedral. This wrought in a manner Miracles among the Inferiour Clergy and Monks, who left their Monasteries, were married, and became Ministers in the Protestant Churches.

The Protestant Religion Established in Sweden.

But the Bishops and their party entred into an Association with some of the dissatisfied Lords in *West Gothland,* who accused the King of Heresie and other Crimes, renouncing their Allegiance to him. These were Headed by *Thuro Johanson* the Rix Marshal,[20] who raised an Insurrection among the *Dalekerls,* and endeavoured also to stir up the West and East *Gothes,* whom he persuaded to make *Magnus Brynteson,* a Man in great Authority among them, their King. But the King having again appeased this tumult by granting his Pardon to them, *Magnus* the Bishop of *Skara* and *Thuro Johanson* fled into *Denmark,* but *Magnus Bayteson, Nils Olofson* and *Thuro Erickson* having been Convicted of High Treason at the Dyet held at *Strengness,* the two first were Executed, and the third paid a considerable Fine.

The King then, to settle the minds of his Subjects having renewed his Pardon, caused the superfluous Bells to be taken out of the Steeples, the same being granted to him by the Estates towards the payment of a Debt due to the *Lubeckers.* Which proved a new Subject for an Insurrection; for the *Dale-*<496>*kerls* not only seised upon some of these

20. *Riksmarskalk, Reichsmarschall,* or chancellor of the realm.

Bells, but also pretended to hold an Assembly at *Arboga,* to consult about the Deposing of King *Gustave,* which obliged the King to call together the Estates at *Upsal,* whither he came in person with a good Army, and meeting with great opposition from the mutinous People, ordered his Soldiers to fire among them, which so terrified them that upon their Knees they begged his Pardon, promising to be more Obedient for the future.

Things being thus pretty well settled the King married *Catharine* the Daughter of *Magnus* Duke of *Saxe*[*n*] *Lauenburgh,* and having received intelligence that King *Christian* was landed in *Norway* with a considerable Force, he sent some Troops under the Command of *Lars Sigeson* the Rix Marshal to the Frontiers of *Norway,* who having been joined by some *Danes,* forced King *Christian* to raise the Siege of *Babus,* \A. 1533\ who at last surrendring himself to the *Danes,* was by *Frederick* King of *Denmark,* committed to Prison, where he died after twenty seven years imprisonment.

But no sooner was this storm over, but the *Lubeckers* raised another against *Sweden.* For, they having demanded from the King, to grant them the whole Trade on his Northern Sea Coasts, which he refused to consent to, peremptorily demanded their Debt, and having joyned with a great many Refugies of King *Christian's* party, and made *John* Earl of *Hoya,* who had married King *Gustave's* Sister, their Head, did propose to themselves no less than the Conquest of the Northern Kingdoms, having inticed some Citizens of *Stockholm* under pretext of making that City a free Hanse Town, to lay violent hands on the King: And after the death of *Frederick* King of *Denmark,* when that Kingdom was divided into several Factions[,] persuaded the Senate of *Copenhagen* and *Malmoe* to enter into the Confederacy of the Hanse Towns. Being thus strengthened by a considerable party within that Kingdom they had great success against the *Danes,* till these having declared *Christian* III. their King, and being assisted with Money, Ships, and Forces by King *Gustave*[,] beat the *Lubeckers* near *Helsinburgh,* and afterwards in a Sea-Fight defeated their whole Fleet, and carried a great many of their Ships into *Denmark.*

Soon <497> after King *Gustave* to strengthen himself the better at

Home, married *Margaret* the Daughter of *Abraham Erickson*, Governor of *West Gothland*, which Alliance stood afterwards his Son Duke *John* in great stead against King *Erick*. King *Gustave* having also conceived a jealousie against the Emperour *Charles* V. whom he suspected to be for making *Palls Grave* [*Pfalzgraf*, Count Palatine] *Frederick*, Son in Law of the imprisoned King *Christian*,[21] King over the Northern Kingdoms, took a resolution to strengthen himself with the Alliance of *France*. To put this design in execution he sent his Secretary into *France*, who having first made a Treaty of Commerce betwixt these two Crowns, did also afterwards conclude a defensive Alliance betwixt them.

    Gustave+ having thus settled his Affairs called a Dyet to be held at *Westeraas*, where the Estates of the Kingdom declared the Succession Hereditary for the future, Constituting *Erick Gustaveson*, who was then but eleven years old, his Father's Successor. \A. 1544\ At the same Dyet the Popish Religion was quite abolished, and the *Lutheran* Religion Established in *Sweden*, the King and the Estates having obliged themselves by a Solemn Oath to maintain the same with all their power. In the year 1551. King *Gustave*, after the death of his Queen *Margaret*, married *Catharine* the Daughter of *Gustave Olufson*, and ruled the Kingdom of *Sweden* with great Tranquility, except that the *Russians* had faln into *Livonia* and *Finland*, with whom having made a Peace, and being now grown very old[,] he by his Testament \A. 1556\ gave to *John* his second Son the Dukedom of *Finland*, to the third Son *Magnus* the Dukedom of *East Gothland*, and to *Charles*, the youngest of all, the Dukedom of *Sudermanland*, *Nericke* and *Wermeland*, which Countries they were to hold in Fief from the Crown.

[margin note:] The Kingdom of Sweden made Hereditary, and the Popish Religion abolished.

    But his eldest Son *Erick*, who was to succeed him in the Kingdom, having been persuaded by his Tutor, *Dionysius Beurraeus* a *Frenchman* to make his Addresses to *Elizabeth* Queen of *England*, thereby to strengthen his Interest against his Brothers, sent the said *Dionysius* into *England*, who having writ to his Master that nothing was wanting to make up the Match but his presence, the Prince would have gone forthwith into *En-*

---

21. Frederick II the Wise (1482–1556), Elector Palatine from 1544 to 1556, introduced the Reformation into the Palatinate.

gland, if <498> his Father had not opposed it, who sent in his stead his second Son *John,* and Steen Sture. These being very civilly entertained by Queen *Elizabeth,* at their return Home told the Prince that they believed nothing to be wanting to compleat the Marriage but his presence, which was very joyfully received by the Prince. But the old and wise King, who soon perceived, that they had mistaken Complements for Realities, thought it advisable to Communicate the business with the Estates Assembled at *Stockholm,* who after having confirmed the former Hereditary Union and the King's Testament, at last gave their consent to this Marriage, granting a considerable Supply towards the defraying of the charges of this Marriage. But whilst the Prince was preparing for his Voyage, part of his Baggage having been sent before, he being near ready to follow in person, King *Gustave* dyed at *Stockholm,* \A. 1559\ and King *Erick,* not thinking it advisable to trust his Brother with the Kingdom, was forced to put by his Journey into *England.*

Erick XIV. §10. King *Erick* was twenty seven years of age when he succeeded his Father in the Kingdom. His first business was to prescribe certain new Articles to his Brothers, thereby to maintain the Royal Authority against them, which though sorely against their will, they were forced to subscribe at the Dyet held at *Arboga.* \A. 1561\ At his Coronation he first introduced the Titles of Earls and Barons into *Sweden,* alledging that in an Hereditary Kingdom there ought to be also Hereditary Dignities among the Nobility. At his very first Accession to the Crown he was engaged in the Troubles, which then sorely afflicted the *Liflanders* [Livonians]. For some of them having put themselves under the Protection of *Denmark,* some under the Crown of *Poland,* those of *Reval* and the Nobility of *Estbenland,* that were nearest to *Sweden,* sought for Protection to King *Erick.* Whereupon the King having sent an Army under the Command of *Claes Horn* (who was joyfully received at *Reval*) took them into his Protection, and confirmed to the City and Nobility their former Privileges. As soon as the *Poles* heard of the arrival of the *Swedish* <499> Army at *Reval,* they sent an Ambassadour to demand *Reval* from the *Swedes,* who having received no other answer, but that the *Swedes* had at least as good a Title to *Reval,* as the *Poles,* returned

The Titles of Earls and Barons introduced.

Home again, and the *Swedish* Garrison that was besieged by the *Polish* Forces in *Reval*, forced them to quit that Enterprise.

Soon after, the King being fully resolved to pursue his intentions concerning the Marriage with Queen *Elizabeth* of *England*, Embarked at *Elshorgth* to go thither in person, but was by a violent Tempest forced to return. As he was very inconstant in his Temper, and very Superstitious, being much addicted to Astrology, so after this misfortu[n]e he laid aside the thoughts of this Marriage for a while, making his Addresses by his Ambassadours, and with great Presents, to *Mary* Queen [of] *Scotland*, and the Princess of *Lorain*[22] both at one time, and not long after to *Katharine* the Daughter of the *Landgrave* of *Hessen*, but succeeded in neither. In the mean while his Brother *John* had married *Katharine* Daughter of *Sigismund* King of *Poland*, which having been done without King *Erick's* good liking, who was both mistrustful of the *Poles* and his Brother, put him into such a rage, that he besieged his Brother in the Castle of *Aboa*, which having been taken by Strategem, he caused him to be sentenced to death, which Sentence he however changed into a perpetual Imprisonment for that time, but seemed to repent of it afterwards, when the *Russians* demanded the said *Katharine*, his Brother's Wife, in Marriage for their Great Duke. The *Poles* to revenge this Affront, stirred up the *Danes* and *Lubeckers* against the *Swedes*, and the *Danes* having affronted the *Swedish* Ambassadours at *Copenhagen*, preparations were made on all sides, which soon broke out into a War, wherein the *Swedes* routed the *Danes* and *Lubeckers* in several Sea Engagements, but also lost their Admiral (which Ship carried two hundred Brass Guns)[,] and by Land there was great havock made on both sides, with almost equal Fortune, except that the *Swedes* had pretty good success in *Livonia*.

But whilst King *Erick* was engaged in War with all his Neighbours round about him, the inward discontents began to increase more and more among his Subjects by the ill management which <500> he had shown both in his Affairs and Amours, being surrounded with a Sera-

22. Renata of Lorraine (1544–1602), maternal granddaughter of Christian II of Denmark.

glio of Mistrisses, (among whom one *Katharine,* an ordinary Country Wench had the greatest sway over him, whom he also married afterwards, whereby he lost his Authority among the Nobility). Besides this, he was guided in most concerns of moment by one *Joran Paerson* his Favourite, and his former Tutor *Dionysius Beurraeus,* who fomented a continual jealousie betwixt him and the Family of the *Stures,* which at last broke out into a fatal revenge. For there having been Witnesses suborned against *Suarte Sture* and his Son *Erick,* they were with several others of that Family not only committed to Prison, and miserably murthered there by the King's command, but he also with his own hands stab'd *Nils Sture,* and repenting soon after of so barbarous a Fact caused his former Tutor *Dionysius,* who advised it, to be slain by his Guards.

A[+] great part of the Kingdom, having been put into confusion by these enormous cruelties, of which the King feared the consequences, he thought it his best way, to prevent further inconveniencies, to set his Brother *John* at Liberty under certain conditions, and to lay the blame of these barbarities upon *Joran Paerson* his Favourite, who having been committed to Prison the Intestine Commotions seem'd to be appeased for the present. But the King having not long after been very succesful in several Engagements against the *Danes,* whom he beat quite out of *Denmark*[,] he soon after released his Favourite, and not only declared him free from any imputation, but also justified the death of those Lords formerly murthered at *Upsal.* By his advise also he would have taken from his Brothers those Provinces which were allotted them by their Father's Testament, in exchange of which he proffered them some Possessions in *Livonia.* But the Brothers having refused this proffer, he again resolved to make away [with] his Brother *John* at the [Erick's] Nuptials which were to be celebrated at *Stockholm* betwixt his Mistress *Catharine* and himself, and to give his Widow[23] in Marriage to the Grand Duke of *Russia.*

But the Brothers having been advertised [advised] of the King's sinister intentions, did not appear at the Wedding, and having made an

23. John's widow, also named Katharine.

Association with several of the Nobi-<501>lity, that were Kindred of
the Lords murthered at *Upsal,* they resolved to dethrone King *Erick.*
The better to execute their intentions, they had by the intercession
of the King of *Poland* procured a Truce with *Denmark,* and having
gathered what Forces and Mony they could among their Friends, and
brought over some *German* Forces, that were in King *Erick's* service[,]
to their side, as also engaged *Charles,* King *Erick's* Brother, to join in
the Confederacy, they seised upon the Castles of *Stockeburgh, Lackoe*
and *Wadstena,* in the last of which they found a great Treasure. Then
they published their Reasons for taking up Arms against the King and
his evil Counsellours, and marched directly with their Forces towards
Stockholm, near which place having fixed their Tents, they attacked the
City on the side of the *Brunckehill;* King *Erick* on the other side defended himself valiantly for a while, and by frequent Sallies did great
mischief, and being mistrustful of the Citizens of *Stockholm,* he sent a
Messenger into *Denmark,* to crave assistance from King *Frederick;* but
this Messenger having been taken and killed by the way[,] the Senate
of that City, who despaired to hold out much longer against the Dukes
Forces, and also were favourers of their party, would have persuaded
the King to a surrendry; which proposition having been rejected by
the King, they whilst the King was at Church opened the Gates to
his Enemies, so that he narrowly escaped into the Castle. The Dukes
[Charles's] Forces laid then close Siege to the Castle, so that King *Erick,*
having first received Hostages, was forced to come out, and after having
resigned the Crown to surrender himself a Prisoner to his Brother Duke
Charles. The Estates then assembled at *Stockholm* having also jointly
renounced their Obedience to him, he was made a close Prisoner, and
committed to the care of some of the Friends of the murthered Lords,
who used him most barbarously.

§11. After the Deposition of King *Erick, John* was by the Estates then   John III.
assembled at *Stockholm* proclaimed King of *Sweden* \A. 1568\, who having caused some of those that had been instrumental in the Murther of
the Lords at *Upsal,* to be Executed, sent his Ambassadour to *Roeshild*
<502> to treat with the King of *Denmark* either concerning a Peace or

at least the prolongation of the Truce; But these Ambassadours having exceeded their Commission, and agreed to such articles as were very prejudicial to *Sweden*, the whole Transaction was declared void at the next Dyet, and King *John* sent other Ambassadours to desire more moderate propositions of Peace from the King of *Denmark*. And to give some sort of satisfaction to his Brother *Charles*, unto whom he had formerly promised a share in the Government, he put him in the Possession of *Sudermannia*, *Nericke* and *Wermeland*, which Provinces were granted him before pursuant to his Father's Testament.

Then he was Crowned at *Upsal*, and having sent back the *Russian* Ambassadours, he sent also some of his own into *Moscovy* to prolong the Truce betwixt them, but no sooner were they arrived there, but the *Moscovites* took them into custody, and perceiving that the *Liflanders* would in no ways submit themselves under their Yoak, they found out this expedient[:] to put *Magnus* Duke of *Holstein* into the Possession of that Country, with the Title of an Hereditary King, paying only some small acknowlegement to the Grand Duke of *Moscovy*.[24] This Proposition having been approved of by the King of *Denmark*, Duke of *Holstein*, and all the *Liflanders* in general[,] who were very willing to live under the jurisdiction of a *German* Prince, the *Moscovites* to put their design in execution advanced with a great Army, which obliged King *John* to make Peace with the *Danes*, at *Stetin*, upon very disadvantageous terms. But whilst the *Moscovites* had employed all their Forces in *Livonia* and *Finland*, the *Tartars* being set on by the *Poles*, fell into *Moscovy*, and having taken and burnt the City of *Moscovy*, cut above thirty thousand of the Inhabitants to pieces. \A. 1571\ This misfortune proved a main obstacle to their [Moscovites] design upon *Livonia*, yet having made a Truce with the *Tartars* and *Poles* for some years they again entred *Livonia* with 80.000 Men, and committed most inhuman barbarities, which the *Swedes*, who were much inferiour in number, could not prevent at that time. But a *Swedish* party of 600 Horse and 100 Foot, that were faln in with the *Moscovites*, having routed 16.000

War with the
Moscovites.

24. Livonia was still under Swedish control, and Magnus's new realm had still to be conquered with Russian assistance.

Mos-<503>*covites,* killing 7000 of them upon the spot, the *Czar* of *Moscovy* was so dismayed that he of his own accord offered a Treaty of Peace to be set on Foot at *Newgarten,* which place being disliked by King *John,* the War began a fresh, which was carried on but with very indifferent success on the *Swedish* side, they having been repulsed before *Wesenbergh* and *Telsburgh.*

There happened also another misfortune in the *Swedish* Camp, which proved not a little prejudicial to their Affairs; for the *German* Horse and *Scotish* Foot that were in their Service came to handy blows, upon some distaste taken against one another, wherein 1500 *Scotish* Foot were all cut to pieces by the *Germans,* except 80 that escaped their fury, and the *Russians* not long after surprised the *Swedes* and *Germans,* that were drunk in their Camp (and killed a great many of them upon the spot); and because the *Swedes* were also not idle on their side, but made frequent inrodes into the *Russian* Territories, a Truce was concluded betwixt them for two years. Most of the *Swedes* are of opinion that King *John* might have prosecuted this War with more vigour if he had not been more intent upon a Religious design, than upon warlike preparations.

The⁺ business proceeded thus: King *John,* though he was Educated a Protestant, yet having been very conversant with a great many learned *Roman* Catholicks, and influenced by his Queen,[25] had resolved to restore by degrees the *Roman* Catholick Religion, under pretence of making a Reformation in the lately introduced Protestant Religion. To effect this, he intended to follow the footsteps of *Georgius Cassander,* that was employed by the Emperours *Ferdinand* I. and *Maximilian* II. to unite and compose the Religious differences in *Germany,* and having called in some Jesuits disguised in Laymens Habits to be assisting to his Secretary Mr. *Pieter Fretenius,* who was to be the chief manager of the business, he at the Convocation of some of the Bishops and Clergy at *Stockholm* proposed to them a new form of a Liturgy, wherein a great many of the Popish Ceremonies were to be used in the Administration

25. The Catholic Catherine Jagiellon, youngest daughter of Sigismund I the Old (1467–1548) of Poland.

of the Sacraments, and Consecration of Bishops and Priests, as also the
Mass was again introduced; which new <504> Liturgy he got subscribed
by the new Consecrated Bishops and some of the inferiour Clergy, and
was called the Liturgy of the *Swedish* Church, conform to the Catholick
and Orthodox Church. This Liturgy having been published under the
new Archbishop's name in the *Swedish* and Latin Tongues, the Mass
and other *Roman* Catholick Hymns were again sung in the *Swedish*
Churches (except in the Territories belonging to Duke *Charles*[,] the
King's Brother) and the Celibacy of Priests and other Popish Doctrines
mightily extolled in the Pulpits by these disguised *Roman* Catholicks.

The next thing to be done was to try whether he could bring over his
Brother *Charles* to his party[,] whom he sollicited by his Delegates to
introduce the Liturgy into his Territories, who having made answer that
it was, (according to their Father's Testament) neither in his, nor in the
King's power to make any Innovation in Religion, this proved the subject of a great misunderstanding betwixt them. Next the King had his
recourse to the Pope, who also having disapproved his undertaking,[26]
he demanded from the Clergy at *Stockholm* to give their approbation of
the said Liturgy, but these answered that thereby a door was opened for
the *Roman* Catholick Religion to be re-established in *Sweden,* and having made their Appeal to a General Synod of that Clergy in the Kingdom, a Convocation of the Clergy of the Kingdom (except those in the
Duke's Territories) was held by the King's Authority \A. 1577\, where
New Liturgy   the King's party prevailed, so, that the Liturgy was confirmed not only
introduced.   by the said Clergy, but also by the Temporal Estates, who declared all
such Traitors as should for the future oppose the same. The King having
gained this point banished and imprisoned some of those, that would
not conform to the said Liturgy, notwithstanding which a great many of
the Clergy that were professed Enemies of the said Liturgy, and upheld
by Duke *Charles*[,] did not only boldly discover the deceitful snares of
the adverse party, but also sent [correspondence] to the *German* Universities of *Wittembergh, Leipzick, Helmstad, Francfurt* [on the Oder] and

26. Gregory XIII refused because John insisted on retaining clerical marriage,
vernacular masses, and communion under both forms.

others, where their Zeal for the *Augsburg* Confession was approved, and the said Liturgy condemned as dangerous to the Protestant Religion.

Hitherto King *Erick* had <505> suffered a very hard imprisonment during the space of nine years, but he having in the mean while by several ways endeavoured his delivery, and King *John* now fearing, that perhaps these Intestine Divisions might furnish him with an opportunity to make his escape, he sent his Secretary to give him his last Dose, which he did accordingly, having poisoned him in a Pease Soop. The King being rid of this danger began now to act more barefaced than before; for now the Invocation of Saints was publickly taught in the Pulpits, those that contradicted it were imprisoned, a new University of Papists was to be erected at *Stockholm,* he sent his Ambassadour to reside at *Rome,* and the Pope had his Nuncio at *Stockholm,* and to compleat the matter, a great many young Scholars were sent to the Jesuits abroad, to be duely instructed in their Principles.

In the mean while the War betwixt the *Swedes* and *Moscovites* was carried on without any remarkable advantage on either side, till it was agreed betwixt the two Kings of *Poland* and *Sweden,* that each of them should act separately against the *Moscovites,* and what either of them could gain by his Sword, should remain in his possession. Then it was that *Stephen* King of *Poland* having attacked the *Moscovites* vigorously on his side, the *Swedes* also under the Command of *Pontus de la Gardie* took from the *Moscovites* the strong Fortress of *Kekholm,* the Castle of *Padis, Wesenburgh, Telsburgh, Narva,* (where 7000 *Moscovites* were killed) *Jawmagrod* and other places of note, which raised such a jealousie in the *Poles* that they not only made a separate Peace with the *Moscovites,* \A. 1582\ but also demanded several of those places, taken from the *Moscovites* by the *Swedes,* for their share, which put a great stop to the *Swedish* progresses, and occasioned a Truce of two years (which was afterwards prolonged for four years longer) betwixt them and the *Moscovites.*

Whilst these things were transacting the misunderstanding betwixt the King and his Brother *Charles* could not be removed, notwithstanding that the Duke had shown his inclination of having these Differences composed, but the King having called together a Dyet at *Wadstena,* sent a summons to the Duke to appear there in person. The Duke on the other hand, <506> who did not altogether trust the King, having assembled some Forces in his Territories, did not appear at the said Dyet, but lodged himself in some of the adjacent Villages, where at last by the mediation of some of the Senators, the Brothers were reconciled, \A. 1587\ the Duke having begged the King's pardon, and referred the Differences concerning the Liturgy to the decision of his Clergy, who at an Assembly held at *Strengness* rejected the aforesaid Liturgy.

In the mean while died *Stephen* King of *Poland*, and his Widow *Anna* being Aunt of Prince *Sigismund*[,] the Son of King *John*,[27] she prevailed with some of the great Men in *Poland* to make him their King, which was done accordingly, tho' not without great difficulty on the *Swedish* side, who could not for a great while agree to the several Propositions made to them by the *Poles*, and King *Sigismund* himself seemed soon after to repent of it. As soon as *Sigismund* had left *Sweden*, his Father King *John* began to renew his Care for establishing the new Liturgy in the Duke's Territories; but the Clergy there trusting upon the Duke's Authority and Protection, remaining stedfast in their Opinion; the King at last being tired out by their constancy, sent for his Brother *Charles* to *Stockholm*, where a hearty reconciliation being made betwixt them, *Charles* was so dear to him ever after, that he did nothing without his Advice or Consent, which Friendship continued betwixt the two Brothers till a little before the King's death, when *Charles* having married *Christina* the Daughter of *Adolph* Duke of *Holstein*, the former jealousy was renewed in some measure in the King, which soon ceased by his death, which happened a few Months after at *Stockholm*. \A. 1592\

§12. After King *John's* death had been kept secret for two days, the same having been notified to Duke *Charles*, he forthwith came to *Stockholm*, and having sent a Messenger to King *Sigismund* in *Poland*, he in the mean while took upon him the Administration of the Government

Sigismund.

27. Sigismund III Vasa (1566–1632) was the son of Catherine Jagiellon, whose sister Anna was married to Stephen Bathory of Transylvania (1533–86), who had attained the Polish throne through his wife.

with the Consent of the Senate, which was confirmed to him by King *Sigismund* for that time. Soon after, he called together the *Swedish* and *Gothick* Clergy at *Upsal* (the *Finns* refusing to appear) where the *Augs-* <507> *burgh* Confession was confirmed, and the Liturgy, as also Popish Ceremonies newly introduced quite abolished. This Decree having been approved of by the rest of the Estates, they also made another, wherein was declared, That no body should appeal out of *Sweden* to the King in *Poland,* and that the King should subscribe these Decrees before his Coronation.

This proved the subject of great broils afterwards, for the King having understood what had passed at *Upsal,* he declared, that he being a hereditary Prince in *Sweden,* would not oblige himself to any thing before his Coronation, and as to the Decrees made at *Upsal,* he declared them void, which the Estates looked upon as an ill Omen for the Protestant Religion in *Sweden.* Their jealousie was also not a little augmented when they saw King *Sigismund* come into *Sweden* accompanied by the Pope's Nuncio, by whose advice the King demanded a Church for the Roman Catholicks in each City, that the new Archbishop should be deposed, and that he would be Crowned by the Pope's Nuncio, which obliged the Estates to send their Deputies to Duke *Charles,* to desire him to interpose his Authority with the King. *Charles* therefore having in conjunction with the Estates, in vain endeavoured to perswade the King to a compliance with the Estates, entred into an Association with them for the defence of the Protestant Religion, and mustered his Troops near *Upsal.* The King perceiving them to be in earnest, thought it his best way not to let things run to extremity, but having consented to most of their Propositions, which he surrendred to them the same morning when he was to be crowned, the Coronation was performed by the Bishop of *Strengness.* \A. 1594\ But no sooner was he returned to *Stockholm,* but he took a resolution quite contrary to his Promise, with an intention to obtain by force what he could not get by fair means. Wherefore having sent for some Forces out of *Poland,* he hoped to terrifie the Estates into a compliance at the next Dyet, but these being backed by Duke *Charles,* and having raised the *Dalekerls,* remained stedfast in their Resolution. The King seeing himself disappointed again in his Design, resolved upon the advice of the *Poles,* to leave the Kingdom and the Government in an unsettled <508> Condition, hoping thereby to oblige them to be more pliable for the future.

But as soon as the Senators understood that he was sailed towards *Dantzick,* they in conjunction with Duke *Charles,* took upon themselves the administration of the Government, deposed the King's Governour of *Stockholm* (he being a Papist) and forbid [forbade] the exercise of the Romish Religion. And soon after a Peace having been concluded with the *Muscovites,* a Dyet was held at *Sudercoping,* where after the Estates had justified their proceeding in a Letter to the King, the *Augsburgh* Confession was again confirmed, the Popish Religion abolished, and all *Swedes* that adhered to the same, declared incapable of any Employments in the Kingdom, and several other Decrees were made against the Papists, and for the maintaining of the Privileges of the Subjects. Then they constituted Duke *Charles* Regent of the Kingdom to govern the same with Advice of the Senate, and the whole Transaction was published in the *Latin, Swedish* and *German* Tongues.

This having occasioned a general flight among the Roman Catholicks out of *Sweden;* King *Sigismund* was so dissatisfied thereat, that he quickly sent some Commissioners out of *Poland* to disswade the Duke from these proceedings, but also when this proved ineffectual[,] by his Letter to the Estates he committed the whole management of Affairs to the Senate, excluding the Duke from the Regency. In the mean while some Senators either to curry favour with the King, or upon some distaste taken against Duke *Charles,* had shewn themselves great Favourers of the King, and declined to appear at the Dyet, which was appointed to be held under the Duke's Authority at *Arboga.* Notwithstanding which, the few Senators and the Estates there present did again confirm the Decrees lately made at *Upsal* and *Sudercoping,* declaring Duke *Charles* sole Regent of *Sweden.* But *Niclaco Flemming* the King's General, being in Arms, and having lately killed a great number of the Boors, the Duke also thought it not fit to sit still, but having gathered what Troops he could, possessed himself first of *Gothland,* and not long after of the whole Kingdom of *Sweden,* the King's Governours and those of the

Senators, that had not appeared at the last Dyet held at *Arboga,* flying <509> in great numbers to the King in *Poland.*

King *Sigismund* then perceiving that his presence was absolutely necessary in *Sweden,* resolved to go thither in Person with 6000 Men, which the Duke having been advertised of, called together the Estates of the *Gothick* Kingdom at *Wadstena,* and having made known to them the King's intention, it was unanimously resolved to meet the King with an Army near *Calmar.* \A. 1598\ But the *West-Goths* and *Smalanders* having taken up Arms for the King, and the *Finns* equipped some Ships for this Service, the former were beat back by the Boors, headed by two Professors of *Upsal,* and whilest Duke *Charles* was sailed with his Fleet to reduce the latter, which he did with good Success, the King without any opposition arrived at *Calmar.* Several Treaties were then set on foot to endeavour the settlement of the Kingdom, and to reconcile Matters betwixt the King and Duke, which proving ineffectual, both Parties had recourse to Arms. The first encounter happened near *Stegeburgh,* where the Duke's Forces being surrounded, were quickly put to the rout, but laying down their Arms, obtained Pardon from the King; but the Duke soon made amends for this Misfortune, at *Stangbroo,* where having surprised part of the King's Army, he killed 2000 of them upon the spot, with the loss of 40 Men on his side. This Defeat occasioned an agreement betwixt the King and Duke upon certain Articles, of which the Estates were to be Guarrantees, and the King promised to come forthwith to *Stockholm* to settle the Affairs of the Kingdom, whither he would needs go by Sea, tho' it was in *October,* but in lieu of sailing to *Stockholm,* [he] directed his Course from *Calmar* (where he was droven in by contrary Winds) to *Dantzick.*

The Duke being surprised at this unexpected departure, called together the Estates of the Kingdom \A. 1599\, who having once more constituted him Regent of *Sweden* at their second meeting at *Stockholm,* renounced their Obedience to King *Sigismund,* offering at the same time the Crown to his Son *Vladislaus,* in case he would come within a twelve Months time into *Sweden,* and be educated in the *Lutheran* Religion, but in case of failure he and his heirs [were] to be excluded from the Crown. Duke *Charles* thereupon marched against the *Finns*, <510> whom he quickly forced to Obedience, and having made an Alliance with the *Russians*, convened the Estates of the Kingdom in the next following year \A. 1600\ at *Sincoping*, where some of the Lords that were here, having before fled into *Poland*, were condemned of High Treason and executed accordingly, and not only King *Sigismund* declared incapable of the Crown, but also his Son *Vladislaus* (because he had not appeared within the limited time) excluded from the Succession.

Sigismund deposed.

About the same time the Duke being certified [assured] that the *Eastlanders* [Estonians], and especially those of *Reval* were inclined to his side, he marched thither with a great Army, and being received very joyfully by the Inhabitants of *Reval*, the *Polish* Governours left the rest of the places of *Esthland* voluntarily to the disposition of *Charles*. The same fortune attended him at first in *Livonia*, where he took several places of note without much opposition, but was forced to raise the Siege of *Riga* upon the approach of the *Poles*, who retook *Kakenhausen* and some other places thereabouts. *Charles* having in the mean time got notice how the *Poles* had set up the false *Demetrius*,[28] and assisted him against the *Muscovites*, under pretence of being afraid of the designs of the *Poles* against *Sweden*, desired to resign. But these[29] having first offered the Crown to *John*[,] King *Sigismund*'s half Brother, who refused to accept of the same, they bestowed it upon *Charles*, who being the only Son left of King *Gustave*, and by his Valour and Prudence having deserved so well of the Kingdom, the Crown was confirmed to his Heirs[,] even to the Females. \A. 1604\

Charles IX.

No sooner was *Charles* declared King, but he undertook an Expedition into *Livonia*, where he received a signal overthrow from the *Poles*, which might have proved of very ill consequence to *Sweden*, if King *Sigismund* had not been prevented by the intestine Commotions of the *Poles* to pursue his Victory. The *Russians* also had slain the false *Demetrius*, and having made one *Suski* their Grand Duke, craved As-

28. See above, at X.10, pp. 387–92, and XI.3, pp. 408–9.
29. The Swedes, presumably, though the passage is not clear about Charles's strategem here, probably because of omitted material.

sistance from King *Charles*, who sent some Thousand Auxilaries under the Command of *James de la Gardie*, with whose Assistance they were very successful against the *Poles*. But in *Lifland* the *Poles* got the better of the <511> *Swedes* in several encounters, and the *Danes* seeing the *Swedes* engaged on all sides, began to make great preparations against them. The *Muscovites* also had delivered their Grand Duke *Suski* up to the *Poles*, and offered that Crown to *Vladislaus* the Son of *Sigismund*, so that the *Swedish* Affairs looked with an ill face at that time, if Prince *Gustave Adolph*, King *Charles*'s Son[,] by his extraordinary Valour had not upheld their drooping Courage. For whilst the *Danes* were busy about *Calmar*, he with 1500 Horse, not only surprised their chief Magazin in *Blekingen*, which is now called *Christianstad*, but also took from them the Isle of *Oeland* and the Castle of *Borkholm;* and whilst he was busy in putting his Forces into Winter-Quarters his Father King *Charles* died at *Nycoping* in the 61 year of his age. \A. 1611\

War betwixt the Swedes and Poles in Livonia.

§13. *Gustavus Adolphus* being at the time of his Father's Death, yet under age, was under the Tuition of his Mother *Christina*, Duke *John* and some of the *Swedish* Senators. But the *Swedes* being at that time embroiled in the *Polish* and *Russian* Affairs, and the *Danes* pressing hard upon them, it was concluded at the Dyet at *Nycoping*, that King *Gustave Adolph*, notwithstanding he was not 18 years of age, should take upon himself the administration of Affairs. The King immediately applied all his Care to the *Danish* War, which was carried on but with indifferent Success on the *Swedish* side especially by Sea, where the *Danes* played the Masters, the *Swedish* Fleet being but in a very ill condition; and the *Danes* having taken besides *Calmar*, also *Risbyfort* and *Elffesburgh*, two considerable places in *Sweden*. King *Gustave* finding this War very grievous to the Kingdom, and the *Muscovites* having about the same time declared themselves very favourably in behalf of his Brother *Charles Philip* (unto whom they offered that Crown)[,] a Peace was concluded with the *Danes*, the *Swedes* being obliged to pay them a Million of Crowns for these three places above-mentioned. \A. 1613\

In the mean while *James de la Gardie* had so well managed his Affairs in *Muscovy*, that the Chiefest among them desired King *Gustave*

Gustavus Adolphus.

Adolph, and his Brother *Charles Philip* to come into *Muscovy,* but King *Gustave Adolph* who had more mind to <512> unite that Crown with *Sweden* than to leave it to his Brother, was not only very slow in his Resolution, but also at last, in his Answer to the *Muscovites* only spoke of his own coming thither, without mentioning his Brother, which having been interpreted by the *Muscovites* as if he intended to make their Country a Province of *Sweden,* they made one *Michael Foedorowitz Romano* their Grand Duke, and when Prince *Charles Philip* afterwards came into *Muscovy,* some of them for a while adhered to him, but the new Grand Duke having the stronger Party, the rest also at last left the *Swedish* side, who vigorously attacked and beat the *Muscovites* in several Engagements, and took from them some of their Frontier places, till at last a Peace was concluded betwixt both Partys at *Stolbova,* by the mediation of the *English,* by vertue of which, the *Swedes* got *Kexholm* and *Ingermanland.* \A. 1617\

Peace with the Muscovites.

In⁺ the mean while a Truce had been concluded with *Poland* for two years, but the same being near exspiring, King *Gustave Adolph* resolved to pursue the War against the *Poles* with more vigour than before. The better to put this Design in execution, he after his Coronation had been performed at *Upsal* \A. 1617\ with an universal Joy of the People, paid to *Christian* King of *Denmark* the residue of the sum due to him by vertue of the last Treaty of Peace; and having married *Mary Eleonora* the Daughter of *John Sigismund* Elector of *Brandenburgh,* \A. 1620\ he attacked the City of *Riga,* which defended it self for six weeks bravely, but being reduced to the last extremity, surrendred it self upon very honourable Terms. From hence he sailed towards *Dantzick,* to carry the War into *Prussia,* but King *Sigismund* being then at *Dantzick,* the Truce was renewed for two years longer. During the time of the Truce a Peace was proposed betwixt these two Crowns, which the *Polish* Estates were very desirous of, notwithstanding which, King *Sigismund* persisted in his former Resolution of pursuing the War.

King *Gustave* therefore again entred *Livonia* with a good Army, where having defeated 3000 *Lithuanians,* who under the Command of *Stanislaus Sariecha* would have disputed his Passage, *Kakenhausen, Dorpt,* and other places of less note, surrendred themselves to the King. From hence he advanced into *Lithuania*, and took *Bir-*<513>*sew*, and tho' the *Poles* had nothing left in *Livonia*, but only *Duneburgh*, and the *Lithuanians* were again defeated by the *Swedes* near *Walsow* in *Sem-Gallia*; King *Sigismund* persisted in his Resolution of carrying on the War, being encouraged by the Emperour, who then was very successful in *Germany*. \A. 1626\ King *Gustave* then resolving to give the *Poles* a home-stroke, sailed with a Fleet of 80 Ships and 26.000 Landmen towards the *Pillaw* [Pillau], where by Order of the Elector of *Brandenburgh*, having been received without opposition, he landed his Men, and without any resistance took *Brandenburgh* and *Frauenburgh*. The next was *Elbingen*, where the Citizens having made some shew of resistance, the Senate surrendred the City without making as much as a Capitulation. The same good Fortune attended him before *Marienburgh, Meve, Dirshaw, Stum, Christburgh* and other places in *Prussia*, which all fell into his hands, before the *Poles* had notice of his arrival. Soon after the *Poles* sent 8000 Horse and 3000 Foot into *Prussia*, who had formed a design to surprise *Marienburgh*, but were repulsed with the loss of 4000 Men, and were also forced to raise the Siege of *Meve*. And *Stanislaus Koniecpolski* with his *Podolians* also besieged *Dirshaw* in vain, but re-took *Pautske* from the *Swedes*, and dispersed some *German* Troops that were lifted [raised] in *Germany* for the Service of King *Gustave*.

> The War carried on against the Poles in Prussia.

In the next Spring \A. 1627\ the *Swedish* King having received new Supplies out of *Sweden*, intended to attack *Dantzick*, but having received a shot in the Belly before one of their out-works, he desisted for that time, but soon after made himself Master of the said Fort, having first beaten the *Poles* that came to its relief, who nevertheless, in the mean while had forced *Meve* to a surrendry. Soon after, both Armies encamped near *Dirshaw*, where King *Gustave* having drawn out his Forces in Battel array, the *Poles* did the like, having a boggy Ground before them, which the King did not think fit to pass with his Army; but when the *Poles* began to draw off again into their Camp, the King falling into the Rear, killed them a great number of Men. But some days after, attacking them in their Camp, he received a shot in his left Shoulder with a Musquet Bullet, which his Forces being dismayed at, <514> they returned without any further Action into their Camp.

Towards the latter end of the year, a new Treaty having been set on foot betwixt the two Kings, the Treaty was so far advanced, that King *Sigismund* had resolved to sign it the next day, if the *Austrians* (who did promise to send 24 Men of War and 12.000 Men to his assistance) had not prevented it. After the Treaty was broke off, King *Gustave,* before his Army went into Winter-quarters, took several places from the *Poles,* and at the beginning of the year next following, attacked a Fort near *Dantzick,* but was repulsed with loss. Soon after he had a smart Engagement with the *Poles,* wherein 3000 of them were killed upon the spot, the *Swedes* having taken four pieces of Cannon, and fourteen Standards, tho' not without great blood-shed on their side. Then the King advanced nearer unto *Dantzick,* having sent eight Men of War to block up that Harbour, but the *Dantzickers* with ten Men of War having attacked the *Swedish* Squadron, they killed the *Swedish* Admiral *Nils Sternshield,* took his Ship, forced their Vice-Admiral to blow up his own Ship, and put the rest to flight, tho' the *Dantzickers* also lost their Admiral and 400 Men in this Engagement. King *Gustave* then having detached 1000 foot Souldiers, who passed the *Veixel* in Boats, they surprised *Niewburgh,* which being a Magazin of the *Poles,* they took most of their Baggage and 600.000 Crowns in Money. \A. 1629\ But in the year next following, he gave them more work; for *Herman Wrangel* raised the Blockade of *Brodnitz* where 3000 *Poles* were killed, 1000 taken Prisoners, with five Pieces of Cannon and 2000 Waggons with Provision.

The *Poles* being frightened at this Defeat, were very desirous then to receive the Imperial Forces which were sent to their Assistance under the command of *Arnheim,* who with 5000 Foot and 2000 Horse, joined *Koniecpolski,* the *Polish* General near *Graudentz.* King *Gustave* on the other hand encamped with an Army of 5000 Horse and 8000 Foot near *Quidzin;* and tho' the *Swedes* were much inferiour in number, yet did they not refuse the Combate; and both Armies soon after having met near *Stum,* there happened a brisk Engagement betwixt them, wherein the *Swedish* Horse were first repulsed, <515> with the loss of five Standards, but the King coming up in Person with more Forces, soon forced the *Poles* to retreat, who would have passed over a Bridge which they were laying over the River of *Nogat*. But King *Gustave* endavouring to cut off their retreat that way the Fight was renewed on both sides with great fury, so that the King venturing himself too far, was taken hold of by his Shoulder-belt, which he slipping over his head got free of them, leaving his Hat and Belt behind him. But immediately after, another catching hold of his Arm, would have carried him off, if one *Erick Soop* had not shot the *Polander*, and delivered the King. In this Action the *Swedes* got seventeen Colours and five Standards, the Imperial Forces having received the greatest damage.

Not long after, there happened another Engagement about the same Bridge, where the *Poles* were again repulsed, and in the attack of *Stum*, they lost 4000 Men of their best Forces. The *Poles* having imputed these Losses chiefly to *Arnheim* the Imperial General (who being a Vassal of the Elector of *Brandenburgh*, was suspected by them to hold a correspondence with the said Prince) and being grown quite weary of the Imperial Forces, being also pestered with Famine and the Plague, by the mediation of *France*, *England*, *Brandenburgh* and *Holland*, a Truce was concluded for six years, by vertue of which, King *Gustave* was to restore to *Poland*, *Brodnitz*, *Wormdit*, *Melsack*, *Stum* and *Dirshaw*, *Marienburgh* was committed to the custody of the Elector of *Brandenburgh*, King *Gustave* kept the Castle and Harbour of *Pillaw* and *Memel*, as also *Elbingen* and *Braunsbergh*, besides all what he was possessed of in *Livonia*[,] so that King *Gustave Adolph* had ended both the *Russian* and *Polish* War to his eternal Honour and the great Advantage of his Kingdom.

Truce with Poland.

§14. But he was not long at rest before *Germany* was the Scene where he acquired everlasting Glory to his Nation, and performed some of the greatest Actions that were ever seen in *Europe*. As soon as the Protestants in *Germany* began to be jealous of the Roman Catholicks sinister Intentions against them, they were then for bringing King *Gustave* over to their Alliance; but he being at that time entangled in the *Polish* Affairs, was <516> not at leisure to engage himself with them. \A. 1626\ But *Christian* IV. King of *Denmark* who was ambitious of that Honour, having in the mean while received a great Defeat from the Imperialists, who since that had made themselves Masters of the *Lower Saxony*,

German War.

and got footing on the *Baltick,* King *Gustave* fearing the consequence
of it, pressed the harder upon the *Poles* to oblige them to a Peace or
Truce; and having called together the Estates of *Sweden,* \A. 1628\ he
represented to them the danger which threatened *Sweden* from the *Imperialists,* who had not only got footing on the *Baltick,* but also made
themselves Masters of a part of *Denmark;* whereupon it having been
resolved by the Estates, that it was not advisable to stay till the Enemy
should attack them at home, but to meet him abroad and to keep him
from getting footing on the Borders of the *Baltick,* the King only waited
an opportunity to put this Design in execution, which presented it self
in the same year.

For *Albert Wallenstein,* Duke of *Friedland,* the *Imperial* General, having laid a Design against the City of *Strahlsund,* the King who was then
in *Prussia,* offered his Assistance to that City, and having sent them
voluntarily some Ammunition, and exhorted them to a vigorous Defence; the Citizens accepted of the King's offer, making an Alliance with
him for the Defence of their City and Harbour, and to maintain their
Commerce in the *Baltick.* Pursuant to this Treaty, the King sent some of
his Forces to their assistance, who were very instrumental in defending
that City against the *Imperialists,* but he did not think fit to attempt
any thing further at that time, because *Wallenstein* and *Tilly* were with
two considerable Armies not far off. But as soon as the *Polish* War was
ended, he resolved not to make any further delay. Having therefore in
vain proffered his mediation for the procuring of a Peace in *Germany,*
and represented again to the Estates of *Sweden* the necessity of meeting
the *Imperialists* with an Army abroad, he with all expedition prepared
himself for the next Campagne, \A. 1630\ and having sent *Alexander
Lesley* with some Troops before, to drive the *Imperialists* out of the Isle
of *Rugen* (which he effected)[,] and settled his Affairs at home, he embarked with 92 Companies of Foot, and 16 <517> of Horse (which were
however considerably augmented afterwards by some Regiments raised
in *Prussia*) and landed the 24 of June at *Usedom.*

Upon his arrival the *Imperialists* having left their Forts thereabouts
and at *Wollin,* he re-embarked his Souldiers with a Train of Artillery
in some small Vessels and directly took his course towards *Stetin,* and

Charles Gus-
tave lands with
his Forces in
Germany.

having obliged the Duke of *Pomerania* to receive him and his Forces into that City, he made a defensive Alliance with him. From hence he marched to *Stargard, Anclam, Uckermund* and *Wolgast,* all which places he took without much opposition. And whilest King *Gustave* acted with such Success against the *Imperialists* in *Pomerania, Christian Wilhelm* administrator of *Magdeburgh* (who had been deposed by the Emperour) had got into the possession again of the City and Territories of *Magdeburgh,* whither King *Gustave* sent *Diedrich* of *Falckenburgh* to be assisting to the said Administrator in settling his Affairs that were then in great confusion. In the mean while several Regiments of *Liflanders* and *Finlanders* were arrived under the Command of *Gustave Horn,* these having been joined by such Troops as were lately come out of *Prussia,* the King left his Camp near *Stetin,* he himself marching with his Army into *Mecklenburgh.* In his absence the *Imperialists* had endeavoured to force the *Swedish* Camp near *Stetin,* but were vigorously repulsed, and at his return he also beat them out of *Greiffenhagen* and *Gartz*[,] nay, even out of the furthermost parts of *Pomerania,* and the *New Marck.* The Archbishop of *Bremen,* Duke *George* of *Lunenburgh,* and *William* Landgrave of *Hesse,* then entred into an Alliance with the King, and the Protestant party in general being encouraged at the Success, began to consider of ways and means to rid themselves of the Roman Catholick yoke.

At[+] the beginning of the next ensuing year, \A. 1631\ King *Gustave* at last concluded the so long projected Alliance with *France,* by vertue of which he was to receive a yearly Subsidy of 400.000 Crowns from the *French* King. Having thus strengthned himself, he notwithstanding the Winter Season, took *Lokenitz, Prentzlow, New Brandenburgh, Clempenow, Craptow* and *Leitz,* without much opposition. *Demmin* also, where the Duke of <518> *Lavelli* was in Garrison with two Regiments, was surrendred after a Siege of three Days, and *Colberg* surrendred after a Blockade of five Months.

Alliance made with France.

The Emperour in the mean while perceiving that his Generals were not able to cope with King *Gustave Adolph* had given to *Tilly* the *Bavarian* General the supreme Command over his Forces, who being an antient experienced and renowned Captain marched directly to the relief

of *Demmin,* but having received intelligence that the place was surren-
dred before, he fell with great fury upon *Kniphausen* who lay with two
Regiments of *Swedes* at *New Brandenburgh,* which being a place of no
defence, he forced after a brave resistance, killing most of the Common
Souldiers. But perceiving that King *Gustave* being strongly entrenched,
was not to be forced in his Camp[,] he directed his march upwards to
Magdeburgh, in hopes to draw the King out of his advantageous Post.
But King *Gustave* marched directly towards *Franckfort* upon the *Oder,*
where the Earl of *Shaumburgh* lay with a small Army, notwithstanding
which, he took the place by Storm after a Siege of three Days, slew 700
of the Enemies and took 800, among whom were a great many Officers
of note. From hence he sent a Detachment to *Landsbergh,* to endeavour
to drive also the *Imperialists* from thence.

About the same time a general meeting of the Protestant *German*
Princes was held at *Leipzick*[,] where a League was proposed to be made
in opposition to the demanded restitution of the Church-Lands.[30]
Thither King *Gustave* sent some of his Ministers to exhort them to a
mutual Union against the Emperour, and to demand some assistance
from them of Men and Money. But the Elector of *Saxony* was very
backward in declaring himself positively, pretending several reasons,
but in effect intended to make himself head of the Protestant League,
and in the mean while to take this opportunity of putting the Protestants in a good posture, and to keep the ballance betwixt the Emperour
and the *Swedes.* King *Gustave* therefore perceiving that the Protestants
in *Germany* were so very cunning and overcautious, thought it his best
not to venture his Army at the discretion of others, wherefore tho' he
was very willing to have relieved the City of *Magdeburgh,* which was
<519> reduced to extremity, yet did he not think it advisable to march
thither before he had secured his retreat. To render therefore his design
effectual, he marched with his Army strait to *Berlin,* and having obliged
the Elector of *Brandenburgh* partly by fair words, partly by threats, to

30. The Edict of Restitution, imposed by Ferdinand II in 1629, sought to reverse
the loss of Catholic properties (through secularization and conversion) that had
occurred since 1555 in violation of the Ecclesiastical Reservation of the Peace of
Augsburg (1655). See VIII.16, p. 344, above.

put into his hands the Forts of *Spandau* and *Custrin* for the security of a retreat over the two Rivers of the *Havel* and *Oder,* he would have straitways marched to the relief of the City of *Magdeburgh* if the Elector of *Saxony* would have joined him, but whilest the said Electors made a great many tergiversations, the said City was taken by Storm by General *Tilly,* who miserably burnt the City, and killed most of the Inhabitants, there having been but 400 left of a great many thousands. \10. May, 1631\

The City of Magdeburgh taken by the Imperialists.

After this Disaster, King *Gustave* having published his Reasons, why he could not timely enough relieve that City, and having cleared the whole *Pomerania* of the *Imperialists,* he divided his Army, and having sent part of his Forces to the assistance of the Dukes of *Mecklenburgh,* he marched with the rest into *Marck* and encamped at *Werben* near the River *Elbe,* to observe *Tilly,* who having received Intelligence of the King's arrival near that River, was obliged to alter his march (which he intended to have directed towards *Saxony*) in hopes to force the King to a Battel. But the King surprised his Avaint-Guard near *Wolmerstadt,* where he totally ruin'd three Regiments of Horse. Notwithstanding which, *Tilly* approached near the King's Camp at *Werben,* but the King refusing to fight, and he not daring to attack him in his Camp, he was for want of Forage, obliged to march back to his former Camp at *Wolmerstadt.* In the mean while the Dukes of *Mecklenburgh* had with the assistance of the *Swedish* Auxiliaries driven the *Imperialists* out of their Territories, except *Domitz, Wismar* and *Rostock,* which places they also kept block'd up. And about the same time *James* Marquis of *Hamilton* came with 6000 *English* and *Scots* into *Pomerania,* but stood the King in no great stead, most of them dying in the same year by several Diseases. But *Tilly* seeing that he could not attack the King near *Werben,* decamped from *Wolmerstadt* and marched to *Eisleben,* and from thence to *Halle,* from whence he marched with 40.000 Men <520> to *Leipsick,* which he took soon after.

The Elector of *Saxony* being thus put to a nonplus, was then forced to send to King *Gustave,* and to desire him to join his Army which lay encamped near *Torgau,* the King who had foreseen what would befal him, being already advanced near *New Brandenburgh;* and tho'

the King was very glad of this opportunity, yet because the Elector being now put to a nonplus, now desired what he had refused before, he
proposed to him certain Conditions, which the Elector having readily
granted, he passed the River *Elbe* near *Wittenbergh* with 13.000 Foot
and 9000 Horse, and joined the Elector near *Dieben.* Then a Council
of War having been called (where the Elector of *Brandenburgh* also was
present) the King, who did not exspect that the old cunning General
[Tilly] would give them any opportunity to fight, was for acting very
cautiously; but the Elector of *Saxony* was not for protracting the War,
telling them that if the rest refused he would fight alone: This opinion
at last prevailed, the King then thought it most convenient to attack
him [Tilly] immediately before he could be joined by the Generals
Altringer and *Tieffenbach,* the first of which was already arrived near
Erffurt, the second being on his march out of *Silesia.*

Thereupon the command of the right Wing being left to the King,
that of the left to the Electors, they marched towards the Enemy. *Tilly*
Battle near had no sooner been informed of their approach, but he began to fortifie
Leipzick. himself in his Camp near *Leipzick.* But *Pappenheim* and the rest of the
Imperial Generals trusting too much upon the bravery of their *Veteran*
Bands, and despising the new Levies of the *Saxons* and the *Swedes* that
were tired out by long march[,] would by all means fight the Enemy in
the Plains near *Breitenfeld* \7. Sept., 1631\, where *Tilly* lost the fruits of
his former Victories. He had possessed himself of all the rising Grounds
where he had planted his Cannon, and had also the advantage of the
Wind; but King *Gustave* who had put some Battalions of Foot among
the Squadrons of Horse, by wheeling about, got the advantage of the
Wind from him, and having obliged the *Imperialists* to open their left
Wing, *John Banner* fell in among them and brought them into confusion. But the greatest force of the *Imperialists* fell upon the *Saxons,*
<521> whose Infantry and some of the Militia Horse were put to flight,
which obliged the King to fall with his Wing upon the Enemy's Horse
that were in pursuit of the *Saxons,* whom he quickly also forced to fly.
But the Imperial Infantry still held out, till *Gustave's* Horse with some
Squadrons of the right Wing fell into their Flank; and the King about
the same time having taken all the Enemy's Artillery, they were put to

an entire rout on all sides, leaving 7600 Men dead upon the spot, besides what was killed in the pursuit, 5000 Prisoners took Service under the King. *Tilly* himself who refused Quarter, was likely to have been killed by a Captain of Horse, if *Rudolf Maximilian* Duke of *Saxon-Lauenburgh* had not delivered him by shooting the Captain thro' the head. The *Swedes* took above 100 Standards and Colours, but lost 2000 Men most of them Horse; the *Saxons* lost 3000, who quickly retook *Leipzick,* whilest the King marched towards *Merseburgh,* where he cut to pieces 1000 of the Enemies, and took 500 Prisoners.

Then it was resolved at a Council of War held at *Halle,* not to follow *Tilly,* who was retired towards the River of *Weser,* but to carry their victorious Arms into the Emperour's hereditary, and other Roman Catholick Countries thereabouts. After some dispute it was agreed that the King should march towards *Franconia,* whilest the Elector of *Saxony* entred the hereditary Countries of the Emperour. Pursuant to this agreement, the King marched towards *Erffurt,* (where *William* Duke of *Weimar* was received without opposition) and from thence into *Franconia,* where he took *Konigshofen* and *Schweinfurt* without any opposition, and the Castle of *Wurtzburgh* after some resistance. In the mean while *Tilly* the Imperial General having been reinforced by several Troops that were before dispersed in *Germany,* was come to the relief of *Wurtzburgh,* but coming too late, marched toward the River of the *Tauber* to cover the *Bavarian* and the Emperour's hereditary Countries on that side, but in his march the *Swedes* falling into his Rear, cut off four entire Regiments. The King having then made an Alliance with the Marquis of *Anspach* marched towards the *Rhine,* surprised *Hanau,* but *Franck-fort* on the River of *Mayn* surrendred voluntarily, and having possessed him-<522>self of the whole Country of *Ringau* [*Rheingau*], directed his march into the Palatinate, which was then in the possession of the *Spaniards.* Soon after entring the *Bergstrasse* he took *Gernsheim,* and passed the *Rhine* near *Stockstadt,* having defeated the *Spaniards* that would have disputed his Passage, and at *Oppenheim* he cut 500 *Spaniards* in pieces, but the Garrison of *Mayence* surrendred upon Articles, and *Landaw, Spiers* [Speyer], *Weissenburgh* and *Mannheim,* fell soon after into the King's hands. *Rostock* also and *Wismar* having in the mean while been surrendred, the *Baltick* Sea-Coast was cleared from the *Imperialists.* And the Members of the Circle of the *Lower Saxony* at an Assembly held at *Hamburgh,* had resolved to levy 6000 Foot and 500 Horse for the defence of that Circle.

The Elector of *Saxony* in the mean while having refused the offers made to him by the *Spanish* Ambassadour, had sent his Army under the command of Lieutenant General *Arnheim* into *Bohemia,* where among other places they had taken the City of *Prague;* but having conceived a jealousy against the King (whom he suspected to aim at the Imperial Crown) he could not be prevailed upon to march further into *Moravia* and *Austria.* And the Imperial Court seeing that *Tilly* was no more able to cope with the King, resolved to give the supreme Command of the Imperial Forces to *Wallenstein,* who being an old experienced Souldier, and in great Authority among the Souldiers, had besides this gathered such riches that he was able to raise an Army at his own charge. He having been at last prevailed upon to take upon him the supreme Command, raised an Army of 40.000 Men against [for] the next Spring. \A. 1637\

But whilest these Preparations were making at *Vienna,* the King's Forces, notwithstanding the Winter Season, having beaten the *Spaniards* upon the *Moselle,* had taken *Creutznach, Braunfels Kobenhausen* and *Kirchbergh,* and the King having left the supreme direction of Affairs on the *Rhine* to *Axel Oxenstirn,* he himself towards the Spring marched into *Franconia.* But *Tilly* at his approach, retired on the other side [of] the *Danube,* the King possessed himself of all the places along that River as far as *Ulm,* from whence he marched towards the River of *Lech,* where *Tilly* had entrenched himself in a Forest on the other side of that River. Here it was <523> that General *Tilly* was wounded by a Canon Bullet, of which he died in a few days after at *Ingolstadt.* His Army being dismayed at the loss of their General left their advantageous Post, and the *Swedes* having cut 1000 of them in pieces in their retreat marched straightways into the Country of *Bavaria,* where they took possession of *Rain,* and *Niewburgh* upon the *Danube. Augsburgh* surrendred without much resistance. But their design upon *Ingolstadt* and *Ratisbonne* [Regensburg] miscarried, being repulsed at the first, where the King's Horse was shot under him, and *Christopher* the Marquis of *Baden* killed by his side, but the latter the Elector of *Bavaria* had secured by throwing some of his Forces into the place. The King therefore returning into *Bavaria* set that Country under Contribution, and the City of *Municken* [Munich] opened its Gates to the King.

In the mean while General *Wallenstein,* having left the Elector of *Bavaria* a while to shift for himself, had driven the *Saxons* out of *Bohemia,* by the treachery of their General *Arnheim,* who was an utter Enemy of King *Gustave,* and the *Imperialists* under Lieutenant General *Pappenheim* had made considerable progresses in the Circle of the *Lower Saxony, Wallenstein* also had taken a resolution to fall with all his Forces upon the King in the Country of *Bavaria.* Pursuant to this resolution, the Elector of *Bavaria* having left a sufficient Garrison at *Ingolstadt* and *Ratisbonne,* marched towards *Egen* to join *Wallenstein,* whom the King pursued in hopes to hinder their conjunction, but coming too late, he encamped near *Nurembergh,* till he could be joined by his Forces that were dispersed in several parts of *Germany. Wallenstein* then made a shew as if he would turn his Arms against the Elector of *Saxony,* thereby to draw the King out of his advantageous Post near that City; but the King remaining in his Post[,] he marched towards him, spreading his Cavalry all round about, which occasioned a great scarcity of Forage in the King's Camp, but as for Provisions he was sufficiently supplyed withal from *Nurembergh.* Whilst the King was reduced to these Straits he received a reinforcement of 15.000 Foot, and 10.000 Horse from several places, so that being now superiour in number he attacked *Wallenstein* in his Camp, <524> who being strongly Entrenched repulsed the *Swedes* with the loss of 2000 Men.

In the mean time the *Imperial* General *Pappenheim* had beat the *Hessians* near *Volckmarsen,* had forced the Duke of *Lunenburgh* to raise the Siege of *Callenbergh,* had beat General *Baudist* from before *Paterborn* and *Hoxter,* had relieved *Wolffenbuttel,* and taken *Hildesheim,* from whence he was marched into *Thuringia,* to join *Wallenstein.* On the other hand the *Saxons* were entred [into] *Silesia* with an Army of 16.000 Men, where meeting with no opposition, they might have carried all before them, if their General *Arnheim* had not been treacherous to King

Gustave, whom he hated, and was for working [toward] a reconciliation betwixt the Emperour and the Elector of *Saxony.* The King therefore, not to lose any more time, having put a good Garrison into *Nurembergh,* resolved to send part of his Army into *Franconia,* and with the main Body to return towards the *Danube* into *Bavaria,* where he had taken several places on the River of *Lech.*

But whilst he was carrying on his victorious Arms among the *Roman* Catholicks, frequent Messengers were sent to him by the Elector of *Saxony* craving his assistance against *Wallenstein,* who was with all his Forces entred into *Misnia* [Meissen]. The King though he had great reason to be dissatisfied with the Elector, yet fearing he might be forced to make a separate Peace with the Emperour, if he did not come to his assistance; he having left some Forces in *Bavaria* and *Suabia,* under the Command of *Pfaltsgrave Christian* of *Berckenfeld,* and commanded *Gustave Horn* to remain in *Alsatia,* where he forced *Benfelden* to surrender (as *Franckenthal* was about the same time forced to surrender by Famine), himself marched with the Army towards *Misnia.*

Being arrived at *Nauenburgh* he received information that the Enemies had raised the Siege of *Weissenfels,* and that they had detached *Pappenheim* with some Forces upon another design. Having therefore resolved not to stay for the Duke of *Lunenburgh,* who being already arrived at *Wittenbergh,* was to have joined him, but to fight the Enemy before he could be rejoined by *Pappenheim.* Pursuant to this resolution he marched to the great Plains near *Lutzen,* where a most bloody Battel was fought betwixt them \Nov. 6, 1632\, <525> in which the *Swedish* Infantry fell with such fury upon the *Imperial* Foot that they routed them, and made themselves Masters of their Cannon. But the *Swedish* Horse being stopt by a broad Ditch (that was cut cross the Plains for the conveniency of floating of Wood), the King put himself at the Head of the *Smaland* Regiment of Horse, encouraging the rest by his example to follow him. Thus furiously advancing before the rest, and being only accompanyed by *Francis Albrecht* Duke of *Saxen Lauenburgh,* and two Grooms, he there lost his life. Concerning his death there are different opinions, but the most probable is, that he was shot by the said Duke of *Lauenburgh,* who was set on by the *Imperialists* that had their only

Battel near Lutzen.

hopes in the King's death. The *Swedes* were so far from being dismayed at the King's death, that they fell with great fury again upon the Enemy, whom they routed on all sides. The *Imperialists* having been rejoined by *Pappenheim,* would have rallied again, but *Pappenheim* having also been killed, they were routed a second time, leaving an entire Victory to the *Swedes,* which was nevertheless dearly purchased by the death of so great a King.

King Gustave Adolfe killed.

§15. The death of this great King caused great alterations in *Europe,* for, though the *Imperialists* had lost the Battel and a great many brave Officers, yet were they in no small hopes that the *Swedish* Affairs would now sink under their own weight, and therefore made great preparations against them [for] the next Campagne. The Protestants in *Germany* were by his death divided into several Factions, not knowing whom they should choose for their Head, and the *Swedes* overwhelmed with troubles, his Daughter *Christina* being then but six years of Age. \A. 1633\ Nevertheless, having settled their Affairs at Home, and committed the Administration of the Kingdom to the five chief Officers of the State, the chief management of the Affairs in *Germany* was committed to the care of the Lord Chancellour *Oxenstirn*[a], who having been sent by the King's order into the higher[31] *Germany,* received this sad News at *Hanau.* The Chancellour did not so much fear the Power of his Enemies as their constancy and unanimous Resolution, whereas <526> the Protestants were divided in their Counsels and Opinions, and were not likely to follow his directions after the King's death, it being not probable that the Electors and Princes of the Empire would be commanded by a Foreign Nobleman; nevertheless he thought it not advisable, by leaving their Conquests, to ruin at once the Protestant Cause and the Interest of *Sweden,* but rather to endeavour by a brave resistance to obtain an honorable Peace.

Christina.

Having therefore sent some Regiments back into *Sweden,* he divided his Army, and having sent 14.000 Men under the Command of *George* Duke of *Lunenburgh* into the Lower *Saxony* and *Westphalia,* the last

---

31. That is, upper or southern Germany.

were ordered into *Franconia,* and some Forces were also detached towards *Silesia.* These Forces acted with good success against the *Imperialists,* especially in *Westphalia,* where the Duke of *Lunenburgh* took several places, defeated the Earl of *Mansfeld* near *Rinteln* and besieged the City of *Hamelen.* But in *Silesia* the Common Cause was not carried on with the same forwardness, by reason of the misunderstanding betwixt the *Swedish* and *Saxon* Generals, the latter of which keeping a secret Correspondency with *Wallenstein,* left the *Swedes* in the Lurch, who were at last miserably beaten by the said *Wallenstein.* But in all other places they had better success, where their Generals took several places of note, and the Duke of *Lunenburgh* had also retaken the strong City of *Hamelen* by accord, after having defeated 15.000 *Imperialists* that were coming to its relief, whereof 2000 were killed upon the spot, and as many taken Prisoners. Thus the *Swedish* Army were every where flourishing but in *Silesia,* nevertheless the burthen of the War grew heavier upon them every day, most of their Confederates being grown weary of the War, and willing to be rid of the *Swedes.*

Whilst they laboured under these difficulties, *Wallenstein* being faln in disgrace and killed by the Emperour's order, they hoped to reap some advantage by this Change, but the Emperour having made the King of *Hungary* (his Son)[32] General of his Army, who having taken *Ratisbonne,* and being joined by the *Spanish* Forces that were marching towards the *Netherlands,* besieged *Nordlingen,* where the *Swedish* Avantguard intending to possess themselves of <527> a Hill near that City, were engaged with the *Imperialists,* which occasioned a Battel betwixt the two Armies, \A. 1634\ and the *Swedish* Left Wing having been brought into disorder by the *Polish, Hungarian* and *Croatian* Horse, was forced back upon their own Infantry, which also were brought into Confusion and totally routed, 6000 having been slain upon the spot, a great number taken Prisoners, among whom was *Gustave Horn,* and 130 Colours were lost, besides the whole Artillery and Baggage. After this Battel the whole Upper *Germany* being over-run by the *Imperialists,* and the Elector of *Saxony* having made a separate Peace with the Emperour, the *Swedish*

Battel of Nordlingen.

32. Ferdinand III (1608–57).

Affairs seem'd to be reduced to a very ill condition, especially since the Elector of *Brandenburgh* also had sided with the *Saxons,* and the Truce with the *Poles* was near expired about the same time, which made the *Swedes* very desirous of a Peace; but the same not being to be obtained in *Germany* they were fain [obliged] to prolong the Truce with the *Poles* for twenty six years, and to restore to them their so dearly beloved *Prussia,* and [in order] to draw *France* into *Germany* to their assistance, to put them in the Possession of *Philipsburgh.*

Truce prolonged with the Poles.

Thus having in a manner settled their Affairs, the War broke out betwixt them and the Elector of *Saxony,* who offered them a recompence of mony for the Archbishoprick of *Magdeburgh,* which the *Swedes* refusing to accept of, there happened a sharp Engagement betwixt them near *Allenburgh* upon the *Elbe,* where of 7000 *Saxons,* one half were killed, and the rest taken Prisoners. Notwithstanding this advantage the *Swedes* had no small obstacles to surmount, since the Emperour was in Possession of the whole Upper *Germany,* and had besides this set the Elector of *Saxony* upon their Back, which obliged the *Swedes* to take new Measures, and being now left by all their Confederates, they were at liberty at least to act more unanimously, though perhaps with less force, the effects of which appeared soon after; for though the Elector of *Saxony* had the good fortune to retake *Magdeburgh* from the *Swedes,* yet they soon after revenged this loss near *Perlebergh* where they attacked the said Elector with a less number in his fortified Camp, and having routed his Army killed 5000 <528> upon the spot, besides what were killed in the pursuit, 1100 being killed on the *Swedish* side, and 3000 wounded, and having soon after driven the *Imperialists* out of *Hessia* into *Westphalia,* and regained *Erffurt,* they were again in a fair way to get footing in *High* [Upper] *Germany.* \A. 1637\ They had also in the next ensuing year several Encounters with the *Imperialists* and *Saxons,* which proved most to their advantage, *Banner* having defeated eight *Saxon* Regiments near *Edlenburgh,* and soon after 2000 [troops] more near *Pegau,* and when the *Imperialists* thought to have got him with his whole Army into their Clutches near *Custrin,* he got off with great dexterity, but could not prevent, but that the *Imperialists* took several places in *Pomerania,* as also near the Rivers of *Havel* and *Elbe; George* Duke of

War betwixt the Swedes and Elector of Saxony.

Lunenburgh having also declared against the *Swedes,* who also began to
be extremely jealous of [the Elector of] *Brandenburgh* by reason of his
pretension upon *Pomerania,* after the death of *Bogislaus* XIV. the last
Duke of *Pomerania,* (who dyed this year)[,] an Alliance was concluded
betwixt them and *France* for three years.

Alliance with
France.

The⁺ *Swedes* having been brought the year before somewhat in the
straits, they now \A. 1638\, after having received fresh Recruits began
to recover what they had lost the year before, *Banner* having driven
Gallas the *Imperial* General back even into the Hereditary Countries
of the Emperour. And *Bernhard* Duke of *Weimar* had the same success
on the *Rhine,* where having besieged *Rhinefelden,* he fought twice with
the *Imperialists,* that came to its relief, and having routed them in the
second Engagement took *Rhinefelden, Kuteln* and *Freiburgh* in *Breisgau.*
After this exploit having blocked up *Brisack* [Breisach] so closely that
it was reduced to the utmost by Famine, the *Imperialists* endeavoured
to relieve it with 12.000 Men, which were so received by the said Duke
that scarce 2500 escaped. And not long after the Duke of *Loraine* having
attempted its relief with 3500 Men, the same were also cut in pieces, and
the place surrendred to the Duke [of Weimar].

The *Imperialists* having been thus routed both near the *Rhine* and in
the *Lower Saxony,* the Duke and *John Banner* had both taken a resolution to carry the War into the Emperour's Here-<529>ditary Countries,
and *Banner* marched straitways (after several Defeats given to the *Imperialists* and *Saxons*) into *Bohemia,* where he in all likelihood might have
had great success if the untimely death of Duke *Bernhard* (who was
to join him) had not broke his Measures. This Duke being sollicited
by the *French* to surrender *Brisack* [Breisach] into their Hands (which
he refused), was Poisoned by them, and his Army with great promises
and mon[e]y debauched to submit under the *French* Command. The
Imperialists then growing too strong for *Banner* alone in *Bohemia,* he
marched back into *Misnia* [Meissen] and *Thuringia,* and having been
joined by the Duke of *Longueville,* who Commanded the Army of the
lately deceased Duke of *Weimar*[,] and by some *Hessians* and *Lunenburghers* near *Erffurt* (which made up an Army of 21 Brigades and 2000

Horse)[,] he would fain have Fought the *Imperialists,* but these avoiding to come to a Battel the Campagne was most spent in marching up and down the Country.

But at the beginning of the next ensuing year \A. 1641\ *Banner* had very near surprised the City of *Ratisbonne,* where the Emperour and the Estates of the Empire were then assembled, if the Ice which was by a sudden Thaw loosned in the River, had not hindred them from laying a Bridge of Boats, which design having miscarried, *Banner* resolved to carry the War again into *Moravia, Silesia,* and *Bohemia.* But the *Weimarian* Forces under the Command of the *French* General having left him thereabouts, the *Imperialists* had so closely beset him, that there was no way left to retreat but through the Forest of *Bohemia,* which was done with all expedition, having left Colonel *Slange,* with three Regiments of Horse behind, who after a brave resistance were all made Prisoners of War, but saved the *Swedish* Army, which would else have been in great danger if they had not detained the *Imperialists,* the *Swedish* Army being arrived but half an hour before them at the Pass of *Presswitz,* where they stopt the Enemies march.

Not long after dyed the famous *Swedish* General *John Banner* \May 10\, whose death caused some dissatisfaction in the Army, notwithstanding which they beat the *Imperialists* near *Wolffenbuttel* at two several times, and *Torstenson* (who was made General)[,] <530> being arrived in the Camp, directed his march into *Silesia,* where he took *Great Glogau* with Sword in Hand \A. 1642\, and a great many other places, the chiefest of which was *S*[ch]*weinitz,* where he defeated the *Imperialists,* that came to its relief, under the Command of *Francis Albert* Duke of *Saxon Lauenburgh,* who was killed himself and 3000 Horse. Afterwards he besieged *Brieg,* but was forced to raise that Siege, the *Imperialists* being superiour in number, who also prevented him from marching into *Bohemia.* Wherefore having directed his March towards the *Elbe,* and passed that River at *Torgaw,* he straightways went to besiege the City of *Leipzick.* But the *Imperialists* under the Command of the Arch Duke, and General *Piccolomini* coming to its relief, a bloody Battel was fought in the same Plains near *Breitenfeld,* where King *Gus-*

Battel fought near Leipzick.

tave Adolf before had obtained a signal Victory against the *Imperialists.*
\Oct. 23\ In this Battel the Left Wing of the *Imperialists* having been
brought into confusion, the Left Wing of the *Swedes* underwent the
same fate, but the *Swedes* Left Wing rallying again and falling in the
Flank of the *Imperialists* Right Wing, they put them to the rout, 5000
being killed upon the spot, and 4500 taken Prisoners. The *Swedes* lost
2000 Men, and had a great many wounded. After the loss of this Battel
Leipzick was soon forced to surrender, but *Freybergh* (which was soon
after besieged by *Torstenson*) defended it self so well, that the *Swedes,*
upon the approach of the *Imperial* General *Piccolomini,* were forced to
raise the Siege with the loss of 1500 Men. And the *Weimarian* Army
under the Command of the *French* General *Gebrian* was for the most
part ruined by the *Bavarians.*

War with   In⁺ the mean while *Torstenson* had received Orders to March with his
Denmark.   Army into *Holstein,* the *Swedes* provoked by a great many injuries, having resolved to turn their Arms against *Denmark;* \A. 1644\ which was
executed with great secresie, so that the *Swedes* coming unexpectedly
upon the *Danes* took the greatest part of *Holstein,* beat their Troops in
Jutland and *Schonen,* and ruined their Fleet; made themselves Masters
of the whole Bishoprick of *Bremen,* and the Isle of *Bernholm,* which
obliged the *Danes* to make a disadvantageous <531> Peace with them at
Bromsebroo, giving to the *Swedes Jempteland* and *Herndalen, Gothland*
and *Oesel,* besides other advantages.

Peace with   *Torstenson* having then made a Truce with the Elector of *Saxony*
Denmark.   \A. 1645\ marched again into *Bohemia,* where another Battel was fought
near *Janowitz* betwixt the *Imperialists* and *Swedes,* wherein the first were
routed with the loss of 8000 Men, one half of whom were killed [and]
the rest taken Prisoners. The *Swedes* had 2000 Men killed. The *Swedes*
then marched through *Bohemia* into *Moravia,* and from thence into
Austria, where having been joined by [Prince] *Rago*[z]*zi* they were
in a fair way of making greater progresses, if *Ragoz*[zi], who had received satisfaction from the Emperour, had not left the *Swedish* Army,
and marched Home with his Forces. The *French* also under the Command of *Turenne* having been again routed by the *Bavarians, Torstenson*
marched back into *Bohemia,* who having put his Forces into Winter

Quarters near the River of *Eger,* and growing very crazy[33] left the Supreme Command of the Army to *Wrangel,* who finding the Enemy too strong for him thereabouts, marched further back into *Misnia* [Meissen], and from thence towards the *Weser.* But having not long after been joined by *Turenne* near *Giessen*[,] they attacked *Augsburgh* which being reinforced with 500 Men, they were forced to quit the Siege upon the approach of the *Imperialists,* who also retook several places in the Hereditary Countries of the Emperour.

Not long after[,] *Wrangel* also made a Truce with the Elector of *Bavaria,* which however lasted not long, the said Elector having upon the persuasion of the Emperour broke the same a few months after, and joined his Forces with the *Imperialists.* \A. 1648\ But *Wrangel* marching early out of his Winter Quarters, in conjunction with *Turenne,* pressed so hard upon the *Bavarians* that they were forced to retire to *Saltzburgh,* leaving a great part of the Country to the discretion of the Allies, where these burnt a great many Houses, because the Inhabitants refused to pay Contribution. \July 16\ About the same time *Koningsmark* had surprised the Suburbs of *Prague,* where he had got a prodigious Booty in the *Imperial* Palace, and other Noble-Mens Houses which are all built on that side of the River, but could not take the City, which was defended <532> by 12.000 Citizens, so that having sent his Forces into their Winter Quarters thereabouts, whilst *Wrangel* was marching into the *Upper Palatinate*[,] they received the News of a Peace being concluded at *Munster.*

This⁺ Peace had been long in agitation before it was brought to perfection, the *Imperialists* having endeavoured, after they saw the *Swedes* recover themselves so bravely after the Battel of *Nordlingen*[,] to persuade them to a separate Peace without including the Protestant Estates in *Germany.* But the *Swedes* having refused these offers as being neither honourable nor secure, seven years were spent in the Preliminaries, and these having been adjusted[,] the Treaty it self was begun at *Osnabrug* and *Munster,* where the Emperours, *Spanish,* and *Dutch* Ambassadours, as also those of the most *Roman* Catholick Estates, and the Popes *Nuncio* were Resident, but in the first the *Imperial* Ambassadours also, and

Peace made at Munster and Osnabrug.

33. Lennart Torstenson (1603–51) was plagued by gout.

those of most of the Protestant Estates were assembled,[34] where at last a
Peace was concluded, by vertue of which *Sweden* got the Dukedoms of
Bremen and *Veerden,* the greatest part of *Pomerania,* the Isle of *Rugen,*
and the City of *Wismar,* to hold these Countries in Fief of the Em-
pire, with all the Priviledges thereunto belonging, and five Millions of
Crowns towards the payment of their Armies. Besides this they had the
Honour of having been instrumental in re-establishing several *German*
Princes in their Territories, and settling both the Quiet and Protestant
Religion in *Germany.*

The War being thus ended to the great Honour of the *Swedes,* the
Queen, who had already then taken a resolution of surrendring the
Crown to her Nephew *Charles Gustave,* would willingly have put an
end to the Differences betwixt *Sweden* and *Poland,* which were likely
to revive again after the Truce expired, but the *Poles* were so haughty
in their Behaviour, and refractory in their Transactions that no Peace
could be concluded at that time. Having therefore settled her Affairs
and reserved a certain yearly allowance for her self during her life, she
surrendred the Crown to the said *Charles Gustave* her Nephew at the
Dyet at Upsal, \1654, Jun. 6\ where he was Crowned the same day when
she resigned the Government.[35] <533>

Charles   §16. *Charles Gustave,* finding the Treasury exhausted, obtained at the
Gustave.   first Dyet from the Estates that the fourth part of such Crown Lands
as had been granted away since the Reign of *Gustave Adolfe,* should be
reunited with the Crown, and having again settled the Military Affairs,
which were somewhat decayed since the last Peace, resolved to force
the *Poles* to an honourable Peace. The better to execute his design, he
The War   marched in Person into *Poland,* where he met with such success, that af-
with Poland   ter having defeated some that would have opposed his passage, not only
renewed.   the *Polanders,* but also the *Lithuanians* submitted voluntarily, swearing
Allegiance to him, and *John Casimir,* their King, was forced to fly into

34. Catholics and Protestants would not meet directly with one another, so the
former (including France) met at Münster, while the latter (including Sweden) met
at Osnabrück.
35. Charles X Gustav (1622–60) reigned from June 5, 1654, until his death.

Silesia. But whilst the King of *Sweden* was marched into *Prussia,* the *Poles,* with the assistance of the House of *Austria,* having with the same readiness again forsaken his Interest, were faln upon the *Swedes* in their Quarters, of whom they killed a great many, especially in *Lithuania,* forcing the rest to seek for shelter in some strong Holds which were in their possession. The King having put an end to the differences betwixt him and the Elector of *Brandenburgh* concerning *Prussia,* in conjunction with the said Elector, marched back towards *Warsaw,* where he obtained a signal Victory over the *Poles* and *Tartars;* \A. 1656\ and being in the beginning of the next year joined by *Bogislaw Radzivil,* Prince of *Transylvania,* would in all likelyhood have humbled the haughty *Poles,* if the *Danes* had not threatened a dangerous diversion near Home, and actually denounced War to *Sweden.*

This[+] obliged the King to draw his main Army that way, where he not only made great progresses both in *Holstein* and *Bremen;* but also by a prodigy scarce to be believed by Posterity[,] marched over the Ice into the Island of *Fuhnen,* \A. 1658\ and from thence to other Islands, and at last into *Sealand,* where he carried all before him, which brought the King of *Denmark* to such a distress, that he was forced to clap up a sudden Peace at *Roschild* [Roskilde], giving to the *Swedes Schonen, Halland* and *Bleckingen,* the Isle of *Bernholm,* besides several other Possessions in *Norway.* But this Peace was of no long continuance, <534> for the King having again conceived a jealousie at the *Danes,* Embarked his Forces in *Holstein,* and under pretence of going towards *Dantzick* landed in *Sealand,* and besieged *Copenhagen,* whilst *Wrangel* reduced the strong Fortress of *Cronenburgh.* But the *Danes* being chiefly encouraged by their King's presence defended themselves bravely, till the *Dutch* Fleet gave them relief, which obliged the King after having attempted, but in vain, to take it by Storm, to raise the Siege. But the greatest misfortune befel the *Swedes* in the Island of *Fuhnen,* where being over numbred by the joint Forces of the *Imperialists, Poles, Brandenburghers* and *Danes,* they were totally routed near *Nyborgh,* \A. 1666\ their Infantry being most cut to pieces, and the rest made Prisoners. The King being busie in repairing this loss, was seized with an Epidemical Fever, of which he dyed on the 23. of *February.*

War with Denmark.

Siege of Copenhagen.

Battel in Fuhnen.

§17. *Charles*[36] being but five years old when his Father dyed, the *Swedes* applyed all their care to obtain an honourable Peace, which was concluded with the *Poles* in the Monastery called *Oliva,* near *Dantzick* \May 3\, wherein were also included the Emperour and [the] Elector of *Brandenburgh,* and King *John Casimir* resigned his pretension to the Crown of *Sweden,*[37] and the *Poles* to *Livonia.* In the same month a Peace was concluded with *Denmark* \May 23\, much upon the same conditions, which were agreed on formerly at *Roschild,* except that the *Danes* kept the Isle of *Bornholm,* and *Druntheim* in *Norway.*

For the rest, the *Swedes* were for preserving Peace with their Neighbours during the minority of the King,[38] till having broke off the Triple Alliance made betwixt them, and the *English* and *Dutch*[,] they sided with *France* against the Elector of *Brandenburgh,* \A. 1674\ whom they pretended [attempted], by sending an Army into his Territories, to draw from the Interest of the Empire. But this occasioned a heavy War to the King, at the very beginning of his Reign, wherein the Elector having routed the *Swedish* Army, took all what the *Swedes* were possessed of in *Pomerania,* as the *Lunenburghers* got into their possession the Dukedoms of *Bremen* and *Veerden,* and the King of *Denmark* the City of *Wismar,* <535> and several considerable places in *Schonen,* but the *Danes* having at last been routed at two Battels in *Schonen,* the King after the Treaty of *Nimeguen,* by a particular Peace was put again into the possession of his Countries in *Germany,* very few excepted, and *Denmark* was forced also to restore the places taken from the *Swedes* in *Schonen.* This Peace having been again settled in *Sweden,* the King married *Ulrica Eleanora*[39] the present King of *Denmark*'s Sister, since which time the King has chiefly applied himself to settle his Military Affairs and Revenues, and to maintain the Peace with his Neighbours. \A. 1678\

Marginal notes: Charles IX. Peace made with the Poles. Peace made with Denmark. The Swedes routed by the Elector of Brandenburgh.

---

36. Charles X Gustav's son, Charles XI (1655–97).

37. John II Casimir (1609–72) was the son of Sigismund III (1566–1632), who had been deposed as king of Sweden in 1599.

38. The regency ended in 1672.

39. Ulrika Eleonora (1656–93), to be distinguished from her daughter by the same name (1688–1741) and from her mother-in-law, Hedwig Eleonora (1636–1715), whom Pufendorf served as secretary.

§18. The *Swedish* and *Gothick* Nation has antiently been famous for Warlike Atchievements, and is very fit to endure the Fatigues of War; yet were their Military Affairs in former times but very indifferently ordered, their chiefest Force consisting in the Boors, till *Gustave* and his Successours with the assistance of some *Scotch* and *German* Officers and Souldiers have introduced such a Discipline as that now they do not stand in so much need of foreign Souldiers, except it be to make up the number of Men, wherewith they are not overstock'd, especially since the late great Wars. As in most other Kingdoms of *Europe,* by reason of the multitude of their populous Cities, the Estate of the Citizens is the fundamental part of the State, so is in *Sweden* that of the Boors, who enjoy more liberty in *Sweden* than in other Kingdoms, and also send their Deputies to the Dyet, where their consent is requisite to any new Taxes to be levied upon the Subjects.

This[+] Nation loves to shew a great deal of gravity and reservedness, which if not qualified by conversation with other Nations, often degenerates into mistrustfulness. They generally are apt to think very well of themselves, and to despise others. They have sufficient Capacity to attain to the first Principles of any Art or Science, but commonly want Patience to attain to the perfection of them. Their inclination is not much to Trade or Handy-work, and therefore Manufacturies are but little encouraged among them.[40] <536>

§19. The Kingdom of *Sweden* is of a great extent, but full of great Forests and innumerable Lakes, and the Sea-Coast surrounded with many Rocks. But deeper into the Country, there are a great many fertile tracts of Ground, the Forests furnish them with Fuel, and the Lakes with great store of good Fish, which also contribute much to the easie transportation of the Native Commodities from one place to another. The Country produces Corn sufficient for its Inhabitants, neither is there any want of Cattel or Horses. *Sweden* produces more Copper

The nature and qualification of the Swedish Nation.

Condition of the Country and its Strength.

40. These somewhat briefer comments correspond to §83 of the *Continued Introduction* (see Pufendorf [1692], p. 858), where Pufendorf characterizes the Swedes as good warriors but also as envious, conceited, and too impatient to perfect the various arts, sciences, and crafts.

and Iron than any other Kingdom in the World, and their Mines are fitted by nature for that purpose, being surrounded with Woods and Rivulets. There is a Silver Mine in *Westmanland*. *Finland* brings forth Pitch, and Tar, and Deal [softwood]; and *Wermeland* [a] good store of Masts. The Native Commodities of *Sweden* are Copper, Iron, Tar, Pitch, Masts, Boards &c. In lieu of which, *Sweden* receives from abroad Wine, Brandy, Salt, Spices, Cloaths, Silk and Woollen Stuffs, fine Linnen Cloath, *French* Manufactories of all sorts, Furs, Paper and such like, all which in some years surpasses in value the Commodities fit for exportation here. To recompence this, Navigation and Commerce has been encouraged of late years among the Natives, and several sorts of Manufactories, whereof those made of Copper, Iron and Brass would questionless turn to the best account, if these Artists were duely encouraged to settle themselves in this Kingdom, Copper and Iron being the foundation of the *Swedish* Commerce abroad.

This present King has put their Forces both Horse and Foot in a better Condition than ever they were before, which are maintained in *Sweden*, with a small charge to the Crown, the Foot being maintained by the Boors, but the Horsemen have for the most part some Farms in their possession belonging to the Crown, the Revenues of which are their pay. But the King's Guards are paid out of his Treasury. Formerly the station of the Royal Navy was at *Stockholm*, but since [then] a new Harbour has been made in *Bleckingen*, where the Ships may be put to Sea sooner, and with more conveniency. Besides this, *Sweden* has this advantage, that it is covered on the side <537> of *Norway* with inaccessible Rocks, besides the three strong Fortresses of *Bahus*, *Marstrand* and *Gothenburgh*, and the *Swedish* and *Finland* Coasts are so well guarded by innumerable Islands, that it is very difficult to approach the shoar.

Neighbours of Sweden.

Muscovites.

§20. As to the Neighbours of *Sweden*, it borders on the East side upon *Muscovy*, with whom the *Swedes* in former times were often at War, but since *Finland* is now well covered against them by the Fortresses of *Narva*, *Kexholm* and *Noteburgh*, and they have learn'd by experience that the *Swedes* are better Souldiers than they, there is nothing to be feared from thence. And since the *Swedes* have no great reason to covet

any further Conquests on that side, they may be taken now for good
Neighbours. With the *Poles* the *Swedes* used formerly to have no differ- Poles.
ence at all, except when in outrage that Nation espoused the quarrel of
their King concerning his Title to *Sweden*. But since *Charles Gustave* a
little humbled their pretensions upon *Livonia,* as the *Swedes* have done
upon *Prussia,* the *Poles* for the future may in all likelihood prove good
Neighbours to *Sweden*.

The *Swedes* have had antiently a great Communication with the *Ger-* Germany.
mans, by reason of their Commerce with the *Hanse* Towns. But since
the *Swedes* have by the *Westphalia* Treaty been put into possession of
two Provinces in *Germany,*[41] they enjoy the same right with the rest of
the Estates, and the King of *Sweden* is now to be considered as a Member, and not as a Neighbour of the Empire, whose Interest therefore is
to see, that the *Westphalia* Treaty be kept in vigour. There is some jealousy betwixt the *Swedes* and the Elector of *Brandenburgh,* about some
part of *Pomerania,* which would else have fallen to that Elector's share,
and besides this, he is obliged to keep up a constant standing Army
against so considerable a Neighbour, but since *Sweden* has preserved
Brandenburgh and the rest of the Protestant Estates, and the said Elector has received a triple equivalent[42] for this loss, it is but reasonable
that something of allowance should be given as to this point, especially
since it is not for the Interest of *Sweden* to make any further Conquests
in *Germany*.

But betwixt the *Swedes* and the House of <538> *Lunenburgh,* there
ought to be a good understanding, since they are able to do one another great Service against *Denmark, Brandenburgh* and the *Westphalian*
Bishops. Since *Sweden* by making the Sea the borders betwixt them
and *Denmark,* has put a stop to those troubles which formerly used to Denmark.
proceed from the too near neighbourhood of the *Danes,* and secured
their Trade, it ought not to make any attempt of further Conquests in

41. The Swedes received western Pomerania, including Stettin and the island of
Rügen, as also the port of Wismar and the bishoprics of Bremen and Verden.
42. Brandenburg received the bishoprics of Halberstadt, Minden, and Camin,
and the bishopric of Magdeburg (after the death of its administrator, August of
Saxe-Weissenfels, in 1680).

Denmark, it being [in] the interest of most Estates of *Europe,* to take care that neither of the two Northern Kings become sole Master of the Sound. Wherefore *Swedes* ought to endeavour to keep the present limits betwixt them and *Denmark,* and to live in amity with those Estates in *Germany,* who are jealous of the Neighbourhood of *Denmark.*

France. The foundation of the good Correspondency betwixt *France* and *Sweden* was built upon the common agreement of keeping under the overgrown Greatness of the House of *Austria,* but since the case is now altered, the King of *France* now pretends to play the Master over Princes.[43] *Sweden* ought not to assist *France* in those Designs which overturn the *Westphalian* Treaty, or are intended against the Protestants

Holland. in *Germany* and *Holland.* The good understanding betwixt *Sweden* and *Holland* is chiefly founded upon this bottom, that as *Sweden* cannot be glad to see *Holland* ruined, so the *Hollanders* are obliged to prevent the King of *Denmark* from making himself sole Master of the passage of the *Sound* or the *Baltick.*

England. *England* has hitherto had so little concern with those Northern parts, that their greatest Correspondency has been transacted by way of con-

Spain and templating with very little Reality. *Spain* is considered by the *Swedes* as
Portugal. a part of the House of *Austria,* tho' the *Swedes* have so far a concern in the *Spanish Netherlands,* as from their preservation depends the welfare of *Holland.* But the good understanding betwixt *Sweden* and *Portugal* depends only from the mutual Commerce of these two Nations, who else by reason of this great distance can scarce be serviceable to one another. <539>

FINIS

43. See V.29, pp. 270–71, above, for Pufendorf's contrasting assessment.

A Brief Publication History of the
Introduction and Its Descendants

Like several of his other works, including *The Present State of Germany* (1667), *On the Law of Nature and of Nations* (1672), and *On the Duty of Man and Citizen* (1673), Pufendorf's *Introduction to the Principal Kingdoms and States of Europe* (1682) began a publishing tradition that continued long after his death, well into the second half of the eighteenth century.[1] Its final editions during that period appear to be those, in English and German, of 1782 and 1783. Yet even those dates may not reflect the end of the work's pedagogical influence, even at Königsberg, where the new, metaphysical enlightenment of Kant was about to eclipse the civic enlightenment of Pufendorf and Thomasius.[2] For instance, Riccardo Pozzo has shown on the basis of recently discovered course announcements that in the 1790s the University of Königsberg curriculum still contained courses, in both History and Law faculties, on "the history of European empires and states," on "modern history of the sixteenth and seventeenth centuries," and on "the history of the German Empire and of the individual states thereof."[3] Given the

---

1. On the dissemination of Pufendorf's main natural law works in Europe through the French translations of Jean Barbeyrac, see Othmer (1970).

2. Hunter (2001) and Hochstrasser (2000).

3. Pozzo (2000), 121–24. Lectures on the history and current condition of the main "European states," based on pedagogical compendia with similar names, were offered frequently throughout the eighteenth century at many other universities, particularly at Göttingen. The latter was known for its historical studies and the new discipline of *Statistik* which—through Achenwall, Gebauer, Schlözer, Spittler, and others—"built on" and "continued" the "intellectual legacy of Pufendorf" and

work's prominence during the preceding century, it is reasonable to assume that Pufendorf's *Introduction* continued to feature prominently in courses with such titles. Furthermore, Kant's own *Anthropology from a Pragmatic Point of View* (1797), which was based on some thirty years of teaching that subject, still contains philosophized remnants of the end-of-chapter analyses in Pufendorf's *Introduction*, particularly in the section on "the Character of Nations," where Kant generalizes about different European peoples, including the French, English, Spanish, Italians, Germans, and Russians.[4]

Pufendorf's *Introduction* originated in his lectures at the University of Lund—that is, before 1676, when the *Carolina* was forced to close because of the Danish occupation—and perhaps even earlier at Heidelberg.[5] It seems he had no plans to publish this material, at least in such a form.[6] However, in 1680 an unauthorized Swedish version by Petrus Brask appeared in Stockholm, based on one or more of the student transcripts that had been circulating.[7] So to gain control over the work, Pufendorf was forced to revise and publish it on his own. It appeared in 1682 while he was royal Swedish historiographer and deeply immersed in preparing his history of Gustavus Adolphus.[8] The first official edition of the work contained, as Chapter 12, Pufendorf's essay on the papacy, which had been separately published several years earlier, also in German, under the Latin pseudonym Basileus Hypereta.[9]

---

others. See Valera (1986), pp. 129 and 135, and Jarausch (1986), especially pp. 37–42; Vierhaus (1987), Behnen (1987), Pasquino (1986), Van der Zande (2010), and Koskenniemi (2007, 2010); also the Editor's Introduction above, p. xvi, note 27, and p. xxiv, note 57.

4. Kant, *Anthropology*, Part II.C, trans. Gregor (1974), 174–82. Of course, it was this historical-political tradition that Kant ultimately rejected, as reflected in his dismissive "sorry comforters" remark in *Toward Perpetual Peace* (1795), sect. 2, art. 2. See Devetak (2007) and Koskenniemi (2009).

5. Döring (1996a), p. 21, note 54.

6. Malmström (1899), p. 41; Niceron (1732), col. 249.

7. Martinière, "Éloge historique," in Pufendorf (1753), p. xv; Malmström (1899), p. 42. On Petrus Brask, see *Svenskt Biografiskt Handlexikon* (1906), vol. 1, p. 133.

8. Pufendorf (1686).

9. Siebenkäs (1790), p. 51, identifies the Hamburg imprint of 1679 as the first edition. According to Niceron (1732), col. 248, the work was incorporated into the *Introduction* "with some changes." He notes as well that a few years later a similar

However, it did not yet include the short history of Sweden that we find in Crull's edition as Chapter 13. Instead, in 1686 Pufendorf issued an account of Swedish history that rivaled the entire *Introduction* in length. This *Continued Introduction* had a long life of its own, and it was often bundled with the *Introduction* and its descendants, both in German and in the other European languages into which the two works were repeatedly rendered. The only exception to the general pattern was Swedish, ironically, which saw no further editions of either the *Introduction* or the *Continued Introduction* (also translated by Brask, in 1688) until Jacob Wilde's two-part edition of the *Continued Introduction* in 1738 and 1743.[10]

The German text of the *Introduction* was quickly translated into Dutch (1684), French (1685), Latin (1687), and English (1695), followed by long publication histories in the original and the latter three languages.[11] For more than half a century, there was a steady stream of new editions and imprints, with Pufendorf's account typically corrected, improved, continued, expanded, or entirely recast by a series of translators, editors, and compilers—sometimes unknown—who appropriated the work for their own purposes. Pufendorf's original was typically retained in some form (albeit linguistically doctored at times) and his Preface often reprinted, but the work was constantly adapted to the changing national and international circumstances in which it appeared. Moreover, the national publication streams interacted and influenced one

work appeared with the title *Theodosii Gibellini Caesareo-Papia* (Frankfurt, 1684), whose unknown author, some thought, was Esaias Pufendorf. See the Editor's Introduction, p. xiv, note 17.

10. On Jacob Wilde, see *Sammlung russischer Geschichte*, Bd. 9 (1764), pp. 25–56; *Svenskt Biografiskt Handlexicon* (1906), vol. 2, p. 732; Malmström (1899), p. 42; and Siebenkäs (1790), p. 52.

11. Ludwig's "Vorrede" (1700), p. 19, mentions Spanish and Italian translations, but I have not found these. Also, there is no evidence of any Polish or Danish versions. A direct Danish edition may have been preempted by Ludvig Holberg's (1684–1754) *Introduction til de fornemste Europaeiske Rigers Historier* [*Introduction to the Histories of the Foremost European States*], in 1711, which was based on Pufendorf. Another work by Holberg, *Synopsis historiæ universalis* (1733), was translated into English in 1755 as *An Introduction to Universal History*. See Robertson (1916), and the Editor's Introduction, p. xl.

another, sharing their respective emendations and additions and indicating thereby the transnational status of Pufendorf's work. For much
of the eighteenth century it was the French and the English editions
that carried the work forward, though the German versions also continued to come thick and fast and, in fact, constituted the *Introduction*'s
final phase.

The first real "addition" was to the German text of the *Continued
Introduction* (1686), which received an appendix (*Anhang*) in its second
edition of 1689. This essay of some sixty pages, first published in 1688,[12]
presented Pufendorf's relentless critique of Antoine Varillas (ca. 1620–
96), *Histoire des revolutions arrivées dans l'Europe en matière de religion*
(Paris, 1686), a work dedicated to Louis XIV and reputedly subsidized
by the French clergy.[13] In it Varillas accused sixteenth-century Protestant
reformers of having had political motives—a position directly contrary
to Pufendorf's own characterization of those events[14]—and purport-
edly made some ninety-one errors about Swedish history in particular
that Pufendorf sought to expose.[15] Like the chapter on the papacy, the
response to "Varillas's thousand lies"[16] became a permanent feature of
the *Continued Introduction* and the defense of political Protestantism.

A further enlargement of Pufendorf's original *Introduction* came with
Crull's 1695 English translation thereof, which contained a new Chapter
13 similar in size to the other chapters and devoted to Swedish history.
This condensation of the *Continued Introduction* was later attributed to
Pufendorf's Latin translator, Johann Friedrich Cramer (1664–1715).[17]
That is unlikely, however, for the chapter did not appear in Cramer's

12. Niceron (1732), col. 250, dates the *Anhang* to (Frankfurt, 1687), though the
catalogs give no evidence of this. The piece also appeared in Brask's 1688 Swedish
translation of the *Continued Introduction*.

13. Martinière, "Éloge historique," in Pufendorf (1753), vol. 1, p. xvi; Siebenkäs
(1790), p. 53. The work appeared one year after Louis XIV had revoked (1685) the
Edict of Nantes and sent even more Huguenot refugees into Europe.

14. See XII.25–28.

15. Niceron (1732), p. 250; *Hamburgische Bibliotheca* (1729), art. 42, p. 147. The
errors were numbered in the margins of the various editions.

16. *Anhang der Continuirten Einleitung* (Frankfurt, 1688 [1689]), p. 62.

17. Martinière, "Éloge historique," in Pufendorf (1753), vol. 1, p. xv. On Cramer,
see *Allgemeine Deutsche Biographie*, vol. 4, p. 548.

translation until the third edition (1702/3);[18] and it is not found in the "longe emendatior" second edition of 1693, nor in the imprint of 1700. Barring the assumption that there were two independently produced versions of the chapter, by different translators, or that Crull had access to Cramer's chapter some seven years before Cramer published it himself, it seems instead that Cramer (1702) translated Crull (1695). Indeed, this is supported by a comparison of the two texts.[19] The Latin version of Crull seems also to have been quickly assumed into Rouxel's 1703 French edition of the *Introduction*, again with no acknowledgment of its English original.[20]

Cramer's Latin translation of the German *Einleitung* appeared first in 1687 and was supposedly reviewed by Pufendorf himself.[21] The second edition came out in 1693, and the third (with the compendium) in 1702/3; its final imprint was in 1704. The *Continued Introduction*, and its later expansions in the other languages, never made it into Latin.

The early eighteenth century saw a number of multivolume editions (often over several years) that greatly increased the scope of Pufendorf's original. The first of these was in German, and it established the scheme

18. The date is 1702, though the engraved title leaf has 1703; Niceron (1732), col. 251.

19. For instance, Crull's section numeration mistakenly repeats §9 (see pp. 541 and 553 above), and Cramer (1702) has the same error. Moreover, the Latin follows Crull's English presentation fairly closely, though it sometimes omits sentences and even paragraphs—perhaps for contemporary political reasons. Also, the 1702 edition does not attribute the new compendium to Cramer (d. 1715) himself, and the printer's foreword to the reader ("Typographus Lectori") says only that "redigi in ordinem & contrahi Historiam Suecicam jussi, ut prioribus capitibus brevitate sua respondeat . . . ," with no indication of how this abbreviation came about.

20. The "Avis au Lecteur" in Pufendorf, *Introduction à l'histoire* (1703) says that Rouxel (or someone else: that is, the reference is not specific) "received" (*reçu*) the *abrégé* of the Swedish history only a short time before publication, suggesting that it came from the just issued (1702) Cramer edition. Meusel (1782), p. 198, says only that Rouxel's edition was polished and continued by an anonymous person, who also added the epitome of the Swedish history. Selective comparison of passages (from chap. 13) in Rouxel (1703) with both Cramer (1702) and Crull (1695) shows it to be sometimes closer to one or to the other: specifically, some clauses in Rouxel appear in Crull but not in Cramer. A definitive answer would require a more thorough comparison of the three texts.

21. Martinière, "Éloge historique," in Pufendorf (1753), vol. 1, p. xv.

often used to refer to the work from then on.[22] The *Introduction* was henceforth called "Part 1" (*erster Teil*), and the *Continued Introduction* "Part 2" (*zweiter Teil*). In 1706, an entirely new portion was added as "Part 3" (*dritter Teil*), comprising a history of various Italian states—particularly Venice, Genoa, Florence, and Savoy—as well as Austria, the Turkish empire, and the main ruling houses of Germany. This new work consisting of fifteen chapters is attributed to Christian Gottfried Franckenstein (1661–1717), "doctor juris et scabinus" at Leipzig, who not only retained Pufendorf's method but also imitated his style.[23] Franckenstein's contribution was acknowledged by Bruzen de la Martinière (pseud. Estienne de la Chambre), editor of the great French edition of 1721, though he also faulted him for having a pro-Austrian bias and speaking always as a "court councillor."[24] Part 3 soon took on a life of its own (appearing in a "second edition" already in 1709), even while it constituted part of the larger, comprehensive editions. Three of these, in German, came out early in the century: the first between 1705 and 1707, the second in 1709–10, and the third between 1715 and 1719. During these spans, the individual volumes were not always issued in the order in which they were originally written.

"Part 4" (*vierter Teil*) of the now much-enlarged "Introduction" (*Einleitung*) was added to the set in 1707, when it was translated into German from the original of a "learned Englishman" by an unknown *Theotiscus* (that is, *Teutonicus*) identified only as C. J. W[ilke]. The Englishman was none other than Jodocus Crull, who first published his continuation in 1705 as *An Introduction to the History of the Kingdoms and States of Asia, Africa and America, both Ancient and Modern, According to the Method of Samuel Pufendorf.*[25] Crull's new work soon acquired

22. The scheme is used explicitly by Meusel (1782) in discussing the *Introduction*'s publication history.

23. *Hamburgische Bibliotheca* (1729), art. 43, p. 147; and Meusel (1782), p. 197. On Franckenstein, see Zedler, vol. 9 (1735), cols. 1713–14; and Michaud, vol. 14 (1856), p. 654. A *scabinus* was a legal expert who advised the court.

24. Martinière, "Avertissement," in Pufendorf (1721). On Martinière, see Michaud, vol. 27, pp. 160–61; and Zedler, vol. 19 (1739), col. 1845.

25. Wilke identifies Crull as the original author in his "Translator's Preface," reprinted in the 1732 German edition. Also see Meusel (1782), p. 195; and *Ham-*

an identity of its own, in both German and English, where it appeared in many distinctly sequenced editions.[26] Moreover, his original *Introduction* (Part 1) was in turn enlarged by the Franckenstein edition's Part 3, which was added to the sixth edition (1706) as an "Appendix" and regularly accompanied the work from then on, at least through the eleventh edition of 1753.[27] Thus, two new additions (Parts 3 and 4) to the *Introduction* were exchanged quickly across the Channel in the space of about two years.

Readers of French encountered the *Introduction* and the *Continued Introduction* through the translations of Claude Rouxel,[28] which were frequently printed between 1685 and 1720, both separately and together. The former work included Crull's version of the short Swedish history, at least by 1703. As noted, the year 1721 saw a major revision of Rouxel by Martinière, in six volumes. Martinière not only corrected the stylistic and factual infelicities of Rouxel's "monstrous translation" but also greatly expanded the work's contents, reorganizing them into a "more natural" order. He continued the various chapters up to 1720 and added accounts of the ruling houses of Germany and Italy that had "any distinction" at the time. Moreover, he provided two sets of notes, one of which indicated changes in states' interests since Pufendorf's time.

---

burgische Bibliotheca (1729), art. 43, p. 148. The work was discussed in the *Journal des Savants* 45 (November 5, 1708), pp. 719–22, where the reviewer praises its clarity but complains that more than half is devoted to Asia. Also, he says, it does not include any discussion of states' interests, like Pufendorf's original, since many of these states are too far removed from Europe for such things to be known or of use. See Appendix 2, list, pp. 624–25, below, and the Editor's Introduction, p. xxxviii.

26. See the English sixth edition in 1736, and Faßmann's German version (mentioned by Meusel [1782], p. 199) in 1738.

27. The English version contained only five chapters, however, devoted to Venice, Modena, Mantua, Florence, and Savoy, with the short account of Mantua (not in Franckenstein [1706]) presumably added by Crull himself.

28. Rouxel also authored *Le grand dictionnaire françois et flamend* . . . (Amsterdam: Halma, 1708). Further biographical details are hard to come by. There is mention of a Claude de Rouxel de Blanchelande (d. 1740) in Lainé (1834), under the entry on "Berault de Billiers," p. 7, note (2). This Rouxel entered French military service in 1686 and fought in Germany, Piedmont, and Italy, retiring in 1722 due to injuries. His travels suggest that he may have had some facility in German, but the entry lists no publications.

Acknowledging his own dependence on "the German continuer" (that is, Franckenstein, who had added Part 3), Martinière went considerably beyond him, including, for instance, both the short (in vol. 4, chap. 6) and the long (vols. 5–6) Swedish histories within the set. As a whole, his voluminous edition exhibits well the metamorphosis of Pufendorf's work into an international collaboration relevant to the Europe of that time—a fact suitably announced by its new title: *Introduction à l'histoire generale et politique de l'univers, ou l'on voit l'origine, les revolutions, l'état present, & les interêts des souverains*. Part 4 (on Asia, Africa, and America) was omitted from the 1721 edition because of pressure to publish, but it joined the set as vol. 7 in the following year. Both versions included Martinière's informative "Avertissement sur cette nouvelle edition" and the briefer "Memoires pour servir à la vie de Mr. le Baron de Pufendorff."[29]

Martinière's grand edition, which also contained many charts, was reissued in whole or part during each of the next three decades. In 1732 came a seven-volume update notable mainly for the first appearance (in vol. 1) of the long "Eloge historique de Monsieur Le Baron de Pufendorff"—a substantial expansion of the earlier "Mémoires." It also encompassed (as vols. 5–7) a newly corrected and continued (to 1730) edition of the long Swedish history prepared by Martinière's collaborator, Jean-Baptiste Desroches de Parthenay, which was sometimes issued separately thereafter. Martinière (d. 1746) updated his work into the 1740s, as did de Parthenay. Interestingly, the latter's 1748 revision of the *Histoire de Suède* included—apparently for the first time—his French translation of Pufendorf's critique of Varillas, some sixty years after its initial publication in German.[30] The years 1753–59 saw another large

29. Martinière's "Avertissement," in Pufendorf (1721), contains his severe criticisms of Rouxel. Also, the 1721 "Memoires" became the 1732 "Éloge historique," which was reprinted in Pufendorf (1753), vol. 1, pp. i–xviii.

30. See de Parthenay's "Preface de l'Editeur" (partly carried over from the 1732 edition) in *Histoire de Suède* (1748), p. xi. According to Michaud, vol. 10 (1855), p. 553, de Parthenay (1690–1766) worked closely with Martinière in Holland, even residing in the same house. He also published histories of Denmark and Poland, and after moving to Copenhagen produced there several translations of Danish works,

revision of Martinière, by Thomas-François de Grace, who expanded the work to eight volumes and corrected and continued it to 1750. This version, which appeared again in 1763, was apparently the last French edition of the century.[31]

Martinière served as the basis of a new English edition by Joseph Sayer in 1748, which was reissued in 1764.[32] Sayer explicitly acknowledged the debt, even as he sought to reduce Martinière's complexity and return to "the original Plan of Puffendorf" by omitting many of the smaller states "not of Consequence enough," and others that had "lost their Independency."[33] Interestingly, this new English version of the *Introduction* did not replace Crull's, which saw its eleventh edition in 1753 after a gap of twenty-four years (since the tenth edition in 1729). Thus, there were two separate English editions in print at mid-century. All English editions and printings, it should be noted, were satisfied with the short (chapter-length) Swedish history, and none included the *Continued Introduction*—as in the comprehensive German and French editions—even when the European coverage was expanded with the 1706 *Appendix* (Part 3) and the independently published *Supplement* of 1710 and 1726 (apparently a broader version of Franckenstein going well beyond Italy). The *Continued Introduction* did appear in English in 1702, translated (and continued to 1701) by Charles Brockwell as

including Holberg's *Pensées ou réflexions morales* (1749), Norden's *Voyage d'Égypte et de Nubie* (1752), and Egède's *Description et histoire naturelle de Groenland* (1763).

31. On Thomas-François de Grace (1714–99), see Michaud, vol. 17 (1857), p. 299. Michaud says that de Grace's edition is "the only one of Pufendorf's works [the *Introduction*] that one still finds," and he comments ironically that "it is a pity that a work intended to serve as an introduction to history has acquired an extent that makes it useless for that purpose." This assessment is somewhat at odds with the favorable reviews of the first two volumes in the *Journal des Savants* (1754: Janvier, pp. 30–35; and Novembre, pp. 743–48), which note the "reasonable length, the avoidance of both the dryness common to these sorts of works and the prolixity of some of our histories," and refer to the edition as "an entirely new work, a new introduction to history formed according to the plan laid out by Pufendorf" (Novembre, p. 747). (Translations by M.J.S.)

32. Interestingly, the 1748 Dedication to Sayer's edition (reprinted in Pufendorf [1764]) was to "Prince George" (1738–1820), who became King George III in 1760.

33. "Translator's Preface" in Sayer (1748), p. xii.

The Compleat History of Sweden.[34] This was reissued once more in 1704 in a second, corrected edition, but it saw no further printings after that—perhaps in part because of the severe demands made on readers by Brockwell's dense, run-on text, but more likely because of limited English interest in Swedish history.[35]

The German publishing stream culminated in 1763 in the substantially reworked edition (Parts 1 and 2) of the imperial councillor, Johann Daniel von Olenschlager.[36] After this each of the four Parts had a separate issue at least once more, until 1783, which saw the final publication of Part 1 (the original *Introduction*) more than a century after its first appearance.

As noted above, the long essay on the papacy preceded the *Introduction*, into which it was incorporated as Chapter 12 in Pufendorf's first edition (1682). It retained that place throughout the revisions and expansions in the various languages, where its content was sometimes presented in two chapters respectively devoted to the pope's worldly and spiritual authority.[37] However, the essay also had a brief life on its own, including Cramer's Latin translations of 1688 and 1693—though

34. According to Allibone (1902), vol. 1, Brockwell also published *A Church* [*chronological*] *History of Great Britain: or an impartial abstract of the most remarkable transactions, . . . a supplement to Mr. Pointer's Chronological history,* 8 vols. . . . (London, 1716–21), and *The natural and political history of Portugal, from 1090 down to the present time, to which is added the history of Brazil and all other dominions subject to the crown of Portugal in Asia, Africa, and America* (London, 1726). Biographical information is scarce, and the only other record is of a Charles Brockwell, M.A. (d. 1755), assistant rector of King's Chapel and chaplain to King George II, and to the English troops stationed at Boston, who gave a sermon to Boston area Freemasons on December 27, 1749.

35. This raises an interesting question: given Sweden's decline as a European power after the Great Northern War (1700–1721), why did the interest of French and German readers continue to support (updated) reprintings of the *Continued Introduction*, while the interest of English readers did not? Very briefly on Sweden's new status, see Lockhart (2004), chap. 9, pp. 145–52.

36. Meusel (1782), pp. 196–97. On Olenschlager, see Michaud, vol. 31, p. 239; and *Allgemeine Deutsche Biographie,* vol. 24, pp. 285–86.

37. See Sayer (1748), vol. 2, chaps. 12–13 ("Rome" and "Of the Pope's Spiritual Monarchy"); Sayer (1764), vol. 2, chaps. 4–5 ("The Pope's Dominions" and "The Pope's Spiritual Monarchy").

these listings may refer to separately titled (and paginated) parts of the *Introduction*, which was also issued in those years.[38] English readers first encountered it in 1691 as *A History of Popedom*, translated by John Chamberlayne, some four years before the appearance of Crull's (separate) version in the *Introduction*.[39] Most significant were the heavily annotated German editions produced by Christian Thomasius in 1714 and 1717, which enlisted Pufendorf's anti-Catholic account into Thomasius's own polemic against Protestant papalism.[40] This version, including some of Thomasius's notes, also saw a French translation in Amsterdam in 1724.[41] There were no independent editions after that until more than a century later (1839), when the work—again with some of Thomasius's notes—was reissued at Leipzig by Carl Hermann Weise.

Pufendorf's *Introduction* also received several commentaries. Thomasius's extensive annotations, along with the introduction to his edition, fall into this category. Most notable, however, was Johann Peter Lud[e]wig's *Erleuterung*, which appeared in 1695 and 1700, aiming explicitly to document Pufendorf's historical account.[42] Unlike Pufendorf himself, Ludwig did not rely merely on one national historian in each instance but sought instead to support everything by going back to original sources (*cooevos*). The result was a work of amazing erudition, albeit one whose eight hundred pages managed to cover only the first four chapters of Pufendorf's work: the ancient empires, Spain (including Naples), Portugal, and England. A similar, albeit less thorough treatment is found in Gundling's *Academischer Discours* (1737),

38. In Cramer's 1693 edition of the *Introduction*, the *De monarchia . . . liber singularis* is separately paginated and indexed.

39. On John Chamberlayne (1688/89–1723), see *Oxford Dictionary of National Biography* (2004), vol. 10, pp. 966–67.

40. See Thomasius's (1714) lengthy "Zuschrift"; also, Ahnert (2006), chaps. 3–4, pp. 43–68; and Hunter (2007), chap. 2, pp. 51–93.

41. Martinière, "Éloge historique," in Pufendorf (1753), vol. 1, p. xiv; Denzer (1972), p. 371.

42. See Ludwig's "Vorrede" to the *Erleuterung* (1700), pp. 17–24, and Meusel (1782), p. 198. On Ludwig (also Ludewig, Ludovicus, etc.), see Zedler, vol. 18 (1738), cols. 954–69; and *Allgemeine Deutsche Biographie*, vol. 19, p. 379.

which was written earlier in the century but emerged only as part of the *Gundlingiana* issued at that later date.[43] Considerably shorter than Ludwig's commentary, it covered eight of Pufendorf's original chapters, from Spain through Poland.[44] Finally, there were Christoph Friedrich Ayrmann's two editions (1744 and 1752)[45] of Christian Gottfried Franckenstein's *Erleuterung*—also produced earlier in the century—and the Swedish historian Jacob Wilde's *Praeparatio hodegetica* (1741), issued between the split publication of his two-part edition of the long Swedish history (1738, 1743).

43. On Nicolaus Hieronymus Gundling, see Zedler, vol. 11 (1735), cols. 1399–1401; and *Allgemeine Deutsche Biographie*, vol. 10, pp. 129–30. The collection of Gundling's writings known as *Gundlingiana* appeared between 1715 and (his death in) 1729, in forty-four parts. In 1732 a forty-fifth part was added, consisting of material from unpublished manuscripts and including a general index of all his publications. It also brought to light some longer discourses such as the one about Pufendorf's *Introduction*.

44. See Meusel (1782), p. 19, who says that Gundling's *Discours* is "hardly worth mentioning" and that it is one of those academic works that printers demand from authors against their will or after they are dead.

45. On Ayrmann (1695–1747), see *Allgemeine Deutsche Biographie*, vol. 1, 1875, p. 711. The 1752 edition was posthumous.

APPENDIX 2

A List of Early Modern Editions and Translations

The following list has been years in the making and is based on a variety of sources, including extensive hands-on research[1] in the British Library, the Herzog August Bibliothek Wolfenbüttel, the Library of Congress, and the University of Helsinki Library. In addition, I have utilized select microforms obtained from many other libraries, and benefited from the generous assistance of well-positioned colleagues, who are mentioned in the Acknowledgments. Of course, given the necessary limitations of direct access (in view of the wide dispersal of editions) it has also been necessary and helpful to utilize various online catalogs and collections, particularly the *Karlsruhe Virtueller Katalog KVK* <http://www.ubka .uni-karlsruhe.de/kvk.html>, *Early English Books online* <http://eebo .chadwyck.com/home>, *Eighteenth Century Collections Online* <http:// www.gale.cengage.com / DigitalCollections / products / ecco / index .htm>, the *OCLC World Catalogue* <http://www.oclc.org/worldcat>, and the printed *National Union Catalog, pre-1956 imprints* (vol. 475). Furthermore, downloadable copies of works in the public domain, such as those in the *Gallica* collection <http://gallica.bnf.fr> at the Bibliotheque Nationale de France (BnF), have been very helpful as well. In all such cases, the dedications, prefaces, introductions, and other frontal materials to the various volumes have been carefully examined and combed for details. Also, and at all stages of the work, I have consulted

---

1. Works directly examined are indicated by the notation *⁾ preceding the title of the work.

the various early modern bibliographical accounts of Pufendorf's works in general, and of the *Introduction* in particular (listed in the "Bibliographical Entries" section of the Bibliography). Needless to say, given the variety of sources and the impossibility of examining each work firsthand, the following list cannot claim to be comprehensive. It does, however, provide an initial overview, a general map, and a guide for further research; that is, like Pufendorf's original, it invites correction and continuation.

Swedish and Danish Versions

*) *Samuelis Pufendorf Inledning til historien, angående the förnähmste rijker och stater, som för tijden vthi Europa stå oprätte,* translated into Swedish by Petrus Brask. Stockholm: Keyser, 1680.

*) *Innledning till swänska historien, med där till fogad ökning ställt emot en fransos, Antoine Varillas benämd, under authoris egen censur uttålkad af Petro Brask.* 2 vols. Stockholm: Eberdt, 1688.

[Holberg, Ludvig.] *Introduction til de fornemste Europaeiske Rigers Historier, fortsat indtil diss sidste Tider, Med et tilstraeckeligt Reg.* Kopenhagen: Kruse, 1711.

Inledning til swenska statens historie med wederbörlige tilökningar, bewis och anmerkningar försedd af Jacob Wilde [first half of Part 2]. Stockholm: Hartwig Gercken, 1738.

Inledning til swenska statens historie med wederbörlige tilökningar, bewis och anmerkningar försedd af Jacob Wilde [second half of Part 2.] Stockholm, Hartwig Gercken, 1743.

German Versions

*) *Einleitung zu der Historie der vornehmsten Reiche und Staaten in Europa.* Frankfurt: Knoch, 1682.

Einleitung . . . , zum andern mal gedruckt und verbessert. Frankfurt: Knoch, 1683.

*) *Einleitung . . . ,* zum andern mal gedruckt und verbessert. Frankfurt: Knoch, 1684.

Continuirte Einleitung zu der Historie der vornehmsten Reiche und Staaten von Europa, worinnen des Königreichs Schweden Geschichte und dessen mit auswertigen Cronen geführte Kriege insonderheit beschrieben werden. Frankfurt: Knoch, 1686.

*) *Anhang der Continuirten Einleitung . . . einem neuen Frantzösischen Scribenten, Antoine Varillas, entgegen gesetzt.* Frankfurt: Knoch, 1688.[2]

Einleitung . . . , zum andern mal gedruckt und verbessert. Frankfurt: Knoch, 1689.

Continuirte Einleitung . . . , zum andern mal gedruckt und mit einem *Anhang* vermehrt. Frankfurt: Knoch, 1689.

Einleitung . . . , zum dritten mal gedruckt und verbessert. Frankfurt: Knoch, 1693.

*) *Continuirte Einleitung . . . ,* zum dritten mal . . . mit einem *Anhang. . . .* Frankfurt: Knoch, 1693.

Einleitung . . . , zum dritten mal gedruckt und verbessert. Frankfurt: Knoch, 1695.

Continuirte Einleitung . . . , zum dritten mal . . . mit einem *Anhang. . . .* Frankfurt: Knoch, 1695.

Einleitung . . . , zum vierdten mal gedruckt und verbessert. Frankfurt: Knoch, 1699.

Continuirte Einleitung . . . , zum vierdten mal gedruckt . . . und mit einem *Anhang. . . .* Frankfurt: Knoch, 1699.

Einleitung . . . , von neuem getruckt und biß auf das Ende des vorigen Seculi vermehrt [Part 1].[3] Frankfurt: Knoch, 1705.

Continuirte Einleitung . . . , von neuem gedruckt, und mit einem Anhang vermehret [Part 2]. Frankfurt: Knoch, 1705.

Einleitung . . . , darinnen sonderlich die Republiquen Venedig und Genua, die Groß-Hertzoge von Florentz, Hertzoge von Savoyen, das Türckische Reich . . . kürtzlich abgehandelt und beschrieben [Part 3] [first German edition of this part]. Frankfurt: Knoch, 1706.

Einleitung zu der Historie der vornehmsten Reiche und Staaten von Asia, Africa und America, nach der Methode Herrn Samuel Frey-Herrns von Puffendorff, welche ein gelährter Engelländer [Jodocus Crull] kürtzlich abgehandelt und beschrieben, anjetzo aus dem Englischen ins Hoch-Teutsche

2. Niceron (1732), cols. 249–50, says (Frankfurt, 1687).

3. Here the numeration of editions is replaced by the more general "von neuem gedruckt." Since new printings were typically "improved" and "continued," there may be little distinction between printings (*Drucke*) and editions (*Auflagen*—as in Part 3, 1709).

übersetzt von C. J. W[ilke] [Part 4] [first German edition of this part].
Frankfurt: Knoch, 1707.

Einleitung . . . , von neuem getruckt und biß auff das Ende des vorigen Seculi vermehrt [Part 1]. Frankfurt: Knoch, 1709.

Continuirte Einleitung . . . , von neuem gedruckt und mit einem Anhang
vermehrt [Part 2]. Frankfurt, 1709.

Dritter Theil zu . . . Einleitung . . . , darinnen die Republiquen Venedig . . . ,
die zweyte Aufflage durchauß vermehrt und verbessert [Part 3]. Frankfurt, 1709.

*Vierter Theil zu . . . Einleitung zu der Historie der vornehmsten Reiche und
Staaten von Asia, Africa und America, wie solche so wohl vor alten Zeiten,
als auch noch jetzo in diesen Ländern sich befinden,* welche nach dessen
Methode ein gelährter Engelländer . . . , die zweyte Aufflage durchauß
vermehrt und verbessert [Part 4]. 1710.[4]

*Einleitung zu . . . , darinnen sonderlich die Republiquen Venedig und Genua, die
Groß-Hertzoge von Florentz, Hertzoge von Savoyen, das Türckische Reich, inglei-
chen das Ertz-Hauß Oesterreich, die Chur und Fürstlichen Häuser, Bayern, Pfaltz,
Sachsen, Brandenburg, Braunschweig, Lüneburg, Würtenberg, Hessen, Baaden,
Mecklenburg und Anhalt, kürtzlich abgehandelt und beschrieben werden,* von
neuem wiederum auffgelegt und verbessert [Part 3]. Frankfurt: Knoch, 1715.

Einleitung . . . , von neuem gedruckt, und biß auf den Baadischen Frieden
[1714] abermahl fortgesetzt und vermehrt, deßgleichen mit neuem Vorbericht versehen, darinnen des Authoris *Politische Anmerckungen* nach
dermahligem geänderten Zustand der Sachen erläutert sind [Part 1].
Frankfurt: Knoch, 1718.

Continuirte Einleitung . . . , aufs neue nebst ehmahligem *Anhang* gedruckt
und biß auf den Todt König Carl des XII. und an die Regierung Ulricae
Eleonorae fortgesetzt und vermehret, aufs neue . . . gedruckt [Part 2].
Frankfurt: Knoch, 1719.[5]

*Einleitung zu der Historie der vornehmsten Reiche und Staaten von Asia, Africa
und America,* welche . . . , die dritte Auflage durchauß verbessert [Part 4].
Frankfurt: Knoch, 1719.

Einleitung . . . , von neuem gedruckt, und biß auf den Baadischen Frieden
abermahl fortgesetzt und vermehrt, deßgleichen mit neuem Vorbericht
versehen, darinnen des Authoris *Politische Anmerckungen* nach dermahli-

---

4. Meusel (1782), p. 197, says (1709).
5. Meusel (1782), p. 197, mentions another edition at (Hamburg, 1722).

gem geänderten Zustand der Sachen erläutert sind [Part 1]. Frankfurt: Knoch, 1728.[6]

*) *Einleitung* . . . , von neuem gedruckt und biß auf gegenwärtiges Jahr fortgesetzet und vermehret, desgleichen mit Anmerckungen versehen, darinnen des Authoris *Politische Gedanken* nach dermahligen. . . . [Part 1]. [There is no chap. 13 on Sweden.] Frankfurt: Knoch, 1733.

*) *Continuirte Einleitung* . . . , aufs neue nebst ehmahligem *Anhang* gedruckt, und bis auf den Tod König Karl des XII. und an die Regierung Königin Ulrica Eleonora fortgesetzet und vermehret . . . [Part 2]. Frankfurt: Knoch, 1730.

*) *Dritter Theil zu . . . Einleitung . . . darinnen sonderlich die Republiquen Venedig und Genua* . . . , von neuem wiederum aufgelegt und biß auf gegenwärtige Zeiten fortgesetzet . . . [Part 3]. Frankfurt: Knoch, 1732.

*) *Vierter Theil zu . . . Einleitung zu der Historie der vornehmsten Reiche und Staaten von Asia, Africa und America*, welche . . . , die vierte Auflage durchaus verbessert und biß auf gegenwärtige Zeiten fortgesetzet . . . [Part 4]. Frankfurt: Knoch, 1732 [1731].

Continuirte Einleitung . . . , aufs neue nebst ehmaligem Anhang gedruckt, und . . . biß auf unsere Zeiten fortgesetzet und vermehret. Frankfurt: Knoch, 1733.

Continuirte Einleitung . . . , aufs neue nebst ehemaligem Anhang gedruckt, und . . . biß auf unsere Zeiten fortgesetzet und vermehret. Frankfurt: Knoch, 1735.

David Fassmann, *Herkunfft, Leben und Thaten, des Persianischen Monarchens, Schach Nadyr vormals Kuli-Chan genannt, samt vielen historischen Erzehlungen und Nachrichten, so das weitläufftige Persianische Reich, und seinen gehabten Fata . . . aus glaubwürdigen Autoribus, und gepflogener eigener Correspondentz, sorgfältigst zusammen getragen von Pithander von der Quelle, samt einer Vorrede Herrn Joh. Christian Clodii . . . von der Beschaffenheit der Persianischen Sprache, und andern hierzu gehörigen Nachrichten.* Leipzig and Rudolstadt: Deer, 1738.[7]

Einleitung . . . , fortgesetzt biß auf gegenwärtige Zeiten, mit Anmerckungen, worinnen des Autoris *Politische Gedancken* nach dermaligem geänderten Zustand der Sachen erläutert sind, neue und verbesserte Ausgabe [Part 1]. Frankfurt: Knoch and Eßlinger, 1746.

6. Reprint or misprint of 1718?
7. Meusel (1782), p. 199, lists this version of Part 4 as (1739).

Einleitung in die Geschichte des Königreichs Schweden, nebst einer Fortsetzung dessen neuerer Historie vom Jahr 1679 bis zum Jahr 1750 [Part 2]. Frankfurt: Knoch and Eßlinger, 1750.

Einleitung in die Historie und Gerechtsamen der besonderen Staaten des Römischen Reichs in Teutschland und Italien, oder Dritter Theil zu der Puffendorfischen *Einleitung in die Historie der Europäischen Staaten* [Part 3]. Frankfurt: Knoch and Eßlinger, 1748.

Einleitung zu der Historie der vornehmsten Reiche und Staaten von Asia, Africa und America, . . . die fünfte Auflage, durchaus verbessert und biß auf gegenwärtige Zeiten fortgesetzet [Part 4]. Frankfurt: Knoch and Eßlinger, 1746.

Einleitung zu . . . , vermehrt und fortgesetzt von Joh. Dan. von Olenschlager [Part 1]. Frankfurt and Leipzig: Knoch and Eßlinger, 1763.

Continuirte Einleitung . . . , fortgesetzt von Joh. Dan. von Olenschlager [Part 2]. Frankfurt and Leipzig: Knoch and Eßlinger, 1763.

Einleitung . . . [Part 3]. Frankfurt: Knoch, 1766.

Einleitung . . . [Part 4]. Frankfurt: Knoch, 1768.

Einleitung . . . [Part 2]. Frankfurt: Knoch, 1780.

Einleitung . . . [Part 1]. Frankfurt: Knoch, 1783.

Latin Versions

Introductio ad historiam praecipuorum regnorum et statuum modernorum in Europa, latio donata a Jo. Friderico Cramero [Johann Friedrich Cramer]. . . . Frankfurt: Knoch, 1687.

Introductio . . . , latio donata à Jo. Friderico Cramero. . . . Frankfurt: Knoch, 1688.

*) *Introductio ad historiam Europaeam*, latine reddita a Jo. Fr. Cramer, editio secunda longe emendatior. 2 vols. Utrecht: van de Water, 1693. [The engraved title-leaf has 1692.]

Introductio . . . , latio donata a Jo. Friderico Cramero. Frankfurt: Knoch, 1700.

*) *Introductio ad historiam Europaeam*, latine reddita a Jo. Frid. Cramero, editio tertia a multis erroribus emendata, et *Compendio Historiae Sueciae* aucta. [The *Compendium* is the *short* history of Sweden in Crull's chap. 13.] Utrecht: van de Water, 1702. [The engraved title-leaf has 1703.]

Introductio ad historiam Europaeam, latine reddita à Joh. Frid. Cramero, a multis erroribus emendata, nunc vero *Supplemento* usque ad initium seculi decimi octavi, itemque *Compendio Historiae Suecicae* aucta. Frankfurt: Knoch, 1704.

French Versions

Introduction à l'histoire des principaux etats, tels qu'ils sont aujourd'hui dans l'Europe, traduite de l'original allemand par Claude Rouxel. 2 vols. Utrecht: Ribbius, 1685.

Introduction à l'histoire . . . vol. 1 (1685), vol. 2 (1686). Cologne: Marteau, 1685–86 [fictive location, actually printed in Holland].

Introduction à l'histoire. . . . 2 vols. Frankfurt: Knoch, 1687.

Introduction à l'histoire. . . . 2 vols. Utrecht: Ribbius, 1687.

Suite de l'Introduction à l'histoire des principaux etats de l'Europe, qui comprend l'histoire de Suede, les guerres qu'elle a euës avec ses voisins; & où l'auteur fait voir quels sont les interêts de ce roiaume à l'égard des autres puissances de l'Europe. 2 vols. Utrecht: Ribbius, 1687 [title page of vol. 2 dated 1688].

Introduction à l'histoire. . . . 2 vols. Utrecht: Ribbius, 1688.

Suite de l'Introduction. . . . 2 vols. Utrecht: Ribbius, 1688.

Introduction à l'histoire. . . . 4 vols. Frankfurt: Knoch, 1688.

Introduction à l'histoire. . . . Frankfurt: Knoch, 1689.

Suite de l'Introduction. . . . Frankfurt: Knoch, 1689.

Suite de l'Introduction. . . . 2 vols. Utrecht: Ribbius, 1689.

Introduction à l'histoire. . . . 2 vols. Leyden: Haring, 1697.

) *Introduction à l'histoire.* . . . 2 vols. [includes chap. 13 on Sweden]. Utrecht: Schouten, 1703.

) *Introduction à l'histoire.* . . . Vols. 1 and 2. Amsterdam: aux dépens de la société,[8] 1710.

) *Introduction à l'histoire . . . , qui comprend l'histoire de Suede.* . . . Vols. 3–4 [containing the *long* history of Sweden]. Amsterdam: aux dépens de la société, 1710.

Introduction à l'histoire. . . . 2 vols. Leiden: van der Aa, 1710.

8. "Aux dépens de la compagnie" [or "aux dépens de la société"] could refer to the "compagnie des libraires" of the city in which the work was published. That is, the book may have been copublished by the booksellers belonging to a local booksellers & printers guild, whose individual members did not have their own presses." [Post by Eva Guggemos to *ExLibris:29628,* at http://palimpsest.stanford.edu/byform/ mailing-lists/exlibris/2005/03/msg00394.html, last accessed on 9.13.2008].

*) *Introduction à l'histoire générale et politique de l'univers, ou l'on voit l'origine, les révolutions, l'état present, & les interêts des souverains* . . . , nouvelle édition, où l'on a continué les anciens chapitres jusqu'à présent et ajouté l'histoire des principaux souverains de *l'Italie, de l'Allemagne &c.*, le tout dans un ordre plus naturel, avec des notes. . . . 6 vols. Amsterdam: aux dépens de la Compagnie, 1721. [Dedication signed by Estienne de la Chambre (pseud. for Bruzen de la Martinière).] [Contains "Avertissement sur cette nouvelle edition" and "Memoires pour servir à la vie de Mr. le Baron de Pufendorf."] [There are two accounts of Sweden: the short chapter in vol. 4, chap. 6, and the long account (= *Suite de l'Introduction*) in vols. 5–6.]

Introduction à l'histoire générale et politique de l'univers, . . . 7 vols. Amsterdam: aux dépens de la Compagnie, 1722.

Introduction à l'histoire générale et politique de l'univers, . . . nouvelle édition, plus ample & plus correcte que les précedentes [publiée par Bruzen de La Martinière, d'après la traduction de C. Rouxel et avec les additions de J.-B. Desroches de Parthenay]. On y a continué tous les chapitres jusqu'à présent et ajouté un *Éloge historique de l'auteur.* 7 vols. Amsterdam: Chatelain, 1732.

Histoire de Suède avant et depuis la fondation de la monarchie . . . , nouvelle édition, plus correcte que les précédentes et continuée jusqu'à l'année 1730 [publiée par J.-B. Desroches de Parthenay, d'après la traduction de Claude Rouxel, remaniée par Bruzen de la Martinière]. 3 vols. Amsterdam: Chatelain, 1732.

Introduction à l'histoire de l'Asie, de l'Afrique et de l'Amérique, pour servir de suite à *l'Introduction à l'histoire* de Pufendorff, par M. Bruzen de La Martinière. 2 vols. Amsterdam: Chatelain, 1735.[9]

Introduction à l'histoire générale et politique de l'univers, . . . nouvelle édition, plus ample & plus correcte que les précédentes [publiée par Bruzen de La Martinière, d'après la traduction de C. Rouxel et avec les additions de J.-B. Desroches de Parthenay]. On y a continué tous les chapitres jusqu'à présent, & ajouté un *Éloge historique de l'auteur.* 7 vols. Amsterdam: Chatelain, 1738.

Introduction à l'histoire de l'Asie, de l'Afrique et de l'Amérique, pour servir de suite à *l'Introduction à l'histoire* de Pufendorff, par M. Bruzen de La

---

9. Meusel (1782), p. 199, says that this item was reprinted in (1748).

Martinière, seconde édition revue & corrigiée. 2 vols. Amsterdam: Chatelain, 1739.

Introduction à l'histoire générale et politique de l'univers . . . , commencée par le baron de Pufendorff, complétée et continuée jusqu'à 1743 par Bruzen de la Martinière. 10 vols. Amsterdam: Chatelain, 1739–43.

Introduction à l'histoire générale et politique de l'univers . . . , commencée par Mr. le baron de Pufendorff, complétée et continuée jusqu'à 1743 par Bruzen de la Martinière. 8 vols. Amsterdam: Chatelain, 1743–45.

Histoire de Suede, avant et depuis la fondation de la monarchie, nouvelle edition, plus correcte que les précédentes, & continuée jusqu'à l'année 1743. 3 vols. Amsterdam: Chatelain, 1743.

*) *Histoire de Suède, avant et depuis la fondation de la monarchie*, nouvelle edition, plus correcte que les precedentes, et continuée jusqu'à l'année 1748. 3 vols. Amsterdam: Chatelain, 1748.[10]

*) *Introduction à l'histoire moderne, générale et politique de l'univers, où l'on voit l'origine, les révolutions & la situation présente des différens états de l'Europe, de l'Asie, de l'Afrique & de l'Amérique, commencée par le Baron de Pufendorff, augmentée par M. Bruzen de la Martinière*, nouvelle édition revûe, considerablement augmentée, corrigée sur les meilleurs auteurs, & continuée jusqu'en mil sept cent cinquante [1750] par M. de Grace [avec la collaboration de Meusnier de Querlon]. 8 vols. Paris: Mérigot et al., 1753–59.

Introduction à l'histoire moderne, générale et politique de l'univers. . . . Vol. 3 [complete set?]. Amsterdam: Chatelain, 1763.

English Versions

*) *An Introduction to the History of the Principal Kingdoms and States of Europe, by Samuel Puffendorf, Counsellor of State to the Present King of Sweden, made English from the Original* [dedication signed by J[odocus] C[rull] M.D.] [contains chap. 13 on Sweden]. London: Gilliflower and Newborough, 1695.

*) *An Introduction* . . . , made English from the Original, the High-Dutch, the second edition, with additions. London: Gilliflower and Newborough, 1697.

10. Meusel (1782), p. 199, refers to a complete edition in 10 vols. at (Amsterdam, 1743–48).

*) *An Introduction* . . . , the third edition. . . . London: Gilliflower and New-borough, 1699.

*) *An Introduction* . . . , the fourth edition. . . . London: Newborough and Gilliflower, 1700.

*) *An Introduction* . . . , the fifth edition. . . . London: Newborough and Gilliflower, 1702.

*) *The Compleat History of Sweden, from its Origin to this Time* . . . *written by the famous Samuell Puffendorf, faithfully translated from the original High-Dutch, and carefully continued down to this present year* [by Charles Brockwell]. [Dedication signed by Charles Brockwell of Catharine Hall, Cambridge.] London: Brudenell, 1702.

The Compleat History of Sweden . . . , the second edition, corrected. London, 1704.

*) *An Introduction to the History of the Kingdoms and States of Asia, Africa and America, both Ancient and Modern, according to the Method of Samuel Puffendorf.* . . . London: Newborough et al., 1705.[11]

A Continuation of Samuel Puffendorf's Introduction to the History of the Principal Kingdoms and States of Europe, brought down [from 1680] to this present year by J[odocus] C[rull] . . . who publish'd Mr. Puffendorf's *Introduction* in English. London: Churchill and Bassett, 1705.

*) *An Introduction* . . . , the sixth edition . . . with an *Appendix*[12] never printed before, containing *An Introduction to the History of the Principal Soveraign States of Italy, particularly Venice, Modena, Mantua, Florence, and Savoy.* London: Newborough and Midwinter, 1706.

A Supplement to Mr. Samuel Puffendorf's Introduction to the History of Europe: containing A Succinct, but most Exact Historical Account of Several European States and Countries, not Inserted in the said Introduction, viz. The Lives of the Popes, the Turkish Empire, An Historical Account of the European Tartars and the Cossacks, with some Historical Observations of Lapland and Greenland, by J[odocus] C[rull] M.D., . . . who oblig'd the Publick with Puffendorf's *Introduction* and *Continuation* [a version of Part 3?]. London: W. Taylor, 1710.

*) *An Introduction* . . . , the seventh edition, . . . with an *Appendix*. . . . London: Midwinter and Atkins, 1711.

---

11. Meusel (1782), p. 197, calls this the first edition and attributes it to J. Crull. See Appendix 1, Publication History, pp. 608–9, above, and the Editor's Introduction, p. xxxviii.

12. From here on, in titles like this, "Appendix" refers to "Part 3."

*) *An Introduction* . . . , the eighth edition . . . with an *Appendix*. . . . London: Took et al., 1719. [The *Appendix* has a separate title page dated 1718.]

An Introduction . . . , the eighth edition . . . with an *Appendix*. . . . London: J. Peele, 1719.

A Supplement . . . , the second edition. . . . London: Ward, 1726.

*) *An Introduction* . . . , the ninth edition . . . with an *Appendix*. . . . London: Knapton et al., 1728.

An Introduction . . . , the tenth edition . . . with an *Appendix*. . . . London and Dublin: Samuel Fairbrother, 1729.

The History of the Kingdoms and States of Asia, Africa and America, both Ancient and Modern, the sixth edition with additions. . . . London: Knapton, 1736.

*) *An Introduction* . . . , begun by Baron Puffendorf, enlarged and continued down to the year 1743 by M. Martinière . . . , improved from the French by Joseph Sayer. 2 vols.[13] London: Knapton et al., 1748.

*) *An Introduction* . . . , the eleventh edition . . . with an *Appendix*. . . . Dublin: William Williamson, 1753.

*) *Introduction* . . . , begun by Baron Puffendorf, continued by Mr. de la Martinière, improved by Joseph Sayer . . . , a new edition revised and corrected. 2 vols.[14] London: Wilde et al., 1764.

An Introduction . . . , begun by Baron Puffendorf, continued by M. de la Martinière, improved by J. Sayer . . . , a new edition revised. . . . 2 vols. London, 1774 [misprint for the 1764 edition?].

An Introduction. . . . London, 1782.

Dutch Versions

Inleydingh tot de historien der fornaemste Rycken en Staten in Europa . . . , trans. S[wen] de Vries.[15] Utrecht, 1684.

Inleydingh tot de historien der fornaemste Rycken en Staten in Europa . . . , trans. S[wen] de Vries, second edition. Utrecht, 1686.

---

13. This is an abbreviated version of Martinière, containing portions of Parts 1 and 3.

14. See note 13 above.

15. Based on Niceron (1732), p. 252. Like Le Clerc, de Vries objected in his commentary to Pufendorf's criticism of religious diversity in the Netherlands. See Döring, in Pufendorf (1995), p. 467, note 59, and the Editor's Introduction, p. xviii.

Vervolgh van dae Inleydingh tot de historie der vooraemste rijcken en staten van Europa, insonderheyd beschrijvende de geschiedenissen des koninghrijcks Sweeden . . . , trans. S[imon] de Vries. Utrecht: Ribbius, 1687.

Historie de voornaemste Rycken en Staten, welke tedeser tijd in Europa gevonden worden, . . . tweede deel [*Inleydingh tot de Sweedsche Historie*], trans. Simon de Vries. Utrecht, 1703.

Russian Versions

Einleitung . . . , trans. Ilya Kopiewitz. St. Petersburg, 1718.[16]

Einleitung . . . , trans. Ilya Kopiewitz, second edition. St. Petersburg, 1723.

Einleitung . . . , trans. Boris Volkov. St. Petersburg, 1767.[17]

Einleitung . . . , trans. Boris Volkov. St. Petersburg, 1777.

Spiritual Monarchy (all languages)

*) *Basilii Hyperetae* [pseud.] *historische und politische Beschreibung der geistlichen Monarchie des Stuhls zu Rom.* Leipzig: Wittigau; Franckfurt: Knoch, 1679.

Basilii Hyperetae [pseud.] *historische und politische Beschreibung der Geistlichen Monarchie des Stuhls zu Rom*, von den vielen Druckfehlern der ersten Edition aus des Autoris Manuscripto gesäubert und zum andernmahl gedruckt. Hamburg: Lichtenstein, 1679.[18]

Tractatus historicus de monarchia pontificis Romani [trans. Johann Friedrich Cramer]. Frankfurt: Knoch, 1688.

*) *The History of Popedom, Containing the Rise, Progress, and Decay Thereof, &c. written in High Dutch by Samuel Puffendorff*, trans. by J.C. [John Chamberlayne]. London: Hindmarsh, 1691.

De monarchia pontificis Romani, liber singularis [possibly a reference to chap. 12 in Cramer's 1693 edition of the *Historia*]. Utrecht, 1693.

16. This translation was based on Cramer's Latin edition. Ilya Kopiewitz (1651–1714) died four years before the 1718 publication, which is presumably the first edition.

17. Mentioned by *Hamburgische Bibliotheca* (1729), p. 145, and by Meusel (1782), p. 200, who describes it as a two-part edition (half in 1767, half in 1777) of Part 1, based on a German version at (Frankfurt, 1741).

18. Siebenkäs (1790), p. 51, calls this the first edition.

*) *Des Freyherrn von Pufendorff politische Betrachtung der geistlichen Monarchie des Stuhls zu Rom, mit Anmerckungen, zum Gebrauch der Thomasischen Auditorii.* Halle: Renger, 1714.

Des Freyherrn von Pufendorff Politische Betrachtung der Geistlichen Monarchie des Stuhls zu Rom, mit Anmerckungen, zum Gebrauch der Thomasischen Auditorii. Halle: Renger, 1717.

Description historique & politique de la monarchie spirituelle du pape [with Thomasius's notes], trans. by Jean de Long. Amsterdam, 1724.[19]

*) Samuel von Pufendorf, *Über das Pabstthum*, neu bearbeitet von Carl Hermann Weise [with some of Thomasius's notes]. Quedlinburg-Leipzig: Basse, 1839.

Commentaries

Johann Peter Ludwigs Erleuterung über Herrn Samuel von Pufendorf Einleitung zur Historie der vornehmsten Reiche und Staaten so jetziger Zeit in Europa sich befinden, in vollständigen Allegaten und nützlichen Anmerckungen bestehend. Leipzig: Zeidler, 1695.

*) *Johann Peter Ludwigs Erleuterung über Herrn Samuel von Pufendorf Einleitung zur Historie der vornehmsten Reiche und Staaten so jetziger Zeit in Europa sich befinden, in vollständigen Allegaten und nützlichen Anmerckungen bestehend,* zum andern mahl gedruckt und verbessert. Leipzig and Halle: Zeidler and Musselius, 1700.

*) *Des Freyherrn von Pufendorff Politische Betrachtung der geistlichen Monarchie des Stuhls zu Rom, mit Anmerckungen, zum Gebrauch der Thomasischen Auditorii.* Halle: Renger, 1714.

Des Freyherrn von Pufendorff Politische Betrachtung der geistlichen Monarchie des Stuhls zu Rom, mit Anmerckungen, zum Gebrauch der Thomasischen Auditorii. Halle: Renger, 1717.

*) *Nicolaus Hieronymus Gundlings academischer Discours über des Freyherrn Samuel von Pufendorffs Einleitung zu der Historie der vornehmsten Reiche und Staaten, so jetziger Zeit in Europa sich befinden,* aus richtigen und unverfälschten MSCtis ans Licht gestellet. Frankfurt: Varrentrapp, 1737.

Jacob Wilde, *Praeparatio hodegetica ad introductionem Pufendorffii in suetici status historiam ex regni tabulariis accurandam, ex versione Andreae Wilde,*

19. Based on Denzer (1972), p. 371, and Martinière, "Éloge historique," in Pufendorf (1753), vol. 1, p. xiv.

Jacobi filii, accesserunt acta publica de novissimo successionis jure et auctoris notae criticae & politicae cum appendice de praejudiciis circa regalia. Stockholm, 1741.

Christian Gottfried Franckenstein, *Erleuterung über des Freyherrn von Pufendorff Einleitung zu der Historie der vornehmsten Reiche und Staaten, so jetziger Zeit in Europa sich befinden,* aus einem vollständigen und vorlängst zum Druck zubereiteten Exemplare an das Licht gestellet von Christoph Friedrich Ayrmann. 2 vols. Hamburg: Brandt, 1744.

Christian Gottfried Franckenstein, *Erleuterung über des Freyherrn von Pufendorff Einleitung zu der Historie der vornehmsten Reiche und Staaten, so jetziger Zeit in Europa sich befinden,* aus einem vollständigen und vorlängst zum Druck zubereiteten Exemplare an das Licht gestellet von Christoph Friedrich Ayrmann, second edition. 2 vols. Hamburg: Brandt, 1752.

Editions and Translations:
Specific Publication Dates (Chart 1)

Multi-year editions are listed in every year that at least one volume appeared. Multiple same-language editions in one year are indicated by small letters (a, b, c . . .). Superscripted numbers after a left parenthesis [$^{(n)}$] indicate consecutive same-language editions (e.g., $^{(2}$ = second edition). The following abbreviations are used: Pt-1 = *Introduction;* Pt-2 = *Continued Introduction;* Pt-3 = *Italy;* Pt-4 = *Asia, Africa, America;* C1 = Ludewig; C2 = Thomasius; C3 = Gundling; C4 = Wilde; C5 = Franckenstein. Different-language editions for the "Spiritual Monarchy" are indicated explicitly on the chart: De = German, Lt = Latin, En = English, Fr = French. Shaded entries identify works that have been directly examined.

	Monarchy	Swedish	German	Dutch	French	Latin	English	Russian	Commentaries
1679	De (a,b,c)								
1680		Pt-1^(1							
1682			Pt-1^(1						
1683			Pt-1^(2						
1684			Pt-1	Pt-1					
1685					Pt-1^(1 (a,b)				
1686			Pt-2^(1	Pt-1	Pt-1				
1687				Pt-2	Pt-1 (a,b), Pt-2^(1	Pt-1			
1688	Lt	Pt-2^(1	Pt-2		Pt-1 (a,b), Pt-2	Pt-1			
1689			Pt-1, Pt-2^(2		Pt-1, Pt-2 (a,b)				
1691	En (J.Ch.)								
1693	Lt		Pt-1^(3, Pt-2^(3			Pt-1^(2			
1695			Pt-1, Pt-2				Pt-1^(1		C1
1697					Pt-1		Pt-1^(2		
1699			Pt-1^(4, Pt-2^(4				Pt-1^(3		
1700						Pt-1	Pt-1^(4		
1702						Pt-1^(3	Pt-1^(5, Pt-2^(1		CI^(2
1703				Pt-2	Pt-1				

Year							
1704							
1705	Pt-1, Pt-2		Pt-1	Pt-4[1], (Pt-1)	Pt-2[2]		
1706	Pt-3[1]			Pt-1[6], Pt-3[1]			
1707	Pt-4[1]						
1709	Pt-1, Pt-2 Pt-3[2]						
1710	Pt-4[2]	Pt-1 (a,b), Pt-2		(Pt-3)[1]			
1711				Pt-1[7], Pt-3			
1714	De						C2
1715	Pt-3						
1717	De						C2[2]
1718	Pt-1					Pt-1	
1719	Pt-2, Pt-4[3]			Pt-1[8] (a,b), Pt-3 (a,b)			
1721		Pt 1-4					
1722		Pt 1-4					
1723						Pt-1	
1724	Fr						
1726				(Pt-3)[2]			
1728	Pt-1			Pt-1[9], Pt-3			
1729				Pt-1[10], Pt-3			

continued

Monarchy	Swedish	German	Dutch	French	Latin	English	Russian	Commentaries
1730		Pt-2						
1731		Pt-4[4]						
1732		Pt-3		Pt 1-4, Pt-2				
1733		Pt-1, Pt-2						
1735		Pt-2		Pt-4[1]				
1736						Pt-4[6]		
1737								C3
1738	Pt-2	(Pt-4)		Pt 1-4				
1739				Pt-4[2], Pt 1-4				
1740				Pt 1-4				
1741				Pt 1-4				C4
1742				Pt 1-4				
1743	Pt-2			Pt 1-4 (a,b), Pt-2				
1744				Pt 1-4				C5
1745				Pt 1-4				
1746		Pt-1, Pt-4[5]						
1748		Pt-3		Pt-2		Pts 1&3		
1750		Pt-2						
1752								C5

Year					
1753		Pt-1$^{(1)}$, Pt-3	Pt 1-4		
1754			Pt 1-4		
1755			Pt 1-4		
1756			Pt 1-4		
1757			Pt 1-4		
1758			Pt 1-4		
1759			Pt 1-4		
1763			(Pt 1-4)	Pt-1, Pt-2	
1764		Pts 1&3		Pt-3	
1766					
1767	Pt-1 (1st half)			Pt-4	
1768					
1774		Pts 1&3			
1777	Pt-1 (2nd half)				
1780				Pt-2	
1782		Pt-1			
1783				Pt-1	
1839					De

Editions and Translations:
Temporal Overview (Chart 2)

NOTE: Different same-language imprints during a particular year are not distinguished here. Multivolume editions appearing over several years are listed every year that at least one volume was published. Different-language editions of the essay on the papacy are not noted.

	Monarchy	Swedish	German	Dutch	French	Latin	English	Russian	Commentaries
1679	o								
1680		o							
1682			o						
1683			o						
1684			o	o	o				
1685					o				
1686			o	o	o				
1687				o	o	o			
1688	o	o	o		o	o			
1689			o		o				
1691	o								
1693	o		o			o			
1695			o				o		o
1697					o		o		
1699			o				o		
1700						o	o		o
1702						o	o		
1703				o	o		o		
1704						o	o		
1705			o				o		

Year						
1706			o		o	
1707					o	
1709					o	
1710			o	o	o	
1711			o			
1714	o					o
1715					o	
1717	o					o
1718		o			o	
1719					o	
1721			o	o		
1722				o		
1723		o				
1724						o
1726			o			
1728			o		o	
1729			o			
1730					o	
1731					o	
1732				o	o	
1733					o	

continued

Year	Monarchy	Swedish	German	Dutch	French	Latin	English	Russian	Commentaries
1735			o		o				
1736							o		
1737									o
1738		o	o		o				
1739					o				
1740					o				
1741					o				o
1742					o				
1743		o			o				o
1744					o				
1745					o				
1746			o						
1748			o		o		o		
1750			o						
1752									o
1753					o		o		
1754					o				
1755					o				
1756					o				
1757					o				

1758					o				
1759					o				
1763			o		o				
1764							o		
1766			o						
1767								o	
1768			o						
1774							o		
1777								o	
1780			o						
1782							o		
1783			o						
1839	o								

BIBLIOGRAPHY

The bibliography does not repeat all of the items listed in the Publication History (Appendix 2).

Primary Sources

WORKS BY PUFENDORF

"Pufendorfs Vorträge vor dem *Collegium Anthologicum* in Leipzig" [1655–58]. In Pufendorf (1995), 1–86.

"Gundaeus Baubator Danicus, sive Examen nugarum atque calumniarum . . . " [1659]. In Pufendorf (1995), 125–55.

Dissertationes academicae selectiores. Lund: Haberegger, 1675.

"Brevis commentatio super ordinum religiosorum suppressione ad Bullam Clementis IX P.M. emissam anno 1668 d. 6 Decembris" [1675]. In Pufendorf (1995), 218–33.

"Discussio quorundam scriptorum Brandeburgicorum, quibus partim publico nomine . . . " [1675]. In Pufendorf (1995), 281–327.

Basilii Hyperetae historische und politische Beschreibung der geistlichen Monarchie des Stuhls zu Rom. Leipzig: Wittigau; Franckfurt: Knoch, 1679.

"De occasionibus foederum inter Sueciam et Galliam et quam parum illa ex parte Galliae observata sint" [1681]. In Pufendorf (1995), 360–85.

Einleitung zu der Historie der Vornehmsten Reiche und Staaten so itziger Zeit in Europa sich befinden. . . . Franckfurt am Mayn: Knoch, 1682.

Commentariorum de rebus Suecicis libri XXVI ab expeditione Gustavi Adolfi regis in Germaniam ad abdicationem usque Christinae. Utrecht: Ribbius, 1686.

"Epistolae duae super censura in Ephemeridibus Parisiensibus, et Bibliotheca Universali de quibusdam scriptorum locis lata, ad virum celeber-

rimum Dn. L. Adamum Rechenbergium P.P.I.A.L." [1688]. In Pufendorf
(1995), 488–506.

*Continuirte Einleitung zu der Historie der vornehmsten Reiche und Staaten
von Europa, worinnen deß Königreichs Schweden Geschichte, und dessen mit
auswärtigen Kronen geführte Kriege insonderheit beschrieben werden,* zum
dritten mal gedruckt, und mit einem Anhang vermehret. . . . Franckfurt
am Mayn: Knoch, 1692.

*An Introduction to the History of the Principal Kingdoms and States of Eu-
rope,* by Samuel Puffendorf, Counsellor of State to the present King of
Sweden, made English from the Original. London: M. Gilliflower and
T. Newborough, 1695a.

*De rebus gestis Friderici Wilhelmi Magni, Electoris Brandenburgici commen-
tariorum libri novendecim.* Berlin: Schrey & Meyer, 1695b.

*De Rebus a Carolo Gustavo Sueciae Rege Gestis Commentariorum Libri Sep-
tem. Elegantissimis Tabulis Aeneis Exornati, Cum Triplice Indice.* Edited by
G[ottfried] Thomasius. Nüremberg: Christopher Riegel, 1696.

*Freyherrn von Pufendorff Politische Betrachtung der Geistlichen Monarchie des
Stuhls zu Rom,* mit Anmerckungen [by Christian Thomasius] zum Gebrauch der Thomasischen *Auditorii.* Halle: Regner, 1714.

*Introduction à l'histoire generale et politique de l'univers, où l'on voit l'origine, les
révolutions, l'état present, & les interêts des souverains,* par Mr. Le Baron de
Pufendorff, nouvelle édition, où l'on a continué tous les anciens chapitres
jusqu'à present, & ajouté l'histoire des principaux souverains de l'Italie,
de l'Allemagne, &c., le tout dans un ordre plus naturel, avec des notes
historiques, géographiques, & critiques, & les cartes nécessaires. . . .
6 vols. Amsterdam: aux dépens de la Compagnie, 1721.

*Introduction à l'histoire moderne, générale et politique de l'universe; où l'on
voit l'origine, la révolution & la situation présente des différents états de
l'Europe, de l'Asie, de l'Afrique & de l'Amerique,* commencé par le Baron de
Pufendorff, augmentée par M. Bruzen de la Martinière, nouvelle édition,
revûe, considérablement augmentée, corrigée sur les meilleurs auteurs, &
continué jusqu'en mil sept cent cinqante [1750], par M. de Grace. 8 vols.
Paris: Mérigot &c., 1753–59.

An Introduction to the History of the Principal States of Europe, begun by
Baron Puffendorf, continued by Mr. de la Martinière, improved by Joseph Sayer . . . in two volumes, a new edition revised and corrected. London: A. Wilde et al., 1764.

De rebus gestis Friderici Tertii, Electoris Brandenburgici, post primi Borussiae regis commentariorum libri tres, complextentes annos 1688–1690. Fragmentum posthumum ex autographo auctoris editum. Edited by E. F. de Hertzberg. Berlin: Decker, Georg Jacob, 1784.

Über das Papstthum, neu bearbeitet von Carl Hermann Weise. Quedlinburg & Leipzig: Gottfried Basse, 1839.

De officio hominis et civis juxta legem naturalem libri duo. Vol. 1: The Text. Edited by James Brown Scott. The Classics of International Law. New York: Oxford University Press, 1927a.

De officio hominis et civis juxta legem naturalem libri duo. Vol. 2: The Translation. Edited by James Brown Scott. Translated by Frank Gardner Moore. The Classics of International Law. New York: Oxford University Press, 1927b.

Elementorum jurisprudentiae universalis libri duo. Vol. 1: The Text. Edited by James Brown Scott. The Classics of International Law. Oxford: Oxford University Press, 1931a.

Two Books of the Elements of Universal Jurisprudence. Vol. 2: The Translation. Edited by James Brown Scott. Translated by William Abbott Oldfather. The Classics of International Law. Oxford: Clarendon Press, 1931b.

De jure naturae et gentium libri octo. Vol. 1: The Text. Edited by James Brown Scott. The Classics of International Law. Oxford: Clarendon Press, 1934a.

De jure naturae et gentium libri octo. Vol. 2: The Translation. Edited by James Brown Scott. Translated by C. H. Oldfather and W. A. Oldfather. The Classics of International Law. Oxford: Clarendon Press, 1934b.

The Compleat History of Sweden. Translated and continued by Charles Brockwell. Norwood, Pa.: Norwood Editions, 1976 and 1978; reprint of London: J. Budenell, 1702.

Samuel Pufendorf's "On the Natural State of Men." The 1678 Latin Edition and English Translation. Translated by Michael Seidler. *Studies in the History of Philosophy.* Lewiston: Edwin Mellen, 1990.

The Political Writings of Samuel Pufendorf. Edited by Craig L. Carr. Translated by Michael J. Seidler. New York: Oxford University Press, 1994.

Kleine Vorträge und Schriften. Texte zur Geschichte, Pädagogik, Philosophie, Kirche und Völkerrecht. Edited and introduced by Detlef Döring. Frankfurt am Main: Vittorio Klostermann, 1995.

Briefwechsel. Edited by Detlef Döring. Vol. 1 of *Samuel Pufendorf: Gesammelte Werke,* edited by Wilhelm Schmidt-Biggemann. Berlin: Akademie Verlag, 1996.

Eris Scandica und andere polemische Schriften über das Naturrecht. Edited by Fiammetta Palladini. Vol. 5 of *Samuel Pufendorf: Gesammelte Werke,* edited by Wilhelm Schmidt-Biggemann. Berlin: Akademie Verlag, 2002a.

The Divine Feudal Law: Or, Covenants with Mankind, Represented. Edited by Simone Zurbuchen. Translated by Theophilus Dorrington. Indianapolis: Liberty Fund, 2002b.

Of the Nature and Qualification of Religion in Reference to Civil Society. Edited by Simone Zurbuchen. Translated by Jodocus Crull. Indianapolis: Liberty Fund, 2002c.

The Whole Duty of Man, According to the Law of Nature. Edited by Ian Hunter and David Saunders. Translated by Benjamin Tooke. Indianapolis: Liberty Fund, 2003.

The Present State of Germany. Edited by Michael J. Seidler. Translated by Edmund Bohun. Indianapolis: Liberty Fund, 2007.

Two Books of the Elements of Universal Jurisprudence. Edited by Thomas Behme. Translated by William Abbott Oldfather. Indianapolis: Liberty Fund, 2009.

WORKS BY OTHER AUTHORS

Theodosii Gibellini [Matthäus Göbel, 1630–98] *Caesareo-Papia Romana: darinnen die Begebnisse, Gelegenheiten und Geheimnisse des Päbstl. Stuhls zu Rom, durch welche sich der Pabst zum Herrn der Christenheit gemachet, auch sich annoch in seiner Hoheit erhält, wie auch die Päbstische Römische Staats-Religion der Christl. Welt politisch vorgestellet werden.* Frankfurt and Leipzig: Weidmann, 1684.

Grotius, Hugo. *Commentary on the Law of Prize and Booty.* Edited and with an Introduction by Martine Julia van Ittersum. Indianapolis: Liberty Fund, 2006.

Gundling, Nicolaus Hieronymus. *Academischer Discours über des Freyherrn Samuel von Pufendorffs Einleitung zu der Historie der vornehmsten Reiche und Staaten, so jetziger Zeit in Europa sich befinden,* aus richtigen und unverfälschten Msctis ans Licht gestellet. Franckfurt am Mayn: Varrentrapp, 1737.

Kant, Immanuel. *Anthropology from a Pragmatic Point of View*. Translated with an Introduction and Notes by Mary J. Gregor. The Hague: Nijhoff, 1974.

Ludewig, Johann Peter. *Erleuterung über des Freyherrn von Pufendorf Einleitung zur Historie der vornehmsten Reiche und Staaten so jetziger Zeit in Europa sich befinden*, in vollständigen Allegaten und nützlichen Anmerckungen bestehend, zum andern mahl gedruckt und verbessert. Leipzig and Halle: Zeidler and Musselius, 1700.

Simonetti, Christian Ernst. "Beilage II: Die neunzehn Eigenschaften eines pragmatischen Geschichtschreibers" (1746). In Blanke (1991), 350–69.

Temple, William. *Works of Sir William Temple, Bart. complete in four volumes, to which is prefixed, The Life and Character of the Author, considerably enlarged*, a new edition. Vol. I. London: S. Hamilton, 1814.

Thomasius, Christian. *Essays on Church, State, and Politics*. Edited, translated, and with an Introduction by Ian Hunter, Thomas Ahnert, and Frank Grunert. Indianapolis: Liberty Fund, 2007.

Valla, Lorenzo. *On the Donation of Constantine*. Translated by G. W. Bowersock. The I Tatti Renaissance Library. Cambridge, Mass.: Harvard University Press, 2008.

Westphal, Andreas. "Beilage I: Kurtze Anleitung zur Erlernung der Historie" (Greifswald, 1729). In Blanke (1991), 290–347.

Bibliographical Sources

Adlemansthal, Petronius Harteviggus [Peter Dahlmann]. "Vita, Fama, et Fata Literaria Pufendorfiana, oder denckwürdige Lebens-Memoire des weltberuffenen Herrn Autoris." In *Samuels Freyhrn. von Puffendorff kurtzer doch gründlicher Bericht von dem Zustande des H. R. Reichs teutscher Nation*. . . . Leipzig: Weidmann, 1710.

Collijn, Isak. *Sveriges Bibliografi 1600–Talet*. Vol. I:3, cols. 748–50. Uppsala: Almquist & Wiksellis, 1944.

Glafey, Adam Friedrich. *Vollständige Geschichte des Rechts der Vernunft . . . nebst einer Bibliotheca Juris Naturae et Gentium*. Leipzig, 1739.

Hamburgische Bibliotheca, der studierenden Jugend zum besten zusammen getragen, die zehnte Centuria. Articles 42–43, pp. 143–49. Leipzig: Gleditsch, 1729.

Ludwig, Johann Peter von. "Eulogium Esaiae ac Samuelis Pufendorfiorum, laconice scriptum." In *Opuscula Oratoria . . . ob argumentorum praestan-*

tiam nunc primum cum auctibus edita, cum indice instructissimo, 463–88, esp. 480–82. Halle, 1721; orig. 1700.

————. "Vorrede an den günstigen Leser." In Ludwig (1700), 17–24.

Malmström, Oscar. *Samuel Pufendorf och Hans Arbeten i Sveriges Historia,* 41–44. Stockholm: Nordin & Josephson, 1899.

[Martinière, Bruzen de la.] "Avertissement sur cette nouvelle édition." In Pufendorf (1721), vol. 1.

————. "Memoires pour servir à la Vie de Mr. Le Baron de Pufendorff." In Pufendorf (1721), vol. 1.

————. "Éloge historique de Monsieur Le Baron de Pufendorff." In Pufendorf (1753), vol. 1, pp. i–xviii.

[Meusel, Johann Georg.] *Bibliotheca Historica, instructa a Bucardo Gotthelf Struvio, aucta a Christi. Gottlieb Budero, nunc vero a Ioanne Georgio Meuselio ita digesta, amplificata et emendata, ut paene novum opus videri possit.* Vol. I, Part 1, section on "Compendia historiae universalis," 196–200. Leipzig: Weidmann and Reich, 1782.

Niceron, Jean-Pierre. "Samuel de Pufendorf." In *Mémoires pour servir à l'histoire des hommes illustres dans la republique des lettres, avec un catalogue raisonné de leurs ouvrages.* Vol. 18, cols. 224–56, esp. cols. 248–52. Paris: Briasson, 1732.

Othmer, Sieglinde C. *Berlin und die Verbreitung des Naturrechts in Europa. Kultur- und Sozialgeschichtliche Studien zu Jean Barbeyracs Pufendorf-Übersetzungen und eine Analyse seiner Leserschaft.* Berlin: Walter de Gruyter, 1970.

Pufendorf, Samuel. "Dedication to Ernst-Ludwig." In *Einleitung zu der Historie . . .* , zum andernmal gedruckt und verbessert. Franckfurt: Knoch, 1684.

————. "Dedication to Charles XII" [dated 1685]. In Pufendorf (1692).

Sayer, Joseph. "Mr. Serjeant Sayer's Preface." In Pufendorf (1764), vol. 1, pp. xi–xiii. (The Preface is carried over from the 1748 edition.)

Siebenkäs, Johann Christian. "Von den Schriften des Freyherrn Samuel von Pufendorf." In *Historisch-Litterarisch-Bibliographisches Magazin.* Edited by Johann Georg Meusel [Hofrath und Professor der Geschichte in Erlangen], Sweytes Stück, 22–64, esp. 51–53. Zürich: Ziegler u. Söhne, 1790.

Sitwell, O. F. G. *Four Centuries of Special Geography. An annotated guide to books that purport to describe all the countries in the world published in English before 1888, with a critical introduction,* 174–75 (Crull), and 483–84 (Pufendorf). Vancouver: UBC Press, 1993.

Thomasius, Christian. "Zuschrift" to Pufendorf (1714).

Warmholtz, Carl Gustav. *Bibliotheca Historica Sveo-Gothica.* Vol. 5, nos. 2522 and 2523, pp. 75–81. Kopenhagen: Rosenkilde og Bergger, 1967–68; reprint of Stockholm: Nordström, 1790.

Reviews of the *Introduction*

This list was compiled mostly from Zurbuchen (1991), Palladini (1978), and Döring in Pufendorf (1995).

Acta Eruditorum 1 (1682), pp. 336–37:
   Einleitung zu der Historie der vornehmsten Reiche und Staaten so itziger Zeit in Europa sich befinden. Frankfurt am Main, 1682.
Nouvelles de la Republique des Lettres (Avril 1685):
   Introduction à l'Histoire des principaux États, tels qu'ils sont aujourd'hui dans l'Europe. Traduit de l'original Allemand de Samuel Pufendorf, par Claude Rouxel. 2 vols. in 12. A Utrecht chez Jean Ribbius, 1685.
Journal des sçavans 13 (1685), p. 298:
   Introduction à l'histoire des principaux États dans l'Europe, trad. par C. Rouxel. Amsterdam, 1685.
Acta eruditorum V (1686), pp. 381–82:
   Continuirte Einleitung zu der Historie der vornehmsten Reiche. . . . Frankfurt am Main, 1686.
Journal des sçavans 15 (1687), pp. 112–20 (by Abbé de la Rocque):
   Continuirte Einleitung . . . (1686).
Bibliothèque universelle et historique 7 (1687), pp. 205–11 (by Jean Le Clerc):
   Introductio ad historiam praecipuorum regnorum et statuum mod. in Europa, latine donata a Jo. Frid. Cramero. Frankfurt am Main, 1688.
Nouvelles de la republique des lettres (Fevrier 1688):
   S. Puffendorfi Introductio ad Historiam praecipuor. Regnor. et statuum modernorum in Europa. Francof. ad Moenum sumpt. Fr. Koch, 1688 in 8. Pag. 887.
Histoire des ouvrages des sçavans (Novembre 1688, Article V):
   Suite de l'Introduction à l'histoire des principaux États de l'Europe, qui comprend l'Histoire de Suede, les guerres qu'elle a eues avec ses voisins, et où

*l'Auteur fait voir quels sont les intérêts de ce Royaume à l'égard des au-
tres Puissances de l'Europe:* traduite de l'original Allemand de Samuel
Puffendorf, par Claude Rouxel. I. et II. Partie. A Utrecht, chez Jean
Ribbius, 1689, in 12. pagg. 624 et 525.

Bibliothèque universelle et historique 8 (1688), pp. 249–56:
　　*Introductio ad historiam praecipuorum regnorum et statuum mod. in Eu-
　　ropa,* latine donata a Jo. Frid. Cramero. Frankfurt am Main, 1687.

Bibliothèque universelle et historique 12 (1689), pp. 472–86:
　　*Epistolae duae super censura in Ephemeridibus Eruditorum Parisiensibus
　　et Bibliotheca universali de quibusdam suorum scriptorum locus lata ad
　　Dn. L. Adamum Rechenbergium.* Lipsiae, 1688. [Le Clerc's response to
　　Pufendorf's *Epistolae duae,* esp. Epistle 2.]

Journal des Sçavans 45 (November 5, 1708), pp. 719–22:
　　*An Introduction to the History of the Kingdoms and States of Asia, Africa,
　　and America both Ancient and Modern, According to the Method of
　　Samuel Puffendorf Counsellor of State to the late King of Sweden.* . . .
　　London: T. Newborough, &c., 1705.

Journal des Sçavans (Janvier 1754), pp. 29–35:
　　Introduction à l'histoire moderne, générale & politique de l'Univers; . . . par
　　M. de Grace, Tome Premier. Paris: Merigot et al., 1753.

Journal des Sçavans (Novembre 1754), pp. 743–48:
　　Introduction . . . , Tome Second (1754).

Biographical Entries

[Zedler, Johann Heinrich. *Grosses vollständiges Universal-Lexicon aller Wis-
senschafften und Künste* . . . *nebst einer Vorrede, von der Einrichtung die-
ses mühsamen und grossen Wercks* [von] *Joh. Pet. von Ludewig.* . . . 64
vols. Vols. 19–64 edited by Carl Günther Ludovici (1707–78). Leipzig,
1732–54; online version, München: Bayrische Staatsbibliothek, 2004–7,
<http://www.zedler-lexikon.de>.]

[Michaud, Louis-Gabriel. *Biographie universelle ancienne et moderne,* nouvelle edition. 45 vols. 1843–65; microform reprint at Leiden, 1983; online version at *Gallica,* Bibliotheque Nationale de France: http://gallica
.bnf.fr.]

"Ayrmann, Christoph Friedrich." *Allgemeine Deutsche Biographie.* Vol. 1
(1875), p. 711.

"Brask, Petrus." In *Svenskt Biografiskt Handlexikon*, new ed., vol. 1, p. 133. Stockholm: Bonniers, 1906.

"Brockwell, Charles." In S. Austin Allibone, *A Critical Dictionary of English Literature and British and American Authors, Living and Deceased, . . . ,* vol. 1. Philadelphia: J. B. Lippincott, 1902. Also see Albert C. Mackey, M.D., *Encyclopedia of Freemasonry and Its Kindred Science,* at http://www .phoenixmasonry.org/mackeys_encyclopedia/s.htm, under letter *S* (Sermons), last accessed September 20, 2009.

"Chamberlayne, John (1668/9–1723)" (by Reavley Gair). In *Oxford Dictionary of National Biography,* edited by H. C. G. Matthews and Brian Harrison, vol. 10, pp. 966–67. Oxford University Press, 2004. Also see "Chamberlayne, John (1666–1723)" (by Francis Watt). In *The Dictionary of National Biography,* edited by Leslie Stephen and Sidney Lee, vol. 4, pp. 9–10. Oxford University Press, 1993.

"Cramer, Johann Friedrich." *Allgemeine Deutsche Biographie,* vol. 4, p. 548. Leipzig, 1876.

"Franckenstein, Christian Gottfried." In Zedler (1735), vol. 9, cols. 1713–14. Also see "Franckenstein, Chrétien-Fréderic." In Michaud (1856), vol. 14, p. 654.

"Grace, Thomas-François de." In Michaud (1857), vol. 17, p. 299.

"Gundling, Nicolaus Hieronymus." In Zedler (1735), vol. 11, cols. 1399–1401. Also see *Allgemeine Deutsche Biographie,* vol. 10, pp. 129–30. Leipzig, 1879.

"Kramer, Johann Friedrich." In Zedler (1737), vol. 15, col. 1735.

"Ludewig, Johann Peter von." In Zedler (1738), vol. 18, cols. 954–69. Also see *Allgemeine Deutsche Biographie,* vol. 19, p. 379. Leipzig, 1884.

"Martinière, Antoine-Augustin Bruzen." In Michaud, vol. 27, pp. 160–61. Also see "Martinière, Augustin Bruzen de la," in Zedler (1739), vol. 19, col. 1845.

"Olenschlager, Johann Daniel v." In *Allgemeine Deutsche Biographie,* vol. 24, pp. 285–86. Leipzig: van Noort and Ovelacker. Also see "Olenschlager, Jean-Daniél d'." In Michaud, vol. 31, p. 239.

"Parthenay, Jean-Baptiste Des Roches de." In Michaud (1855), vol. 10, p. 553.

"Rouxel, Claude de." In Lainé (1834), "Berault des Billiers," p. 7, note (2).

"Wilde, Jacob." In *Sammlung Russischer Geschichte,* vol. 9, pp. 250–56. St. Petersburg: Kayserl. Academie der Wissenschaften, 1764; reprinted Elibron Classics, 2002. Also see "Wilde, Jakob." In *Svenskt Biografiskt Handlexikon,* new ed., vol. 2, p. 732. Stockholm: Bonniers, 1906.

"Wilke, Christoph Johann [?]." In Zedler (1756), vol. 56, cols. 1658–59.

Secondary Literature

Ahnert, Thomas. *Religion and the Origins of the German Enlightenment. Faith and the Reform of Learning in the Thought of Christian Thomasius.* Rochester, N.Y.: University of Rochester Press, 2006.

Baena, Laura Manzano. "Negotiating Sovereignty: The Peace Treaty of Münster, 1648." *History of Political Thought* 28, no. 4 (2007): 617–41.

Barudio, Günter. "Im Zeichen des Goticismus—Schweden zu Beginn der Frühzeit." In *Pipers Handbuch der politischen Ideen,* vol. 3: *Neuzeit: Von den Konfessionskriegen bis zur Aufklärung,* edited by Iring Fetscher and Herfried Muenkler, 179–89. München: R. Piper, 1985.

Bazzoli, Maurizio. "La concezione pufendorfiana della politica internazionale." In *Samuel Pufendorf Filosofo del diritto e della politica,* edited by Vanda Fiorillo, 29–72. Milan: La Città del Sole, 1996.

Bedford, R. D. "Jodocus Crull and Milton's *A Brief History of Moscovia.*" *Review of English Studies,* New Series 47, no. 186 (1996): 207–11.

———. "Crull, Jodocus (d. 1713/14)." In *Oxford Dictionary of National Biography,* ed. H. C. G. Matthews and Brian Harrison, vol. 14, 534. Oxford: Oxford University Press, 2004.

Behnen, Michael. "Statistik, Politik und Staatengeschichte von Spittler bis Heeren." In Boockmann and Wellenreuther (1987), 76–101.

Behnke, Andreas. "'Eternal Peace' as the Graveyard of the Political: A Critique of Kant's *Zum Ewigen Frieden.*" *Millenium: Journal of International Studies* 36, no. 3 (2008): 513–31.

Blanke, Horst Walter, "Von Chyträus zu Gatterer. Eine Skizze der Historik in Deutschland vom Humanismus bis zur Spätaufklärung." In *Aufklärung und Historik: Aufsätze zur Entwicklung der Geschichtswissenschaft, Kirchengeschichte und Geschichtstheorie in der Deutschen Aufklärung,* edited by Horst Walter Blanke and Dirk Fleischer, 113–38. Waltrop: Spenner, 1991.

Bödeker, Hans-Erich, and Georg G. Iggers, Jonathan B. Knudsen, and Peter Reill, eds. *Aufklärung und Geschichte. Studien zur deutschen Geschichtswissenschaft im 18. Jahrhundert.* Göttingen: Vandenhoeck & Ruprecht, 1986.

Boockmann, Hartmut, and Hermann Wellenreuther, eds. *Geschichtswissenschaft in Göttingen. Eine Vorlesungsreihe.* Göttingen: Vandenhoeck & Ruprecht, 1987.

Boucher, David. "Pufendorf and the Person of the State." In *Political Theories of International Relations,* 223–54. New York: Oxford University Press, 1998.

————. "Resurrecting Pufendorf and Capturing the Westphalian Moment." *Review of International Studies* 27 (2001): 557–77.

————. *The Limits of Ethics in International Relations. Natural Law, Natural Rights, and Human Rights in Transition.* New York: Oxford University Press, 2009.

Burke, Peter. "Cultures of Translation in Early Modern Europe." In *Cultural Translation in Early Modern Europe,* edited by Peter Burke and R. Po-Chia Hsia, 7–38. Cambridge: Cambridge University Press, 2007.

Cavallar, Georg. *The Rights of Strangers. Theories of International Hospitality, the Global Community, and Political Justice since Vitoria.* Burlington, Vt.: Ashgate, 2002.

————. "Vitoria, Grotius, Pufendorf, Wolff and Vattel: Accomplices of European Colonialism and Exploitation or True Cosmopolitans?" *Journal of the History of International Law* 10, no. 2 (2008): 181–209.

Christov, Theodore K. "Liberal Internationalism Revisited: Grotius, Vattel, and the International Order of States." *The European Legacy* 10, no. 6 (2005): 561–84.

————. *Leviathans Tamed: Political Theory and International Relations in Modern Political Thought.* Chap. 3: "The Anti-Hobbesian Camouflage: Pufendorf and the Paradox of International Sociability," 85–174. Ph.D. Thesis UCLA, 2008.

————. "The Federal Idea of Europe: Late Eighteenth-Century Debates." In *Europavorstellungen des 18. Jahrhunderts—Imagining Europe in the 18th Century,* edited by Dominic Eggel and Brunhilde Wehinger, 63–79. Hannover: Wehrhahn Verlag, 2009.

DeBujanda, J. M., and Marcella Richter. *Index Librorum Prohibitorum 1600–1966,* edited by J. M. DeBujanda et al., Index des Libres Interdits, vol. 11, 731–32. Montreal: Mediaspaul, 2002.

Denzer, Horst. *Moralphilosophie und Naturrecht bei Samuel Pufendorf: eine geistes- und wissenschaftsgeschichtliche Untersuchung.* Aalen: Scientia Verlag, 1972.

Devetak, Richard. "Between Kant and Pufendorf: Humanitarian Intervention, Statist Anti-Cosmopolitanism and Critical International Theory." *Review of International Studies* 33 (2007): 151–74.

Döring, Detlef.[1] "Samuel Pufendorf (1632–1694) und die Leipziger Gelehrtengesellschaften in der Mitte des 17. Jahrhunderts." *Lias. Sources and Documents Relating to the Early Modern History of Ideas* 15 (1988): 13–48.

1. Many of Döring's essays have now been gathered in Döring (2012).

————. "Samuel von Pufendorf als Verfasser politischer Gutachten und Streitschriften. Ein Beitrag zur Bibliographie der Werke Pufendorfs." *Zeitschrift für historische Forschung* 13, no. 2 (1992a): 189–232.

————. *Pufendorf-Studien. Beiträge zur Biographie Samuel von Pufendorfs und zu seiner Entwicklung als Historiker und Theologischer Schriftsteller.* Berlin: Duncker & Humblot, 1992b.

————. "Das Lebensende Samuel von Pufendorfs (26.10.1694)." *Forschungen zur brandenburgischen und preussischen Geschichte. Neue Folge der Märkischen Forschungen des Vereins für Geschichte der Mark Brandenburg* 2 (1994): 195–210.

————. "Einleitung" to "Brevis commentatio super ordinum religiosorum suppressione ad Bullam Clementis IX P.M. emissam anno 1668 d. 6 Decembris." In Pufendorf (1995), 196–217.

————. "Einleitung" to "Epistolae duae super censura. . . . " In Pufendorf (1995), 450–87.

————. "Samuel von Pufendorfs Berufung nach Brandenburg-Preußen." In *Samuel Pufendorf und die Europäische Frühaufklärung (1694–1994)*, edited by Fiammetta Palladini and Gerald Hartung, 11–28. Berlin: Akademie Verlag, 1996a.

————. "Das Heilige Römische Reich Deutscher Nation in der Beurteilung Samuel von Pufendorfs." In *Samuel Pufendorf. Filosofo del Diritto e della Politica*, edited by Vanda Fiorillo, 73–106. Napoli: Instituto Italiano per gli Studi Filosofici, 1996b.

————. "Samuel Pufendorf und die Heidelberger Universität in der Mitte des 17. Jahrhunderts." In *Späthumanismus und Reformierte Konfession. Theologie, Jurisprudenz und Philosophie in Heidelberg an der Wende zum 17. Jahrhundert*, edited by Christoph Strohm, Joseph S. Freedman, and Herman J. Selderhuis, 293–323. Tübingen: Mohr Siebeck, 2006.

————. *Samuel Pufendorf in der Welt des 17. Jahrhunderts.* Frankfurt am Main: Vittorio Klostermann, 2012.

Doyle, Michael W., and Geoffrey S. Carlson. "Silence of the Laws? Conceptions of International Relations and International Law in Hobbes, Kant, and Locke." *Columbia Journal of Translational Law* 46, no. 3 (2008): 648–66.

Droysen, Johann Gustav. "Zur Kritik Pufendorfs." In *Abhandlungen von Joh. Gust. Droysen zur neueren Geschichte*, 307–86. Leipzig: Veit & Comp., 1876.

Drury, Marjule Anne. "Anti-Catholicism in Germany, Britain, and the United States: A Review and Critique of Recent Scholarship." *Church History* 70, no. 1 (2001): 98–131.

Dufour, Alfred. "Tradition et modernité de la conception Pufendorfienne de l'état." *Archives de Philosophie du Droit* 21 (1976): 55–74.

————. *Droits de l'homme, droit naturel et histoire. Droit, individu et pouvoir de l'école du droit naturel à l'école du droit historique.* Paris: Presses Universitaires de France, 1991a.

————. "Les ruses de la raison d'état, ou histoire et droit naturel dans l'œuvre et la pensée des fondateurs du droit naturel moderne." In *Droit de l'homme, Droit naturel, et histoire,* 125–48. Paris: Presses Universitaires de France, 1991b.

————. "Pufendorfs föderalistisches Denken und die Staatsräsonlehre." In *Samuel Pufendorf und die Europäische Frühaufklärung. Werk und Einfluß eines deutschen Bürgers der Gelehrtenrepublik nach 300 Jahren (1694–1994),* edited by Fiammetta Palladini and Gerald Hartung, 105–22. Berlin: Akademie Verlag, 1996.

————. "La pensée politique de Pufendorf et la permanence de l'idée luthérienne de l'état." In *Dal "De Jure Naturae et Gentium" di Samuel Pufendorf alla Codificazione Prussiana del 1794,* edited by Marta Ferronato, 7–39. Milan: Casa Editrice Dott. Antonio, 2005.

Friedeburg, Robert von. "Church and State in Lutheran Lands, 1550–1675." In *Lutheran Ecclesiastical Culture, 1550–1675,* edited by Robert Kolb, 361–410. Boston: Brill, 2008.

Glozier, Matthew. *Marshal Schomberg, 1615–1690, "the Ablest Soldier of His Age": International Soldiering and the Formation of State Armies in Seventeenth-Century Europe.* Brighton: Sussex Academic Press, 2005.

Goodwin, Gordon. "Crull, Jodocus, M.D. (d. 1713?)." In *The Dictionary of National Biography,* edited by Leslie Stephen and Sidney Lee, vol. 5, 262. Oxford: Oxford University Press, 1993.

Grafton, Anthony. *What Was History? The Art of History in Early Modern Europe.* Cambridge: Cambridge University Press, 2007.

Grunert, Frank. "'Händel mit Herrn Hector Gottfried Masio.' Zur Pragmatik des Streits in den Kontroversen mit dem Kopenhagener Hofprediger." In *Appell an das Publikum. Die öffentliche Debatte in der deutschen Aufklärung,* edited by Ursula Goldenbaum, vol. 1, 119–74. Berlin: Akademie Verlag, 2004.

Haakonssen, Knud. *Natural Law and Moral Philosophy: From Grotius to the Scottish Enlightenment*. Cambridge: Cambridge University Press, 1996.

Hammerstein, Notker. *Jus und Historie: Ein Beitrag zur Geschichte des historischen Denkens an deutschen Universitäten im späten 17. und 18. Jahrhundert*. Göttingen: Vandenhoeck & Ruprecht, 1972.

Hochstrasser, T. J. *Natural Law Theories in the Early Enlightenment*. Cambridge: Cambridge University Press, 2000.

Hont, Istvan. *Jealousy of Trade. International Competition and the Nation-State in Historical Perspectives*. Cambridge, Mass.: Belknap Press of Harvard University Press, 2005.

Hüning, Dieter, ed. *Naturrecht und Staatstheorie bei Samuel Pufendorf*. Baden-Baden: Nomos Verlag, 2009.

Hunter, Ian. *Rival Enlightenments. Civil and Metaphysical Philosophy in Early Modern Germany*. Cambridge: Cambridge University Press, 2001.

———. *The Secularisation of the Confessional State. The Political Thought of Christian Thomasius*. Cambridge: Cambridge University Press, 2007.

———. "The Law of Nature and of Nations." In *The Routledge Companion to Eighteenth-Century Philosophy*, edited by Aaron Garrett. New York: Routledge, 2011.

Jägerskiöld, S. "Samuel von Pufendorf in Schweden, 1668–1688. Einige neue Beiträge." In *Satura Roberto Feenstra*, edited by J. A. Ankum, J. E. Spruit, and F. B. J. Wubbe, 557–70. Friburg, Switzerland: University Press, 1985.

Jarausch, Konrad H. "The Institutionalization of History in 18th-Century Germany." In Bödeker (1986), 25–48.

Kelley, Donald J. "Between History and System." In *Historia. Empiricism and Erudition in Early Modern Europe*, edited by Gianna Pomata and Nancy G. Siraisi, 211–37. Cambridge, Mass.: MIT Press, 2005.

Klippel, Diethelm. "Das Deutsche Naturrecht am Ende des 18. Jahrhunderts." In *Das Naturrecht der Geselligkeit. Anthropologie, Recht und Politiki im 18. Jahrhundert*, edited by Vanda Fiorillo and Frank Grunert, 301–25. Berlin: Duncker & Humblot, 2009.

Koskenniemi, Martti. "'Not Excepting the Iroquois Themselves. . . .' Machiavelli, Pufendorf and the Prehistory of International Law." Max Weber Lecture No. 2007/07. Florence: European University Institute. Available:

http://cadmus.eui.eu/bitstream/handle/1814/7632/MWP_LS_2007_07
.pdf?sequence=1 [accessed July 14, 2011].

———. "Miserable Comforters: International Relations as New Natural
Law." *European Journal of International Relations* 15, no. 3 (2009): 395–422.

———. "International Law and *raison d'état:* Rethinking the Prehistory
of International Law." In *The Roman Foundations of the Law of Nations:
Alberico Gentili and the Justice of Empire,* edited by Benedict Kingsbury
and Benjamin Straumann, 297–339. New York: Oxford University Press,
2010.

Kraus, Hans-Christof. "1837 als Krisenjahr des politischen Konfessionalis-
mus in Deutschland." *Historisches Jahrbuch* 127 (2007): 465–85.

Krieger, Leonard. "History and Law in the Seventeenth Century: Pufendorf." *Journal of the History of Ideas* 21 (1960): 198–210.

———. *The Politics of Discretion. Pufendorf and the Acceptance of Natural
Law.* Chicago: University of Chicago Press, 1965.

Lainé, M., *Archives généalogiques et historiques de la noblesse de France.* Tome
Quatrième. Paris, 1834.

Lockhart, Paul Douglas. *Sweden in the Seventeenth Century.* New York:
Palgrave-Macmillan, 2004.

Meinecke, Friedrich. "Pufendorf." In *Die Idee der Staatsräson in der neueren
Geschichte,* 279–303. Berlin: R. Oldenbourg, 1925.

———. "Pufendorf." In *Machiavellism: The Doctrine of Raison D'état and Its
Place in Modern History,* 224–43. New Brunswick: Transaction Publish-
ers, 1998 (a translation of *Die Idee der Staatsräson*).

Moraw, Peter. "Kaiser und Geschichtschreiber um 1700." *Die Welt als Geschichte* 22 (1962): 62–203, and 23 (1963): 93–136.

Muhlack, Ulrich. *Geschichtwissenschaft im Humanismus und in der
Aufklärung. Die Vorgeschichte des Historismus.* "2. Spezialgeschichte und
Universalgeschichte," 97–150. München: C. H. Beck, 1991.

Neiman, Susan. *Evil in Modern Thought: An Alternative History of Philosophy.* Princeton, N.J.: Princeton University Press, 2002.

Neville, Kristoffer. "Gothicism and Early Modern Historical Ethnography."
Journal of the History of Ideas 70, no. 2 (2009): 213–34.

Niléhn, Lars. "On the Use of Natural Law. Samuel Von Pufendorf as Royal
Swedish State Historian." In *Samuel Von Pufendorf 1632–1982. Ett Rätts-
historiskt Symposium I Lund 15–16 Januari 1982,* edited by Kjell Ä. Modéer,
52–70. Lund: Bloms Boktruckeri, 1986.

Olden-Jorgensen, Sebastian. "Robert Molesworth's *An Account of Denmark as It Was in 1692:* A Political Scandal and Its Literary Aftermath." In *Northern Antiquities and National Identities. Perceptions of Denmark and the North in the Eighteenth Century,* edited by Knud Haakonssen and Henrik Horstboll, 68–87. Copenhagen: The Royal Danish Academy of Sciences and Letters, 2007.

O'Neill, Charles E., and Joaquín María Domínguez. *Diccionario histórico de la Compañía de Jesús: biográfico-temático.* 4 vols. Roma: Institutum Historicum; Madrid: Universidad Pontificia Comillas, 2001.

Palladini, Fiammetta. *Discussioni seicentesche su Samuel Pufendorf. Scritti Latini: 1663–1700.* Milan: Societa d'Editrice il Mulino, 1978.

———. "S. Pufendorf lettore di Guicciardini." *La Cultura* 22, no. 1 (1984): 44–93.

———. *Samuel Pufendorf discepolo di Hobbes. Per una reinterpretazione del giusnaturalismo moderno.* Bologna: Il Mulino, 1990.

———. *La Biblioteca di Samuel Pufendorf.* Vol. 32, *Wolfenbütteler Schriften zur Geschichte des Buchwesens.* Wiesbaden: Harrassowitz Verlag, 1999a.

———. "Poesie satiriche sulla Storia del Grande Elettore di S. Pufendorf." In *Neulateinisches Jahrbuch—Journal of Neo-Latin Language and Literature,* edited by Marc Laureys and Karl August Neuhausen, vol. 1, 171–88. New York: Georg Olms Verlag, 1999b.

———. "Ein Vergessener Pufendorf-Übersetzer: Der *Réfugié* Antoine Teissier." In *The Berlin Refuge 1680–1780. Learning and Science in European Context,* edited by Sandra Pott, Martin Mulsow, and Lutz Dannenberg, 113–35. Boston: Brill, 2003.

———. "Pufendorf Disciple of Hobbes: The Nature of Man and the State of Nature: The Doctrine of *Socialitas.*" *History of European Ideas* 34 (2008): 26–60.

Pasquino, Pasquale. "Politisches und historisches Interesse 'Statistik' und historische Staatslehre bei Gottfried Achenwall (1719–1772)." In Bödeker (1986), 144–68.

Piirimäe, Pärtel. "Official Historiography in Seventeenth-Century Europe." Unpublished manuscript.

———. "Politics and History: An Unholy Alliance? Samuel Pufendorf as Official Historiographer." In *Rund um die Meere des Nordens. Festschrift für Hain Rebas,* edited by Michael Engelbrecht, Ulrike Hanssen-Decker, and Daniel Höffker, 237–52. Heide: Boyens Buchverlag, 2008.

Pozzo, Riccardo. "Kant's *Streit der Fakultäten* und Conditions in Königsberg." *History of Universities* 16, no. 2 (2000): 96–128.

Pursell, Brennan C. *Frederick V of the Palatinate and the Coming of the Thirty Years' War.* Burlington, Vt.: Ashgate, 2003.

Reibstein, Ernst. "Pufendorfs Völkerrechtslehre." *Österreichische Zeitschrift für öffentliches Recht* 7, no. 4 (1955): 43–72.

Reill, Peter Hanns. *The German Enlightenment and the Rise of Historicism,* 9–47. Berkeley: University of California Press, 1975.

Robertson, J. G. "Review of *Ludvig Holbergs Samlede Skrifter.* . . . " *Modern Language Review* 11 (1916): 109–14.

Rödding, Hans. "Pufendorf als Historiker und Politiker in den *Commentarii de rebus gestis Friderici Tertii.*" Halle: Max Niemeyer, 1912.

Salzer, Ernst. *Der Übertritt des grossen Kurfürsten von der schwedischen auf die polnische Seite während des ersten nordischen Krieges in Pufendorfs "Carl Gustav" und "Friedrich Wilhelm."* Heidelberg: Carl Winter, 1904.

Saunders, David. "Hegemon History: Pufendorf's Shifting Perspectives on France and French Power." In *War, the State and International Law in Seventeenth-Century Europe,* edited by Olaf Asbach and Peter Schröder, 211–30. Burlington, Vt.: Ashgate, 2009.

Saunders, David, and Ian Hunter. "Bringing the State to England: Andrew Tooke's Translation of Samuel Pufendorf's *De officio hominis et civis.*" *History of Political Thought* 24, no. 2 (2003): 218–34.

Scherer, Emil Clemens. *Geschichte und Kirchengeschichte an den deutschen Universitäten. Ihre Anfänge im Zeitalter des Humanismus und ihre Ausbildung zu selbstständigen Disziplinen.* Freiburg: Herder & Co., 1927.

Schilling, Heinz. *Konfessionalisierung und Staatsinteressen. Internationale Beziehungen 1559–1659. Handbuch der Geschichte der Internationalen Beziehungen,* vol. 2, edited by Heinz Duchhardt and Franz Knipping. Paderborn: Schöningh, 2007.

Schneewind, J. B. "Pufendorf's Place in the History of Ethics." *Synthese* 72 (1987): 123–55.

———. "The Central Thesis: Pufendorf." In *The Invention of Autonomy: A History of Modern Moral Philosophy,* 118–40. New York: Cambridge University Press, 1998.

Seidler, Michael J. "'Turkish Judgment' and the English Revolution: Pufendorf on the Right of Resistance." In *Samuel Pufendorf und die europäische Frühaufklärung. Werk und Einfluß eines deutschen Bürgers der Gelehrten-*

republik nach 300 Jahren (1694–1994), edited by Fiammetta Palladini and Gerald Hartung, 83–104. Berlin: Akademie Verlag, 1996.

———. "Natural Law and History. Pufendorf's Philosophical Historiography." In *History and the Disciplines. The Reclassification of Knowledge in Early Modern Europe,* edited by Donald R. Kelley, 203–22. Rochester, N.Y.: University of Rochester Press, 1997.

———. "Qualification and Standing in Pufendorf's Two English Revolutions." In *Widerstandsrecht in der frühen Neuzeit. Erträge und Perspektiven der Forschung im deutsch-britischen Vergleich,* edited by Robert Von Friedeburg, 329–51. Berlin: Duncker & Humblot, 2001.

———. "'Wer mir gutes thut, den liebe ich': Pufendorf on Patriotism and Political Loyalty." In *'Patria' und 'Patrioten' vor dem Patriotismus. Pflichten, Rechte, Glauben und die Rekonfigurierung europäischer Gemeinwesen im 17. Jahrhundert,* edited by Robert von Friedeburg, 335–65. Wiesbaden: Harrassowitz Verlag, 2005.

———. "Introduction." In *Samuel Pufendorf: The Present State of Germany,* edited by Michael J. Seidler, ix–xxvii. Indianapolis: Liberty Fund, 2007.

———. "'Monstrous' Pufendorf: Sovereignty and System in the *Dissertations.*" In *Monarchism and Absolutism in Early Modern Europe,* edited by Cesare Cuttica and Glenn Burgess, 159–75. London: Pickering & Chatto, 2011.

Tamm, Ditlef. "Pufendorf und Dänemark." In *Samuel Von Pufendorf. 1632–1982,* edited by Kjell Ä. Modéer, 81–89. Lund: Bloms Boktryckeri, 1986.

Toyoda, Tetsuya. *Theory and Politics of the Law of Nations. Political Bias in International Law Discourse of Seven German Court Councilors in the Seventeenth and Eighteenth Centuries.* Boston: Martinus Nijhoff, 2011.

Tuck, Richard. *Natural Rights Theories. Their Origin and Development.* New York: Cambridge University Press, 1981.

———. "The 'Modern' Theory of Natural Law." In *The Languages of Political Theory in Early-Modern Europe,* edited by Anthony Pagden, 99–119. New York: Cambridge University Press, 1987.

———. *Philosophy and Government 1572–1651.* Cambridge: Cambridge University Press, 1993.

———. *The Rights of War and Peace. Political Thought and the International Order from Grotius to Kant,* chap. 5, 120–65. New York: Oxford University Press, 1999.

Valera, Gabriella. "Statistik, Staatengeschichte, Geschichte im 18 Jahrhundert." In Bödeker (1986), 119–43.

Van der Zande, Johan. "Statistik and History in the German Enlightenment." *Journal of the History of Ideas* 71, no. 3 (2010): 411–32.

Vierhaus, Rudolf. "Die Universität Göttingen und die Anfänge der modernen Geschichtswissenschaft im 18. Jahrhundert." In Boockmann (1987), 9–29.

Wegele, Franz X. von. *Geschichte der deutschen Historiographie seit dem Auftreten des Humanismus,* on Pufendorf: 499–523, 535–41. München: R. Oldenbourg, 1885; reprinted New York: Johnson Reprint Co., 1965.

Woolf, Daniel. "From Hystories to the Historical: Five Transitions in Thinking About the Past." In *The Uses of History in Early Modern England,* edited by Paulina Kewes, 31–67. San Marino, Calif.: Huntington Library, 2006.

Wrede, Martin. "*L'état de l'empire empire?* Die Französiche Historiographie und das Reich im Zeitalter Ludwigs XIV.—Weltbild, Wissenschaft und Propaganda." In *Imperium-Romanum—Irregulare Corpus—Teutscher Reichs-Staat. Das Alte Reich im Verständnis der Zeitgenossen und der Historiographie,* edited by Matthias Schnettger, 89–110. Mainz: Philipp von Zabern, 2002.

Wright, Martin. "De systematibus civitatum." In *Martin Wright: Systems of States,* edited with an introduction by Hedley Bull, 21–45. London: Leicester University Press, 1977.

Zedelmaier, Helmut. "'Im Begriff der Geschichte': Zur Historiographiegeschichte der frühen Neuzeit." *Historisches Jahrbuch* 112 (1992): 436–56.

Zurbuchen, Simone. *Naturrecht und natürliche Religion. Zur Geschichte des Toleranzproblems von Samuel Pufendorf bis Jean-Jacques Rousseau.* Würzburg: Königshausen & Neumann, 1991.

THE TABLE[1]

A.

1. The page numbers in this Table are those of the original 1695 edition of Crull's translation, which are enclosed in angle brackets in the text.

I.

N.

O.

P.

INDEX